THE REAL ROCKYS

Rolando Vitale

First published 2014
by RV Publishing

British Library Cataloguing in Publication Data
A catalogue record for this book is available
from the British Library

Library of Congress Cataloging-in-Publication Data
A catalog record has been requested for this book

ISBN: 978-0-9929822-0-1

The book is available through the usual retail outlets. Further copies can also
be ordered by visiting the www.therealrockys.com website.
For further book enquiries please email rv1publishing@aol.com

Every effort has been made to trace the owners of copyright material
displayed in this book. Where this has not been possible the author
and publisher will correct this by making complete acknowledgments
in future reprints of the book.

Front cover: Pete Herman on the left (*Sussman Studio*) and Rocky
Kansas on the right. Unless otherwise stated, all photographs
are courtesy of Vincent Colitti photo archives.

Typeset in Janson Text 10½ pt by
www.chandlerbookdesign.co.uk

Printed in Great Britain by
Berforts Group Ltd

THE REAL
ROCKYS

A HISTORY OF THE GOLDEN AGE OF ITALIAN AMERICANS IN BOXING 1900–1955

ROLANDO VITALE

RV

To my beloved son and inspiration Giovanni,
whose presence kept me focused and
distracted in equal measure and made sure
it was never boring.

Contents

List of appendices

Acknowledgments

The Real Rockys: A History of the Golden Age of Italian Americans in Boxing 1900–1955 would not have been possible without the co-operation, support and encouragement of many individuals along the way in this lonely and exhaustive process. What began as an undergraduate dissertation and for years lay on a shelf gathering dust metamorphosed into this book. Following several encounters with Dennie Mancini,* one of Britain's most respected boxing figures, and someone I knew from my days working as a sports journalist, I rediscovered the motivation to rewrite the original manuscript. I began by culling facts and background material from newspapers, magazines and record books and from personal interviews. The research mission also included several visits to the United States of America. I owe the biggest debt of gratitude to Dennie for his friendship and for his belief in my ability. His passion for boxing was second to none, and he knew that no one had written a fitting story encapsulating the Italian American contribution to boxing. At times he despaired and was left wondering whether I would ever complete the task, but in spite of life's complications and some wrong turns I reached the finishing line. Unfortunately Dennie never got to see the realization of my dream as he passed away on September 10, 2004. Not only did I win the bet with you but wherever you are, my friend, I hope you enjoy the read!

I would also like to express my sincerest gratitude to Vincent Colitti, former International Boxing Research Organization (IBRO) member, and perhaps the most eminent authority on Italian American prizefighters, who provided me with much research and photographic material from his personal collection, as well as historian Hank Kaplan* for his invaluable insight and words of wisdom and for allowing access to his impressive boxing archives, and Peter Heller, of New York, the sports producer at ABC News television network, for providing a list of contacts that paved the way to a number of important interviews. Also to Harry Mullan,* former editor of *Boxing News*, for his support in permitting access to the substantial and specialist archives, and to his assistant Mark Butcher, and to British boxing historian Barry Hugman and Herb Goldman of New York, historian and former editor of *Boxing Illustrated*, for their expertise on all things boxing. Thanks to Angelo Prospero, boxing writer and historian and George Randazzo, founder of the Chicago-based National Italian American Sports Hall of Fame. I would like to thank historian and retired lecturer Professor Lucio Sponza of the Italian Department at the University of Westminster for the time spent mentoring and supervising my thesis and for his continued support. A special mention is reserved for the numerous archivists who helped me at the University of Westminster Library, University College London Library, the British Newspaper Library, the Hoddesdon Public Library and the New York Public Library. Special thanks go to George Rugg of South Bend, Indiana, head curator at the University of Notre Dame's Joyce Sports Library archives for his professionalism and patience in locating specialist material. To Maurizio Bruni from CONI, The Italian National Olympic Committee archives, who supplied six rare articles on Italian American prizefighters and *to La Gazzetta dello Sport* archives section in Milan, Italy for their assistance. I would also like to acknowledge the numerous sports writers, commentators, chroniclers, columnists, academics, authors and researchers who covered the period under review, whose work enabled me to extract useful nuggets of information.

Boxing managers and trainers Al Certo, John De John,* Angelo Dundee,* Joey Fariello,* boxing official Steve Acunto and renowned boxing referee Arthur Mercante Senior,* Dan Muscato from the Buffalo fighting dynasty, Ralph Citro,* boxing trainer, record keeper and former director of the International Boxing Record Organization, and Steve Corbo, boxing announcer and judge, all offered their knowledge. Of course, without the heroic sporting deeds of the boxers we would have no project and world champions Carmen Basilio,* Tony De Marco, Joey Giardello,* Jake La Motta and Willie Pep* willingly gave up their valuable time to be interviewed. Not only was it a personal honor for me, but I will always be indebted to them for their help. To those names that do not appear, forgive me and please understand that I have appreciated your assistance. I would like to thank copy-editor Ian Howe for his thoroughness and expert guidance in ensuring that I crossed the T's and dotted the I's, and adhered to the house style of American English spelling, staying faithful to the source material used and subject matter discussed. Finally I would like to thank my family, who have been a solid rock of support: my mother Giannina, father Giovanni and sister Carmela, who have loved me through some difficult times. Last but not least to my wife Cinzia for her devotion, understanding and patience so I could complete this book.

* Denotes person now deceased

Author's note

Positioning the Italian American boxer at the heart of this manuscript has not been without complication, and research has been hampered by dubious written records contained in old newspapers and venerable publications upheld as standard-bearers of the sport. Whilst there is no doubting that Nat Fleischer, founder and editor of *Ring Magazine*, made a valid and unique contribution in spreading the pugilistic gospel, his record keeping and in particular the data held on fighters' nationalities was less desirable and rather erratic. To make matters worse, errors made by the great man were usually left unchecked and disseminated by hordes of syndicated writers across America, leading to widespread inaccuracy and misinformation. Hence it is not uncommon to see rival publications refer to the same boxer as having different ethnic backgrounds. With such inconsistencies rife even today it has almost become the accepted norm for writers to deal with these associated research and journalistic hazards. Against this backdrop it is my belief that champions and title claimants referred to in this book have been correctly identified and matched to their respective ethnic group. Interviews with historians, former boxers, trainers and managers have been a valuable source of cross reference and wherever possible families of boxers have been contacted and the boxer's personal details verified. This is especially important as often the "exotic" sounding Italian cognomens were savagely butchered in the American press. All data used in this work has been checked against multiple sources and it is believed to be reliable and accurate.

Introduction

When Sylvester Stallone portrayed Rocky Balboa in the award-winning film *Rocky* (1976), it raised the profile of a hungry Italian fighter conquering the world with his fists. Rocky's fictional heroics served to remind us that ordinary Italian Americans with extraordinary athletic abilities had once occupied a prominent role inside the ring, and in the course of my research for this book I discovered that this success was one of the best-kept secrets in boxing, and most definitely not common knowledge. The dearth of information in this subject area is evidenced by the fact that there is no record book chronicling this important slice of boxing history. Several sports encyclopaedias briefly note an Italian American presence in boxing, but most texts gloss over this contribution. The only other book on the topic, entitled *The Italian Stallions: Heroes of Boxing's Glory Days* (2003), written by Stephen Brunt and Thomas Hauser, delivers a narrative restricted to the period between 1945 and 1959, and is largely comprised of *Sport Magazine* articles. *Sport* began in 1946 and was the *Sports Illustrated* of its day.

This glaring omission in sports research has presented an opportunity to set the record straight. The more I dug into archives and old newspaper accounts, the more fascinated I became. Many of the greatest moments in boxing in the first half of the twentieth century were, I discovered, attributed to men of Italian lineage. Italian Americans not only captured more world boxing titles, but the sustained longevity of their success occurred in the most competitive era, when there was generally one world champion in each of the traditional eight weight divisions and a larger proportion of great fighters competing. Boxers' names were not always great indicators of this, as boxers appropriated Irish or anglicized monikers, with the unintended consequence being that the true extent of their contributions was concealed from the outside world.

The story aroused my interest on three levels. Professionally speaking, it offered an unfamiliar and unconventional view of the Italian immigrant experience in the United States, one that featured triumph and pride at a time of maladjustment, exploitation and societal alienation. Secondly, as an avid boxing aficionado I found the project had instant appeal. I fell in love with the sport from the moment I sat beside my father to watch my first televised boxing match, the 1974 *Rumble in the Jungle* between Muhammad Ali and George Foreman. Since then, I have been spellbound by the compelling unpredictability of outcome and by the boxer's level of sacrifice and professionalism, seldom matched by other competing disciplines. Finally, as a proud son of Italian immigrants, I felt a kinship with these boxers' struggles, having witnessed my own parents' fight for assimilation, survival and recognition, and their selflessness and sense of purpose and stubborn resoluteness to drive forward, without which many opportunities would have been lost.

Boxing served as a sort of wider societal metaphor in the fight to make it outside your comfort zone, and taken together these concurrent themes were a no-brainer, warranting deserving attention. When I asked friends, family and work colleagues to recall past Italian American boxing champions, the names of Rocky Marciano, Jake La Motta and Rocky Graziano were frequently cited. Beyond those three well-known fighters, however, a massive chasm in knowledge existed, and I therefore felt an enormous responsibility to bring to life the forgotten golden age of the Italian American boxing experience. I have included biographies of all 51 champions and recognized title claimants, as well as listing the hundreds of boxers of elite standing who belonged to a cohort of thousands who reached for the stars. The book is exhaustively researched and contains an impressive list of famous and lesser-known Italian American prizefighters plus a list of interviews with boxing legends Hank Kaplan, Arthur Mercante, Carmen Basilio, Angelo Dundee, Jake La Motta, Willie Pep and Tony De Marco. The reader will learn about Italian American involvement in boxing beginning in the 1880s, and the growth in participation which triggered unrivaled success in the first half of the twentieth century. We carefully analyze the socio-economic, cultural and political factors behind the cohort's rise to the top by exploring comprehensive data on inter-ethnic rivalry within the sport, and the intertwined themes of Italian American ethnicity, ethno-racial identity in boxing and, more broadly, mid-twentieth-century Italian American immigrant culture, which helps our existing understanding of the place of Italian Americans in boxing and in American culture. Despite their having arrived in the United States without any modern pugilistic tradition, the collective success of Italian Americans in the boxing ring was met with little fanfare, and this slice of American popular culture appeared lost in the ether. Significantly, successive generations of Italian Americans also bear responsibility, either too ignorant or too embarrassed to remember the many decorated antecedents in the manly art of boxing. Upon landing in the New World, Italians labored for a stake in the American Dream; and within the confines of bustling and colorful Italian wards most occupations were represented, and the image of the saloonkeeper, barber, organ grinder, street peddler and musician rapidly became synonymous with the Italian newcomer.

Although the role of the Italian American prizefighter is often dismissed from general and intellectual discourse, the most prominently projected *paesani* from the earliest days of settlement through the Depression years and the Second World War were frequently connected to boxing. In an era when boxing films primarily explored working-class masculinity and ethnic assimilation, the film *Kid Galahad* (1937) portrayed a corrupt Italian American fight promoter, Nick Donati, who sees the error of his ways before being shot and killed in this tragic drama. In *Golden Boy* (1939), a film adapted from a Clifford Odets play, Italian culture and American culture is brought into conflict, and a struggle ensues between the father who wants his son to play the violin and further his musical career and his son's ambition to be a prizefighter. In the same year a little-known film entitled *Winner Take All* reinforced the closeness between boxing and Italian Americans. The plot is simple. The Gambinis run a delicatessen store in New York City and as members of the Sons of Garibaldi Social Club they need $5,000 to fund the building of a new recreation hall. The local sportswriter suggests they stage a boxing show and the family agree to the problem-solving proposal. In the post-war period when boxing films began to focus more on racial integration, *Kid Monk Baroni* (1952) is a film drama about the leader of a street gang who becomes a professional boxer to escape his troubles in Little Italy. Directed by Harold Schuster, it features a disfigured central character who finds redemption through boxing, funding the local church's social programs. His generosity wins him back his family, friends and girlfriend, and eventually he becomes the center's new physical education director. This was followed by the box office hit *Somebody Up There Likes Me* (1956), which tells the life story of world champion boxer

Rocky Graziano, and drives home the message that the American Dream is possible, even for a petty criminal no-hoper like Graziano.

During this period, classic American literature also included references to Italian Americans and boxing. In the summer of 1919, Ernest Hemingway, a self-proclaimed boxing fan, wrote an unpublished short story entitled "The Passing of Pickles McCarty." The text refers to a an imaginary character called Nick Neroni, aka Pickles McCarty, a courageous preliminary level Italian American prizefighter who leaves behind the rough and tumble world of the boxing ring to enlist with the *Arditi*, an elite Italian army corps, and help his brethren on the Austro-Italian front of the Great War. The Arthur Miller play *A View from the Bridge*, first published in 1955, confronts the American Dream. Miller wrote about a Brooklyn longshoreman, Eddie Carbone, who welcomes his Sicilian cousins to his American home, giving them refuge and a new start. In the play Eddie's wife refers to Eddie "as a good boxer." Eddie welcomes Rodolpho to attend one of the local fight clubs. He spars with Rodolpho to show him his pugilistic skills, further confirming the familiarity between Italian American working-class culture and boxing. Italian American boxers did not exist in a vacuum, and contrary to the popular depiction that all prizefighters were hordes of semi-literate, anti-intellectual raging dead-end kids the Italian experience revealed something less sinister. Predominantly of Southern Italian origin, the majority, in fact, were honest, upright children of immigrants, stuck between old country attitudes and traditions and the aspirations and ambitions connected to the New World. Many young men boxed to alleviate family poverty. For some, boxing was an add-on to a regular job, but for a large proportion, boxing represented a sporting chance to make quick money. Those who were good enough to reach the top of their profession usually gained a level of financial independence and freedoms not available to the vast majority, and friends and family all benefited from a fighter's progress. Importantly, success in the ring imbued Italian American communities with a sense of pride that one of their own could make it big in America at a time when vertical social and economic mobility was difficult. The growth of television, radio and the print media turned ambitious folk into national heroes, and Italian American fighters became role models for a younger generation of athletes, who marveled at their physical feats and enjoyed a sense of ethnic glorification at a time when "dagoes" were as unpopular as blacks.

This is their story: *The Real Rockys: A History of the Golden Age of Italian Americans in Boxing 1900–1955*. Chapter One presents a general historical overview of pugilistic activity on mainland Italy and evaluates whether any direct correlation existed between boxing success in the United States and these ancient origins. It also introduces the demographic characteristics of the Italian migrant, his passage to the New World in an era dominated by nationalism and xenophobia, and his struggle for assimilation. Chapter Two examines the cultural mentality of the Italian immigrant and the importance for children to undertake paid work, and how the financial lure of boxing brought many into the fold. The pre-boxing occupations of Italian American boxers are studied, and a comparison is made between boxers' purses and wages received from other forms of employment. Chapter Three looks at the thorny question of racial identity inside the boxing ring, tracing the evolution of the name-changing process and how Italian boxers coped with this tradition, and includes one of the biggest collections of Italian American boxers with adopted Irish ring monikers ever assembled.

Chapter Four traces the pre-1900 Italian involvement in an American ring with the emergence of Casper Leon, the first professional boxing icon of Italian heritage. It also chronologically details the milestones and significant events in the success story of the Italian American boxer and presents the elite band of men who became world champions and title claimants. Chapter Five evaluates the ascendancy of the Italian American boxer and inter-ethnic rivalry using yardsticks such as world titles, recognized title claims won, and the total top ten world rankings achieved in each division and in each decade. Chapter Six considers the main recruitment pathways of boxing among Italian American boys and probes these influences in relation to the popularity and success experienced by this ethnic group. Chapter Seven looks at whether the foundation of this success was the result of genetic advantages or a by-product of dedication and hard graft. Chapter Eight assesses Italian involvement in other American sports at a time when boxing and baseball rivaled each other for the country's attention, and asks in which field of sporting activity the Italian emerged as the most successful. Chapter Nine provides the conclusion of the study findings, evaluates life after boxing for the Italian American athlete, and outlines the narrative for what happened next once the golden age of the Italian American boxer ended.

Finally, if anyone is left wondering about the catchy book title and how it relates to the subject matter, let me enlighten you. *The Real Rockys* encapsulates the close association between Italian Americans and boxing as well as managing to embrace their actual achievements in the most competitive of pugilistic époques. Over time the Rocky name became a byword for grit, toughness, determination and courage, a battler who never knows when he's beaten, all traits closely identified with the Italian American boxer, and ubiquitously depicted and described this way by the American media and by Hollywood. It has resonance and symbolism for Italian Americans. There have been three Italian American world boxing champions who have sported the Rocky name, most famously heavyweight champ Rocky Marciano (1952–56) and middleweight champion Rocky Graziano (1947–48), and the lesser-known lightweight titleholder, Rocky Kansas (1925–26). Interestingly, there have been over eighty Italian American fighters that have adopted the Rocky name. This is not a chance occurrence as Rocco is a popular Italian forename, and translates into English as Rocky.

The Real Rockys title pays tribute to fictional boxer Rocky Balboa, the Italian Stallion, perhaps the most famous "boxer" of them all. Some say that Stallone's creation was inspired by African American Joe Frazier, but this is not entirely true. Stallone actually borrowed many elements and influences from a number of real-life boxers to construct a fictional amalgam, a composite of characters. When Rocky Balboa is seen working in a meat-packing plant and part of his training consists of running up the steps of the Philadelphia Museum of Art Stallone is referencing Joe Frazier. That's not all. In a 2005 interview Chuck Wepner, a tough journeyman boxer of German–Ukrainian–American extraction, claimed that Stallone made the original *Rocky* movie based on his 1975 world heavyweight title fight against Muhammad Ali, about his heroics as an underdog who nearly causes a sensational upset. Most importantly the actor pays homage to Rocky Marciano in his films. He copies his fighting style of an awesome brawler who always keeps coming forward, hooking and undercutting. Even Frazier's all-action swarming style earned him the sobriquet in boxing circles of the "Black Marciano." The 1954 Ezzard Charles–Rocky Marciano world title rematch is reportedly the inspiration behind Balboa's win over Apollo Creed in *Rocky II*. Bleeding from a nasty gash on his nose and moments away from the fight being stopped, Marciano turns the tide by scoring a desperate knockout victory over master boxer Charles. Real-life drama transferred onto the big screen by a talented actor/writer. In another blink-and-you'll-miss-it scene, Balboa stares at a wall mirror in his bedroom and the viewer gets a glimpse of Marciano's picture on Balboa's bedside cabinet. Former middleweight champion Joey Giardello is also referenced. When Balboa stops at the church to light a candle to pray for good health and to make it through another fight, well, funnily enough, that's just what Giardello did. The transplanted New Yorker who fought out of Philadelphia often popped into St John's Cathedral to light a candle. Just like Balboa, Giardello lived in the predominantly Italian enclave of South Philadelphia and, similar to another trademark Rocky scene, he frequently completed his training by running up and down the city's market section, being greeted warmly by his friends and neighbors. Giardello, like many of the great Italian American fighters such as Carmen Basilio and Willie Pastrano, routinely knelt in his corner and engaged in prayer and made the sign of the cross before each contest. Rocky Balboa, America's best-loved "boxer," was a fictional creation based on different boxing experiences with the Italian influence never far away. *The Real Rockys* ignores fiction and film. Instead it gives you the straight facts about a long overlooked story in sporting history. Enjoy the book!

1

The beginning
Pugilism in Italy and New World discovery

The golden age of the Italian American prizefighter in the twentieth century has its beginnings loosely rooted in Roman antiquity. These origins date back to the Hellenistic colonization of Southern Italy and gladiatorial combat in ancient Rome, and pugilatus, the forerunner of modern professional boxing, first appeared at the Greek-staged Olympic Games in 688 BC. Back then there were no rings to keep the athletes in a confined space, no weight classes, no rounds and no time limits. Boxers fought in all weather conditions as pugilatus lacked the controls and organization associated with its modern cousin.

At these festivals of sport, where only Pan Hellenic Empire athletes competed, Olympic boxing champions emerged from the Aegean and Ionian Islands, Sparta, Turkey, Macedonia and Southern Italy. Diappos of Kroton (Crotone), Calabria was the first Italo-Greek pugilistic hero, winning the Olympic boxing tournament in 672 BC. Philytas of Sybaris (Sibari), Calabria came next, clinching his title in 616 BC. Tisander of Naxos (Taormina), Sicily won the Olympics and Delphi tournament four times each between 572 and –560 BC. Italian-based Greeks from the Calabria region continued their triumphant tradition when Euthymos of Lokris (Locri) captured a trio of Olympic championships in 484 BC, 476 BC and 472 BC. The Etruscans and the Greeks, both with a strong predilection for physical exercise, introduced boxing to the Romans, and for a time it remained fashionable. Tarquinius Priscus (616–579 BC), the fifth King of Rome, demonstrated the beauty of pugilatus by inviting Etruscan exponents to perform at athletic festivals. The *Ludi Romani* (Roman Games), launched by Tarquinius, mainly consisted of boxing and chariot racing. Boxing became a valued activity for Romans and was even recommended as a cure for vertigo and headaches. Statesman Cato the Elder (234–149 BC) was so fond of the combat discipline he taught it to his son. Virgil, the greatest Roman poet and writer of his generation, introduced boxing in his literary masterpiece. In Book V of the *Aeneid*, a passage contains a vivid description of the fierce boxing match waged between the Trojan Dares and the brave Sicilian Entellus. Boxing was also the preferred sport of Emperor Augustus (27 BC–AD 14), and according to Suetonius, author of the important book *The Twelve Caesars*, Augustus was especially stirred when Italian fighters were pitted against Greek or African rivals. Emperor Caligula (AD 37–41) openly encouraged the recruitment of the best and bravest pugilists from the Campania region and rounded up African slaves in preparation for gladiatorial combat inside the amphitheaters of ancient Rome. Both Emperor Nero (AD 54–68) and Titus (AD 79–81) promoted athletics and boxing. Emperor Maximinus (AD 235–238), a fighter of Herculean strength, is said to have dispensed with rules when fighting his adversaries. Whilst boxing flourished during the classical era it never came close to replacing the Roman national sports of gladiatorial contests and chariot racing.

Medieval and Renaissance period

Strong religious authority combined with the deeply deteriorating living conditions for the masses during the early Middle Ages and medieval period relegated the importance of games and sports to that of frivolous pastimes. Boxing ceased to be important and disappeared from normal view. However, sports were not completely eradicated and fist-fighting activities continued exclusively in Northern Italian cities and their hinterlands between the twelfth and seventeenth centuries. In 1100 Saint Ubaldo, the Bishop of Gubbio, who saved the city from the threatened destruction by German Emperor Frederick Redbeard, openly encouraged boxing in public areas, describing it as "a very useful natural defense," without resorting to weaponry. He recognized the protective element of boxing. Rules were not fixed, and there was no governing body. The Medieval to Renaissance period was characterized by the organization of team boxing matches between rival factions, with famous battles staged in Gubbio, Siena, Cremona, Lucca, Busto Arsizio, Milan, Genoa and Venice. The most famous of these fistfights were held on the isle of Torcello, ten kilometers from Venice, where fights were held on bridges over streams and rivers. In 1420 Saint Bernardino of Siena made his mark when he expressed concern over frequent knife-related deaths and preached the virtues of bare-knuckle fighting. He urged his parishioners to learn about the scientific art of boxing and to use various maneuvers, aimed at blocking incoming blows. Saint Bernardino's notable contributions earned him recognition as the patron saint of boxing.

Three years later Vittorino da Feltre, a humanist scholar, openly preached the virtues of physical exercise. He opened a "playhouse" in Mantova in the northern region of Lombardy where boxing was instructed, but it failed to ferment widespread interest. Unlike England and Russia, where a sporting mentality flourished among the nobility and the country's rulers, development in Italy was slow and sporadic. During the fifteenth century Siena hosted public festivals, which witnessed the involvement of hundreds of contestants in a ritual boxing game called *le pugna* (fists). Despite its popularity the authorities enforced banning orders on participation because of the fatalities and riots it provoked. The existence of *le pugna* is also documented in a Gentile Sermini short story written in 1424. On his visit to Siena in 1494, the Cardinal of San Malo wrote of being entertained by the *pugna* games.

In the early sixteenth century guilds of dyers and weavers in Florence met in specially organized fistfights, usually lasting thirty minutes. In Pisa, the city square staged spectacles which were used as a form of martial exercise as well as sport.[1] Similar events staged in Tuscany were held in North Eastern Italy as Renaissance Venice became quickly associated with the notorious "bridge wars" fought between rival groups using sticks, stones and other armaments. By 1600 the stick fights were replaced by unarmed brawls called *guerre di pugni* (fist wars) which attracted thousands of fighters and tens of thousands of spectators. By 1660 group brawling was substituted with single combat, allowing the Venetian bridge battle contestants to develop and hone fine pugilistic skills in one-to-one boxing contests. The shift in emphasis from armed combat to fisticuffs proved very popular with most of the bridge battle warriors drawn from a pool of working class artisans and laborers. The best champions attracted fame and fortune all over the city.[2] Despite these documented episodes of pugilistic activity, dueling in Italy was still primarily settled with weapons, with preferences extending to using a sword, a pistol, a knife or the stiletto.

Whilst Italy established itself as a world leader in the art of fencing, with schools set up in Naples and in Sicily and with sword masters in demand across Europe, it was England that experienced a meteoric rise in pugilism. England was firmly placed in the vanguard of organized boxing, with an established set of governing rules and the rise of popular champions. It is unclear when controlled boxing matches in Italy began. Some research source material points to around 1720. Pierce Egan wrote in the *Sporting Anecdotes* that "Boxing in Italy began to make its appearance in the crudest form between 1728 and 1732."

Then, in 1731, Italy discovered Tito Alberto Di Carini, a 6-foot 3-inch, 240-pound Venetian giant with a big reputation, who emerged from the same fighting subculture that for almost a century had produced "bridge war" champions in the north eastern region of Friuli Venezia Giulia. In one evening at a European boxing tournament staged in Venice, Di Carini knocked out three adversaries. By chance William Pulteney, the first Earl of Bath, who was traveling through Italy, found himself at ringside. The Earl was thrilled by what he saw and promptly dispatched his observations to Jack Braughton, inventor of the first set of boxing rules. Captain John Godfrey, a boxing writer, alerted James Figg, a master in the art of self-defense and champion boxer, of the threat, and to find a man capable of competing against Di Carini, who was widely known for breaking his opponent's jawbone.

Di Carini was invited to London in 1733 to meet Bob Whitaker, a Yorkshire student of Figg, in what was reportedly the first international boxing match. They met at Figg's amphitheater in Oxford Street, central London. After a promising start, Carini discovered that not all opponents could be silenced with one heavy blow, and the Englishman's body-punching ultimately proved too much for the "Venetian Gondolier." Di Carini returned home and made successful ring appearances in Venice, Milan and Rome before disappearing from the international scene. Di Carini was widely recognized as Italy's first professional boxer. Further evidence of boxing in mainland Italy is contained in the London-based *Sporting Magazine* published by John Wheble in 1793. The journal wrote that "a form of sport, which combined boxing and wrestling, is being fostered in certain hamlets in Italy." In 1820 Egan's *Sporting Anecdotes* printed a story under the caption of "Pugilism in Italy," based upon a publication called *Letters from Italy* written by Stewart Rose, a poet, translator and politician. Egan reported that "boxing in different forms, is now common all over Tuscany, but is reduced to least perfection in the capital."

The town of Siena projected a more "scientific" form of boxing, with its academies schooling converts in pugilistic exercises and a code of rules. Whilst Vicenza and Florence also witnessed contests with unarmed fists the same could not be said for Pisa and Livorno, which saw fist duels where rivals wore sharpened sticks strapped to their clenched hands. Each blow delivered was designed to inflict maximum damage to an opponent, evoking the era of the gladiatorial cestus.[3] In the nineteenth century notable author, journalist and critic, Niccolò Tommaseo defined pugilism as a "game played in the style of *pugna*: much used among the Greeks and carried on up until the recent years among the Sienese." His description confirmed that it was a primitive activity, lacking the science and subtleties associated with English-style boxing.[4]

In the last decade of the nineteenth century Italian newspapers reflected a growing interest in boxing, referring to the sport as "virile" and "extraordinarily exciting." In 1897 an "English boxing" gymnasium was set up in Milan. The Paris-based venue La Salle Wagram staged English-style boxing matches, featuring Italian boxers, which was particularly fashionable with well-heeled Italian patrons traveling to the French capital. Boxing clubs appeared and promotions were staged, but it wasn't until the First World War that the sport spread to the rest of the Italian peninsula. Pietro Boine, the Italian heavyweight boxing champion, was the main instigator behind the structured activity. In 1912 he founded the National Boxing Club in Milan, and a year later Boine traveled across the country staging exhibition bouts. Boxing in Italy remained a northern-dominated sport, evidenced by the number of champions hailing from the regions of Friuli Venezia Giulia, Lombardy, Tuscany and Emilia Romagna.

In 1916 the Italian Boxing Federation was founded. European heavyweight champion Erminio Spalla became the first big international box office star, and he campaigned during the First World War through to the twenties. The advent of Fascism thrust sport to the forefront of popular culture as athleticism, physicality and strength were fundamental elements vigorously promoted and propagandized by Benito Mussolini. The dictator saw boxing as "an exquisitely fascist means of self-expression" and even compared boxing to war.[5] In 1928 the first live radio broadcast of a sports event was a boxing match held in Milan. Mussolini's desire to project an image of a strong and dynamic nation abroad, able to compete against other superpowers, bore fruit through the regime's athletic programs. Italy won boxing medals at successive Olympiads and throughout the twenties and thirties produced world-class fighters like Saverio Turiello, Aldo Spoldi, Enrico Venturi, Cleto Locatelli, Bruno Frattini and Michele Palermo. Mussolini used sport to glorify his fascist ideals, and he presided over the export of a number of Italian behemoths to America designed to capture the world heavyweight title. Although the likes of Roberto Roberti,

Riccardo Bertazzolo, Arthur DeKuh, Salvatore Ruggirello and Innocente Baiguera were stunning examples of masculinity, it was not until 1933 that Primo Carnera of Sequals, Udine lifted the heavyweight championship, becoming the first Italian to win a world professional boxing title. Repeated world championship success eluded Italy until the late fifties and sixties.

From a historical perspective, besides the distant heritage of ancient Greek combatants, born and raised in the regions of Calabria, Puglia and Sicily, and Roman pugilists pooled from the ancient tribes of Southern Italy, boxing development in Italy was uniquely a Northern Italian sporting and cultural phenomenon. Significantly, Southern Italians arrived in the United States with no modern pugilistic tradition or experience. Within a generation they developed a sporting interest and subsequently emerged from behind the shadows of Irish American hegemony to occupy the most prominent position in boxing. This was exclusively a New World discovery, rooted in the difficult transition from life as an uprooted migrant to a besieged settler in the towns and cities of America.

Uprooted migrant to besieged settler

So how did this happen? Well, before we analyze the Italian entry into the world of American pugilism it is important to establish a general framework for the story, and acknowledge that without large-scale Italian emigration many heroes of American sport and culture would never have surfaced. The main characteristics of the Italian exodus to the United States, the migrant's overall socio-economic and political position, his profile, settlement and employment patterns and anti-Italian sentiment offer a vital insight into the social origins of the Italian American boxing experience and the subsequent proliferation of these sportsmen, who were not immune from the collective struggles and sustained persecution. Decades after his arrival the uprooted Italian migrant still faced the harsh realities of a besieged settler, and assimilation into the mainstream was beset with problems and complications.

Italian emigration in the late nineteenth century and the early part of the twentieth century is characterized by multiple mass movements of people to the New World. Whilst there were large migratory shifts in continental Europe, namely to France, it was the Northern Italian-led immigration to Latin American countries like Argentina and Brazil and the Southern Italian exodus to the United States that defined this period of Italian migration. The mass flight from the Southern Italian provinces began in the 1880s, and by 1914 over three million migrants had left *Il Mezzogiorno* (Southern Italy) for the United States. A series of crucial factors triggered this migratory shift. Overpopulation placed great demands on meager resources and between the mid and late 1880s the natural birth rate quadrupled. Despite the safety valve of emigration the population increased by six million between 1860 and 1910. Agriculture underpinned the Southern Italian economy, and the exploitative and efficient Northern-dominated government strangled the South with onerous tax and state tariffs, forcing small landholders to the wall.

There were additional strains on the Italian economy. American competition hampered the fruit-growing regions of Southern Italy. The olive fly repeatedly destroyed crop harvests, and outbreaks of malaria wrecked lives. Disease, pests and acts of God all contributed to a prevailing sense of desperation. A series of natural disasters culminating in the 1908 earthquake and tidal wave which struck Sicily and the Italian mainland, killing one hundred thousand people, convinced many to prepare for a new beginning. Decisions to leave were made easier as news filtered through to family and friends in Italy that vastly higher salaries in agriculture and across the employment spectrum were possible in the United States.

Migrant profile

The image of impoverished peasants from the lowest depths of Italian society leaving for the United States has dominated scholarship on this subject, but closer analysis reveals that the extremely poor seldom left. Historian John Bodnar argues that it was members of the middle and lower middle levels of the peasantry, artisans, craftsmen and others with skills rendered obsolete by rapid commercialization and industrialization that contributed to the mass flight.

The academic John Briggs studied three American cities—Rochester, Utica and Kansas City—and concluded that those likely to emigrate were agriculturists or townsmen who held a "stake in society" in the form of property. The lower strata day laborers were least likely to leave because either they couldn't afford to, or they were contracted to work the estates of the landowners. Briggs found that 54 percent of Sicilian passports checked between 1901 and 1914 were either fishermen or skilled tradesmen.[6] Of those entering New York City, an above average number were small landowners, artisans and petty merchants. Over half of those leaving from Abruzzi and Molise were from construction and excavation, and the figure for the trades among departures from Sicily and Calabria was over 30 percent.[7] Southern Italians resisted emigration, remaining longer in the face of adversity. They were more conservative and poorer than their Northern cousins and originally intended to earn enough money to return home with an enhanced status. This affinity and deep attachment was reflected in repatriation rates. Between 1892 and 1896, 43 out of every 100 Italians immigrating to the United States returned home, and this figure rose to 73 between 1907 and 1911. The sex ratios also pointed to a temporary sojourn. During peak Italian migration 80 percent were male and over 83 percent fell into the productive 14-to-44 age category, whereas Jewish migration, the other mass influx of this period, revealed that the group emigrated as a family unit. Italian settlement became more permanent after 1910.[8]

Settlement and employment patterns

The geographical dispersal of Italian settlement leant heavily on the points of entry, and commonly this was New York, Boston and New Orleans. Since 97 percent landed in New York, and many had used up all their savings, immigrants found shelter and work there, chiefly in Lower Manhattan, and it remained the most densely populated Italian metropolitan area in the United States. The expansion of the railroads and the demands of industry influenced settlement patterns, and it was through the *padrone* (employment agents) that unskilled Italians were transported across the country to work on railroads, in mines and in agriculture.

In Massachusetts they worked in the shoe factories of Brockton and in the woolen mills of Lawrence. They were represented in the silk dyers of New Jersey, and in the mines of Pennsylvania and Illinois. They invaded the garment industry of New York and Philadelphia, and established dominance in the hairdressing trade with over half the barbershops in Philadelphia, Buffalo, Pittsburgh and St Louis being Italian.[9] In Louisiana, Nevada and California, sons of Italian immigrants were most numerous as farmers and agricultural laborers, but this represented only 1 percent of the overall national occupational total. In Colorado and Alabama, they mostly occupied roles in manufacturing and mining and served as miners, quarrymen and iron and steel workers. By 1910, most Italian males were pick and shovel laborers, with thousands sent to railroad construction camps, and in all major cities Italians were involved in the construction of streets, sewers, bridges and subways, and any large-scale building project that required heavy-duty excavation.

Whilst past occupational studies routinely show an overwhelming presence of the Italian laborer in all areas of the reconstruction process, closer scrutiny of the social origins of the Italian American boxer reveals a distinct pattern found within two sectors of employment. In a sample of 295 fathers of Italian American pugilists, the largest single group of 44 percent predictably comprised of laborers engaged in construction, railroad work, mining and agriculture, as well as operatives working in factories and manufacturing plants. Like other newly arrived ethnic groups, Italians, and specifically the Italian boxers' fathers, found jobs in the expanding sectors of manufacturing and construction. However, the second largest group of 33 percent were involved in locally based small business ventures, occupied in running saloons, restaurants, farms, grocery stores, shoe shops, barbershops and jewelers. The occupational sample shows that Italian boxers' fathers formed part of a category of small businessmen providing services to their wards and districts. They displayed a degree of ambition and single-minded individualism and captured the mood and spirit of the age in attempting to deliver better futures for their families. Interestingly, the third largest group is filled by artisan/traders, representing 9 percent of the total sample. (See Appendix I.)

So the overriding perception that boxers primarily emerged from the *lumpenproletariat* or the social underclass, and the belief that only deprived youth turned to boxing because of its violent and brutal nature, is not so clear cut in relation to the Italian American cohort. Italian boxers' families essentially belonged to a materialistic working class that usually owned some property. Many were middle class in aspiration if not by income, as small business owners were still relatively poor. To some extent the sample data debunks the age-old thesis that the Italian American boxer emanated solely from the social underclass, one where the familial structure was based on the father being inactive or restricted to toiling as either a laborer or a factory hand. Generally speaking, Italian immigrants were not beggars, outcasts or unemployed. They were neither destitute nor from the lowest depths of society, and compared to poor Americans of white stock, Italians that settled in the United States found work. Of those that lost their jobs and struggled to find new employment it usually resulted in a return to the old country. In fact, over half of those who traveled to the United States returned home, and it is unlikely that Italian immigrants living in the United States formed part of a recognized urban underclass. What is irrefutable is that the position of the Italian in American society was rendered burdensome by large families and the many mouths to feed in each household. This inevitably placed a strain on overall family expenditure. Evidence also shows that Italian artisans and shopkeepers were not wealthy. They were more comfortable than most, and most definitely not desperate. Although my occupational sample size is relatively small, it still presents a fascinating picture of the structure and mobility of employment, and it shows that perhaps conventional wisdom has exaggerated the link between pugilism and the underclass, especially among Italian American boxers' families in the first half of the twentieth century.

Anti-Italian sentiment

Prevalent discrimination throughout American society was responsible for slowing down the degree of acculturation and assimilation and exacerbating tensions among Italian Americans. The Italians experienced one of the vilest and most racist campaigns ever targeted against any ethnic group, where prejudice turned to lynching. The emotive question of race and immigration provided the ruling elites with a subtext to browbeat the most vulnerable, and the continuous influx of Italian migrants disconcerted many who feared for the very foundations of White Anglo-Saxon Protestant (WASP) society. Their response was strange because, on the one hand, a booming economy required Italian muscle and subservience to fuel the extraordinary growth story, but on the other they complained about the very people underpinning such progress.

The Italian immigrant was no stranger to intellectual criticism, having been subjected to special treatment by the race theorists back home. Criminologist Cesare Lombroso and sociologist Alfredo Niceforo were among the best-known scholars of nineteenth-century Italy, and their work illustrated that people from *Il Mezzogiorno* were racially inferior to their Northern cousins. Lombroso held the view that delinquency was hereditary and theorized that Southern Italians possessed the physical hallmarks of criminals. Racial science established a momentum among the leading thinkers of the age and the controversial establishment of a hierarchical structure of human races was developed, placing the Nordic and Teutonic peoples at the head of these race classifications.

At the highest levels of American society the perceived threat posed by the Italian to the status quo produced a hysterical response based on deeply rooted stereotypes of the *meridionali* (Southern Italians). The Dillingham Commission refused to classify Italians as white and academics labeled them an "in-between" race. During the Great War era, the *Saturday Evening Post*, a mouthpiece of disgruntled intellectuals called Southern Europeans "a hybrid race of good for nothing MONGRELS . . ." This publication was generally credited to have contributed to the slowness of acceptance of the

Italian in American society. In 1916 Madison Grant, the founder and chairman of the New York Zoological Society, echoed similar themes in *The Passing of the Great Race*. David Starr Jordan, Stanford University President, referred to Southern Italians as "biologically incapable" in the *Congressional Record,* and just for good measure added: "There is not one in a thousand from Naples or Sicily that is not a burden on America. Our social perils do not arise from the rapacity of the strong, but from the incapacity of the hereditarily weak."[10]

Not even the Church safeguarded them from overt forms of racism. Whether it be the predominantly Irish-controlled Catholic Church or the Protestant equivalent, Italians were frequently denounced as "dagoes" and made to sit at the back with black people. Between 1921 and 1922, following a sustained public backlash, immigration quota controls and discriminatory "Mental Tests for Immigrants" became part of the legal apparatus, which especially penalized Italian migrants, curtailing this source of migration to a manageable figure of ten thousand per year. Aryan purity was now safeguarded from the Italian menace. A staple diet of powerful stereotypes depicting the Italian as violent, corrupt, lazy and untrustworthy fueled the insecurities of ordinary Americans. Was any of this rooted in fact or was it just plain fiction?

Organized crime

The murder of New Orleans police chief David Hennessy in 1891 sparked the largest lynching in American history. Following the acquittal of eleven innocent Italians, a mob of hundreds broke into the jail and murdered them. An unrepentant *New York Times* fumed:

> These sneaking and cowardly Sicilians, the descendants of bandits and assassins, who have transported to this country the lawless passions, the cutthroat passions and the oath bound societies of their native country, are to us a pest without mitigation. Lynch law was the only recourse open to the people of New Orleans.[11]

Episodes like this helped to establish and spread the most pervasive myth that the Italian was a gangster and pivotal in organized crime, a view that became firmly embedded in the American psyche and confirmed their dread about the Southern Italian immigrant. The authorities reacted with hysteria and violence to a fear of a supposed Italian criminal conspiracy. The reality told a different story, one which presented the Italian as the victim. In 1894 in Altoona, Pennsylvania two hundred Italians were driven out by an armed mob. Five years later a mob dragged and lynched five Italians in Tallulah, Louisiana because three Sicilian shopkeepers permitted blacks equal status in their shops. Between 1885 and 1915, some fifty Italians were murdered in Colorado, Florida, Illinois, Kentucky, Louisiana, Mississippi, New York and Washington.[12]

There was no rational justification for these actions. Heightened public anxieties unfairly placed the Italian in the eye of the storm, but the facts pointed elsewhere. In 1903 police reports filed in Boston and New York City indicated that Italians were no more a criminal threat than any other foreign-born group, with most crime Italian upon Italian, and violence rarely spread outside their city enclaves.[13] In 1910 the Report on Immigration and Crime stated that Italians were responsible for the highest number of violent personal offences in New York City, but there was nothing unusual about this as these crimes were relative to population size.[14] The report suffered from uncorroborated press reports and dubious police data, at a time when inter-ethnic societal feuding between the Irish and Italian was rife. Objectivity was in short supply within the New York City Police Department, largely made up of Irish officers, and all criminal acts involving Italians were seen to have a direct link to organized crime. This enduring stereotype obsessed the nation, and the activities of notorious figures such as Al Capone, Lucky Luciano and Frank Costello during the twenties and thirties pushed Hollywood into making the image stick permanently.

Sacco and Vanzetti injustice

In the pre-First World War era Italians in the United States championed the need to stand up for improved pay and conditions. They played a central role in the founding of unions and were actively engaged in the bloody West Virginia Mine Wars. Unfairly painted as anarchists who sought to start a revolution, undesirable Italians were rounded up and deported upon the orders of attorney general Mitchell Palmer, whose job it was to stop the "Red Scare." In April 1920, legal political events took a nasty turn when two innocent men, Nicola Sacco and Bartolomeo Vanzetti, were arrested over the murder of two guards in South Braintree, Massachusetts. Despite frequent protests and appeals, and still without a shred of evidence, the men were executed by electric chair in August 1927. A merciless anti-Italian bias dogged any chance of a fair trial for the accused. The state-approved slaughter of Sacco and Vanzetti sent shock waves among Italian communities, particularly in Brockton's Ward Two Italian neighborhood, only a mile away from the alleged crime, where Rocky Marciano's family lived. Like many Italians, Marciano's grandfather Luigi Picciuto was enraged by the outcome, which only confirmed the deep Italian mistrust of authority. "These bastards, they make us suffer. They have no love," he exclaimed.[15]

Four months after Sacco and Vanzetti were arrested Italian people of all ages living in the mining town of West Frankfort, Illinois were dragged out of their houses, beaten and their homes burnt to the ground. The besieged Italian community fought back though, and it took five hundred law enforcement officials three days to restore order. Historian John Higham wrote: "no pogrom has ever stained American soil, nor did any single anti-Jewish incident in the 1920s match the violence of the [mob-led] anti Italian riot."[16] These events left many Italians angry, unprotected and with a sense that fighting back was the only way forward. Sam Tornatore came to the United States as a ten-year-old to work in the cotton fields of Louisiana. After witnessing the lynching of three Italians in nearby Mississippi he pledged to fight prejudice "with his fists."[17] This combative streak was replicated nationwide. Enrico Vecchione grew up in New York's Lower East Side Manhattan district during the twenties. He recalled the inter-ethnic tensions:

> When I was a little boy the Irish ran everything. They used to make fun of the Italians. They had an attitude. As we grew older we realized that we would have to protect ourselves and our property, and most of us decided to take up boxing as a way of protecting ourselves. Not all of us became professional boxers or amateurs but we could all fight. The neighborhood I grew up was strictly controlled by the Irish. St Patrick's Church is still here and is a testament to the days the Irish were on top but we stood up and changed all that.[18]

None of the events or anti-Italian fever that swept across the country singularly contributed to a wholesale shift in mentality among young men. However, seen in the context of a period where economic hardship and legitimate business and political opportunities were scarce, Italians realized early on that sport, particularly prizefighting, was one way to bring about economic gain and freedom from societal constraints. It became an asset to be good with your fists, especially when family livelihoods depended on it.

2

The dollar is king

Most Italians, irrespective of occupational background, began life in the lower levels of the American economy. Life was a struggle and paltry wages shattered expectations of upward mobility. For example, among Buffalo's Italians in the early 1900s a family of four needed $650 to $772 per year on which to subsist, but between 1890 and 1916 the average Italian laborer earned $364 to $624.[1] In 1912 the Immigrant Commission's Report documented that the Southern Italian earned $600, one of the lowest yearly incomes out of sixty ethnic groups in the United States with only the African American and Serbian on lower wages. Supportive government data showed that the Italian made around $12.50 per week.[2]

Faced with this stark reality it wasn't difficult to figure why so many Italian Americans chose prizefighting. Young men of all races stepped into the boxing world incentivized by the promise of fortune. "There was an easier way," says boxing historian Hank Kaplan. "You could work all week long for five dollars or you could fight, get a professional fight and bring home $20–$25 in one night."[3] For the less educated money was the catalyst. The attraction was easily sold even though boxing did not offer a safety net of medical provision or pension entitlement.

In 1894 Casper Leon picked up a purse of two hundred dollars, following his twenty-eighth-round world title defeat to Jimmy Barry. His purse equated to about $7,813 in 1998 values. Hardly a king's ransom, but it's worth remembering that the vast majority paid no income tax back then and all income was generated from gate receipts only. There were no additional income streams from film, radio, television or pay-per-view services.[4] Boxers of this era also supplemented their purses by wagering side bets on the outcome of fights. In comparison with other fields of employment in the American labor market, Leon's purse illustrates the financial standing of prizefighting. In 1900 the average schoolteacher in the United States made $330 a year, and those that completed a university education struggled to command an annual salary upwards of a thousand dollars.

In baseball the average salary awarded to stars of the diamond in 1901 stood at $2,000 per season and a decade later had increased by 50 per cent. Good salaries for the era, but way off the level of earnings set by boxing champions, contenders and Class A pugs over the same period.[5] In a headline bout staged on September 29, 1903 between Benny Yanger (Benjamin Angona) and Eddie Hanlon, the *Chicago Daily Tribune* reported that the Italian received 35 percent of gross box office receipts totaling $7,500.[6]

It was clear that high-ranking pugilists made more money in one major bout than the average worker grossed in a single year. Former heavyweight champion James Corbett, turned influential paper columnist, openly declared that the balance of power during the decade from 1900 to 1910 had shifted towards the prizefighter, with contenders demanding a larger cut before appearing. In December 1908, Hugo Kelly (Ugo Micheli) fought Billy Papke in one of the decade's middleweight super fights, and the Italian netted over $2,000 in their twenty-five-round drawn bout.

It was a similar story elsewhere (see Appendix II). Professional boxers benefited even in the provincial localities of New York. In 1914 headline boxers made between $250 and $300 per fight on Rochester boxing cards. Four-round preliminary fighters drew between $10 and $20 based upon an average attendance of 500 to 1,200 people. In 1915 news spread like wildfire through Italian colonies in the United States that Johnny Dundee (Giuseppe Carrara), a leading fighter of his era, was raking in between $25,000 and $30,000 per year. Five years later Dundee reportedly amassed an estimated fortune of $250,000, having competed in hundreds of bouts, sometimes as many as five a month.

The twenties represented an era of prosperity for boxers as they achieved higher purses across all weight divisions, reflecting a more commercialized orientation characterized by the first million-dollar gate. The *National Police Gazette*, long regarded as the most populist supporter of boxing, reported in the winter of 1920 that "pugilism is now the highest paid of all vocations. In the race for wealth today brawn wins over brains.

The present crop of boxers are in the moneyed class." The editorial summed up the importance of money in an age of fun and frivolity, and poked fun at the educated elites, pointing out that "bank presidents work for less in a year than some of the first class boxers get in a single night."

The paper proclaimed that boxers and promoters had never had it so good, adding that whilst $10,000 purses were rare in bygone ages contenders were now turning up their noses at such figures in ten-round no-decision contests. Middleweight champion Johnny Wilson (Giovanni Panico) refused to defend his title in Boston against Mike O'Dowd for a $25,000 purse. He was accused of playing hardball and holding out for more. During this period Italian champions and contenders benefited from the rich pickings. Pete Herman, world bantamweight champion, was said to be worth $125,000 and fellow bantamweight rival Little Jack Sharkey (Giovanni Cervati) made $75,000.[7]

The Great Depression took its toll at the box office, however. Declining attendances resulted in a drastic cut in purse money, especially at smaller boxing venues, paying as little as $20 for a preliminary and semi-wind-up category fighter, representing an average fall of between 50 and 60 percent. Madison Square Garden in New York retained its luster, though, and every boxer in the country still aspired for a slot on a boxing card there. After all, that's where the real money was. A main eventer was still guaranteed thousands of dollars per fight. Other top fight venues in the Big Apple paid a main event pugilist between $500 and $600. Not in the same league, but in troubled times top-ranking prizefighters were rewarded for their abilities, and fighters generally earned larger sums than their fellow brethren stuck on poverty-level wages.

Depression-era boxing compared favorably to other sports. In January 1937 Joe DiMaggio of the New York Yankees was reportedly awarded a $10,000-a-year contract. His teammate, Tony Lazzeri had been on a $12,000-a-year rolling contract since 1931, and six years later, following his Most Valuable Player performances, he was given a one-thousand-dollar-a-year top-up. Whilst boxing custom ensured the heavyweights commanded the highest purses, a simple comparison between baseball's elite set against three Italian American headliners reveals the pay gap. At just one New York boxing promotion, billed the Carnival of Champions, staged on September 23, 1937 at the Polo Grounds, Lou Ambers, lightweight champion, received $65,000 in a title defense. Fred Apostoli, middleweight title challenger, got $5,000 against Marcel Thil and Harry Jeffra received $2,500 in winning the world bantamweight championship. All three fighters closed out the year by appearing twelve, eight, and eleven times respectively, having grossed far more in one year than DiMaggio and Lazzeri. These fighters were by no means the most famous in circulation either. The financial appeal of boxing was undeniable.[8]

The forties brought a return to larger purses, with additional increments derived from television money. Italian Americans were prominent fixtures. Contenders Tony Janiro and Joe Miceli never captured world boxing titles but their earning power was impressive. Between 1942 and 1951 middleweight aspirant Janiro grossed $650,000 in 125 bouts, appearing in sixteen big Madison Square Garden contests. Joe Miceli, perennial welterweight contender of this period, averaged $50,000 to $60,000 per year.

The champions were on a higher pay scale. Middleweight champion Joey Giardello made over one million dollars in 139 fights. In retirement Rocky Graziano confessed to being a millionaire. Jake La Motta amassed an estimated half a million dollars, and in seven world title fights between 1952 and 1955 Rocky Marciano made $1,460,388 from combined purses and television money. Carmen Basilio collected his biggest purse of $215,639 when he beat Sugar Ray Robinson in September 1957. Amazing sums at a time when National Boxing Association President Fred Saddy observed that the "average pay of the average man doesn't amount to $20 a week in US currency. The lad who becomes a pro fighter can earn twice or three times that amount for a six round bout."[9]

Illiteracy and child labor

It wasn't difficult to understand the allure of boxing within tightly knit and heavily populated Italian enclaves where news of success traveled fast. Of course, there were other underlying social problems that provided fertile ground for boxing recruitment. Southern Italians were handicapped by illiteracy. A report documenting the period between 1899 and 1909 illustrated that 54.2 percent of Southerners fourteen years or over could not read or write. Given that the educational system in Italy was the preserve of the affluent, and that government disinterest was matched by derisory expenditure in the South, this is a rather predictable outcome.[10]

The first problem the American educational authorities encountered was the extent of child labor among Italian families. Children had aided the process of subsistence farming in Southern Italy and Sicily, and now fulfilled their labor obligations in the New World by working before and after school hours. Italian boys were commonly engaged as shoe shiners, rag pickers, newsboys and general and domestic cleaners. New Orleans boxer Pete

Herman (Pietro Gulotta), a two-time world bantamweight champion in 1917 and again in 1921, represented a familiar story. He recalled: "When I was twelve years old, my daddy looked at me and he said, 'Twelve years lost.' I knew what he meant by that. He meant to go to work, find yourself a job, and go to work." Herman found employment as a shoeshine boy inside a barber shop and before long was earning ten dollars a week, enough to support his family. Soon afterwards his father quit his job as a banana carrier on the Mississippi river. A source of much satisfaction for Herman, but he wanted a lot more. He liked boxing and saw it as his passport to better things. At the age of sixteen he turned professional.[11]

The downside of working had a marked effect on progress in school—or lack of it. In 1902, the Chicago-based *L'Italia* newspaper wrote that as a result of an "old country attitude" Italian children were put to work at the first opportunity, and they secured jobs after school to an "alarmingly high degree."[12] In 1908 a survey of fifteen Manhattan schools in New York showed that 36 percent of Italians were left behind compared to 23 percent of Jews who had arrived in the same numbers at the same time. The study showed that none of the Italians who entered high school graduated, while 16 percent of Jews received a diploma.[13]

Battling Reddy (Luigi Nobile) from New York's Lower East Side fought in over one hundred and fifty professional bouts between 1910 and 1923. He summed up the importance of paid work to the Italian:

> When I was a kid school was a nuisance. Unless he wanted to become a doctor, or a lawyer or a civil engineer the average kid couldn't see the sense in going to school. Once he learnt to read and write and add two and two that was all the education he needed. Folks used to raise big families in those days and it was a tough grind on the old man to support a wife and an army of kids. So the kids would quit school when they could and hustle around for jobs to help out at home. If they could fight a bit there was always a chance to pick up an extra buck or two at night, boxing in preliminaries at many clubs around. It was nothing for some of us to fight three or four nights a week, and if we had ten dollars or fifteen dollars clear for ourselves at the end of the week that was a lot of money in those days. Aside from money boxing was a sport to us. We enjoyed it and we were always trying to learn and improve. That's why we'd never pass up a chance to see the headliners either in the ring or in the gym always studying and practising.[14]

The lack of progress in education extended nationwide. Between 1890 and 1920 the Italians of Tampa, Florida saw schooling as representing a significant loss of earnings. Parents looked at the prosperity of the cigar-making industry and as far as they were concerned it made no sense to educate their sons and daughters.[15]

John De John (Di Gianni), boxing manager and trainer, highlighted the need of Italian boys to work during the twenties. He explained:

> They can talk about Hell's Kitchen in New York, but we came from the toughest neighborhood any kid could imagine. We came from North Franklin Street in Syracuse, surrounded by railroad tracks and factories. Only a quarter of a block and we must have been over one hundred kids living in a small block. The kids would fight on the streets. Then they got smart and they used to go and box and pick up a few bucks. It was better than swinging a pick and shovel or working in a dirty factory. In them days you had a lot of fight clubs. Also when we were growing up you think they sent us to school. The minute we got to be twelve or thirteen we had to get a job. It's all changed now.[16]

Most Southern Italians, especially from Sicily, arrived between 1900 and 1914, and they grew to maturity at a time when educational requirements were important when qualifying for jobs in public as well as in private employment. The political, social and financial patterns which sped the assimilation of Germans, Irish, Bohemians, Swedes and Norwegians grew more rigid as earlier immigrant attitudes hardened. The early arrivals established barriers preventing later migrants from challenging their position and early Northern Italian settlers did not consider "Southerners to be of their own."[17] The sons of Italians fared little better, and though statistically fewer, they were still concentrated in manual labor. First-generation Italians continued to stand out in the domestic and personal category in New York where as common laborers they constituted about half of the total Italian workforce.[18]

Pre-boxing occupations of boxers

The occupational activities of Italian American professional boxers either before or alongside their fighting careers are consistent with the old country view that children best served the interests of the family by contributing towards the family economy. Out of a study sample of 172 children, 21 percent found employment within the manufacturing sector. The next biggest contribution came from helpers in the family business, representing 10.5 percent of the total sample. Ten percent worked as newsboys, and 7 percent worked as either bootblacks or general laborers. Six percent of the total sample worked as newly qualified tradesmen. This experience was indicative of a nationwide phenomenon of work culture and ethic. The Italian simply did not take advantage of the new opportunities in education in a resurgent America, and fell behind in the race to join the expanding middle classes as accomplished by the established ethnic groups and education savvy Jewish cohort. (See Appendix III.)

For decades urban slum living worsened the alienating school experience for Italian-born and second-generation Italian American children. Some reported their anxieties and inferiority as being linked to the Italian language and general appearance, finding the school environment "strange and unfamiliar, disturbing and disquieting."[19] The early years were characterized by high drop-out rates and rampant truancy as children looked to earn a living. Not even federal labor legislation of 1916, designed to extend the education of immigrant children, changed much, and for Southern Italian children living in New York City during the twenties and thirties it was still a "heroic struggle" to get a college education.[20] The truancy and dropouts among Italian American males were still several times higher than for other students in the thirties and forties.[21]

Boxing's extraordinary social and cultural ascendancy coincided with the Italian's zest for quick monetary gain. Angelo Dundee, boxing manager, described the attractiveness of boxing to the Italian.

> It was everything. It was a way of life. Boxing got them away from being the shoeshine boy or the guy digging trenches. It was tough working, tough getting a job. You had to have a college education and most Italian kids didn't have a college education. They barely were able to get out of high school. They had to learn a new language. I mean it was tough.[22]

Options were limited without further educational qualifications. When champion boxer Tony De Marco started out his professional career in 1948 he picked up between $75 and $100 for six-round contests and made between $2,500 and $15,000 as a main event fighter. He said: "I made good money in those days. Where could I have earned as much money if I wasn't boxing?"[23]

Young men entering boxing was consistent with the thesis that Italian American boys left school or worked part time to support the family's aspiration for wealth, primarily manifested through property ownership. In 1888 novelist Giovanni Verga captured this mood in his literary masterpiece *Mastro Don Gesualdo*, in which he details the Sicilian admiration and near obsession for *l'accumulo* (the accumulation of riches) and holding on to and expanding *la roba* (property and possessions) to ensure societal status and power. This desire for individual and familial prestige and progress was not a New World discovery but was one deeply entrenched in the Italian psyche, especially among Sicilians and Southern Italians. The frontier mentality prevalent in America merely provided immigrants and their offspring a greater freedom of individual adventure to steadily build family businesses and personal fortunes. The ineffectiveness of the education system combined with the pressing demands placed on Italian children to exit school and enter the labor market was an uncomfortable reality, and for some this experience meant that the economics of boxing was unrivaled.

3

When a Mick is a Dago

Identity crisis or badge of convenience?

In professional boxing the running gag was: "When is an Irishman not an Irishman?" Answer: "When he is Italian." The intention is to be neither facetious nor deliberately misleading, but to highlight the questionable practice that prevailed during the early part of the twentieth century when most boxers of Italian ancestry assumed an Irish *nom de guerre*. To the untrained eye, it seemed that there were no noteworthy American fighters of Italian origin, and overall they had a rather limited presence in the noble art prior to the twenties, but this would be wrong. Behind an Irish name there frequently stood an olive-skinned, dark-haired battler with matching Italian identity. The industrial scale of this nationwide phenomenon is represented in a table showing hundreds of fighters with their Hibernian boxing monikers and real cognomens. (See Appendix IV)

So why did so many Italian American fighters change their names? One explanation is that during the period from 1880 to 1910, which was marked by mass Italian immigration to the United States, the Irish dominated boxing and the heavyweight title and John L. Sullivan and Jim Corbett were among several champions who established the Irish as all-conquering. A sort of false tradition lingered that nobody could be successful in the ring unless they had an Irish name. Very simplistic stuff, but this view was widely peddled and supported at the time. Italian fighters warmed to the idea and the superstitious among them didn't want careers to stall even before they had set foot in the ring.

Others preferred camouflage as it avoided the attentions of disapproving parents, especially from their mothers, who might be distressed about their son's career choice and the fear of injury. Unlike Jewish mothers who considered boxing activity shameful, the Italian was primarily concerned about overall safety.

Many careers were interrupted and short-lived. Joey Cilione was an aspiring amateur boxer from Hester Street on Manhattan's Lower East Side, and a good friend of Ben Jeby, the world middleweight champion. Cilione taunted the Jewish boxer in training that he would seize his title one day. He boxed briefly during the thirties, but Cilione did not turn professional.

> I missed out on becoming the middleweight champion. I became interested in boxing and took up the sport under an assumed name. I kept it away from my mother because she was a worrier. My father had an idea but [he] didn't worry about it. I went to [New] Jersey to try out with manager [Babe] Orlando] I was told, "Don't leave your fighting in the amateurs, you'll burn out." I went along. My father didn't say no or yes. "Whatever you do don't get in trouble."
>
> A couple of months before Primo Carnera killed Ernie Schaff [February 10, 1933], my mother is all ears. I tell her that I will be gone for a couple of weeks, you don't have to worry. I'm going to box on a show. She said: "You are going to fight?" I said: "Listen, Mum, I'll make enough money to take care of you. You don't have to worry." She said: "I don't want your money. I want you as you are." Holy Gosh! I damn well knew that if I was to go under those conditions, it wouldn't do either of us any good. Should she have a stroke what would happen to the family? I couldn't sleep nights. What am I gonna do with my mother? I'm not broke. My father's in business and the family is together. I might start something that could create an argument. Is it worth it? I gave it up.[1]

It's easy to see here how much parental disapproval caused personal turmoil and uncertainty for the boxer. It's hardly surprising Italian boxers chose to hide their pugilistic activities from their mothers because careers would not have got off the ground. Italian sons held a special bond with their mothers. They were devoted and tried hard not to upset or disappoint them, fully aware of the tough daily grind of looking after large families. Boxing participation tested these relationships, and in such cases the protection of a boxer's anonymity was vital. In many instances the mother only became aware of her son's participation when he was firmly established and brought home relatively large sums, which he handed over to her.

Adopted names were also applied for practical reasons. Newspaper reporters were guilty of gross ineptitude and poor spelling and made no apologies for it. Similarly referees, ring announcers, managers and promoters were often guilty of illiteracy. Some boxers grew frustrated and resented their names being butchered in a hundred different ways and so agreed to a name change. In the early days American promoters who sensed the potential of riotous behavior in hostile arenas placated mobs by asking Italian boxers to adopt "Irish" handles. In one instance Joseph Valenti, a top bantamweight during the 1900s, became known as Joe Wagner, after his favorite baseball player Honus Wagner. Ridiculous and farcical really, as the baseball legend was in fact German!

Old-time heavyweight contender Andrew Chiariglione, better known as "Fireman" Jim Flynn, claimed his Irish moniker on a Utah boxing card. Irritated by the announcers' inability to pronounce his surname correctly and anxious to get the proceedings under way, the fighter bellowed contemptuously: "Oh, hell, just call me Jim Flynn." It didn't matter to the Hoboken-born prizefighter. He was immensely proud of his Italian heritage.[2]

As strangers in a foreign land their philosophical approach was born out of far bigger issues, with money in the pocket an essential driver. Angelo Dundee, the legendary boxing manager, rejected the notion that Italian Americans were coerced into adopting an Irish identity in order to get regular billing in fight clubs. He explained:

> There was no reason, no rhyme or reason to it . . . The Italians got everything they wanted. They did it by hard work and desire. It was not by a name change. I don't buy that. They couldn't pronounce the Italian names. So they changed them. It was easier to pronounce Irish names.

Dundee was more hard-hitting in his autobiography *I Only Talk Winning*, and pointed to societal tensions and deep-rooted anxieties held by northern Europeans towards Italians.

> In the early 1900s it wasn't advantageous to have an Italian name. Italians were not held in high esteem by the host population. We lived in Italian ghettos, held menial jobs, spoke funnily and ate spaghetti and ice cream and were considered by the average American to be "gangsters" and members of crime societies.[3]

Carmelo Bazzano, Professor Emeritus of Physical Education at the University of Massachusetts, has argued that commercial considerations pressurized Italians into adopting non-Italian names. As Irish or English promoters considered themselves superior they sought to cosmetically arrange the infiltration of Italians into the sport, producing an army of "ready-made Irish" boxers palatable to the mainly Irish patrons. During this period of dwindling Irish fighters the newcomer was conveniently positioned to fill the void. Although some Italians organized boxing shows in the early 1900s, most could not afford ticket prices, and devoted a lot of energy to saving for a return to Italy.[4] In addition, when Italians entered boxing societal conditions presented fertile terrain for extreme anti-immigrant proclamations. Madison Grant singled out the Italian cohort and under the headline "Keep Out Foreigners and Restore Real Americanism," Grant asserted that under the 1917 Literacy Test most Southern Italians and Sicilians would be kept out, describing them as "largely descended from the old slave population of the Roman Empire."[5] The Sacco and Vanzetti case convinced Italian Americans that their position in American society was at best tenuous, and the perpetuation of persistent and erosive stereotypes might have been sufficient motive for the Italian not to box under the family name.

John De John (Di Gianni) was a member of the famous fighting clan from Syracuse, New York and the eldest son of sharecroppers from Avellino, Campania. He grew up during the twenties and remembers the strain on his fellow countrymen to conform. "The Italians were forced to change their names because the Irish and the Germans were running everything. They had to change their names otherwise they would have got the worst of it. They got better jobs."[6]

In the era of the adopted Irish ring tag, Tony Caponi was a rarity. This capable middleweight from St. Paul, Minnesota boxed during the 1900s under his family surname. He battled to change people's perceptions, but complained at the lack of regular fights. Caponi blamed it on his surname, believing that to boxing promoters his real name sounded "more like a music master than a prizefighter." For a time he changed his name to T.C. O'Brien.[7]

Whilst these findings make for interesting reading they do not present a uniform overall picture. Firstly discrimination, prejudice and hostility were not solely experienced by the Italian cohort. Secondly the practice of assumed names was not exclusively reserved for the Italian or restricted to boxing. The Italian followed an earlier trend with both the Jewish and German cohorts embracing Irish and anglicized ring tags. The changing and altering of ethnic names was rife throughout society and indicated a willingness and acquiescence on the part of the immigrant to speedily integrate and assimilate into the host society. Others countered that full integration and participation could still occur without compromising national identity.

Professor Bazzano has argued that most promoters were Irish or English and they were directly responsible for the implementation of assumed names. Whilst it is true that Irish managers predominated there were numerous fight managers and several high-profile promoters of Italian extraction during the First World War era. These men used adopted names. Mike Criss (Crisalfi) managed fighters out of Boston and Silvey Burns (Bernei), Jimmy Kelly (Di Salvio), Tony Kelly (Lento) and Phil De More did the same out of New York, while Harry Lenny (Setaro) operated out of Philadelphia and New York. New Orleans-based Dominic Tortorich (Tortorice) was one of the biggest boxing promoters during this period, staging many high-profile events.

In the early 1900s, a sizable proportion of Italian fighters were also handled by fellow compatriots and by family members. Hugo Kelly was managed by businessman Silvio Ferretti, Frankie Conley (Conte) by his brother Joseph and Benny Yanger (Angona) by John Hertz, a Jewish entrepreneur. These examples illustrated that the picture was not homogeneous and depended upon personal experiences, childhood associations, the ethnic composition of a neighborhood, your position within the urban enclave, and the part of country you lived in.

New ring tags were preferred by those requiring anonymity. Others acquiesced if it permitted regular work and higher billing on a boxing card, and some abhorred the irritating and disrespectful practice of mispronounced and misspelt family names. The commercial motive was a driver in the name-changing process, and this did not always mean switching to an Irish name. The 1900s featherweight Benny Yanger and 1926 lightweight champion Sammy Mandell adopted a Jewish *nom de guerre* in a marketing ploy designed to capture the large concentrated Jewish boxing fan base in the state of Illinois.

The name-changing process threw up a number of wonderful curiosities. One in particular involved Johnny Dundee (Giuseppe Carrara). His iconic status during the second decade of the twentieth century spawned a generation of Italian boxers parading the Dundee moniker as their own. To some extent Dundee's impact inside a boxing ring neutralized any negative associations connected to the use of an Irish or Americanized name. It ironically helped make the Dundee fighting name into a recognizable

Italian American boxing brand. It was possible for scores of Italian fighters to comfortably command a lofty position in the ring with an anglicized name yet still project their ethnicity. Later world champions, top-notchers and fight managers, all Italian Americans, sported the *nom de plume* proudly. To them it no longer sounded Irish or English but exhibited a magical transcendent quality. Nevertheless, some prominent Italians could not accept the sacrifice of giving up one's personal and cultural identity. Famous Italian wrestler Renato Gardini spoke on behalf of many when he declared: "I am Italian proud too. Why not keep glory, if any is to be made in Italian names?"[8] The twenties ushered in a more bullish generation of Italian American boxers and champions such as Genaro, Canzoneri, La Barba, La Morte, Ballerino and Battalino were clear opponents of the Irishized ring name tradition. Not all were like-minded and there were still individuals clinging on to the strong tradition of assumed names well into the forties.

Two of the biggest Italian American boxing heroes were Willie Pep and Rocky Marciano. They approached the name-changing dilemma from different perspectives. Willie Pep (Guglielmo Papaleo), from Hartford, Connecticut gave an insight into what was considered in the adoption of a ring alias. "How could I fight with such a name [Papaleo]? It wasn't a fighting name. I agreed with it. It worked out well for me. We changed our names to fit our [boxing] styles." An adamant Pep reiterated that he was never leaned upon to change his name. His manager was Lou Viscusi, a fellow Italian. When Pep ruled the featherweight ranks in the forties there was an established presence and dominance of Italian American promoters, managers and trainers operating nationwide.[9]

Champion heavyweight Rocky Marciano (Rocco Marchegiano), from Brockton, Massachusetts, resisted all attempts by his manager to box under a non-Italian moniker. Marciano was a fiercely proud Italian who understood the importance of his heritage and identity. In March 1947 he rejected the name Rocky Mack because it wasn't Italian. His real name had been carved up repeatedly in the local and national press, and his Jewish manager, Al Weill, favored a name change, arguing it would create popular appeal. Weill suggested Rocky March but the boxer slammed the idea. Manny Almeida, a top promoter in Providence, Rhode Island intervened and manufactured a new name simply by deleting a few letters to form his surname. At first the boxer wasn't enamored of this selective tinkering but eventually agreed. He reacted: "I guess if it's got to be done, Marciano will be all right. It's Italian all right. It's almost my real name. Who'd have thought they'd make me change my name. How do you think Pop's gonna feel?"[10]

There's no question that the damaging forces of patriotism and racism, combined with ethno-racial conflict within American society, particularly prominent between the Italian and Irish working classes, brought enormous pressure on the Italian newcomer to conform. From the moment the Italian immigrant landed at Ellis Island those forces became apparent. Civil servants deliberately changed or simplified passenger names. Among the new arrivals there were some who believed a fresh start required a new name and opted for transliterations. In the wider context and at different stages of the adjustment process, persons of Italian origin changed their names to avoid identification with what Emma Lazarus characterized in her famous poem as "the wretched refuse." The rationale behind taking up American-sounding names was primarily seen as speeding up assimilation in their new homeland and to appease the Irish foreman at the workplace. The Italians, like the Jews, changed their names so that they wouldn't be identified by society at large for fear of discrimination. Its existence was real and pervasive in all socio-economic and political spheres.

No area remained untouched, not even sport, and especially boxing, which was controlled by Irish promoters and politicians and predominantly patronized by Irish fans. The organizers dictated the terms of engagement and recruited from the vast pool of new immigrants, and having an Irish moniker was a necessary evil just to get a foothold in the boxing arena. This was supposed to offer more prominent billing on boxing cards and ensure wider appeal to audiences expecting to see men with crowd-pleasing qualities, synonymous with the old-time Irish American prizefighters. The inter-ethnic street conflict between the Irish and Italian was transferred into the boxing ring. Famous rivalries developed and the first nationally identifiable match-up began in the 1890s between Casper Leon (Gaspare Leone) and Jimmy Barry. They fought for the world title and met each other six times. Middleweight Hugo Kelly (Ugo Micheli) shared a ring with Philadelphia Jack O'Brien on four occasions in the 1900s. In New York, neighborhood bantamweight rivals Little Jack Sharkey (Giovanni Cervati) and Joe Lynch fought in five torrid action-packed thrillers in the post-First World War era through to the mid-twenties. Featherweight Steve "Kid" Sullivan (Stefano Tricamo) tangled with Brooklyn Irish rival Vincent "Pepper" Martin in five scintillating encounters. Johnny Wilson (Giovanni Panico) spoiled the 1921 St Patrick's Day celebrations when he successfully defended his world title by outpointing Mike O'Dowd in New York. In Boston Sammy Fuller (Sabino Ferullo) met Irish North End rival Andy Callahan six times. Despite the Irish-sounding names the fighter's Italian neighborhood all turned out to cheer their favorite, cognizant of his ethnic origin and his family name.

Italian boxers were never isolated or removed from the name-changing process and in some instances held the power of veto. When it was fashionable to use an Irish or anglicized boxing name they followed the established trend. Greater participation and frequent championship success brought with them rising levels of confidence and visibility. The improving economic position of Italians in society translated into vigorous support from the fighter's local community who clamored to see their hero box under his real name. The twenties especially witnessed this breakthrough as shrewd promoters exploited neighborhood inter-ethnic rivalries in order to boost ticket sales.

In 1933 Primo Carnera of Italy knocked out Jack Sharkey in six rounds in Long Island, New York to capture the world heavyweight title. The magnitude of this event, the powerful symbolism of masculinity of an Italian winning the biggest prize in boxing, influenced Italian American boxers to believe that success was appropriate under the family name. Henry Louis Mencken, an influential literary figure in the first half of the twentieth century, found that the adoption of Irish or anglicized names to disguise an Italian identity had virtually ceased during this period, and attributed the change in behavior to the rise in Italian national pride and the international role of Benito Mussolini.[11] Although this point is difficult to substantiate, what is true is that the process of assumed names diminished in importance without entirely extinguishing itself.

The changing of names formed part of the overall process of American conformity and in many fields of employment Italians were rendered virtually invisible to the outside world by the adoption of Irish or WASP names, and some of the worst examples were recorded in politics, trade unions, trades associations and law enforcement. This custom was also pervasive in the world of entertainment. Jerry Vale, Alan Dale, Vic Damone, Frankie Laine, Johnny Desmond, Bobby Darin, Don Cornell, Tony Bennett, Dean Martin and Guy Marks were some of the famous crooners of the forties and fifties who adopted anglicized pseudonyms. Band leaders and composers included Harry Warren, Tony Pastor, Jerry Gray, Paul Creston, Sal Carson and Ray Anthony. The world of jazz was similarly affected and notable Italian American performers included Nick Lucas, Lenny Peyton, Eddie Lang, Flip Phillips, Willie Dennis, Lee Castle, Teddy Powell, Carmen Mastren, Laurie Bellson and George Wallington.

Whilst there was Italian opposition, with some describing this tradition as a "perverse habit" that would have a "bad outcome" for all Italians, the majority saw it as primarily a symbolic gesture, and a way to avoid discrimination and racial intolerance and achieve social acceptance. For all the admonishments centring on humiliation and the struggle for identity it did not stop Italian boxers from speaking Italian at home, eating pasta and drinking wine, or from participating in cultural and religious *feste* (feasts). They still maintained close family ties and developed and consolidated their neighborhood relationships within their peer groups.[12] At heart Italian American boxers never lost sight of who they were, and they were mindful of their heritage. Their acceptance of the need to integrate into American society and embrace the host culture did not mean that they traded in their core Italianate beliefs and values.

4

Trailblazer Casper Leon, title claimants and contenders

Boxing had existed in the United States in its crudest forms since the eighteenth century, and in the early to mid-nineteenth century the English were the first to export a brand of pugilism. After the Great Migration the Irish came with a boxing tradition, and by 1850 the bulk of American prizefighters were of either English or Irish extraction.[1] New York and Philadelphia became recognized hives of activity, and boxing prospered through transport and technological improvements. The growth of prizefighting did not please everyone and a Puritan backlash triggered anti-fight legislation that stifled any further development. The sport remained locally based and primarily the preserve of young males of the urban streets, which became a battleground for neighborhood and ethnic rivalries. In 1882, when John L. Sullivan gained the heavyweight championship, he presided over the transition from bare-knuckle combat to glove contests and Marquis of Queensberry rules, and his championship reign was further evidence that the Irish were the dominant presence in boxing.

Spectacular large-scale migration from Southern and Eastern Europe changed the sport, with Irish domination experiencing its stiffest challenge from the Italian and Jewish newcomers. It's fair to say that the early Italian appearances in the world of American professional boxing were undistinguished. With large-scale transatlantic migration still in its infancy, a dearth of competitors ventured onto the dangerous fight club circuit, and those that dared to do so discovered that competition was an onerous task. Scan any of the major newspapers of the 1880s and you will struggle to find boxers of premier standing. The unsung and largely obscure names of Brooklyn lightweights Joe Milletecchia and Theodore Angelo and Philadelphia's Charles "Bull" McCarthy (Montagasini) were possibly the first Italian prizefighters to take center stage in America. Against a backdrop of prejudice and tough living conditions, extended newspaper coverage and advertising from profit-seeking promoters elevated the importance of boxing. By the close of the nineteenth century Italian involvement was gathering momentum, and not only were Italian boxers competing in the major boxing arenas against the best practitioners of the manly art, but they were also fighting for Italian colony titles disparagingly referred to as "spaghetti championships." It was commonplace for Italian fighters from different parts of an American city or state to contest these titles. In 1895 bantamweight Frank Pinto was referred to as the "Italian Champion of New York." In 1898 featherweight Andy Cuneo was also accorded the same recognition and Dago Mike (Michael Mongone), from the railroad camps, annexed the Colorado featherweight title in 1898. Flyweight Kid Bernasconi and lightweight Kid Williams (Ted Di Donna) campaigned to packed auditoriums in Philadelphia boxing circles.

At the height of Italian immigration the largest proportion of Italian boxers hailed from the Upper West Side and Lower East Side sections of Manhattan, New York. The Five Points Bowery enclave, a notorious hangout for general low life, was also a traditional area for boxing recruitment. Despite their mainly Irish-sounding names Jim Burke, Kid Curley, Jack Lowery, Al and Tommy Ginger, Chick Tricker, Patsy White, Johnny Keyes, Tony Moran, Packey Hommey, Kid Murphy and Andy Thomas were all notable Italian fighters who walked the streets of Mulberry Bend, Worth, Leonard Park, Baxter Street, Pell Street and Mott Street in the early part of the twentieth century. Paul Kelly (Paolo Vaccarelli), a product of this environment, was a promising bantamweight who was well schooled in the art of boxing science. He later courted widespread public notoriety as the leader of the Five Points Gang, the largest criminal group in the city. Kelly was a capable boxer among the underworld fraternity and was rivaled only by Jewish gang leader Monk Eastman. Their regular territorial gang spats came to a head in the winter 1903 when the two agreed to settle their differences by way of a marathon prizefight. Both chieftains were accompanied by fifty of their best fighters and after two hours of milling, the rumble in a Bronx barn was declared a draw.[2]

Others plying their trade included the unflatteringly named Goose the Dago (Gus Marino), a popular figure in Rochester and Syracuse athletic clubs. Buffalo lightweight Roxy Kanell (Rocco Canelli) performed regularly at venues all over New York State. Headliners Kid Thomas (Joseph Tomasulo) and bantamweight Jimmy Kelly (John Di Salvio) were main eventers on New York City fight cards, as was Brooklyn's hard-hitting lightweight Mike Tuths.

Eddie Lenny (Edward Setaro) was a top-notch featherweight of his era. The Philadelphian made his professional ring debut in the autumn of 1896, and under the stewardship of hotel owner "Baron" Jimmy Dougherty Lenny rapidly developed a national reputation as a skillful and tough competitor. He was a clever defensive fighter with a jab-and-move style that befuddled many great boxers. Following impressive displays against main contenders and future champions Harry Forbes and Joe Bernstein, Lenny earned a world title shot. On November 21, 1899 Lenny lost a hard-fought twenty-five rounds decision to Nova Scotian ring legend George Dixon at the Broadway Athletic Club in Brooklyn, New York. In January 1902 Lenny got even with "Little Chocolate" Dixon when the former champion was knocked out in nine rounds. A subsequent match-up staged in Chester, Pennsylvania ended in a draw.

Casper Leon the pioneer

Of all the men that risked life and limb in the brutal pre-1900 world of American prizefighting, one boxer stood out. Virtually forgotten today, Casper Leon was the first Italian to gain distinction as a top-notch fighter. Old record books show that Leon was born Gaspare Leone in Palermo, Sicily on December 8, 1872. He was brought to the United States as a two-year-old and his family settled in the part of Manhattan nicknamed Goatsville, a remote area of the city where the landscape was dominated by wooden houses and open spaces. His brothers Benny and Jack followed him into boxing.

Leon began his professional career in 1891. He fought as a bantamweight and only weighed 105 pounds. Today he would be classified as a mini-flyweight, and if the flyweight division had been in existence Leon would have certainly been the universally acclaimed world champion. He was untouchable at his weight. Very often Leon conceded considerable weight to his rivals, sometimes by as much as ten to fifteen pounds, but amazingly this physical handicap did not compromise his status as one of the best boxers in circulation.

When George Dixon moved up to featherweight Jimmy Barry of Chicago claimed the world championship. As Leon was considered the best fighter in the East, having mopped up all before him, he disputed Barry's claim by meeting him under a large tent in the scenic setting of a picnic grove in Lamont, Illinois on September 15, 1894. With honors even after eleven rounds, the hard-hitting Barry dropped Leon for a six count and the tide swung the Irishman's way. Only Leon's bravery and ring stewardship kept him upright in the face of a heavy tirade of punches. Leon was a beaten man in the twenty-third round but refused to quit and fought on for another five stanzas before finally caving in to Barry's power. The two boxers locked horns on five other occasions, four of them ending in draws with one no decision. When Barry retired Leon mounted two subsequent title attempts, drawing the first encounter with Harry Forbes and losing the rematch on points. It signaled the end of Leon's top-flight career, which had seen him engage in over two hundred fifty fights.

Leon campaigned inside the ring at a time of vehement anti-Italianism. It didn't get much better when Jacob Riis, a prominent social reformer, concluded that New York Italians were criminals and tramps incapable of hard work and of controlling their masculinity, and were prone to antisocial violence. The weighty matter of group alienation, unfair criticism and the ever-present threat of lynch mobs did not deter him. Leon bore the brunt of racist epithets, boos and jeers from the predominantly Irish and English club patrons. By the time he retired the derision and intimidation associated with these hate-filled cauldrons had not diminished. In 1903 the *National Police Gazette* captured this mood, reporting:

> It is amusing to note the way in which the crowd at ringside receives the different nationalities of fighters. There is always a hearty cheer and earnest backing for the Irishman; grins and good-humored tolerance for the German and virulent hostility to the Italian and the Negro. Put a boy of any race in with an Italian and everybody in the house who is not himself of Italian origin at once begins to root frantically against the son of ancient Rome. It is to the credit of the Italians that they have pushed so far forward against such adverse influences.[3]

For Casper Leon this was the least of his troubles as he risked arrest and imprisonment for plying his trade when boxing was fighting for its very survival. The anti-boxing crusaders argued that the sport acted as a magnet for objectionable types and promoted gambling, which, they believed, triggered disorder and rioting. The lack of control and the corruption prevalent during the unregulated era gave the lobbyists the upper hand when the Horton Law was repealed in 1900, four years after it had legalized the sport. Notwithstanding the boxing ban in New York, the sport thrived, with new clubs opening in Brooklyn, Queens and Long Island City, and contests were staged much to the disapproval of the Puritans. Fighters were frequently arrested and charged, only released on payment of fines and sometimes imprisoned too. Despite the socio-legal constraints Leon managed to establish himself in the ring. He was a cagey operator and known for his clever ducking and lateral ring movement. He could turn a bout with solid right-handers and rapier-like jabs, which earned him the nickname of the "Sicilian Swordfish." He fought *la crème de la crème* in the shape of Patsy Haley, Johnny Connors, Jack McKeck, Steve Flanagan, Torpedo Billy Murphy, Morris Rauch, "Terrible" Terry McGovern, Harry Harris, Harry Forbes, Jimmy Barry and George Dixon. Leon was always in superb physical condition. Fight followers admired his courage, and the way he battled against featherweights and even lightweights. His title bout with Jimmy Barry in 1894 was one of the most grueling in boxing history. In 1899 he fought McGovern for the title, bowing to defeat only after suffering two broken ribs.

Although he never won an official world boxing title in the ring his supporters pressed Leon's bantamweight and paperweight claims in 1894, 1896 and again in 1899. When Jimmy Barry relinquished his title in 1896 he designated Leon and Johnny Connors to contest the 105-pound Championship of America. Leon knocked Connors out in nine rounds in Niagara Falls, New York and these claims gained credence in some quarters. In 1897 respected boxing writer Sam Austin wrote that Leon had legitimate claims to the American bantamweight title. Even Jimmy Barry's manager Charles Parson Davies agreed that Leon had a technical claim to the 105-pound championship because his charge could no longer make the weight. In 1899 Leon finally lost his claim when McGovern dispatched him in twelve rounds.

For much of his career Leon remained a world championship-caliber boxer and on average grossed $500 for a single fight; his biggest purse was $800. Leon lived lavishly and squandered most of his money on fancy clothes and a racy lifestyle. At one time he owned a cigar store. He briefly instructed boxing to budding recruits at a local New York gymnasium. He worked in a variety of other jobs, which included racking up balls in a billiard parlor and digging trenches as part of a construction crew. In May 1926 he lost his most important battle in Harlem hospital, succumbing to a series of complications following a knee injury after slipping on a piece of ice three months earlier. Gangrene set in and his leg was amputated. He never recovered and died aged 54.[4]

Leon is sometimes referred to as the father of all Italian American boxers, and was a trailblazer of his time. Despite the lack of a modern sporting heritage, with one essentially centered on *bocce* (bowls) and card games, Leon showed the first wave of young Italian boys that American pastimes offered real financial possibilities. He proved that size was no barrier to sporting success, and any psychological hang-ups Italians might have had about competing in the manly art were quickly dispelled by his much-publicized victories. His sterling feats later culminated in mass group participation and tremendous triumphs across all weight categories.

Heroes and hard men

During tough and troubled times heroes and hard men were needed and the rise of the Italian American prizefighter represented the group's precarious position in American society. With so few success stories and a distinct lack of civic and political leaders, influential clergymen or eminent businessmen that Italians could look up to, professional boxers alongside baseball players and gangsters occupied these voids as alternative role models. Between 1900 and 1955 a richly versatile and talented fighting cohort emerged, encompassing the unregulated era to the establishment of state governance, in which 51 Italian American champions and title claimants rose to the top of their respective weight classes. Pete Herman, Johnny Dundee, Tony Canzoneri, Lou Ambers, Willie Pep, Rocky Graziano, Jake La Motta, Rocky Marciano and Carmen Basilio were among illustrious champions who were instrumental in many of the sport's golden moments. (See Appendix V.)

There were numerous contenders worthy of consideration, and a list containing one hundred outstanding Italian American boxers reveals that this deep pool of pugilistic talent stretched far and wide (see Appendix VI). The geographical distribution of the best Italian American boxers, drawn from these two tables, shows that 40 percent, the largest proportion, came from New York State and 74 percent of these fighters hailed from Little Italies located in Brooklyn, Manhattan, Bronx and Harlem; the rest came from towns in upstate New York. Pennsylvania and specifically the South Philadelphia enclave supplied the next highest proportion of fighters followed by New Jersey State, Boston, Chicago, Cleveland and San Francisco.

The exploits of Italian American champions were a source of great encouragement to other members of the group. At a time when the stamp of *campanilismo* (parochialism), which had governed Italian cultural thought and behavior for centuries, began to lose its luster, their involvement in big-time fights drew people of different Italian regions to unite together under a single Italian identity. Americanized Italian boys preferred New World expectations and attitudes over *la via vecchia* (the old way). They viewed rural traditions marked out by local divisions and the notion of loyalty to a particular clan as an outdated mode of survival that had little meaning or merit in their new urban realities.

Their increasing fascination with competitive organized sport directly challenged the authority of the Italian patriarch for the very first time, and as they pushed for greater assimilation the fathers' diminishing power failed to halt the wave of dissension and they eventually bowed to their sons' wishes as mass participation in boxing became a reality. The elders drew some comfort from the observation that their offspring used their purse money to zealously contribute to the familial economy.

Italian fervor found its voice and expression in boxing through widespread support of one of their own competing as an equal, especially against his hated Irish rival, something that was still not possible in the workplace or in any other field. Particularly great champions like Johnny Dundee and Tony Canzoneri were shadowed wherever they went and typically throngs of fans patiently awaited their arrival at train stations and accompanied them back following their ring battles. Banquets and ceremonies held in their honor were organized by Italian businessmen and community groups nationally. Italian ethnic pride extended to the boxing arena, where fans were among the most passionate and routinely unfurled and waved the Italian green, white and red tricolor flags. The Italian American boxers projected a spirit of adventure, strength of individualism and physical endeavor at a time when progress for the ordinary working man was made difficult, with most legitimate pathways blocked off. By confronting the physical hazards of a brutal sport, they showed a determination to aspire to a better future rather than passively accept their fate. Their heroic deeds in one of America's most popular sports symbolically restored pride in a group that had been declared inferior and undesirable by the enactment of immigration quotas and stripped of dignity by prolonged Italian stigmatization.

The regularity of boxing success in the first half of the twentieth century struck a hammer blow against the advocates of Nativist ideology and Teutonic superiority and also facilitated a unifying and patriotic Italianate feeling, something that did not exist among Southern Italian immigrants who arrived at Ellis Island. In fact they did not think of themselves as Italian. The remote hilltop village was the center of their universe. The Italian unification of 1861 was an alien concept and the overwhelming majority did not speak or write Italian and only communicated in local dialects. By the twenties there was no longer any ambiguity associated with being Italian in the United States. During the inter-war period Italy had fought alongside its American allies in the First World War and 10 percent of the American soldiers were of Italian origin. The rise of fascism and Mussolini's stirring speeches, extensively publicized on American radio and in newspapers, promising to reclaim the former glories of the Roman Empire, and the international legitimacy afforded to his regime fostered pride in a single Italian identity. But it was the struggle against discrimination and social bigotry particularly during these years that gained impetus, and the determination to gain equality and respect in every walk of American life that bound together people from different Italian regions.

Although the Italian American boxer did not deliberately set out to be a bigot buster or a patriot, his winning displays, at least at a visceral level, imbued a degree of confidence and new found optimism, and in some small way contributed towards the formation and consolidation of a solid identity for the newly defined Italian American group. In an age of group vilification and hostility, representations of Italian success were woefully deficient in other areas of American society, and Italian American boxing champions were a welcome beacon of light projecting a positive force as role models. They were headline makers within the enclaves they inhabited, and the impact of certain personalities and triumphs even transcended neighborhood boundaries.

Not even the political imposition of the Lewis Law, which made prizefighting illegal in New York in 1900, could deter the Italian fighter from participating in an era when the sport remained active on a club membership basis. In 1905 the *National Police Gazette* reported the changing cultural habits within the Italian colonies of New York City. It wrote

> Of the pugilists at the present time, however, the great majority of them are young Italian Americans who, for convenience or for other reasons have taken Celtic names. Immigrants from Italy coming into New York have had the name of being inclined to use knives when they fought instead of their fists. This was true of the Italian immigrants but it does not apply to the second generation born and reared in the city of New York. Unlike the older Italians they have developed here a strong partiality for American athletics and the number of amateur boxers and professional fighters among the children of Italian parents

residing here is very large. It is increasing too, so much so that a special designation for them has become current. In the same way that there has been a change in the fighting proclivities of Italians, the stiletto of one generation is being superseded by the hard knuckles of the next.[5]

Faced with challenging socio-economic problems, a scarcity of Italian promoters with mainstream influence and a limited managerial presence, both Italian-born and second-generation fighters emerged against the odds. In 1907 standout performer Kid Murphy (Peter Frascella) achieved world bantamweight title claimant recognition, and earned a reputation as one of the most fearsome hitters among the little men. He was supported by the Boston bantamweight contender and title claimant Al Delmont (Alberto Delmonti) and world-rated Philadelphia featherweight, Eddie Lenny (Edward Setaro), all of whom staked title claims. In 1902, Benny Yanger (Benjamin Angona), a ferocious body puncher from Chicago, was proclaimed as the new 122-pound world champion by the West End Athletic Club in St. Louis, Missouri. Yanger's opponent, the great Jewish fighter Abe Atell, was floored five times before succumbing to a devastating knockout in the nineteenth round. Yanger's claim was not universally accepted and unsurprisingly Atell refused to give the Italian a rematch. Whilst Atell went on to rule the featherweight division, Yanger could not persuade the titleholders of his era to defend their crowns even though he had beaten champions Joe Bernstein, George Dixon, Young Corbett and Harry Forbes in non-title contests.

In the heavyweight ranks "Fireman" Jim Flynn (Andrew Chiariglione) of Pueblo, Colorado was broadly accepted as one of the best "white hopes" in an era packed with great African American boxers, and later became the only man to knock out the great Jack Dempsey. Flynn began boxing in 1901 and became known as the "Fighting Fireman" from the time he worked as a locomotive fireman on the Denver and Rio Grande railroad. He was a rough, tough, big-hitting fighter, who twice fought for the world heavyweight title. In 1906 he challenged Tommy Burns for the title in Los Angeles and lost on a fifteen-round stoppage. When Burns suffered defeat to Jack Johnson the black boxer dominated the division to the abhorrence of white America, whose hysterical reaction in racially charged times was summed up by the clamor for a white boxer to usurp the "black menace." For his part Flynn developed a reputation as a destroyer of "white hopes," and when he beat lauded title aspirants Carl Morris and Al Kaufmann in 1911 Flynn earned a second world title shot a year later. In an ill-tempered

Las Vegas bout with Johnson, the referee stopped the contest in the ninth round with Johnson declared the winner. Flynn eventually retired in 1925.

In New York alone, Manhattan bantamweight Joe Wagner (Joseph Valenti) and Brooklyn featherweights Joe Coster (Giuseppe Agnello) and Young Wagner (Anthony Sarubbi) made their mark, as did lightweight title aspirants Terry Young (Anthony Samperi) and Johnny Marto. Hugo Kelly (Ugo Micheli) was one of the biggest drawing cards of his era. Although the Italian-born campaigner was never recognized as world middleweight champion, he was the perennial title claimant and his titular status was supported vigorously from 1905 to 1907 and again in 1910. In an era of newspaper championship claims and counter claims between prominent rival camps, the retirement of ring immortal Tommy Ryan created a fragmented picture and one of Ryan's final acts before hanging up his gloves was to publicly anoint his stablemate Kelly as his successor. In the spring of 1905, the Chicago-based Kelly cemented his status by winning a ten-round decision over highly rated Philadelphia Jack O'Brien in Indianapolis, taking over O'Brien's claim to the 158-pound middleweight title. Kelly stayed on top by outboxing the leading contenders. When Ryan returned and boxed a six-round draw with Kelly, he again declared Kelly a worthy successor. Despite these proclamations Californian boxing writers ignored Kelly's entitlement, preferring Stanley Ketchel. In July 1908 the question of supremacy among the middleweights was finally settled when Kelly met Ketchel for the undisputed crown. A left hook from the "Michigan Assassin" resolved the subject once and for all. Despite the setback Kelly maintained an elevated position as a main contender until 1912.

1910–19: Demigod Johnny Dundee surfaces in a claimant's world

In the absence of strict regulations and no official controlling body, pre-1920 champions were generally accepted if they were recognized by Richard Kyle-Fox's *National Police Gazette* newspaper. Hence title claims were commonplace and disputed, with "undesirable" contenders often shunned by titleholders through the implementation of imaginative contractual get-out clauses and catchweight bouts staged to maintain their title stranglehold. Only three world titles changed hands in the first seven years of this decade. With this seemingly immovable picture, newspapermen pledged their support to alternative champions known as claimants. Some of them were outstanding boxers who had previously trounced champions in non-title matches. Misplaced political influence also seriously undermined the standing of the sport. In 1911 the Frawley Law legalized ten-round no-decision exhibition bouts between affiliated "members" of boxing athletic clubs and the act inadvertently plunged the sport into disarray with points decisions forbidden and victory only possible via a knockout. A chaotic system emerged whereby a winner was declared by a "newspaper decision" based on the collective opinions of the majority of ringside writers, but unanimity was seldom reached, and contests often produced two winners depending on the newspaper account.

The problematic and inflexible nature of this system ruined the titular ambitions of Patsy Kline (Pasquale Gengaro). The Italian-born featherweight contender of Neapolitan parentage was one of the most feared boxers of his age, possessing a famed left hook knockout punch that had flattened half of his one hundred and fifty opponents. For the best part of his career Kline was forced to fight considerably heavier boxers when featherweights and lightweights ducked him. Boxing out of Newark, New Jersey, Kline tangled with 126-pound champion Abe Atell on four separate occasions but the cautious Jew never risked his title. Many remember Kline for the way he battered Johnny Kilbane in Vernon, California on July 15, 1911. In the eighth round Kline connected with his trademark left hook, sending the Irishman sprawling to the canvas. He was up at nine when the bell sounded, rescuing the stricken Kilbane from defeat. The Irish fighter stayed out of reach for the remainder of the contest, winning a debatable twenty-rounds decision. Seven months later Kilbane wrested the featherweight title from Atell. He held onto his belt until June 1923, but he refused to meet Kline again. In 1938, several decades after Kline had retired, *Ring Magazine* paid tribute to the fighting qualities of the Italian campaigner by comparing him to the great Henry Armstrong, the triple world champion. The editorial refused to pass judgment as to who would have won that match-up.

Despite this intractable system overall Italian American participation increased, with numerous contenders and world title challengers moving to the forefront in each category. Bantamweights Frankie Conley (Francesco Conte) and Pete Herman (Pietro Gulotta) and flyweight Young Zulu Kid (Giuseppe Di Melfi) were accepted as leaders in their respective classes. In 1910 Kenosha's pride Frankie Conley won the bantamweight title by stopping Monte Atell, brother of Abe, after 42 rounds of mayhem in one of the longest title matches on record. In 1917, Pete Herman of New Orleans became the first Italian American to be recognized as undisputed world professional boxing champion. On May 3, 1919, Herman was involved in the first all-Italian American world title fight when he faced Patsy Wallace (Pasquale Appalucci) in Philadelphia. Young Zulu Kid was generally recognized as the best flyweight in the United States and international recognition was only resolved when he met Welshman Jimmy Wilde.

For all the early exploits of the Italian prizefighter it was the arrival of New York featherweight Johnny Dundee (Giuseppe Carrara) that catapulted the cohort to a higher level. Dundee, the Sicilian-born son of a fisherman, regularly headed boxing cards nationwide, entertaining legions of fight fans. His achievements in the ring encouraged a new generation of Italian American boxers. Known as the "Scotch Wop," his fighting style was unique and full of trickery and his trademark move of bouncing off the ropes to launch into a flurry of punches was later copied by many of his admirers. Dundee maintained the highest level of consistency against the very best opposition in a range of weight classes, and his longevity was just as remarkable, spanning an extraordinary 22 years. He was unfortunate to have campaigned in the no-decision era, which made winning a title difficult, and had to wait until 1921 before annexing the world junior-lightweight title. He lost it and regained it in 1923, and in the same year collected the 126-pound title. Dundee was a consummate and hard-working professional, who made frequent ring appearances. In his first ten days in the paid ranks he fought five times, and in his first two years made an astonishing 59 appearances. He racked up an amazing 340 career bouts.

1920–29: Gladiators of the Golden Age

Sport was integral to the general health of the nation, the government's promise to build sport venues, gymnasiums and arenas was honored, and thousands including the great and the good flocked to boxing. In 1920 the call for stricter regulation ushered in the Walker Law, and the legalization of boxing returned New York to the apex of world boxing. It was the home of more fighters, the center of the boxing publishing business, and significantly the base of the largest Italian community. A distinguished scribe noted the impressive growth in Italian American boxing participation and concluded in November 1921 that there were "over a thousand Jew and Italian boxers in New York City alone." At preliminary entry level Italians and Jews outnumbered the Irish by five to one. Journalist Wilbur Wood reported that overall numbers were ten times those of the previous generation. The predominance of the Italian American fighter in New York brought a mass of new patrons through the turnstiles.[6] Increased participation equated to major success as boxing promotion became a vast American industry. Purses increased and overall boxing show receipts swelled.

With the enlargement of its borders, boxers from around the world were invited to the United States, and one inevitable repercussion was the intensification of competition. This did not halt the gladiatorial advance of the Italian American prizefighter, and one of the best of an outstanding crop was ironically a non-world champion. His name was Billy Petrolle (William Michael Petrolla). Petrolle had been campaigning at the pinnacle of boxing since the mid-twenties but was quite simply too dangerous an adversary and lightweight champions Rocky Kansas and Sammy Mandell refused to defend their titles. By the time Canzoneri gave him a title chance in 1932, it had come a few years too late for the aging warhorse, who struggled to make the 135-pound limit. Petrolle, the son of a railroad employee, was no ordinary fighter. On turning professional in 1922, the "Fargo Express" wooed crowds with displays of powerful body punching and breath-taking toe-to-toe exchanges. His fearlessness and fighting courage, epitomized by his refusal to yield even when the battle seemed forlorn, influenced literary authors of the period. Joseph Heller referred to the boxer in his award winning novel *Catch-22*, and Nat Fleischer, *Ring Magazine* editor, reported that "if Petrolle were a heavyweight he would be worth his weight in gold. He would be a second Jack Dempsey. Fighters of his ability come but once in a lifetime." Petrolle racked up an awesome record of conquests over ring champions Jackie "Kid" Berg, Tony Canzoneri, Ray Miller, Battling Battalino twice, Sammy Fuller, Jimmy McLarnin, Jimmy Goodrich, and held a newspaper decision over Sammy Mandell before bowing out of the sport in 1934. He was elected into Boxing's Hall of Fame in 1962. In retirement Petrolle opened a gift shop and invested some of his accrued wealth into buying a bank and an iron foundry in Duluth, Minnesota.

The Italian American overran the flyweight class with Frankie Genaro and Fidel La Barba both winning Olympic gold medals and world boxing titles—the first boxers in history to achieve this. In 1929, Willie La Morte also clinched the New York version of the 112-pound crown. The Italian American was also the protagonist in the Golden Age of Bantamweight Boxing, with the illustrious Eddie Martin (Eduardo Martino), Tommy Ryan (Angelo Marino), Mike Ballerino, Carl Tremaine (Carmelo Cantalupo), Vic Burrone, Andy Martin (Andrea Magri), Terry Martin (Francesco Martino), Earl Mastro, Emil Paluso, Joe Ryder (Giuseppe Gargiulo), Willie Spencer (William Sperico), Eddie Shea (Eduardo D'Onofrio) and Little Jack Sharkey (Giovanni Cervati).[7] Bushy Graham (Angelo Geraci) of Utica, New York chipped in with a bantamweight title, joining Eddie Martin at the top of the 118-pound weight class. The featherweights were blessed with six consistently top ten ranked boxers, of whom Carl Duane (Carlo Iacconetti),

Johnny Dundee, Tony Canzoneri and Battling Battalino later won titles. In the lightweight division, Rocky Kansas (Rocco Tozzo) and Sammy Mandell (Samuele Mandala) struck gold, with Steve "Kid" Sullivan (Stefano Tricamo) and Mike Ballerino annexing the junior-lightweight crown. Baltimore's welterweight champion Joe Dundee (Salvatore Lazzara) led the way from contenders Jack Perry (Antonio Perri) and Paul Doyle (Paul San Filippo). Johnny Wilson (Giovanni Panico) ruled the middleweights between 1920 and 1923 and Frank Carbone, Caveman Fisher (Charles Fazio) and title claimant Lou Bogash (Luigi Buccassi) were good enough to make it onto the list of the world's best 160-pound fighters.

The Italians finished the decade spearheading the flyweight, bantamweight and featherweight divisions, with old-timer Johnny Dundee passing the baton of greatness to Tony Canzoneri of New Orleans. Canzoneri won world championships at three different weights and was lightweight champion in arguably the best era in the division's history. In 1928 he confirmed his potential by winning the featherweight title, the first of his professional titles. Two years later, the 22-year-old captured the lightweight title by flattening Al Singer in one round, paving the way for a period of dominance in the 135-pound category, which lasted for six years and spread over two title reigns. In that time he successfully defended against the great Jack "Kid" Berg of England and Cuban legend Kid Chocolate and also outpointed the indomitable Billy Petrolle. Canzoneri won and lost his title to Lou Ambers, and ended on the wrong side of two controversial split points decisions to tough Chicago Jew Barney Ross. He reigned supreme at a time of great champions and contenders and was lauded for being a true fighting champion.

Like Johnny Dundee before him, he was a busy fighter who did not discriminate or hand-pick his opponents, and over his career he met the most important fighters of his generation. Between 1925 and 1939, he met eighteen world champions and six Hall of Famers and he appeared in 21 world title fights. He won 143 of 175 fights, scoring ten draws, and was only knocked out once, in his last fight.

1930–39: The glory years of the Depression

Hard times lifted the bar of competition higher as mass unemployment pushed men into prizefighting, with over eight thousand registered boxers on the pro circuit.[8] Amidst the economic gloom and heightened political tensions abroad, particularly the aggressive foreign policies of Mussolini and Adolf Hitler, heavyweight boxer Primo Carnera became Italy's first world champion in 1933. Although Carnera cannot be considered an Italian American, having learnt his trade in France and boxed in Italy before landing in New York, his standing as world champion bolstered self-esteem among Italian Americans. Acknowledged by the Fascist dictator as a hero, he was always warmly greeted in Little Italies throughout the country. He motivated a generation of Italian American children towards a boxing vocation and future champion Rocky Marciano cited him as his earliest hero.

In an era when heavyweight boxing bouts became overtly politicized Joe Louis single-handedly defeated Nazism and Fascism inside a boxing ring with triumphs over Max Schmeling and Primo Carnera respectively. But perhaps Louis's biggest test came against an unlikely star of this period: Tony Galento, a balding and rotund bartender from Orange, New Jersey. Galento stood 5 feet 9 inches and weighed 230 pounds and he didn't look much like a fighter. He made no secret of his love for beer and Italian food, preferring the nightlife to the boxing gymnasium, but when Galento stepped inside the ring he represented an uncompromisingly aggressive force and armed with a pulverizing left hook he left nothing to chance. He would do anything to win and Galento's use of elbows, eye gouging and blows below the belt made him one of the most feared heavyweights. In a fifteen-year career stretching back to 1928 he toppled most of the main contenders to become one of boxing's top drawing cards. Significantly he never drew the color line and met and beat most of the top African Americans of the thirties.

He came closest to winning the title from the great Louis. Galento was an abrasive larger-than-life character; brash and self-confident, he got under the skin of the normally demure Joe Louis with taunts delivered in his thick New Jersey drawl of "I'll moida da bum!" They met on June 28, 1939, and before a crowd of 35,000 people in Yankee Stadium, Galento, a six-to-one underdog, made his intentions clear from the outset, bullying Louis around the ring with a succession of left hooks. In a dramatic fight of changing fortunes Louis was staggered in the second round before retaliating to inflict upon Galento his first career knockdown. A determined Galento responded in the third by landing a stunning left hook that sent Louis to the canvas. A shocked and weary Louis survived Galento's onslaught, and recovered his composure to stop Galento in the fourth round. Galento retired with impressive career figures of 74 wins, 8 draws and 22 losses, scoring 51 knockouts.

In a talent-laden era more Italians broke into the world's top twenty rankings and achieved undisputed recognition in the most popular divisions compared to the previous decade, which included victories in junior weight classes. Tony Canzoneri augmented his reputation as pound for pound the best boxer around. For much of the decade he and Lou Ambers (Luigi D'Ambrosio) shared the lightweight crown between them.

Ambers ruled the lightweight division between 1936 and 1938 and again in 1939 and 1940, and no one ever begrudged the two-time champion his place at the summit of world boxing. Lou Ambers was the archetypal "hungry fighter." He was malnourished, his brothers and sisters needed food, and when his father lost his saloon business during prohibition and later died suddenly, Ambers' family, comprising nine other siblings, faced financial ruin and a fight for survival. Ambers felt a personal obligation to look after his family. He drifted from one odd job to another, and when he discovered he could make a lot more money by appearing in bootleg fights he chose it as his vocation. He left his hometown of Herkimer and traveled to New York City in search of the big fights. He hooked up with influential manager Al Weill, who instantly recognized promise in Ambers and set about making him into a champion.

After three years as a pro he made his debut at Madison Square Garden in 1935. Old patrons marveled at his work rate, mobility and endurance. In the same year he fought for the world title against his idol Tony Canzoneri, whom Ambers described as the "President of the United States." Ambers dropped the decision but later avenged it and confirmed his superiority over the old master in the rubber match. Ambers was a tough competitor and typified a never-say-die spirit, which helped him to navigate through troubled waters. In his bout with Fritzie Zivic he demonstrated real gutsiness, and in the seventh round he fought on despite sustaining a broken jaw. Bleeding profusely from the mouth, he refused to let his corner throw in the towel, boxing on to complete a courageous victory. During his career, Ambers graduated from making a few dollars in bar-room smokers to receiving $80,000 against Pedro Montanez in 1937. He resolved his family's economic woes, and the once half-starved kid from Herkimer lived out a comfortable retirement.

Other champions included the colorful Midget Wolgast (Joseph Loscalzo), a dazzling Philadelphia flyweight who stayed on top for five years, and no less amazing is that he achieved this with very little training and a combined love of women and alcohol. Lou Salica of New York, Tony Marino of Duquesne, Pennsylvania and Baltimore's Harry Jeffra (Ignazio Guiffi) held the 118-pound title. Battling Battalino (Christopher Battaglini) of Hartford, Connecticut began the decade as the undisputed featherweight champion. Buffalo's Tommy Paul (Gaetano Papa) and Mike Belloise of

Brooklyn, New York joined him at the top, winning other versions of the 126-pound title. Boston's Sammy Fuller (Sabino Ferullo) claimed the junior-welterweight crown and Young Corbett III (Raffaele Giordano) of Fresno, California briefly held the welterweight title. Baltimore's Vince Dundee (Vincenzo Lazzara) and San Francisco's Fred Apostoli confirmed their superiority at middleweight, and three men—Buffalo pair George Nichols (Phillip Nicolosi) and title claimant Lou Scozza and Melio Bettina of Beacon, New York—established their titular credentials in the light-heavyweight category.

1940–49: First class combatant, second class citizen

During the war years, which were characterized by frozen titles and mass recruitment of professional and amateur boxers into the armed forces, a trio of masterclass Italian American fighters stormed to the front of their profession. Featherweight Willie Pep (Guglielmo Papaleo) brought a dash of genius and craft and middleweight Rocky Graziano added brute force, excitement and color. His slugfest trilogy with Tony Zale ranked as the most savage and breath-taking duels ever witnessed inside a boxing ring. Jake La Motta, tormented by inner demons and obstructed by racketeers, was the essence of toughness and driving force. The Italian dominated the featherweight division for the third successive decade, and in a supporting cast of champions, including Petey Scalzo and Phil Terranova from New York, Sal Bartolo of Boston and title claimant Jimmy Perrin from New Orleans, it was the star of Willie Pep that shone the brightest.

Pep was pure unadulterated boxing genius, a featherweight boxer with a heavyweight reputation. He was adored by fans and acclaimed by writers. His sublime boxing skills, cunning, elusiveness, speed of thought, rapidity of fistic delivery and general mastery around the ring made him one of the greatest boxers ever to lace a pair of gloves. Boxing legend Sugar Ray Robinson described the Hartford fighter as the best boxer he ever saw. Mike Gibbons, former world middleweight champion from St. Paul, Minnesota said: "I'd pay to watch Willie [Pep] shadow box." Pep held the featherweight title from 1942 to 1948 and again in 1949 and 1950 and effortlessly swept aside all his rivals.[9] Pep was an outstanding boxer even among champions and his achievements transcended the ring. The 5-foot 5-inch frail-looking son of a Sicilian construction worker was propelled forward as an unlikely standard bearer for Italian American communities in the United States, who regarded his sporting accomplishments and unique skills as a spur to make it in America. Millions watched his fights on television and each time he fought in the Big Apple thousands of supporters left Pep's hometown of Hartford to support him.

Pep was raised during the Depression era and learnt the basics of his trade in the streets working as a shoeshine boy. For five years he defended his turf from older and bigger boys before choosing boxing. He had a stellar amateur career, and when his father's illness forced him to stop work, Pep turned professional at seventeen years old. He won his first 54 bouts before outclassing Mexican heavy hitter Albert "Chalky" Wright over fifteen rounds to win the New York State Athletic Commission (NYSAC) featherweight belt at Madison Square Garden, New York. Pep continued his winning habit until March 1943, when he dropped a ten-round decision to Sammy Angott, ending Pep's remarkable sequence of 62 consecutive victories. He then went undefeated in his next 73 fights before Sandy Saddler dethroned him of his title in October 1948. He avenged the loss in what Grantland Rice, eminent sports writer, described as the greatest boxing exhibition he had ever seen in more than fifty years of covering boxing. Pep retired from the sport in March 1966, having won a staggering 229 fights. He was elected into the Boxing Hall of Fame in 1963 and into the International Boxing Hall of Fame in 1990.

There were other first-rate boxers who earned their place in the sun, such as doughty Louisville lightweight Sammy Angott (Samuele Angotti), who grabbed the 135-pound crown on two separate occasions. Tippy Larkin (Antonio Pilleteri) of Garfield, New Jersey was crowned the junior-welterweight titleholder. Marty Servo (Mario Severino) of Schenectady, New York clinched the world welterweight title and Izzy Jannazzo, the New York-based Alabaman seized the Maryland title version at the same weight. Rocky Graziano and Jake La Motta confirmed their elevated status among the middleweights. Graziano achieved it in 1947 and La Motta followed suit two years later.

The success enjoyed by La Motta and Graziano also confirmed that the overall picture had changed from a physiological perspective. An increasing number of world-ranked Italian Americans appeared in heavier weight categories, a trend that continued into the next decade and beyond, severing any connection with the past. The average Italian American was now bigger than his grandfather and father and found it virtually impossible to comfortably make the flyweight and bantamweight limit, leaving traditionally successful categories to the Hispanic and Asian boxers. During the Second World War Italians accounted for 10 percent of American manpower, a total of 1.5 million men, and one effect of the war was its impact on their pre-eminence in boxing. This is borne out by the impressive number of world championship bouts involving Italian fighters prior to the United States' entry into the war.[10] Between 1940 and 1942 he fought in 36 world title fights but appeared in only 27 title showdowns between 1943 and 1949. The resumption of activity was challenging and most returnees experienced problems with balance, speed, snap, accuracy, timing and delivery of punches, essential elements to ring success. Seen in the context of a wider picture, these practical problems were the least of their worries. A by-product of international hostilities culminated in the internment of Italians living in the United States. Over 600,000 carried identity cards and some of these "resident aliens" were forcibly removed from their properties. Hundreds were held in military camps for up to two years, with Italian-language schools and newspapers closed. Despite the extraordinary courage and sacrifice of young Italian American servicemen in the United States military this cohort was still viewed with suspicion.

1950–55: Colossus Marciano and new horizons

Millions were transfixed by the pugilistic exhilaration of televised boxing in the fifties and for a time, at least in the minds of the people, the notion that Italian Americans held the upper hand in the boxing ring was real enough. The aura of indestructibility surrounding Rocky Marciano (Rocco Marchegiano) influenced public sentiment despite the fact the numbers simply didn't stack up, In September 1952, Marciano became the first and only American of Italian origin to win the biggest prize in sport. Four years later he retired as the only undefeated heavyweight champion in history, having knocked out former champions Joe Louis, Ezzard Charles and Jersey Joe Walcott. An unblemished record, a model of consistency, a paragon of decency and generosity, Marciano distinguished himself not only as a champion but also as an ambassador, enjoying the acclaim that accompanied his title.

Carmen Basilio demonstrated unparalleled warrior-like qualities that made him a box-office star. Between 1955 and 1959 he appeared in five championship contests, each one voted *Ring Magazine's* Fight of the Year. Basilio also captured three world titles and beat the legendary Sugar Ray Robinson. He held the welterweight crown between 1955 and 1956 and 1956 and 1957 and the world middleweight championship between 1957 and 1958. Only three other Italian American champions were crowned during this era. These included Cleveland's Joey Maxim (Giuseppe Berardinelli), who held the light-heavyweight title from 1950 to 1952, New Yorker Paddy De Marco (Pasquale De Marco), the 1954 world lightweight titleholder, and Tony De Marco (Leonardo Liotta) of Boston, who captured the welterweight title in 1955.

Bizarrely, though, it is the fifties that are best remembered as evoking the most poignant memories of Italian American boxing glory. One explanation is the perception perpetuated by Hollywood films of champions Graziano and La Motta. This left a lasting mark on the public psyche and engendered a distorted impression that this era was the pinnacle of greatness for the Italian American fighter. The widespread popularity of television boxing also extended this idea. Marciano emerged as an invincible fighting machine at a time when boxing styles changed drastically to meet the demands of television, with a greater emphasis placed on all-out two-fisted onslaughts. Numerous Italian American fighters of this era possessed crowd-pleasing qualities considered vital by television executives and they were given prominent billing. In this setting the Italian American secured his place in the forefront of this high-tempo blood-and-thunder ring warfare. Between 1945 and 1959 at least one Italian American boxer featured in the best boxing matches voted by *Ring Magazine* in thirteen out of fifteen years.[11] Tough Brooklyn-born street fighter Joe Miceli was hot property in New York arenas and a star of televised boxing in the fifties, featuring in 37 screenings with only Kid Gavilán and Ralph Jones appearing more times. Miceli, a genuine welterweight contender, scored victories over four world champions—Wallace Bud Smith, Virgil Akins, Ike Williams and Johnny Saxton—and only his recklessness and indifference towards training prevented the left-hooker from being world champion. Exciting middleweight contender Joey Giambra appeared on national television 33 times, and big names like Tony Janiro, Rocky Castellani, Enrie Durando and Chico Vejar were other marketable notables making frequent appearances on the small screen.

In reality the number of contenders declined as the barriers of ghettoization of an entire community crumbled and favored an exodus to the city suburbs. Sporting tastes changed and evidence of this transformation began happening at ground level ten to fifteen years earlier when everybody wanted to be like baseball legend Joe DiMaggio. American football also vied for the attentions of the second generation as a greater number of Italian Americans entered universities. Education widened horizons and with greater possibilities in the post-war era through initiatives like the GI Bill many Italian males sought to improve their individual positions by following alternative and less arduous pursuits. With better political organization and awareness young Italians aspired to more and exercised their right to social change in a more assimilated setting. The net result was a decline in overall participation, and the impact of this was that Italian American titular glory receded in the face of stiff competition from the African American. These were undoubtedly thrilling times but essentially it was the last hurrah of the Italian American as a mass fighting force. In 1958 only 15 percent of active fighters were Italian. They had been usurped by the African Americans, and as their participation steadily faded, the new ethnic on the block, the Mexican fighter, also supplanted him. There was no going back to the halcyon days of the previous decades.[12]

5

Ascendancy and inter-ethnic ring rivalry

The question of Italian American ascendancy and inter-ethnic competition in professional boxing is a neglected area of sports research. It's almost as if Italian American participation and subsequent accomplishments never happened and are not worthy of note. Two academic boxing papers with differing remits of study lend a hand as a starting point in our attempt to unravel the truth about the standing of the Italian American inside a boxing ring. In 1952 Kirson Weinberg and Henry Arond looked at the occupational culture of the boxer. In their essay, they identified the recruitment of young boxers most prevalent among Italians, Jews and Irish and African American communities in inner city areas of Chicago. They suggested that the rank order of prominent boxers closely matched ethnic urban groupings. Based upon data tabulated from listings contained in boxing record books, they concluded that the Irishman was dominant in 1909 and in 1916. The Jew replaced him in 1928, and the Italian usurped the Jew in 1936 before the African American assumed top spot in 1948.[1]

Three years later Thomas Jenkins wrote a sociological paper which focused on the changes in ethnic and racial representation among professional boxers, and produced findings on the pattern between ethnic succession in American professional boxing and immigration. Jenkins astutely traced the history of dominant nationalities in boxing, concluding that the second generation of most urban immigrant groups was more than likely drawn to boxing, and the rise of these groups was attributed to the natural demographic expression of large-scale migration.[2]

A comparison between the Italian migratory experience and championship boxing success show that those belonging to the three main influxes of Italian immigration to the United States, namely 1890–99, 1900–09 and 1910–19, registered the most world boxing titles. Interestingly, of the Italian American world champions, all were children of immigrants, with 84 percent of the Italian American world titlists born in the United States. It is possible to extrapolate from migration and year of birth data that, on average, the Italian boxer was under 24 years old when he won a world title (see Appendix VII).

Whilst the studies by Weinberg and Arond and Jenkins are valuable sources and broadly reflect ethnic succession outcomes in boxing, neither specifically addressed the question of ethnic group participation and boxing success. Significantly, not a single cohort or nationality was examined as a case study. In addition several methodological concerns arose, especially relating to ethnic group predominance. Weinberg and Arond's rankings were not indicative of ability or actual performance, and the random sampling of data picked from six single years and used to illustrate group participation over a fifty-year period is somewhat chancy and open to question. There is some potential for confusion with the Jenkins outcomes too. For instance, where an ethnic group produced outstanding boxers, who during their career won several titles at different weights or regained old titles, an unbalanced impression was created that overall one ethnic cohort produced innumerable champions. By his own admission Jenkins found that ethnic data on boxers was "spotty" and data hard to come by, with Nat Fleischer, editor of *Ring Magazine*, central to much of the data kept on boxer nationalities. This presented problems that allowed erroneous data to be recorded. Jenkins also made no distinction for boxers of other countries, describing them only as "others."

Unlike past academic forays my investigation brings together comprehensive data on boxer ethnicity. In addition, in a bid to avoid any distortion of data, only first titles won and not multiple titles captured by great boxers are considered. We also include the most deserving and recognized title claimants, which reveal a more accurate world championship picture. It's important to understand that between 1909 and 1930 almost two thousand no-decision contests were fought, and disputes over legitimacy in the era of press recognition and the validity of no-decision bouts are still the subject of contentious debate. With this type of research still a work in progress some contests have assumed greater significance and certain boxers have been credited with titular recognition, with revisionist historians particularly favoring this approach today.[3]

Set in this historical context the exploits of the Italian American boxer are an unfamiliar story. In contrast the tale of the fighting Irish is central to countless manuscripts. The Jewish boxer is remembered for hitting the heights in the prize ring and establishing periodic dominance. The myth of timeless African American hegemony in boxing prevails due largely to the popularity of television sports coinciding with the pinnacle of African American sporting accomplishments, and the image of triumphant black American heavyweight champions left a lasting impression that it had always been this way. Yet, during the fiercest period of inter-ethnic ring rivalry the Italian American laid claim to 51 world professional boxing titles—one-third greater than the Irish and African American cohort and more than double the Jewish tally. Even Thomas Jenkins, who used an altogether different computation method, wrote that between 1920 and 1949, Italian Americans crowned more champions than any other American cohort, leading the way with 34 titlists. This statistical superiority is important as these titles were amassed at a time when each weight category produced an infinite array of talented fighters regularly engaged in once monthly fights. For long intervals there was generally just one recognized titleholder and a situation developed where many great boxers simply never held world titles (see Appendix VIII).

A summary breakdown of overall world titles won shows that the Italian boxer achieved two recognized world title claims in the first decade of the twentieth century. During the époque from 1910 to 1919 the fighting Irishman maintained championship dominance with seven champions, the German American followed in second place with five champions, and tied in third were the Jew and Italian with three titles apiece. In the twenties both Italian and Jew multiplied the number of individual world boxing champions with the Italian capturing sixteen titles, the Jew with twelve and the Irish with eight titlists. The Italian led the way during the Depression era with fourteen world champions, exhibiting an overall two-to-one superiority over his closest rivals with the African and Jewish cohort both claiming six crowns in the same period. Between 1940 and 1949 there were eleven Italian American world champions, counteracting a downward trend in the overall number of Italian boxers of contendership ability, and finishing the decade in pole position having crowned champions at a disproportionately higher rate. He was followed by the African American on nine, the Irish on three and the Mexican American on two titles. The Irish managed one title and the Jew vanished without trace. Declining overall participation, which had begun a decade earlier, saw a marked fall in the number of Italian American champions crowned in the first half of the fifties. He still mustered five titleholders, which positioned him second behind the African American with nine champions.

The Italian consolidated a strong presence among leading contenders in the official world top ten boxing rankings. He rose from second spot in the twenties to lead these classifications in the thirties, producing the largest proportion of contenders in seven out of the ten weight categories He succumbed only to the Jew in the light-welterweight class, to the Irishman in the middleweight class and to the African American in the light-heavyweight division. Between 1940 and 1955 he occupied second place behind the African American (see Appendix IX). During the forties the African American cohort generated the highest number of contenders, yielding 97 boxers, which comprised 60 percent of the five thousand professional fighters in circulation.[4]

Between 1900 and 1955 the Italian American cohort competed in 371 world title fights including title claim bouts, of which 49 were all-Italian American title showdowns. Between 1900 and 1909 there were a total of 32 "world title" fights involving at least one boxer of Italian ancestry and this total increased to 43 boxers in the next decade. Between 1920 and 1929 he appeared in 93 world title fights, more than doubling the previous ten-year period. The apex of world title appearances materialized in the next decade when the Italian appeared in a staggering 107 world title matches and the overall quality of protagonists boosted the total of all-Italian American world title bouts to sixteen. Although further championship success followed in the forties, the rate of new contenders steadily declined and the Italian engaged in 63 world title contests, a significant decrease from the zenith of the Depression era. These figures continued to slide in the first half of the fifties (see Appendix X).

Nevertheless, the Italian American was the sole cohort to unveil champions in all eight traditional divisions as well as junior classes and achieve undisputed distinction in all categories. Italian American ring achievement is crystallized by the fact that between 1920 and 1955 a new boxing champion was crowned in every year, with the sequence interrupted in only seven of those years. None of his rivals matched this consistency and glory. Both the Irish and African cohort missed out in two divisions, with the Irishman failing to register a single champion at flyweight and at junior-lightweight. The African American was unproductive at flyweight and at junior-welterweight. The Jewish American failed to crown a recognized champion in the heavyweight class. Some pointed to Max Baer lifting the crown in 1934, but Jewish organizations and the International Jewish Sports Hall of Fame have omitted him from their list of past world boxing champions. Bernard Postal, who compiled an authoritative list of great sportsmen of Jewish descent, disregarded Baer's claims, as have experts Ken Blady and Allen Bodner. *Ring Magazine* listed Baer as being of mixed German–Scottish background.[5]

With no boxing ratings available prior to 1924, many boxers worthy of their place among the world's elite have also been excluded from this period of boxing history. I have included a list of contenders and title claimants of Italian origin based on merit, and had such a classification been in existence these boxers would have charted prominently (see Appendix XI). Neither Weinberg and Arond nor Jenkins highlighted any prominent activity by Italian American boxers in the first two decades of the twentieth century.

Ring Magazine's annual world top twenty rankings between 1924 and 1955 adds further evidence of this cohort's prominence over three decades, revealing the names of numerous fringe contenders (see Appendix XII). Prolonged activity and success did not signify that Italian champions emerged from an unlimited supply of participants. At least four thousand Italian Americans appeared on professional boxing cards between 1900 and 1955. According to boxing historian Mike Silver this figure is dwarfed by their Jewish counterparts, where an estimated twenty thousand were in circulation between 1910 and 1940. Silver states that almost one-third of professionals in the twenties and thirties were of Jewish background. Author Allen Bodner wrote that Jewish world championship success was not proportionate to the mass participation and may have been under-represented. Strong competition, particularly from the Italian cohort, thwarted a greater number of Jewish world title challengers.[6]

The question of cohort success would not be complete without some kind of ratio analysis determining "wastage" among professional boxers from the main ethnic cohorts, i.e., those that succeeded and those that failed from overall participation figures. Obtaining data proved awkward and overall boxer totals from the main ethnic cohorts is based purely on speculative figures. Prior to 1920, there was no official regulatory body holding records on boxers and on results. Research on the overall numbers of Italian American professional boxers is taken from scores of local and national American newspapers. Data on Jewish and African American boxers was derived from estimates supplied from books, journals and old newspapers. Unfortunately no data was available on the overall totals of Irish American boxers for this period. Furthermore this task was hampered by the custom of boxers' adoption of ring pseudonyms and it was not always possible to identify the ethnicity and nationality of relatively unknown boxers. Another problem was defining success and the establishment of boxing failure, especially among the very large category of preliminary/ semi-wind-up professional boxers. A boxer's inability to advance to contendership or headliner status was affected by so many variables, and without the relevant resource of mass testimonies this task was deemed impractical and abandoned. With particular focus given to the Italian American boxer, additional yardsticks examine in greater detail his importance inside the boxing ring.

Inter-ethnic ring rivalry

The Italian versus Jew confrontations was legendary, and the greatest were the Benny Leonard and Johnny Dundee contests during the no-decision era. Other notable pairings included four meetings between Eddie Martin and Charley Phil Rosenberg, and five explosive matches featuring Benny Bass and Johnny Farr during the twenties. The Barney Ross versus Tony Canzoneri and Sammy Angott against Davey Day lightweight title encounters featured prominently in the thirties. With both cohorts of similar physical size and build they regularly fought each other, especially in the lighter weight categories. They obstinately competed over world titles, title claims and title eliminators, and national and state recognized belts, and most of the 499 meetings between world-ranked contenders occurred between 1924, the inaugural year of the world rankings system, and 1940, when the Jew ceased to be a force in boxing.

Subsequent top ten showdowns featured Italian and African American fighters, disproving the fallacy that blacks were avoided. Between 1924 and 1955 the Italian fighter met his black opponent almost as often as his Jewish rival, and in the head-to-head showdowns success was finely balanced. Out of a total of 484 recorded professional bouts, the African American won 237 contests (49%) and the Italian 223 (46%) with 24 drawn bouts (5%). When you consider that Sugar Ray Robinson, arguably the greatest pound-for-pound boxer ever, won 23 of his 25 fights against a top-ranking Italian opponent up to the year ending 1955, performance levels were startlingly similar in the most compelling of pugilistic époques.

The Italian versus Irish American rivalry was bitterly competitive but the match-up was the least frequent rivalry, chiefly due to two reasons. The heyday of the Irish American pug had come and gone prior to a significant Italian American breakthrough, and when the Italian was on top overall, world-ranked Irishmen dwindled in number. Secondly, Irish American contenders were concentrated in the middleweight and heavyweight categories where there were fewer combatants of Italian origin, particularly during the early twenties when the Irish celebrated a greater share of champions at these weights. The two cohorts engaged in 342 contests featuring world-ranked boxers with the spoils of victory remarkably even, with the Italian winning 156 bouts, the Irish 157 and with 29 drawn encounters (see Appendix XIII).

Analysis of world title fights between 1900 and 1955 revealed the African American winning thirty matches with the Italian triumphing eighteen times with one bout drawn out of 49 championship bouts between them. The Italian held the initiative over the Irish boxer and was evenly matched with his Jewish rival (see Appendix XIV). A composite analysis of the aggregate tenure of world title reigns (duration in years) from the main ethnic American groups showed that the African American possessed the longest title reign of two and a half years. He was followed by the Jewish, the Irish and the Italian boxer (see Appendix XV).

With reference to the American boxer scoring the most annual world top ten rankings between 1924 and 1955, 40 percent of those listed are Italian American, with only the African American yielding a higher total of ranking years. Featherweight Willie Pep, light-heavyweight Joey Maxim, lightweight Tony Canzoneri and bantamweight Lou Salica were the fabulous four on the list (see Appendix XVI).

Analysis and interpretation

What does this reveal about levels of success between the main ethnic groups? At face value the hard data simply conveys that once the African American fighter captured a title he held it the longest, and not much else. There are some problems with this type of quantitative analysis and interpretation. For example, as the Italian American cohort produced the greatest proportion of champions, so there exists a greater likelihood that variation and distortion will affect the data representation. By examining specific points we can establish a better understanding of the data. Strangely, the Italian American championship reigns were characterized by brief tenures, and this did not always mean titles were surrendered in ring battles.

In actual fact the opposite was true. For example, Lou Bogash won the NYSAC middleweight title but he did not defend his claim, and by the end of 1923 he had been stripped of the title and general recognition accorded to Johnny Wilson. In the early forties featherweight Jimmy Perrin and welterweight Izzy Jannazzo won the Louisiana and Maryland recognized world title versions respectively. Perrin made no defenses and Jannazzo gave it up voluntarily after one successful defense. Carl Duane won the newly introduced junior-featherweight title from Jack "Kid" Wolfe, but he never defended it and the weight category fell into disuse. Mike Belloise defended his NYSAC featherweight crown once, but after contracting pneumonia, which kept him out of the ring for eleven months, he was unable to meet further obligations and was stripped of his title. In 1946 Tippy Larkin won the junior-welterweight title and after one defense he abandoned the title. Sammy Angott won the lightweight title in December 1941. Soon afterwards he was forced into early retirement due to hand injuries. He later resumed his career and regained his championship laurels. Bushy Graham won the bantamweight title but outgrew the 118-pound weight limit and was forced to relinquish his title without making a title defense. Johnny Dundee also gave up his featherweight title. Pete Herman, former world bantamweight champion, retired in 1922, seven months after losing the title for a second time due to a detached eye condition. He was just 26 and in his prime. Welterweight Marty Servo was perhaps the most unfortunate of all. He was forced into early retirement due to a nose injury, seven months after winning the title, having made no title defenses.

The data relating to the overall tenure of world championships significantly obscures the fact that the majority of world titles won by Italian Americans occurred during the twenties, thirties, forties and fifties. They did not draw any advantage from the no-decision era, prevalent in the first two decades of the twentieth century, which produced a stalemate where champions locked titles away indefinitely. A championship belt could not be lost unless the titleholder agreed to put his title on the line and made the stipulated weight, and even when these conditions were met he would still have to be stopped to be dethroned. Often a bizarre situation occurred where a champion lost a newspaper decision but still held onto his crown. Only five Italian Americans won title claims before 1920. The Irish champions particularly benefited from this system as they churned out the greatest number of contenders, closely followed by the Germans and the Jews. Featherweight champion Johnny Kilbane held onto his title for eleven years, making only eight title defenses. It's worth remembering that this happened when it was customary to appear in two to three bouts per month. The boxing authorities acquiesced, while he handpicked his opponents. He appeared in exhibitions and countless non-title bouts, seldom risking his title. He was not alone. Fellow Irish American Philadelphia Jack O'Brien had one of the longest reigns on record, holding the light-heavyweight title between 1905 and 1912, but he never defended the championship and moved up to heavyweight to challenge for that title. Other long-reigning champions included Jewish lightweight champion Benny Leonard. He ruled between 1917 and 1924 and defended his title on only nine occasions.

Data available on the tenure of world championships for this period portrays a distorted representation of ethnic ring success. Italian and African Americans won titles *en masse* at a time of open international competition, closer scrutiny and greater pressure applied by boxing commissions, compelling boxers to defend titles in stipulated time limits or risk losing their title. Two decades later Joe Louis reigned as heavyweight champion for twelve years, but was the lengthy tenure simply down to pugilistic greatness or did it arise from something else? Without question Louis was a talented boxer and history will judge him as one of the best, but his grip on the major prize was extended in no small part by several significant factors. The Second World War interrupted regular competition and his title was frozen for several years. Secondly, whilst America lauded Louis as a superhero when he trounced Max Schmeling, and greeted him as a true patriot when he served his country, this did not mean that the racial landscape had changed. It hadn't and the heavyweight title was not risked against a select band of dangerous black heavyweight contenders. Instead Louis was served white fighters of average ability in what became labeled as the "bum of the month" competition. This arguably boosted the length of his title reign.

The Italian American boxer successfully coped in the most competitive weight divisions. He was a major player in the bantamweight class and in the ultra-competitive featherweight and lightweight categories. An almighty struggle for domination ensued for two consecutive decades between the Jew and the Italian, and when the Jewish presence dissipated the African American moved up. In stark contrast the same period threw up fewer premium level contenders and less overall quality in the heavier divisions, at light-heavyweight and heavyweight where Italians were less visible.

Another significant factor is whether titleholders were "fighting champions." Only by evaluating a champion's ring activity can an accurate assessment be made about his worthiness as a titlist. Pete Herman, Johnny Dundee, Frankie Genaro, Battling Battalino, Tony Canzoneri, Lou Ambers, Harry Jeffra, Pete Scalzo, Sammy Angott, Willie Pep, Jake La Motta and Rocky Marciano all deserved reputations as "fighting champions." They encountered the best in their respective divisions and risked being stripped of their belts if they refused to meet the number one challengers, something that seldom happened prior to the twenties. At face value a boxer who held a title for years might have conveyed an impression of exceptional ability, but this was not always the case. For example, prolonged championship tenure might have been forged through the unscrupulous avoidance of leading contenders, and long intervals between title defenses may have characterized a title reign adding up to fewer title defenses. This approach prompts an obvious poser, that is whether a champion making a quick title defense against a leading light and who subsequently loses is less worthy than someone who successfully defends his belt frequently against inferior rivals, but holds onto it for years. Former champions, bantamweight Eddie "Cannonball" Martin and welterweight Young Corbett III lost in their first defenses against number one contenders Charley Rosenberg and Jimmy McLarnin respectively. Despite these losses, both Martin and Young Corbett III were outstanding performers. They were not flash-in-the-pan boxers and had established solid reputations in the sport, having beaten contenders and champions alike.

To muddy the waters further a boxer's pre-championship experience is another factor to consider when establishing the merits of the published data. Welterweight Joe Dundee's tortuous eight-year wait before capturing the title left him scarred and embittered. For years he battled against the top men in his division and beat champions Mickey Walker and Tommy Freeman in non-title contests, but was cruelly denied a title opportunity. When he eventually won the title he opted for easier purses and unashamedly traveled to where the money was, relying on imaginative excuses to avoid commission-appointed mandatory challengers. He was vehemently criticized for this behavior. The above-mentioned yardsticks demonstrate qualitative evidence of the Italian American's boxing ability and the general impact made in the sport. By itself the data does not wholly explain his sustained longevity and prolific success. For this we need to look further afield and draw comparisons between the main ethnic groups and evaluate attitudes, habits and expectations and how this changed over time.

The Jewish American

As much as the Jewish contribution to boxing was notable so was its sudden decline. By 1940, the Jewish role in boxing was confined to involvement as managers and promoters. Most second-generation Jews opted for conventional avenues such as education as a ticket to success in American society. No group participated more fully in the attendance increase at American colleges than the children of East European Jewish immigrants. They flocked to private and public colleges, far exceeding their proportion of the general population. By 1920 Hunter and City Colleges of New York revealed 80 percent Jewish enrolments. Prior to the First World War

Columbia's Jewish enrolment had reached 40 percent and Harvard's 20 percent.[7] The Jewish culture and religious ties had assisted in the smooth process of adjustment to American society. Greater emphasis was placed on intellect and business. Physical pursuits, ruthless force and sensuality were deemed to be "unjewish" and shunned. However, Jews broke with some of their cultural values and sought ways to make money and earn self-respect. Boxing was seen in the larger process of acculturation. As Jews grew more mobile, gaining access to higher education institutions, they changed their focus away from boxing to basketball and baseball. For many Jews baseball became a way to a larger American society.[8]

The Irish American

Between 1846 and 1870 over three million Irish emigrated, and decades later the majority of Irish males had advanced both socially and economically, joining the exodus to the suburbs. The Irish working class held better-paid jobs in the industrial sector compared to other ethnic cohorts, and they jealously guarded political control from the "new" immigrants. Between 1900 and 1930 the Irish were in charge of the distribution of municipal employment. Jobs and contracts were awarded through a system of patronage.[9] Irish rule in Boston, New York and Jersey City had secured and controlled public services, police, dockyard activities and construction services, and this widespread effect was similar in other North East cities.

Irish ring supremacy was at its peak during the bare-knuckle era and the transition to the Marquis of Queensberry rules. Some writers such as Bob Waters looked at this period and supported the argument that Irish success had lasted for almost a century. Whilst this appears statistically unequaled there were few challengers to this mantle who emanated from outside the Irish sphere. The "old" immigrants of Germany, Sweden and the other Scandinavian countries predominantly settled into agriculture and industry in equal numbers. Unlike the Irish and later immigrants who vied for the only available positions in industry and manufacturing in the decaying slums of American cities, these migrants were not confined to urban zones.[10] The next large-scale migration did not occur until the period between 1880 and 1910, which witnessed the settlement of Eastern European Jews and Italians. The argument of Irish ring supremacy is further weakened by the lack of opportunities afforded to African American fighters. The English, despite their boxing tradition, did not produce an abundance of combatants and the natives were slow to generate interest. Therefore contests were usually disputed by Irish-born or first generations of Irish parentage. The growth of organized sport in the late nineteenth century and early twentieth century, combined with the move to settle on the city outskirts, saw a drift into American football and baseball. By the thirties and forties Irish boxing involvement had petered out.

The African American

Large waves of African Americans migrated to northern cities in the inter-war period, and again after the Second World War as boxing became a symbol in their struggle for assimilation. The African American filled the void left by the Jew and the Irishman, and some of the most memorable matches in boxing history between Italians and African Americans developed over the next two decades as they vied for ring supremacy. In the late thirties Lou Ambers and triple titlist Henry Armstrong twice locked horns over the world lightweight title with each fighter registering a thrilling points victory. Between 1948 and 1951 the inimitable Willie Pep and the tough Sandy Saddler engaged in four tempestuous and action-packed featherweight title encounters. Middleweight Jake La Motta tangled with the great Sugar Ray Robinson on six occasions and it was the "Bronx Bull" who inflicted on Robinson his first professional loss. In the early to mid fifties Rocky Marciano swept aside legends Joe Louis, Ezzard Charles twice, Jersey Joe Walcott twice and Archie Moore in exhilarating slugfests en route to retiring as undefeated heavyweight champion. These celebrated pairings represented a taster of the many Italian versus African American pugilistic tussles that laced each division.

Proponents behind the notion of African American hegemony direct particular focus to the imposition of the color bar, which prevented black boxers from competing for the world heavyweight title for over two decades. During the First World War era, a quartet of exceptional black heavyweights—Sam Langford, Joe Jeanette, Bill Tate and Sam McVey—were denied initially by champion Jack Johnson, who refused to meet them, and once he was ousted the white establishment froze them out too. *Ring Magazine* editor Nat Fleischer later trumpeted the candidacy of Harry Wills for a match with Jack Dempsey. Promoter Tex Rickard reportedly scoffed at these suggestions and turned the offer down. What is clear is that Wills was not a world-beater. In 1926 he succumbed to a thirteenth-round defeat to eventual champion Jack Sharkey, and a year later Spain's title challenger Paulino Uzucdun knocked him out in four rounds. George Godfrey was touted as the next African American sensation, but even with widespread support he incurred losses to champions in waiting Jack Sharkey and Primo Carnera, and also to main contender Johnny Risko as well as fringe contenders Jack Gross and Walter Cobb, hardly a ringing endorsement of one harboring titular aspirations.

Did this exclusion materially advantage other ethnic cohorts? Arguably the Irish American cohort benefited most from this enforced absence as three champions were crowned: Jack Dempsey, Gene Tunney and James Braddock. Other winners were Jess Willard, a Scottish–Native Indian American, Jack Sharkey, a Lithuanian American, Primo Carnera an Italian national, Max Baer, a Scottish–German American, and Max Schmeling representing Germany. The exclusion of black competitors did not advantage Italian Americans as few of them actually made the heavyweight poundage and those that did were not of a high standard. They were neither big enough nor possessed the pugilistic armory to mount a major challenge. "Fireman" Jim Flynn, who campaigned in the first two decades of the twentieth century, was relatively small, weighing 180 pounds and only 5 feet 9½ inches in height. He was essentially a light-heavyweight. Even Rocky Marciano, who emerged victorious in the fifties, tipped the scales at only 184 pounds and stood 5 feet 11 inches tall, making him one of the lightest and shortest world heavyweight champions on record.

The superimposed exclusion did not apply to black boxers in lower weight categories. Joe Gans held the lightweight title between 1902 and 1908. Theodore Flowers took the middleweight title in 1926 and Young Jack Thompson the welterweight title in 1930. William "Gorilla" Jones won the middleweight title in 1932 and John Henry Lewis seized the light-heavyweight belt in 1935. Whilst some states outlawed mixed-race fights, the record books show that the most frequent opponent for the African American was the Italian, who cared little about the political repercussions of the color line. Barely known African American contenders like George Robinson, Jack Green, Ansell Bell, Wilbur Cohen, Allentown Joe Gans, Chick Suggs and Danny Edwards regularly swapped punches with Italian Americans during the no-decision era and the twenties.

Although boxing was generally the most meritocratic of sports the fortunes of an African American fighter were often hindered. Whilst it became accepted to see a black American compete at weights outside the heavyweight division, the path to the top was fraught with difficulties and obstructed by the prevailing social and political conditions of the day. According to historian Hank Kaplan, if there had been a level playing field for the African American there would have been fewer champions from other ethnic groups. He explained:

Prejudice was so strong that they never allowed the African American to develop into contendership. That is important. Boxing is the only sport where you cannot possibly become really good at what you're doing until you have had the experience, the practice. Theoretically you can take a big six-foot-tall kid, comes off the farm, comes to the big city and you put him on the field, you hand him a baseball bat and you say "Look! Kid, that guy is going to pitch a ball to you and when you see that ball coming just swing with the bat at the ball." Theoretically he could hit that ball and put it right out of the park. But in boxing you cannot become good until you have the experience. You know why I say that? Because nobody ever has. So particularly with black American kids, you say: "OK, kid, you wanna be a fighter? OK come on." They put him in over his head and got him beat. They use him as an opponent, as a body to build the white guy. This is what they did throughout the twenties and thirties whenever a little black kid showed up in the neighborhood and wanted to earn a few bucks. That existed from the turn of the century to the mid-thirties.

He continued:

Some fighters made it, got past those barriers of being knocked off. Some guys made it despite the fact they were using them as opponents. They still made it. They ascended and got to a certain point, and at that point when they were competitors they couldn't get work. Then they got fights and they used to fight with handcuffs on. I hate to say this but if we could start again now beginning with the 1900s the [world championship] picture would be different.[11]

The arrival and impact of Joe Louis in the thirties, and a general softening in attitude, opened the floodgates of large-scale African American participation. In 1937 a *Ring Magazine* survey confirmed the presence of 1,800 African Americans in the professional ranks and 1,500 represented at amateur level.[12] As a mass participant, the black fighter churned out a greater number of world-ranked professionals in the forties, but was unable to replicate this success into proportionate championship wins.

One possible explanation is the bitter rivalry with the Italian, which continued unabated into the next decade. Italian success would not have been possible without great fighters and it was particularly fantastic boxing talent; Willie Pep, Sammy Angott, Jake La Motta, Rocky Graziano, Joey Maxim, Carmen Basilio and Rocky Marciano were arguably champions built for any era. Italian fighters were born and bred in cities and towns located on the Eastern seaboard of the United States, where many of the fight clubs and boxing venues were situated. With New York City, the Mecca of boxing, within close vicinity it made commercial sense for shrewd boxing promoters to exploit large fan bases from long established partisan communities ready to rally behind one of their own. If it meant packing arenas and lifting revenue yields then this was a no-brainer for a promoter. Interestingly, at this time African Americans did not benefit from an established boxing infrastructure or a large fan base.

Influence of racketeering

Another theory presupposes that the foundation of the disproportionate Italian American championship success was based on the increasing role of Italians in positions of authority. Italians succeeded the Irish and the Jews in becoming an established and dominant force in boxing administration, management and promotion, and coupled with a pronounced criminal involvement the implication is that these connections helped Italian American fighters obtain the big fights and lucrative paydays. Acceptance of such a premise would mean the erasure of all boxing championship history, since the sport has traditionally been associated with mob elements dating back to the bare-knuckle era. "Mr Grey" aka Frankie Carbo was widely reported as the man from the underworld who influenced the fight game from behind the scenes. He reportedly took cuts from fighters' purses, appointed managers as his stooges and controlled the destinies of fighters. Carbo, who was involved in boxing in some guise since 1933, controlled boxers in the middleweight, welterweight and lightweight divisions. He represented the latest addition to a racketeer's roll of honor stretching back to the turn of the century. From Monk Eastman to Arnold Rothstein, Legs Diamond to Dutch Schultz, Al Capone to Johnny Torrio and Owney Madden to Waxey Gordon, all had declared interests in the fight game. Carbo established important connections with Jewish promoters including leading figure Mike Jacobs. The incorporation of the Boxing Managers Guild of New York in 1944 assured Carbo's direct control over most managers and indirect influence over the fighters. By 1949 he had secured a virtual national monopoly of the sport through his promotions group, the International Boxing Club. Between 1949 and 1953 he held the promotional rights to 36 out of 44 championship fights staged in the United States, including all heavyweight and middleweight divisions.

If the mob had concocted a masterplan to enhance the prospects of Italian American boxers then their actions betrayed their intentions. In 1947 Rocky Graziano was suspended after admitting under oath that he had been offered one hundred thousand dollars to throw a fight. He also testified that bribes were offered on three other occasions.[13] Jake La Motta, long considered the "uncrowned middleweight champion," attributed his predicament to his unwillingness to co-operate with underworld figures. After years out in the cold he tried cutting a deal by promising to lose to Tony Janiro in exchange for a title shot. The mob refused and La Motta won the fight. Less than a year later Felix Bocchicchio, Philadelphia's leading promoter, guaranteed La Motta a long-awaited title chance as long as La Motta "threw'" his fight with African American Billy Fox. In November 1947 La Motta tamely surrendered in four rounds. The New York boxing commission withheld purses and began an investigation, which led nowhere. Sugar Ray Robinson, the welterweight champion, reported that he had been offered a bribe not to fight Marty Servo. Carmen Basilio, the perennial number one welterweight contender, was brushed off for years because he wouldn't do business with the mob, leaving celebrated author and writer Budd Schulberg indignant at such treatment. Welterweight contender Vince Martinez was disliked by Carbo and frozen out until 1958 when he got a world title shot against Virgil Akins. Middleweight Joey Giardello was also shut out of the title picture until he switched camps. Mob intervention also impacted on champions and contenders of the ilk of Rocky Castellani, Paddy De Marco, Tony De Marco and Joey Giambra, who joined a lengthy list of disgruntled and dispirited professionals on the wrong end of questionable verdicts.

As far back as the summer of 1925 talented Chicagoan Eddie Shea had pulled the short straw in challenging Charley Rosenberg for the world bantamweight title. He was unexpectedly knocked out in four rounds in what NYSAC commissioner William Muldoon described as an "outrageous fake." Rosenberg's manager was notorious gangster Champ Segal. Many years later Battling Battalino, featherweight champion, revealed that he was supposed to take a dive in his January 1932 title defense against Freddie Miller in Cincinnati. It went against everything he stood for and the farcical encounter was declared a no contest. Three months later Battalino relinquished his title.

The extent of mobster involvement in boxing was so prevalent in the careers of many boxers of different ethnic backgrounds since many grew up as children in the same streets and in the same wards. Barney Ross, the Jewish lightweight champion, worked as a messenger for Al Capone. Capone enjoyed his victory over Tony Canzoneri. Ross was never accused of rigging fights. Capone bet on their outcome and offered Ross his company. Capone was heavily involved in boxing, controlling Irish and African American fighters. The relationship between boxer and gangster was evident throughout the careers of Jewish boxers Benny Leonard, Abe Atell and Ruby Goldstein.[14] Jewish mobster Arnold Rothstein was an avid fightgoer and socialized with many champions. Harry "Champ" Segal managed Dave Rosenberg, 1922 middleweight title claimant. Members of Detroit's Jewish-led Norman Purple gang muscled their way into the boxers' training camps prior to the Primo Carnera versus Jack Sharkey heavyweight title fight in 1933.[15]

Moreover, claims abound that the involvement of *la mano nera* (Black Hand) somehow influenced the decision making process of referees and judges in favor of the Italian cohort. In short, numerous boxers across the racial divide were victims of unfair decisions during this period. The subjective nature of judging contests has caused frustration and rancor among fight followers since time immemorial. Dennie Mancini, the late and distinguished British boxing manager and trainer, refuted the suggestion that organized crime had manufactured a world championship picture dominated by Italian Americans:

> I can't accept that. It's like everything, all promoters need great fighters and vice versa. Jake La Motta tried to avoid working with the system and for many years he was kept out. Other guys who were more co-operative had opportunities before La Motta. History tells us that it's a maneuvering. If you're in with a certain crowd your boxer will get his chance before some other boxer who is not. That's always been part of boxing politics.[16]

The infiltration of organized crime into boxing was omnipresent and did not begin or end with the Italian American involvement in the sport. Some boxers from different ethnic backgrounds were rapidly elevated to championship prominence and others were held back. This was the general experience and accepted standard in the underbelly of professional boxing. The central issue for racketeers, who were usually of a multi-ethnic composition, was financial and not racially motivated. Their overriding aim was to promote a fighter who could generate a maximum return on their investment. Jewish mobsters controlled Italian and Irish fighters. Al Capone handled fighters of diverse backgrounds, and English American Owney Madden is said to have run boxing in the twenties. High-profile African American fighters Ike Williams, Johnny Bratton, Jersey Joe Walcott, Johnny Saxton and Wallace Bud Smith were all controlled by Carbo Incorporated. Yet all of them became world champions.

Pioneer Casper Leon, the Palermo-born title claimant, fought between 1891 and 1904 and is generally considered the father of all Italian American prizefighters.

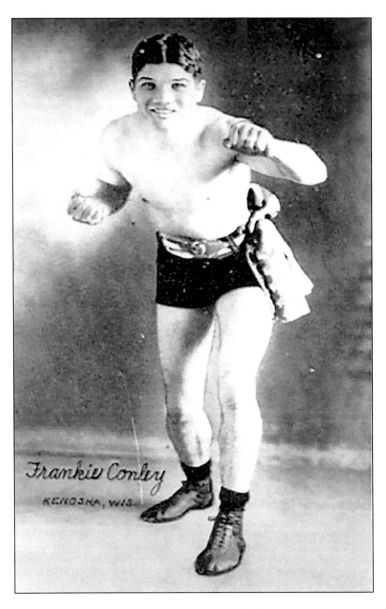

Spirited Frankie Conley laid claim to the world bantamweight title in 1910 when he knocked out Monte Atell in the 42nd round of their title bout in Vernon, California.

Mighty midget Young Zulu Kid (left) of Brooklyn stood less than
five feet tall, but what he lacked in height he made up in persistent
aggression. In 1916 he fought Britain's Jimmy Wilde for the inaugural
world flyweight title. Indefatigable Sicily-born Johnny Dundee (right)
was one of the greatest boxers of his era. He campaigned from 1912 to
1932, fought in 340 recorded bouts and won three world titles.

Harlem middleweight Johnny Wilson won the title in 1920. He was
no stranger to controversy. His boxing style was lambasted and claims
were made about nefarious associations.

Carl Duane was known as the "Bronx Steamroller" He won the newly created junior-featherweight title in 1923.

Sammy Mandell of Rockford, Illinois was a cool and stylish boxer
who was lightweight champion between 1926 and 1930. He also beat
Hall of Famer Jimmy McLarnin.

Indomitable Fargo lightweight Billy Petrolle (left) beat eight world
champions in his career, but ironically never held the title. Battling
Battalino (right) of Hartford captured the featherweight title in 1929
by outpointing Andre Routis of France. He also bested the great
Cuban Kid Chocolate.

Joe Dundee (left) and Vince Dundee (right) are generally considered
the first siblings to win world titles. Joe won the welterweight title in
1927 and Vince captured the NYSAC middleweight title in 1933.

Legendary Tony Canzoneri won world titles at three different weights
(featherweight, lightweight and junior-welterweight) in the twenties
and thirties in arguably the most competitive era.

100-1 underdog George Nichols of Sandusky, Ohio, shocked the
boxing world in 1932 by winning the NBA light heavyweight title.
(Courtesy of *Ring Magazine*)

Sammy Fuller of Boston (left), a rugged and cagey fighter, won the *Ring Magazine* sponsored junior-welterweight title in 1932 beating Jack "Kid" Berg of England. Midget Wolgast (right) of Philadelphia ruled the flyweights between 1930 and 1935. In his prime, Wolgast's reflexes and neat footwork were so quick nobody could lay a glove on him.

Flashy Bushy Graham (left) of Utica, New York won the NYSAC world bantamweight title in 1928. Industrious Young Corbett III (right) of Fresno, California captured the welterweight title in 1933.

Marty Servo (left) of Schenectady, New York dethroned Freddie Cochrane to win the welterweight title in 1946, but his ambitions were thwarted by a nasty nose injury sustained in his next fight. Sammy Angott (right) was a tough and clever ring tactician who won the lightweight title twice. He was the first boxer to beat Willie Pep in the paid ranks.

Rocky Graziano (left) of Brooklyn won the middleweight title in 1947 in an amazing slugfest with Tony Zale. For a long time, Jake La Motta (right) of the Bronx was recognized as the uncrowned middleweight champion. After making a deal with the mob he captured the title in 1949. Both boxers' legacies endure thanks to two memorable films.

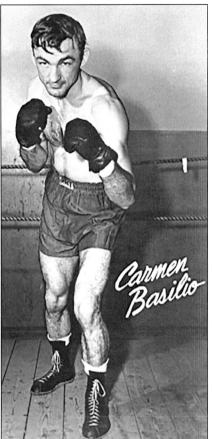

Sublime Willie Pep (left) of Hartford possessed dash and craft, helping him stay on top of the featherweight division for most of the forties. No boxer gave up more in the pursuit of glory than the courageous Carmen Basilio (right). He won the welterweight crown twice and the middleweight title by beating Sugar Ray Robinson.

Invincible Rocky Marciano of Brockton, Massachusetts is still the only heavyweight boxer in history to retire undefeated. He stopped 43 of his 49 opponents including ex-champions Ezzard Charles, Jersey Joe Walcott twice and Joe Louis.

6

God, the gang, the club and the settlement house

For a while in the twentieth century the role of the Catholic Church was influential in spreading the popularity of boxing among Italian American boys. The impact of street-corner societies and athletic clubs and the establishment of the settlement house movement provided recruitment pathways which accelerated and consolidated the Italian American boxing experience. Traditionally, the Church has been a vehement opponent of boxing, questioning the moral purpose and the inherent brutishness and violence associated with this blood sport. But as the moral and ethical arguments became blurred both Protestant and Roman Catholic clergy occupied a central role in promoting the sport among newly arrived immigrants. The change in attitude in American society had happened long before, and previous opponents of sporting pastimes now argued that athletics was character building, permitting organized sport to make its mark. Boxing, a primary example of working-class recreation, was seen by many as the sport of choice for ghetto boys, and one way to lift the hopes of aberrant youths who might otherwise lean towards delinquency and the insidious influence of organized crime.

To counter the ethos of "Muscular Christianity" and organizations like the YMCA and the Boy Scout movements, as well as Protestant influence in public schools, the Catholic Church created parochial schools and opened up athletic and social clubs. These clubs provided unassimilated immigrant urban dwellers with Bible classes and they became centers of learning and congregation, with team athletics sanctioned and with its most notable presence in boxing with the staging of local and national tournaments. In some inner city neighborhoods it became an integral part of structured parish life.

As early as 1900, Italian amateur boxers were generating headline news. One A. Padrucco of St. Bartholomew Athletic Club in Manhattan, New York reached the semi-final of the 158 pound category at the National Amateur Athletic Union boxing championships.[1] In 1903 a boys' club was set up at the Our Lady of the Holy Rosary Church in East Harlem's Little Italy in New York City, where Irish priests taught boxing to the predominantly Italian members. It was a similar story in other Italian enclaves, with church facilities and back rooms accommodating boys' clubs that featured a variety of athletic activities. On the Upper West Side, the Catholic Church of the Holy Name of Jesus organized the Holy Name Boxing Club, and in the post-First World War era the club captured ten out of twelve Golden Gloves amateur titles with numerous champions of Italian background. Its most celebrated members were Melio Bettina and Pete Scalzo, who later won world titles. Two other high-profile Catholic-affiliated boxing clubs were situated on the Upper West Side Manhattan district. The Church of the Ascension supported the highly regarded Ascension Parish House and this outfit produced the area's best amateur and professional boxers. The Paulist Athletic Club, which was connected to the Catholic St. Paul the Apostle Church, was one of the oldest of the local sports organizations. It used its basement for boxing matches and many of its star Italian American athletes enlisted for service in the First World War.

The Knights of Columbus, the large Catholic fraternal service organization, founded in New Haven, Connecticut in 1882, later spread nationally and was actively engaged in the sponsorship of athletic contests. Derelict buildings were converted and vacant lots put into use as boxing was supported in inner city wards. The American Catholic Church continued to support important basketball tournaments, athletics meetings and boxing shows, and during the twenties the Catholic Boys' Club network in New York strengthened the link between the Catholic Church and boxing. During the same period St. Anthony's Church in the Italian West Side section of Buffalo boasted 26 societies including state-wide acclaimed sports teams, and the pool of sporting talent from this area was especially characterized by top Italian boxers. In the Hell's Kitchen district of West Side Manhattan, a notorious breeding ground for boxers, St. Raphael Catholic Church developed a recreation center for boxing with St. Vincent De Paul gymnasium on 53rd Street, also popular with local Italians. At the

1929 New York Metropolitan Amateur Boxing Championships one-quarter of the 120 title aspirants were of Italian background and half of the eight championship class winners were Italian. Many trained in church-sponsored clubs such as Ascension Parish, Trinity Athletic Club and the Holy Name Boxing Club.

So, to what extent did the Catholic Church's involvement in boxing boost Italian American participation and resultant success? The church provided a vital function in parish life in all things fraternal, educational and spiritual and through sporting provision the clerics hoped it would eventually win the trust of its parishioners and turn them into "good Catholics." On the one hand the formula proved successful when membership among boys skyrocketed. On the other hand these sportsmen had little desire to offer themselves up as dutiful and subservient churchgoers. Unlike their fathers, who were emotionally torn between Italy and their adopted home, the sons exhibited a willingness to participate in American society. In religious outlook these males manifested starkly similar views to their fathers, and an old-country attitude based upon suspicion and mistrust of the clergy and Papacy prevailed. They inherited a hybrid religion combining Catholicism and superstition, where patron saints of Italian villages were celebrated with annual festive processions in Little Italies. The Irish–German ecclesiastical axis denounced their traditions, criticized poor Italian church attendance, especially among males, and questioned their commitment to the Catholic faith. There was a partial improvement when Italian churches were established, but the Italian felt alone and misunderstood, and self-reliance through work was seen as the only way forward for himself and for his family. The Italian tradition of secularism and church indifference continued and by accepting the American way he developed a sense that uninterrupted material progress was possible. By 1918 less than one-third of the 600,000 Italians in New York City were practicing Catholics, and children best served their family by their economically productive role in a booming American economy.[2]

The 1916 Child Labor law, designed to combat the evils of child labor, extended the education of immigrant children and theoretically, at least, gave boys more time for sports and leisure activities. Church-run sports activities provided facilities within parish boundaries, and church appearances were necessary to take advantage of training and competing in sporting fixtures. During the thirties Yogi Berra, the famous baseball star who considered a professional boxing career, confirmed that sporting competition compelled boys to attend Mass every Sunday. "It didn't pay to fake," Berra recalled. "If you were too sick to go to Mass in the morning, you can bet your life you were going to be too sick to go out and play ball in the afternoon."[3] Just like St. Ambrose Parish in St. Louis's Italian quarter, boys from other Italian enclaves remained loyal to their parish guardians as long as athletic provision and instruction were guaranteed.

It didn't matter much whether leadership came from a Catholic voice or a Protestant one. Take the case of St. Ann and the Holy Trinity Church in Brooklyn and its auxiliary the Trinity Athletic Club, which operated from a building to the rear of the church. During the late twenties this club was popular among Italians and produced some of the finest amateur boxers such as Joe Siclari, Tony Scarpati and Vince Pimpinella, all of whom went on to box professionally. These men were unconcerned with the club's Episcopalian roots and were just pleased that a boxing club was conveniently situated on the North West corner of Clinton and Montague Streets in their Brooklyn neighborhood.

Catholic Youth Organization

Although displays of organized recreation were significant they were dwarfed by a bigger Catholic-inspired social and recreational program. Under the leadership of Bishop Bernard James Sheil of Chicago's Roman Catholic archdiocese this encouraged supervised recreation for older boys in various sports. The first CYO (Catholic Youth Organization) boxing tournament was staged on December 4, 1931 at the Chicago Stadium. Later other sports were introduced, but boxing was the headline-grabber, seen as ideal to replace gangster role models with legitimate heroes from the boxing world.[4] Its impact was far-reaching, managing to recruit thousands of people into its orbit. Bishop Sheil hoped that, through sports and games, a better acculturated and more Americanized urban youth would be encouraged to prayer and a fuller religious participation.

Whilst some non-Catholics converted to the new faith it was the sport of boxing that appealed to the Italian. He represented one of the largest inner city groups where the CYO was most active, and with mass Italian immigration to the United States occurring between 1880 and 1910, it entailed that sons of immigrants reached adulthood in the twenties, which coincided with increased interest and investment in sports. Furthermore, boxing was a handy skill to have on the mean streets of overcrowded tenement blocks. The Catholic Church tapped into the inner city populations of North American cities, a trend that began with the Irish, followed by the Poles, the Italians, the Mexicans and the Puerto Ricans. These groups did not flee their original point of settlement, and territorial affinity meant they inhabited the same "blighted" areas for decades, supplying recruitment potential to the boxing industry. In this regard the factor of "organizational efficiency and direction, as in the case of the CYO among Catholics" played its part in the process of group boxing experience and success. Without question the Roman Catholic Church used sport and recreation to bring individuals into the fold, motivating them to become boxers, and with its annual boxing tournaments it offered them a potential pathway towards a professional boxing career.[5]

Catholic Youth Organization boxing was important because instruction was offered by professional fighters. Legendary old-timer Packey McFarland headed up the CYO team in the thirties and former world welterweight champion Jack Britton supervised the New York-based Catholic organization. For ambitious and talented aspirants it provided a stepping stone to greater things: CYO members made it onto United States Olympic boxing teams and their champions qualified for the Golden Gloves tournament of champions. The most talented to make CYO teams were rewarded with perks such as free healthcare, clothes, jobs or college scholarships and all-expenses-paid international trips.[6]

Chicago's CYO established branches all over the country and its boxing tournaments were popular spectacles, with fan interest exceeding many professional boxing cards. In its fifth year of activity, the CYO boasted a membership of 230,000, and when most other gymnasiums disappeared from Chicago's inner city landscape the Catholic Church continued to be a major sponsor of amateur boxing throughout the forties. By the early fifties there were four CYO gyms in central Chicago, and five out of the seven remaining gyms pooled boxers from these deprived areas.[7] The momentum of Bishop Sheil's sporting crusade was unstoppable, and in 1952 he oversaw a structure of CYO centers throughout the United States and a staff of five hundred people. Numerous projects were supported and the CYO spent $1.5 million in Chicago alone on two community centers in Black and Italian districts as well as providing social assistance to Puerto Ricans.[8]

Elsewhere boxing clubs sprung up and were independently run by local parishes. Father Vincent Verderame led one of the most famous, and having assumed parish control in 1939, he was instrumental in setting up the St. Mary's Italian Parish boxing gymnasium in New Orleans' old French quarter. He worked alongside famous boxing trainer and director of the club "Whitey" Ernest Esnault, and during the thirties and forties many professional and amateur boxers emerged including notable Italians Augie La Para, Jerome Conforto, Vince Bonomo and Willie Pastrano.

Broadly speaking the Catholic Church promoted general athletic recruitment, organized competitions and is credited with instigating the overall development of American sport. It assisted the process of Americanization and acculturation of newly arrived immigrant children. However, its part is less clear cut in the context of the Italian cohort's overall boxing success. An examination of the CYO project showed that its epicenter of activity was based in Chicago and stretched outwards to neighboring Mid-Western states, but rather curiously no Chicago-based Italian fighter surfaced as a world professional champion during its period of influence. In 1940 Joey Maxim of Cleveland won the national amateur title and later captured the world light-heavyweight title in 1952. Besides Maxim only two other champions of Italian origin are known to have graduated to the top of boxing via the CYO route. By the time of the inaugural CYO tournament in December 1931, twenty-two Italian Americans had already been crowned world champions. Furthermore, the appeal and inclusiveness of the CYO sports program extended to other religions, faiths, races and nationalities, permitting African Americans and Jews to participate. For example, Joe Louis, world heavyweight champion, Jimmy Carter, former lightweight titleholder, Harold Dade, the 1947 bantamweight champion, and title claimant Luther Rawlings all prospered from these facilities. Polish middleweight champion Tony Zale was another, as were Leo Rodak, Ukrainian American featherweight champion, and Davey Day, Jewish lightweight contender.

The Catholic Church's commitment to sports increased participation, and championship glory cut across the racial divide. With specific reference to the Italian cohort the Catholic factor provided an effective tool of recruitment and played a vital part in the accelerated growth of participation and in the attainment levels of boxing outcomes at amateur level, reflected in the number of Italian American winners of CYO, local, state and national Golden Gloves titles. Somehow this did not translate over to the paid ranks as many distinguished Italian American amateur competitors did not turn professional.

Notwithstanding, some boxing careers were touched by the hand of God. For instance, Jake La Motta came across Father Joseph whilst serving a three-year term at the Coxsackie State reform school. The cleric proposed boxing as an outlet and assigned him to the gymnasium, booking him onto the reformatory fight program. On leaving the facility La Motta joined a boxing club in the Bronx. He never forgot Father Joseph, and in 1949 he invited him to be at ringside for his triumphant world middleweight title contest with Marcel Cerdan. At the age of nine, Fred Apostoli, the 1937 world middleweight champion, was sent to an all-boy Catholic orphanage. After six years inside the San Francisco youth directory run by Father John Crowley, Apostoli left the institution having learnt how to box and set about joining a boxing club. Lou Ambers first learnt how to box from parish priest Gustavo Purificato in the basement of his local church in his native Herkimer. They remained close and the priest is said to have attended all of Ambers' fights. Champions with high-profile religious convictions included Carmen Basilio. He practiced daily communion and prayer before his fights and after his encounters dropped to his knees and blessed the Lord for his having come through another contest safely. Sammy Mandell attended church every Sunday, and was also able to reconcile the violence of his sport with his Catholic faith.

The street gang

The scarcity of resources inside and outside the home created intensely competitive Italian boys with a tendency for physical aggression, underpinned by the anger and rage they felt at their lack of progress. All over America Italian boys gravitated towards a dynamic street gang culture where the street became the playground, the battleground and a place of congregation. Skills developed in boyhood games were later transferred into professional sports. Although the formation of street gangs was widespread in every slum of American metropolises, the city streets of Italian American neighborhoods were the "public arena of male authority", where the informal education of the street replaced the shortcomings of formal education.[9] The culture of each gang depended on influences within that group. Some were overrun by criminals actively occupied in the rackets, but many were sports oriented and dominated by baseball players or boxers who divided their time between the bowling alley, the poolroom, the recreation center and playground, and the staging of fights was commonplace.

The famous baseball player Joe Garagiola, from St. Louis's Italian district of "Dago Hill," summed up the realities of the twenties and thirties: "You either belonged [to a gang or club] or were out of the action."[10] Confined to the margins of mainstream society at a time when the changing notion of manhood was shifting towards violence and independence, Italian defiance built up through displays of aggression resulting in street gang violence, acts of criminality and sports like boxing.[11] Italian youths became self-reliant and boxing was perceived to be a useful skill to have in warding off the unwanted attentions of rivals inside and outside territorial boundaries. It was cheap and accessible, and the knowledge that relatively large sums of money were obtainable sold it to disenfranchised youths chasing the quick buck.

Sociologist Frederick Thrasher observed the popularity of boxing among Italian boys. His 1927 study on Chicago street gangs found that Italian groups appeared on the South Side of the city, as well as on the West Side, and dominated in the North. In the North Side district known as "Little Sicily," numerous gangs extended their admiration to pugilists, and out of a ten-member Italian gang called Clutchy-Clutch founded in 1915, one was a fight referee, a quarter were trained pugilists, and two or three were well-known prizefighters who instructed younger boys to take lessons from them.[12] It was no different elsewhere. Famous singer Frank Sinatra, who grew up in the town of Hoboken, New Jersey in the twenties and thirties, found that fraternal subdivisions in his Italian community were divided up between those that became boxers and factory workers and groups that sang on street corners.[13] In 1943 William Foote Whyte concluded that boxing was still widespread among Italian boys in Boston's North End. The sociologist, who had lived among Italian street gangs, discovered that the problem of being Italian and living in an urban slum meant that it was a struggle for many just to get onto the ladder of social mobility. In an area densely populated by the least desirable immigrants occupying the worst housing, hope was in short supply in Boston's Little Italy. Whyte noted that there were no Italians running established businesses and those that managed to form their own enterprises were effectively ruined when the prosperity of the twenties ended, making it difficult thereafter.[14]

Born and raised on Fleet Street in the heart of Boston's North End, boxer Tony De Marco knew more than most about these conditions. He recalled "tough times" during the Depression. He explained:

> Education didn't dominate our lives. One went for where the money was. Boxing had a lot of exposure. Boys' clubs were scattered throughout the city. They gave you accessibility to the sport. In my circle of friends boxing was the most popular sport. Boxing made ordinary men recognized. It made them feel somebody. For some it was an extra, who continued to work.[15]

Nationwide Italian adolescents found a sense of belonging and self-esteem through street-corner societies, and successful displays of manliness in inter-ethnic street feuds or inside a boxing ring raised your profile; it restated your machismo within the gang and generated feelings of instant gratification and self-worth. The street gang experience provided a platform for the Italian culture of male exhibitionism, strength and sexual potency, which needed a proper audience. By day it came from family and relatives and at night among street corner boys indulging in a variety of activities, ranging from romancing females, street singing or fighting each other.[16] Joey Fariello, a former boxing trainer who grew up in the Bronx during the forties, and whose father boxed as a professional featherweight, stated "Italian guys hung out together and boxing added notoriety to friendships."[17]

Dennis Marconi, a Los Angeles attorney, who grew up in the South Philadelphia Italian enclave during the fifties, came from a boxing family with his uncle doubling up as a plumber and a professional boxer. He spoke of ethnic pride and the appeal of boxing in Italian inner city areas:

> If you could box and take care of yourself, you were in with the guys, and you could hang out on the best corners where you gained status. Once in a while, you would fight an Irish corner or a Polish corner, and it was no big deal back then as we didn't use guns or weapons. When I joined the corner, I had to fight a black kid who was handpicked by my peers. My neighborhood was Italian. It was huge. When I was a kid and Marciano was fighting, every radio in the street was turned on to the fight. It gave you prestige if you could fight, the higher level of recognition you got from some guys and girls.[18]

Athletic clubs

As big as the street gang phenomenon and Catholic sporting initiatives were, just as many start-ups came through non-secular boxing clubs run by politicians, businessmen or retired boxers of multi-ethnic composition. A large proportion of fighters were products of Italian American athletic and social clubs and the settlement house movement. In the 1900s there was sufficient evidence of Italian organization of sports and social clubs with boxing a prominent fixture among activities. This was not a local phenomenon but a nationwide expression of Italian organization and a desire for entertainment when sports and games were assuming greater importance in American popular culture. Privately run sports societies sprung up, and in Harlem's Little Italy the Italian American Athletic Club churned out athletes in different sporting fields from track and field to boxing: R. Arizoni represented the team at the 1900 National Amateur

(AAU) Boxing Championships. In September 1902, the Delmonico Club was formed in Chicago, Illinois, sponsoring and promoting new Italian prizefighters. The inaugural show staged at the Aurora Hall featured world-rated middleweight Tony Caponi and every contest included boxers squaring off for Italian colony titles. Following a string of shows events took a dramatic turn that November when a riot ensued following a controversial decision in the Sammy Phillips (Paretto) versus Tony Caponi six-round contest, which also witnessed the referee being attacked and Caponi's supporters drawing their revolvers.[19]

In 1904 the *Bridgeport Herald* reported that the 20th Century Athletic Club in the Connecticut town had staged an all-Italian boxing card, and in the same issue revealed that a wrestling show at the Italian Hall in New Haven comprised Italians competing for colony championships. In May 1905 a boxing tournament was organized by the Italian community in Newcastle, Pennsylvania. In the same year the *National Police Gazette* reported that the 138-pound boxer Joseph Sacco, a former United States Navy Fleet boxing champion, had appeared under the auspices of the Utica-based Italian Empire Athletic Club. Sacco served in the United States Navy during the Spanish–American War and upon honorable discharge he continued boxing in the New York area.[20] Italian sports and social clubs multiplied. In 1912, an Italian organization called the Busti Social Athletic Club in Buffalo opened its doors to members aged between eighteen and twenty-six and offered incentives by waiving membership joining fees. Middleweight contender Al Rogers (Angelo Christiano) was one of the star boxers to appear on their cards. The Italian Athletic Club in Schenectady, New York also recruited and showcased boxing talent. The East End Italian Athletic Club in Pittsburgh entertained its members by regularly staging boxing, wrestling and fencing bouts. Patsy Wallace (Pasquale Appalucci), a multi-tournament winner in the amateur ranks and later a world-rated professional flyweight, began boxing as a fourteen-year-old for the Italian American Athletic Club in South Philadelphia. In 1920 he represented his Philadelphia team at the amateur inter-city meeting staged in New York. At the same time the Brooklyn Italian American Athletic Club produced its own recruits at boxing shows staged in the predominantly Italian section of Bensonhurst.

In 1917 the Cuckoos Boxing Club in South Philadelphia's Italian enclave was founded, and it primarily comprised active Italian American professional boxers including headliners Johnny Mayo, Frankie Howell and Chick Carsey. The *Philadelphia Evening Public Ledger* described the band of brothers as an "organization of staunch rooters" and "great fans of boxing."

On the night the inimitable Italian Johnny Dundee was poleaxed by Jewish battler Willie Jackson, the Cuckoos made sure their man was not left in the lurch. The Cuckoos rallied together and 300 paraded up Broad Street behind "the great Johnny Dundee."

The Nutmeg Athletic Club in New Haven, Connecticut donated funds to the Italian military cause during the First World War by promoting a boxing night featuring top Italian American fighters.[21] Italian sports groups surfaced elsewhere and through organized recreation top athletes were discovered. In the twenties the Kent Athletic Association in the Italian district of Chambersburg in Trenton, New Jersey established itself as one of the earliest and largest athletic clubs in an area renowned for Italian American pugilists like Tommy "Kid" Murphy, Paulie Walker, Johnny Brennan and Young Terry. Yet historian and social activist Caroline Farrar Ware wrote in 1935 that social clubs among Italian slum children "were of comparative recent date" and only flourished in the thirties.[22]

Settlement houses

The settlement house movement was another key recruitment pathway among Italian boys, which first sprung up in Chicago, New York, Cleveland and Boston. The settlement houses were mainly run by Protestant educators and social reformers, and their residents were primarily Catholic or Jewish working-class immigrants. Generations of children were helped to adapt to the American way of life and offered sanctuary from the risks of street crime. Services varied from the provision of English language classes and general education to children of elementary and high school age, to marriage parties for adults, to day care centers whilst mothers worked. Popular among boys was the implementation of physical education programs, with boxing a major attraction.

Chicago's Hull House was the first to open its doors in 1889, and its activities included sponsored gymnastics and team sports. A year later, one of its co-founders and sociologist Jayne Addams placed an advert in the *Chicago Daily Tribune* inviting the predominantly Italian group from Taylor Street on Chicago's West Side to join up. By 1911 Hull House had taken over and renovated thirteen buildings as well as establishing the first public playground and gymnasium in Chicago. Revered amateur boxers emerged from this setting, including Nick Fosco. Italian boys found favor with the settlement house movement because its flexible approach enabled working boys not in school to simultaneously continue in employment and benefit from sports training and competition in the evenings. In 1902 athletics provision began in New York, and it attracted seventeen settlements to compete in various sports including baseball, track and field, gymnastics and wrestling.[23]

From the establishment of the Brooklyn Italian Settlement Society in 1901, which professed to work "for the moral and social advancement of the Italian residents" of the neighborhood, other New York Little Italies embraced this extension of support. In the pre-First World War One era settlement houses like the Riverside House, Recreation Rooms and Settlement, Warren Goddard House, Union Settlement and Doe Ye Next Thynge House became distinctly Italian. Other houses like Maxwell House, Clark House and Hudson Guild showed sizable Italian contingents, and in the post-war period settlement house physical education programs gained in popularity with Italian boys. Some produced amateur boxers who competed in the New York Golden Gloves Championships throughout the twenties and thirties. By 1920 almost five hundred settlement houses were active nationally, but what became apparent is that whilst young boys willingly came to use athletic equipment they were less enthusiastic about accepting core moral and religious inclinations.[24]

Other channels of recruitment

New York bars regularly staged boxing matches in the 1880s. Many bars freely circulated sporting newspapers and the hard-living reputation of boxers like John L. Sullivan, the world heavyweight champion, will not have escaped the attentions of young men impressed by their working-class ring hero. In 1902 Robert Woods, a Boston-based settlement house director, noted that Italians, like Jews, were "habitual gamesters." They were traditional frequenters of bars, taverns and cafés, and cultural pastimes included the enjoyment of drinking wine and playing Italian card games and *morra*, a game of chance played with the hands. Hence it was no surprise to find that the Italian quickly established himself as one of the main players in bar-owning, with establishments across America, and these saloon-based environs stirred and stimulated competing sporting passions among proud and virile men. Chicago-based boxer Hugo Kelly (Micheli), a world middleweight title claimant during the 1900s, worked inside a bar, and began boxing professionally in bar-room smokers.[25]

In 1914 the Police Athletic League (PAL) began in the Lower East Side section of Manhattan, New York. The stated aim of this social movement was to target boys and girls in deprived areas of cities and channel their energies into recreational and athletic programs. It relied on members of the police to coach young people into learning a sport and to assist them with school-related activities. The most popular sporting program was its boxing tournaments and it experienced rapid expansion during the thirties, bolstered by Work Project Administration (WPA) staff. New York and Philadelphia were two of the largest cities to exhibit an enlargement of boxing activity.

Newspaper-sponsored boxing tournaments typically appealed to first and second-generation Italian boys who hawked newspapers on street corners and their work frequently saw them engaged in street battles in defense of their pitch. Boys like Young Zulu Kid (Di Melfi), Rocky Kansas (Tozzo), Fidel La Barba and Young Corbett III got started this way. In the early to mid twenties Golden Gloves boxers were recruited from American colleges, private gymnasiums, parks departments, municipal playgrounds and YMCAs. Later boxers entered the Golden Gloves from the United States armed forces with top representatives from the Department of Aviation and United States Coastal Guards and the infantry divisions. During the Depression the government's New Deal program and the WPA and the Civilian Conservation Corps (CCC) found work for unemployed males. Between 1933 and 1941 more than three million Americans served in the CCC with some camps offering men aged between sixteen and twenty-four regular basketball, baseball and boxing matches.

Big business also boosted boxing organization and participation. During the twenties and thirties American football, baseball, soccer and bowling teams were governed by industrial sports leagues and amateur boxing was supported by industrial sponsorship. For example, in the Pennsylvanian mining and manufacturing area of Erie, Scranton and Allentown, with their sizable Italian populations, fighters of professional, semi-pro or amateur backgrounds became involved as they could hold down a regular job and still engage in night-time boxing competition. In Erie, boxing profited from the town's biggest employer, the General Electric Company (GEC), which was committed to staging regular shows, and for six days a week provided boxing training for its predominantly ethnic workforce. These boxers prepared for matches with GEC rivals from other towns in company-sponsored tournaments.[26]

7

Italian American boxing success
Genetic superiority or sculptured talent?

Historically the Italian American boxer has been perceived as a pugnacious and fearless competitor. Throughout the 1900s and the no-decision era, the *New York Times* frequently depicted the Italian as "sturdy," "tough," "rugged" and "aggressive." There was some basis to the exaggerated generalization as the first wave of Italian American prizefighters suffered from inexperience and improper tutelage, and some had no choice but to rely on exceptional bravery. It's easy to understand how the exigencies of their plight combined with the overriding attraction of boxing were enough for early entrants to throw caution to the wind.

Yet the overall tenor of press reports and the residual implication that the Italian was "made of steel," possessed "a granite chin" and "could absorb punishment" cemented the perception of Italian hardiness and endurance for the longer term. In 1836 French anthropologist Louis Pierre Gratiolet wrote that the skull of white men "is a temple divine but that of the Brutish race is merely a helmet constructed to ward off heavy blows." In twentieth-century America, where the Italian was disparagingly described as an "in-between" race, this perception found its adherents.[1]

Joe Grim (Giuseppe Griminelli, also known as Saverio Giannone) reinforced these wayward depictions on the way to becoming the most famous pugilistic strongman ever. Born in Avellino in the Campania region of Southern Italy, Grim never aspired to major honors, but between 1900 and 1913 he became every bit as famous and popular for his ability to take a punch. The newspapermen loved his showmanship and bravery and duly dubbed him with a variety of exotic sobriquets including "The Iron Man," "The Pugilistic Wonder of the Nineteenth Century," "The Indian Rubber Man," "The Indestructible Man of Pugilism" and "The Human Punching Bag." Grim floated between the 147 and 160-pound weight limits, and in an estimated three hundred contests recorded only ten official victories. He threw down the gauntlet to all challengers and bet that they would not flatten him. Grim met the most dangerous and heaviest hitters, light-heavyweights, heavyweights, and he never drew the color line. He traveled all over the United States and even ventured abroad with his unique brand of entertainment. Grim's stubbornness, recuperative powers and mighty resolve made him a top drawing card for promoters, who fought over his signature, and curious spectators flocked to see whether he would be knocked out. In particular he became a hero to the colony of Philadelphia Italians who staked their meager wages praying he would preserve his special record. They enthusiastically waited for telegram notification outside post office and newspaper buildings for news of his big-ticket clashes. World champions Bob Fitzsimmons, Philadelphia Jack O'Brien and Battling Levinsky all failed to stop him. The best black fighters of his generation— Joe Walcott, Joe Gans, Sam McVey, Dixie Kid, Jack Johnson, Dave Holly and Jack Blackburn—could not silence him. In his bout with Jack Johnson, Grim was floored eighteen times but still managed to preserve his status of "indestructibility," proclaiming that no man on earth could stop him. *Ring Magazine* editor Nat Fleischer described his raw courage as "incomparable."

Grim's durability became the subject of fascination in an age when Aryan America felt uneasy with the masculine ring exploits of the so-called "inferior races." Physicians examined him and concluded on rather shaky medico-scientific grounds that his powers were the result of possessing a small-sized brain, producing an unresponsive nervous system, which blocked the transmission of hurt or pain. Grim was reported as having a skull twice the thickness of an average man's. Dr Carleton Simon wrote:

> Joe Grimm, the Italian pugilist is able to stand the terrific beatings to which he has lately been subjected simply owing to the fact that he is in possession of a very small brain. He is of such a low order of intelligence that his nerves, which carry the news to his brain when he is hurt, find a very chilly reception. Slow to grasp the idea he has been hurt at all, and then not able to take hold of it with one-half the some of pain of a human being of ordinary intelligence. Grimm will have to be almost killed before beaten into insensibility.

Dr Simon's expert medical assessment revealed:

> The fact that this man Grimm can't grasp the idea that he has been hurt when subjected to physical abuse that an ordinary man could not endure does not necessarily mean that he is not as intelligent as the ordinary human being in other respects. Just as the "human pin cushion" of the circus side show can stand up and have pins jabbed into his anatomy all day long without feeling pain, so probably is Mr Grimm constituted. A heavy blow on the jaw, which touches the nerves that take the quickest route to the brain cells has no apparent effect upon Grimm, because his nerves are abnormally sluggish. The same is true of the other nerves of his body. The nerves which are ordinarily so sensitive to a blow in the pit of the stomach are all but dead in the case of Grimm. Grimm is certainly a physical marvel. There is nothing in the build of the man to lead to the belief that he is capable of standing any abnormal amount of pain. He has not the appearance of an athlete. The muscles of his body do not cover him well, his stomach is pudgy and his flesh flabby.[2]

The lack of sophistication in the discourse was akin to the myths perpetuated about black sportsmen possessing innate physiological and biological advantages such as harder and thicker skulls, large and thicker bones, larger muscles and tougher elasticated skin, making them impervious to pain, immune to heat, and with faster overall reflexes. The academics argued that whilst this guaranteed athletic superiority the Anglo-Saxon asserted racial superiority in intelligence.[3] Despite these ingrained ideas it was ultimately Grim's blind courage that proved his downfall. In an era of lax regulations, medical controls and longer fights, Grim should have been offered protection and advised to retire, but the money-spinning circus rolled onwards. By the end of his career Grim manifested severe symptoms of punch-drunk syndrome, paying a heavy price for his reckless displays of manliness.

The overall belief that somehow Italians were blessed with unnatural punch resistance, endurance and courage gathered momentum. It was almost as though these were the only qualities required in ascending the ladder of pugilistic success. In May 1921 Jack Skelly, former lightweight contender turned writer, described Italian Americans as "a small race of men chiefly Southern Italian possessing the essentials of vigor, stamina, endurance, all qualifications and physical requirements for strenuous fistic combat."[4] In 1923, *Ring Magazine* published an article revealing Italians to be "the gamest" fighters in circulation, with boxing critic DeWitt Van Court remarking: "I will take my hat off to the Italians, the boys who never know the word quit."[5] In January 1924, *New York Herald* journalist Wilbur Wood wrote an article along similar lines. He declared Italians to be a sturdy and durable race, furnishing the example of middleweight contender Frank Carbone, who had fought in over two hundred bouts, faced five world champions and had never been knocked out. The paper reported: "We doubt if the game has produced a more durable warrior. Frank has taken enough punishment to sink the combined Atlantic and Pacific fleets. But he is still going along."[6]

Elmer Mitchell, a University of Michigan American football and basketball coach, offered an alternative interpretation of the Italian's physical abilities. In 1922, a series of articles entitled "Racial Traits in Athletics" were published, and Mitchell argued that Italians were not actually suited to sports like boxing, describing them as "better fitted for games of quickness, dexterity, and skill, rather than of rugged strength." Mitchell identified the Italian as being "fearless" and "daring" but lacking self-discipline, and "too fiery and impulsive of feeling" for contact sports compared to American athletes. The overall success of the Italian boxing cohort demonstrated substantive and fundamental flaws in Mitchell's racial arguments, and with each passing decade both his archaic and overgeneralized description of the Italian American sportsman and his reputation was blown out of the water.[7]

In contrast boxing writer Thomas Hauser asserted that Italian American boxers were unquestionably the hard men of boxing. Looking at the career records of fifteen Italian American world champions from Johnny Dundee (1910–32) to Joey Giardello (1948–67), they suffered only 44 knockout losses in 2,101 professional bouts. Incredibly, eighteen of these knockouts occurred only in the twilight years of the boxer's career.[8] Although stoicism and toughness were important characteristics, Italian American boxers demonstrated a tapestry of pugilistic skills acquired through knowledge, habit and hard work.

Focus on the Italian American's so-called natural advantages masked the stark reality for these boxers. Often they were faced with an uncomfortable truth, one in which their physical stature influenced their mental approach and boxing style. Of the 51 world titlists only light-heavyweight Joey Maxim was over six feet in height. They were frequently shorter, lighter and gave away inches in reach (arm length). History has shown they worked tirelessly in overcoming their physical handicaps with efficiency, skill and risk taking.

Almost half achieved glory by not conforming to the archetypal Italian American stereotype of the perpetually rugged, mauling, brawling Joe Palooka-type prizefighter. This group generated some of the best ring technicians and shrewd ring operators that ever set foot inside the squared circle. Diminutive flyweight Young Zulu Kid possessed lightning reflexes and from a defensive semi-sitting position would spring into action to launch his fistic flurries. Middleweight Johnny Wilson was a wily southpaw who worked off the back foot and jab and backed this up with effective body punching. Johnny Dundee was fleet-footed and slick and used his guile to avoid being hit. Frankie Genaro was a superb boxer with dazzling hand speed and nimbleness and equipped with a wonderful defense. Fellow flyweight Fidel La Barba was his equal in the defensive art, using his agility and powerful left hook to great effect. Lightweight Sammy Mandell was a ring wizard. He used his speed, accurate punching, a winning left jab and quick reflexes to befuddle the best boxers of his era. Bushy Graham, the classy showboating bantamweight, achieved stunning results with tremendous mobility and consummate jab-and-move technique.

Tony Canzoneri was a fusion of skill and bravery and his cockiness and split-second timing was the foundation of his fantastic success. In the thirties flyweight Midget Wolgast was one of the fastest boxers of his generation and in the main his opponents struggled to land a punch. Bantamweight Lou Salica possessed fine boxing ability at long range and he was just as effective as an in-fighter. Featherweight Mike Belloise was a clever counter puncher who was the personification of poise and power. Lightweight Lou Ambers was a thoughtful ring tactician who altered his style to suit the opponent. He fought with boundless energy and mobility and delivered accurate punching in a whirlwind fashion. Forties featherweight champion Pete Scalzo blended astuteness and big hitting. He worked off the jab and his quick feet enabled him to land his trademark strong right hand. Title claimant Jimmy Perrin was a skillful solid puncher. Willie Pep was a boxing genius with the most sublime defensive and technical skills. Sal Bartolo, one of Pep's rivals, was a clever ring technician and a fine practitioner of the jab and hook technique. Junior-welterweight Tippy Larkin was the classic exponent of the noble art, a talented ringster who possessed agility, slippery moves and a fair punch.

Television exposure influenced boxing styles, with performers pressurized into substituting boxing science with a slam bang approach, and youngsters were thrust in at the deep end having not fully polished off their ring craft. Against this backdrop of toe-to-toe slugfests and exhibitions of raw power, light-heavyweight Joey Maxim stuck to his principles and became known as a great ring tactician. His accurate jab underpinned his consistency and enduring standing in the world's elite for over a decade. In short, the Italian American boxer exhibited confidence, poise and coolness under pressure. He demonstrated mental agility, superior ring generalship and intelligence, equipping him to survive the rigors of boxing.

Attributes like gameness and courage formed part of his overall gamut of fighting qualities. Boxing manager Angelo Dundee believed that strength of character, dedication and hard graft were the fundamental building blocks of Italian American ring success:

> They were talented. You gotta have talent to be a fighter. You gotta have good balance . . . good reflexes. So much goes into it, not anybody can be a fighter. That's why fighters are special in my eyes. To this day I respect the fighters. They gotta pay their dues. They gotta train hard. It's a heartless thing. You don't make money early on. You don't make money. You gotta scrub. You can't support a family. They [Italian boxers] gotta have a certain strength, a personality to endure, to take adversity because you're not bringing money to the table. It's a tough profession. They [Italian boxers] were talented. Not everybody can be a champion. Not everybody can be a fighter. God gave them the talent and they utilised it, very simple. They could hang in there, take adversity, broken hands, arthritis . . . [Carmen] Basilio had arthritis in his hands and elbows. He was an onion picker and he used to work around water all the time. He had dry skin and used to bust up all the time.[9]

Despite these handicaps Basilio became world champion in two divisions.

Historian Hank Kaplan explained the context of the Italian American success story:

> As history proves, Italians had a great aptitude for the sport. They had the agility, they developed the ring wisdom, and they became very cagey operators in the ring. Some of them became great punchers. Italians were always great physical specimens, especially the kids who were raised doing labor. They had big labor force in this country when they first came in. It was just a natural sport for them to get into.

He added that ring success was based on the manifestation of special qualities.

> Not just Italians, other ethnic groups too, had this unique kind of courage that you don't find in hardly any other sport. The kind of courage that it takes to stand in front of another opponent who is going to whack you right in the mouth in any second. If you throw a punch at him you are going to get hit in return. The greatest defensive fighter that ever lived can hardly avoid getting hit. I am telling you it takes a Willie Pep to avoid getting hit, and there weren't too many of those developed. This is a very important factor. Those that didn't have that could have had all kinds of ability, flashiness, speed, power, everything. If they didn't have that ability they fell by the wayside. Not only fighters but also a lot of people don't have that. That's why it takes a special breed of person to become a boxer. That special kind of unique courage is not required in any of the other sports, not quite to that extent. That is one of the reasons for their [Italian Americans'] successes. They had that, without doubt. It was just a characteristic that belonged to the Italians, which was common to their athleticism, which they had in copious quantities. They seemed to have a little more than the average group of people. Within that fifty-year period there existed conditions where the immigrant was coming into the country. Those were very hungry kids reared in the streets of America. The economic status they were in bred this kind of courage to some extent. You also had to have it as one of your characteristics. You had to be born with that instinct, that bravery, that courage that we are talking about. It wasn't something manufactured. In some cases it helped but in most cases what is required is a natural form of courage. This was very evident in Italian [American] boxers. That is why their [Italian Americans'] styles had so much variation. Some were very aggressive. Some were slightly aggressive. Some were very smart, brilliant boxing styles. Some had very brilliant defensive skills and some were very powerful punchers like Eddie Shea for example. A great puncher! In order to land those punches you have to be in the danger zone, and not everybody has the courage to be in the danger zone.

Kaplan contrasted the Italian American's pugilistic expression with that of his rivals.

> The Jewish boxers tended to depend on their headiness. They became good boxers, skillful and developed good defenses so that they didn't have to get into the fire. Why? Well, because they had some fear of the fire. Irish boxers, a lot of them were crafty boxers. They [Irish] were the progenitors of the sport. The early ones were crude and they used their muscle. They depended on their muscle but later on they became very crafty and they developed what I like to call the Irish style of boxing. Mike Gibbons, Packy McFarland, Jimmy Slattery, Tommy Loughran and Jack Britton were brilliant, brilliant boxers.[10]

The weird fascination with Italian American toughness and fearlessness, as if they were natural gifts bestowed by God, is an unsafe and haphazard line to pursue. These traits were not exclusively Italian American characteristics. Rival African, Irish and Jewish American boxers displayed similar combativeness, grit and resilience in triumph and the implication that somehow Italian American athletic performance and success was underlain by biodeterminist considerations is unfounded. The Italian, like the Eastern European Jew, the Irish and the African American, emerged from physiological hazards associated with turbulent pasts. The Southern Italian overcame enslavement, oppression, invasion and tragedy. The Irish fled from English occupation and the potato famine, the Jew from persecution, prejudice and the Russian pogroms and the African from the unimaginable horrors of the slave trade. This is certainly a thought-provoking line of enquiry and one that requires further research.

The question remains, however, to what extent was Italian American boxing success connected to a genetic predisposition to unquestionable toughness, or a by-product of migration to a hostile foreign land and exclusively learnt behavior inside American gymnasiums? One suspects that the truth lies somewhere between nature and nurture. Whilst the majority of these boxers were Southern Italian, and the ancestors of what the ancient Romans astutely observed as *genus acutum*—a combative people—this story of boxing achievement is made possible by a particular time and place in American social, political and economic history which, combined with the experience of mass Italian immigration, produced generations of tough men with heightened desires. Economic historian Arnold Toynbee argued that hardier and more capable children were produced from "new" immigrant communities in the United States rather than those born in their homelands. He presented the history of civilizations in terms of challenge and response and asserted that fighters were produced by their environment and not by nationality. "Had warriors like Battling Nelson, Frank Mantell, Johnny Dundee and Frank Erne remained in the land of their birth, the chances are they would have lived and died unsung without ever lacing a glove," *Ring Magazine* reported.[11] He may have a point as his European cousins, or for that matter those born and raised in Italy, did not replicate the boxing triumphs of the Italian American cohort. Despite the rule of Fascism (1922–43), which placed enormous emphasis on muscle and strength, Italy produced just one world champion in the first half of the twentieth century.

The Italian immigrant came with the impression that the streets in the United States would be paved with gold, and on discovering that his hope for a better life was based on overinflated reports, he became resentful. The challenges, hardships and uncertainties associated with immigrant life were characterized by relative deprivation and prolonged social bigotry. A shift in political ideology on what constituted American manhood further complicated the position. Theodore Roosevelt, prior to his appointment as American president in 1901, pulled no punches in singling out the hordes of Southern Italians as a real menace to the American way of life. Using clear social Darwinist evolutionary terms wrapped up in a language of hate, Roosevelt warned in his speech entitled "The Strenuous Life" that if White (Anglo-Saxon) Americans did not act manlier and become more "strenuous" to procreate faster, the "battle" would be lost and "race suicide" was a distinct possibility. He espoused the "masterful virtues" of greater physicality as a way for the American middle classes to respond to the challenges of the modern era.[12] Roosevelt's ideas carried momentum beyond the First World War and into the twenties.

In an age when strength and masculinity were celebrated, power found a new outlet in the celebration of men's bodies, as healthy, muscular and physical sporting manifestations were seen as a crucial antidote in a world dominated by economic uncertainty, rapid urbanization and industrial developments.[13] Notwithstanding the plethora of contrasting displays of Italian American masculinity in twentieth-century America—like the notorious Italian mobster, the Italian political agitator and the gallantry and sacrifice of hundreds of thousands of Italian American servicemen who contributed to the American military effort in both world wars, through to the icons of popular culture like Hollywood lothario Rudolph Valentino and bodybuilder Charles Atlas (Angelo Siciliano), crowned "the world's most perfectly developed man" in 1921, and to Joe DiMaggio, the archetypal all-

American hero, and Frank Sinatra, the voice of his generation who epitomized coolness—nothing better illustrated the physicality of Italian American masculinity than his role in the world of professional boxing.

Rocky Marciano cemented the reputation of the Italian American prizefighter by winning the world heavyweight title. His unrelenting aggression and remarkable determination to win at all costs encapsulated Italian American manliness—a powerful survival instinct, a tireless work ethic and a strength of individualism to cope with adversity—and emphasized that ordinary Italian males could acquire strength and shape through dedication and hard training in order to beat poverty and anonymity. Italian individualism, which for centuries had resisted the feudal and aristocratic abuses of power and foreign invasions, found expression within the new setting of a hostile and dominant American culture. The Italian cohort excelled in individual sports well before they made a dent in team sports, and in the wider context Italian immigrants and their offspring demonstrated potent examples of individualism and independence through their involvement in family business and enterprise. They were pivotal in the formation of thousands of firms across America, establishing dominance and control in numerous sectors like barbering, stone masonry, wholesale food distribution and food production, trucking and removals, and took up a pre-eminent position in the catering and hospitality area.

The force of Italian individualism was evident in other forms of cultural participation. Historian Robert Foerster observed that they were more likely to be an opera singer than a member of a gospel choir and in show business the majority of the best-known and most talented male singers were of Italian origin. A similar situation registered among bandleaders and composers. However, it was in the world of professional boxing that Italian individualism and masculinity blossomed. There was no better place for the Italian fighter to disprove the Nativist notion of the "enfeebled Mediterranean Race," and in the arena of open and fair competition the Italian more than any other race and nationality was driven by a strong sense of duty, a vision and a desire to resolve familial hardship. The sad reality for the majority of young Italian males living in America in the first decades of the twentieth century was that wealth and political influence was a distant mirage, and they had to fight a lot harder to make gains. They occupied low-status, poorly paid jobs for longer, many of which were physically challenging and damaging to personal health. For Italian American boxers, failure was not an option and a combination of adherence to the family cause and tough masculinity got their loved ones out of a hole.

When Tony Vaccarelli's father died suddenly in 1923, the Harlem boxer assumed responsibility as the main breadwinner. He said: "It never occurred to me in my boyhood days that I would become a professional fighter when I grew older." Vaccarelli fought in over one hundred amateur contests but had been considering a career in business. He supported four brothers, two sisters and his mother, and in just six years as a professional he earned $60,000, helping the family buy a house.[14] Philadelphia's Midget Wolgast (Loscalzo) was responsible for some heroic deeds of his own. He began boxing at the age of fifteen and rapidly developed into the most dominant flyweight of the Depression era. He was the eldest of a family of eleven, and when his father, a carpenter, became too sick to work, Wolgast, aged 21, single-handedly supported them from his ring earnings.

Rocky Marciano, the son of a Brockton shoe factory worker, who ruled the heavyweight division from 1952 to 1956, was particularly disturbed by the strong smell of leather and the stench of his father's breath from working in a sweatshop. Marciano idolized his father and would deliver lunch daily so that he could continue to slave away at his bed-laster machine. He remembered his father, covered in sweat, telling him: "Be somebody Rocky. Don't never work in a factory." Marciano never forgot the advice, his father's dreary existence or the lack of money. Like many Italian immigrant families Marciano's father owned his own two-storey house, had a steady job and a loving and healthy family. But Marciano wanted financial success for himself and for his family. As the eldest son of a traditional Italian family unit, Marciano felt an enormous responsibility to improve his family's lot and to make sufficient money to stop his father from working at the godforsaken factory.[15] Marciano worked odd jobs to help the family but quickly realized he did not want to return to manual labor or a life of financial struggle.

Rocky Castellani, fifties middleweight title contender, worked alongside his father in a Pennsylvania mine for a twelve-month period. Castellani's father, originally resistant to his son's enthusiasm for boxing, came around to the idea when he advised his son to stop mining:

> See, in these mines, we all get destroyed, sooner or later. Either we die like my friend, Jugus…, or like many others who get sick—miner's disease! But I, I don't want you to die like the rest of us. Do you understand! I don't like it [fighting], but if that will get you out of this miserable place—I don't even feel like a human being here—then go ahead.[16]

It bothered Carmen Basilio that his father worked like "a slave" in all weathers and at all hours on his onion farm in Canastota, upstate New York.

Basilio turned professional in 1948 and his tough masculinity was underlined by a tender and noble objective: to deliver on a promise he made to his parents:

> I am going to be a world champion. I am going to pay off your mortgage and you aren't going to owe anybody anything. If I didn't do anything the rest of my whole career I did that for my mother and father. I took them out of debt. When I made enough money boxing I walked into the house, and I laid down the mortgage and the deeds. My dad had tears in his eyes.[17]

The demonstration of tough Italian masculinity was also an expression of the fight against personal chaos and violence, and there is no question that tenement living, particularly in New York City during the thirties and forties, was grim. Jake La Motta and Rocky Graziano were Italian boys who symbolized the struggle against desperation and hopelessness. They had much in common. They were born in New York City, La Motta in the Bronx and Graziano on the Lower East Side. They were boyhood buddies, juvenile delinquents and perceived unsympathetically by the authorities as dead-end kids with no future. They also suffered from complicated relationships with their fathers. These patriarchal figures were weakened by the demands of the New World and emasculated by their failure to meet the core aims associated with Italian culture of nurturing and safeguarding family honor and public reputation, and both frequently lashed out at their families. For example, Graziano's father, a former prizefighter, was frequently drunk and struggled to find regular employment at the docks, so home relief was the order of the day. La Motta's father never held down a steady job and he was unambitious to learn the language or train for a vocation, and struggled to make ends meet from his horse-drawn wagon peddling groceries. A boxing career was the farthest thing from Graziano's mind, and he actually hated it as it reminded him of those frequently uncomfortable moments when he was forced to fight his older brother Joe for the amusement of his father and his old-time friends, which usually ended with a bloody nose for Graziano. When Graziano wasn't running wild on the streets with his cronies, stealing from pushcart peddlers, candy stores and other soft targets, he hung out with the rest of his crew as part of the Tenth Street Gang. Several of his friends were trained professional boxers and Terry Young (Angelo De Sanza), a highly regarded lightweight boxer, tried convincing Graziano to commit himself to the sport. When a fellow club member failed to turn up for the New York Metropolitan

Amateur Championships, Graziano filled the empty berth and won the area title. By now he had become a father and the belated realization that there was nothing promising about a life dominated by incarceration led him to professional boxing.

La Motta's formative years were also blighted by violence and brutality. Along with the rest of his family, he was frequently beaten and taunted by his father, who often referred to his son as a failure. La Motta was teased at school and set upon by older children in his neighborhood. He learnt early on that to survive he would need to embrace his father's adage of "hit 'em first and hit 'em hard." La Motta described this as the only piece of sound advice he ever picked up from his father. In his autobiography, La Motta revealed he had been fighting for money since he was eight years old. His father routinely took him to social clubs where adults played cards and drank alcohol with children encouraged to fight for money. Sometimes, he fought two or three times a week.[18]

La Motta turned to professional boxing following the numbness of the jail experience and an unpleasant time in solitary confinement. There was no mileage in being a lousy second-rate thief, so he became a fighter. "Hunger drove me to boxing. It was a way of making a living. It was the only alternative to me. The neighborhood I grew up in you either went to jail or you became a fighter," La Motta said.[19]

Italian American boys reacted to their individual tensions and frustrations and developed a strong sense of purpose to make something happen. In many examples families were rescued from relative poverty, further proof that *familismo* (family togetherness) gave these boys a great sense of pride. The Italian American boxer embodied the survivalist mentality of his forefathers who had been betrayed by the land and by successive governments. He demonstrated an ability to overcome each crisis with a resourcefulness and an adaptability to his environment that were the cornerstones of Italian individualism. His strength of character and sense of altruism in meeting the unmet needs of those around him were powerful motivating drivers to get the job done inside a boxing ring. Self-reliance, self-control, hard work, firmness of spirit and determination were vital components of Southern Italian manliness and illustrative of the Italian American boxer's character in realizing social status and power, an essential criterion of Italian American masculinity.[20]

Boxing participation also tapped into the Italian cultural philosophy of *fare la bella figura* (cutting a fine image). This wasn't just about appearance or dress code but a cultural mind-set based upon the premise of keeping one's reputation intact. For the newcomer the possibilities of scaling the heights in professional boxing, the second most popular sport in America, created quite a stir among friends, family and Italian neighborhood dwellers. Adulation, admiration and adoration are prerequisites coveted by all Italians, especially those in the public eye. Italian American boxers were no different, eager for acceptance and recognition. This national compulsion of *la bella figura* along with the changing cultural perceptions of manhood was intertwined with the strong emphasis in Italian culture on manliness and exhibitionism. Italian manliness and more specifically survival instincts and individualism lay at the core of the cohort's success in professional boxing.

The idea of hard work, physical sacrifice, the countless hours of dedication to training and the associated risks of boxing were viewed as a price worth paying. To some extent the childhood experiences of mental and physical hunger influenced their brutal style of fighting, and enduring physical pain was seen as a necessary evil in order to succeed. The Italian's driving intensity, unquenchable thirst for battle and an implacable willpower to wade through buckets of his own blood reinforced his image of pugilistic heroism. Carmen Basilio referred to the motivational driving force and the tough environmental conditions behind Italian American success. "It was a desire to win. The days of the Depression were about survival. Most fought for survival. Hunger, the ingredient which makes great fighters, was the trademark of many Italian fighters."[21] Dennie Mancini, former boxing manager and trainer, reinforced this point:

> They [Italians] had a determination to win. Nobody could ever fault the heart or courage of the Italian American fighters. They stood favorably with any of the ethnic groups. They got great support in their neighborhoods. What could you do in a neighborhood? You would be lucky to be an iceman. If you were a boxer you were something special in the community. Boxing is the ultimate challenge. It gave them a sense of achievement that ordinary people never enjoyed. Italian people had to fight for everything. It [the United States] was a new country, a new language, they had to battle for everything.[22]

Steve Corbo, Illinois boxing judge and ring announcer, agreed:

> It was "Great heart! Great heart! Courage!" When Sylvester Stallone put together the movie series about boxing he used the name Rocky. Rocky implies heart and courage, the will to prevail over adversity. Rocky Graziano and Rocky Marciano—both

these fighters prevailed over great adversity both in and out of the ring. Marciano with that nose split pleading to let the [Ezzard Charles II] fight go on one more round and miraculously coming back with a knockout win. Graziano, the adversity he faced even before he got in the ring. The trilogy with Tony Zale, getting stopped in the first fight and coming back and stopping Zale in the second fight. The Italian American contribution is heart with a capital H.[23]

Herb Goldman, historian and researcher, explained that an integral part of Italian American boxing success was based on the expression of manliness and racial pride:

> Machismo—the Italian responded to ethnic rivalry in the ring. The Italian came from a "masculine" culture and coupled with extreme hardship and economic strife in Sicily and Southern Italy where most of the Italian American fighters originated they were eager and hungry to succeed.

He stressed that Italians possessed psychological advantages over other rival ethnics. "The lack of fear; centuries of having lived side by side with other nationalities had reduced the fear of the unknown of ethnic opposition."[24]

Another point to consider is the idea that success bred success. So when the likes of Casper Leon (1891–1904), Johnny Dundee (1910–32) and Tony Canzoneri (1925–39) scaled the summit of world boxing a powerful message filtered down to young aspiring urban males that money, fame and prestige were attainable. The image of success accompanying numerous Italian boxers in every decade effectively pulled others forward. The strong momentum seen in New York's Italian districts and wards was evidenced in other city enclaves. Albert Bandura, a Canadian social psychologist, agreed that role modeling was possible when individuals observed and imitated those with status and power. He believed that depictions of aggression reinforced by family members or by the media or in the environment supported aggressive behavior in children. In such environments conflicts were usually resolved by fighting, especially when aggression possessed an element of reward. The influences of street slum culture combined with the attractiveness of tough masculinity allowed for role emulation to flourish in the Italian American boxing experience.

Manhattan's Lower East Side, East Harlem, Brooklyn's Williamsburg and Bensonhurst sections, and Bronx's Arthur Avenue and Tremont Avenue were some of the numerous enclaves that became synonymous with Italian American fighters. The growth in popularity of boxing ensured that, by the thirties, smaller Little Italies such as Baltimore's Stiles Street had also become known for their boxers. Children from slum areas developed a close personal attachment to their heroes. In Hartford's Little Italy Willie Pep grew up worshipping nationally established neighborhood boxing heroes Battling Battalino, the 1929 world featherweight champion, and Bobby Ivy (Sebastian Di Mauro), a prominent contender in the 126-pound class in the early forties. Later, when Pep trained at the nearby gymnasium he shared the locker room and training facilities with Ivy and plucked up the courage to ask for advice on ring moves and technique. Take the example of Tony Canzoneri, a starry-eyed eleven-year-old boy from New Orleans who donned a pair of boxing gloves for the first time and began fighting on the street for nickels and dimes. He dreamt of emulating local boxing hero Pete Herman (Gulotta). Canzoneri closely identified with Herman. He was a neighbor and, like him, a Sicilian. After each of Herman's fights he would cut out fight reports and photographs. He regularly joined thousands to greet the returning champion after each of his ring battles. It was hero worship on a grand scale. Canzoneri eventually got spotted by Herman, who had been alerted to the youngster's promise. Between 1916 and 1919 Herman taught his protégé the finer points of the manly art in their twice weekly sessions staged at the local gymnasium. When Herman discovered that Canzoneri's family were upping sticks to seek their fortune in the Big Apple, Herman offered Canzoneri a way into the big time by writing a letter of recommendation to top boxing manager Sam Goldman. Canzoneri fulfilled his potential and became a champion at three different weights.

These relationships with heroes and icons were not always close and personal, and it didn't always follow that role modeling would only work if the hero was an outstanding performer. During the thirties Nicky Castiglione was a Chicago boxer of only moderate ability and yet he created quite an impression on the children in his district. A sociologist who came from the same Near North Side enclave explained:

> He [Nick Castiglione] got to be quite a famous guy, headlined at the [Chicago] Stadium a few times . . . Blackie [Nick Castiglione] was really a big shot in the neighborhood and these guys were really fed on that recognition, you know. People around here would read his name in the paper a lot and everybody would know him when they see him. He used to walk around with his

jacket on, with his name on it. You could hear the kids saying, "Hey, look across the street, there's Nicky!" or "You see that guy; that's Blackie Castiglione!"[25]

How much importance should be attached to Bandura's theory is open to interpretation, but what we do know is that, over and beyond other social psychological theories, sanctioning of boxing legitimized aggressive and violent behavior, and in that environment the Italian American cohort generated repeated success.

As well as the cohort's strong identification with role models and tough masculinity, the large-scale presence of family members supported the Italian American boxer's phenomenal rise to the top. Between 1900 and 1955 more brothers of Italian origin fought in professional boxing than from any other ethnic group, with 120 families identified (see Appendix XVII). The Italians, more than any other group, embraced boxing as if it were some sort of family enterprise. They entered this world as fighters, managers, trainers, promoters, cutmen and seconds. It's no accident or coincidence either that the first brothers to win a world professional boxing title were Italian: Baltimore's Joe and Vince Dundee (Lazzara). Joe won the world welterweight title in 1927 and his younger brother Vince annexed the world middleweight crown six years later.

Sibling rivalry drove forward intense competition and major outcomes. We find that younger brothers in particular were overly ambitious and aspired to displace older siblings. Fidel La Barba, Phil Terranova, Tony Marino, Sammy Mandell, Tommy Paul, Tippy Larkin, Lou Bogash and Rocky Kansas were all the younger brothers of established professional boxers who went on to claim world titles. Their natural competitive nature was first tested in impromptu sparring sessions at home or in makeshift rings erected in tenement back alleys. The younger siblings possessed the advantage of learning the tricks of the trade, and they copied moves and techniques. They became immersed in the family's involvement in this boxing subculture before heading to the gymnasium where formalized supervised boxing training was offered. They discovered a sheltered meeting place, the opportunity to freely mingle and establish meaningful associations and companionship with family and other members of the same cohort. Similar to the *padrone* system, which grouped fellow *paesani* in the workplace, it was no different in the boxing world. The Italian culture of closeness extended to boxing participation and socializing with people from your own background; competing and training side by side with boxing champions intensified Italian pride and identity. Rivalry in the gymnasium boosted self-improvement and overall performance levels, and later champions trained in the same spaces as their heroes and some even hung out together. A sporting culture developed where training and intimacy promoted confidence and a winning mentality. Recognition from the local community was important too, which by the twenties and thirties was openly supportive of local boxers by buying tickets, attending fight venues and betting on fight outcomes. Support from these Italian strongholds assisted the overall process of mass boxing recruitment and lasting success.

Finally, the genetic question not only overlooks the possibility that traits such as bravery and fearlessness might have been instinctive responses to the challenges faced from a brutalizing environment; it also negates and undermines the work ethic and diligence shown by Italian Americans, who were passionately immersed in the boxing lifestyle within an established framework. The thousands of gym hours that sculpted body and mind and honed boxing technique and strategy should not be undervalued. For example, both Carmen Basilio and Rocky Marciano embodied the idea that success could be achieved through hard training and motivation. Basilio, one of ten children, never forgot his tough upbringing. For six months of the year he helped out alongside the other siblings on his father's farm. He was in the fields every day on his hands and knees planting onions. He hated it, but these early childhood experiences served to develop his legendary discipline for order and structure in boxing. During training Basilio worked out seven days a week. Basilio believed in gaining a mental edge over his opponent, no matter how small, and he was always up at 5.30 a.m., running the miles when everybody else was asleep. Inside the gymnasium Basilio displayed a meticulous attention to detail and never left anything to chance. He always did more than was expected of him and he regularly ran out of sparring mates. Basilio lived and breathed the training and his relentless drive to be in the best physical condition for his fights made him a formidable foe.

Nobody could have foreseen Marciano as a future world heavyweight champion. There was nothing natural about him. He was a late starter at 23, clumsy and heavy legged, but he was eager and willing to learn from top trainer Charley Goldman, who sharpened his assets of punching power and body strength. Marciano approached his training and preparations with a religious zeal, leaving nothing to chance, and always presented himself in the best physical shape for every fight. The concluding thought goes to Hank Kaplan, the "Godfather of all Boxing Historians."

Boxing is the only sport where you cannot possibly become really good at what you're doing until you have had the experience, the practice . . . In boxing you cannot become good until you have had the experience. You know why I say that? Because nobody ever has.[26]

8

Boxing versus baseball and American football

It has been suggested that Italians have made a greater collective contribution in the quintessential American sports of baseball and football than in boxing. In my view much of the ballyhoo surrounding baseball has centered on sport's intrinsic place in American society and its attached cultural value, and in particular the impact of Joe DiMaggio, who led the New York Yankees to ten pennants and nine World Series over a glorious thirteen-year period, and so has remained in the public consciousness for longer, creating a misleading impression.[1] Actually baseball did not prove to be an effective source of vertical mobility for the sons of Italian immigrants.

Between 1901 and 1906 no Italian players were involved in baseball's major leagues and in the twenties only two Italian rookies broke onto the circuit out of a total of 133 first-year men.[2] Although this is technically inaccurate because Lou Schiappacasse played two games for the Detroit Tigers in the 1902 season, and Edward Abbaticchio spent the decade at the Philadelphia Phillies and at the Boston Beaneaters and Doves, and was part of the 1909 Pittsburgh Pirates World Series winning team, the overall figures are evidence of low participation levels. Fast forward two decades and participation was still nothing special. By 1926, only nineteen Italian Americans had played in the Major Baseball League with mixed success. Contrast this with professional boxing, where twenty-one Italian Americans won world boxing titles and an army of fighters of contendership quality appeared in the world rankings. It was a mismatch plain and simple. Boxing success measured in terms of overall participation levels, individual prominence and status acquired, reputations established and national and international championships won outstripped anything the Italian could muster on the diamond at this stage of American sporting history. Baseball was fraught with difficulties as Italians and Jews encountered discrimination from veteran players who resented their presence and worried over job losses, salary levels dropping, and having the prestige of their occupation destroyed. In this sporting field lift-off was not wholly dependent on whether you possessed the raw materials and pure sporting talent. Ethnic newcomers required opportunities and the sport's top brass was unwilling to loosen the reins of power. In a sport long considered exempt from societal prejudices this caused rancor and hostility too.[3]

Restricted access to baseball during the first two to three decades of Italian settlement in the United States strengthened the attraction of individual sports, and the ring, in particular, served as a springboard for success. Boxing, seen to be a natural choice for urban children, was also popular in outlying areas. In Ybor City, an industrial suburb of Tampa, Florida, where baseball was the national game, boxing challenged its popularity in the twenties and thirties, and out of a list of fifty local boxers 30 percent were Italian.[4] The thirties witnessed the first significant presence of Italian American players in the major leagues, and by 1936, even though the Slavs and Italians together comprised just 7 percent of all major leaguers, they were scoring notable achievements. Of the top 32 batting averages in the National League six belonged to Italian Americans; Gus Mancuso, Dolph Camilli and Ernie Lombardi in the National League and Joe DiMaggio and Zeke Bonura in the American League received Most Valuable Player (MVP) votes.[5]

They walked off the sandlots of California straight into the major leagues with a quarter of the 199 Italian American ball players hailing from San Francisco, Oakland and Los Angeles and their hinterland areas. By 1941 Italians represented 8 percent of major leaguers—more than double their share of the national white population—and now most major league sides possessed star-studded Italians; The Boston Braves fielded five, the Chicago Cubs three and the New York Yankees had Joe DiMaggio, Phil Rizzuto and Frank Crosetti. Of the fifteen teams listed, nine included at least one player of Italian origin.[6]

Whilst these gains translated into progress it is important to remember this occurred at a time of racial segregation in the game, when African American players were excluded from the world of organized white baseball. It was not until April 1947, when Jackie Robinson made his professional major league baseball appearance for the Brooklyn Dodgers, that the color line was officially ended. Integration was slow and by 1953 only six of the sixteen major league baseball teams had black players on their rosters.[7] The forties were the pinnacle of Italian American baseball achievement. In 1941 Joe DiMaggio of the New York Yankees was jointly named the Sports Athlete of the Year and the American League's MVP for his 56-game hitting streak. DiMaggio won the MVP on two other occasions, finishing 1937 and 1948 as the Home Run leader in the American League. Yogi Berra, like DiMaggio, captured three American League MVP titles in 1951, 1954 and 1955. Phil Rizzuto won the MVP award in 1950.

Boston's Dom DiMaggio, brother of Joe, finished top twice for the best hitting streak in 1949, and secondly for the most stolen bases in 1950. Vic Raschi of the New York Yankees ended the 1950 season as the most successful pitcher. Frank Crosetti secured recognition for the most stolen bases in 1938. Phil Cavarretta was voted the National League's MVP in 1945, finishing top of the batting averages. Roy Campanella clinched a hat-trick of MVP titles in 1951, 1953 and 1955. Dolph Camilli finished the 1941 season as the home run table topper. Ernie Lombardi twice topped the batting average charts in 1938 and 1942. Carl Furillo emulated him in 1953. In 1950 Sal Maglie topped the best pitcher rankings, with Johnny Antonelli coming out on top in 1954. Augie Galan achieved the most stolen bases in 1935.

With few Italian American children finishing high school, let alone achieving college entry qualifications, the university sport of American football remained inaccessible. There were some examples of talented players from the semi-pro circuit gaining places on National Football League (NFL) teams but the game was essentially closed off to outsiders, and a notable Italian American presence was delayed until the forties. The process of recruiting college football's most exceptional players became formalized in 1936 under a system which became known as the NFL annual player selection draft. This allowed NFL franchises to cherry-pick the best American footballers in the amateur game. Between 1900 and 1955, over 440 Italian American gridiron players, including NFL draftees, either appeared professionally or made the team roster. Some players drafted made neither. It is certainly not an insignificant figure, but neither is it a force of presence.

To put this into some sort of perspective, between 1936 and 1945 Italian American footballers accounted for 5 percent of the total number of NFL draft recruits, about the same as their share of the national white population. In the first three decades of the twentieth century fewer than fifty players of Italian background made the ranks of pro football. It increased slightly a decade later, but the apex of Italian American presence in football is defined by a fifteen-year period from 1941 to 1955. This accounted for a staggering 75 percent of Italian American participation in professional American football between 1900 and 1955. The increase in Italian males attending university led to participation in college football, and the majority of NFL footballers emerged from smaller semi-rural towns and hailed from 33 states, with Pennsylvania producing the largest share of players of Italian origin, more than double that of California, Massachusetts, Ohio, New York and New Jersey.

The number of individuals included into the sport's hall of fame is a further yardstick of success. Research has shown that there were no Italians in the College Football League Hall of Fame between 1900 and 1910, only one player a decade later, and between 1920 and 1930 just two players. These figures doubled between 1930 and 1940, and doubled again between 1940 and 1950, with one player winning the Heisman Trophy for his outstanding contribution. In the fifties five Italians gained entry into college football's elite, with Wisconsin's Alan Ameche clinching the Heisman Trophy. In the NFL Professional Hall of Fame only seven players made it onto the celebrated list for the same period.

Sport was a powerful medium in which performers of Italian descent demonstrated that, given a level playing field, they could excel. Whilst some successes were undoubtedly observed in All America selections, first draft picks, Heisman Trophy triumphs and the like, these did not represent a dominant position on the gridiron for the Italian American. Growth in participation and stories of individual success in college football and in the NFL were not commonplace until the late thirties. And only when the criteria for entry into further education loosened, and a greater importance was attached to learning, did the glory days of Italian American football (1941 to 1955) happen.

In baseball Italian American progress was sluggish and hindered in no small part by the prejudice that was rife in the game, and whilst the earliest ball players were denied their chance, 75 percent of Italian Americans represented in Major League Baseball (MLB) were not products of the college system at all. Instead they were products of semi-professional and minor-league teams, spotted by talent scouts.[8] The thirties marked a breakthrough for some Italian baseball players, and 1941 represented the first year in which two Italians captured MVP titles in both American and National League baseball. Between 1945 and 1955 Italian Americans consolidated their new eminence on the diamond with five players (Cavarretta, Joe DiMaggio, Rizzuto, Berra and Campanella) capturing nine

MVP titles between them, more than any other ethnic American cohort for this period. Above all, it confirmed baseball's new era of openness.

It wasn't always like this, and the slowness to integrate the Italian cohort is magnified by one cold, hard fact drawn from comparative sporting experiences. In 1938 Ernie Lombardi of the Cincinnati Reds became the first Italian American in major league baseball to win the MVP, the highest individual accolade in the sport. A splendid achievement and a real boost to the Italian presence in baseball, but by the time Lombardi completed his award-winning season, 34 Italian American professional boxers had already been acclaimed world titlists with scores riding high in the world rankings.

It was in the world of boxing that Italian American youth achieved success with the greatest consistency, and most importantly it was the first high-profile sport to give the Italian a platform on the national stage. This is an uncomfortable truth for some, as boxers were depicted as "toughs," immoral and unruly, but in reality this portrayed more the bias of the sport's detractors than it said about the enthusiasm, courage and discipline exhibited by thousands who found refuge and meaning inside the boxing gymnasium. These athletes were supported by city neighborhoods and by the provincial backwaters they hailed from, and their success whipped up a sense of ethnic euphoria and attracted large audience figures.

One of the most striking features of the Italian American boxing experience in the first half of the twentieth century that has thus far been overlooked is this cohort's involvement in amateur boxing. So what was the appeal of amateur boxing? Significantly the sport was popular and attracted huge fan interest, and except for world championship fights amateur boxing drew larger crowds than professional bouts in the United States. For example, 22,234 spectators attended to see the eight Chicago area Golden Gloves winners take on a European select boxing team at the Chicago Stadium in 1938, twice the total that turned up to see the Joe Louis versus Harry Thomas world heavyweight title fight in January 1938.[9]

At first glance it seems implausible that amateur boxing without financial reward could exist, let alone thrive, in these tough times. Whilst it is true that young boxers received pleasure from the glory, the public gaze and the importance attached to their athletic displays, any sporting passion or obsession with masculinity were secondary considerations. During an era when amateur boxing was not strictly controlled and open to regulatory abuse, boxers, especially the most gifted, always got paid. This was especially true during the Depression years and in some instances amateurs earned more than their professional counterparts. Amateur rules forbade boxers to fight in more than two contests per week. The boxer's card was stamped as proof of participation after each ring appearance, but many boxers flouted these lax impositions, claiming a lost or stolen card. Duplicate cards allowed individuals to make four appearances a week and earn between four and fifteen dollars each time. This practice continued without enforcement. A professional boxer might appear once or even twice monthly. So, based upon regularity of appearances, some amateurs earned more than professional boxers.[10] Moreover, triumphant amateurs were also awarded gold watches, diamond pins, trophies, medals and new boxing equipment, which was often later sold on and converted into money. Boxing shows sponsored by local businessmen encouraged fee-based performances with such matches hastily arranged for a private audience at the back of a saloon or at an athletic club.

The thirties represented the pinnacle of attainment levels for the Italian American cohort in amateur boxing. Between 1931 and 1935, Italians contributed nineteen out of a possible forty national boxing champions, accounting for 47.5 percent of the overall titlists. They were runners-up seven times, with another seven boxers making it to the semi-finals stage, and figured prominently in the Golden Gloves city and state championships staged around the country (see Appendix XVIII). These boxers were just as consistent when taking a bow for their country in international competitions and between 1920 and 1936 Italian American boxers contributed seven out of the twenty Olympic boxing medals gained by the United States boxing teams. What makes these images of triumph even more astonishing is that they occurred at a time of intense ethnic rivalry and red-hot competition. For example, the 1938 Chicago Golden Gloves winners were survivors from 26 Mid-West and Southern states who had entered the first preliminaries four months before the cream of the crop were left to battle it out for prizes. The sheer size of the challenge can be gauged via the 1941 Golden Gloves tournament, where 33,000 entrants vied for just sixteen titles, comprising the open and novice categories. Whilst the Golden Gloves, which began in 1927, and the Catholic Youth Organization (CYO) tournaments were usually seen as stepping stones to a professional boxing career, a large number of aspirants did not sign professional contracts. Many of the boys held regular jobs and trained and competed in their spare time. So once competition finished they hung up their gloves and returned to their families and communities. The boxer's personal obligations and the adverse publicity surrounding the shady characters and crime syndicates inhabiting professional boxing may have pushed some to reach for the exit door. Fate also played a part in some of the boxers' careers, but on a more practical level the tangible differences between the boxing codes may help explain the loss of so many talented men. Amateurs trained for three, four and six rounds, with each stanza lasting two minutes, whereas professionals trained for longer twelve and fifteen-round fights, with each round lasting three minutes. In the early part of the century fights lasted even longer. Amateur fighters used to technical rapid-fire battles soon discovered that a different breed of animal was suited to the pros, with stamina, endurance and courage the essential prerequisites. For those brave enough to cross the divide the majority could not deliver the same outcomes in the professional code and the chance of an amateur boxing champion winning a world professional boxing title carried the long odds of ninety to one.[11] It was quite evident that an extraordinary level of effort and skill was needed to scale the championship heights and achieve the promised riches. Genaro, La Barba, Battalino, Apostoli, Salica, Maxim and title claimant Tommy Paul were the magnificent seven from the Italian cohort to accomplish this feat. Perhaps the realization of this difficult undertaking, combined with a greater commitment of their time, exertion and the loneliness associated with this vocation persuaded the faint-hearted to stop at amateur level.

Of course, professional boxing was not immune to the improving socio-economic conditions and it is noticeable that a number of prominent Italian American amateur boxers decided to concentrate on other activities. In the twenties Nick Fosco, a superlative amateur welterweight boxer, won the Chicago Golden Gloves title and represented Chicago in the Inter-City Golden Gloves Championships. He turned his back on a professional boxing career, preferring the security of regular employment, and worked as a foreman in the pottery kilns. Between 1927 and 1929 Brooklyn-born Anthony Rudolph Curreri was thrice crowned All University Tournament boxing champion in the 128–135-pound category, and as an eighteen-year-old, the University of Wisconsin undergraduate was of Olympic class ability. He ignored the overtures of boxing promoters, preferring to complete his medical studies, eventually becoming an internationally known chest surgeon and oncologist. Louis Fugazi won the 1935 New York City Golden Gloves flyweight title and later added the United States Navy title but gave it all up to pursue a high-flying business career. In 1936 Danny Farrar (Donato Ferrara), the son of a shoemaker in Youngstown, Ohio, won the national amateur welterweight title in St. Louis and was destined for great things, but instead of following fellow tournament winners Joe Louis and Fred Apostoli into the paid ranks Farrar accepted an athletic scholarship at Duke University. He later worked at Sperry Gyroscope, a company specializing in manufacturing navigation equipment and aircraft components.

In 1936 Arthur Mercante, who later became a famous boxing referee, wanted to turn professional having reached the quarter-final of the New

York Golden Gloves tournament, but his father insisted his son aim higher for a college education. The Brockton-born Mercante had been introduced to boxing by his uncle, Joe Monte, a good professional heavyweight boxer who had reached the light-heavyweight final of the 1926 National amateur championships. Monte was forced to quit the sport suffering a detached retina and his damaged eye was removed for a glass replacement. This episode was a painful reminder of the dangers of boxing, and the Mercante family remained vehemently opposed to their son's involvement. Mercante recalled:

> Not very much was said about boxing. He [father] knew it was a Golden Gloves tournament and it would end in six weeks. That was the extent of it. He never cared about boxing and he discouraged it. Managers would come and knock at the door and ask him if he was interested in his son turning pro. My father would virtually kick them out of the house.[12]

In 1942 Mercante graduated from New York University in physical education. After the war he obtained his Master's degree and combined working in the sales and promotion department for a brewery with his international refereeing duties.

Rochester's Nello Nucelli was widely recognized as the best amateur lightweight in the United States and yearned to represent the country at the 1940 Olympics, but the outbreak of the Second World War disrupted his plans. He was eventually drafted in 1941 and spent the next five years in military service. Upon discharge he belatedly joined the paid ranks as a welterweight, but after twelve fights and aged just 26 he quit boxing to concentrate on a business career. In the forties Al Weill, Rocky Marciano's manager, was alerted to the stellar collegiate feats of Syracuse's John Mastrella. Weill gave him a try-out and offered him a four-round bout at Madison Square Garden. Mastrella refused to sign forms and went to law school, becoming a lawyer and in later years serving as a district attorney and judge.[13] Vince Palumbo was another boxer whom Weill tried to lure with a lucrative contract. The Georgetown dental student, who began boxing at fourteen years old in Golden Gloves competitions in Newark, New Jersey, twice captured the national intercollegiate boxing championships in 1954 and 1955. Palumbo briefly flirted with the paid ranks before completing his dentistry course with high grades. He later served as Chair of Oral Surgery at Southern Maryland Hospital and South East Community Hospitals.

The importance of sports in the immigrant experience was especially promoted by Italian and Slavic newspapers in the late thirties. New York-based Italian dailies like *Il Progresso Italo-Americano* and *Corriere d'America* were instructive in spreading this message, and although 25 percent of Italian papers were printed in English in whole or part, they included columns usually written in Italian and sometimes in English eulogizing the new age heroes of boxing, baseball and American football.[14] Generoso Pope Senior, a Bronx construction millionaire and proprietor of *Il Progresso Italo-Americano* newspaper, was a boxing aficionado, who often treated politicians to the major cards at Madison Square Garden. On March 5, 1937 Pope sponsored a boxing extravaganza at the St. Nicholas Arena in New York City, which featured three of the biggest-named Italian imports, Enrico Venturi, Italo Colonello and Aldo Spoldi, watched by five thousand predominantly Italian fans. *Il Progresso Italo-Americano* occupied a leading position in the United States and at the height of its popularity it sold 175,000 copies daily. Along with *Corriere d'America* it provided boxing coverage and the major stars were profiled as paragons of success. Italian newspapers across America forged close ties with boxers. It was a mutually rewarding partnership as readers welcomed news on their heroes' every move and the publicity injected interest and generated ticket sales among Italians. Fresno's Young Corbett III was one of many Italian boxers to benefit from this sporting media connection. His manager, Larry White, established an informal working relationship with *La Voce del Popolo* and throughout the twenties and thirties he provided them with a constant stream of stories. This unrestricted access equated to huge ticket sales as Fresno's Italian section turned out in droves to support their hometown hero. He repaid their faith by capturing the world welterweight title. Elsewhere *Il Corriere del Connecticut* was another Italian publication that reported on the role of the Italian boxer and his commitment to the First World War effort by enlisting for Uncle Sam. During this period Ferdinando Scutari, a United States-based Italian journalist and friend of many of the pioneering Italian boxers, performed a vital function as his series of articles on Hugo Kelly, Joe Grim, Tommy Daly, Johnny Dundee, Fireman Jim Flynn and Jimmy Murray were published in *Lo Sport Illustrato* and in *La Gazzetta dello Sport*, illuminating Italy about how her sons had created solid reputations in the most American of sporting pastimes.

The socio-cultural importance of boxing was clear for all to see. It was definitely not a niche or minority sport. Unlike baseball, where advancement was compromised by the political and racial landscape, boxing possessed a more meritocratic quality. An Italian could walk into an athletic club, show the promoter his wares, engage in a stint of training and be given a date on a boxing card. He did not have to jump through hoops to secure paydays. He stood alone in the ring, and knew that by developing a winning habit there was a good chance of becoming a main attraction, ultimately leading to larger purses and title chances. There were no educational entry criteria to satisfy.

On the issue of race in sport, over half a century of racial segregation in baseball simultaneously created a distorted and unholy representation of what was considered the national pastime, ruining the prospects of talented African American ball players who were forced to compete against each other in Negro leagues. American football stayed relatively integrated until the early thirties. Ohio's Charles Follis (1902–06) was the first African American professional in the pre-NFL era. Only fifteen black footballers played pro football through to the early thirties and their prospects worsened once George Marshall, the owner of the Boston Braves and Washington Redskins refused to select black players. This had widespread repercussions as other franchises followed suit and no black players took part in the NFL until after the Second World War. Although not immune to similar strife, boxing proved to be the most inclusive and egalitarian of American sports. In the post-Jack Johnson era a color bar kept the world heavyweight title out of reach, but black boxers were still able to fight for other championships, to win titles and to make a living in the most competitive of all sports. As we have seen, set in the context of this period Italian Americans made sterling contributions in the field of baseball and American football, but any comparable gains and achievements came much later, and were obtained without a significant African American presence.

9

Conclusion

The defining feature of the Italian American boxing experience is that this cohort produced more professional world boxing champions and title claimants than any other nationality in the first half of the twentieth century. It would be foolhardy to suggest that this pugilistic supremacy ran the entire fifty-five year course. It didn't, and success was shared with several other ethnic American groups. Unrivaled world championship success primarily lasted for three decades between 1920 and 1950. In this most competitive era, it was the only ethnic group to crown undisputed world champions in every division including the junior weight categories, and generated more leading contenders in the thirties. Italian Americans maintained second place in the overall world rankings throughout the twenties, forties and between 1950 and 1955. During the twenties they dominated the flyweight, bantamweight and featherweight classes. In the thirties they supplied the most leading contenders in seven out of ten weight categories. Between 1920 and 1950 they dominated the featherweight class. In short the Italian American was a champion of small men.

For much of this period the world was largely oblivious to his achievements as he followed the customary practice of adopting an Irish or anglicized ring moniker. Generally migrants making their way to the New World were down on their luck, and Italian immigrants were described as the most impoverished group to enter Ellis Island.[1] But the family profile of the Italian boxer revealed that these young men did not emerge from a social underclass, but were products of an aspirational and ambitious working class.

Whilst academics concur that the Italian laborer played an integral part in the reconstruction of America, closer scrutiny of his boxing experience shows two distinct routes of employment, with fathers just as likely to be tradespeople or to run small businesses as be a factory hand or laborer. The initial constraints and complications arising from new beginnings forced migrants to accept boundaries imposed by geography and those erected by the group. Since only the youngest men from the poorest city neighborhoods became prizefighters, Italians were obvious candidates, representing one of the largest predominantly young male urbanized groups. The spatial patterns of these densely populated areas influenced sporting choice. Boxing required little space and a network of established city-wide sporting structures and facilities supported by government agencies and the Church enabled these boys to develop athletic skills.

Opponents of boxing lambasted the sport as uncivilized and argued that it debased the human condition. Very noble and altruistic sentiments, but ghetto living and labor conditions were perceived negatively by Italian immigrants. Jobs in mines, railroads, in factories and in construction had notoriously poor health and safety records with many incidences of work-related death or injury. Immigrant labor was often unprotected by unions and prone to gross exploitation characterized by long hours and low pay. Ambitious Italian boys recognized early on that, provided they graduated to a competent standard of boxing they could comfortably double or treble their income and sometimes yield larger annual sums compared even to college-educated counterparts.

The harsh realities in the New World often resulted in Italian children forsaking a high school education to facilitate the family economy. The situation worsened as most Southern Italians, especially those from Sicily, arrived between 1900 and 1914, and the children grew to maturity when educational requirements for jobs were important. Established groups built barriers against the new arrivals, thwarting competition for jobs. For Italians rooted in blue-collar labor the cataclysmic effects of the Great Depression destroyed the prosperity of the construction industry and their new status. Unlike Western Europe, the United States had no federal system of unemployment insurance and relief, and where it was offered responsibility fell on the state and on municipal authorities working alongside charities. By 1933 nine out of ten companies had cut wages by as much as 50 percent, and more than half of all employers put their workers onto part-time work. The Depression era witnessed an upsurge in interest in boxing participation, especially among Italian Americans.

The subject of sporting success is a similar story of limited opportunities. Boxing aside, big-league participation in American football and baseball was obstructed as established ethnic groups safeguarded their vested interests. Steven Riess, sports historian, has noted that between 1900 and 1919 major league baseball players were primarily college men. The social origins of professional ball players were definitely not lower class and most definitely not from Italian backgrounds. Baseball was the favored pastime of world champions Eddie "Cannonball" Martin, Mike Belloise, Rocky Marciano and Joey Giardello, and only when their dreams went up in smoke did these multi-talented athletes turn to boxing. Baseball was a source of mobility for the Irish, who generally had a lower rate of vertical mobility than rival Northern Europeans, and for the Italian American advances on a grand scale did not appear until the late thirties and forties.

The social mobility movements of other urban ethnic groups reveal that at the time of Italian championship dominance the Irish had vacated the inner city slums, consolidated their social standing and modified their pastimes. The Jews had made the greatest leap of all, transforming their position in society within a generation, and this partly explained why there were no Jewish champions after 1940. It was a different story for the African Americans, who were permanently rooted to the bottom. In 1900 African Americans comprised the least urban of ethnic groups and boxing was an urban sport. Inter-war migration to the northern cities saw 70 percent of African Americans settle in urban ghettos, fewer than the Italians and Jews. By 1920 migration from the Southern states had boosted the African American population in New York to 150,000 people.

Suggestions that mobster activity unduly placed Italians at an advantage have little qualitative merit. Frankie Carbo did not obtain exclusive control of championship fights until the period between 1949 and 1953 and only after 1954 did his power dramatically escalate, which ironically coincided with a marked decline in the number of Italian titleholders. Italians were not awarded title shots because they were of the "preferred" ethnic orientation. Actually many highly touted individuals had their titular ambitions thwarted. Mobsters were in the business of reaping huge rewards and were not sentimentally obliged to promote fighters by virtue of their race. It did not make commercial sense, nor did it reflect the realities of the period. Due to the fact that Italians achieved a slower rate of vertical social and economic mobility and were disproportionately disadvantaged by a scarcity of opportunities in other spheres of society they offered promoters a precious commodity: a supply of hungry white fighters at a time when Irish and Jewish prizefighters had all but disappeared.

Whilst no single factor can solely account for the longevity of Italian American boxing success, prolonged ghetto living prevented assimilation, and the slowness to naturalize and register to vote hampered political fortunes, depriving them of a voice in education and the distribution of municipal employment. Under this system, young Italian males without influence and intellectual or monetary assets were unable to take advantage of traditional routes for social advancement. They were restricted to going it alone or tied to the manual labor sector for longer periods. They had a harder time of it and the precariousness of their position always left them exposed to economic fluctuations. The popularity of boxing and the potent imagery of repeat success made it a natural choice for risk takers as it not only offered social honor and access to areas previously barred, but most importantly the associated money-making potential appealed to the Italian blessed with individualism and enterprise.

In the aftermath of the Second World War his socio-economic position changed. Widespread discrimination was a lesser problem and new occupational and educational opportunities followed, and like other Americans he shared in the post-war economic boom. In an era when the majority of new housing was erected outside the main cities the Italian cohort left behind the declining urban enclave, transferring *en masse* to their castles in the suburb. The wind of change sweeping across the country influenced the decision-making process as they discovered that there were easier ways to move forward than having to fight with your fists. Prominent amateur boxers of this period were now more reticent about joining the paid ranks and readily brushed aside lucrative professional contracts. The sacrifice and loyal service of the Italian American soldier in the war made him feel a greater sense of belonging in a more assimilated setting, as ethnicity as a social, economic and cultural force began to recede. Education assumed a greater importance, evidenced by the rising numbers completing further education courses and attending university and, as new pathways opened up, he extricated himself from the past, from that particular time and place in American social and sporting history, which gloriously placed him in the forefront of the manly art.

Life after boxing

The general consensus among twentieth-century academics is that sport was a powerful means of social advancement since most respectable opportunities were restricted to urban youth. So what actually happened to the Italian American boxers in the post-boxing aftermath? Aside from the inherent difficulties associated with the definition of success we will look at the extent of vertical mobility achieved in retirement as well as life expectancy.

In 1952, Kirson Weinberg and Henry Arond wrote a paper that became the accepted gold standard in this area of research. Based upon a random sample of 95 boxers taken from different nationalities, and with career earnings above one hundred thousand dollars, the researchers concluded that the best a boxer could hope for was a boxing-related position or to become a tavern keeper. They surmised that even the most successful fighters went broke and seldom secured respectable jobs. In short they experienced a rapid decline in status in life after boxing.[2]

These findings were put to the test using the Italian American boxer as a case study. I discovered that 39.5 percent secured jobs in boxing-related employment or ran a small business and sometimes both. Secondly, these boxers were active in the catering and hospitality service sector, managing cafés, restaurants, taverns, bars, clubs and dance halls. They successfully operated in other sectors of the small business world as proprietors of grocery stores, delicatessen shops, barbershops, confectionery stores, games rooms, auto supplies dealerships, gymnasiums and ice cream parlors. One even ran a macaroni factory and several were bail bondsmen. In other words, out of a comprehensive sample of 862 retired Italian American boxers 341 either pursued an involvement in small business or maintained an interest in boxing-related activities. Of the overall sample, 11.6 percent worked in manufacturing and factory work, 5 percent were represented in the transport sector, working either as bus drivers, chauffeurs or teamsters, 4.6 percent were involved in law enforcement, and construction workers primarily consisting of semi-skilled and skilled workers accounted for a 3.9 percent representation. Traders and artisans represented 3 percent. Dock and shipping work, salesmen and security personnel closely followed in the occupational table rankings. Interestingly, criminal activities accounted for only 1.3 percent of post-boxing involvement, clearly demonstrating that although boxers and criminals came from similar ghetto environments there wasn't the much publicized overlap, and the tarnished image of the Italian male is not actually based on hard evidence.

Unlike Weinberg and Arond's study, my findings are based on a survey sample which is over nine times bigger and restricted to the occupational activities of a single ethnic American cohort. Secondly, boxers listed were not discriminated on the grounds of ability or by career earnings. Whilst the researchers concentrated on champions and contenders, my survey used professional boxers of varying abilities, ranging from preliminary category fighters to A-list competitors and champions. A footnote to the inclusion of preliminary and semi-wind-up level competitors is that these boxers would not have commanded large purses and frequently worked a second job and retired earlier from the sport. With that in mind the data reveals that the Italian cohort displayed a significantly higher number of aggregate businesses compared to the general representations made by Weinberg and Arond. A detailed and comprehensive listing of these prizefighters is included in Appendix XIX. Aside from the sample size differentiation, there are other notable differences with Weinberg and Arond. They found that 27.3 percent of the retirees worked or owned taverns whereas my data points to a far lower proportion of 13 percent. Whilst the former study found that 18.9 percent were involved in boxing-related jobs and a similar number worked in unskilled jobs, my survey showed that 8.5 percent of Italian Americans held boxing-related positions. However, 128 individuals listed as having a main job across various fields of employment were also identified to having some degree of boxing involvement. The former study noted only a paltry 2.1 percent representation in other business activities whereas I found that Italian American boxers registered an impressive 18 percent involvement in non-catering businesses, the largest single representation of employment in the overall sample. Furthermore, major participation in boxing-related positions, namely as managers, promoters, trainers and even as state boxing commissioners is consistent in the wider context of the cohort's closeness to business and entrepreneurial activity, a feature particularly noticeable during the forties and fifties.

Weinberg and Arond concluded that, overall, boxers suffered a marked deterioration in post-boxing status with many occupying low-status jobs. In contrast my findings show qualitative evidence of progress among Italian American boxers, revealing a strong presence in the catering and hospitality sector. They set up numerous establishments and generally they fed off their fame and in most cases operated relatively successful businesses. Without boxing it is unlikely they would have had access to capital or the bullishness to open high-profile, lavishly furnished city center-located businesses. Boxing provided them with the opportunity to experiment with new business ideas and within a generation they had transformed themselves into recognized and established community figures. It was not unusual for these boxers to have bought their own home and have sizable savings deposits too. Very few retreated to laboring jobs. Their temperament and transferable skills were used in various fields of employment like law enforcement and personal security. Some strayed on the wrong side of the law and earned reputations in the rackets. The Volstead Act, which outlawed the distribution and sale of alcohol, fueled a new demand throughout society in the twenties at a time when Italians were excluded from the American mainstream. The Italian newcomer together with established Irish and Jewish crime syndicates worked in unison to fill the void in the marketplace, making substantial revenue from their illicit bootlegging operations. Others reverted to being ordinary Joes on Main Street and got used to picking up a weekly wage as factory hands. They joined construction crews as semi-skilled and skilled men filling in as bricklayers, foremen and highway supervisors. Some made a big splash in union activities and in politics. One ex-boxer used his spare monies to train as a flight instructor and another took up his $85,000-a-year post as a boxing commissioner, whilst several swapped punches for grappling in the competitive world of professional wrestling.

New wealth brought with it new perils. Wily managers frequently grabbed onto more than their entitlement. An infinite stream of hangers-on expected the champion to bestow riches on those who massaged his ego. An added problem for boxing's high earners was the family drain on resources with many loans made to relatives simply forgotten about. Some fighters struggled when the lights dimmed, with the absence of constant adrenaline rushes associated with the training regimen, the competition, the purpose of fixed objectives, and the preparation for boxing matches together with the public adoration. When all that was gone they pursued alternative addictions. Some found solace inside a bottle, took drugs or squandered their hard-earned riches on roaming from one racetrack to another and being comforted by unscrupulous ladies in what the great Willie Pep described as falling victim to "fast women and slow horses." Then there were factors beyond anyone's control. The 1929 stock market crash and the ensuing international crisis deprived millions of people of their savings and investments. Champions Sammy Mandell, Fidel La Barba, Rocky Kansas and contenders Cuddy De Marco and Caveman Fisher were some of the big names robbed of their fortunes. Not all descended down the doom-laden slippery slope. Some managed self-restraint and smartly turned a profit. Take the case of Joey Maxim, underrated light-heavyweight boxer, who epitomized frugality and ordinariness. In January 1941, Maxim turned professional, and by the time he enlisted into the United States Army in December 1943 he had developed a fine savings habit, paying off the mortgage on his first home. Cuddy De Marco, lightweight contender, displayed admirable concern and selflessness, spending over thirty thousand dollars trying in vain to restore the eyesight of a blind brother. Without a second thought, Italian American fighters supported the family's value that was placed upon home ownership. They supported their parents financially and it was commonplace for big earners to purchase properties for their siblings too. There were those that simply reintegrated into their communities and carried on as normal.

In comparison to their fathers, greater opportunities were available to these young boxers, and they could achieve a higher level of wealth creation and enhanced recognition. Although usually confined to their local neighborhoods, a significant proportion, notably champions and contenders, were able to transcend the boundaries of their enclaves, receiving national and even international prominence. At times some of them mixed with politicians, Hollywood actors and chief executives of large American corporations. This attainment of social prestige and recognition was unattainable to fellow members of their cohort and was certainly not accessible to their immigrant fathers. With success came increased knowledge and awareness. A boxing career was short-lived. With this in mind men pursued a variety of business interests. Of course, some did better than others, and for the least successful it usually ushered in a period of blue-collar employment.

Many Italian American boxers remained in boxing after retirement. They administered their skills as managers, promoters and trainers, revealing individual and group progress, and a willingness to integrate in American society. No working-class job or for that matter middle-class occupation matched the level of passion, status and income stream associated with boxing's high achievers. Boxers were consumers. They spent extravagantly on big-ticket items, acquiring luxury cars, expensive clothes, and homes in salubrious surroundings, and in-between fights enjoyed their freedom and companionship. Yet this line of enquiry is largely ignored, and the intangible nature of these benefits and the combined difficulty in quantifying them has, perhaps, pushed it to the margins of this discourse. One should not let the degree of analytical difficulty stand in the way of an appreciation of the excess and action-packed lives they experienced during their time as prominent sportsmen.

The Italian American boxer attained some level of prosperity and satisfaction, but social mobility was still out of reach for this cohort as it was for the vast majority, with wealth controlled by the few. The general feeling of optimism that anything was possible following the First World War reached its apex in the post-Second World War era when America transformed itself into a suburban nation with home ownership encouraged. The growth of the entertainment industry propelled the boxer into the limelight in the new age of mass consumerism. They purchased homes and completed house purchases on behalf of their parents when most were struggling to pay their mortgage. Generally speaking the Italian boxer ensured that his family was always safeguarded and familial requirements like children's college fees were paid. His efforts launched his family towards middle-class respectability, challenging the damaging stereotype that depicted boxers as self-destructive individuals consumed by emotional problems, as being uneducated and obtuse, and as lower-class folk likely to fritter away their hard-earned gains.

Life expectancy

Without satisfactory general health, retirement for the Italian American boxer would have been a very distressing and lonely existence. By crudely examining the ages of 429 deceased boxers, the average life expectancy of the Italian cohort was found to range between 70.1 years of age for champions and title claimants to 72.1 years of age for contenders right up to 72.9 years of age for other professional boxers. Although the latter group possessed a higher overall average age by nearly two years compared to the champions they invariably had shorter and far less competitive careers. An overview of a five-decade breakdown by boxer births revealed boxers born in the 1880s and who fought in the 1900s had the shortest longevity at 69.7 years. Those born in the 1910s era and who competed during the thirties had the longest at 73 years. The thirties birth data has not been taken into account, as it is based on just one boxer and is therefore statistically insignificant. Despite nine recorded boxing fatalities in this sample between 1918 and 1940, and the wide variation in sample size for the respective decades the longevity data of the Italian American is uncannily similar, scoring an average age for the period of 72.4 years.

Moreover, when you consider that these boxers fought in the most competitive age, with boxing matches far more frequent, bouts longer, and referees a lot more lenient inside the ropes, his longevity compares remarkably well with the average life expectancy of an American male for the same period (see Appendix XX). What isn't known is whether these boxers experienced any major quality of life issues and boxing-related co-morbidities. Although it is accepted that permanent and irreversible neurologic dysfunction does not occur in the majority of boxers, concerned academics report an association between the number of fights and the development of neurological disorders such as Parkinson's disease.

The basis of future research might consist of accessing detailed health profiles of the retirees and studying the effects of boxing-related injury or disablement and how, or if, any of these impact overall quality of life in retirement. Such a study might also analyze the four major cohorts (African, Irish, Jewish and Italian) to ascertain whether a single group possessed longer life expectancy and improved health outcomes in retirement. For a long time now the debate about the value of professional boxing as a source of vertical mobility has solely focused on the question of direct outcomes from participation. Hence if a retired boxer failed to improve his position from the lofty heights of iconoclastic status he was judged to have experienced a rapid descent in terms of social-economic mobility. Further detail is required on retirees to accurately determine post-retirement societal positions. Negotiating access to private financial records relating to business activity, salary, levels of savings and investments, extent of property interests and the duration of financial wellbeing are all possible indicators in determining the full extent of socio-economic status attained through boxing. Subsequent studies might wish to pursue other lines of enquiry and examine the question of vertical mobility achieved by rival ethnic cohorts in boxing during the same period and ask how successful were the African, Jewish and Irish groups following boxing retirement. Did they also manifest similar traits of individualism in post-boxing occupations or was this purely an Italian phenomenon?

Postscript

In the post-1955 aftermath Italian American boxers did not altogether vanish from circulation. Champions Joey Giardello, Willie Pastrano and Carmen Basilio, who belonged to the last wave of boxers of the golden age of Italian American boxing, continued to fly the flag in the late fifties and early sixties. Against a backdrop of dwindling numbers of Italian American boxers and a dearth of championship contenders, Basilio appeared in eight more world title fights, winning both the welterweight and middleweight titles before retiring in 1961. Pastrano and Giardello captured their world titles in 1963. The best of the Italian American contenders was energetic puncher Joey Giambra. Between 1952 and 1962 the Buffalo-born fighter of Sicilian origin maintained a prominent world ranking among the middleweights, amassing victories over top fighters, twice beating Rocky Castellani and Ralph "Tiger" Jones, while others to fall included Joey Giardello and Gil Turner. In August 1955 Giambra lost a televised ten-round non-title fight to middleweight champion Carl "Bobo" Olson on a controversial split points decision. Millions watched Giambra beat the champion to the punch, repeatedly stunning and shaking Olson. The outrageous decision started a riot and it received front-page coverage, with many hailing him as the new king of the 160-pounders and Hall of Fame sports presenter Bill Stern declaring Giambra the "uncrowned champion." Despite the widespread attention Giambra never got a shot at the world middleweight title. He blamed the mob for his predicament. Aged 31, and seemingly destined never to compete for a world title following his eighth-round knockout of Florentino Fernandez, the number one contender, he eventually signed to meet Denny Moyer for the newly created junior-middleweight crown in 1962. Giambra narrowly lost the fifteen-rounder in Portland, Oregon. A year later Giambra retired.

The seventies were a lean period, with only Billy Backus and Mike Rossman, Italians of mixed parentage, registering world title wins. The fortunes of this cohort stood on the precipice of irreversible decline, but an unexpected fillip to overall group participation came from an influential source—Hollywood. In 1976 the *Rocky* saga, written by and starring Sylvester Stallone, told a popular rags-to-riches tale. This struck a chord with many, and its impact was widely felt, re-igniting a mini-revival in the fortunes of the Italian American boxer. Ray Mancini of Youngstown, Ohio, Vinny Pazienza of Cranston, Rhode Island, New Jersey's Bobby Czyz and New Yorkers Billy Costello and Vito Antuofermo headed a new generation of fine glove-wielders, recording the most significant post-fifties ring achievements during the eighties and early nineties. In more recent times Pittsburgh's Paul Spadafora and New Yorker Paulie Malignaggi and Long Island's Chris Algieri have joined the ranks as champions. This did not equate to the heightened group success of their predecessors, but it once again illustrated that even in times of elevated socio-economic prosperity and a powerful political voice in American society Italian Americans shared a special affinity with boxing (see Appendix XXI).

Although victories and titles diminished with each passing decade, the Italian Americans' connection with boxing continued in a different guise and their fighting role was substituted with an equally prominent one outside the ropes. They appeared as boxing commissioners, deputy commissioners, inspectors, judges and physicians—important functionaries responsible for regulation, safeguarding and maintaining standards in the sport. But it was in the realm of boxing management and the entrepreneurial side of boxing where Italian Americans made their biggest impact. In the post-1955 world of boxing, behind every great ring artisan of the modern era stood an Italian guardian who dispensed knowledge, invaluable experience and wisdom. Angelo Dundee followed his brother Chris into the boxing business and developed into the incomparable motivator-manager of nineteen world champions, and among his recruits instructed ring icons

Muhammad Ali and Sugar Ray Leonard. In the sixties Lou Viscusi managed world champions Joe Brown and Bob Foster. Johnny Duke trained Marlon Starling, the 1987 world (WBA) welterweight champion. Ritchie Giachetti guided Larry Holmes, Goody Petronelli influenced Marvelous Marvin Hagler, and Buddy De Rosa was behind Aaron Pryor. Lou Duva managed a galaxy of boxing stars as well as successfully steering Evander Holyfield's career. Not forgetting too that Cus D'Amato discovered and nurtured the two youngest heavyweight champions in boxing history. He first achieved this accolade with Floyd Patterson in 1956 and then his protégé Mike Tyson stormed to the title thirty years later.

The overall improvement in the cohort's socio-economic position in American society created a situation where the Italian American was no longer prepared to risk life and limb to become a prizefighter. In December 2010, veteran Paulie Malignaggi appeared on a BBC (British Broadcasting Corporation) radio program to mark the thirtieth anniversary of the film *Raging Bull*, and when asked about the demise of the Italian American fighter, he casually remarked: "They [Italian families] would rather his son went into pizza than pugilism." Whilst it doesn't offer too much of an insight it does show that attitudes have changed and boxing as a vocation is no longer appealing. Malignaggi added:

> When the pizza business started doing good in America there was no need to fight. Italians have been immigrants, goal getters . . . Italian immigrants wanted to make a better life for themselves and succeed. Second, third and fourth generations are established in all industries. If you can do it with your brain, intellectually there's no need to fight. Italians are making a good life for themselves. Italians now belong in the top half of American society. They are established now.[3]

Low levels of boxing recruitment among Italian Americans in the post-1955 period did not equate to a declining sporting presence. It was quite the opposite, directly boosting Italian American involvement and triumph in baseball and in American football. The group consistently produced a galaxy of major league players in subsequent decades. In American football Joe Montana, Dan Marino, Joe Flacco, Nick Buoniconti, "Duke" Cappelletti and legendary full back Franco Harris are just some of the leading lights to have stamped their mark on the gridiron. The same is true for other sports, and if you scratch beneath the surface you will invariably find that numerous American sportsmen have Italian lineage. In boxing today Italian Americans are primarily sports consumers, vociferous and knowledgeable spectators and television viewers, with celebrities like actors Al Pacino, Joe Mantegna and Sylvester Stallone passionate ringside observers. In the eighties Stallone set up a promotions outfit called Eye of the Tiger Productions with the aim of finding new talent. He struck up a friendship with heavyweight boxer Lee "Italian Stallion" Canalito, steering him on a championship course only for Canalito to turn his back on the sport after an unbeaten sequence of twenty fights. In the last decade Stallone has been pivotal in the successful *Contender* television series, which has showcased some of the country's most promising boxers. Mario Cuomo, former Governor of New York, is a big fight fan as is Lou DiBella, vice president of HBO (Home Box Office), who grew up watching the big fights. He is now instrumental in transmitting today's boxing spectaculars into our homes.

Appendices

Chapter 1

APPENDIX I: FATHERS' OCCUPATIONS OF ITALIAN AMERICAN PROFESSIONAL BOXERS 1900–55

Fathers' occupations of Italian American professional boxers

EMPLOYMENT STATUS	TOTAL
Other small business owner	86*
Laborer	69**
Factory/manufacturing	48***
Artisan/tradesman	26
Small business owner (catering & hospitality)	11x
Miner	9
Transportation	7
Docks/shipyard worker	5
Retail shop work	4
Professional	3
Deceased	2
Disablement/Illness	2
Law enforcement	2
Laundry operatives	2
Racketeer	2
Artist/sculptor	1
Chef	1
Clerical & admin	1
Fireman	1
Junkman	1
Military	1
Milkman	1
Postman	1
Public/municipal sector	1
Salesman	1
Unemployed	1
TOTAL	**295**

Notes

* The other small business category consists of shopkeepers and self-employed individuals such as grocers, shoeshine stand proprietors, liquor store, barbershop, baker, soft drinks storekeepers, games' room proprietors, auto supplies dealer, gymnasium, hotel, ice cream parlor, delicatessen and macaroni factory owner, polisher and shop owner, jewelry shop owner, fishmonger, onion farm owner plus self-employed food peddlers, blacksmiths and boxers.

** The laborer category pools individuals from the construction sector, water and sewerage labor, agriculture and from the railroads with the largest group classified as general and odd job laborers.

*** The factory & manufacturing category also includes dye house workers and mill hands.

x Denotes restaurant, tavern, saloon, bar, café or nightclub establishments.

A carpenter listed also boxed professionally.

A longshoreman listed also boxed professionally.

For the purpose of this analysis the father's occupation of identified sibling grouping is registered once per family and not for each sibling recorded. Eleven brothers have been identified in this study. They are Joe & Vince Dundee, Ralph & Al Tribuani, Sledge & C.M. McCarthy, Pal and Vic Moran, Tommy & Al Murray, Ralph & Jackie Brady, Paul & Al Carr, Jimmy & Packey O'Gatty, Jake & Joey La Motta, Sam & Phil Muscato and Roland & Jerry La Starza.

Chapter 2

APPENDIX II: ITALIAN AMERICANS AND PRIZE MONEY IN PROFESSIONAL BOXING 1900–55

DATE	WEIGHT	BOXING CONTEST		PURSE RECEIVED ($)	VENUE
15/09/1894	Bantamweight*	Casper Leon	Jimmy Barry	Leon – 200	Lamont, IL
29/09/1903	Featherweight (1)	Benny Yanger	Eddie Hanlon	Yanger – 2,625	San Francisco, CA
14/04/1905	Featherweight	Benny Yanger	Young Mowatt	Yanger – 750	Kalamazoo, MI
15/12/1908	Middleweight*	Hugo Kelly	Billy Papke	Kelly – 2,500	Los Angeles, CA
26/02/1911	Bantamweight*	Frankie Conley	Johnny Coulon	Conley – 3,500	New Orleans, LA
03/02/1912	Bantamweight*	Frankie Conley	Johnny Coulon	Conley 2,000	Vernon, CA
20/03/1912	Middleweight	Hugo Kelly	Eddie McGoorty	Kelly – 1,260	Kenosha, WI
29/04/1913	Featherweight*	Johnny Dundee	Johnny Kilbane	Dundee – 5,000	Vernon, CA
18/12/1916	Flyweight*	Young Zulu Kid	Jimmy Wilde	Young Zulu Kid – 2,750	London (England)
09/01/1917	Bantamweight*	Pete Herman	Kid Williams	Herman – 1,500	New Orleans, LA
05/11/1917	Bantamweight*	Pete Herman	Frankie Burns	Herman – 6,500	New Orleans, LA
24/03/1919	Bantamweight	Pete Herman	Memphis Pal Moore	Herman – 1,000	Memphis, TN
12/04/1920	Flyweight	Young Zulu Kid	Jimmy Wilde	Young Zulu Kid – 2,500	Ontario (Canada)
06/05/1920	Middleweight*	Johnny Wilson	Mike O'Dowd	Wilson – 1,200	Boston, MA
13/01/1921	Bantamweight*	Pete Herman	Jimmy Wilde	Herman – 3,500	London (England)
17/03/1921	Middleweight*	Johnny Wilson	Mike O'Dowd	Wilson – 50,000^	New York City
25/07/1921	Bantamweight*	Pete Herman	Joe Lynch	Herman – 22,500	Brooklyn, NY
05/09/1921	Middleweight*	Johnny Wilson	Bryan Downey	Wilson – 35,000	Jersey City, NJ
30/12/1921	Featherweight	Johnny Dundee	Willie Jackson	Dundee – 7,740.41	New York City
26/12/1921	Lightweight	Rocky Kansas	Johnny Ray	Kansas – 5,000	Pittsburgh, PA
04/07/1922	Lightweight*	Rocky Kansas	Benny Leonard	Kansas – 15,000	Michigan City, IN
24/03/1923	Bantamweight	Bobby Wolgast	Pancho Villa	Wolgast – 3,000	Philadelphia, PA
18/07/1923	Bantamweight	Eddie Martin	Joe Ryder	Martin - 300	Brooklyn, NY
09/07/1923	Bantamweight	Bobby Wolgast	Joe Lynch	Wolgast – 2,500	Philadelphia, PA
19/12/1924	Bantamweight*	Eddie Martin	Abe Goldstein	Martin – 2,100	New York City
01/04/1925	Jr-lightweight*	Steve Sullivan	Mike Ballerino	Sullivan – 4,000	Philadelphia, PA
10/08/1927	Middleweight	Italian Joe Gans	George Courtney	Italian Joe Gans – 2,000	Brooklyn, NY
03/06/1927	Welterweight*	Joe Dundee	Pete Latzo	Dundee – 10,000	New York City
21/05/1928	Lightweight*	Sammy Mandell	Jimmy McLarnin	Mandell 49,000	New York City
11/10/1928	Featherweight	Eddie Guida	Carl Duane	Guida – 1,500	New York City
25/07/1929	Welterweight*	Joe Dundee	Jackie Fields	Dundee – 50,000	Detroit, MI
25/06/1929	Featherweight	Earl Mastro	Fidel La Barba	Mastro – 2,250	Los Angeles, CA
23/08/1929	Featherweight	Earl Mastro	Eddie Shea	Mastro – 11,000	Chicago, IL
20/05/1930	Middleweight	Young Terry	Joe Reno	Young Terry – 7,000	Newark, NJ
29/01/1930	Featherweight	Earl Mastro	Kid Francis	Mastro – 3,500	Los Angeles, CA
04/07/1930	Welterweight	Young Corbett III	Young Jack Thompson	Young Corbett III – 7,754.20	San Francisco, CA
07/08/1930	Featherweight	Earl Mastro	Fidel La Barba	Mastro – 5,800	Chicago, IL
03/11/1930	Featherweight	Fidel La Barba	Kid Chocolate	La Barba – 15,000	New York City
13/11/1930	Lightweight*	Tony Canzoneri	Al Singer	Canzoneri – 7,250	New York City
27/05/1931	Lightweight	Billy Petrolle	Jimmy McLarnin	Petrolle – 9,500	New York City
22/02/1933	Welterweight*	Young Corbett III	Jackie Fields	Young Corbett III – 3,869	San Francisco, CA
29/05/1933	Welterweight*	Young Corbett III	Jimmy McLarnin	Young Corbett III – 35,000	Los Angeles, CA
14/08/1934	Welterweight	Young Corbett III	Mickey Walker	Young Corbett III – 7,641.30	San Francisco, CA
11/09/1934	Middleweight*	Vince Dundee	Teddy Yarosz	Dundee – 25,000	Pittsburgh, PA
22/09/1936	Heavyweight	Al Ettore	Joe Louis	Ettore – 37,276+	Philadelphia, PA

DATE	WEIGHT	BOXING CONTEST		PURSE RECEIVED ($)	VENUE
23/09/1937	Lightweight*	**Lou Ambers**	Pedro Montanez	Ambers – 65,000	New York City
23/09/1937	Middleweight*	**Fred Apostoli**	Marcel Thil	Apostoli – 5,000	New York City
23/09/1937	Bantamweight*	**Harry Jeffra**	Sixto Escobar	Jeffra –2,500	New York City
24/02/1938	Heavyweight*	**Nathan Mann**	Joe Louis	Mann – 12,158+	New York City
01/04/1938	Middleweight*	**Fred Apostoli**	Glen Lee	Apostoli – 10,000	New York City
03/02/1939	Light-heavyweight*	**Melio Bettina**	Tiger Jack Fox	Bettina – 600	New York City
28/06/1939	Heavyweight*	**Tony Galento**	Joe Louis	Galento – 50,000+	New York City
13/07/1939	Light-heavyweight*	**Melio Bettina**	Billy Conn	Bettina – 15,000	New York City
22/08/1939	Lightweight*	**Lou Ambers**	Henry Armstrong	Ambers – 23,398	New York City
24/09/1940	Bantamweight*	**Lou Salica**	Georgie Pace	Salica – 1,200	New York City
14/03/1941	Middleweight	**Steve Belloise**	**Tami Mauriello**	Belloise – 6,000, Mauriello – 6,000	Bronx, NY
08/04/1941	Heavyweight*	**Tony Musto**	Joe Louis	Musto – 8,734	St Louis, MO
07/08/1942	Bantamweight*	**Lou Salica**	Manuel Ortiz	Salica – 6,000	Hollywood, CA
20/11/1942	Featherweight*	**Willie Pep**	Chalky Wright	Pep – 7,000	New York City
05/02/1943	Middleweight	**Jake La Motta**	Sugar Ray Robinson	La Motta – 10,000	Detroit, MI
19/03/1943	Middleweight	**Jake La Motta**	Jimmy Reeves	La Motta – 6,000	Detroit, MI
30/03/1943	Middleweight	**Jake La Motta**	Ossie Harris	La Motta – 9,000	Pittsburgh, PA
11/06/1943	Lightweight	**Sammy Angott**	Henry Armstrong	Angott – 20,000	New York City
07/01/1944	Lightweight	**Lulu Constantino**	Beau Jack	Constantino – 8,000+	New York City
08/03/1944	Lightweight*	**Sammy Angott**	Juan Zurita	Angott – 17,500	Hollywood, CA
10/03/1944	Featherweight*	**Sal Bartolo**	**Phil Terranova**	Bartolo – 19,250, Terranova – 12,500	Boston, MA
17/07/1944	Featherweight	**Willie Pep**	Manuel Ortiz	Pep – 20,000	Boston, MA
08/03/1946	Welterweight	**Tony Pellone**	Bob Montgomery	Pellone – 8,513	New York City
29/03/1946	Welterweight	Marty Servo	**Rocky Graziano**	Graziano – 12,090	New York City
08/07/1946	Lightweight	**Sammy Angott**	Beau Jack	Angott – 6,987.39	Washington DC
18/09/1946	Heavyweight*	**Tami Mauriello**	Joe Louis	Mauriello – 38,854+	New York City
27/09/1946	Middleweight*	**Rocky Graziano**	Tony Zale	Graziano – 78,892	New York City
18/01/1947	Heavyweight	**Tami Mauriello**	Jimmy O'Brien	Mauriello – 10,000	Chicago, IL
14/03/1947	Middleweight	**Jake La Motta**	Tommy Bell	La Motta – 21,000	New York City
16/07/1947	Middleweight*	**Rocky Graziano**	Tony Zale	Graziano – 70,341	Chicago, IL
10/06/1948	Middleweight*	**Rocky Graziano**	Tony Zale	Graziano – 120,000	Newark, NJ
24/01/1950	Light-heavyweight*	**Joey Maxim**	Freddie Mills	Maxim – 19,000	London (England)
08/09/1950	Featherweight*	**Willie Pep**	Sandy Saddler	Pep – 92,889++	New York City
26/10/1951	Heavyweight	**Rocky Marciano**	Joe Louis	Marciano – 24,000	New York City
24/09/1953	Heavyweight*	**Rocky Marciano**	**Roland La Starza**	Marciano – 175,000	New York City
17/06/1954	Heavyweight*	**Rocky Marciano**	Ezzard Charles	Marciano – 89,000	New York City
05/03/1954	Lightweight	**Paddy De Marco**	Jimmy Carter	De Marco – 14,000	New York City
11/04/1955	Welterweight*	**Tony De Marco**	Johnny Saxton	De Marco – 21,220	Boston, MA
16/05/1955	Heavyweight*	**Rocky Marciano**	Don Cockell	Marciano – 130,000	San Francisco, CA
30/11/1955	Welterweight*	**Carmen Basilio**	**Tony De Marco**	Basilio – 69,000	Boston, MA

Notes

Italian American boxers are in bold.

Purse figures cited are derived from various newspapers and periodicals and in some cases it is not always clear whether these are gross or net figures.

Asterisk denotes world professional boxing title bout.

(1) denotes contest billed as for the 130-pound world title.

# denotes that in addition to Young Zulu Kid's purse of $2,500 he also received $200 in training expenses and 25% of the moving picture money.

+ denotes the boxer's largest payday.

^ denotes that Johnny Wilson received an additional $2,500 in expenses, not included in the above-mentioned purse.

++ denotes that at the time this was the biggest boxing purse ever awarded to a fighter below the lightweight division.

APPENDIX III: PRE-BOXING OCCUPATIONS OF ITALIAN AMERICAN PROFESSIONAL BOXERS 1900–55

Pre-boxing occupations of Italian American professional boxers

EMPLOYMENT STATUS	TOTAL
Factory/manufacturing operative	36
Family business helper	18
Newsboy	17
Bootblack	13
Laborer - (construction & railroad)	12
Artisan/trade	11
Sport & leisure related	9*
Further education	7
Retail shop work	7
Transportation	7
Docks/shipyard worker	6
US armed forces	5
Mining & quarrying	4
Service sector employees	4**
Office clerk	3
Salesman	3
Criminal/delinquent	2
Iceman	2
Janitorial & cleaning services (including mill sweeper)	2
Farm labor	1
Laundry helper	1
Petrol station attendant	1
Postman	1
TOTAL	**172**

Notes

* Sport & leisure-related occupation category includes horse racing groom, golf caddy, and bowling pin boy and street fighter etc.

**The service sector employee category includes those working as a bartender, cinema camera operator and hotel bellboy

No data available for sixteen of the world boxing champions included.

Chapter 3

APPENDIX IV: ITALIAN AMERICAN PRIZEFIGHTERS USING IRISH AND ANGLICIZED NAMES 1900–55

RING MONIKERS & REAL NAMES	IN BRIEF	ERA BOXED	BIRTHPLACE & HOMETOWN
Flyweight (112 pounds)			
Young Fox (Frank Volpe)		1900s	Newark, NJ
Joe Clark (Verna)		1900s/10s	Philadelphia, PA
Young Sieger (Dominic Garaventi)	1912 Jersey City 105-pound champ		Hoboken, NJ
Al Murphy (Alex Triano)		1900s/10s/20s	Manhattan, NY
Phil Carmine		1910s	Brooklyn, NY
Jimmy Curtis			Manhattan, NY
Young Dundee (Mike Pellegrino)			Manhattan, NY
Young Francher			Syracuse, NY
Johnny Keyes (Andrea Canonico)	"Chinatown 110-pound champ". "Chinatown Jabber"		Manhattan, NY
Corona Kid (James La Gattuta)			Queens, NY
Young Jimmy Murray			New York
Joe Ross			BP: Italy HT: Oswego, NY
Bobby Doyle (Girolamo Santucci)	1922 New York National Guard flyweight title challenger.	1910s/20s	Manhattan, NY/ Philadelphia, PA
Tommy Dundee (Passarella)			Camden, NJ
Battling Kiddy (John P. Romano)	Contender. Bantamweight champ of the 27th Division		Brooklyn, NY
Terry Miller (Paul Milo)	"Italian flyweight champ of New York"		Brooklyn, NY
Mickey Nelson (Mike Colletti)	1922 junior-flyweight world title claimant		Brooklyn, NY
Spike Sullivan (Michael Lobello)	1916 "Italian bantamweight champ of Syracuse"		Syracuse, NY
Smiling Willie (Leonardo La Basso)			Manhattan, NY
Patsy Young (Martarire)			Pittsburgh, PA
Sam Anch (Gangi)		1920s	Kansas City, MO

RING MONIKERS & REAL NAMES	IN BRIEF	ERA BOXED	BIRTHPLACE & HOMETOWN
Stevie Cole (Stephen Columbo)			Allentown, PA
George Fitzsimmons (Ignatius La Placa)			BP: Italy HT: Brooklyn, NY
Fighting Pete Harmon (Peter Morocco)			Auburn, NY
Jimmy Jackson (Joseph Valicenti)			Brooklyn, NY
Little Jeff (Tony Angelo)			Atlantic City, NJ
Mickey Lewis (Michael Mancini)	1926 Hudson County bantamweight champ		Jersey City, NJ
Charlie Martin (Carmine Maurone)			Philadelphia, PA
Tommy Milton	Contender		BP: Messina, Sicily (I) HT: Harlem, NY
Bobby Myson (Pete Aiello)			Philadelphia, PA
Tony Norman (Bova)	"Harp Wop"		Pittsburgh, PA
Al Ray (Mastripolito)	Brother of Charlie Ray		Philadelphia, PA
Paddy Reade AKA Patsy D'Andrea (Pasquale Luigi Andrea)			BP: Italy HT: Manhattan, NY
Al Segar (Joseph Rocco)			Utica, NY
Pee Wee Ross (Alfred Rossi))			Camden, NJ
Young Slate (Charles Saletta)			Newcastle, PA
Little Jeff Smith AKA Joe Burman (Joseph Cosentino)	World title challenger. 1922, 1924 & 1925 Southern flyweight champ.		Baltimore, MD
Joey Wallace (Appalucci)			Philadelphia, PA
Kid Wolfe (Henry Graio)	Contender		Philadelphia, PA
Ray Belmont (Raymond Lauria)	Of mixed Italian-Slovak origin. He won the Val Barker trophy at the 1936 Berlin Olympics for being the most scientific boxer.	1920s/30s	Cleveland, OH
Mickey Farr (Farinacci)	Brother of Johnny Farr		Cleveland, OH/ Oakland, CA
Kid McCoy (Francis D'Alessandro)			BP: Vineland, NJ HT: Philadelphia, PA
Frankie Murray (Frank Carrozza)	World title challenger		Stockton, CA

RING MONIKERS & REAL NAMES	IN BRIEF	ERA BOXED	BIRTHPLACE & HOMETOWN
Gig Rooney (Oswald Rodia)	Brother of Teddix Dix		Chester, PA
Joey Ross (Joseph Nisivoccia)	Contender		Hoboken, NJ
Jimmy Wallace (Mario Gendracri)			Chester, PA
Bushy Brooks (Gerard Radice)		1930s	Trenton, NJ
Sammy Dalton (Sabino D'Alto)			Los Angeles, CA
Al Little (Navo)			Philadelphia, PA
Harry Little (Navo)			Philadelphia, PA
Johnny Nate	Brother of Georgie Nate		South Bend, IN

Bantamweight (118 pounds)

RING MONIKERS & REAL NAMES	IN BRIEF	ERA BOXED	BIRTHPLACE & HOMETOWN
Paul Kelly (Paolo Antonio Vaccarelli)	Leader of the notorious Five Pointers street gang in New York City.	1890s/1900s	BP: Naples, (I) HT: Manhattan, NY
Dago Mike (Michael Mongone)	1898 Colorado featherweight champ. 1900 Colorado bantamweight champ.		BP: Italy HT: Denver, CO
Tommy "Kid" Ginger		1900s	Brooklyn, NY
Johnny Oliver (Anthony Fertitta)			No data
Chick Tucker (Giuseppe Purgi)			Utica, NY
Billy Brannon		1900s/10s	San Francisco, CA
Andy Costello	Ex-New Haven bantamweight champ		New Haven, CT
Harry Dell (Albert Papa)			San Francisco, CA
Kid Murphy (Michael Canzanella)	1906 New England bantamweight champ		BP: New Haven, CT HT: Queens, NY
Kid Peterson (Virgil Sorri)			San Francisco, CA
Tom Sharkey (Gaetano Caggio)	Ex-Pennsylvania bantamweight champ		BP: Italy HT: Reading, PA
Frankie Stinger (Francis Napoli)			Philadelphia, PA
Kid Williams (Dominic Incerto)	Ex-New England bantamweight champ		BP: Scilla, Calabria (I) HT: Norwalk, CT
Willie Rock (Rocco Scala)	Baltimore's former "Little Italy" bantamweight champ.	1900s/10s/20s	Baltimore, MD

RING MONIKERS & REAL NAMES	IN BRIEF	ERA BOXED	BIRTHPLACE & HOMETOWN
Young Barnes (Bernardo Nardiello)		**1910s**	Syracuse, NY
Tony Baron (Barrone)	Outpointed Johnny Ertle, bantamweight claimant		Pittsburgh, PA
Willie Burns (William Salomone			Jersey City, NJ
Jack Casey (Ray Marchi)	"Brownie"		Milwaukee, WI
Frank Conway (Nicholas Iacovelli)			Camden, NJ
Jerry Dalton			Indianapolis, IN
Baltimore Dundee (Salvatore Ranzino)	1917 Maryland bantamweight champ. 1918 US Navy bantamweight champ.		Baltimore, MD
Nick Gans	Brother of Italian Joe Gans		Brooklyn, NY
Joe Monroe (Joseph Cognate)			Brooklyn, NY
Young Palmer	"Italian bantamweight champion"		New York City
Kid Ryan (Piano)			Syracuse, NY
Mike Wagner			Manhattan, NY
Dave Astey (Asti)		**1910s/20s**	Manhattan, NY
Willie Astey (William Asti)			BP: Italy HT: Manhattan, NY
Bill Bandy (William Bandiere)			Philadelphia, PA
Danny Brown (Michael Credico)	1920 Central New York bantamweight champ.		Syracuse, NY
Jersey Jimmy Carter (James Corrado)			Newark, NJ
Mike Clancy (Michele Catanzaro)			BP: Italy HT: Manhattan, NY
Joe Clifford (Joseph Ingenito)	Contender.		Elizabeth, NJ
Benny Coster AKA Young Benny (Cosimo Aidala)	"Chinatown Flash"		BP: Italy HT: Manhattan, NY
Joe Coster (Michael Migliaccio)			Philadelphia, PA
Frankie Curley			Brooklyn, NY
Young Dundee (Frank Maglione)			Syracuse, NY
Frankie Fay (Frank Farina)	1921 New York State National Guard bantamweight champ		Albany, NY

RING MONIKERS & REAL NAMES	IN BRIEF	ERA BOXED	BIRTHPLACE & HOMETOWN
Billy Hill (Fazzone)			Newcastle, PA
Young Battling Hurley (Michael Salitto)			Syracuse, NY
Young Jaggie (Frank Carricato)			Pittsburgh, PA
Patsy Johnson (Pasquale Petta)	Contender		Trenton, NJ
Young Al Kale (Paul Marconi)			Buffalo, NY
Marty O'Brien (Anthony Martin Sinatra)	Father of singer Frank Sinatra		BP: Catania, Sicily, (I) HT: Hoboken, NJ
Al Paul (Alfonso Papa)			Buffalo, NY
Charlie Ray (Charles Mastripolito)	1921, 105-pound American title claimant		Philadelphia, PA
Young Ritchie (Anthony Riccio)			Auburn, NY
Happy Smith	Brother of "Terrible Mike"		Manhattan, NY
Jimmy Taylor	1915 world title challenger		Manhattan, NY
Kid Tony (Anthony Sisti)			Buffalo, NY
Chick Tucker (Louis Medicina)			Utica, NY
Patsy White (Pasquale Revelli)	"Mulberry Bend Belter"		Manhattan, NY
Frankie Barnes (Al Valentino)		**1920s**	Philadelphia, PA
Frankie Bell (Frank De Leo)			New York
Danny Brooks (Fornatara)			Manhattan, NY
Jimmy Burns (James De Fagio)			BP: New York HT: Bridgeport, CT
Johnny Cobb (Chemello)			Grand Rapids, MI
Kewpie Collins (Albert De Pace)	"Bronx Chicken"		Bronx, NY
Al Cook (Peter Cucuzzella)			Newark, NJ
Frankie Coster (Francis Costelli)			Brooklyn, NY
Connie Curry (Curcio)			Sioux City, IA
Johnny Curry			Brooklyn, NY
Mickey Delmont (Michael Molinaro)	Contender		Newark, NJ
Danny "Kid" Dix (Daniel Rodia)			Philadelphia, PA

RING MONIKERS & REAL NAMES	IN BRIEF	ERA BOXED	BIRTHPLACE & HOMETOWN
Frankie Dundee (Frank Carlucci)			Port Chester, NY
Joe Dundee (Charles Marchetta)			Hoboken, NJ
Frankie Evans (Frank Ferrara)			Manhattan, NY
Willie Farrell (Michael J. Ferrulo)			Poughkeepsie, NY
Bobby Gleason (Robert Gagliardi)	Founder of the world famous Gleason's Gym in New York City		Bronx, NY
Johnny Gray (Grado)			Brooklyn, NY
Young Jeff (Michael Papa)			Canton, OH
Bucky Josephs (Joseph Barone)	Ex-New Jersey flyweight champ		Nutley, NJ
Mike "Kid" Julian Michael Juliano)			Kenosha, WI
Lou Kemp (Louis Carangio)			Syracuse, NY
Young Andy Ketchel (Andrew Crisco)			New York City
Midget Kilburn (Frank Lagona)			BP: Naples, (I) HT: Philadelphia, PA
Joey Leon (Joseph Liani)			Harlem, NY
Kid Leonard (Leonard Dramesi)			BP: Italy HT: Philadelphia, PA
Pete Lucy (Lucci)	Ex-Worcester County bantamweight champ		Clinton, MA
Eddie Mack (Angelo Marrucco)	1924 New England bantamweight champ		Stamford, CT
Tony Mandell (Anthony Mandella)	"Worcester Firecracker"		Worcester, MA
Harry Martin (Martino)	Contender. Brother of Terry Martin. Ex Rhode Island State bantamweight champ		BP: Susquehanna, PA HT: Providence, RI
Johnny Mason AKA Ralph J. Pilgoste (Paligostri)			Bridgeport, CT
Frankie Moran (Joseph Cucurullo)			BP: New Orleans, LA HT: Gulfport, MS
Mike Moran	"Midget"		Pittsburgh, PA
Jackie Murray			Brooklyn, NY

RING MONIKERS & REAL NAMES	IN BRIEF	ERA BOXED	BIRTHPLACE & HOMETOWN
Tommy Murray (Thomas Di Renza)	Brother of Battling Al Murray		Philadelphia, PA
Johnny Nelson (Anthony Simonelli)			Stamford, CT
Mickey Nelson (Pizzulo)			New Jersey
Kid Palmer (Nicholas Palmieri)			Newark, NJ
Patsy Paschal AKA Young Paschal (Pasquale Marziotti)			Marcus Hook, PA
Jimmy Regan (James Rago)			Oakland, CA
Joe Reid (Joseph Abbruzzi)			Brooklyn, NY
Kid Reynolds (Joe Governale)			New York City
Babe Rivers AKA Joe Nell	Brother of Pete Mazzeo		Newcastle, PA
Spark Plug Russell (Joseph Restivo)	Contender		Newark, NJ
Jimmy Stone (Rappisi)			Garfield, NJ
Kid Thomas (Tommy Iacono)	Ex-Utica featherweight champ		Utica, NY
Kid Tony (Anthony Peluso)			New York
Patsy Willard (Antonio Apice)			Providence, RI
Jimmy Wilson (Vincent Silvano)			Philadelphia, PA
Buddy Young (Andrew Cipolla)			Yonkers, NY
John Young (Ianno)			Schenectady, NY
Jimmy Zill (Ziella)			Youngstown, OH
Jimmy Bagley (Baglio)		1920s/30s	Washington DC
Johnny Brennan (Ralph Dotina)	Contender. "Trenton Firecracker"		Trenton, NJ
Frankie Brown AKA Nick Alexander (Nicholas Alessandro)	Former Utica bantamweight champ		Utica, NY
Tony Cal (Anthony Pintaro)			Fairview, NJ
Jimmy Dugan (Vincent Esposito)			Philadelphia, PA
Midget Mike Dundee (Dominic Girardi)			Brooklyn, NY

RING MONIKERS & REAL NAMES	IN BRIEF	ERA BOXED	BIRTHPLACE & HOMETOWN
Young Dundee (Carl Fiorini)			Reading, PA
Johnny Erickson (Angelo Azzolina)	Contender. World title challenger. "Swedish Wop"		BP: Catania, Sicily (I) HT: Brooklyn, NY
Jimmy Ireland (De Fonzo)			BP: Wilmington DE HT: Glen Falls, NY
Chick Kansas (Anthony Chichricco)	1924 Southern featherweight champ		BP: Italy HT: Baltimore, MD
Battling Mack (Matthew Fanelli)			Camden, NJ
Mike Marcells (Macaluso)	"Scrap Iron"		Rochester, NY
Georgie Nate	Contender		South Bend, IN
Tony Palmer (Anthony Palmieri)			Newark, NJ
Frankie Paul (Papa)	Brother of famous Tommy Paul		Buffalo, NY
Harry Roberts (Dominic Ricercato)			Boston, MA
Young Joe Roche (Basil Puglisi)	Nephew of 1920s middleweight Joe Roche. 1939 California bantamweight title challenger		San Francisco, CA
Young Tony Ross (Joseph Barranco)			Baltimore, MD
Dick Welsh (Di Matteo)			Philadelphia, PA
Mike Valentine	"Italian Flash"	1920s/30s/40s	Duluth, MN
Johnny DeFoe	1932 Golden Gloves & Inter-City bantamweight champ	1930s	West Side, NY
Johnny Clark (Basile)			Philadelphia, PA
Joe Nelson (Oriolo)			Philadelphia, PA
Billy Passan (William Passanante)			Philadelphia, PA
Babe Kelly		1930s/40s	Beverley, NJ
Al Mandell (Albert S. Cimino)			Scranton, PA
Tony Brooks (Anthony Bochicchio)		1940s	Worcester, MA
Johnny Wolgast (John Cristaldi)			Philadelphia, PA

RING MONIKERS & REAL NAMES	IN BRIEF	ERA BOXED	BIRTHPLACE & HOMETOWN
Featherweight (126 pounds)			
Phil Demore AKA (Phillip Damore)	"Phil the Dago"	**1890s/1900s**	Syracuse, NY
L. G. Flint	"Utica Kid"		Utica, NY
Benny Leon (Leone)	Brother of Casper Leon		Manhattan, NY
Jack Leon (Leone)	Brother of Casper Leon		Manhattan, NY
Charles McCarthy (Montagasini)	"Bull"		Philadelphia, PA
Tony Moran	Contender		Brooklyn, NY
Buck Lincoln (Franchetti)		**1900s**	Philadelphia, PA
Nick "Kid" Kline (Nicholas Gengaro)	Brother of famous Patsy Kline	**1900s/10s**	Newark, NJ
Jimmy Moran (Vincenzo Marrone)			Brooklyn, NY
Kid Pantz (Charles Campana)			Boston, MA
Frankie Pass (Achille Antonelli)	"Ninth Ward Terror"		BP: Washington DC HT: Brooklyn, NY
Chick "Kid" Rose (Pasquale Vellana)			Brooklyn, NY
Jimmy Sheppard (Dr. Vincent Nardiello)			New York
Kid Stinger (Frank Caputo)	Former Pennsylvania featherweight champ		BP: Brooklyn, NY HT: Philadelphia, PA
Jackie Sanders (Frank Sanders)	"Dixie Cyclone"	**1900s/10s/20s**	BP: Italy HT: Elizabeth, NJ
Kid Alberts (Felice K. Alberti)		**1910s**	Frederick, MD
Kid Andrews (Anthony Andruccia)			Buffalo, NY
Lew Cardell (Louis Lawrence Cardell)	"Young"		BP: Montclair, NJ HT: Newark NJ
Charley J. Costello (Virgullo)			BP: Naples (I) HT: New Haven, CT
Taddo Coster (Salvatore Agnello)	Brother of famous Joe Coster		Brooklyn, NY
Tommy Dixon	Ex-Rochester featherweight champ		Rochester, NY
Pete Doyle			Brooklyn, NY
Young Driscoll (Anthony Padovano)			Brooklyn, NY
Young Dundee (Domenico Boschetti)			BP: Italy HT: North Adams, MA
Tony Fair			Newcastle, PA

RING MONIKERS & REAL NAMES	IN BRIEF	ERA BOXED	BIRTHPLACE & HOMETOWN
Johnny Ford (Eugene Del Bianco)			Oakland, CA
Young Griffo AKA Kid Griffo (Giovanni Cucco)			Chicago, IL
Young Jasper (Richard Jasper)			BP: Italy HT: Boston, MA
Young Joret (Al Reggio)			New Orleans, LA
Bobby Lincoln (Nick Franchetti)			Philadelphia, PA
Italian Joe Miller			Rochester, NY
Young Morrissey			Rochester, NY
Patsy Murphy (Charles Zingaro)			Newcastle, PA
Young Murphy (Thomas Ciraulo)			Syracuse, NY
Young Otto			Rochester, NY
Young Papke (Emilio De Vincenzo)			San Francisco, CA
Freddie Russell (Alfred Cinquina)			No data
Kid Stevens (Cardella)			Niles, OH
Battling Victor (Victor Cargiullo)			Utica, NY
Kid Stone			Providence, RI
Young Sylvester			Chicago, IL
Frankie White (Thomas Labratti)			Philadelphia, PA
Willie Ames (William Iamme)	Contender, ex-Ohio featherweight champ	1910s/20s	Akron, OH
Al Blades (Robert Di Fruscio)			BP: Caserta, (I) HT: Lawrence, MA
George Brown (Barone)			Rochester, NY
Paul "Red" Carr (Carriero)			BP: Avigliano, Potenza (I) HT: Buffalo, NY
Mike Castle (Joseph Casella)			Lawrence, MA
KO Circus (Michele La Duca)			BP: Italy HT: Belaire, OH
New Haven Joe Currie (Paul Acampora)	"New Haven Bearcat"		BP: Italy HT: New Haven, CT
KO Joe Daly			Brooklyn, NY

RING MONIKERS & REAL NAMES	IN BRIEF	ERA BOXED	BIRTHPLACE & HOMETOWN
Brooklyn Joe Dillon (De Trano)			Brooklyn, NY
Patsy Dugan (Pasquale Fusco)			BP: Italy HT: Niles, OH
Battling Dundee (Carmelo Lazzara)	Brother of world champions Joe and Vince Dundee		Baltimore, MD
Dickie Dundee			Buffalo, NY
Jimmy Dundee (Rinaldo D'Annunzio)	"Kid Lucky". 1920 Pacific Coast featherweight champ		Oakland, CA
Young Dundee (Alberto R. Corbi)			Providence, RI
Tommy Elm (Thomas Pisacreta)			Paterson, NJ
Bobby Ertle (Vincent Carvello)			BP: Nebraska HT: Oakland CA
Ted Frenchie (Theodore La Barba)	Brother of famous Fidel La Barba		BP: New York HT: Los Angeles, CA
Mike Frisco (Michael Russo)			New Orleans, LA
Battling Gabe (Gabriel Lawrence)	1919 Central New York featherweight champ		Little Falls, NY
Joe Garry (Giuseppe Fischelli)			Brooklyn, NY
Al Ginger (James Damis)			Brooklyn, NY
Andy Gorman (Andrew Pizza)			Brooklyn, NY
Happy Gorman	"Wolf"		Brooklyn, NY
Jimmy Herman AKA Young Bungo (James Bongo)			BP: Italy HT: Syracuse, NY
Billy Hines (Joseph Garofalo)			Philadelphia, PA
Society Kid Hogan (Salvatore De Lorenzo)			BP: Palermo, Sicily (I) HT: Chicago, IL
Bobby Hollis (George Giannini)	"Hunk", 'Fighting Newsboy'		San Francisco, CA
Joe Kelly (Joseph Analore)			Des Moines, IA
KO Kid Kelly (Calisto Rondoni)			Rochester, NY
Spider Kelly II (Henry Albert)			BP: Coal City, IL HT: Red Lodge, MT
Kohoma Kid (Marino Snello)			Queens, NY

RING MONIKERS & REAL NAMES	IN BRIEF	ERA BOXED	BIRTHPLACE & HOMETOWN
Young Limbo (Charles Bellucci)			Brooklyn, NY
Frankie Mack (Francis Monacchio)			Hartford, CT
Joe Mandell (Joseph Mandala)	Brother of Sammy Mandell		Rockford, IL
Johnny Mayo (De Maio)			Philadelphia, PA
Frankie McFarland (Bevilacqua)	"Kid"		Boston, MA
Kid Terry McGovern AKA Skeets (Joseph Di Leo)			Philadelphia, PA
Joe Moran (Joseph Barsa)			Philadelphia, PA
Vic Moran (Victor Louis Miorana)	1919 Southern welterweight title challenger		New Orleans, LA
Eddie Pinchot (Angelo Biagini)	Twice challenged for Canadian bantamweight & featherweight titles		BP: Gallatin, PA HT: Charleroi, PA
Jimmy Powers (Giovanni Vincenzo)			Hoboken, NJ
Frankie Rex AKA Young Rex (Romeo Cerniglia)			BP: Louisiana HT: Sacramento, CA
Young Ross (Nick Ficaro)			BP: New Orleans, LA HT: Syracuse, NY
Phil Ross AKA Young Dilly (Phillip Rossi)			Newark, NJ
Charlie Sheppard (Miraglia)			Manhattan, NY
Georgie Spencer (Dispensa)			BP: Buffalo, NY HT: San Francisco, CA
Dummy Thomas (Negri)			San Francisco, CA
Joe Thomas (Charles Joseph Tomasulo)			Rochester, NY
Jimmy Travers (Mario Tromnini)			Milwaukee, WI
Johnny Victor (Victor Vigorito)			Manhattan, NY
Tony Vincent (Vincent Mattioli)			Rochester, NY
Al Wagner (Albert Campoli)			Philadelphia, PA

RING MONIKERS & REAL NAMES	IN BRIEF	ERA BOXED	BIRTHPLACE & HOMETOWN
Bobby Wagner (Sarubbi)	Member of famous Wagner fighting family		Manhattan, NY
Frank Susnell (Frank Cucinelli)	"Young"	**1910s/20s/30s**	BP: Caserta (I) HT: Rochester, PA
Billy Baxter (Gus De Lamo)		**1920s**	Utica, NY
Jimmy Bones (Mastriani)			Bridgeport, CT
Young Britton (Frank D'Alba)			Bayonne, NJ
Billy Brown (Dominic Nardini)			BP: Naples, (I) HT: Syracuse, NY
Frisco Frankie Brown (Frank Ferrando)			San Francisco, CA
Kid Burns (Joseph Glorioso)			Trenton, NJ
Oakland Bobby Burns (Johnny Dalto)			Oakland, CA
Jack Coburn (Ned Rini)			Brooklyn, NY
Johnny Coney (Tony Zaccone)			Manhattan, NY
Benny Cross			Newark, NJ
Frankie Curry (Nunzio Carrozza)			Manhattan, NY
Danny Dillon AKA Young Tennessee (Joseph Pascarella)			BP: Slate Run, PA HT: Newcastle, PA
Teddy Dix (Alfred Rodia)			Leiperville, PA
Kid Dooley (Salvatore Buggica)			Tampa, FL
Patsy Doyle			New York
Joe Dundee (Joseph Galliano)			Philadelphia, PA
Sammy Dundee (Randesi)			Detroit, MI
Joe Flynn (Lester Vozzolo)			Manchester, CT
Jimmie Foley (Vincent Vecchio)			Brooklyn, NY
Young Frenchy (Aristide Granatelli)			BP: Italy HT: Bronx, NY
Mickey Greb (Ferrari)			Pennsylvania
Babe Griffin (Victor Galiotto)			San Jose, CA

RING MONIKERS & REAL NAMES	IN BRIEF	ERA BOXED	BIRTHPLACE & HOMETOWN
Eddie Griffin (Martin Galiotto)			San Jose, CA
Mickey Griffin (De Luca)	Brother of Philly Griffin		Newark, NJ
Midget Guery (Frank Guerrea)			Newport, KY
Kid Harvey (Migliacci)			Trenton NJ
Johnny Hayes (Ferrara)	Brother of featherweight contender Petey Hayes.		Brooklyn, NY
New York Joe Herman (Pasquale Catti)			Brooklyn, NY
Bobby Higgins (Albert Siciliano)			New Orleans, LA
Lew Hurley (Ludovico Suraco)	Contender		BP: St. Alpine, Naples, (I) HT: Harlem, NY
Nick Johnson (Nicholas Petta)			Syracuse, NY
Rocky Joyce (Rocco Rotunno)			Chicago, IL
Sid Kelley (Sam Gaudesi)	Member of fighting family		BP: Winnipeg (CA) HT: Milwaukee, WI
Battling Joe King (Robert Bonamici)			BP: France HT: Bridgeport, CT
Eddie Lenny (Peter Massino)			Philadelphia, PA
Jack Lester (Bennetti)			Philadelphia, PA
Skelly Lewis (Louis Petrozelli)			Hoboken, NJ
Harlem Willie Mack (Granieri)			Harlem, NY
George Malone (Avallone)			Brooklyn, NY
Jimmy Mars (Maurice James Marsanico)	"Ravenswood Kid"		Queens, NY
Billy Marlowe			Brooklyn, NY
Joey Mastrion			Brooklyn, NY
Pete Murphy AKA Sam Mallett AKA Kid Casey (Malatesta)			Albany, NY
Johnny Nash (Angelo Stinconi)			Queens, NY
Battling Peach (Giovanni Salerno)			New York
Paulie Porter			Brooklyn, NY

RING MONIKERS & REAL NAMES	IN BRIEF	ERA BOXED	BIRTHPLACE & HOMETOWN
Billy Prince	Later became Connecticut State boxing commissioner		Bridgeport, CT
Frankie Ritchie (Florio)	"Fighting Fool of Fordham"		Bronx, NY
Kid Ritchie (Richard Fazio)	Brother of Caveman Fisher		Syracuse, NY
Young Joe Rivers (Vincent Fasano)			Brooklyn, NY
Steamboat Sam (Sam Tubolino)			Watertown, NY
Young Peter Sharkey (Peter Piraino)			Syracuse, NY
Italian Joe Thomas			Rochester, NY
Jimmy Trannett	"Cleveland Toothpick"		Cleveland, OH
Mickey Travers (Michael Traversano)	Brother of Tony Travers		New Haven, CT
Pee Wee Valentine (Sammy Sacco)			New York
Young Veter (Barbano)			Leavenworth, WA
Harry Virgets (Verdichizzi)	Member of Virgets fighting family		New Orleans, LA
Nick Virgets (Nicholas Verdichizzi)	1926 Southern junior-lightweight champ, Brother of Phil Virgets		New Orleans, LA
Baby Willard (Alfonso Apice)			Providence, RI
Kid Williams (Vigliotti)			Reading, PA
Kid Willis (Louis Caputo)	1924 National Guard New York bantamweight champ		BP: Baltimore, MD HT: Syracuse, NY
Young Yippo (James Carnevale)			Troy, NY
Charlie Young (Charles Ciaccio)			Brooklyn, NY
Charlie Young (Dominick Gentiluomo)			BP: Bagnara Calabro, Reggio Calabria (I) HT: New York
Jimmy Zill AKA Jack White (Ziella)			Youngstown, OH
Louis Avalon (Avallone)		**1920s/30s**	New York
Sil Barry (Silvio Olivi)			Alpha, NJ
Joe Belmont (Felix Vitacollona)			Philadelphia, PA
Bobby Bennett (Bonetti)			New York
Charlie Blood (Charles Benanti)			Garfield, NJ

RING MONIKERS & REAL NAMES	IN BRIEF	ERA BOXED	BIRTHPLACE & HOMETOWN
Young Bobby Burns (Joseph Castranda)	Of mixed German-Italian origin		Baltimore, MD
Jimmy Burns (George Santa Maria)			Philadelphia, PA
Nick Christy (Nicholas Cristafoni)			Bristol, CT
Young Dempsey (John Licari)			Newark, NJ
Johnny Dixon (Rizzo)			Newark, NJ
Johnny Dodge (Zelano)	Brother of Joey Dodge		Sacramento, CA
Kid Douglas (Frank Nanci)			Swissvale, PA
Mickey Doyle (August Rodola)	"Italian bantamweight champ"		Pittston, PA
Midget Doyle (Mike Dolcemascolo)			Passaic, NJ
Frankie Edwards (Frank Micelli)			Brooklyn, NY
Chick Emmons (Crisco)			Trenton, NJ
Frank Erne (Frank Fagnano)			Williamsport, PA
Bobby Flynn (Mario La Guardia)			Philadelphia, PA
Joe Folins Sr (Joseph Folino)	Brother of Herman Folins		BP: Sellia, Catanzaro (I) HT: Ambridge, PA
Joe Geno (Joseph Genovese)			Boston, MA
Tony George (Antonio Giorgi)			Buffalo, NY
Frankie Graham AKA Frankie Garcia (Francesco Geraci)	Brother of famous Bushy Graham		Utica, NY
Jersey Mickey Greb (Orlando Luzzi)			Nutley, NJ
Oakland Billy Harold (Vito Fabrizio)			Oakland, CA
Johnny Hayes (Luciano Mancuso)			Brooklyn, NY
Willie Joyce (William Schiavo)			Philadelphia, PA
Frankie Lands (Frank Aquivania)			Newcastle, PA

RING MONIKERS & REAL NAMES	IN BRIEF	ERA BOXED	BIRTHPLACE & HOMETOWN
Kid Lux (Lou Centolella)			Utica, NY
Georgie Mack (De Matteo)	Brother of Petey Mack		Jersey City, NJ
Petey Mack (Peter De Matteo)			Jersey City, NJ
Joe Malone (Miloni)			Bronx, NY
Nick Malone	Of mixed Italian Irish origin		Wellsville, OH
Ernie Mandell (Ernest Mendillo)			Providence, RI
Brooklyn Frankie Martin (Salvaggio)			Pittsfield, MA
Eddie Mason (Angelo Scalze)	"Wildcat"		BP: Italy HT: St Paul, MN
Patsy Mayo (Collura)			Trenton, NJ
Patsy Michaels (Pasquale Vercillo)	Brother of Nick Michaels		Syracuse, NY
Ray Mitchell (Johnny Lombardo)			Milwaukee, WI
Frankie Murphy (Lazzari)	Brother of Joe "Dynamite" Murphy.		Los Angeles, CA
Joe Murphy (Alfonso Lazzari)	"Dynamite"		Sacramento, CA
Johnny Naples			Portland, ME
Johnny Nelson (Caesar Gesario)			Belleville, NJ
Willie Oliver (Oliveri)			BP: Italy HT: Harlem, NY
Terry Parker	1923 National AAU featherweight champ		Boston, MA
Joe Peach (Giuseppe Labruzzo)			BP: Ybor City, FL HT: Tampa, FL
Kid Polo (Paul Salerno)			Syracuse, NY
Frankie Rapp (Rapini)			Camden, NJ
Phil Raymond (Raimondi)			Baltimore, MD
Babe Ruth (Anthony Schettini)			Philadelphia, PA
Charlie Ryder (Charles Fiumano)			Staten Island, NY
Tony Shea (D'Onofrio)	Brother of famous brother Eddie Shea		Chicago, IL
KO Sweeney AKA Sammy Bronco (Salvatore Branca)			Utica, NY

RING MONIKERS & REAL NAMES	IN BRIEF	ERA BOXED	BIRTHPLACE & HOMETOWN
Young Patsy Wallace			Atlantic City, NJ
Matty White (Americo Bianchi)			Philadelphia, PA
Battling Wop (August Nanello)			Bakersfield, CA
Johnny Andrews (Serafino Vitale)		**1930s**	New Haven, CT
Louis August	1931 Pacific Coast featherweight champ. Brother of Joey.		BP: Italy HT: Spokane, WA
Bobby Augustine (Agostino)			Stockton, CA
Monty Blue (Mario Guliuzza)			Marion, OH
Tony Brown AKA Jimmy Marsh (Frank Aiello)			BP: Haverhill, MA HT: New York City
Toppy Cal (William Calcagni			Elizabeth, NJ
Young Chippy (Anthony Avello)			Poughkeepsie, NY
Al Daley (Alexander Di Salvio)			Camden, NJ
Bobby Dean (Anthony Di Cesare)			Philadelphia, PA
Jack Dempsey (Nicholas Gencarelle Sr)			Westerly, RI
Joe Dempsey (Joe Gerace)			Buffalo, NY
Young Dillon (George Radice)			Wilkes Barre, PA
Joey Dodge (Giuseppe Zelano)			BP: Rowelsburg, WV HT: Sacramento, CA
George Dundee (Generoso Caggiano)	Became top boxing promoter in Boston area.		Boston, MA
Young Frenchy (Joe Forchione)			Cleveland, OH
Henry Gowatch (Enrico Iacovacci)			BP: Colorado HT: Detroit, MI
Pete Herman II			Brooklyn NY
Young Kelley (Joseph Lazzaro)			Portsmouth, NH
Mohican Kid (Frankie Del Ragno)			Pittston, PA

RING MONIKERS & REAL NAMES	IN BRIEF	ERA BOXED	BIRTHPLACE & HOMETOWN
Jackie LaSalle (John Gherlone)			BP: Pittsfield, MA HT: Hartford, CT
Johnny Lombard (Lombardi)			Vallejo, CA
Charles Manley (Annunziato)			Stamford, CT
Jackie Martin (Salvatore Scribetta)			Boston, MA
Jimmy Martin (James Lombardi)	1932 National AAU bantamweight champ		Manhattan, NY
Ralph Morgan (Raffaele Morganelli)	Ex-Massachusetts featherweight champ		BP: Boston, MA HT: Roxbury, MA
Mickey O'Day (John Pepe)			Newark, NJ
Frankie Paul (Frank Pellegrino)			Philadelphia, PA
Frankie Ross (Frank Ronzano)			San Jose, CA
Sammy Scully (Scoglio)			Chicago, IL
Mickey Summers	Brother of Frankie Bove		Newark, NJ
Kid Torpedo (Cavalli)	Brother of Young Battling Nelson		Walla Walla, WA
Jimmy Valentine (Salvatore)			Omaha, NE
Frankie Bove (Bova)		**1930s/40s**	Newark, NJ
Joey Brown (Arpino)			Syracuse, NY
Johnny Brown (Marelli)			Chicago, IL
Lou Camps (Luigi Castelgrande)	Great amateur		Bronx, NY
Lou Dell (Louis Della Ripa)			Hartford, CT
Bobby Ivy (Sebastian Di Mauro)	"Poison". Contender & title challenger		Hartford, CT
Nicky Jerome (Nicola Girolamo)	"Machine Gun"		Brooklyn, NY
Pete Kelly			Beverley, NJ
Frankie Mandell			San Francisco, CA
Willie Oliver (Oliveri)			Queens, NY
Danny Russell (Parillo)			BP: Naples, (I) HT: Philadelphia, PA
Tommy Ryan (Giaimo)			New Haven, CT
Larry Teene (Nick Tarentino)	"Southington Flash"		Southington, CT

RING MONIKERS & REAL NAMES	IN BRIEF	ERA BOXED	BIRTHPLACE & HOMETOWN
Frankie Wallace (Angelora)	Contender & title challenger		BP: Campobasso, (I) HT: Cleveland, OH
Hank Cisco (Ciacco)		**1940s**	Philadelphia, PA
Johnny Dell (John M. Del Giorno)	Crowned South Pacific featherweight champ during World War II		BP: Fulton, NY HT: Brooklyn, NY
Joe Fratt (Fratarola)			Chester, PA
Tony Gartex (Joseph A. Marvella)			Poughkeepsie, NY
Joe Liddy (Lipari)			Jersey City, NJ
Norman Mastrian	Of mixed Austrian-Italian origin		BP: Duluth, MN HT: Minneapolis, MN
Petey Virgin (Vergine)	"Young Jimmy Cagney"		Schenectady, NY
Joey Cam (Joseph Camiolo)	1951 New England featherweight champ	**1950s**	Boston, MA

Lightweight - (135 pounds)

RING MONIKERS & REAL NAMES	IN BRIEF	ERA BOXED	BIRTHPLACE & HOMETOWN
Roxy Kanell (Rocco Canelli)	"Dangerous Dago"	**1890s/1900s**	Buffalo, NY
Jimmy Kelly (Giovanni Di Salvio)			Manhattan, NY
Jack Lowery			Brooklyn, NY
Harry Smith	"Italian champion of Chester"		Chester, PA
Mike Tuths (Tony Cio)			Brooklyn, NY
Kid Williams (Ted Di Donna)			Philadelphia, PA
Joey Angell (Angeli)		**1900s**	San Francisco, CA
Jim Burke (James Valentino)			Manhattan, NY
Young Crosta (Anthony Costolia			Philadelphia, PA
Mike Dalton			Los Angeles, CA
Jimmy Dunn (Vincent Zito)			Bronx, NY
Jack Galligan (Filippo S. Serritella)			Chicago, IL
Kid Kirby (Eugene Presti)			BP: Italy HT: Prescott, AZ
Fred Landers			San Francisco, CA
Paul Martin (Paolo De Martini)			San Francisco, CA
Charles McCarthy AKA C.M. McCarthy (Angelo Buscaglia)			BP: Montemaggiore Belsito, Palermo, Sicily HT: Buffalo, NY

RING MONIKERS & REAL NAMES	IN BRIEF	ERA BOXED	BIRTHPLACE & HOMETOWN
Sledge McCarthy (Serafino Buscaglia)			BP: Montemaggiore Belsito, Palermo, Sicily HT: Buffalo, NY
Joe Argen	"Human Toothpick"	**1900s/10s**	Utica, NY
Jack Clifford (Virgilio Montani)			BP: Genoa (I) HT: New York
Freddy Corbett (Alfred Stipa)			Philadelphia, PA
Charlie "Kid" Dalton (D'Alto)			BP: Italy HT: Los Angeles, CA
Bobby Evans (Augustine Ardiss)			BP: Paterson, NJ HT: Portland, OR
Freddie Kelly (Ferdinando D'Alfonso)			BP: Italy HT: Philadelphia, PA
Jack Lee (Humbert Fugazy)	Later became top boxing promoter		Manhattan, NY
Gus Lenny (Raimo)			Boston, MA
Harry Lenny (Enrico Setaro)	Brother of Eddie Lenny		Chester, PA
Frankie Madden (Sperduto)	"Bowery Bhoy"		BP: Staten Island, NY HT: Manhattan, NY
Denver Mike Malone (Miglionico)	"Dago Mike"		Pueblo, CO
Jack Martin (Joseph Grecco)			Buffalo, NY
Frankie Nelson (Michael Valerio)	1914 New Jersey lightweight champ		BP: Italy HT: Hoboken, NJ
Joe Phillips (Ferdinando Gagliardo)	1912 Rhode Island lightweight champ		BP: Italy HT: Providence, RI
Young Robideau (Vincent D'Anella)			Philadelphia, PA
Kid Scaler (Louis Scalero)	1909 North West lightweight champ		BP: Luzzi, Cosenza (I) HT: Spokane WA
Al Schumacher (Salvatore Scimeca)	"Doc Schumacher"		BP: Palermo, Sicily, (I) HT: Manhattan, NY
Lou Sheppard (Louis F. Inno)			BP: Italy HT: Manhattan, NY
Battling Terry (Eugene Peluso)	1913 Western Pennsylvania lightweight champ		BP: Cosenza, (I) HT: Pittsburgh, PA
Chick Tricker (Tricarico)			Manhattan, NY
Bobby Wilson (Robert Sequino)	Former Canadian lightweight champ		BP: Montreal, (CA) HT: Utica, NY
Pat Bradley (Rocco De Carlo)	Contender	**1900s/10s/20s**	Philadelphia, PA

RING MONIKERS & REAL NAMES	IN BRIEF	ERA BOXED	BIRTHPLACE & HOMETOWN
Frankie Maher (Maurice Marra)			Elmhurst, NY
Tony Adams	1917 Rochester lightweight champ	**1910s**	Rochester, NY
Jimmy Barry (Felice Callavolo)			Newark, NJ
Charlie Bergen	"Italian Bearcat"		New Haven, CT
Danny Churue (Tortorice)			Boston, MA
Mike Daley (Bolletino)			Philadelphia, PA
Frankie De Meyer (Francis De Maio)	"Red Hook Bearcat"		Brooklyn, NY
Fighting Eagan			New York
Dummy Evans (Paul Marchese)			Brooklyn, NY
Young Josie (Giuseppe Varuzzo)			North Adams, MA
Joe Kattell (Joseph Cataldo)			Pittsburgh, PA
Joe Kansas (Joseph Tozzo)	Brother of Rocky Kansas		Buffalo, NY
Pete Kelly (Mechella)			Philadelphia, PA
Battling Kelman AKA Joe Killem (Puzzillio)			Utica, NY
Joe Lawrence (Joseph Lotta)			Rochester, NY
Joe Masterpole			BP: Italy, HT: Lima, OH
Young Terry McGovern (Frank Di Leo)			BP: Naples, (I) HT: Philadelphia, PA
Tommy Moore			Providence, RI
Joe Moran (Avallone)			Harlem, NY
Jimmy Murphy			Chicago, IL
Johnny Nelson (Oriolo)			Philadelphia, PA
Jimmy Peters	US lightweight title claimant.		Chicago, IL
Joe "Kid" Post (Giuseppe Esposito)			BP: Avellino, (I), HT: Olean, NY
Battling Jim Reilly			Albany, NY
Tony Ross (Alex Basile)			Boston, MA
Kid Ruell (Ralph Inverso)			BP: Italy HT: Pittsfield, MA
Frankie Russell (Frank Merenda)	Contender		New Orleans, LA

RING MONIKERS & REAL NAMES	IN BRIEF	ERA BOXED	BIRTHPLACE & HOMETOWN
Al Severs (Albert Serino)			No data
Jack Sheppard	"Italian lightweight champion of East Side"		East Side, NY
Harry Tracey			Philadelphia, PA
Leo Tracy	Brother of Harry		Philadelphia, PA
Young Victor (Victor Tataseo)			Jersey City, NJ
Young West (Anthony Brocagne)			Queens, NY
Harry Williams			Hartford, CT
Tommy Young (Joe D'Amico)			Boston, MA
Johnny Alberts (Alberto Izzo)	"Clever"	1910s/20s	Rochester, NY
Kid Black (Joseph Paccione)			Buffalo, NY
Ralph Brady (Ralph Pizzica)	"Syracuse Flash"		Syracuse, NY
KO Brennan (Charles Barbanti)			Boston, MA
Terry Brooks (Leonard Battaglia)			New York
Chic Brown (Antonio Amato)	1916 Connecticut state lightweight champ		New Haven, CT
Chubby Brown (Louis Anthony Cuva)	1922 Rochester lightweight champ. "Chesterfield of the Ring"		Rochester, NY
Billy Burke (Raymond Privitera)			Rochester, NY
Young Carmen (Carmine Manafort)	Contender		BP: Charleroi, PA HT: San Jose, CA
Kid Chicago	"Rochester Assassin"		Rochester, NY
Hugo Clements (Clemente Malatesta)	"Fighting Wop"		BP: Italy HT: Albany, NY
Jimmy Coffey (Vincenzo Foglietto)	"Mohawk Indian"		BP: Naples, (I) HT: Harlem, NY
Willie Curry (Luigi Molinari)			Staten Island, NY
Mickey Dell (Michele Del Bagno)			BP: Salerno, (I) HT: Newark, NJ
Young Dennis (Tony Dentis)			Milwaukee, WI
Dick DeSanders (Richard Dasandro)			Pittsburgh, PA

RING MONIKERS & REAL NAMES	IN BRIEF	ERA BOXED	BIRTHPLACE & HOMETOWN
Jimmy Dundee (Dominick Di Marzo)	Johnny Dundee's cousin. 1922 Mexican lightweight champ		Los Angeles, CA
Philly Battling Dundee (Herman Bozzi)			Baltimore, MD
Paul Edwards (Paul Micelli)			Brooklyn, NY
Jimmy Farren (Luigi Talamini)			Boston, MA
Joe Farren (Joseph Faretra)			New York
Joe Flynn (Clemente)			Boston, MA
Joe "Wop" Flynn (Fico)			Denver, CO
George Fox (Nicholas Riometti)			Manhattan, NY
Charley Griffiths (Perelli)			Yonkers, NY
Kid Hindoo (Henry Masterpole)			Lima, OH
Battling Hogan (Nick Ferrante)			Utica, NY
Battling Hurley AKA Robert Hurley (Nicholas Parella)			Syracuse, NY
Battling Jimmy (James Scarpone)			Newark, NJ
Young Joey (Joseph Emma)			Utica, NY
Battling Johnson (Florine Petta)	Brother of Patsy Johnson		Syracuse, NY
Frank Landers (Dante Landucci)			San Francisco, CA
Young Lawrence (Lorenzo Giacomo Alemi)	1920 Central New York lightweight champ		BP: New York HT: Philadelphia, PA
Louis Kid Lewis (Laudani)			Lawrence, MA
Johnny Lisse (Lisi)			Philadelphia, PA
Bobby Lyons (Nunzio Ramunto)			Bronx, NY
Johnny Martin	"Italian lightweight champion of New York"		New York City
Patsy Masterson (Pasquale Mastantonio)			BP: Italy HT: Altoona, PA
Josh Matthews (Joseph Veripapa)			Bronx, NY
Young Maxwell (Ernest M. Farina)			Albany, NY

RING MONIKERS & REAL NAMES	IN BRIEF	ERA BOXED	BIRTHPLACE & HOMETOWN
Mike Mazie (Mario Bessi)			Staten Island, NY
Young Joe McCarthy (Joe Russo)			Syracuse, NY
Tommy McFarland (Carmine Bevilacqua)			BP: Italy HT: Boston, MA
Nick "Young" Michaels (Nicholas Vercillo)	1922 Central NY lightweight title challenger		Syracuse, NY
Charlie Chick Miller (Giulio Puzano)	"KO"		Boston, MA
Jesse Morey (Caesar P. Tronolone)	Ex-Buffalo featherweight champ		Buffalo, NY
Kid Napoleon (Napoleon Gentile)			BP: Italy HT: Utica, NY
Joe Nelson (Matteo Seminara)			BP: Louisiana, HT: Philadelphia, PA
Sailor Packie	Navy champ of Panama Canal Zone		Rochester, NY
Young Papke (Orfeo Arpea)			BP: Italy HT: Los Angeles, CA
Joe Perry (Joseph Sangimino)			San Francisco, CA
Kid Pershing (Anthony Di Lego)	1919 Berkshire County featherweight champ		North Adams, MA
Kid Roberts (Adam F. Diorio)			Worcester, MA
Mike "Young" Rogers (Fazio)	Brother of Young Fisher		Syracuse, NY
Terrible Mike Smith	1917 "Italian welterweight champion of New York"		New York City
Kid Stanley (Charles Genaro)			Brooklyn, NY
Frankie Sullivan (Frank Vienna)			Los Angeles, CA
Charlie Trabon (Trabona)	Brother of Joe Trabon		New Orleans, LA
Kid Twist (John Pizzo)			Brooklyn, NY
Phil Virgets (Felix Peter Verdichizzi)	Recorded wins over Abe Atell, Joe Mandot, Gene Delmont and Pal Moore		New Orleans, LA
Eddie Wagond			Philadelphia, PA
Chick West (Charles Della Penna)	1913 Connecticut lightweight champ		BP: Middletown, CT HT: Holyoke, MA
Eddie White (Bianchi)	1920 Pacific Coast lightweight claimant		San Francisco, CA

RING MONIKERS & REAL NAMES	IN BRIEF	ERA BOXED	BIRTHPLACE & HOMETOWN
Red Cap Wilson (Giovanni Giuseppe Terranova)			BP: Italy HT: Manhattan, NY
Babe Wolf (William Marsillo)			Philadelphia, PA
Tony Zill (Antonio Ziella)			Youngstown, OH
Tony Ross (Anthony Russo)			BP: Italy HT: Carnegie, PA
Nick "Young" Susnell (Nicholas Cucinelli)		**1910s/20s/30s**	Rochester, PA
Joey Baker (Campione)		**1920s**	Syracuse, NY
Jack Barry	"Italian Kangaroo"		Kansas City, MO
Lou Bates (Louis Sorrento)			Brooklyn, NY
Jack Belford AKA Jack Belden (Emilio Belfatto)			Watertown, NY
Young Berry (Sam Alioto)			Brooklyn, NY
Sammy Black (Panzella)			New York
Canastota Bob AKA Joe Kanafolo (Canasolla)	1924 Central New York lightweight champ		Solvay, NY
Young Kid Broad (Pasquale Ancone)			Philadelphia, PA
Pete Cannell (Canale)			Youngstown, OH
Frankie Carter (Salamone)			San Francisco, CA
Original Joe Carter (Salvatore Frescice)			New York
Lulu Clements (Ralph Griello)			Brooklyn, NY
Sam Cole (Samuel Latragna)			Rochester, NY
Wee Jimmy Collins (Al Nuzzelli)			Brooklyn, NY
Johnny Cooney (Ciccone)			Queens, NY
Tommy Darcy (Thomas Cardamone)			Bradford, PA
Joe Devine (Dave Cipriano)			Queens, NY
Jimmy Dixon (Nicholas Marotta)			Brooklyn, NY
Tom Dorsey (Nick Amano)			Bridgeport, CT
Eddie Duane (Anthony Basilone)			Bronx, NY

RING MONIKERS & REAL NAMES	IN BRIEF	ERA BOXED	BIRTHPLACE & HOMETOWN
Kid Dundee (Joseph Rollino)	Later became famous strongman		Brooklyn, NY
Kid Emmons (Episcopo)			Trenton, NJ
Johnny Fay (Paul Failla)			Chicago, IL
Frank Fields (De Feo)			No data
Nick Foley (Nicholas Ilvento)	"Young"		Brooklyn, NY
Tommy Foley (Tom Foti)			West Side, NY
Al Frazee (Naddeo)			New Jersey
Charlie Frisco (Friscia)			Brooklyn, NY
Jimmy Gaudy (Guardino)			Manhattan, MY
Jimmy Greb	Brother of Young Chappie		Binghamton, NY
Benny Harvey (Bernardo Ventola)	"Italian Tornado"		New Orleans, LA
Midget Herman (Herman Campanelli)	Ex-New Jersey state champion		Orange, NJ
Tommy Herman			BP: Italy HT: Dayton, OH
Young Jackson (Gasper Schalfani)			Brooklyn, NY
Sailor Jeff (Ralph Caramante)			Brooklyn, NY
Tony Julian (Juliano)			Brockton, MA
Jackie Lewis (Sam La Rocca)			New Orleans, LA
Jimmy Lewis (Lou Speziale)			Yonkers, NY
Johnny Lewis (Louis Cascarelli)			Brooklyn, NY
Philly Lewis (Phillip Falcetano)			Newark, NJ
Joe Martin (Joseph J. Magri)			Boston, MA
Robert Martin (Albert De Paula)			New York
Gooch Masterpole (Mastropaolo)			Lima, OH
Guy Mastrion	Brother of Joey		Brooklyn, NY
Italian Joe McCarthy			Long Branch, NJ
Harry Miller (Almerico)			Tampa, FL
Italian Terry Mitchell			Binghamton, NY

RING MONIKERS & REAL NAMES	IN BRIEF	ERA BOXED	BIRTHPLACE & HOMETOWN
Jack Moochy (Mucciacciaro)			Wisconsin
Tommy Moran	Brother of Midget Mike Moran		Pittsburgh, PA
Joe Morey (Tronolone)	Brother of Jesse Morey		Buffalo, NY
Ray Morrell (Mauro)			Spokane, WA
Battling Murphy (Emil Schiavone)			BP: West Virginia HT: Miami, FL
Spider Naples (Louis Napolitano)			Portland, ME
Joe Palmer (Joseph Palmieri)			White Plains, NY
Mickey Papner (Papaneri)			Philadelphia, PA
Joe Peppers (Joseph Albondante)			Cleveland, OH
Lefty Peters (Peter Pugliese)			Geneva, OH
Frankie Pitcher (Piccirillo)			Philadelphia, PA
Frank Posey (Pozzi)			Solvay, NY
Wisconsin Johnny Reno (Regalbuto)			Wisconsin
Johnny Reynolds (Louis De Bartolo)			New York
Jimmy Rivers	Of mixed Italian-Creole origin. "Dixie Flash"		BP: New Orleans, LA HT: Tacoma, WA
Kid Roberts (Francis John Pirlozzi)	"Sheik"		Youngstown, OH
Frankie Ross			Newcastle, PA
Nick Sanders (Santoro)			Reading, PA
Young Shannon (Neno Di Maggio)			Pittsburg, CA
Joey Silvers (Joseph Silverman)	Contender. Of mixed Italian-Jewish origin		Brooklyn, NY
Tony Silvers			Syracuse, NY
Joe Summers (Joseph Aiello)			Utica, NY
Andy Thomas (Antonio Perrini)	"Pride of Mulberry Bend"		BP: Calabria, (I) HT: Brooklyn, NY
Joe Thomas (Joseph Scoppetone)			Bronx, NY
Lefty Thomas (Anthony Tomasino)			Rochester, NY
Mickey Travis (Michael Aiello)			BP: Frankfort, NY HT: Utica, NY

RING MONIKERS & REAL NAMES	IN BRIEF	ERA BOXED	BIRTHPLACE & HOMETOWN
Young Freddie Welsh (Andy Sartelli)			Atlantic City, NJ
Willie Wiggins (Radice)			Baltimore, MD
Joe Bell (Belleci)		1920s/30s	Pittsburg, CA
Tony Blond (Anthony Suraci)	"Pride of Cotton Hollow Factory Chain Gang"		Schenectady, NY
Benny Britt			Philadelphia, PA
Matt Brock (Matteo Picataci Sr)			BP: Morgan City, LA HT: New Orleans, LA
Bristol Brown (Nicholas Ruggiero)	"Brownie"		Bristol, RI
Buster Brown (Sebastian Catanzaro)	Two times world title challenger		Baltimore, MD
Ernie Caesar (Di Cesare)			Philadelphia, PA
Paris Cangey	"Kid Poison"		Newcastle, PA
Tony Celmars (Paparino)			Akron, OH
Young Chappie (Angelo Capolupo)	"Charlie Chappie"		Albany, NY
Carmen Cook (Cocco)			Bridgeport, CT
Johnny Costello (Ernest Marinoni)			Berkeley, CA
Georgie Day (Pasquale Bagnano)	1926 Connecticut lightweight title challenger		New Haven, CT
Joey DeBell (Carmen Stracuzzi)	1929 Illinois lightweight boxing champ		BP: Lockhaven, PA HT: Beloit, WI
Al Delmont (Dominic Villanova)	Fought Jack "Kid" Berg for light-welterweight title in 1930		Newark, NJ
Danny Delmont			Chicago, IL
Mickey Diamond (Porreca)			Philadelphia, PA
Mickey Dodge (Zelano)			Sacramento, CA
Pat Duffy			Bridgeport, CT
Herman Folins (Armando Folino)			BP: Catanzaro (I) HT: Ambridge, PA
Patsy Gilmore (Pasquale Cioffi)			Pittsfield, MA
Battling Gizzy (Mike Urilli)	"Donora Windmill". Contender		Donora, PA
Fighting Johnny Glynn (Edward Mandola)	Of mixed Italian-Irish descent		Buffalo, NY
Philly Griffin (Phillip De Luca)	World title challenger		Newark, NJ

RING MONIKERS & REAL NAMES	IN BRIEF	ERA BOXED	BIRTHPLACE & HOMETOWN
Tommy Harper (Sebastian J. Cianci)			BP: Canicattini Bagni, Siracusa, Sicily (I) HT: Medford, MA
Joey Harrison (Joe Barcellona)			Harrison, NJ
Mike Hogan (Michael Laquatra)			Pittsburgh, PA
Jack "Kid" Hurk (Nuzzi)	1928–32 New York National Guard lightweight champ		Brooklyn, NY
Mickey Jones (Dom St Angelo)			Newark, NJ
Young Rocky Kansas (James Stopielo)			BP: Danby, VT HT: Troy, NY
Al King (Passanante)			Manhattan, NY
Charlie Klause (Cangelosi)			Passaic, NJ
Ralph Lenny (Lanni)	"Pride of the Dardanelles"		BP: Hoboken, NJ HT: Union City, NJ
Al Letty (Arthur Letteriel)			Staten Island, NY
Jackie London (Charles Battaglia)			Chicago, IL
Johnny Mack (John Libretti)			New Haven, CT
Joey Manuel	"Fighting Pressman"		BP: Fort Allegheney, PA HT: Rochester, NY
Joe Marsh (Joseph Del Santo)	"Gentleman Joe", "Battling Windmill"		Auburn, NY
Richie Martell			Philadelphia, PA
Jackie Mason (Nocera)			Staten Island, NY
Young Al Mellow (Louis C. Iezzi)			Portland, ME
Frankie Moore (Michael Forti)			Boston, MA
Danny Morgan (Puglia)			Syracuse, NY
Larry Murphy (Lazzari)	Brother of Joe "Dynamite" Murphy		Los Angeles, CA
Tommy "Kid" Murphy (Thomas Frascella)	"Trenton Lightning Rod". Son of old timer Kid Murphy		Trenton, NJ
Young Battling Nelson (Ernesto Cavalli)			Walla Walla, WA
Young Frankie Nelson (Frank Gano)			Brooklyn, NY
Pep O'Brien (Joseph Mattioli)	1922 Central New York lightweight title challenger		Scranton, PA

RING MONIKERS & REAL NAMES	IN BRIEF	ERA BOXED	BIRTHPLACE & HOMETOWN
Civi Osborne (Mike Civiletto)			Cleveland OH
Mickey Paul (Papa)			Buffalo, NY
Ernie Ratner (Anthony Nardiello)	Contender		BP: Montclair, NJ HT: Newark, NJ
Baby Jack Renault (Rinaldo Trementozzi)			BP: Italy HT: Cambridge, MA
Joe Rivers (John Arpino)			Auburn, NY
Tony Rose (La Rosa)			Cincinnati, OH
Tony Sanders	"Tough Tony"		Chicago, IL
Louis "Lew" Skymer			Camden, NJ
Mike Sarkis AKA Mike Sarko (Salvatore Saccuzzo)	Former New York National Guard lightweight champ		BP: Sicily (I) HT: Lawrence, MA
Frankie Stetson (Frank Pudeaux Jr)	Of mixed French Italian and Irish origin		San Francisco, CA
Al St John (John Corso)			Sandusky, OH
Jimmy Sullivan (James Lazzara)			Rochester, NY
Tommy Syracuse			Bronx, NY
Mickey Terry (Tirro)	"Punchin Poem"		BP: Bound Brook, NJ HT: Jersey City, NJ
Joe Trabon (Giuseppe Trabona)	"Kansas City Cyclone"		BP: New Orleans, LA HT: Kansas City, MO
Bobby Tracey AKA Young Diamond (Carlo Boncore)			BP: Campobello di Licata, Agrigento, Sicily HT: Buffalo, NY
Frankie Vincent (Frank Di Vito)			Chester, PA
Harry Wallace	1928 New York National Guard lightweight champ. 1929 New York National Guard welterweight champ		Philadelphia, PA
Billy West (Siino)			Pittsburg, CA
Mickey White (Petrullo)			Brooklyn, NY
Jackie Williams AKA Al Tripoli (Salvatore Tripoli)	Member of the 1924 USA Olympic team		Yonkers, NY
Larry Williams (Errico)			Mount Vernon, NY
Joey Wilton (Joseph Papalini)			Philadelphia, PA
Joey August		**1930s**	Spokane, WA

RING MONIKERS & REAL NAMES	IN BRIEF	ERA BOXED	BIRTHPLACE & HOMETOWN
Phil Baker (Filippo Matro)	Contender. Ex-New England lightweight champ. "Busy Bee"		BP: New York City HT: Norwalk, CT
Frankie Blair (Frank Tennerelli)	Contender. "Tarzan", "The Upset Kid"		Camden, NJ
Frankie Boyle (Fred Fasano)			Chicago, IL
Sam Calvin (Calvagno)			Queens, NY
Al Carr (Alfredo Tramontano)			New Haven, CT
Solly Carter (Salvatore Carta)			Middletown, CT
Tommy Corbett (Romeo Buzzello)			BP: Douglas, NE HT: Omaha, NE
Freddie DeFoe			Manhattan, NY
Lou Dell (Louis Della Ripa)			Hartford, CT
Mickey Devine (Joey Cintorino)			BP: Brooklyn, NY HT: Rochester, NY
Teddy Edwards Louis Calisanti)			Philadelphia, PA
Joe Erne (Ennius Pier Leoni)	1934 Rochester lightweight champ. "Butcher Boy"		BP: Italy HT: Rochester, NY
Midget Fox (Anthony Rossi)			Reading, PA
Bucky Keyes (Angelo Zimbardo)			Jersey City, NJ
Eddie Kline (Phillip Pugliese)			North Adams, MA
Jack Lapel (Michael La Bagnara)			Paterson, NJ
Bobby Larkin (Frank Pilleteri)	Brother of world champion Tippy Larkin		Passaic, NJ
George Levy (Paglione)			Trenton, NJ
Frankie Litt (Littriello)			BP: Newark, NJ HT: Baltimore, MD
Johnny Mack (Monacchio)			BP: Boston, MA HT; Hartford, CT
Al Manley (Annunziato)			Stamford, CT
Paul Martin (Maroni)			Lebanon, PA
Eddie Mason (Vento)			Boston, MA
Al Masty (Steve Donofrio)			Schenectady, NY
Teddy Mays (Marino Curzi)			BP: Teramo (I), HT: Waterbury, CT

RING MONIKERS & REAL NAMES	IN BRIEF	ERA BOXED	BIRTHPLACE & HOMETOWN
Billy Nolan (Natale)			Brooklyn, NY
Jerry Paul (Paolucci)			Providence, RI
Tony Paul (Vito Antonio Papa)			Buffalo, NY
Billy Petrolle II (John Raymond Scarmana)			Torrington, CT
Joey Pierce (Giandria)			Philadelphia, PA
Mickey Regan (Ragaglia)			New Britain, CT
Midge Renault (Salvatore Annunziata)			New Haven, CT
Frankie Smith (Johnny Troncone)			Norwalk, CT
Kid Wolf (Wilfred Ramella)			Youngstown, OH
Joey Allen (Auletto)		1930s/40s	Camden, NJ
Willie Andrews (Oresteus Vitale)			New Haven, CT
Teddy Baldwin (Joseph Bologna)			Philadelphia, PA
Phil Cardy			Brooklyn, NY
Marty Celeste (Martin Agricola)			Binghamton, NY
Dom Coll AKA Dom Colan (Dominic Colantonio)			Walpole, MA
Jimmy Cook (James Rossi)	Former New England featherweight champ & Maine State lightweight champ		Rumford, ME
Alfred Croat (Alfredo Pasquale Croce)			BP: Mechanicsville, NJ HT: Plainfield, NJ
Ace Dundee (Angelo Meola)			Baltimore, MD
Patsy Gall (Pasquale Gallucci)			BP: Freeland, PA HT: Hazelton, PA
Joey Greb (Joseph Greco)			BP: Brooklyn, NY HT: Herkimer, NY
Michael Julian (Juliano)			Paterson, NJ
Mickey La Marr (Michael La Macchia)			BP: Italy HT: Bronx, NY
Johnny Mack (De Stefano)			Syracuse, NY
Honey Melody (Joseph Ferrante)	1936 New England lightweight champ		Boston, MA
Pete Metro (Peter Demetrio)			New York City

RING MONIKERS & REAL NAMES	IN BRIEF	ERA BOXED	BIRTHPLACE & HOMETOWN
Mickey Page (Michele Pazienza)			Providence, RI
Kid Sal (Carabetta)			Meridien, CT
Jack Sharkey Jr (Cervati)	Son of Little Jack Sharkey		Union City, NJ
Charley Varre (Varrecchio)	"Brooklyn Whirlwind"		Brooklyn, NY
Mickey Williams (Mike Landino)			New Haven, CT
Terry Young II (Angelo De Sanza)	Contender	1930s/40s/50s	Manhattan, NY
Jeep Anderson (Louis Bocchicchio)		1940s	Los Angeles, CA
Marty Bell AKA Marty Burns (Martin Iacobelli)			Newark, NJ
Billy Brown (Frank Zezima)			Stamford, CT
Al Celey (Celli)			Long Island, NY
Johnny Gall (Gallucci)			Freeland, PA
Mike Konnors	Of mixed Italian-Austrian origin		Manhattan, NY
Willie Leo	1948 Maine lightweight champ		Portland, ME
Pal Moran Jr (Maiorana)			New Orleans, LA
Ross Moran (Rosario Iannolo)			Syracuse, NY
Paul O'Hara (Paul Papesca)			Bronx, NY
Johnny Priest (Prete)			Cambridge, MA
Johnny Virgo	Contender		Rochester, NY
Ossie Andrews (Nazzareno Vitale)		1940s/50s	New Haven, CT
Joey Barnum (Giuseppe Roselli)	Contender		BP: Chicago, IL HT: Culver City, CA
Frank De George	"Chippie"		Manhattan, NY
Tommy Greb (Carmelo Consolo)	1946 New England lightweight champ		Boston, MA
Tommy Monty (Monti)			Brooklyn, NY
Frankie Steele (Frank Stellato)			Salem, MA
Basil Marie (Miragliotta)		1950s	Philadelphia, PA

Welterweight (147 pounds)

Fred Wright		1900s	Philadelphia, PA
Young Evans (Peter Giudice)		1900s/10s	New York

RING MONIKERS & REAL NAMES	IN BRIEF	ERA BOXED	BIRTHPLACE & HOMETOWN
Joe Grim AKA Giuseppe Di Severio and Saverio Giannone (Giovanni Griminelli)	Dubbed the Iron Man for his fearlessness and durability. A major boxing attraction		BP: Avellino, (I) HT: Philadelphia, PA
Young Hugo Kelly (Frank De Rice)			Portland, ME
Joe O'Brien (Joe Valesano)			BP: Italy HT: Milwaukee, WI
Sammy Phillips (Shanghi Paretto)			Buffalo, NY
Fighting Joe Bob (Nicola Barbella)	Father of Rocky Graziano	**1910s**	Manhattan, NY
Frankie Diamond	"Bananas"		Pittsburgh, PA
Jack Hogan (Sebastian Paris)			Brooklyn, NY
Chuck O'Connors (Mazza)	Father of Jerry Mazza.		Brooklyn, NY
Willie Schaeffer (Vito Caponegras)			Bronx, NY
Italian Jack Smith			Brooklyn, NY
Young Tack (Davey Formica)			Brooklyn, NY
Tony Verne	"Italian Terror"		Watertown, NY
Frankie Wagner (Frank Ferraro)	"Jersey City Cyclone"		Jersey City, NJ
Italian Joe York			Orange, NJ
Johnny Baker AKA Kid Baker (Guy La Bruzzo)		**1910s/20s**	Harlem, NY
Frankie Berry (Frank Alioto)			Milwaukee, WI
Young Joe Borrell	World title challenger		Philadelphia, PA
Luke Carr (Domenico Carriero)	Brother of Paul Carr		BP: Avigliano, Potenza (I) HT: Buffalo, NY
Mickey Carroll (Charles Nucito)			Bronx, NY
Syracuse "Kid" Carter (Nicholas Di Lulio)			Syracuse, NY
Pete Daley (Peter Spatafore)			San Francisco, CA
Steve Dalton (Steven D'Alto)	"Iron Man"		Los Angeles, CA
Joe Denny (Di Ienno)			BP: Caldori, Abruzzi, (I) HT: Wilmington, DE
Danny Dillon (Daniel Tripoli)			Pittsburgh, PA

RING MONIKERS & REAL NAMES	IN BRIEF	ERA BOXED	BIRTHPLACE & HOMETOWN
Joe "Wop" English (Serafino Sinatra)			Toledo, OH
Young Frank AKA Kid Frank			Erie, PA
Frankie Howell (Lauletta)	Brother of Tommy Howell		Philadelphia, PA
Young Leonard AKA KO Leonard (Frank Valenti)			BP: Italy HT: New Orleans, LA
Mickey McDonough (Michael Di Giacomo)			Philadelphia, PA
Bad News Murphy (Jimmy Buzzello)			Denver, CO
Jimmy O'Gatty (Vincenzo Agati)	Contender. "East Side Assassin"		BP: Scilla, Reggio Calabria (I) HT: New York
Willie Ritchie (Louis Sposato)			Scranton, PA
Reb Russell (Louis Rigoni)			Chicago, IL
Kid Savage (Michael Vito Cazzato)	"Seneca Falls Wildman", "White Battling Siki"		BP: Italy HT: Seneca Falls, NY
Johnny Saxon (Anthony Retarta)	1925 Connecticut state welterweight title challenger		BP: Italy, HT: Bridgeport, CT
George Texas (Cava)			Brooklyn, NY
Young Freddie Welsh (Palermo)			Trenton, NJ
Joe Wopp AKA Kid Ryan (Patsy Ciacco)			Seattle, WA
Billy Gannon (William Cimini)		1910s/20s/30s	Philadelphia, PA
Patsy Bogash (Pasquale Buccassi)	Brother of Lou Bogash	1920s	BP: Faeto, Foggia (I) HT: Bridgeport, CT
Jackie Brady (Adam Pizzica)	Contender. 1926 Central New York lightweight champ		Syracuse, NY
Willie Cadore AKA Charley Kid Williams (William Cordaro)			Queens, NY
Mike Carrier (Michele Carrieri)			BP: Italy HT: Bronx, NY
Soldier Patsy Cline (Frank Sposeto)			Des Moines, IA
Mike "Young" Coogan (D'Amore)			Utica, NY
Eddie Dempsey (Armando De Pasquale)			Philadelphia, PA

RING MONIKERS & REAL NAMES	IN BRIEF	ERA BOXED	BIRTHPLACE & HOMETOWN
Mike Dempsey (Joseph Amodio)			Rochester, NY
Joe Donley (Bozza)	Brother of Mickey Donley		Newark, NJ
Jack Duffy (Alfred Serfine)			Rochester, NY
Johnny Fields (John Sarno)			Newark, NJ
Frankie Ford (Frank Azzoli)			Brooklyn, NY
Joe Jackson (Vincent Franchetti)			Philadelphia, PA
Oakey Keyes (Daniel Mucerino)			Staten Island, NY
Tony Lyons	"West Side Cyclone"		Manhattan, NY
Sailor Mack (Salvatore Di Atello)			New York
Mickey Maff (Mafetone)			Brooklyn, NY
Mickey Martell			Philadelphia, PA
Johnny Martin (Joseph Marcello)			Wilmington, DE
Jack McGurn (Vincenzo Gibaldi)	Also known as "Machine Gun" Jack McGurn, one of his several aliases		BP: Licata, Agrigento Sicily, (I) HT: Chicago, IL
Frankie Murphy (Frank Civarola)			Boston, MA
Johnny Murphy (John Peretto)			Chicago, IL
Young O'Connor (Caesar Campana)			BP: Italy HT: Camden, NJ
Johnny O'Keefe (John Gatta)			Philadelphia, PA
Jack Palmer (Anthony Farinella)			Philadelphia, PA
Joe Patrice			Chicago, IL
Mike Peters (Michael Pederzolli)			BP: Italy HT: Solvay, NY
Sammy Phillips (Filipelli)			Utica, NY
Kid Preston (Joseph R. Pusateri)			Worcester, MA
Jack Reno (Onorato)			Trenton, NJ
George Russell (La Rocco)			Wilkes Barre, PA
Jimmy Ryder			Brooklyn, NY
Battling Sal (Billeci)			Pittsburg, CA

RING MONIKERS & REAL NAMES	IN BRIEF	ERA BOXED	BIRTHPLACE & HOMETOWN
Harry Simon (Simone)			Cleveland, OH
Frankie Tierney (Frank Latano)			Los Angeles, CA
Frankie Thomas (Negri)			San Francisco, CA
Dan Alexander (De Nucci)		**1920s/30s**	Newton, MA
Roxy Allen (Rocco Auletto)			Camden, NJ
Paulie Andrews (Chris De Levo			Springfield, MA
Pete August (Peter La Quessa)	Contender. 1922 Connecticut lightweight champ. Ex New England welterweight champ		BP: Italy HT: Bridgeport, CT
Nick Bass (Basciano)	1930 Southern middleweight champ		BP: Philadelphia, PA HT: Baltimore, MD
Johnny Bennett (Benedetto)			San Jose, CA
Patsy Bradley (Ray Basciano)			Philadelphia, PA
Al Britton (Alex Dibrizzi)			New York
Eddie Burry (Edward Barraco)	1926 Nevada welterweight champ		Pittsburg, CA
George Carney (Anthony Indelicato)			Boston, MA
Marty Collins (Ettore Collucci)			Philadelphia, PA
Jack Delaney (John Di Lella)			BP: Buenos Aires (ARG) HT: Syracuse, NY
Pat Dundee (Pasquale De Mera)			Fresno, CA
Soldier Frank (Frank Joseph Vento)			Providence, RI
Jack Hoskey (Steve Colletti)			Newark, NJ
Tommy Malco (Thomas Macaluso)			Pittsburgh, PA
Young Mandell (Pete Petrolle)	Brother of Billy Petrolle		Schenectady, NY
Teddy Martin (Louis Stolfi)			Manhattan, NY

RING MONIKERS & REAL NAMES	IN BRIEF	ERA BOXED	BIRTHPLACE & HOMETOWN
Frankie Miller (Frank L. Pernice)			BP: New York HT: Los Angeles, CA
Lou Nickolette (Luigi Nicoletti)			Lorain, OH
Benny Palmer AKA Joey Palmer (Pagliaro)			Mechanicsville, NY
Tony Palmer (Palermo)			East Side, NY
Jimmy Phillips (James De Fillipis)			Bernardsville, NJ
Lew Raymond (Luigi Raimondi)	Contender. Fought for Maryland welterweight title		Baltimore, MD
Rocky Rayo (Ernest Faccinto)			BP: Hamden, CT HT: Hartford, CT
Joey Reynolds (Joseph M. Russo)			Atlantic City, NJ
Billy Rhodes (Joseph M. Di Conza)			Worcester, MA
Tony Ross			Brooklyn, NY
Tommy Skymer	Brother of Lew Skymer		BP: Lycoming County, PA HT: Camden, NJ
Battling Spag AKA Sailor Spag (Carmen Spagnoli)			BP: Italy HT: Philadelphia, PA
Sammy Tarzan (Bongiorno)			McKeesport, PA
Joe Terry (Joseph Impelleteri)			New York
Frankie Thomas (Negri)	Brother of Dummy Thomas		San Francisco, CA
Tony Travers (Traversano)	1925 Connecticut lightweight champ		New Haven, CT
Bobby Vernon AKA Kid Champs (Joseph P. Vaccarella)	Elected Mayor of Mount Vernon in 1951		Mount Vernon, NY
Pete Wagner (Anthony C. Tomasco)			Philadelphia, PA
Johnny Lucas (Carmelo Di Biasi)	1936 District of Columbia welterweight champ	**1920s/30s/40s**	BP: Italy HT: Camden, NJ
Jersey Johnny O'Keefe (Silvestri)			Garfield, NJ
Jimmy Abbey (Vincent Abbagliato)		**1930s**	Bronx, NY
Freddie Bernard (Bernardi)			Flint, MI
Charley Brown	Nephew of Chic Brown		New Haven, CT

RING MONIKERS & REAL NAMES	IN BRIEF	ERA BOXED	BIRTHPLACE & HOMETOWN
Joey Brown (Joseph Di Carlo)			Rochester, NY
Lem Collett			Ogdensburg, NY
Eddie Dempsey (Peter Palumbo)	1932 United Federation lightweight champ. "Syracuse Thunderbolt"		Syracuse, NY
Dynamite Dominick (Dominic Carelli)			Troy, NY
Pat France (Franco)			Roseburg, OR
Eddie Frisco (Anthony J. Curro)	1934 Nevada welterweight champ		BP: Mussomeli, Sicily (I) HT: Albany, NY
Ralph Fulton (Mangiapane)			Trenton, NJ
Tommy Grady (Albert Tancredi	"Shoemaker Grady"		Springfield, MA
Tony Greb (Scala)			Hoboken, NJ
Johnny Hazel			Pittsburgh, PA
Nick "Kid" Hogan (Ferrante)			Syracuse, NY
Jack Laverne (Louis Lavargna)			Boston, MA
Tony Mandell	Nephew of Sammy Mandell		Rockford, IL
Sammy Manley (Annunziato)			Stamford, CT
Sammy Martin (Salvatore Polese)			Lawrence, MA
Larry Napp (Lorenzo Napadano)	Later became recognized baseball umpire in American League		Brooklyn, NY
Sonny O'Day AKA Charles George (Carlo Giorgi)	"Kid from Meaderville", "Butte's Boxing Star"		BP: Lucca (I), HT: Butte, MT
Louis "Kid" Oswald AKA Larry Bell (Louis Belli)			Watertown, NY
Young Papke (Arpea)	Younger brother of Young Papke, the lightweight from the post WW1 era		Los Angeles, CA
Al Parell (Parelli)			Lyndhurst, NJ
Johnny Pastor			Hightstown, NJ
Tony Rock (Roccaforte)	1933 Nevada welterweight champ		BP: Italy HT: Mayfield, PA/ Reno, NV.
Phil Ross (Centracchi)			Chicago, IL

RING MONIKERS & REAL NAMES	IN BRIEF	ERA BOXED	BIRTHPLACE & HOMETOWN
Young Sappo (Salvatore Cardillo)			Amsterdam, NY
Billy Sullivan (Armando De Petrillo)			BP: New York City HT: Tampa, FL
Sam Terry (Alfano)			Chicago, IL
Danny Ventry			Niagara Falls, NY
Johnny Bell (John Bellu)	1948 New England welterweight champ	**1930s/40s**	New Britain, CT
Dave Bungy (David Buonagurio)			Yonkers, NY
Pete Cappy (Peter Caprotti)			Kingston, NY
Pat Casey (Pasquale Casserino)			Hartford, CT
Carl Dell (Delberta)	Contender		Oneonta, NY
Rego Dell			Dunmore, PA
Frankie Duane (D'Antico)			Elizabeth, NJ
Al Dundee (Dominic Geraci)			BP: Lawrence, MA HT: Hartford, CT
Philadelphia Joe Dundee (Mirena)	Brother of trainer Angelo Dundee		Philadelphia, PA
Eddie Ganns (Gannucci)			Sacramento, CA
Nickie Gerard (Giannuzzi)			Queens, NY
Ralph Gizzy (Ralph Urilli)			Donora, PA
Bucky Jones (Roberto Caravaggio)			BP: New Jersey HT: Philadelphia, PA
Al Nettlow (Alfred Nittlo)	Contender		BP: Pennsylvania HT: River Rouge, MI
Carmen Notch (Pernatozzi)	Contender. "East Liberty Wildcat"		Pittsburgh, PA
Johnny Phillips (Fillizola)			Paterson, NJ
Tommy Roman (Romano)			Bayonne, NJ
Carmen Silvers (Di Silva)	"Kid"		Syracuse, NY
Mickey Vance (Cianci)			Philadelphia, PA
Vinnie Vines (Vincenzo Semprevino)	Contender		BP: Elizabeth, NJ HT: Schenectady, NY
Frankie Wills (Francesco Guido)	Contender		BP: Morgantown, WV HT: Washington DC
Jimmy Anest	Of mixed Italian-Greek origin	**1940s**	Hackensack, NJ
Johnny Brenda (Imbrenda)			BP: Italy HT: Chester, PA

RING MONIKERS & REAL NAMES	IN BRIEF	ERA BOXED	BIRTHPLACE & HOMETOWN
Young Chappie (Charles Bianchino)			Albany, NY
Alex Doyle (Dolcemascolo)	Ex-New Jersey welterweight champ. One of five boxing brothers		BP: Garfield, NJ HT: Passaic, NJ
Lou Dundee (Lazzara)	Son of world champion Joe Dundee		Baltimore, MD
Johnny Duke (Giulio Gallucci)			Hartford, CT
Ernie Frank (Bernice)			Philadelphia, PA
Richie Gibbons (Ercole A. De Bonis)			Springfield, MA
Joe Griffo (Joseph V. Agrifoglio)			Newark, NJ
Johnny "Bo" Harris (Guerriero)			Brooklyn, NY
Smokey Joe (Joseph Ventafido)			Auburn, NY
Tony Junior (Anthony Di Nardo)			Berlin, NH
Jay Macks (John Magaletta)			Newark, NJ
Mickey Oliver (Oliveri)			Jersey City, NJ
O'Neil Pepe	Of mixed Italian-Irish origin		New Haven, CT
Goody Peters (Guerino Petronelli)	Later became top boxing trainer		Brockton, MA
Tony Ross Jr	Son of heavyweight Tony Ross		Pittsburgh, PA
Jackie Tarzan (Anthony Cerruto Sr)			BP: Brooklyn, NY HT: Bantam, CT
Bee Bee Wright (James Maletta Jr)	Contender. Of mixed Italian-African American origin)		BP: Waterloo, IA HT: Clairton, PA
Vic Cardell (Victor S. Cardelli)		**1940s/50s**	Hartford, CT
George LaRover (Peter Prosper)			Philadelphia, PA
Bobby Lloyd	Of mixed Italian-Irish origin		BP: Ashley, PA HT: New York/ Wilkes Barre, PA
Sammy Mastrean			Pittsburgh, PA
Frankie Ross (Frank Toscano)			Boston, MA
Sammy Secreet (Salvatore Secreti)	Contender		Bingham, WV

RING MONIKERS & REAL NAMES	IN BRIEF	ERA BOXED	BIRTHPLACE & HOMETOWN
Jimmy Sullivan AKA Rocky Sullivan (James J. Salamone)			Boston, MA
Ross Virgo (Rosario Virgo)	Contender. In March 1950 rated 8th best welterweight in the world by *Ring Magazine*		Rochester, NY
Jerry Naples		**1950s**	Chicago, IL
Johnny Pape (Pepe)			Miami, FL

Middleweight (160 pounds)

Tommy Gavigan (Cavigna)		**1900s/10s**	Cleveland, OH
Fred Lucas (Anthony Policastro)			New York
Jimmy Bush	"Italian champion of Williamsburg"	**1910s**	Brooklyn, NY
Joe West (John Martini)			New York
Willie Baker (Michael Fanelli)		**1910s/20s**	Philadelphia, PA
Johnny Burns	Pacific Coast contender		San Francisco, CA
Jimmy Dime			Oswego, NY
Jimmy "Kid" Doyle (Di Leo)			Massachusetts
Jimmy Gray (James Christiantiello)			Auburn, NY
Zulu Kid (Michael Flammia)	Contender		Brooklyn, NY
Tommy Littleton (Sam Impastato)			Mobile, AL
Kid Manuel	"King"		Erie, PA
Andy "Kid" Palmer (Andrea Palermo)	"Oklahoma Cowboy". Contender		Douglas, AZ
Young Remsey AKA Jack Renzo (Lorenzo Totoro)			BP: Sicily, (I) HT: Bethesda, WA
KO Sullivan (Peter Mirarchi)			BP: Catanzaro (I) HT: Allentown, PA
Pat Walsh	Of mixed Italian-Scottish origin		Philadelphia, PA
Johnny Cline (Nicholas Dionisio)	"Tiger"	**1910s/20s/30s**	BP: Hoboken, NJ. HT: Fresno, CA
Joe Roberts (Clement Lombardi)	"Racehorse"		BP: Italy HT: Alameda, CA

RING MONIKERS & REAL NAMES	IN BRIEF	ERA BOXED	BIRTHPLACE & HOMETOWN
Jimmy Bove (Bova)		**1920s**	Utica, NY
Dago Joe Gans (Joseph Costanzo)			St Paul, MN
Johnny Hart (Michael Crusco)			Brooklyn, NY
Sammy Howard (Samuel Ciminelli)			Canton, OH
Frankie Kramer (Aliano)			Philadelphia, PA
Charley Martin (Martino)			San Francisco, CA
Jimmy Oakland (Vincent Ochiuto)			Philadelphia, PA
Mickey Oliver (Oliveri)			BP: Sicily (I) HT: Brooklyn, NY
Jack Perry (Ralph Perri)			BP: Long Branch, NJ HT: Philadelphia, PA
Charley Picker (Charles Picora)			Mineola, NY
Joe Pledge (Emetio Polizio)			Queens, NY
Mike Ruby (Mike Pasquale)			Dunbar, PA
Frankie Theodore	"Tiger"		Philadelphia, PA
Ralph Thomas (Tommaso)			BP: Cleveland, OH HT: Bronx, NY
Mickey Wallace (Tony Amadio)			Reno, NV
Jimmy White (Amato)			Boston MA
Babe Amos (Emilio Antonacci)		**1920s/30s**	Syracuse, NY
Jack Avalon (Herbert Avallone)	Brother of Joe Moran		San Antonio, TX
Al Diamond (Alfonso Pescatore)	World title challenger		Paterson, NJ
Jimmy King (James Anselmo Sr)			New Orleans, LA
Joey La Grey (Giuseppe La Greca)	1931 New York National Guard middleweight champ		BP: Johnstown, PA HT: Brooklyn, NY
Jean Lester (Eugene Lestardo)			Wilmington, DE
Charlie Miller (Silvio Matteo)			Philadelphia, PA
Nick Palmer (Nicola Palmieri)	"Clinton Street Ironhorse". 1928 New York State National Guard welterweight champ, 1928 middleweight champ & 1932 heavyweight champ		Brooklyn, NY

RING MONIKERS & REAL NAMES	IN BRIEF	ERA BOXED	BIRTHPLACE & HOMETOWN
Joey Raymond (Raimondi)	Brother of Lew Raymond		Baltimore, MD
Joe Roche (Aschero)	Contender. 1926 Pacific Coast middleweight title challenger		San Francisco, CA
Ted Ross (Centracchi)			Chicago, IL
Lew Seltzer	Of mixed Italian Jewish origin		Vineland, NJ
Texas Joe Dundee (Nick Lillo)	1942 Southern middleweight champ	**1920s/30s/40s**	BP: Beaumont, TX HT: Greenville, MO
Jay Macedon			Orange, NJ
Pal Silvers (Silverman)	Of mixed Italian-Jewish origin		Brooklyn, NY
Carmen Barth (Carmine Di Bartolomeo)	Contender & world title challenger. 1932 Olympic middleweight gold medalist	**1930s**	Cleveland, OH
Danny Brooks (Daniel Gentile)			Auburn, NY
Frankie Caris (Francis Di Vicaris)			Philadelphia, PA
Joe Denise (Tony Batarelli)			Syracuse, NY
Joe Desmond (Disperato)	"Desperate", "Tiger"		Mechanicsville, NY
Nick Dorsey			Binghamton, NY
Tony Fedora	"Fulton Plasterer", "Fighting Hatman of Fulton"		Fulton, NY
Tony Fisher (Anthony Pesce)	World title challenger		Newark, NJ
Harry Greb II (Gustavo A. Schiavo)			BP: Philadelphia, PA HT: Vineland, NJ
Hookie Jackson (Alec Panciera)			Boston, MA
Kid Law AKA Joe Lombardo (Joseph L. Ippolito)			Tampa, FL
Solly Louise			Fulton, NY
Lou Savin			San Francisco, CA
Billy Walters (Benjamin Lopata)			Schenectady, NY
Jack White (Michael Palumbo)			BP: Brooklyn, NY HT: Sharon, PA
Nick Basil		**1930s/40s**	Detroit, MI
Italian Jack Dempsey (Victor Palmieri)	1942 New England light-heavyweight champ		New Bedford, MA
Bobby Hagen (Vento)			Boston, MA
Tony Mann (Maniscalco)			Brooklyn, NY

RING MONIKERS & REAL NAMES	IN BRIEF	ERA BOXED	BIRTHPLACE & HOMETOWN
Eddie Steele (Ralph Tiovelli)			Beacon, NY
Frankie Terry (Terranova)			Brooklyn, NY
Paulie Warren (Paul Gullo)			Meridien, CT
Frankie Young (Gesino)			New Haven, CT
Jimmy Young			Dunmore, PA
Tony Brush (Anthony Brescia)		1940s	Cleveland, OH
Charlie Chaney (Passaro)			Baltimore, MD
Paul Coley (Collicci)			Providence, RI
Reggie Cosmo (Cosimo Ruggiero)			Brooklyn, NY
Carmine De John (Di Gianni)			Syracuse, NY
Johnny Ditto (Giovanni Di Tommasi)			Baltimore, MD
Dover Kid			Dover, OH
Eddie Lee (Alfred Baia)			Amsterdam, NY
Jimmy Mandell (Mandolene)			Indiana, PA
Ronnie Mason (Joseph Marino)			Boston, MA
Billy Brown (Baiocchi)		1940s/50s	Hartford, CT
Billy Corbett (Lanza)			Seattle, WA
Andy "Kid" De Paul (De Paolo)	Contender		Pittsburgh, PA
Johnny Driscoll (Dominick Venezia)			Newark, NJ
Mickey DuBerry (Richard J. Da Biere)			Amsterdam, NY
Bobby Morgan			New York
Al "Red" Priest (Alfred Prete)	Contender. 1946 New England middleweight champ.		Cambridge, MA
Benny Urs (Urso)			Shinnston, WV
Tony Wolfe Jr (Anthony Tuzzi)			BP: Norristown, PA HT: Lebanon, PA
Don Lambert (Louis Lamberti)		1950s	New Haven, CT
Pat Lowry (Albert Allyn)	Mother Italian, father of mixed Irish-Italian origin		BP: Sandusky, OH HT: Toledo, OH

RING MONIKERS & REAL NAMES	IN BRIEF	ERA BOXED	BIRTHPLACE & HOMETOWN
Light-heavyweight (175 pounds)			
Ray Carcy (Raymond Carciofini)		1900s	BP: Philadelphia, PA HT: Minneapolis, MN
Mike Sullivan (Ralph Salvati)		1900s/10s	Middletown, NY
Chick Carsey (Anthony Puglio)		1910s	Philadelphia, PA
Young Buffalo (Carl Cialella)		1910s/20s	Newcastle, PA
Eddie Hayes (Frank Comodeca)			Rochester, NY
Big Mike Toronto (Angelo Spigarolo)	"Spiggy"	1920s	Bridgeport, CT
Jimmy White (James Bianchi)			Gloversville, NY
Ray Actis (Raymond Caporali)	Contender. "Excelsior Assassin"	1920s/30s	San Francisco, CA
Tommy Bennett (Benedetto)			San Jose, CA
Frankie Campbell (Francesco Camilli)	Also fought as heavyweight		BP: Glen Park, CA HT: San Francisco, CA
Joe Cavalier (Cavaliere)			Paterson, NJ
Bud Doyle (Louis Oteri)			San Jose, CA
Jimmy Francis (Ghiraldi)	"Jersey Terror"		Union City, NJ
Johnny Mack (Anthony Bondi)	"Bulldog"		Cincinnati, OH
Tony Mike (Anthony De Vincenzo)			Leiperville, PA
Don Petrin (Donald Petrine)	Contender. Competed in the 1931 NBA light-heavyweight elimination tournament		Englewood, NJ
Eddie Priest			Brooklyn, NY
Charles Risko (Nello Gentile)	1930 Pacific NW heavyweight champ		Tacoma, WA
Kid Sullivan (Anthony Leone)	"Caveman"		Watertown, NY
Frankie Arcus (Arcucci)		1930s	BP: Ischia, (I) HT: Chester, PA
Joe Birdie (Giardino)			Rochester, NY
Blackie O'Keefe (Silvestri)			Garfield, NJ
Jack Renault (Annunziata)	"Tiger Jack"		New Haven, CT
Johnny Colan (Collani)	Contender. "Hell's Kitchen Howitzer"	1930s/40s	Queens, NY
Joey De John (Di Gianni)	"Golden Boy". Contender		BP: Syracuse, NY HT: Buffalo, NY

RING MONIKERS & REAL NAMES	IN BRIEF	ERA BOXED	BIRTHPLACE & HOMETOWN
Ralph De John (Di Gianni)	Contender		Syracuse, NY
Pete George (Pietro Giorgi)			Buffalo, NY
Carmen Fredericks (Carmine Frederico)	"Duke"		BP: Cleveland, OH HT: Long Beach, CA

Heavyweight (190+ pounds)

RING MONIKERS & REAL NAMES	IN BRIEF	ERA BOXED	BIRTHPLACE & HOMETOWN
Nick Bennett (Nicholas Panetta)		**1900s**	Chicago, IL
Al Fair			Newcastle, PA
Sam Nolan (Salvatore Franciosa)	Ex-Rochester heavyweight champ	**1910s**	BP: Naples, (I) HT: Rochester, NY
Al Benedict (Albert De Benedictis)	"Brooklyn Thunderbolt". Winner of the 1910 Eastern "White Hope" tournament, stopping three men in one evening	**1910s/20s**	BP: Salerno, (I) HT: Hoboken, NJ
Tony Melchior			BP: Italy HT: Chicago, IL
Johnny Ambrose (Ambrosio)		**1920s**	Bronx, NY
Frankie Mox (Frank Antonio)			BP: Iron Mountain, MI HT: Ironwood, MI
Silent Perry			Trenton, NJ
Franal Ruffles (Cataldo Piarulli)			BP: Bisceglie, Barletta (I) HT: Hanford, CA
Paul Cavalier (Cavaliere)	1929 New Jersey heavyweight champ	**1920s/30s**	Paterson, NJ
Italian Jack Herman (Emilio Buttafuoco)			BP: Italy HT: Yonkers, NY
Joe Oliver (Olivieri)	1927 New York Golden Gloves champion		Brooklyn, NY
Sam Singer (Frank Polacci)			Utica, NY
Harold Scarney (Scarnecchia)	"Young"		Youngstown, OH
Gene Stanton (Jack Mernone)			Cleveland, OH
Mickey Taylor (Michael Consulmagno)	Ex-New York State National Guard heavyweight champ. Boxed in all eight weight categories		Jersey City, NJ
Tony Capps (Cappoletti)		**1930s**	Harlem, NY

RING MONIKERS & REAL NAMES	IN BRIEF	ERA BOXED	BIRTHPLACE & HOMETOWN
Rudy Cavell (Cavazzale)			BP: Italy HT: Pittsfield, MA
Fred Feary (Fioravanti)	1932 National AAU heavyweight champ & Olympic bronze medalist		Stockton, CA
Monty Mark (Marchese)			Troy, NY
Eddie Camps (Campagna)		**1930s/40s**	Detroit, MI
Don Card (Cardorelli)			Providence, RI
Nathan Mann (Natale Menchetti)	Contender & world title challenger		BP: New Haven, CT HT: Hamden, CT
Jack Marion (Marotti)			Silver Lake, NJ
Joe O'Gatty (Guido Gatti)	"Fireplug"		Toms River, NJ
John Petry			Los Angeles, CA
Joe Wagner (Joseph Micatrotto)			BP: Cleveland, OH HT: Newark, NJ
Big Boy Baker (Frank Giannelli		**1940s**	Everett, MA
Jim Costello (Cuccinotti)			Harrisburg, PA
Jimmy Jerome (De Luca)			Brooklyn, NY
Jimmy Letty (Lischetti)			Brooklyn, NY
Mike De John (Michael De Gianni)	Contender	**1950s/60s**	Syracuse, NY

Notes

This table features Italian American world ranked boxers, headliners, top notchers, semi-wind-up category professionals and preliminary fighters that campaigned using an Irish or anglicized *nom de plume*.

The top 150 Italian American boxers i.e. world champions, recognized title claimants and main contenders who used Irish/Anglicized ring tags are not listed in this appendix.

Boxers appear under their respective weight categories and under each category they are arranged alphabetically under their era of participation.

Some boxers fought in several weight categories but they have only been given one listing.

Where possible both birthplace and hometown are included. In many cases the boxer fought from the same location. Many boxers traveled widely and made their home in various locations. Thus a boxer's hometown may vary depending on source checked.

The fighters are listed by weight category and then by era they appeared.

Boxing historian Vincent Colitti assisted in the compilation of this table.

Some data contained in this table is taken from public sources and is believed to be reliable and accurate but it cannot be warranted as to accuracy and completeness.

In the birthplace/hometown column abbreviations (I) = Italy; (CA) = Canada.

Chapter 4

APPENDIX V: ITALIAN AMERICAN WORLD CHAMPIONS AND TITLE CLAIMANTS 1900–55

Weight category	Status	Tenure
Flyweight		
Young Zulu Kid	(Claimant)	1915
Frankie Genaro	(Claimant)	1925
Fidel La Barba		**1925–27**
Frankie Genaro	**(NBA/IBU)**	**1928–29,**
		1929–31
Willie La Morte	(Claimant)	1929–30
Midget Wolgast	(NYSAC)	1930–35
Bantamweight		
Kid Murphy	(Claimant)	1907
Frankie Conley	(California)	1910–11
Pete Herman		**1917–20,**
		1921
Eddie "Cannonball" Martin		**1924–25**
Bushy Graham	(NYSAC)	1928–29
Lou Salica	(NBA)	1935
Tony Marino		**1936**
Harry Jeffra		**1937–38**
Lou Salica		**1940–42**
Junior-featherweight		
Carl Duane		1923–24
Featherweight		
Johnny Dundee		**1923–24**
Tony Canzoneri		**1927–28**
Battling Battalino		**1929–32**
Tommy Paul	(NBA)	1932–33
Mike Belloise	(NYSAC)	1936–37
Jimmy Perrin	(Louisiana)	1940
Petey Scalzo	**(NBA)**	**1940–41**
Harry Jeffra		**1940–41**
Willie Pep		**1942–48,**
		1949–50
Phil Terranova	(NBA)	1943–44
Sal Bartolo	(NBA)	1944–46
Junior-lightweight		
Johnny Dundee		**1921–23,**
		1923–24
Steve "Kid" Sullivan		**1924–25**
Mike Ballerino		**1925**

<u>Lightweight</u>		
Rocky Kansas		**1925–26**
Sammy Mandell		**1926–30**
Tony Canzoneri		**1930–33,**
		1935–36
Lou Ambers		**1936–38,**
		1939–40
Sammy Angott	(NBA)	1940–41,
		1943–44
Sammy Angott		**1941–42**
Paddy De Marco		**1954**
<u>Junior-welterweight</u>		
Tony Canzoneri		**1931–32,**
		1933
Sammy Fuller	(Claimant)	1932
Tippy Larkin		**1946**
<u>Welterweight</u>		
Joe Dundee		**1927–29**
Young Corbett III		**1933**
Izzy Jannazzo	(Maryland)	1940–41
Marty Servo		**1946**
Tony De Marco		**1955**
Carmen Basilio		**1955–56,**
		1956–57
<u>Middleweight</u>		
Hugo Kelly	(Claimant)	1905–07,
		1910
Johnny Wilson		**1920–23**
Lou Bogash	(NYSAC)	1923
Vince Dundee	(NYSAC)	1933–34
Fred Apostoli	**(IBU)**	**1937**
	(NYSAC)	**1938–39**
Rocky Graziano		**1947–48**
Jake La Motta		**1949–51**
Carmen Basilio		**1957–58**
<u>Light-heavyweight</u>		
George Nichols	(NBA)	1932
Lou Scozza	(Claimant)	1932
Melio Bettina	**(NYSAC)**	**1939**
Joey Maxim		**1950–52**
<u>Heavyweight</u>		
Rocky Marciano		**1952–56**

Notes
Boxers highlighted in bold denote universally recognized titleholders.
Boxing authority awarding recognition in brackets
Boxers with credible support to a titular claim are listed as claimants

1900–09
HUGO KELLY [UGO GENO MICHELI]
WORLD MIDDLEWEIGHT CLAIMANT 1905–07, 1910

In an era dominated by newspapers trumpeting the claims of a variety of title claimants, Hugo Kelly was never recognized as the undisputed world middleweight boxing champion. Kelly was one of the best and when the legendary Tommy Ryan retired he was viewed as the logical successor. Kelly established his claims by defeating the best 160-pounders in circulation, notching wins over former and future champions Jack "Twin" Sullivan, Philadelphia Jack O'Brien, Billy Papke and Frank Klaus. He recorded impressive wins over contenders Mike Schreck, Young Mahoney and Tony Caponi, but the question of supremacy was only resolved in July 1908, when Kelly met Stanley Ketchel in San Francisco for the undisputed world middleweight crown. Kelly started well, drawing first blood by opening a cut inside Ketchel's mouth, but he paid the price for his overconfidence by walking into a left hook in the third round and was counted out. There was no shame in losing to the "Michigan Assassin" as Ketchel had knocked out fifty of his sixty-six opponents. In the same year Kelly met Billy Papke, who had won and lost the middleweight title to Ketchel, and following a bruising encounter with the Italian, Papke thought about quitting on his stool before referee Jim Jeffries announced a twenty-five-round controversial draw, allowing Papke to hold onto the title. In 1910, Ketchel, reported to be "resting" from boxing, contemplated handing his title to Kelly, but following his untimely death that year, four contenders were named: Frank Klaus, Billy Papke, Eddie McGoorty and Kelly. The quartet began an elimination series to find the undisputed champion. In December 1912 Kelly defeated Klaus over twelve rounds in Boston and toppled a number of quality opponents to claim the world title again. He defended his claim against Billy McKinnon in Boston and later won a newspaper decision over Cyclone Johnny Thompson, another claimant, in Racine, Wisconsin over ten rounds. In the same year he dropped a decision to Eddie McGoorty, and then lost his middleweight title claim to Jack Dillon when he was dispatched in three rounds.

That was the end of Hugo Kelly as a main attraction. For over a decade Kelly held his own with the world's best middleweights, winning the support of fans, newspapermen and boxing's top brass. He started out as a welterweight and gradually bulked up to fight middleweights and light-heavyweights. He was durable and strong and possessed good in-fighting qualities. Al Lippe, renowned Philadelphia fight manager, described Kelly as a "sweet fighter." In spring 1905, the *Chicago Tribune* described Kelly as a "good conscientious fighter" following his friendly match with Tommy Ryan at Benton Harbor. The paper also reported that the middleweight title would pass to Kelly. Following his memorable win against Philadelphia Jack O'Brien, with the authorities intervening to save O'Brien from a knockout loss, Kelly was described as "one of the shiftiest fighters in the country." In May 1909, prior to the Billy Papke showdown, the *Chicago Tribune* eulogized Kelly as "the cleverest middleweight in the world, feline in movements, knows every turn in the road."

Kelly was born Ugo Micheli in the Village of Vitiana in the province of Lucca, Italy on February 11, 1883. The teenager arrived in Chicago with his parents, Carlo Micheli and Mary Parensi. There was nothing in Kelly's make-up that indicated that he was suited to the fancy. He was well educated, mild mannered and refined. Some reports suggested Kelly had royal blood running through his veins but he played down any aristocratic connections. He scraped a living in his adopted country by working as a bartender, and when he grew tired of the dead-end job his curiosity turned to fisticuffs. He bought a punch bag and had it installed in the basement of his workplace. The saloon owner reprimanded him repeatedly for punching the bag instead of serving customers, at which point the proprietor secured the services of a retired boxer called Henry Lyons. Lyons had formed part of the Joe Gans team and an impromptu bout arranged between the African American and Kelly in the basement left no one in any doubt of Kelly's natural gifts. Kelly whipped the old-timer in front of stunned onlookers. Lyons took him under his wing as a welterweight, giving him the name Kid Kelly. The name stuck, and within one year of setting foot in the United States Kelly had branched out as a prizefighter. In the early days Kelly was poorly promoted and mismatched with seasoned heavier opponents like Buck Montgomery, who flattened Kelly in two rounds. The Italian fighter bounced back to turn the tables on Montgomery in two subsequent contests. In 1901 Kelly was brought under the management of Sylvie Ferretti, a well-connected businessman, who ensured Kelly got the opportunities his talent deserved steering his charge for the remainder of his career. In retirement Kelly made his home in the picturesque setting of Antioch, Illinois and with the proceeds from the fight game he bought a house and hotel and became part owner of a restaurant.

KID MURPHY [PETER FRASCELLA]
WORLD BANTAMWEIGHT CLAIMANT* 1907

Former shoeshine boy Kid Murphy was among a crop of talented and stout-hearted Italian American fighters marching forward in their respective weight categories during the 1900s. Kid Murphy was born Peter Frascella in Boston on May 2, 1886 to Italian immigrants hailing from the village of San Fele in the Southern Italian region of Basilicata. The diminutive boxer blasted a trail of fear in the ranks of the bantamweight division with explosive punching power and with his trademark rushes. With Kid Murphy it was simply a case of have gloves will travel. Once he had beaten all opposition in Boston the headliner set about showing his wares in other cities, topping shows in Baltimore, New York, Philadelphia and in the Mid-Western towns of Wisconsin and Illinois. In 1906 Kid Murphy captured the 105-pound title, after a private fight, from world title claimant Willie Schumacher in Westchester, New York. In the following year he met Chicago-based Canadian Johnny Coulon in Milwaukee, Wisconsin. An aggressive Murphy outpointed him over ten rounds to establish a solid claim to the 105-pound title, and inflict on Coulon his first professional defeat. Coulon paid tribute to Murphy's punching power, saying: "Kid Murphy was the hardest hitter I ever faced, laced me once and nearly put my lights out. If I ever live to be ninety years old the memory of that smasher will make me wince every time I think of it."

Murphy remained unbeaten throughout 1907. He met Coulon three more times and the fight series with Coulon defined his boxing career. Murphy won their first bout and then dropped a decision in the return and his claim to the 105-pound title. Coulon repeated the feat three weeks later. This fight was closer with Murphy making a good showing in the early rounds by holding his ground and striking out with precision. Coulon's telling jab kept Murphy at arm's length, opening up cuts above Murphy's eyes and lips, doing just enough to secure the verdict. Coulon declared himself the master of Murphy for a third time when they met in Albany, New York in January 1908. Murphy was stopped in five rounds but he insisted that he had been fouled by a low blow. He was backed up by his manager and refused to continue, leaving the ring to a chorus of jeers. It seemed to onlookers that Murphy could have continued if he wanted to, but within the context of the fight Murphy was generally acquitting himself well in the face of Coulon's two-fisted attacks and just before the bizarre incident Murphy had sent the champion sprawling to the canvas in the second round. With this walkout Murphy's aspirations of world title glory vanished indefinitely. Failing vision prompted Murphy to retire in 1914. He tried a comeback three years later and was knocked out in one round by Teddy Meyers. He later went blind. Murphy started his professional career in 1903 and finished with a total of 70 recorded bouts, racking up 38 wins, 10 draws, 14 no decisions and 8 losses. On leaving the sport he opened a poolroom in Trenton, New Jersey. He was an inspiration to his son Tommy "Kid" Murphy, who followed his father into boxing and enjoyed partial success as a featherweight in the twenties and early thirties. Kid Murphy was inducted into the New Jersey Boxing Hall of Fame. He died in October 1963.

* Prior to 1909, bantamweights were the lightest boxers but the paperweight category had been in existence since the 1880s and included boxers weighing 95 pounds. At that time bantamweights were 105 pounds and featherweights 115 pounds. In 1909 the National Sporting Club of London devised eight weight categories setting a flyweight limit at 112 pounds and bantamweight at 118 pounds. These weights were adopted by the Commonwealth, Europe and by the NYSAC and NBA.

1910–19
FRANKIE CONLEY [FRANCESCO CONTE]
WORLD BANTAMWEIGHT CLAIMANT 1910

Wisconsin's gritty all-action hero Frankie Conley served notice as a worthy bantamweight contender with two impressive draws with the heavier Ad Wolgast, future world lightweight champion, in 1907 and in 1908. Conley's style of boxing made him a darling of boxing promoters nationwide and his durability and rugged in-fighting qualities ensured packed houses everywhere. He traveled to Missouri and New York before stopping over in California. It was on the West Coast that Conley's moment of glory finally came. Former bantamweight champion Jimmy Walsh of Boston had moved up to featherweight and declared the championship vacant. Whilst most boxing authorities recognized Johnny Coulon as having the best title claim, Conley disputed it. On February 22, 1910, Conley claimed the vacant world bantamweight title by knocking out Monte Atell, brother of Abe, in a titanic clash lasting 42 rounds of a scheduled 45-rounder that was advertised as a world title contest. Before a 7,000 crowd in Vernon, mostly rooting for Atell, the Californian Jew was severely punished and on hitting the canvas for the fifth time his seconds threw in the sponge before the referee had completed the count. Conley's feat was a remarkable display of endurance, doughtiness and strength. Prior to the Atell fight, the longest distance Conley had gone was fifteen rounds. It was generally thought the more experienced Atell would have the advantage the longer the fight went on. When Abe declared that Conley had got lucky, Conley offered him the chance to even the score. Months later in New Orleans, Conley battled the reigning featherweight champion to a fifteen-round draw. Conley pressurized the artful Atell and was unfortunate to fall on the wrong side of the decision, with Conley forcing the pace in every round. Conley lost his title claim in his first defense to Johnny Coulon on a twenty-round decision. He got a rematch with Coulon a year later, but an eight-day fast in order to make the weight, which included Conley running on the morning of the fight to slim down to the stipulated limit, meant that the consequences were devastating for him as the drastic weight loss sapped him of his energy. He again lost on points.

Conley was one of the gamest and most vicious bantamweights that ever stepped into the ring. Known as "Bullet Head" and the "Kenosha Wildcat," Conley never met his match at the toe-to-toe style of milling. He was unbeatable at 118 pounds and he frequently gave away between eight to ten pounds in weight just to get work, with most of his fights fought over the bantamweight limit. According to boxing records, in a thirteen-year fight career which began in 1906, Conley engaged in an estimated five hundred bouts including bootleg contests. Officially though, he is listed as having fought 81 contests, with 37 wins, 11 losses and 31 draws or no decisions with 2 no contests. Conley's record reads like a who's who of legendary old-time fighters, having shared the ring with six world champions and a host of contenders such as Charley White, Joe Mandot, Patsy Kline, Abe Atell, Johnny Coulon, Johnny Dundee, Johnny Kilbane, Mexican Joe Rivers, Owen Moran, Ad Wolgast and Joe Coster. The curtain came down on Conley's career in January 1919. He resumed fighting after four years out of the ring, but was knocked out by Jimmy Hanlon in two rounds, finally retiring aged 29. He became a strong supporter of local Golden Gloves boxing programs, training promising fighters from around the Mid-West at his gymnasium.

Conley was born Francesco Conte in Platania, Calabria in Southern Italy on October 4, 1890, and with his family settled in Kenosha, Wisconsin. He attended St. Mark's Catholic School and it was there that Conley discovered he had what it took to make the grade in boxing when he flattened the school bully. His Irish friends made him an honorary Irishman by bestowing the moniker of Frankie Conley and the name stuck with him. Conley died of a heart attack in August 1952.

YOUNG ZULU KID [GIUSEPPE DI MELFI]
WORLD FLYWEIGHT CLAIMANT 1915

In some quarters Young Zulu Kid was recognized as a legitimate world flyweight title claimant, having taken on all comers at 112 pounds and triumphed. The exotically named Young Zulu Kid was born Giuseppe Di Melfi on April 22, 1897 in the mountainous village of Anzi, 25 miles from Potenza in the Basilicata region of Southern Italy. Di Melfi was seven years old when he left Naples with his parents Domenico and Rosa and younger sister Rosa, on the ship *North America* heading for a new life in the New World. Once they arrived in the United States the family settled in New

York City, where he began working as a newsboy for the *Brooklyn Daily Eagle* newspaper. He quickly became known as the "Fighting Newsboy" from his eagerness to defend his patch from other newsboys peddling their papers.

He turned professional in 1912 and following a series of notable victories he was thrust into the limelight as the clamor grew for a title-defining match with Britain's Jimmy Wilde. During the pre-First World War period, a situation developed where Young Zulu Kid was the premier American flyweight and Britain boasted their champion in Jimmy "Mighty Atom" Wilde. In the newly devised flyweight class, for which the English authorities set the 108-pound weight limit, Young Zulu Kid was the American representative. Their paths crossed on December 18, 1916 at the Holborn Stadium, central London in what was the inaugural world flyweight championship title fight. Young Zulu Kid entered the contest having met first-class bantamweights Kid Wagner, Bobby Burns, Pal Moore, Monte Atell, Johnny Ertle, Jack Rosner and Little Jack Sharkey. In many of these matches the 4-foot 11-inch New Yorker conceded between eight and twenty-four pounds in order to secure fights in the United States.

Although Young Zulu Kid was bereft of punching power, he was a tireless and energetic warrior, and started his fights like an express train, maintaining an eye-catching work rate. Prior to the Wilde contest the Kid had never fought over ten rounds. Wilde didn't reveal much, but people guessed that he was inside the stipulated eight-stone weight limit. In the ring Wilde towered over the Kid, benefiting from a four-and-a-half-inch height advantage and a greater reach. Wilde's supporters bet on an early finish but the Kid surprised the throng by standing upright after ten blistering rounds, proving that he was no walkover, and even managing to shake Wilde once or twice. In the seventh round Wilde was twice jolted. The Kid adopted an astute ducking technique, forcing Wilde to miss on countless occasions. His moves were as quick as lightning and springing upwards from a semi-sitting posture he launched into flurries of punches to the head and to the body. In the ninth round Young Zulu Kid took the fight to Wilde and this brought the fight fans to their feet, as he won the round by a big margin. In the following stanza Wilde rallied hard to keep the pressure on, and in the decisive eleventh round the Kid was pinned in one corner, and under a barrage of blows his corner threw in the towel in an act of mercy just as their man slumped to the canvas. He had put on a wonderful display of gaminess and stamina against one of the best flyweights in boxing history. In 1920 the Kid got another chance to fight Wilde and the Briton scored a ten-round no-decision win in Canada.

During the First World War Young Zulu Kid served a stint in the

United States Navy. He was released in January 1919 and immediately returned to fighting top-notch boxers. In 1921 he fought for the American Flyweight title, dropping a close fifteen-round decision to Johnny Buff, the eventual world flyweight champ. That was the Kid's final fling at the big time. In the final years of his career he lost repeatedly on points right through to 1924. After a three year lay-off he tried another comeback and was promptly dispatched into oblivion. Young Zulu Kid quit the ring in 1927 having fought in over 132 official bouts. Boxing expert Charley Rose rated Young Zulu Kid as the tenth best all-time flyweight boxer. On hanging up his gloves he owned and worked with his brother in a bar and grill establishment in New York City.

PETE HERMAN [PIETRO GULOTTA]
WORLD BANTAMWEIGHT CHAMPION 1917–20, 1921

On January 9, 1917, Pete Herman captured the bantamweight crown from Danish American Kid Williams on a twenty-round points decision in front of his adoring fans in New Orleans to become the first Italian American boxer to win an undisputed world professional boxing championship. This was Herman's second crack at Williams as the first world title match, staged a year earlier, ended in daylight robbery, when referee Billy Rocap, a friend of Kid Williams, declared the bout a draw when most ringside observers made Herman a clear winner. Williams was enticed back into the ring by promised riches as well as the opportunity to pick the referee. Herman left nobody in any doubt the second time around.

Herman, an orthodox hard-hitting and accurate puncher, ruled the 118-pound division for nearly four years. His effective piston-like body punching, speed, toughness and superior inside fighting dazzled former champions, title claimants and contenders. Jimmy Wilde, one of the all-time great flyweights, was knocked out by Herman in the seventeenth round in a catchweight contest held at the Royal Albert Hall in London in 1921. Herman was born Pietro Gulotta on the February 12, 1896 in the French market section of New Orleans to Sicilian parents. The turning point for Herman came when he confronted an older brute forcing shoeshine boys to give up their earnings. He squared up to the bully and put him in hospital. Local promoter Dominic Tortorich and matchmaker Red Walsh, who later became his manager, encouraged Herman to turn professional. Without any amateur boxing experience, the sixteen-year-old joined the paid ranks and adopted the ring name of a popular lightweight, Kid Herman. It was an inauspicious start and after five bouts he ended his first year with an inglorious record of two draws, two losses and one win.

This did not dull Herman's zest. The diminutive 118-pounder's first major opportunity came in June 1914, when he fought Kid Williams in a ten-round non-title contest. Herman won the no-decision contest in the opinion of the newspaper reporters, demonstrating his class. Prior to capturing the world title, Herman mainly fought in New Orleans and Memphis but as champion he took his talents on the road, appearing in New York, Philadelphia, Baltimore, New Jersey, Boston and the Mid-West. He even traveled to London, where following his victory over Wilde he became friends with the Prince of Wales. The Duke of Windsor (later Edward VIII) subsequently visited Herman in New Orleans. Herman lost his title to Joe Lynch but regained it in July 1921, with a fifteen-round points decision over the Irish American at Ebbets Field, Brooklyn, in what was the first world title fight to be broadcast on the radio. Herman received $22,500 and became only the third man in boxing history to recapture his crown after Jack Britton and Stanley Ketchel. Two months later Herman lost it to Johnny Buff.

Failing eyesight forced him to retire prematurely in 1922, eventually going blind. According to the *Ring Record Book 1980*, Herman finished with a career record of 149 bouts, 69 wins, 11 losses, 8 draws, and 61 no decisions. He was stopped only once. Herman supported his parents, buying them a home on Ursuline Street in the Crescent City, and when Herman was drafted into the army during the First World War he was allowed to box on, so that he could provide for them, as he was their sole source of income. In retirement Herman purchased a nightclub restaurant in the French quarter of New Orleans and managed it successfully for the remainder of his life. He also served as a member of the Louisiana State Athletic Commission. Herman was enshrined in the National Boxing Hall of Fame in 1959. Nat Fleischer, former editor of *Ring Magazine*, ranked Herman as the second all-time bantamweight behind George Dixon. Herman was inducted into the International Boxing Hall of Fame in 1997. He died in New Orleans in April 1973.

1920–29
JOHNNY WILSON [GIOVANNI FRANCESCO PANICO]
WORLD MIDDLEWEIGHT CHAMPION 1920–23

On May 6, 1920, Johnny Wilson outpointed champion Mike O'Dowd over twelve rounds to win the undisputed world middleweight title. With archetypal pugilistic looks of flattened nose, square jaw and hair slicked back, Wilson courted controversy and press hostility. Associations with mobsters dogged his reign as champion and unjustly he never got the credit he deserved.

He was a strong, durable and wily southpaw whose stance befuddled many opponents. Wilson carried heavy left-handed punches and boxed on the defensive. He met six world champions and never ducked any of the tough middleweight aspirants and, unlike many top middleweights before and after him, Wilson did not draw the color line, meeting George Robinson five times and Theodore Flowers once. By 1920 he reigned as the New England middleweight champion. He fought and beat Al Rogers, Leo Houck, Augie Ratner, Young Fisher and Pal Reed before getting a tilt at O'Dowd.

The champion entered the contest having stopped eleven of his last fifteen opponents but dropped a lop-sided decision to Wilson, even though O'Dowd's manager had been allowed to appoint the referee. Ten months later Wilson won their rematch. He did most things well inside the ring. He jabbed effectively on the retreat and was a canny body puncher, preferring to wear down his opponent. He also developed a reputation for being a notoriously rough fighter and not always keeping within the rules, being described as a "grizzly bear." The New York scribes especially disliked Wilson, unfairly labeling him a second-rater. When O'Dowd ended up in hospital and underwent hernia surgery following their rematch a vigorous press campaign called for action to be taken to outlaw the use of foul blows. On July 27, 1921, Wilson made a title defense against Bryan Downey in Cleveland and controversy reared its ugly head again. Although Wilson appeared to have fouled his opponent when in trouble he retained his crown when the referee disqualified Downey for hitting his opponent with a foul blow after seven rounds. The Ohio boxing commission refused to acknowledge the referee's verdict and named Downey their champion. Two months later they met again in New Jersey and Downey failed to wrest the title. Although Wilson held the world crown for three years New York reporters described his reign as uninteresting, arguing that the division had fallen on hard times, but none of this was attributable to Wilson.

In 1923, he lost his title to boxing legend Harry Greb over fifteen rounds. Wilson lost their title rematch again on points. He boxed on for another three years before retiring in October 1926. He finished with respectable career figures of 123 bouts, 65 wins, 2 draws, 21 losses, 34 no decisions and 1 no contest. Wilson was born Giovanni Francesco Panico on July 3, 1893 in East Harlem's Little Italy in New York City. He left school to become a postman for Western Union before switching to professional boxing in 1911. In his first fight he picked up a measly $2¼. As champion he received a purse of $13,200 for fighting Mike O'Dowd. In their St Patrick's Day return Wilson netted $50,000 plus $2,500 expenses. Rumor and speculation encircled the boxer for much of his career about his involvement in "fixed fights" but nothing was ever proven. Wilson certainly enjoyed the company of mobsters and made no secret of his associations with bootleggers and gunmen "Legs" Diamond and Owney Madden. It was schoolfriend and neighbor Francesco Castiglia, better known as Frank Costello, the gangster, who introduced him to fight handlers.

Wilson lived out a comfortable retirement. He operated many successful clubs in New York City, including the Silver Slipper, through Prohibition and during the Depression. He managed the Silver Dollar and the Swanee Grill in Roxbury, Boston. Wilson also owned a cigar store and bookstore and he promoted boxing shows. He later managed the Gilded Cage nightclub in Boston. After contracting pneumonia whilst recovering from a broken hip, Wilson died on December 8, 1985 at the age of 92.

JOHNNY DUNDEE [GIUSEPPE CARRARA]*
WORLD JUNIOR-LIGHTWEIGHT CHAMPION 1921–23, 1923
WORLD FEATHERWEIGHT CHAMPION 1923

Johnny Dundee spun some truly unforgettable feats in the boxing ring, maintaining the highest level of consistency against the very best, and his longevity extended for over two decades, registering some 340 bouts. From 1912 right through to 1925, he met every notable featherweight and lightweight, including the legendary Benny Leonard eight times. Dundee turned professional in 1910 and from the start acquired a winning habit and within a year he was boxing main events. His first title shot came on April 20, 1913, when he met the featherweight champion Johnny Kilbane in Los Angeles. The fight ended in a controversial twenty-round draw with most onlookers feeling Dundee had been stitched up. The Irish American refused to meet Dundee again. Undeterred by the setback Dundee piled up the newspaper decision victories but the no-decision era made it awkward for Dundee to win a title as official decisions were prohibited. Without a title to his name friends and admirers of Dundee presented him with an emblematic belt to recognize his feats against the best pugilists.

On November 18, 1921, Dundee finally got hold of a title worthy of his talents when he defeated George Chaney for the newly created junior-lightweight division. Following three successful defenses he lost it to Jack Bernstein. Next he captured the elusive featherweight crown from Frenchman Eugene Criqui, the man who had deposed Kilbane. In December 1923, Dundee continued his run of success by regaining the junior-lightweight title from Bernstein, only to lose it to Steve "Kid" Sullivan a year later. In 1927 Dundee waved goodbye to the big time as his quest to regain the featherweight title faltered against Tony Canzoneri.

Dundee continued to box until 1932. In all he was involved in eleven world championship bouts, he had beaten the best fighters in the world, he held two world titles in different weight classes and, astonishingly, Dundee was knocked out just twice in his entire career. He was a fine athlete, who was just at home on a bike saddle as he was in the ring. He was also a superb race walker, covering the five-mile distance in a time of twenty-eight minutes. Dundee relied on his physical equipment to become a quick-footed, nimble, slick, sharp-hitting, all-action fighter. What he lacked in power he made up for in craft, stamina and durability. His unorthodox style of bouncing off the rope to deliver a flurry of blows and avoid being hit was his trademark move and was later copied by many fighters.

Dundee was an audacious performer who left his jaw unprotected when moving forward in a crouched position. Benny Leonard, who knew him best, described him as "a quick thinker . . . immediately upon seeing an opportunity to land, he grasped it. He used none of the stereotyped system of boxing . . . but had a style of his own." Jimmy Johnston, Dundee's knowledgeable manager between 1920 and 1929, elevated his charge to God-like status and viewed him as a greater fighter than Terry McGovern and equal to the legendary Abe Atell. The Italian never ducked anyone and often challenged Ted Lewis when the Briton was the world welterweight champion. He described Dundee as:

> leathery, elusive, a punishing type of box-fighter combination, the most spectacular man in any class today as well as the most popular boxer of all time and one of the greatest. Years ago the boxing world was electrified by the elusiveness and special boxing of the Belfast Spider Ike Weir, who was known as the dancing master on account of his nimbleness in the ring. Dundee has a lot of Weir's tricks, each one a natural gift.[1]

A fact often overlooked is that Dundee was not just a great sportsman but a gentle, friendly and charismatic man who represented his sport with dignity and poise and his charitable work was recognized universally. Dundee expressed a willingness to take part in entertainment for all kinds of relief work and perhaps his best contribution was for the Milk Fund sponsored boxing shows where the proceeds went to help destitute babies in Italy and to children of the working poor in American cities. In December 1921 Dundee received a gold medal from King Victor Emmanuel III of Italy in honor of his charity work there.

Dundee was born Giuseppe Carrara in Sciacca in the province of

Agrigento, Sicily on November 22, 1893. He arrived with his family in Manhattan, New York City at the age of nine, and as a child worked for his father, who owned a fish store. At sixteen, Johnny was spotted sparring in the street with friends by boxing manager William Scotty Monteith. Dundee was asked to go to the gym for a try-out. Three weeks later he turned professional, making his debut at the Sharkey Athletic Club using the moniker Young Marino. He later dropped it in favor of Johnny Dundee. What isn't well documented is that the Dundee *nom de guerre* wasn't merely an act of chance; it was based upon his mother's maiden name of Dondero and since Monteith was born in Dundee, Scotland the name stuck. In retirement Dundee's wealth was estimated at $400,000. He was selected for the Boxing Hall of Fame in 1957 and the International Boxing Hall of Fame in 1991. Boxing expert Nat Fleischer ranked Dundee as the fourth all-time featherweight and Charley Rose rated him the second all-time featherweight. He lived in East Orange, New Jersey until his death on April 22, 1965.

* American boxing record books record Dundee's family surname as Carrora.

CARL DUANE [CARLO IACCONETTI]*
WORLD JUNIOR-FEATHERWEIGHT CHAMPION 1923–24

"Bronx Steamroller" Carl Duane turned his back on a comfortable life as a jeweler to become a star boxing attraction in the New York clubs during the twenties. His no-nonsense and frenzied style took him to the top of his division, capturing the newly created junior-featherweight title in 1923, outpointing the inaugural champion Jack "Kid" Wolfe after twelve furious rounds in Long Island City, New York. Duane raced to the title in less than three years as a professional. He held onto the junior title without defending it as the division fell into disuse a year later.

Duane perfectly exemplified the spirit that had taken Italians to the fore of the sport, fighting with a win-or-die spirit, never succumbing and always embracing the heat of battle. Duane was a dynamic featherweight puncher with the ability to swarm all over his opponents. In October 1922 Duane boxed preliminaries in New York and outpointed the former bantamweight champion Charley Phil Rosenberg of Harlem over twelve rounds. It was Duane's fight all the way. He hooked rights and lefts to the face and body with telling effect. A right to the jaw in the fourth put Rosenberg down for a nine-count. Duane piled on the pressure for the remainder of the fight at the New York Velodrome. This was Duane's second twelve-rounder of his career and guaranteed him a shot at the world title. One month later he took the championship laurels from Cleveland's Jack "Kid" Wolfe at the

Queensboro Stadium, Long Island City. It was an even-money contest in the betting but Duane's aggressive and relentless rushes, leading with heavy rights, dominated the action in this hard-fought battle. He won by a wide margin and only Wolfe's ring nous saved him from a knockout.

In the autumn and winter months of 1923, the Carl Duane versus Frankie Jerome slugfest was the talk of the town in New York City as the protagonists waited for their chance to fight for the Bronx bantamweight championship. The first contest ended in a slashing six-round draw and was voted one of the greatest ring battles seen since the inception of the Walker Law. Duane won the rematch over fifteen rounds, asserting superiority over his bitter Irish neighborhood rival. Just when things were looking up misfortune beset Duane during 1924 and 1925. Firstly, he was rendered inactive for almost a year having had his jaw broken in a contest with Allentown Johnny Leonard. Then he survived a near-fatal car accident in which one of his lungs was punctured. With his career threatened, Duane fought back and after a string of victories challenged Tod [*sic*] Morgan for the junior-lightweight title on November 19, 1926 at Madison Square Garden in New York. Duane led in the early stages of the contest but ran out of gas late on with Morgan awarded eight out of the fifteen rounds. The bout drew receipts of $50,363, the largest gate for a junior-lightweight title fight. It was to be Duane's first and only title shot at the 130-pound limit.

His crowd-pleasing qualities kept arenas full and gate receipts high. In March 1926, Duane met Bronx Italian rival Joe Malone for the Bronx featherweight title. Duane outpointed his rival over ten rounds before 16,000 fans. In a career spanning nine years he retired with a ring record of 63 bouts, 43 wins, 5 draws, 12 losses and 3 no decisions. Carl Duane was born Carlo Iacconetti on June 25, 1902 in the Fordham section of Bronx, New York soon after his parents arrived from Calabria, Southern Italy. Duane's interest in prizefighting stemmed from his role in street-corner fighting. Carlo's father Salvatore hoped his son would join the jewelry business and reluctantly acquiesced to his son's wishes. Sneaking off to the gym at night was no longer necessary and when boxing manager Mike Valentine needed a sparring partner for welterweight Joe Dundee he took Duane under his wing and nurtured the newcomer's potential. Carlo changed his name in favour of a shorter English sounding *nom de guerre*. Once the boxing board registered his new name Carl Duane was unleashed onto the boxing world.

* Old books show Duane's family name beginning with a Y even though this letter does not exist in the Italian alphabet.

LOU BOGASH [LUIGI BUCCASSI]*
WORLD (NYSAC) MIDDLEWEIGHT CLAIMANT 1923

Lou Bogash was a fearless and uncompromising fighter. He capped a fourteen-year career by gaining recognition as the NYSAC (New York State Athletic Commission) middleweight champion. On January 9, 1923, Bogash stopped Charley Nashert Fitzsimmons in eleven rounds of a scheduled twelve-rounder at the Pioneer Athletic Club in New York, ending an elimination tournament to decide a successor to Johnny Wilson. Bogash was presented with a gold buckle and was recognized as the titleholder by New York, New England and other states. Prolonged inactivity by Wilson had forced the NYSAC into action and when later in the year Wilson defended his linear title against Harry Greb and Greb won, Bogash's claim was ignored. But for a brief period Bogash was a deserving "world champion."

Bogash, known as the "Bridgeport Spoiler," was one of the toughest men in the boxing business. At one time all the American middleweights dodged Bogash and those that did pluck up the courage were beaten. Bogash took the scalps of numerous world champions and title claimants including Tommy Loughran, Mike McTigue, Mickey Walker, Jock Malone, Mike O'Dowd, Bryan Downey, Lou Scozza and Tiger Flowers either by referee's decision or by newspaper decisions. Bogash possessed competent defensive skills, a solid left hand and was a tornado of rapid punches. In August 1920, fighting in his hometown, Bogash was cruelly denied the welterweight title when a controversial draw helped champion Jack Britton maintain his grip on the championship belt. Bogash felt robbed and although the crowd knew who won, the undisputed title remained out of reach. Two months later he gave Marty Cross a terrific beating before the Madison Square Garden patrons and when Ted "Kid" Lewis of England lost in the following year Bogash was seen as the sole outstanding contender for Britton's welterweight title. The Irish American refused to meet Bogash again.

He moved up to the middleweight division and created quite an impression. He triumphed over Mickey Walker, the reigning welterweight champion, in Boston and engaged Harry Greb in a no decision bout. Both were reluctant to meet Bogash again. Greb was the middleweight champion when they met in a non-title no-decision clash in Jersey City. Although the fight is recorded as a newspaper win for Greb, esteemed boxing writer George Underwood confirmed that Greb took a bad beating and was jeered by fans for not coping well with Bogash's style.

Bogash was born Luigi Buccassi in Faeto in the province of Foggia in the Apulia region on February 24, 1901. He arrived in Bridgeport,

Connecticut as a youngster, and at fourteen years old be became an orphan when he lost both his parents. A year later he followed his older brother into boxing. He enlisted in the army during the First World War but once the American military discovered his real age, Bogash was discharged and he went back to boxing. At seventeen he became the youngest ever Connecticut lightweight champion. Two years later he went on to win the Connecticut welterweight title. Bogash started boxing as a featherweight and eventually ended up tangling with light-heavyweights. During his career Bogash fought in 140 bouts, winning 109. He scored 40 knockouts, lost 16 and 15 were draws. Amazingly Bogash was never stopped. On retiring from boxing in 1930 he became a wholesaler liquor salesman and also served as a state boxing referee. Bogash died on March 7, 1978. He was inducted posthumously into the World Boxing Hall of Fame in 2000.

* His family surname regularly appears in record books as either Buccassio or Bogassi.

STEVE "KID" SULLIVAN [STEFANO TRICAMO]
WORLD JUNIOR-LIGHTWEIGHT CHAMPION 1924–25

Steve "Kid" Sullivan waited thirteen years to get a world title shot. On June 20, 1924 he seized it with both hands. Nobody deserved it more than Sullivan, as he took the fight to ring legend Johnny Dundee, winning a spirited ten-round scrap on sheer persistent aggression before a partisan crowd of 12,000 fans in Brooklyn, New York. The popular "Kid" Sullivan became the third junior-lightweight titleholder in the newly created 130-pound weight class. "Kid" Sullivan's victory also brought Brooklyn their first champion since 1917 when Al McCoy had ruled the middleweight class. He was a game fighter and a brutal body puncher who fought the most rugged boxers of his era; he was also the best drawing card in Brooklyn and almost all of his fights were staged in that borough prior to the passage of the Walker Law.

The duels with Vincent "Pepper" Martin captured the imagination of the fight public in the Brooklyn area. Both boxers were exponents of the slam-bang-wallop style and their five-fight series, which began in 1916, ended with Sullivan successfully defending his world title in August 1924. These grudge matches were fueled by bitter neighborhood feuds and ethnic rivalry between the Irish and Italians, and further enmity between them dated back to boyhood street-corner fights. The contests became box office specials with Sullivan winning three and Martin two contests.

"Kid" Sullivan was born Stefano Tricamo to Sicilian parents on May 21, 1897 in South Brooklyn. He began boxing in 1911 as a bantamweight. He achieved recognition as a hard-hitting battler who was unafraid to punch it out with the best of them. His career was interrupted in 1917 when he spent three years as a member of the United States Navy's aviation corps unit at Gulfport, Missouri. He returned in 1920 heavier and stronger and began demolishing the title aspirations of other junior lightweights like Babe Herman and Sammy Sieger. He is remembered as a popular 130-pounder but poor business judgment blighted many paydays, and this at a time when boxing champions were more commercially astute, commanding larger purses and picking future opponents. "Kid" Sullivan made two successful defenses before electing to fight fellow Italian rival Mike Ballerino for his third title argument. They knew each other well, having met on three previous occasions with Sullivan winning one, losing one and one no-decision contest. To make matters worse he opted not to fight in New York, which would have been a guaranteed money-spinner. He could have earned three to four times the sums picked up elsewhere. Yet he took to the road and defended his title in Philadelphia. The overall effect of his decision was not only to lose the title in a sizzling twelve-round contest but the pittance of $4,000 in net receipts meant that the promoters lost money.

A month later "Kid" Sullivan suffered his first career knockout defeat, losing to Louis "Kid" Kaplan. In 1926 he tried to recapture the 130-pound crown from Tod [sic] Morgan but was unsuccessful and retired after the fight. He finished with a career record of 111 bouts, 33 wins, 10 draws and 18 losses and 50 no decisions. "Kid" Sullivan invested his money in property in Brooklyn and lived comfortably outside the ring. He died in Ventura, California in September 1979.

EDDIE MARTIN [EDUARDO VITTORIO MARTINO]
WORLD BANTAMWEIGHT CHAMPION 1924–25

On December 19, 1925, Brooklyn dynamo Eddie "Cannonball" Martin fulfilled a lifelong ambition by winning the bantamweight crown from Abe Goldstein after fifteen grueling rounds in New York City. Martin was a popular and tireless performer, perpetually aggressive with an indomitable fighting spirit. His busy infighting approach and attacks ensured thrilling entertainment. He was courageous, possessed great recuperative powers and a fair punch, but his style of milling rendered him susceptible to incoming blows. He won the title after only three years' campaigning as a professional. At one stage the omens of Martin's career progression looked increasingly unfavorable. He boxed three amateur contests before quitting the unpaid ranks. He made an inconspicuous start as a professional, losing his first two bouts but these setbacks only bolstered his resolve. He plugged away and started a winning streak, which stretched for three years, ending in March

1925 when he lost his title to Charley Phil Rosenberg on points, three months after he had won it from Goldstein. Martin took the loss badly, suffering a nervous breakdown. He never boxed again as a bantamweight.

Following a sixteen-month layoff, Martin returned as a featherweight under the wing of influential manager Johnny Keyes. In 1928 Martin was awarded two shots at Tod [*sic*] Morgan's junior lightweight title and many ringsiders who witnessed the matches were convinced that Martin was the better man in both. Morgan was forced to hold and clinch to stop Martin's whirlwind attacks at the New Garden, New York. Two months later, 15,000 fans witnessed a vicious battle at the Ebbets Field, New York, where Martin looked a sure-fire winner. Martin rocked the champion in the third, fifth and sixth rounds and gave the game champion a thumping in the thirteenth round. From the ninth round onwards Martin's right eye injury hampered his efforts, as it became a target for Morgan's persistent jabbing. Martin doggedly stuck to his battle plan, boring in and shaking his man with a two-fisted attack. His gallant showings against Morgan marked the beginning of the end for Martin as a headliner and he eventually quit in 1932 after a decade of ring battles.

Eddie Martin was born Eduardo Vittorio Martino on February 26, 1903* in the Red Hook section of Brooklyn, New York to Southern Italian parents. He was the sixth of fifteen children. Martin was attracted to sports and he led the baseball and basketball teams whilst at Commercial High School. His early ambition was to be a Major League baseball shortstop. In spite of his family's objections to boxing, Martin cut short his high school career during the second year to follow his chosen career path. He began as an amateur and graduated to the pro ranks in 1922. According to the *1980 Ring Record Book*, Martin appeared in 90 bouts, winning 72, losing 11 and drawing 3. His record also included 3 no decisions and 1 no contest. After boxing he worked on the New York docks as a longshoreman. He died on August 27, 1966 in Brooklyn, New York.

* Old record books record Martin's date of birth as March 3, 1903.

MIKE BALLERINO
WORLD JUNIOR LIGHTWEIGHT CHAMPION 1925

In October 1924 Mike Ballerino was thrust into the limelight of world championship boxing when he challenged Steve "Kid" Sullivan for the junior-lightweight crown at Madison Square Garden. It was an unfortunate experience for the former army soldier as he was stopped in five rounds. With his title dreams seemingly in tatters he was given an unexpected opportunity by his nemesis six months later. On April Fools' Day they met again for the title at the 108th Field Artillery Armory in Philadelphia. After surviving a first round knockdown Ballerino meted out a terrific demonstration of body punching that sent the champion into a tailspin. Ballerino piled on the pressure to capture the 130-pound belt, winning every round before the 4,000 crowd. He became the third Italian American holder of the junior-lightweight after Johnny Dundee and "Kid" Sullivan.

Ballerino's achievement fueled excitement in his hometown of Bayonne, New Jersey and a welcome home victory parade was held. Among the two thousand well-wishers were a brass band and city officials including Mayor Robert Talbot, who greeted their hero as he stepped off the train. Ballerino successfully defended his title in a tough battle with perennial challenger Vincent "Pepper" Martin before 12,000 fans at the Queensboro Stadium in New York. In this slam-bang struggle, Ballerino took eight out of the fifteen rounds and he scored the only knockdown in the second round. Ballerino, known as the "Bayonne Whirlwind," possessed crowd-pleasing qualities. He was a strong, rugged, feisty, iron-jawed rushing fighter, swinging punches tirelessly. He had a habit of demoralizing opponents with his party trick by grinning with mouth agape at his opponents when getting hit. The stronger their punch the wider Ballerino's grin became.

In December 1925 Ballerino surprisingly lost his crown to Tod [*sic*] Morgan by a tenth-round stoppage with Ballerino's seconds throwing in the towel. After this setback he boxed on for two more years. He tried an unsuccessful comeback in 1935 and again in 1936 before hanging up his gloves for good.

Mike Ballerino was born on April 10, 1901 in Asbury Park, New Jersey. At the age of ten his parents moved to Bayonne. He learnt to box in the army during American military involvement in the Philippines. Whilst stationed in Manila he fought as a flyweight and between 1920 and 1921 engaged the great Pancho Villa, future world flyweight champion, in ten bouts over six, ten, fifteen, and twenty rounds. Ballerino's fighting exploits in the Far East were headline news, and it was there that he was dubbed the "Manila Typhoon." On his return to the United States he signed under the management of Frank Churchill and made his American ring debut in December 1921. Ballerino met all the top-notch fighters of his era and retired with a ring record of one hundred bouts, 47 wins, 18 draws, 30 losses and 5 no decisions. In retirement Ballerino worked in various theaters. He lived in Tampa, Florida, where he died on April 4, 1965.

FRANKIE GENARO [FRANCO DI GENNARO]*
WORLD FLYWEIGHT CLAIMANT 1925
WORLD (NBA, IBU) FLYWEIGHT CHAMPION 1928–29, 1929–31

The twenties are generally recognized as the golden age of boxing, and none was greater than the diminutive Frankie Genaro, who as a leading light in the flyweight division fought ten world champions. He was so good that he did most of his fighting against bantamweights, handling them with nonchalant efficiency. Genaro was flyweight champion on and off between 1923 and 1930, winning and losing one or other versions of the title. In 1929 and 1930 he was the idol of America and a major attraction in Europe, especially in France, which celebrated mighty midgets.

How did Genaro manage such a glorious impact? Physically he was an unlikely hero. He stood at just 5 feet 2½ inches and weighed 112 pounds but he more than compensated for this with his masterly boxing exhibitions. He made his professional debut in the autumn of 1920 and within two years was notching wins over the likes of Charley Phil Rosenberg and Pancho Villa. Shortly after Villa arrived from the Philippines in the summer of 1922, Genaro claimed a hat-trick of wins over the flyweight legend, firstly taking a popular newspaper decision in Jersey City. He followed that up with a twelve-round points win in Brooklyn and then outpointed Villa over fifteen rounds in New York to win the American flyweight title. When Villa died suddenly in July 1925 the world title was left vacant. Genaro, in pole position, claimed the world flyweight title. The question of superiority was settled when he met Fidel La Barba on August 22, 1925. After ten rounds Genaro lost both his world title claim and the American flyweight title in Ascot Park, Los Angeles before a crowd of 25,000.

The loss invigorated Genaro in his pursuit of glory. In February 1928 he outpointed Albert "Frenchy" Belanger over ten rounds to win the NBA (National Boxing Association) flyweight crown in Toronto, Canada. Although he lost it to Emile Pladner of France in his first defense, he regained his laurels by defeating the Frenchman a month later. Genaro made three successful defenses of his NBA title before meeting Midget Wolgast, the recognized NYSAC flyweight titleholder. The bout ended in a draw and the champions went their separate ways. Genaro made three more defenses before French Tunisian Victor Perez knocked him out in October 1931. Genaro never fought for a world title again and retired in 1934.

Johnny Rosner, a 1916 flyweight claimant, twice defeated by Genaro, described Genaro as the greatest of them all. Years later in a magazine interview he recalled:

It was like trying to hit a ghost. That little Italian bum was all over the place and his hands flashed in the air like pistons. You couldn't even see his gloves – they were just red blurs under lights . . . look at some of the guys he licked—guys who outweighed him ten, sometimes fifteen pounds—Pal Moore, Carl Tremaine, Bushy Graham, Charley Rosenberg and Bud Taylor.[2]

Frankie Genaro was born Franco Di Gennaro in Brooklyn, New York on August 26, 1901 to Neapolitan parents. He thought of becoming a horse jockey and got a job as a stable boy, but decided boxing would make him the fortune he craved. Genaro was the first Italian American professional world champion to have an exceptional amateur record. At sixteen, the Brooklyn boy entered his first tournament at the Crescent Athletic Club. He graduated to the New York State and national titles before capping his amateur career by winning the flyweight gold medal at the 1920 Antwerp Olympic Games before turning professional under the management of Phil Bernstein. He retired in 1934 with a career record of 130 bouts, 94 wins, 8 draws, 22 losses and 6 no decisions. Genaro was elected into the International Boxing Hall of Fame in 1998. In retirement Genaro was involved in sales and real estate and owned a lake-front property in Cochecton, New York. He also worked for the Department of Marine Aviation in New York for fifteen years. Genaro died in Staten Island, New York on December 27, 1966.

* Old record books spell Genaro's surname as Di Gennara but historian Vince Colitti confirms it is actually Di Gennaro.

FIDEL LA BARBA
WORLD FLYWEIGHT CHAMPION 1925–27

On August 22, 1925, competing in only his eleventh fight, Fidel La Barba outpointed Frankie Genaro over ten rounds in Los Angeles, California to win the American flyweight title and take over Genaro's world title claim. La Barba was a great defensive fighter who possessed nimble footwork together with a good left-hook-and-weave style and a potent left jab to outwit the best of them. Two years later La Barba used his assets to good effect, clinching the vacant undisputed world flyweight title by outpointing Scotland's Elky Clark over twelve rounds at Madison Square Garden before 16,000 fans. La Barba won every round, flooring Clark five times. La Barba blinded the Scotsman with boxing science using left jabs and left hooks. Seven months later La Barba became the first and only champion to give up his title to attend college to study journalism.

In 1929 La Barba was forced back into the ring due to the Stock Market Crash, where he lost $250,000. A heavier La Barba had lost none of the shine that had made him world champion, taking on bantamweights and featherweights. His three-fight series with Kid Chocolate of Cuba confirmed his status as a star performer. The Cuban was considered the best pound-for-pound boxer of his day. In their first fight the record books show Chocolate winning the decision but for the ringsiders the kindest thing they reported was that it was controversial. In the rematch held at Madison Square Garden before 17,000, La Barba gained sweet revenge, piling on the pressure with tireless body onslaughts. Chocolate had no answer to La Barba's attacking style. La Barba became only the second boxer to carry a victory over the Cuban in 170 amateur and professional contests. La Barba fought twice for the featherweight title: once in May 1931 losing to Battling Battalino over fifteen close rounds, and a year later to Kid Chocolate over fifteen hotly contested rounds. Before the Kid Chocolate fight LaBarba accidentally tore the retina in his left eye but still went through with the title clash. Eventually he had the eye removed.

He closed out his career in 1933 with a record of 73 wins, 15 losses and 7 draws. He was one of the very few champions never to be knocked out. Boxing writer Nat Fleischer rated La Barba as the fourth all-time flyweight. He was elected into the Boxing Hall of Fame in 1972 and into the International Boxing Hall of Fame in 1996.

La Barba was born in the Bronx, New York on September 29, 1905 to Italian immigrant parents from the Southern central region of Abruzzi. At age three his family uprooted again, leaving New York for Los Angeles, to join relatives with the promise of work and a better life. His father was a laborer and any money sent was squandered by Fidel's eldest brother, who boxed under the name of Ted Frenchie. Fidel was a newsboy selling newspapers for the *Los Angeles Express*, and supplemented his meager earnings by setting up pins in the local bowling alley. He learnt to fight as a newsboy and later boxed at the athletic club under the tutelage of George Blake, who went onto manage La Barba. Blake steered La Barba to memorable triumphs in the United States amateur flyweight championships as well as the 1924 Paris Olympic Games. In September La Barba turned professional. Life after boxing saw La Barba make full use of his degree in journalism. He found work as a sports writer before entering the army in 1942. La Barba was called up into the United States Army Air Corps during the Second World War, where he served as a staff sergeant. On his return from hostilities, La Barba worked in public relations and was later employed as a screenwriter and technical advisor for boxing movies in Hollywood until a series of heart attacks forced him to retire. La Barba died in Los Angeles on October 3, 1981.

ROCKY KANSAS [ROCCO TOZZO]
WORLD LIGHTWEIGHT CHAMPION 1925–26

"Rock of Gibraltar" Rocky Kansas had the misfortune to run into legendary champion Benny Leonard. He lost each of their four encounters, two of which were world title fights. He never despaired and in the twilight of his career Kansas's persistence finally paid off. On December 7, 1925, Kansas outpointed Jimmy Goodrich over fifteen rounds in Buffalo, New York to win the world lightweight title.

Kansas was a devastating hitter who could stand toe to toe with the best and outlast them in a good old-fashioned tear-up. The short, stockily-built Kansas was a real menace in the 135-pound division and beat a number of highly regarded boxers including Charlie White, Joe Welling, Matt Brock, the inimitable Johnny Dundee, Chilean Luis Vicentini and Jack Bernstein. Ritchie Mitchell, who came within a whisker of wresting the title from Leonard in January 1921, faced Kansas a month later, and in the first round Kansas dismantled him with punishing left–right combinations. Mitchell took a nine count before Kansas unmercifully sent his opponent sprawling outside the ropes to the delight of his Buffalo supporters. After a decade of campaigning in Buffalo the Mitchell victory got people's attention. Mitchell asked for a rematch and he got it nineteen days later. Kansas removed him from the title picture with an easy newspaper decision win in Milwaukee. Kansas was moving into the big time. He was awarded a contract with Tex Rickard, the Madison Square Garden promoter. Next Kansas dispatched Willie Jackson and dropped a newspaper decision to Johnny Dundee. In the first of three encounters with Leonard, Kansas tamely surrendered in the first non-title contest. Kansas returned to winning ways by defeating Philadelphian Lew Tendler on points. In February 1922 Kansas got his first title shot at Leonard. In a grueling fifteen-rounder Leonard was roughed up and bloodied but had enough know-how to turn defeat into victory. Leonard mounted a rally in the ninth, sending Kansas down for an eight count in the eleventh round, the first knockdown of Kansas's career. He regained his poise to go the full fifteen rounds in front of President Theodore Roosevelt at Madison Square Garden.

Kansas got his title rematch five months later, but Leonard did not take any chances and boxed Kansas at distance. When Kansas sustained a broken wrist he stopped trying and was halted in the eighth round with Kansas's manager Dan Rogers throwing in the towel to save his charge from further punishment. Two title losses and with Leonard still at the helm the future looked bleak for Kansas. Kansas was in his thirties and time appeared to be running out. With nothing left to prove, Leonard hung up his gloves and his retirement left the lightweight division wide open. After an elimination tournament, fellow Buffalonian Jimmy Goodrich remained the last man standing to become the newly crowned lightweight titleholder. Kansas got his chance and in the first world title fight to be staged in Buffalo for twenty-three years the veteran Italian made no mistake, securing twelve of the fifteen rounds. Seven months later Kansas lost his crown on points to Sammy Mandell in Chicago and hung up his gloves. He returned for one more fight six years later before retiring permanently.

Kansas was born Rocco Tozzo on April 21, 1895, in Buffalo to immigrants hailing from the village of San Fele in the Southern Italian region of Basilicata. Kansas began working as a newsboy before deciding to follow older brother Joe Kansas into the sport. Frank Erne, former world lightweight champion, discovered Kansas but handed the reins of management over to Dan Rogers. Kansas turned professional in 1911 and in a fifteen-year career fought seven world champions and numerous headliners. He was stopped twice in 165 fights. He won 64, drew 7 and lost 13; 81 were no decisions. Kansas saved over $200,000 in career earnings but the Stock Market Crash in 1929 wiped him out of all his savings. He found work in construction, later working for the city of Buffalo. Kansas died of cancer on January 10, 1954.

SAMMY MANDELL [SAMUELE MANDALA]*
WORLD LIGHTWEIGHT CHAMPION 1926–30

The "Rockford Sheikh" Sammy Mandell is not etched into the collective consciousness of fight fans but perhaps he should be, because for a time in the twenties Mandell was untouchable. He ruled the lightweight division in an era packed with great lightweights. Among the many highlights in an impressive career, Mandell won the lightweight championship on July 3, 1926, from brawler Rocky Kansas, winning almost every one of the ten rounds. In Mandell's first championship defense the tough Ireland-born Canadian Jimmy McLarnin was forced to take a bow to Mandell's ring expertise. The hard-hitting McLarnin, who had pulverized the division's top contenders, simply could not land a telling blow and after fifteen rounds left the Polo Grounds ring bloodied, bruised and battered as Mandell ran out the winner in one of the classiest boxing exhibitions seen in New York since the days of Benny Leonard.

Mandell's speedy and accurate punching, a winning left jab and lightning quick reflexes made it possible for him to slip and slide clear of many oncoming blows. A year later in his second title defense against pressure fighter and two-time world champion Tony Canzoneri, once again Mandell's outstanding defensive work and clever boxing made the difference in a close contest. Speed, youth and an inexhaustible supply of energy were traits Mandell held in abundance. He was unquestionably tough to cope with for the caliber of opposition he faced. From 1926 to 1930 he had sixty-three fights, defeating world-ranked fighters Billy Petrolle, Jackie Fields and Phil McGraw among others in non-title contests.

Mandell's reign came to an abrupt end on July 17, 1930 at the Yankee Stadium when he was knocked out in one round by big-hitter Al Singer. Hurt by this defeat he continued to box, taking beatings from "unknowns." In November 1931 he announced his retirement. Mandell reportedly had an estimated fortune of $125,000 and was the owner of three houses in Rockford. It was a brief sojourn for Mandell, who returned to the ring fighting as a welterweight. He retired permanently in 1934 with a career record of 187 bouts scoring 147 wins, 13 draws, 26 losses and 1 no contest. Most of Mandell's defeats came after losing his lightweight title. In a glittering career, Mandell fought thirteen world champions and title claimants and was inducted into the International Boxing Hall of Fame in 1998.

Mandell was born Samuele Mandala on February 5, 1904 at Piana dei Greci in the Palermo province, Sicily. His mother died when Mandell was nine months old, and at the age of two his father took him to the United States. He was raised in Rockford and attended the local high school. His interest in sports was evident from an early age and he was a keen football, baseball and basketball player before boxing took over. His older brother Joe was a professional boxer and in no time both brothers were competing in boxing exhibitions throughout Illinois and southern Wisconsin. They both weighed 105 pounds. It didn't take long before Sammy Mandell got noticed and fell under the control of managerial duo of Eddie Long and Eddie Kane and trainer Jack Blackburn, later Joe Louis's trainer. Mandell was soon taught many of Blackburn's old tricks inside the ropes and was unleashed into the pro ranks under the modified moniker of Sammy Mandell. Mandell, a softly spoken and cheerful man who possessed film star looks was a clean-living family man, teetotaler and non-smoker who attended church every Sunday. Mandell left boxing with his handsome features intact. In retirement Mandell was involved in boxing promotions and flirted with boxing management, handling rated fighter Billy Celebron. He later worked as a bank security guard until he suffered a stroke. He died in Oak Park, Illinois on November 7, 1967.

* Some record books state that Mandell was born in Rockford, Illinois; others cite Piana dei Greci, which has since been renamed Piana degli Albanesi. Occasionally Mandell's surname appears as Mandella but a genealogy trace reveals that no such surname exists in the Sicilian town.

JOE DUNDEE [SALVATORE LAZZARA]*
WORLD WELTERWEIGHT CHAMPION 1927–29

On June 3, 1927 Baltimore's Joe Dundee became the first Italian American to capture the world welterweight title when he decisively outpointed Pete Latzo over fifteen rounds at the Polo Grounds, New York before 30,000 fans. He had won ten rounds with one even. In the mid-twenties, Dundee established a fearsome reputation in the 147-pound class but repeated overtures to welterweight champion Mickey Walker fell on deaf ears as Walker preferred easier paydays. Dundee, a rugged two-fisted box-fighter, was an effective counter-punching scorer. His left hook was not wasteful, and he was careful and opportunistic in method.

In March 1926, Dundee was the world's outstanding welterweight following his fifth-round knockout of Tommy Freeman, future welterweight champion. This was further supported by a stunning sequence of results over Sailor Friedman, Johnny Clinton, Nate Goldman, Sid Barbarian, Louis Vicentini, Pinky Mitchell, Jack McVey, Joe Simonich and Jimmy Jones. Dundee risked it all for a date with the champ but Walker ignored him and eventually lost his crown to Pete Latzo, who in turn risked it against Willie Harmon. Dundee was frozen out of the title picture. Lesser men would have folded but not Dundee. He outpointed world-rated George Levine and Willie Harmon. With no title in sight, in June 1926 Walker was matched against Dundee in a title eliminator. In what was a savagely contested battle, Dundee took Walker's scalp, stopping him in the eighth round. Bizarrely, the vanquished Walker marched on to become world champion again, this time as a middleweight, with Dundee left in the cold.

One year and seven fights later Dundee eventually got his title shot. As champion, Dundee wanted to savor his moment of glory. When he did not immediately defend his crown he attracted vehement press criticism for not being a fighting champion and meeting the best. He was accused of journeying from town to town hand-picking challengers and using imaginative excuses to avoid boxing commission-appointed challengers. In November 1927, Dundee failed to appear in a first title defense against Ace Hudkins in Los Angeles. Dundee argued he did not receive the guaranteed $60,000 purse from the promoter Dick Donald; 17,000 fans gathered and sections of ringside seats were smashed. A riot was only averted when police reinforcements were called to the scene to quell further trouble. The bout was declared a no contest and the NYSAC suspended Dundee.

In 1928, Dundee reportedly made $100,000 in purse money without facing a contender at title weight, preferring catchweight contests, and following a stoppage loss to Young Jack Thompson, the National Boxing Association stripped him of his welterweight title and matched Thompson with Jackie Fields for their title. Officially, however, Dundee was still champion and it wasn't until July 25, 1929 that Fields dethroned him in Detroit, with Dundee delivering a foul blow in the second round. He boxed until 1931, ending a twelve-year career with 123 bouts, 86 wins, 11 draws, 20 losses, 4 no decisions and 2 no contests.

Dundee was born Salvatore Lazzara on August 16, 1903 in Palermo Sicily and his family moved to Baltimore when he was two years old. They settled in the Belair Market section of the city, where Dundee's father was a wholesale fruit dealer. Dundee never boxed as an amateur but on the back of his street-fighting reputation turned professional as a flyweight in 1919. He bulked up and boxed his way through the higher weight classes. Joe was one of four brothers. Vince became a world middleweight champion and Battling Dundee was a flyweight. In retirement Dundee worked in a shipyard through the Second World War. He later owned a tavern in Baltimore and also worked as a bartender. Dundee died on March 31, 1982.

* Record books state Dundee's family name as Lazzaro and say he was born in Rome. His first name is sometimes seen as Samuel. Dundee's Grandson Robert Lazzara confirmed the boxer's first name is Salvatore and the family name is Lazzara.

BUSHY GRAHAM [ANGELO GERACI]
WORLD (NYSAC) BANTAMWEIGHT CHAMPION 1928–29

Bushy Graham was a classy bantamweight from the Italian enclave of Utica, New York. In a professional career, which began in 1922 and spanned fourteen years, Graham beat five world champions—Abe Goldstein, Bud Taylor, Frankie Genaro, Izzy Schwartz and Johnny Jadick—and scored draws with titleholders Freddie Miller and Leo Rodak. On May 23, 1928 Graham crowned his moment of glory by skillfully outpointing Izzy Schwartz over fifteen rounds at Ebbets Field, New York before 14,000 to win the NYSAC recognized world title. Schwartz was the flyweight champion and despite taking an early lead was hauled back by Graham. He picked up the pace, handing Schwartz a real pummeling in the closing rounds of the contest as the weight advantage enjoyed by Graham as well as the heavier punching began to tell. Graham floored Schwartz for a nine count in the fourteenth round but the brave Jewish boxer survived the hammering, finishing the contest on his feet.

Graham was a showboater; flashy and stylish, he used his exceptional mobility around the ring to outsmart his rivals. Against Bud Taylor, foremost bantamweight contender, Graham boxed rings around him over the full distance. His usual routine consisted of bounding and prancing around the ring as if on loaded springs. Graham was able to slip in and out of the danger zone and earned the sobriquet the "Utica Dancing Master." His tireless energy, agility and sterling boxing ability made him a dangerous opponent for all the leading bantamweights. He was a good two-fisted fighter who could unleash a tirade of blows with startling speed, but his lack of punching power prevented him from finishing an opponent when on top. Graham was very active for five years and justified his credentials as the number one challenger to Charley Phil Rosenberg's bantamweight title by defeating notables Tommy Ryan, Frankie Genaro, Pete Zivic, Abe Goldstein, Bud Taylor, Joe Ryder, Davey Abad, Chick Suggs and Young Montreal. He was given a shot at Rosenberg's crown on February 4, 1927. At the weigh-in Rosenberg was found to be four-and-a-half pounds over the 118-pound limit and the title was declared vacant. Despite the weight infringement, the fight went ahead, with Graham losing on points over fifteen rounds. Graham believed he should have been made champion at the scales but it later transpired that the fighters' managers had come to a secret agreement about the result. Graham received a one-year suspension from the sport, as did Rosenberg and the fight managers.

After the enforced lay-off Rosenberg returned as a featherweight, the bantamweight division became fractured and a number of title claimants appeared between 1927 and 1931. Graham was recognized by the NYSAC as bantamweight champion. By August 1929 the Pennsylvania Athletic Commission also considered Graham their world champion. He never defended his 118-pound title and moved up to the featherweight division where he boxed with some success. In 1932 he lost a ten-round bout on points to Tommy Paul in an elimination tournament sanctioned by the NBA to find a successor to Battling Battalino as the new featherweight champion. After the bout he did not fight again for three years. He returned and boxed on for one more year and was good enough to hold future NBA featherweight champion Leo Rodak to a ten-round draw before retiring in November 1936. He finished with a career record of 127 fights, 101 wins, 6 draws and 14 losses.

Graham was born Angelo Geraci in Utica, New York on June 18, 1905 to parents hailing from the Calabria region, Southern Italy. Old boxing record books incorrectly state that Graham was born in Italy in 1903. Yet it has long been known that Graham told a mistruth in order to obtain a professional boxing license at age seventeen. He was too young under the rules to obtain a permit so he told the New York boxing commission that he had been born in 1903. Graham retired with $40,000 in savings as well as owning two buildings in Utica. He ran a car sales business and kept an interest in boxing by training promising youngsters. He was also a successful chicken farmer. Graham died on August 5, 1982.

TONY CANZONERI
WORLD FEATHERWEIGHT CHAMPION 1928
WORLD LIGHTWEIGHT CHAMPION 1930–33, 1935–36
WORLD JUNIOR-WELTERWEIGHT CHAMPION 1931–32, 1933

At a time when titleholders were savagely attacked by newspapers for not upholding the standards expected of venerable fighting champions by defending their belts against ranked contenders and earning the right to be a real drawing card, up popped Tony Canzoneri, the "perfect fighter." In a professional career spanning fifteen years Canzoneri won three world titles at different weights—featherweight, lightweight and junior-welterweight— and became boxing's third three-division champion. In all Canzoneri appeared in twenty-one world title fights across four divisions from 118 pounds right through to the 140-pound weight class. He met eighteen world champions and six Hall of Famers between 1925 and 1939 winning 143 of his 175 fights.

Canzoneri enjoyed unparalleled popularity and earning capacity and over his career took more than $500,000 in purse money. He was the embodiment of fearlessness and indomitable fighting spirit and his belief never wavered in the face of adversity, questionable refereeing or judges' decisions. In March 1927, Canzoneri got his first taste of title action when his bout with bantamweight champ Bud Taylor was mysteriously declared a draw when most onlookers felt Canzoneri had done enough to win. Three months later they met again and although Canzoneri dropped the decision to Taylor this did not diminish his ambitions. It acted as a spur. In October 1927 the NYSAC version of the featherweight title was up for grabs and facing Canzoneri was the much-loved Johnny Dundee. The youthful Canzoneri triumphed over Dundee's guile and experience, taking a fifteen-round decision at Madison Square Garden. In February 1928, he won the unified featherweight crown by outscoring Benny Bass over fifteen rounds in what ringside veterans deemed to be one of the greatest featherweight battles in boxing history.

Seven months later Canzoneri dropped a stirring fifteen-rounder to Frenchman Andre Routis. He moved up a weight and in August 1929 tried to wrest the lightweight title from Sammy Mandell but lost a close ten-round decision. In November 1930 he conquered Al Singer, Mandell's conqueror, in sixty-six seconds, the fastest ever knockout in a world lightweight title fight. Three months later he added the junior-welterweight crown by knocking out Jackie "Kid" Berg in three rounds. In November 1931, Canzoneri held onto his title by convincingly outpointing Kid Chocolate with a tireless and relentless offensive display. Canzoneri floored the cagey Cuban in the fourth and subjected him to the most severe body drubbing the Cuban had ever experienced.

By the start of 1932 Canzoneri was generally recognized as the best pound-for-pound fighter in the world. After three defenses of the junior-welterweight crown Johnny Jadick outpointed him over ten rounds to win the title in Philadelphia in January 1932. In May 1933 Canzoneri regained the junior welterweight title from the Mexican Battling Shaw. Following two lightweight title defenses he succumbed to Barney Ross over ten rounds in Chicago. He tried to regain his title at the Polo Grounds, New York but was on the wrong side of a fifteen-round split points decision to Ross. In November 1933, Canzoneri again met up with Kid Chocolate and this time after two minutes and thirty seconds of the second round managed the unthinkable, inflicting upon the Cuban his first knockout loss in 211 contests, amateur and professional combined.

In 1934 Canzoneri and Barney Ross were jointly voted *Ring Magazine* Fighter of the Year. When Ross vacated the title in April 1935 Canzoneri fought Lou Ambers in an all-Italian title match. He made history by becoming the first man to win the lightweight title twice when he outpointed Ambers at Madison Square Garden in New York. After one defense he lost his title to Ambers and the new champion also won the rubber match between them in May 1937 by a unanimous decision. This signaled the end of Canzoneri's championship ambitions. He boxed until November 1939, and following his first and only career knockout at the hands of Al "Bummy" Davis he announced his retirement.

Canzoneri was a clever and adaptable boxer. He fought belligerently at close quarters and his hard hitting was a useful antidote in the fire of battle. He was just as comfortable using his superior boxing technique and quick reflexes to cope with durable sluggers. His style was very much his own. He kept his guard down and offered his face as a target. Timing was everything and he knew when to withdraw and seize a chance when it presented itself. Benny Leonard described Canzoneri's uniqueness: "Don't be an imitation of a man like Canzoneri, at least not a bad imitation. His tricks will probably die with him. Some of them will remain but most will vanish."[3] Canzoneri was inducted into the Boxing Hall of Fame in 1956 and into the International Boxing Hall of Fame in 1990.

Canzoneri was born on November 6, 1908 in Slidell, Louisiana, the son of Sicilian immigrants. He was one of six children. He grew up on the streets of New Orleans working as a shoeshine boy and engaging in street fights. His older brother Joe was an amateur boxer and Tony attended the gym with him before hooking up with Pete Herman, who trained him for a period before leaving for New York. As an amateur, Canzoneri won three bantamweight titles in 1924: metropolitan, junior national, and the New York amateur championships. On July 18, 1925 Canzoneri made his professional debut with a stunning one-round knockout. He retired from boxing financially secure and for a time he remained in the limelight by appearing on Broadway shows as an actor, but later through a series of bad investments lost his money. On December 10, 1959, Canzoneri's body was discovered in his hotel room two days after dying of natural causes.

WILLIE LA MORTE
WORLD (NYSAC) FLYWEIGHT CLAIMANT 1929–30

Willie La Morte claimed the world flyweight championship at a time when there was a cluster of formidable fighters in the 112-pound class. By the late twenties the flyweight division had become fragmented and this situation was further complicated by the sudden retirement of undisputed champion Fidel La Barba, which resulted in a number of title claimants pitching for honors. The Californian boxing commission recognized Johnny McCoy and in Great Britain Johnny Hill was their titleholder in 1928–29. The NBA first recognized Albert Belanger in 1927–28, then Frankie Genaro in 1928–29 and Emile Pladner in 1929 and Genaro again in 1929–31. The New York State boxing commission accepted Izzy Schwartz as champion between 1927–29 with Midget Wolgast, Philadelphia's incumbent, picking up the mantle between 1930 and 1935.

Between the reigns of Schwartz and Wolgast, Brooklyn-born Willie La Morte entered the frame and established his claim to the highly contested weight class by outpointing Schwartz over fifteen rounds on August 22, 1929 at Dreamland Park, Newark, New Jersey before 7,500 ecstatic fans. On winning the bout La Morte claimed the world title—at least the New York version of it. Schwartz had got off to a slow start but from the fifth round on he became more aggressive, but La Morte weathered the storm and came back strongly. His best chance of a stoppage came in the ninth and tenth rounds when Schwartz was rocking from his long right swings. The Jewish American fighter came back again and handed La Morte a severe drubbing in the thirteenth, his best round, but it was to no avail as La Morte's industry throughout the contest ensured he had piled up sufficient points to win the verdict. On October 3, 1929, a rematch between the two foes was again staged in Newark. La Morte demonstrated that the first time was no fluke by repeating the feat over the brilliant Schwartz and subsequently strengthened his world title claim. Although the rematch was advertised as a world title fight and has subsequently been recorded in record books as a championship contest, the New York boxing commission refused to recognize La Morte as champion when it emerged that both boxers were handled by the same manager. This was a clear breach of commission rules and the authority proceeded to sign eight contenders to a flyweight elimination tournament to begin the following month. Nevertheless the two victories over Schwartz raised La Morte's profile. Schwartz was an outstanding performer and since the introduction of a world ranking system in 1924 he was the most consistent flyweight having maintained a world top ten ranking in every year except for 1929.

Unperturbed by the political infighting outside the ring, La Morte defended his claim on November 21, 1929 by knocking out Frisco Grande, the world-ranked Filipino, in seven rounds in Paterson, New Jersey. This infuriated the New York boxing commission, who stated that La Morte had forfeited New York recognition in his failure to meet Midget Wolgast. Matters were put to rest when La Morte agreed to meet Wolgast, the number one contender. They met on May 16, 1930, at Madison Square Garden, New York. At the end of the fifth round in a fight that was all one-way traffic for Wolgast, La Morte staggered back to his corner and suddenly collapsed, striking his head on the canvas before a stunned 5,096 crowd. Following an examination by the NYSAC doctor William Walker it transpired that La Morte had suffered a heart spasm. La Morte had been outfought and outscored by Wolgast, who would go on to dominate the 112-pound class for the next five years. For La Morte it virtually signaled the end of his career. Three months later he was back losing an unpopular decision to Frankie Genaro, the reigning NBA and IBU champion, in Newark.

In 1931 La Morte called it a day. He retired with a professional record of 56 bouts, 37 wins, 4 draws, 9 losses, 6 no decisions and 3 no contests. In retirement he was employed by the Passaic Valley Sewer Commissioner. He died in Monmouth, New Jersey on February 6, 1990.

BATTLING BATTALINO [CHRISTOPHER BATTAGLINI]
WORLD FEATHERWEIGHT CHAMPION 1929–32

Battling Battalino was a whirlwind of fistic fury and boxed as if his life depended on it. In the summer of 1929 the rugged fighter with tattooed forearms and a menacing grimace made his mark with a stunning non-title ten-round points win over bantamweight champion Panama Al Brown. A professional for less than two years and having exclusively boxed in the state territories of Connecticut and Massachusetts, Battalino seized his opportunity in September 1929 when he outpointed Frenchman Andre Routis, the world featherweight champion, over fifteen rounds in his hometown of Hartford.

Battalino boasted the distinction of being the first unknown to go from provincial obscurity to worldwide prominence overnight. After a successful defense of the title against Ignacio Fernandez he was matched with Kid Chocolate on December 12, 1930. With Battalino appearing at Madison Square Garden, New York for the first time he started nervously, suffering an eight count in the opening round. Battalino refused to wilt and launched into the Cuban with a frenzied onslaught, displaying the raw courage and recklessness which became synonymous with his fights. By the end of the fifteenth round Battalino's persistent body attacks had earned him a unanimous points decision. Battalino eloquently recalled the battle: "The first round, the first punch, he dropped me, caught me cold, down I went. But when I got up I chased him back to Cuba. I punched the shit right out of his belly."[4] In his next title defense on May 22, 1931, the pugnacious Battalino tore recklessly into Fidel La Barba, who had little time to exhibit his incomparable boxing class, so busy was he on the defense. Battalino clinched a fifteen-round win in New York. He developed a splendid knack of nullifying boxing science and cleverness by staying at close quarters and firing away his best shots at an opponent.

Battalino had been a busy and successful champion, defending his title five times in twelve months against world-class opposition like Kid Chocolate, Fidel La Barba, Freddie Miller, Eddie Shea and Earl Mastro. He ended 1931 by halting contender Bushy Graham's world title aspirations in one round and stopping Al Singer, former lightweight champion, in two rounds. In January 1932 things went into reverse for Battalino when he was involved in a farcical title fight with Freddie Miller in Cincinnati Ohio. With Battalino barely disguising his lack of appetite for the fight, the referee called it a no contest after three rounds. Battalino was fined five thousand dollars. Three months later he relinquished his title, which Miller later won. Battalino revealed that he was supposed to lose the fight so that the racketeers could profit on the outcome.

Battalino could no longer make the 126-pound weight. He boxed with junior-lightweights with varying success but hand injuries, which dogged the fighter throughout his career, began to take their toll. He fought twice in 1933, six times in 1934, remained inactive in 1935 and came back for six more bouts in 1936. He stayed out of boxing for three years and resumed again in 1939 before eventually retiring in January 1940. Battalino finished with a ring record of 88 fights, 58 wins, 3 draws and 26 losses and 1 no contest and was stopped only once.

Battalino was born in Hartford, Connecticut on February 18, 1908 to Carmine and Emilia Battaglini. His penchant for brawling got him into trouble early on. He quit school after the fifth grade to work in a tobacco factory, where he was fired after six weeks for fighting. Self-professed as "tough, rough and hungry," Battalino embarked upon an amateur boxing career and in 59 bouts he knocked out 46 opponents, winning the Connecticut State featherweight title twice and the National AAU featherweight title in 1927. He was called up into the 1928 Olympic boxing team but turned professional instead. Although amateur rules stipulated that fighting for money was illegal Battalino was a real drawing card and in a three-fight series promoters paid him $1,500. He received $600 for his first pro fight and later made $72,000 in 1930 alone. In retirement Battalino worked as a construction laborer. He died at Hartford Hospital on July 25, 1977, leaving behind a wife and two daughters.

1930–39
MIDGET WOLGAST [JOSEPH ROBERT LOSCALZO]
WORLD (NYSAC) FLYWEIGHT CLAIMANT 1930–35

Between 1930 and 1935 South Philadelphia's Midget Wolgast consolidated his status as the best flyweight in the world. The naturally gifted boxer with dazzling hand speed and tremendous dexterity of movement befuddled opponents and entertained fight crowds nationally earning him the sobriquet of "Greased Lightning." He was the fastest boxer in the world and his overwhelming superiority left opponents struggling to land a punch as they were picked off as Wolgast darted in and out, flashing in speedy left hands and left hooks to the body. He had the uncanny habit of making world champions, contenders and headliners alike look like novices. Many years later Philadelphia promoter Jimmy Toppi Junior recalled: "Wolgast was a terrific boxer, very small but as fast as lightning. He was quick if not quicker than Willie Pep." Fight trainer Willie O'Neil enthused:

He was so fast and clever nobody could hit him if Midge didn't want them to. He had moves I've never seen before or since. Willie Pep was a clever kid but if you'd seen Midget Wolgast you'd have to forget Pep.[5]

His achievements were remarkable considering Wolgast's playboy lifestyle and undisciplined attitude to training. The lack of flyweight competition during the thirties often found Wolgast meeting men above his weight and the idea of shedding pounds to make the stipulated championship weight limit didn't sit terribly well with him. He only made cameo appearances at the gym, preferring life in the fast lane, and his sexual exploits and alcohol consumption became legendary. Among his many dalliances he courted Hollywood actress Mae West.

Despite the nocturnal distractions, boxing is what made Wolgast famous and on March 21, 1930 he won the New York version of the title by outpointing Black Bill of Cuba. He defended the title by stopping Willie La Morte in five rounds. He drew with Frankie Genaro and outpointed Ruby Bradley over fifteen rounds. He then embarked on a nationwide and international tour where he showcased his skills in California and Hawaii. He then went to Canada before sailing across the Atlantic, appearing in England and in France before returning to the United States. Wolgast lost his NYSAC title on September 16, 1935 when he was outpointed by Filipino boxer Small Montana over fifteen rounds.

His blatant disregard of training eventually caught up with Wolgast as the added pounds blunted his sharp boxing technique. He continued to box in good company until March 1940, when Wolgast announced his retirement. Wolgast finished with a career record of 130 wins, 16 draws and 36 losses and 20 no decisions. Between 1928 and 1934, Wolgast featured in the *Ring Magazine* world top ten ratings, heading the annual rankings four times. He was enshrined in the International Boxing Hall of Fame in 2001.

Wolgast was born Joseph Robert Loscalzo on July 18, 1910 in the Italian enclave of South Philadelphia and was the eldest son of Michael and Lena. He was only fifteen when he turned professional and took his ring moniker from another Italian boxer, Bobby Wolgast (Giordano), a popular flyweight boxer from the same neighborhood, who had beaten the great Pancho Villa when Midget was starting out. Within two years of turning pro Wolgast had developed into a headliner, earning $200 for a ten-round main event. In retirement Wolgast became a successful trainer, steered lightweight contender Eddie Giosa and briefly showed future middleweight champion Joey Giardello the ropes. He also worked as a bartender and fittingly died in a Philadelphia bar on October 19, 1955.

TOMMY PAUL [GAETANO ALFONSO PAPA]
WORLD (NBA) FEATHERWEIGHT CHAMPION 1932–33

"Buffalo's Tiny Tiger" Tommy Paul rolled off Buffalo's seemingly endless production line of Italian American boxing stars to make it to the top. On May 26, 1932, Paul was crowned world featherweight champion, winning nearly every round against Johnny Pena in their fifteen-rounder staged in Detroit, Michigan. In one of the most competitive eras in the 126-pound division the passage to the top was an arduous one. In a bid to find a successor to Battling Battalino, who had outgrown the featherweight division, the NBA (National Boxing Association) organized an eight-man tournament and the upshot of this was that Paul was the last man standing after hostilities ended. Paul secured his passage to the final by eliminating Utica's skillful Bushy Graham over ten rounds and then with a semi-final victory over Cleveland's Frankie Wallace via the same route.

Paul was a combination boxer-fighter with an uncanny knack of adjusting to his opponent's style. He was blessed with courage, boldness and exceptional stamina and admirers of Paul described him as a miniature [Stanley] Ketchel, always alert and up for the challenge. He possessed a good defensive blocking technique and although not a devastating hitter he carried a hurtful wallop and was able to stop twenty-five of his opponents over a nine-year career. Paul's reign as featherweight champion lasted eight months as he was dispossessed of his title on a split decision over ten rounds by Freddie Miller in Chicago. Miller went on to clean up the division and win undisputed recognition. Despite a top ten rating over the next two years Paul was deprived of another title shot he so badly wanted.

An indifferent sequence of results followed in 1934 and 1935 and a year later Paul hung up his gloves. He retired with a record of 80 wins, 29 losses and 10 draws. In all Paul fought eleven world champions and six Hall of Famers with a record of nine victories, ten losses and four draws against them. Paul was rated in the world's top ten from 1929–34.

Paul was born Gaetano Alfonso Papa on March 4, 1909, in Buffalo's Old Waterfront District, the town's Little Italy. His parents came to the United States from Southern Italy and hailed from the village of San Fele in the province of Potenza, Basilicata. Paul was one of twelve children. His father Tony had been a boxer and his two eldest brothers Al and Mickey were also involved in the sport. Paul's interest in boxing started early and at seventeen years old Paul showed up at Jack Singer's gymnasium on Buffalo's East Side in the Polish colony of the city. He urged Singer to give him a try-out. The manager reluctantly agreed and when the youngster was put through his paces Singer came to the conclusion that Paul was a sure-fire winner. After a distinguished amateur career in which he won three titles in three months in 1927—Niagara District Bantamweight Championship, United States National AAU Championship in Boston and the Empire State Amateur Championship at Madison Square Garden—Paul turned pro. He made his debut in the paid ranks with a four-round knockout over Fred Griffiths and by the time he captured the world crown five years later he had developed into a major box office attraction. In retirement Paul worked and trained boxers in Buffalo. He also owned a dry cleaning shop. Paul died on April 28, 1991.

SAMMY FULLER [SABINO FERULLO]
WORLD JUNIOR-WELTERWEIGHT CLAIMANT 1932

Sammy Fuller, "Boston's Pride of Little Italy," was one of a galaxy of Italian American lightweights campaigning during the twenties and thirties. Lesser known than his more illustrious counterparts Canzoneri, Petrolle and Ambers, Fuller scaled the heights on May 20, 1932, when he laid claim to the world junior-welterweight title following a twelve-round points victory over Jackie "Kid" Berg in New York. A month earlier Fuller had met Berg and was unfortunate to have walked away with only a draw. So impressed were the New York patrons that a rematch was ordered. With the support of *Ring Magazine* the bout took on the significance of a world title fight. Berg continued to claim the 140-pound belt and while both men weighed inside the limit the light-welterweight title was put at risk. The second time around Fuller made sure. Game, rugged and cagey, Fuller used his tremendous upper body strength to his advantage and his effective body punching at close quarters earned him the title, becoming Boston's first Italian world boxing champion.

Fuller's rise to the top was no accident. He had turned professional in 1924 and had become a popular drawing card in his hometown having notched up victories over world ranked African Americans Chick Suggs and Bruce Flowers, tough Carl Tremaine, veteran "Red" Chapman and iron man Johnny Farr. His all-action style had earned him the plaudits of both fans and boxing writers and he was seen as a pocket-sized Harry Greb; his exploits in Massachusetts reverberated down to New York. In February 1931, the *Boston Herald* proclaimed Fuller to be the most popular fighter around and drew comparisons with the great Johnny Dundee. A month later, Fuller took a decisive ten-round non-title victory over Tony Canzoneri before 10,000 fans in Boston. He bobbed and weaved on the inside, piercing Canzoneri's guard at will and unleashing heavy body attacks. Fuller showed ability and style worthy of a crack at Canzoneri's title but the superlative champion, not normally shy of giving rivals a chance, declined another match.

In February 1932 Fuller took on deadly puncher Ray Miller in New York and matched Miller punch for punch. He was the first to execute the delivery and always the last to leave a fistic exchange, walking away with a ten-round points victory. Between March and May, Fuller proved a big hit in Madison Square Garden as he appeared in the arena three times in six weeks. Firstly he knocked out Cleveland's Billy Wallace in seven rounds and then met Jackie "Kid" Berg in two action-packed encounters. A knockout loss to big hitter Jimmy McLarnin and two punishing duels with Billy Petrolle in 1933, one ending in a draw and the other a points defeat, were followed by an unsuccessful attempt to wrest the undisputed junior-welterweight title from Barney Ross.

This signaled a gradual decline in fortunes for the Bostonian. In 1934 he was still good enough to score important victories against headliners Harry Carlton, Eddie Cool and Bobby Pacho as well as a four-round knockout over Johnny Jadick, former world champion. He boxed one bout in 1935 and remained inactive in 1936, and after three winning bouts in 1937 stayed retired for five years before making an ill-advised comeback in 1943. After three more bouts, his last two ending in knockout defeats, he retired.

In a professional career that began in 1924 and ended in 1943 Fuller fought in 74 contests, scoring 53 wins, 4 draws and 17 losses. Fuller was born Sabino Ferullo on June 10, 1906 in Boston's North End district to Neapolitan parents. After graduating from high school Fuller turned to boxing. He took a job as a shoeshine boy in one of the numerous parlors in the city and for one year he skipped food during his lunch hour just to attend the nearby gym and go through some moves and routines. He enlisted as an amateur and after several contests turned professional as a bantamweight under the management of Rip Valenti. He went on to fight as a featherweight, moving up to lightweight and then to the 140-pound division. He died in Revere, Massachusetts on May 30, 1979.

GEORGE NICHOLS [PHILLIP JOHN NICOLOSI]
WORLD (NBA) LIGHT-HEAVYWEIGHT CLAIMANT 1932

George Nichols, a 100-1 underdog, found himself on top of the light-heavyweight pile in March 1932 following a mini-tournament organized by the NBA to find a successor to Maxie Rosenbloom. Nichols, a good workmanlike boxer, met overwhelming favorite Dave Maier of Milwaukee in the final of the NBA-staged competition involving 32 fighters. Nichols outgunned and outslugged Maier to capture the vacant title on a split points decision over ten rounds before 10,000 fans in Chicago.

Ohio-born Nichols boxed out of Buffalo under the stewardship of boxing impresario Jack Singer and wins over a pair of African American light-heavyweight contenders, Jack McVey and Billy Jones, as well as Don Petrin, Charley Belanger and Lou Scozza propelled Nichols into the spotlight. In truth the 175-pound division was thrown into chaos in the middle to late twenties. Firstly Jack Delaney vacated the title and moved up to the heavyweights. The next champion, Tommy Loughran, followed suit when he beat Mike McTigue and after Loughran's departure the NYSAC arranged an eliminator competition. Buffalo Irishman Jimmy Slattery narrowly edged Lou Scozza to win the final. The trouble was that the NBA didn't recognize Slattery as their champion and opted to stage their own tournament. This is when the rugged Nichols appeared on the scene and was able to seize his opportunity. Two-and-a-half months into his reign Nichols was decisively beaten by arch rival Lou Scozza, who was recognized in some quarters as the NBA champion, even though official records state that Nichols never officially defended his NBA title. Reports of a knee injury as well as five non-title losses prompted the NBA to strip Nichols of his title in December 1932.

Nichols kept in good company throughout his twelve-year career. He fought Jack McVey three times, Lou Scozza four times, John Henry Lewis twice and a procession of world-ranked opponents. Most of Nichols's victories came via points decisions. He managed twenty-four knockouts. With his mind elsewhere and his best days behind him Nichols suffered a one-round knockout defeat to headliner Ralph De John in October 1937. He went into semi-retirement for eighteen months. He returned in April 1939 and was promptly dispatched in two rounds by former middleweight champion Fred Apostoli and this time retired for good. Nichols finished with a career record of 108 bouts, 71 wins, 10 draws and 26 losses and 1 no decision.

Nichols was born Phillip John Nicolosi on July 9, 1908 in Sandusky, Ohio to native Italian parents. He began professional boxing aged fifteen, and for the first two years boxed in Sandusky. He moved to Buffalo in December 1925 and joined Jack Singer's stable. In April 1935, Nichols made headlines of a different kind, this time in the gossip columns of national newspapers following revelations that he had secretly married Katherine Kit Klein, Olympic and world speed-skating champion two years earlier. The celebrity sporting couple appeared in a boxing ring, sparring for fun, and as a prank got married in 1933 in Ripley, New York after attending a late-night party. Klein later annulled the marriage to Nichols and remarried.

LOU SCOZZA [LUIGI SCOZZARO]
WORLD LIGHT-HEAVYWEIGHT CLAIMANT 1932

Unheralded Lou Scozza twice claimed the world light heavyweight title. Ask any boxing fan about the Buffalo boxer and the chances are they will draw a blank. Scozza was little known outside of New York State. Yet this industrious and hard-punching combination boxer-cum-fighter fought the best light heavyweights in circulation and rose to prominence when Tommy Loughran relinquished his 175-pound title to compete as a heavyweight. The NYSAC officially sanctioned a tournament designed to find a successor to Loughran. Impressive wins against world-rated Maxie Rosenbloom, Yale Okun, Tiger Payne, Osk Till and George Courtney thrust Scozza into the final of the tournament.

On February 10, 1930, he met fellow Buffalonian Irishman Jimmy Slattery, the NBA champion for undisputed recognition. For Scozza this was his big chance. His camp had tried to entice Slattery into the ring for two years with a ten thousand dollar offer proving fruitless. Over 10,000 fans gathered in Buffalo to see a riveting contest. Hugh Shannon, writing in *Ring Magazine*, declared Slattery "a most fortunate young man. Scozza chased him for fifteen rounds and almost knocked him out in the thirteenth when he pounded the First Ward Irishman for keeps, the bell saving Slattery from a complete knockout." Scozza had saved his best work till the last three rounds with the Irishman managing to hold on desperately in the face of devastating onslaughts. Slattery had outmaneuvered Scozza up to the ninth round. Judge Arthur Donovan, one of the most knowledgeable officials in boxing, called the scrap a draw. Ultimately Scozza was on the receiving end of a split decision. Scozza felt he had "been robbed" and made a claim for the title, which was not taken seriously.

Following wins over contenders Larry Johnson, Charley Belanger, Battling Bozo and Tony Shucco, Scozza again claimed the world title in May 1932 when he outpointed fellow George Nichols, the champion. Although some record books state that Nichols never officially defended the NBA crown, others, including late British historians Gilbert Odd and Harry Mullan, agreed that Scozza had a legitimate title claim based upon the fact that he beat the newly crowned champion. Two months later, in July 1932 Scozza renewed his rivalry with old foe Maxie Rosenbloom in a title match in Buffalo under the auspices of the NYSAC. Scozza came within one second of consolidating his NBA claim with undisputed title recognition, when he sent a crushing right to Rosenbloom's jaw in the fourteenth round, dropping him for a nine count. Rosenbloom survived and managed to keep the remainder of the bout at long range to score a fifteen-round points win.

Between 1929 and 1932 Scozza occupied a top ten rating for four consecutive years. He retired in 1934 with a career record of 118 fights, winning 81, with 9 draws and 28 losses. During his career he met world champions Maxie Rosenbloom six times, George Nichols four times, James Braddock, Mike McTigue, John Henry Lewis and Jimmy Slattery and he was never stopped.

Scozza was born Luigi Scozzaro on April 15, 1903 in Buffalo, New York. He worked in the laundry business, washing linen before turning professional in 1925. He joined forces with Bert Finch and instantly became a big drawing card in Buffalo but he remained a virtual unknown outside the state, never quite attracting the interest of a big promoter to spread the word. After boxing he became a successful boxing referee. Scozza died on November 30, 1967.

YOUNG CORBETT III [RAFFAELE CAPOBIANCO GIORDANO]*
WORLD WELTERWEIGHT CHAMPION 1933

The old adage that patience is a virtue is certainly apt when describing the career of Young Corbett III. For over three years this tough southpaw boxer known as the "Fresno Bee" waited in the wings as the most obvious title contender, but champion Jackie Fields, who dropped a bristling non-title ten-round decision to Young Corbett III in February 1930, went to great lengths to avoid the durable Italian. Young Corbett III rattled off an impressive sequence of victories against past and future world champions and ranked contenders, notching three wins and one draw against Young Jack Thompson. He was a knockout winner over Eddie Roberts and Babe Anderson and outpointed Jack Zivic, Joe Glick and Ceferino Garcia twice. Between 1926 and 1932, Young Corbett III lost only once, to world-rated Sergeant Sammy Baker, an opponent he had previously outpointed.

The clamor for a world title shot grew ever louder. As outside pressure mounted on Fields, the San Francisco Jew finally agreed to a world title match-up. On the February 22, 1933, Young Corbett III outpointed Fields over ten rounds to win the world 147-pound title before 15,000 fans in San Francisco. The Italian with a slashing choppy style beat the best offensive boxer by piling up the points in the early rounds to become California's first Italian American world boxing champion. Unfortunately for Young Corbett III his title reign lasted just three months, before losing to Hall of Famer Jimmy McLarnin. At this point he moved up to the middleweight division, where he gave some of his best performances, beating Gus Lesnevich, future light-heavyweight king, Fred Apostoli, future middleweight champion, and Hall of Famers Billy Conn and Mickey Walker.

At 33, Young Corbett III got a second stab at a world title. On November 18, 1938, he met fearsome Fred Apostoli for a second time and was stopped in eight exciting stanzas. Four fights later Young Corbett III brought the curtain down on a splendid career, finishing with a record of 151 bouts, 123 wins, 17 draws and 11 losses, registering 33 knockouts. Most of Young Corbett III's fights were staged in his hometown of Fresno or San Francisco, where he became a huge favorite, and in a twenty-one-year career he only boxed five times outside the western state. In 1984 a life-sized six-foot bronze statue of him was erected in front of the convention center in Fresno. He was inducted into the International Boxing Hall of Fame in 2004.

Young Corbett III was born Raffaele Capobianco Giordano on May 27, 1905 in Rionero in Vulture in the province of Potenza, Basilicata, Southern Italy. His parents arrived in the United States and made Pittsburgh their home. In 1909, they transferred to Fresno and as a child he helped his parents pick grapes in the San Joaquin Valley. He received a good high school education but soon turned to boxing. He entered the *Fresno Herald* newspaper boy tournament and won the 110-pound category. One Christmas his cousin Ralph Manfredo sold him the idea of fighting for money and in October 1919 he turned professional, aged just fourteen. Corbett was initially guided by Manfredo, who later handed the reins to Larry White. In retirement Young Corbett III opened and managed a bar in Fresno. In 1940 he was involved in a serious car accident that left him with head injuries. He made a partial recovery and in later years was seen working as a pin boy in a bowling alley. He died in Auberry, Fresno on July 20, 1993.

* Some record books incorrectly list Corbett's family surname as Capobianca and state that he was born in Naples, Italy.

VINCE DUNDEE [VINCENZO LAZZARA]
WORLD (NYSAC) MIDDLEWEIGHT CHAMPION 1933–34

There was a perception that Vince Dundee was a "lucky fighter" and well connected, but the facts tell a different story. Firstly, Dundee battled spiritedly for ten years before getting any real recognition and had fought one hundred twenty times before he was awarded a title shot. He started in four and six-rounders in Baltimore in insalubrious surroundings before establishing a base in Newark, New Jersey. He went forty fights before losing his first contest to ranked contender Andy Di Vodi. Dundee continued his winning streak against past and future world champions Ben Jeby, Solly Kreiger and Ken Overlin as well as headliners Willie Harmon,

Young Terry, Pete August, Bucky Lawless, My Sullivan, Franta Nekolny and Abie Bain. He could never be accused of avoiding the toughest opponents. Then in 1931 came two titanic struggles with Britain's Len Harvey in Madison Square Garden. The British champion was a fine boxing artisan and in Dundee he met an intelligent ring general who knew how to maneuver into space and away from dangerous punches. Twice Dundee came out the victor, much to the displeasure of the partisan British press, who claimed their charge had been robbed.

On the back of these two high-profile triumphs Dundee secured a first world title shot. On March 17, 1933 he took on Ben Jeby for the NYSAC middleweight title. The bout with his old foe was declared a draw. Dundee met Jeby four times, winning three of them. Seven months later Dundee earned a second title shot and this time he outpointed Quebec-born cotton mill weaver Lou Brouillard over fifteen rounds to gain the 160-pound title in Boston. He successfully defended his crown twice against Andy Callahan and Al Diamond, in his opponent's backyard, before being outpointed by his ring nemesis, Polish American Teddy Yarosz, in Pittsburgh. Controversial decisions tarnished the image of boxing in the thirties and the title battle with Yarosz, who had twice previously outscored Dundee, left some perplexed. At the end of the fifteen rounds Dundee had been dethroned as champion with most spectators in Yarosz's hometown thought Dundee had won, having witnessed their man collapse and be taken to the dressing room.

Dundee continued to box and outpointed contender Paul Pirrone and Eddie Risko, a future world champion. In July 1935 Dundee ran into Freddie Steele, who knocked him down eleven times, and the Italian suffered brain concussion and a broken jaw resulting in a ring absence lasting eighteen months. After seven more fights, with his skills and speed on the slide, Dundee called it a day. He left the ring with a record of 150 bouts, 112 wins, 13 draws, 19 losses, 5 no decisions and 1 no contest. He hit the road regularly and was never afraid to risk his reputation by traveling to his opponent's hometown. Dundee never shunned an opponent and met the best boxers in the division, and he more than once fell victim to some questionable decisions. He was courageous to a fault. Despite three cracks on his jaw he was on his feet at the end of the third round in his nightmare fight with Freddie Steele.

Dundee was born Vincenzo Lazzara on October 22, 1907, in Baltimore. At fifteen years old Vince followed older brother Joe into the paid ranks, and made a winning start in September 1923 under the tutelage of manager Max Waxman. In retirement Dundee opened and managed a bar in Bloomfield, New Jersey before tragedy struck. He suffered severe head injuries in a serious accident with a passenger train that hurled his car three hundred feet. Not long afterwards he was diagnosed with multiple sclerosis. In 1942 he entered hospital in Glendale, California and a botched operation resulted in him losing the use of both arms and legs. For the last two years of his life Dundee was rendered a helpless cripple. He died in California on July 27, 1949.

LOUIS SALICA
WORLD (NBA) BANTAMWEIGHT CHAMPION 1935
WORLD BANTAMWEIGHT CHAMPION 1940–42

Lou Salica cut a dashing figure with his slick jet-black hair, piercing brown eyes and square jawline. He was quite a fighter and a two-times world champion. He won acceptance as the NBA bantamweight champion in 1935. He regained his crown and universal recognition in September 1940, when he outpointed Georgie Pace over fifteen rounds. Salica successfully defended his title three times in hard-fought points wins over Lou Transparenti and Tommy Forte twice, before losing it to Manuel Ortiz on points in August 1942. He attempted to win back the title for a third time but was knocked out in eleven rounds by Ortiz. After twelve years as a professional, Salica retired from the sport in 1944, finishing with a career record of 90 bouts, 62 wins, 11 draws and 17 losses.

Salica was born on November 16, 1913, in Brooklyn, New York to Southern Italian parents. He attended public school at Coney Island and from the age of ten he was absorbed by the radio boxing broadcasts of his idol Johnny Dundee. Some of Salica's older friends were amateur boxers and at thirteen he saw his first professional fight. From then on he was smitten and joined the First Avenue Boys Club. Evidence of his promise was there for all to see in the amateur ranks, as he won an array of City, State and Inter-City titles. Salica secured a spot on the United States Olympic team at the 1932 Los Angeles Olympic Games. After winning his first two bouts, he met Hungarian Stephan Enekes in the semi-final, dropping a controversial points decision which almost led to an international incident. With his Olympic dream shattered Salica left the arena heartbroken and in tears. A month later he faced Enekes in a post-Olympic international match staged at Madison Square Garden and convincingly defeated the newly crowned Olympic champion.

With nothing left to prove he turned professional just before Christmas. Salica made rapid strides in the pro ranks and victories over headliners Johnny Erickson, Midget Wolgast and Pablo Dano ensured his first title shot on August 26, 1935, against hard-punching Sixto Escobar. Fighting on home turf before 10,000 fans, Salica got the nod after fifteen rounds. Three months later at Madison Square Garden Salica lost to Escobar over the same distance. He was given another stab at Escobar in February 1937. Salica traveled to San Juan, Puerto Rico and despite an earnest attempt Escobar received the decision. In March 1940 he got another crack at the world title after Escobar relinquished the title as he could no longer make the 118-pound limit. Salica was paired against the Alabama-born African American George Pace. They met in Toronto, Canada and after fifteen rounds the fight was declared a draw. Six months later the fighters renewed their rivalry at the New York Coliseum in the Bronx. This time Salica came from behind to beat Pace, winning the unanimous decision. In his first title defense against Philadelphia's Tommy Forte, Salica showed his championship class. Trailing in the tenth and with one eye closed, Salica rallied hard to turn back Forte over fifteen rounds.

Although Salica occasionally dropped overweight decisions when the title was not at risk, he was a real champion. His best work was always to be found at long range but he could also mix it with the hard-punching sluggers. On losing his belt to Escobar in 1935 he showed plenty of pluck after sinking to the canvas for a nine count in round three. Salica's comeback from the dead thrilled the crowd. After his second title loss to Escobar, Salica found that the bantamweight division was no longer popular and lower purses forced him to move to California, where he proved a big box office attraction. Salica was one of the last great Italian American fighters in the 118-pound class. He died in his hometown of Brooklyn on January 30, 2002.

MICHAEL BELLOISE
WORLD (NYSAC) FEATHERWEIGHT CHAMPION 1936–37

A chance event is all it took to convince Mike Belloise that a future in prizefighting awaited him. Street skirmishes were not unusual in the teeming neighborhoods of the Bronx but on discovering that he had trounced a star amateur welterweight boxer who outweighed him by fifty pounds, Belloise recognized that he possessed a special talent. Between the reigns of undisputed champions Battling Battalino in 1932 and Henry Armstrong in 1937 the lack of consensus between rival boxing commissions the NBA and NYSAC produced a plethora of title claimants and Mike Belloise emerged as one of the six recognized titleholders.

A professional since 1932, Belloise hit an impressive two-year winning streak that rewarded him with his first title shot on August 30, 1934, against Alberto "Baby" Arizmendi for the NYSAC title at Dyckman Oval in New

York City. The Mexican champion proved too hot to handle as he bossed the fight, with his greater work rate and eye-catching flurries easily outpointing Belloise over fifteen rounds. Belloise itched to get another chance at Arizmendi but when the California-based Mexican refused to come out East and defend against Belloise he was stripped of recognition. The New York boxing commission launched a mini-elimination tournament and in the final eliminator bout, staged on April 3, 1936, Belloise stopped Everett Rightmire in the fourteenth round. A month later Belloise was officially named world champion by New York. In September 1936, Belloise defended his title, knocking out Britain's Dave Crowley in nine rounds at Madison Square Garden, New York.

After two non-title losses to Henry Armstrong and a defeat to Jackie Wilson, Belloise was struck down by pneumonia, which put him out of action for eight months. Whilst convalescing Belloise was stripped of his title in August 1937 and Armstrong was declared his successor following his victory over Petey Sarron. Belloise returned to inflict on Pete Scalzo his first professional defeat in 38 starts. Following Armstrong's title relinquishment Belloise tried to regain his 126-pound title. In October 1938, the Bronx battler dropped a fifteen-round decision to Joey Archibald for the vacant NYSAC title in New York City. Belloise would not get another chance. After a seven-round knockout to Chester Rico in March 1942 he announced his retirement. He was back in the ring seven months later and ended the year with four consecutive points victories. He continued boxing with mixed results and eventually retired in August 1947, finishing with a career record of 126 bouts, 84 wins, 13 draws, and 29 losses.

"The Bronx Spider," as Belloise was known, was a useful sharp-hitting counter-puncher who displayed poise and power. He won the admiration of boxing critics and fans alike, being voted the "cleverest boxer of 1936" by Nat Fleischer's *Ring Magazine*. His ability drew comparisons with the great Irish old-timer Ike Weir of the 1890s. Belloise was born on February 18, 1911, in the Bronx, New York to Neapolitan parents. He was one of ten children; six boys and four girls. His younger brother Steve became a high-flying middleweight contender in the forties and fifties and another brother, Sal, fought as a light-heavyweight club fighter. Mike joined the Our Lady of Refuge Athletic Club and developed an avid interest in both baseball and boxing but it was in the ring that his career really took off. He became a successful amateur boxer, winning a number of titles, and also traveled to Europe with the United States boxing team, appearing in Copenhagen, Berlin, Paris and London. He would have competed in the 1932 Los Angeles Olympic Games but the temptation of big-money purses proved irresistible. He gave up his job as an assistant camera operator in the nearby movie house and signed pro forms with manager George Hughes. Belloise died on June 2, 1969 in New York City.

LOU AMBERS [LUIGI GIUSEPPE D'AMBROSIO]
WORLD LIGHTWEIGHT CHAMPION 1936–38, 1939–40

Lou Ambers defeated boxing legends Tony Canzoneri, twice, and Henry Armstrong and beat four other world champions: Sammy Fuller, Johnny Jadick, Fritzie Zivic and Baby Arizmendi. He broke into the world's elite in 1933 and stayed there until 1940. He did it by combining toughness and determination with intelligence, making it difficult for opponents to plant a solid blow. He was equally comfortable in slugging and adopting a whirlwind style of non-stop punching.

Ambers was born Luigi Giuseppe D'Ambrosio on November 8, 1913 in Herkimer, New York to Neapolitan parents. He was one of ten children, and lived on the south side of the New York central railroad. Ambers' father Tony ran a large saloon and the family were fairly comfortable until Prohibition and the Great Depression. The prohibition laws forced many small businesses to the wall and when the family lost their saloon it became a struggle. Ambers tried helping out his family. At fourteen he worked in a furniture factory for twelve months and he spent another year in a cotto ı mill making sweaters before entering the world of bootleg fights. In 192), he got his first taste of amateur boxing in his hometown, being paid between a few dollars and fifteen dollars a bout. He traveled to wherever the action was and after scores of bootleg shows the nineteen-year-old Ambers turned professional in 1932. On beating Cleveland's Frankie Wallace, Ambers was convinced better things lay ahead.

Three years and forty-five contests later Ambers achieved a number one rating by the New York boxing commission. Ambers left Herkimer for the Bronx. He found work as a sparring partner to Tony Canzoneri, and when Ambers' father Tony passed away he became the sole breadwinner for his family. His lucky break came when he substituted for Tony Scarpati's opponent. Not expected to win, Ambers caused a shock when he beat his much-touted adversary, who later died from injuries sustained in the fight. The tragedy was a setback for Ambers, who thought about quitting. Boxing manager Al Weill promised to make Ambers a champion and in January 1935 he handed Ambers his debut at Madison Square Garden against top welterweight Harry Dublinsky. His performance sent the boxing press into a frenzy of excitement, describing the new kid on the block as a cross between world champions Harry Greb, Jackie Berg and Maxie Rosenbloom.

The press marveled at his rapid mobility, his incredible work rate and precision punching and endurance. He followed that up with his first fifteen-rounder against the rugged Sammy Fuller by outsmarting and outboxing the Bostonian, winning twelve of the fifteen rounds.

On May 10, 1935 Ambers got his first title shot against Tony Canzoneri, losing the fight on points. On September 3, 1936 Ambers avenged his defeat by keeping Canzoneri at range with his solid jab before 18,000 fans at Madison Square Garden. They met for a third time and again Ambers proved to be the master of the aging Canzoneri. On August 17, 1938 he met triple titlist Henry Armstrong, who narrowly secured a split points decision over Ambers. A year later the Italian American outpointed Armstrong in the Yankee Stadium, becoming only the second boxer to regain the lightweight title after Canzoneri. Ambers was eventually dethroned by Lew Jenkins and after losing again to the hard-punching Texan announced his retirement. Ambers claimed to have had 238 fights including bootleg bouts but the official record reads a total of 102 bouts including 88 wins, 6 draws and 8 losses. All of his defeats came against world champions Henry Armstrong, Tony Canzoneri, Jimmy McLarnin, Lew Jenkins and top contenders Pedro Montanez and Eddie Cool.

In retirement he purchased a home for his mother and invested his money in government bonds and insurance annuities. Ambers opened a restaurant and was later involved in public relations. In 1971 the boxer celebrated the "Lou Ambers Herkimer Hurricane Week." He moved to Phoenix, Arizona with his family and three children. In 1992 Ambers was inducted into the International Boxing Hall of Fame. He died on April 24, 1995.

TONY MARINO
WORLD BANTAMWEIGHT CHAMPION 1936

The unpredictability of boxing is what makes the sport enthralling and produces champions out of ordinary men. Pennsylvanian bantamweight Tony Marino was one boxer who turned the form guide upside down. On June 29, 1936, Marino snatched victory from the jaws of defeat when he knocked out Baltazar Sangchili of Spain in the fourteenth round to win the 118-pound crown at the Dyckman Oval Arena in Brooklyn, New York. Sangchili arrived in New York having just dethroned the great Panama Al Brown and his fight with Marino was supposed to be a tune-up before a meeting with NBA-recognized titleholder Sixto Escobar. Sangchili got the shock of his life. Marino, an unspectacular but good club fighter, was receiving a merciless beating for thirteen rounds, having survived four knockdowns. The brave Marino was still there in the fourteenth, valiantly taking punishment, when he unleashed two damaging punches that turned the tables on the Spaniard with a left to the solar plexus followed by a right cross to the jaw, and Sangchili crumpled to the canvas. He failed to beat the count and was carried out from the ring. Sangchili underwent specialist care. Later Sangchili's handlers tried to take the shine off Marino's victory, suggesting their boxer suffered unexpected leg cramp and that Marino merely knocked him off balance.

Two months later Marino returned to the same arena to meet NBA champion Sixto Escobar to settle the question of undisputed recognition. After thirteen brutal rounds, the ringside doctor entered the ring and advised the referee Billy Cavanagh to halt proceedings. Marino visited the canvas five times in the second round and was bloodied, with both eyes badly cut and swollen, at the time of the stoppage. Marino fought five more times in 1936, winning four of them and losing a ten-rounder to deposed champion Sangchili. On January 30, 1937 Marino met the dangerous Carlos "Indian" Quintana at the Ridgewood Grove in Brooklyn. Marino's attempt to climb back into title contention proved fatal. He not only lost the fight but later died in hospital of a cerebral hemorrhage. Marino's death would be a turning point as the New York boxing commission decided to look at safety procedures and empower referees to stop a contest in which a fighter is knocked down three times in a single round.

Marino was born Antonio Marino on May 18, 1912 in Duquesne, Pennsylvania. At fourteen he expressed a desire to follow in the footsteps of older brother Angelo Marino, better known as Tommy Ryan, a title-chasing bantamweight of the early twenties. Marino began his career as an amateur boxer weighing 105 pounds and won the Pennsylvania flyweight title. He worked as an apprentice in the Pittsburgh steel mills and also as a house painter before turning professional in 1931. He met world flyweight champion Midget Wolgast in an over the weight bout, earning a draw. With little competition in Pittsburgh, Marino moved to California, where he met some of the best Filipino boxers with mixed success. With competition lacking Marino moved back east, but top-notch bantamweights steered clear of him. Charley Cook, his manager, fixed him up to fight featherweights at Ridgewood Grove, where he acquired a reputation as a crowd pleaser, beating fighters who outweighed him by ten pounds. Although he was not a powerful puncher Marino was a persistent warrior who loved to rush his opponents. Marino was firmly catapulted into the spotlight when he achieved a stunning victory over Lou Salica, the former NBA champion. Marino clinched a ten-round win with a closing rally in the final round, rocking Salica with hard rights to head and body. His unanimous victory before 2,000 fans at the Queensboro Arena in Long Island earned Marino a title shot. Twenty-seven days later Marino was unexpectedly crowned world champion. In the space of seven months Marino experienced the highs and lows of this unforgiving sport, from a dramatic and unexpected title conquest to a full-scale tragedy that would rob boxing of one of its bravest gladiators. Marino died on February 1, 1937, aged 24.

FRED APOSTOLI
WORLD (IBU) MIDDLEWEIGHT CHAMPION 1937
WORLD (NYSAC) MIDDLEWEIGHT CHAMPION 1938–39

At seven years old his mother is dead. At nine he is sent off to an orphanage. He drifts from one job to another, eking out a meager existence during the Depression, and is seemingly on the road to nowhere. By 23 Fred Apostoli is world boxing champion. At his peak middleweight Fred "Belting Bellhop" Apostoli had few equals. The handsome, dark-haired, dimpled-chinned boxer from San Francisco was the most fearsome two-fisted pug of his era. He was skillful, driven, punched hard, possessed fast hand and foot movements and had the guts to withstand an opponent's best artillery. Apostoli always came to fight. On September 23, 1937, he claimed the middleweight title on the Mike Jacobs-organized "Carnival of Champions" promotion held at the Polo Grounds in New York. Apostoli met the IBU champion Marcel Thil and stopped the Frenchman on a cut eye in the tenth round. By right Apostoli was the new world champion but pre-fight politicking shrouded the match in confusion, with the NYSAC continuing to recognize Freddie Steele as champion. In later years Apostoli's claim has been accorded titular recognition from the day he beat Thil.

Apostoli continued to impress by twice outpointing Solly Kreiger and picking off the scalps of former world champions Lou Brouillard and Eddie "Babe" Risko, but the man he wanted was Freddie Steele. The clamor for a world title match-up between Apostoli and Steele reached fever pitch, with Steele refusing to be drawn into an NYSAC title defense, agreeing only to a non-title contest. Apostoli's manager Larry White felt an Apostoli win would inevitably force Steele's hand. They met on January 7, 1938, and Apostoli was unstoppable. After eight even and spellbinding rounds Apostoli let rip in the ninth round, landing a merciless tirade of blows that had one reporter counting one hundred sixty five Apostoli punches before the referee halted the fight. When Steele ignored the order to meet Apostoli within thirty days he was stripped of his belt. Apostoli outpointed contender Glen Lee for the vacant title in April 1938 and New York and other states joined

Europe in recognizing Apostoli as the undisputed middleweight champion. Apostoli defended his NYSAC title against his boxing idol Young Corbett III, scoring an eight-round knockout. After two hard-fought contests with light-heavyweight great Billy Conn and much-publicized weight-making problems Apostoli surprisingly lost his middleweight crown to Filipino Ceferino Garcia on a seventh-round stoppage.

In the summer of 1941 he joined the navy and sailed off to the Pacific, where he served three years as a gunner on board the USS *Columbus*. He was involved in enemy combat with the Japanese during the Second World War. *Ring Magazine* named him the 1943 Boxer of the Year for meritorious action in combat and also for his contributions as a boxing coach and staging boxing exhibitions on behalf of servicemen. He returned to the ring in 1946 and continued boxing for two more years in California before retiring in December 1948. He finished with a record of 72 contests, 61 wins, 1 draw and 10 losses.

Apostoli was born on February 2, 1913 in the North Beach district of San Francisco. He discovered boxing inside an orphanage and later joined the Olympic Boxing Club. At fifteen, Apostoli worked at a chicken ranch for two years. He spent a year in high school before beginning a series of odd jobs, working as a plasterer, sheet metal worker, carpenter's assistant and a jeweler's messenger boy before finding work at a hotel as a lift operator, moving up to become captain bellboy. In 1932 he won his first boxing title, a junior welterweight tournament. In April 1934 Apostoli captured the national amateur middleweight title in St. Louis. In October he turned professional. In retirement Apostoli worked as a boxing referee for over twenty years. He opened a restaurant in San Francisco and later worked as a sales executive for a gifts company. He died on November 29, 1973.

HARRY JEFFRA [IGNAZIO PASQUALE GUIFFI]
WORLD BANTAMWEIGHT CHAMPION 1937–38
WORLD FEATHERWEIGHT CHAMPION 1940–41
WORLD (MARYLAND) FEATHERWEIGHT CHAMPION 1941

By his own admission Harry Jeffra was a lousy practitioner of the noble art. Torn between his love of golf and boxing he relinquished the golf clubs and donned the mitts instead. His candid assessment of his ability as a novice emphatically highlighted that in Jeffra's case boxers are made rather than born. Years later he quipped:

> I had twenty-eight amateur bouts and won all but twenty-seven. I couldn't fight, period. I'd get the hell kicked out of me—in the

ring and in the street. Back in those days I was a puncher but I
couldn't knock my mother's hat off!⁶

Jeffra was born Ignazio Pasquale Guiffi on November 30, 1914 in the
Pimlico section of Baltimore. He was the eldest of four brothers, all golf
caddies, and their father worked as a bus conductor for the Baltimore Transit
Company. Jeffra attended Morgan Park School, where he developed an
aptitude for boxing and golf. As boxing was compulsory on the curriculum
Jeffra participated and won the school championship at his weight. At fifteen
Jeffra clinched the Baltimore City and Maryland State Amateur
Championships. In his spare time Jeffra caddied for hotshot golfers but there
wasn't much money in it. So Jeffra turned to boxing, making his professional
debut on September 21, 1933 with a four-round win.

Jeffra was a honed product of gym routines under the tutelage of
Baltimore's best trainer, Heinie Blaustein, the maker of champions Kid
Williams and Joe and Vince Dundee. Things didn't pick up until Jeffra
hooked up with influential manager Max Waxman. Within a year of
switching over, Jeffra was crowned world bantamweight champion. He was
a fine athlete, a fast-moving target who possessed a fair sock in both hands.
On September 23, 1937, Jeffra outclassed Sixto Escobar of Puerto Rico to
win the world title in a surprisingly one-sided fifteen-round contest at the
Polo Grounds, New York. Five months later, before 12,000 fans in San Juan
Puerto Rico, Escobar regained his crown, outpointing Jeffra over fifteen
rounds. Jeffra was knocked down three times, twice in the eleventh and once
in the fourteenth round for nine counts. Jeffra feared he would never fight
again, sustaining a double fracture of the jaw and spending four months in
hospital.

Weight-making difficulties prompted Jeffra to move up to the
featherweight class. In September 1939 he got a shot at Joey Archibald's
crown in Washington but after going the distance Archibald was declared
the winner on a split points decision. Most sports writers and many in the
10,000 crowd felt Jeffra had won. A rematch was called and on May 20, 1940
Jeffra won on points in the Baltimore Coliseum. Archibald was floored three
times as he was hammered for the duration of the fight. After one successful
defense he lost his crown back to Joey Archibald in Washington a year later.
The Maryland Boxing Commission matched Jeffra with Lou Transparenti
for their version of the world title and Jeffra won a twelve-round points
decision. His final fling at the big time ended in June 1942 with a tenth-
round knockout defeat to NYSAC champion Chalky Wright.

Jeffra boxed on and retired in early 1947. He remained inactive for two years and returned briefly in late 1950 before calling it a day. He finished with a career record of 122 bouts, 94 wins, 7 draws and 20 losses and 1 no contest. Jeffra was a double world champion at different weights. He beat five world champions: Phil Terranova, Jackie Wilson, Lou Salica, Joey Archibald and Sixto Escobar. Whilst Escobar had little trouble securing wins against other top bantamweights he found Jeffra a tough nut to crack. They met five times, with Jeffra taking the decision on four occasions. Jeffra was elected into the Boxing Hall of Fame in 1982. He was also inducted into the Maryland Hall of Fame—not bad, really, for a boy thrown out of every gym in Baltimore! In retirement Jeffra bought two houses and sent his four children to college. For a while he worked as a horse jockeys' agent and a horse stable manager at the Pimlico racing track. Jeffra died in September 1988.

MELIO BETTINA [EMILIO ANTONIO BETTINA]
WORLD (NYSAC) LIGHT-HEAVYWEIGHT CHAMPION 1939

Melio Bettina stood no taller than an ordinary welterweight but on February 3, 1939, the New Yorker shot into the big league by stopping "Tiger" Jack Fox in the ninth round, becoming the new world NYSAC light-heavyweight champion. Bettina was born Emilio Antonio Bettina on November 18, 1915 in Little Falls, New York. His immigrant family moved to Bridgeport, Connecticut and then back to New York, where they settled in Beacon, a renowned hat-making centre. He came from a family of five brothers and a sister. At fifteen he left school to work firstly as a caddy and then as a laborer. He gave up his $12-a-week construction job to become a boxer because he saw it as a chance to make real money; more than he ever could by mixing cement as part of a construction crew.

He began as a welterweight in bootleg fights earning $15 a show. Then in 1934 he won the Golden Gloves 160-pound title. In the same year at the Chicago–New York Inter-City tournament Bettina beat Tony Zale, the future middleweight champion. Having survived a first-round knockdown Bettina fought back to teach Zale a lesson in the importance of body punching, hammering Zale around the kidneys, and buoyed on by his success Bettina turned professional. At 5 feet 8½ inches tall he often faced bigger, taller and heavier opponents with longer reach. This didn't prevent him from having a successful career. He was tough, durable and a determined southpaw who possessed stunning hitting power and his southpaw stance proved the great equalizer. But he was in a catch-22 situation: He was too good for ordinary group of opponents and avoided like the plague by top-notchers. In order to find work Bettina traveled first to Miami. After a number of bouts Bettina headed to California and following notable wins over Wallace Bud Mignault and Henry Cooper, Bettina earned a crack at the NYSAC title, which had been vacated by John Henry Lewis, who had stepped up to campaign as a heavyweight. Bettina halted Fox in nine rounds.

His reign was short-lived, however. On July 13, 1939, over 15,000 fans packed into Madison Square Garden, of which five thousand had traveled from Beacon to see Bettina defend his title against Hall of Famer Billy Conn. After fifteen grueling rounds Bettina lost his title but picked up his biggest payday of $15,000. The two men met again in September and Conn repeated the feat. Bettina engaged the dangerous Fred Apostoli in two fights, losing the first on points in a savage battle, but he roared back to win the second with a twelfth-round stoppage. When Conn agreed to meet Joe Louis for the heavyweight crown the Irishman relinquished his 175-pound belt and Bettina was back in the title picture. In January 1941, Bettina was matched against Greek Anton Christoforides in Cleveland, but with only two weeks to prepare he lost the fifteen-rounder on points. He scored wins over Pat Valentino and Jimmy Bivins, but by now Bettina was eyeing the biggest prize of all: the heavyweight title.

In 1942 Bettina was being touted as a veritable challenger to Joe Louis. Promoter Mike Jacobs liked the idea as Louis had not met a southpaw and Bettina's record was the best of any pretender following victories over Harry Bobo twice, Gus Dorazio, Clarence Red Burman, Booker Beckwith, Altus Allen and Mose Brown. Jimmy Grippo, Bettina's manager, a professional magician, tried everything to make it happen. Unfortunately for Bettina the Second World War disrupted his best-laid plans. Both Bettina and Joe Louis were drafted into the army, with Bettina serving as a military policeman. Like many fighters Bettina got dispensation to box, losing once to Jimmy Bivins. He was discharged in 1946 and after five bouts was knocked out in one round by Gus Lesnevich. He retired soon afterwards. He made a comeback and after eight more fights retired permanently in December 1948.

Bettina finished with a career record of 100 fights, 84 wins, 3 draws and 13 losses. He scored 37 knockouts and was stopped 3 times. In retirement Bettina became a successful businessman, working as a car salesman. He died on December 20, 1996 in Poughkeepsie, New York from diabetes complications. He was 80 years old.

1940–49
PETEY SCALZO [PIETRO DONATO SCALZO]
WORLD (NBA) FEATHERWEIGHT CHAMPION 1940–41

As a boy Petey Scalzo dreamed of emulating his idol Johnny Dundee. He listened to radio broadcasts of his fights and trawled through the sports pages of newspapers capturing his every word. Scalzo was inspired to reach the top of his class. Scalzo was born Pietro Donato Scalzo on August 1, 1917, in New York's West Side district, and was one of three boys and two girls. He ran errands for the neighborhood tailor and he sold newspapers as well as dancing on Broadway streets for loose change. At school Scalzo was a talented sporting all-rounder and played for Harlem's metropolitan basketball team. At nine years old he tried boxing and never looked back. At eleven years old he enrolled at the West Side Boys' Club and boxed in a junior tournament as a 65-pounder and also captured the 75–85-pound title. In the following year he won the 85–89-pound title. After changing boxing club Scalzo's amateur career skyrocketed, winning the New York Golden Gloves 118-pound title as well as the New York Metropolitan amateur title. He also represented the United States amateur team in international meetings.

Scalzo turned professional in 1936, one month short of his nineteenth birthday. He went forty bouts undefeated, scoring a high knockout percentage ratio. Scalzo was not only a big hitter but also a defensively astute boxer and, equipped with a strong left jab, quick feet and an effective right-hand punch he climbed to the top of the division in no time. Despite two points losses in 1938, one to former featherweight champion Mike Belloise, he returned on December 5, 1938 to blitz Joey Archibald, the NYSAC featherweight champion, in two rounds in a non-title contest at St. Nicholas Palace, New York. The win gained him popular recognition as the "uncrowned champion." The following year he outpointed Sal Bartolo, the New England titleholder and title claimant, over ten rounds in his backyard and reversed his only points loss to Simon Chavez, the world-ranking Venezuelan. The hard-punching Scalzo ended Allie Stolz's unbeaten sequence by flooring him twice before dispatching him in four rounds. His displays were praised by veteran observers, who marveled at his clever adjustments from defense to attack, boxing coolly on the retreat and when an opening presented itself attacking with real force behind his blows.

He continued his good form into 1940, winning a pair of tough bouts against the heavier Primo Flores. On knocking out Britain's Ginger Foran in five rounds the featherweight menace from Hell's Kitchen had positioned himself as the leading contender and entitled to a title shot but Joey

Archibald, the NBA champion, got cold feet. Harry Jeffra looked in the opposite direction and Jimmy Perrin objected to meeting him in Washington, insisting that the fight take place in his hometown of New Orleans. On May 1, 1940, the NBA President Harvey Miller intervened and proclaimed Scalzo the new NBA titleholder. By now Scalzo was having weight-making problems and struggled before each of his championship contests. He successfully defended his title twice against Bobby "Poison" Ivy and Phil Zwick. In July 1941, Scalzo lost his belt to Ritchie Lemos, who stopped him in five rounds in Hollywood, California.

By 1942 it was apparent that Scalzo had no more appetite for the game. He joined the army and secured dispensation for several bouts but the timing and snap in his performances had gone and he packed it in the following year after three more fights. He finished with a career record of 111 bouts, 89 wins, which included 46 knockouts, 6 draws and 15 losses with most of these in the final year of combat. Once he left the army Scalzo spent several years working in construction and for a while worked as a sales representative for a New York beer company. He was a boxing referee and later served as chief inspector for the NYSAC, a role he assumed in 1958. He had a stab at show business and became known as the "Greek Ambassador" for his ability to impersonate others. Scalzo died on June 15, 1993.

JIMMY PERRIN [JAMES RAYMOND LA CAVA]
WORLD (LOUISIANA) FEATHERWEIGHT CHAMPION 1940

"Crescent City Flash" Jimmy Perrin was the hottest ticket in New Orleans boxing in the late thirties and his ring appearances helped to rekindle an expectant buzz of activity not seen since the days of old-timers Joe Mandot and Pete Herman. In 1939, Perrin confirmed his growing reputation as one of the world's best featherweights after winning twelve of his thirteen bouts with victories over two former champions, Sixto Escobar and Joey Archibald, as well as outpointing the highly touted Al Reid. Perrin was a skillful jab-and-move exponent who relied on speedy footwork developed at a dancing school he attended as a small boy. He possessed solid punching power and his right cross and his left hand were rated with the best of them in the 126-pound weight class.

Perrin's headline performances and large fan base meant that he rarely ventured outside Louisiana, preferring to fight in the Big Easy with all his bouts well supported. Perrin's camp tried luring champions Petey Scalzo and Harry Jeffra away from the big fight centers on the Eastern seaboard to come and defend their respective world titles in New Orleans, but negotiations with rival management factions repeatedly faltered. Frustrated by the lack of progress, the Louisiana Boxing Commission acted fast and matched Perrin against Bobby Ruffin in a face-off for their version of the world title. On May 8, 1940, Perrin laid claim to the inaugural Louisiana-recognized world featherweight championship following a fifteen-round points victory. By the end of the year Perrin displayed a record of 46 victories and only three defeats. A situation developed where there were three reigning "world" featherweight champions: Scalzo, Jeffra and Perrin; interestingly all Italian American.

In the following year, Canadian Italian slugger Jackie Callura, a future featherweight titlist, came along and burst Perrin's bubble. In their meeting on March 10, 1941 in New Orleans they fought out an exciting ten-round draw. A rematch was demanded, and a month later, again in New Orleans, Perrin suffered a fourth-round knockout defeat, which effectively wrecked his title aspirations. According to the *Boxing Record Encyclopaedia*, Perrin retired with a career record of 69 fights, 53 wins, 7 draws and 9 losses. However, Joseph Maselli and Dominic Candeloro, authors of the book *Italians of New Orleans*, reported that Perrin actually won 94 of his 107 professional boxing contests.

Perrin was born James Raymond La Cava on February 3, 1915, in New Orleans to Sicilian immigrant parents, and when his mother later remarried he adopted his stepfather's name and used it throughout his boxing career. He began as an amateur boxer and was hugely successful in Louisiana before making it through to the flyweight final of the 1932 national amateur boxing championships in New York City. There, he lost a closely fought three round battle to Brooklyn-born Lou Salica, a future world bantamweight champion. Perrin also boxed for the United States Olympic boxing team and campaigned as a flyweight before entering the professional ranks. After fewer than a dozen fights Perrin's promise excited boxing aficionados everywhere and as early as 1934 Perrin was seen in some circles as the logical contender to "Panama" Al Brown's 118-pound title. The threat to Brown vanished when Perrin moved up a weight class. It proved the right decision as he captured his first professional title, asserting sectional superiority by winning the Southern Featherweight Championship. Perrin's stay at the top was comparatively brief. He broke into the *Ring Magazine* top ten world annual rankings for the first time in 1939. The following year he earned a fifth spot in the *Ring Magazine* rankings and the NBA allocated him fourth place. Perrin was inducted into the Louisiana Sports Hall of Fame for services to boxing and in retirement he joined the New Orleans Police Department, serving as an officer. He also worked in public relations for an amusement company and later became a member of the Louisiana Boxing Commission. Perrin died in his hometown on April 14 1997.

IZZY JANNAZZO [ISIDORO ANTHONY JANNAZZO]
WORLD (MARYLAND) WELTERWEIGHT CHAMPION 1940–41

A fact often overlooked by the most fastidious boxing historian is that "Birmingham Tiger" Izzy Jannazzo held the world welterweight title under the auspices of the Maryland Boxing Commission. When the Maryland governing body refused to sanction the world welterweight title contest between Henry Armstrong and Fritzie Zivic, Armstrong's title became vacant. Jannazzo and Cocoa Kid of Puerto Rico were nominated to fight for the title. On October 14, 1940, Jannazzo outpointed Cocoa Kid over fifteen rounds in Baltimore. Six months later Jannazzo made his only defense of the title, successfully outpointing Jimmy Leto.

Jannazzo was born Isidoro Anthony Jannazzo on January 31, 1915, in Ensley, an industrial center on the outskirts of Birmingham, Alabama. He studied business at high school but gave it up for a boxing career. In 1932, his family moved to the Bronx, New York. After forty bouts in the amateur ranks he made his professional debut on December 6, 1932 under the management of Guy Anselmi. He lost two of his first four bouts, and won only ten of his first eighteen, but Jannazzo got better with experience and preferred the longer-distance bouts as it allowed him time to find his rhythm and range. He appeared primarily in New York clubs. He fought seventeen times in 1934 and twelve times in 1935. Jannazzo made his big breakthrough in 1936 and following victories over headliners Billy Celebron, Steve Halaiko and Johnny Jadick and a draw with Filipino Ceferino Garcia, future middleweight champion, Jannazzo met Barney Ross for the world title.

They met on November 27, 1936, in New York City, and Ross was awarded a disputed fifteen-round decision. Opinions were divided. Some ruled Jannazzo unlucky and others reported that Ross did enough in each round to get the verdict. Jannazzo knew Ross was a strong counterpuncher and he would not be drawn into leading, preferring to keep the contest at long range. He flicked the jab out to good effect and the back-pedaling Birmingham boxer proved elusive, managing to avoid most of Ross's big punches. He fought boxing legend Sugar Ray Robinson four times, and in one of their contests, staged in October 1942 in Philadelphia, Jannazzo demonstrated real toughness when he took all of Robinson's best punches and still kept coming forward, winning three of the rounds. In the tenth and final round it was Robinson who was hanging on from sheer exhaustion. At the final bell Jannazzo joyously cartwheeled around the ring before 10,000 fans that he had gone the distance with the "Sugar Man."

Jannazzo first broke into the annual *Ring Magazine* top ten rankings in 1936. He remained in the top ten a year later, and following two indifferent years came back to achieve his highest rating in 1940, ending the year at number two behind Fritzie Zivic. In 1941 he finished the year at number eight and after slipping out of the elite he broke back into the top ten in 1943. He boxed until 1947, and after losing to middleweight contender Steve Belloise he retired. In a career spanning fourteen years, the well-traveled boxer finished with a record of 125 contests, winning 67, drawing 14 and losing 44 of them. With only seven career knockouts, Jannazzo was not a big puncher. Instead he was a slick exponent of the jab-and-move style of boxing and relied on outboxing and outwitting his opponents. Jannazzo campaigned at a time when his division was packed with stars. The title switched back and forth between Barney Ross and Jimmy McLarnin before Henry Armstrong took over. Armstrong then lost it to Fritzie Zivic, who in turn fell to Freddie Cochrane. None of the latter trio of champions could be persuaded to put the title on the line. Yet so much more could have been accomplished if Jannazzo had been given the opportunities. Chris Dundee, who took over the reins of management from Anselmi in 1941, remarked a year later that "Izzy had been an unfortunate pawn of fate. A boy of his superlative ability should have held the welterweight title several years ago." Dundee forgot but others later reminded him that Jannazzo was a world champion—at least in the state of Maryland! After Jannazzo retired he worked for the Department of Sanitation in New York City. He died on June 18, 1995 in Franklin, Ohio.

SAMMY ANGOTT [SAMUELE ANGOTTI]*
WORLD (NBA) LIGHTWEIGHT CHAMPION 1940–41, 1943–44
WORLD LIGHTWEIGHT CHAMPION 1941–42

Sammy Angott knew how to win. He made a career out of it. An extremely tough and clever ring tactician, he deployed an effective and awkward boxing style that pushed him to the forefront of the lightweight division during the Second World War era. Angott was born Samuele Angotti on January 17, 1915, in Cleveland, Ohio. The family later moved to Washington, where he was raised, and on turning professional in March 1935 he made Louisville his hometown, becoming an instant favorite. After sixty-three starts he was matched with Chicagoan Davey Day for the NBA lightweight title. They were old rivals with both winning one bout apiece. In their rubber match on May 3, 1940, Angott set a furious pace and left-hooked his way to a fifteen-round points victory before 9,000 fans, on the eve of the Kentucky Derby in Louisville, to win his first world title.

On December 19, 1941, Angott won universal acceptance as world lightweight champion by outpointing big-hitter Lew Jenkins, the NYSAC titleholder, in New York City. He successfully defended his title against Allie Stolz, and later in the year announced his retirement from boxing. Four months later Angott was back in the ring, this time inflicting upon Willie Pep his first professional loss in 63 fights. Pep went on to rack up a longer consecutive victory sequence before tasting defeat again. In three fights with African American Bob Montgomery, future lightweight champ, Angott showed his superiority. In their July 1942 bout, Angott swarmed all over Montgomery, clouting him senseless in Madison Square Garden, winning every round in a one-sided encounter. On October 27, 1943, Angott reclaimed the NBA belt, outpointing African American Luther "Slugger" White in Hollywood, California. In March 1944 he lost his crown to Juan Zurita on points.

After the bout he retired for a third time. This time it lasted nine months. He returned as a welterweight and in 1945 Angott broke back into the world's top ten. He boxed on for a further six years before calling it a day in August 1950. Angott's bobbing and weaving style of boxing from a crouched position proved effective. He safeguarded any advantage by holding onto his opponent whenever he sensed trouble, earning the sobriquet "The Clutch." He was the great exponent of the hit and hold strategy, but in some quarters his style was derided for resembling grappling. Angott's manager Charlie Jones defended his charge from any criticism saying that his boxer was a model of consistency who had traveled across the country packing out arenas in Chicago, Pittsburgh and New York. What's irrefutable is that Angott traded blows with the best ringsters from the featherweight to the welterweight divisions. In total he met an incredible sixteen world champions of whom seven were Hall of Famers like Fritzie Zivic, Bob Montgomery, Sugar Ray Robinson, Willie Pep, Henry Armstrong, Beau Jack and Ike Williams. He beat eleven champions ranging from slick movers, boxing scientists, sure-fire sluggers and stout-hearted brawlers. Between 1938 and 1943 Angott consolidated a top five world ranking, except for 1942 when he was not listed due to temporary retirement. Angott's achievements are all the more remarkable as recurring hand injuries forced him to step out of the limelight whilst he was at his peak. He retired with an overall record of 99 wins, 8 draws and 28 losses. He was elected into the International Boxing Hall of Fame in 1998. After boxing he lent his fame to many noteworthy charitable causes. Washington's finest was acknowledged when they named a street after him: "Sammy Angott Way." He worked for a manufacturing plant in Cleveland but as Angott's arthritis worsened holding down the job became more difficult. After suffering a blood clot on the brain he died in Cleveland on October 22, 1980.

*Old record books state his surname as Engotti. Another source listed Angott's forename as Salvatore.

WILLIE PEP [GUGLIELMO PAPALEO]
WORLD FEATHERWEIGHT CHAMPION 1942–48, 1949–50

Willie Pep dominated the featherweight division in the forties with his superior interpretation of boxing science. He was all about technique and speed and this ingenious, fleet-footed artist used every inch of the ring to showcase his array of beautiful boxing skills, ranging from unerring pinpoint accuracy with both hands and feinting to blocking and countering opponents' punches, and his left jab rates as one of the best, period. Pep could also land a knockout blow when he wanted, evidenced by his 65 career knockouts. In the face of unsporting behaviour he retaliated with interest. In several of his four-fight series with Sandy Saddler he was involved in some of the dirtiest world championship contests ever fought in an American ring.

Pep marked his professional debut on May 3, 1940 with a four-round win. After an unblemished sequence of victories over a two-year period, Pep earned a world title shot against Chalky Wright, the NYSAC featherweight champion, and easily outpointed the veteran Mexican over fifteen rounds at Madison Square Garden, New York. At twenty years old Pep became the youngest fighter to win the 126-pound title since Terry McGovern beat George Dixon in 1900. Pep went on to unify the featherweight title by picking off NBA titlist, Sal Bartolo of Boston. Two former titleholders, Chalky Wright and Phil Terranova, were taught a boxing lesson over the fifteen-round route and contenders Jock Leslie and Humberto Sierra were knocked out in the twelfth and tenth rounds respectively.

Pep held the featherweight title for more than six years and in that time lost only once, to lightweight champion Sammy Angott, in one hundred thirty five professional bouts before relinquishing his crown to Sandy Saddler by a fourth-round knockout. Pep returned in February 1949 and gave a superlative display to reclaim the title from the lanky and hard-punching African American. He successfully defended his world title three more times before meeting Saddler in the rubber match in September 1950. Pep was ahead on points when an injured shoulder prevented him from coming out for the eighth round. Saddler and Pep met for the last time in September 1951, and in an ill-tempered foul-strewn affair both boxers wrestled each other to the canvas twice. Pep, again leading on points, failed to come out for the tenth round because of an eye injury. Pep's New York license was revoked and Saddler was suspended.

Pep continued to fight until 1959, when he announced his retirement. He returned six years later, and after nine more wins retired permanently following a knockout loss on March 16, 1966. He finished with a career record of 241 bouts, a staggering 229 wins, 1 draw, and just 11 losses. Pep was elected into the Boxing Hall of Fame in 1963 and into the International Boxing Hall of Fame in 1990. Pep's other claim to fame was to win a round of boxing without throwing a punch. He met Jackie Graves on July 25, 1946, in a non-title catchweight fight. Prior to the Minneapolis-staged fight, he told *Ring* reporter Dan Riley that he was not going to throw a punch in the third round. Riley eloquently described Pep's astute defensive display as making "Jim Corbett's agility look like a broken down locomotive. He made even Sugar Ray Robinson's fluidity look like cement hardening. Never has boxing seen such perfection." For the record Pep stopped his opponent in the eighth round and Riley discovered that Pep was awarded the third round on all three judges' scorecards. Years later Pep modestly recalled: "I was a hit and run artist. I just made 'em miss a lot out there and lived to tell it all." Eyewitnesses at Pep's fights like ex-Connecticut boxer Bill Corcoran claim that Pep could jab at a ratio of eight to every opponent's one. "Every cell in the guy's hand was made for those furious jabs," Corcoran said. *Los Angeles Times* Pulitzer Prize-winning sports writer Jim Murray ranked Pep among the three greatest fighters of all time.[7]

Pep was born Guglielmo Papaleo on September 9, 1922 in Middletown, Connecticut to Sicilian parents who hailed from the province of Siracusa. The family moved and settled in the "Little Italy" section of Hartford. Pep's father Salvatore had been an amateur boxer and was a keen follower of the sport, seldom missing a local fight and often taking his son along. Pep visited the Hartford gyms where he watched one of his idols, Bobby Ivy. At fifteen, Pep fought in his first amateur bout and he captured the Connecticut flyweight title in 1938. In the following year he added the state bantamweight title. He had 62 amateur bouts, losing three, all to older and heavier boxers. He turned professional, much sooner than he expected because his father, a WPA (Work Progress Administration) construction laborer, became ill. At the time his father's take-home pay averaged $13 a week and Pep made $8–9 a fight; on one night he boxed twice taking home $50 to help his family. He closed out his career having grossed about $1.3

million, but by the end much of it was gone on gambling and five failed marriages. After hanging up his gloves Pep worked as a top boxing referee, tax collector and deputy boxing commissioner and his celebrity status enabled him to pick up fees for delivering after-dinner speeches at public and private functions. Pep died in a Connecticut convalescent home on November 23, 2006, having spent the final years battling against advanced Alzheimer's disease.

PHIL TERRANOVA [PHILLIP JOHN TERRANOVA]
WORLD (NBA) FEATHERWEIGHT CHAMPION 1943–44

New Yorker Phil Terranova typified the "hungry fighter" story. Borne out of poverty and misfortune, he bounced back from the depths of despair to be crowned world featherweight champion in 1943. As a boy he survived a near-fatal accident with a truck and was then dumped on a vacant lot. By the time he was discovered he was in a critical condition. He was taken to a hospital where his chances of surviving were slim and he only pulled through with artificial respiration. Perhaps it was this near-death experience or the harsh environmental surroundings in the South Bronx that made Terranova into what the world would come to recognize as a fierce competitor.

Terranova was born Phillip John Terranova on September 4, 1919 in East Harlem's Little Italy in New York to Sicilian parents. He was one of fourteen children and the youngest of four boxing brothers. He followed Frankie, Jack and Nat into the ring and became the most successful of the Bronx quartet, albeit as a late starter. He began swinging leather at twenty-one years old. In 1941 he won the sub-novice featherweight class in the New York Golden Gloves Championships. He joined the paid ranks in the same year, making his debut in July with a first-round knockout. He was trained and managed by Bobby Gleason (Peter Roberto Gagliardi), who ran the famous Gleason's Gym in South Bronx. Standing at 5 feet 2 inches tall, Terranova was one of the shortest featherweights in history, but what he lacked in height he made up in energy and strength. He impressed with his rushes, always chasing and stalking his foes around the ring, and his aggressive style was matched by an ability to absorb punishment.

On August 16, 1943, the comparatively unknown Terranova bagged the NBA world featherweight title when he stopped champion Jackie Callura in the eighth round in New Orleans before 8,500 patrons. Six weeks earlier he had stopped the Canadian in three rounds in Hartford, Connecticut, instigating Terranova's manager Bobby Gleason to claim the title on behalf of his charge, despite both men scaling over the official 126-pound limit. The resultant fallout enabled Terranova to get a crack at Callura's title. In

December 1943, Terranova gave the former champion a title rematch in New Orleans and he dispatched Callura in six rounds. Three months later Terranova traveled to Boston to defend his title against Sal Bartolo in his opponent's backyard. After fifteen hard-fought rounds Terranova was forced to hand over the crown. They met again two months later in Boston and Terranova again lost out, this time on a dubious split points decision with the referee voting for Terranova. The traveling New Yorker felt a hometown decision had robbed him of the prized belt.

Terranova, who cut a dash outside the ring with his penchant for zoot suits, ended the year losing one of his next ten fights to world-ranked Vince Dell'Orto. His consistently good form secured him another title shot. In February 1945 he squared up to the irrepressible Willie Pep, losing on points over fifteen rounds at Madison Square Garden. Terranova later reversed his loss to Vince Dell'Orto and took the scalp of Maxie Shapiro. Between March 1945 and February 1947 Terranova was at his peak, compiling 22 wins, 1 draw and 1 loss, including a ten-round victory over Sandy Saddler. In the 1946 *Ring Magazine* annual ratings Terranova achieved a number one challenger ranking to Pep's crown. Unfortunately for Terranova he failed to secure another title chance. He continued to box with mixed fortunes and retired in 1949, having lost six of his last twelve encounters.

After nine years in the pro ranks Terranova retired with a record of 99 fights, 67 wins, 11 draws and 21 losses. Terranova invested monies into a bar and grill and in real estate but these decisions proved luckless. In the fifties he went to work in the textile industry and for a time worked as a construction worker and a lift operator. He returned to textiles, where he worked as a fabric inspector in Brooklyn. Terranova was an active member of the Veterans' Boxing Association in New York. He died in the Bronx, New York on March 16, 2000.

SAL BARTOLO [SALVATORE INTERBARTOLO]
WORLD (NBA) FEATHERWEIGHT CHAMPION 1944–46

Sal Bartolo was one of many top-notch Italian American featherweights campaigning during the forties. Add to the list Harry Jeffra, Pete Scalzo, Jimmy Perrin, Bobby Ivy, Mike Raffa, Lulu Constantino, Mike Belloise and Joe Marinelli and you get an idea of the caliber of opposition on parade. Despite the competition Bartolo weaved a path to the championship with his bright and stylish counterpunching style, annexing the NBA version of the title by outpointing Phil Terranova on March 10, 1944. Before 12,000 fans in Boston, Bartolo boxed with machine-like perfection to win a one-sided fifteen-rounder, defeating the aggressive Bronx fighter by jabbing and hooking him at will. Fifty-five days later they were back in the Boston Gardens and again Bartolo carried off the spoils of victory on a close decision.

Bartolo defended his title twice against rugged Willie Roache and the Canadian sailor "Spider" Armstrong, who was stopped in six rounds. Bartolo, the "Pride of East Boston," needed to put one over on his arch rival and NYSAC-recognized champion, Willie Pep, something no other featherweight had managed. Three years earlier the skillful ring technicians had twice clashed in Boston. On both occasions Pep ran out the winner; once over ten rounds in a non-title contest, and on June 8, 1943, Bartolo, appearing in his first world title fight, lost on points to the Connecticut boxer. Talk of a reunification battle gathered momentum and on June 7, 1946 they renewed ring hostilities for a third time in Madison Square Garden. Despite a determined showing, Bartolo was knocked out in the twelfth round, experiencing a broken jaw and his first knockout defeat.

It marked the end of the road for Bartolo, who quit after the Pep fight. He tried a comeback in 1949 and after a couple of points victories retired permanently. He finished with a career record of 97 bouts, 74 victories, 16 by knockout, 5 draws and 18 losses.

Bartolo was born Salvatore Interbartolo on November 5, 1917 in East Boston's Italian section to Sicilian parents. He was one of ten children; eight boys and two girls. All of Bartolo's bigger brothers dabbled with amateur boxing and he followed in their footsteps. He shined shoes and with the proceeds bought some boxing equipment. Whilst in high school he boxed under the name of Dom Salvati to hide it from his family. Despite his family's disapproval Bartolo continued to compete in local arenas. A year later he won the 118-pound Golden Gloves tournament. With Bartolo's father working in a soap factory, Bartolo left school at sixteen to help out. He began working on a baker's truck, delivering bread for $14 a week, and spent all his leisure time in the boxing gym. After six months he left his job to train full-time as an amateur boxer. When he first set foot in the gym he scaled 114 pounds, and with a scarcity of flyweights or bantamweights in local arenas he took on featherweights. Over a three-year period he fought in over one hundred fifty amateur contests, winning fourteen titles.

On the back of his amateur successes the nineteen-year-old made his professional debut in Boston in April 1937. His style and determination made him popular with fight fans. After signing up with New York businessman Lou Schiro he moved to Bensonhurst, New York in 1940. Schiro eventually handed the reins over to Lew Burston, who steered him through to world title glory. In retirement Bartolo opened and ran a bar in his hometown of East Boston. In 1996 *Ring Magazine* ranked Bartolo in the top ten best fighters ever to come out of Massachusetts. Bartolo died on February 19, 2002 in the Sunbridge Nursing Home in Lynn, Massachusetts. Joe De Nucci, former middleweight contender, paid tribute to Bartolo: "This man was a legend, a main figure in Boston sports . . . Sal was one of the biggest names long before guys like me came along. He helped establish the foundations for those of us who followed later."

TIPPY LARKIN [ANTONIO PILLETERI]
WORLD JUNIOR-WELTERWEIGHT CHAMPION 1946

New Jersey's Tippy Larkin was among the most skillful of the Italian American boxers. He may not be as recognized as Willie Pep but he was arguably as talented. Pep was the genuine ring craftsman, Sammy Mandell was a master of the defensive art and Larkin was the possessor of silky moves and consummate boxing skill. He was shifty and agile, dancing and prancing around the ring, carried a good punch and had fighting heart too. He boxed rings around many champions and contenders during the forties. His style of fighting gained him popularity with New Jersey and New York crowds, earning him the nicknames of the "Garfield Gunner" and the "Garfield Ghost." He beat Freddie Cochrane, world welterweight champion five times, Freddie Archer three times and Willie Joyce three times. He asserted himself against men of the caliber of Allie Stolz, Chester Rico, Lulu Constantino, Billy Graham and Leo Rodak.

Despite an unsuccessful attempt at the vacant NYSAC lightweight title in December 1942, losing to Hall of Famer Beau Jack, Larkin redeemed himself on April 29, 1946, capturing the vacant junior-welterweight title by outpointing the hard-hitting Willie Joyce over twelve rounds in Boston. Larkin survived three knockdowns in round three and used his ring savvy, his footwork and his expert jab to gain a unanimous decision. Larkin became the first divisional champion since Battling Shaw dethroned Johnny Jadick in 1933, as the junior-welterweight had fallen into disuse. In September 1946 he defended his title once against Willie Joyce in Madison Square Garden. Larkin boxed on the retreat, peppering the African American with rapid-fire lefts and smart one-two combinations, demonstrating that he was the superior boxer over the rugged Joyce. Larkin's speed and elusiveness gave him an edge with the devastating punchers of his day and he generally outboxed them over the distance. He had many of the attributes of great fighters but durability was not one of them. Veteran Hall of Fame boxing trainer Ray Arcel recalled in 1985 that "If Tippy Larkin had Carmen

Basilio's chin he'd still be champion today." Even so Larkin was stopped only ten times in 154 bouts, and until the last year of competition no ordinary fighters claimed his scalp and he was only stopped by world champions Lew Jenkins, Beau Jack, Henry Armstrong, Ike Williams and contenders Al Davis and Charley Fusari twice.

According to the *1980 Ring Record Book* he finished with a career record of 152 fights, 136 wins, 1 draw, 14 losses and 1 no contest. Between 1943 and 1947 Larkin occupied a top ten ranking in the *Ring Magazine* annual ratings. In 1943 he was the top-ranked welterweight behind champion Cochrane. Fortunately for Cochrane the title was frozen during the war years and he would not defend it until 1946. In that year Larkin was still ranked as one of the top five challengers. A title shot looked a distinct possibility, but with Cochrane having lost all five previous non-title contests to Larkin, the welterweight champion chose a different path instead, deciding to fight Marty Servo.

Larkin was born Antonio Pilleteri on November 11, 1917 in Garfield, New Jersey. He turned professional at seventeen years old and during his early days he kept a busy schedule in and around New Jersey. After four years he was boxing on the undercard at Madison Square Garden. Despite hand injuries and a freak accident involving a rifle Larkin continued to box on. After successfully defending his junior-welterweight crown he lost all interest in being a world champion and went on fighting all comers, traveling everywhere for work until 1952. Larkin grossed over $1 million in his career but after he retired much of the money was gone and he later worked as a highway supervisor for a New Jersey construction company. Larkin died in December 1991.

MARTY SERVO [MARIO SEVERINO]
WORLD WELTERWEIGHT CHAMPION 1946

Fate dealt Marty Servo a bad hand inside and outside the ring. Although Servo took the biggest gamble of his life in securing a world title shot, which he subsequently won, he was never able to cash in. To entice welterweight champion Freddie Cochrane into defending his title, which had been frozen for the duration of the Second World War, Servo's manager Al Weill dangled a lucrative carrot of a guaranteed $50,000 purse. At the time Sugar Ray Robinson was the logical contender for the title, but the inducement from Servo proved irresistible and Robinson was circumvented. Servo met Cochrane on February 1, 1946 at Madison Square Garden and the Italian American won by a fourth-round knockout. Unfortunately for Servo, his purse did not cover his obligation to pay Cochrane his fee. Servo's stated aim was to remain unbeaten and meet Sugar Ray Robinson within a six-month period, ensuring a purse fit for a champion. Things did not go to plan. Seven weeks later Servo rather foolishly agreed to fight Rocky Graziano, a fully-fledged middleweight and the most devastating puncher in the division for a generation. Servo was knocked out in two rounds and, most significantly, sustained a serious nose injury. His injury never healed and he had little choice but to throw in the towel on his career weeks before his first title defense against Robinson. The title was declared vacant, and Robinson went on to win it. The following year Servo tried a comeback and appeared in two bouts but retired permanently when Joe Di Martino knocked him out in one round in Bridgeport, Connecticut in August 1947.

Servo was born Mario Severino on November 3, 1919 in Schenectady, New York to Neapolitan parents. He was one of seven children. As a youngster he was a good sportsman, winning cross-country honors for his high school, and was tempted into boxing when he saw his cousin Lou Ambers become world lightweight champion in 1936. He began amateur boxing at sixteen years old and excelled at it. He captured the Golden Gloves featherweight title in 1937. In the following year he won the Diamond Belt featherweight title and reached the final of the national amateur boxing championships. He completed his amateur career, recording 91 wins in 95 fights. On turning professional he went on a similarly impressive unbeaten streak of 45 fights. Servo rapidly put on weight, bulking up from a featherweight to a welterweight. In September 1941 he met Sugar Ray Robinson in Philadelphia and gave the ring legend one of his toughest fights. Servo, a game and durable fighter, withstood all of Robinson's teeth-jarring blows and came back with blistering body attacks, forcing Robinson to hold on in their close-quarter exchanges. Servo lost a close ten-round points decision. In February 1942 Servo bounced back with a ten-round demolition of Lew Jenkins, former world lightweight champion. Servo, a destructive fighter at close quarters, put the pressure on with his trademark left hook and effective body punching, pounding Jenkins to one of the worst beatings of his career. At the end of the contest Jenkins's face was a gory mess, after he failed to win a round in this one-sided affair. In May 1942 Servo met Robinson for a second time before 15,000 fight fans in Madison Square Garden. It was Servo's last bout before being drafted into the United States Coastguard. Servo impressed the crowd with his unflappable commitment to wearing down his opponent, and did enough to carry the referee's verdict, but he lost on a split points decision, which was greeted with hoots of derision.

For the next three and half years Servo was on active duty on behalf of

Uncle Sam. He returned to boxing on December 10, 1945, and inflicted on Freddy Camuso his first professional defeat, stopping him in five rounds in Providence, Rhode Island. Two months later he was world champion. Unfortunately for Servo it was not the springboard to greater riches. His enforced retirement due to injury meant that he only fought 56 career bouts, winning 49, with 2 draws, 4 losses and 1 no contest. Life after boxing was no picnic either and the luckless Servo fought a long, brave battle with cancer and finally died in Pueblo, Colorado on February 9, 1969.

ROCKY GRAZIANO [TOMMASO ROCCO BARBELLA] WORLD MIDDLEWEIGHT CHAMPION 1947–48

Rocky Graziano was the ultimate crowd pleaser. Armed with an explosive right-hand punch, tremendous pluck and primeval instincts to fight to the death, Graziano brawled and slugged his way to the world middleweight title in the summer of 1947. His slugfests brought excitement and color in what was the golden age of middleweight competition, including the likes of Tony Zale, Jake La Motta, Sugar Ray Robinson and Marcel Cerdan. Graziano's popularity in New York exemplified the general public's affinity with big punchers. He was a throwback to the days of Stanley Ketchel, and his raw power, no-nonsense approach ensured there was never a dull moment as long as Graziano was in the ring.

Little was known about Graziano until spring 1945. Harold Green had outboxed him twice and it was expected to be a stroll for Billy Arnold, the strong-hitting welterweight prospect. Graziano, in trouble in the second round, recovered to poleaxe Arnold in the next stanza. This fight offered a glimpse into what was to define Graziano's career. He finished 1945 by repeating two ten-round knockout victories over Freddie Cochrane, the world welterweight champion, the first of which was voted the 1945 *Ring Magazine* Fight of the Year. In both fights Graziano was trailing by a big margin before the lights went out on Steele. In 1946 he busted up Marty Servo, the newly crowned welterweight champion, in two rounds, forcing him out of the sport. After Joe Louis, the heavyweight champion, Graziano was pound for pound the hardest puncher in boxing.

On September 27, 1946 veteran middleweight Tony Zale risked his crown against Graziano in New York, and the challenger was on the verge of winning the title from his incessant pounding when Zale struck, scoring a dramatic sixth-round knockout to maintain his title. The first Zale–Graziano fight was voted 1946 *Ring Magazine* Fight of the Year. A return match was inevitable, but in early 1947 Graziano got into trouble with the boxing authorities for failing to report a $100,000 bribe to throw a fight with Rueben Shank. He was threatened with a life ban, but the NBA, which controlled boxing outside New York State, did not accept this and the Zale–Graziano rematch was given the green light. The match was staged on July 16, 1947 in Chicago. Sky-high interest guaranteed a $422,918 gate, a record for an indoor boxing contest. In a fiercely contested bout, Graziano stopped Zale in the sixth round in a contest voted the 1947 *Ring Magazine* Fight of the Year. A year later the third Zale-Graziano fight was staged in Newark, New Jersey and Zale regained his title by stopping his foe in three rounds.

Graziano won twenty of his next twenty-one fights to earn a crack at Sugar Ray Robinson in April 1952. He floored Robinson in the third round but Robinson got up to stop the New Yorker in the same round. After losing his next fight to Chuck Davey he retired in September 1952. Graziano's ring achievements are startlingly impressive, considering his gross dislike for training and the glaring technical flaws and lead-laden foot movements. Awesome punching power and effective finishing compensated for these deficiencies. He finished with a career record of 83 bouts, 67 wins including 52 knockouts, 6 draws and 10 losses. He was inducted into the International Boxing Hall of Fame in 1991.

Graziano was born Tommaso Rocco Barbella on New Year's Day 1922 to Neapolitan parents. The family were on home relief and Graziano, a persistent truant, quit school in the sixth grade. He began stealing and continued his petty criminal activities throughout his teenage years. Trouble followed him everywhere, and he served spells in reform school and prison. At nineteen he went to jail and straight into the United States army. After basic training at Fort Dix he punched a corporal and later knocked out the captain. He went AWOL. Short of money, Graziano was persuaded by friends to turn professional.

He began boxing under the name of Tommy Rocky Graziano. His first professional fight was staged in March 1942. Seven fights later he was recognized, court-martialed, dishonorably discharged and sentenced to one year in a military jail. There he joined the boxing team and in spring 1943, still only twenty-one, was released. He left jail with a new outlook on life. Now married and with an extra mouth to feed, Graziano got serious about his boxing. In 1945 he received $50,000 dollars by meeting big timer Al Davis and he never got less for all future contests. Graziano grossed $250,000 from four title fights, a considerable sum more than half a century ago. In retirement Graziano exploited his popularity and when his autobiography was turned into a film called *Somebody Up There Likes Me*, the 1956 production netted Graziano more than $250,000. He appeared in comedy shows, television adverts and films and made after-dinner speeches.

By 1967 Graziano admitted to friends that he was a millionaire. Graziano lost his battle with alcoholism and died on May 22, 1990 of heart and lung failure, two weeks short of his sixty-eighth birthday.

JAKE LA MOTTA [GIACOBBE LA MOTTA]
WORLD MIDDLEWEIGHT CHAMPION 1949–51

From hard-nosed hoodlum to world middleweight boxing champion, that's Jake La Motta's story in a nutshell. Born in Manhattan's Lower East Side on July 10, 1921, to a Sicilian father from Messina and an American-born Italian mother, La Motta was one of five children; two brothers and two sisters. At the age of six the family moved to a Philadelphia slum and then back again to New York, settling in the Bronx. La Motta continued school until the tenth grade. He shined shoes for a while and even thought about becoming a plumber, but gave it all up for a life of crime. He was sent to correctional facilities three times before spending a three-year term at Coxsackie Prison for robbing and beating up a bookmaker. He joined the reformatory boxing programme and on leaving prison walked into the Bronx-based Teasdale Athletic Club, scaling a heavyweight 185 pounds. Watching other gym goers sparring, a curious La Motta approached Mike Capriano, head boxing instructor, saying that he wanted to become a boxer. Under his guidance La Motta tried it for seven months, winning the Diamond Belt light-heavyweight championship. He stayed unbeaten in eighteen amateur bouts and supported his family by selling watches won in amateur competitions.

He turned professional in March 1941. La Motta conquered his battle with the bulge and trimmed down to 160 pounds. He went through his first fifteen bouts undefeated before dropping a controversial points loss to Jimmy Reeves, which sparked a near riot in Cleveland, Ohio. La Motta served notice that he was the real deal. He was a strong and aggressive two-fisted fighter, and could drop his hands, feign injury in order to draw an opponent and then unleash a barrage of blows. Opponents never knew when La Motta was hurt. It helped his cause that he possessed an iron jaw, but La Motta later revealed that he had an uncanny ability to roll with incoming punches, allowing him to draw the sting out of each blow.[8]

In 1942 La Motta broke into the *Ring Magazine* annual ratings world's top ten for the first time. In the same year he met Sugar Ray Robinson in New York City for the first time and the "Bronx Bull" created quite an impression on him. Years later Robinson recalled:

Around the middle of the fight I caught him [La Motta] with a good combination. I had him along the ropes. He had his head down and I was really measuring him. For one of the few times in my career, my arms got weary from throwing so many punches. I stepped back for a breather. Jake had his head down and his gloves were up around his head, protecting himself. I thought, man, he has to fall any moment now. But not Jake, not the Bull. His head popped up and he let go a left hook that almost tore through my stomach. It hurt so much I had tears in my eyes, like a little kid. I got the decision but I learned that Jake La Motta was some animal.[9]

On February 5, 1943, 19,000 fans in Detroit saw clear proof of La Motta's ability as Robinson lost his first ever bout in 121 professional and amateur fights combined. La Motta had Robinson down for a nine count in the eighth round before taking a ten-round decision. La Motta met the African American legend six times, all of them captivating contests pitching La Motta, the masterful inside fighter with a granite chin, against the classy and hard-punching Robinson. La Motta finished 1943 as the top-ranked middleweight contender. In 1944 he was at number two, a year later at number three and in 1946 he was the leading contender again. La Motta beat world-class fighters others avoided, scoring triumphs over Holman Williams, Bert Lytell, Jose Basora, Tommy Bell, George Kochan, Tony Janiro and Fritzie Zivic. He finished 1947 with a top-five world ranking and was back at number three in 1948.

Despite his perennial top ten world ranking La Motta was bypassed for five years, prompting the American press to dub La Motta the "uncrowned middleweight champion." He had seen lesser men in the pecking order given their chance. His earnest endeavors, long-suffering pain and sacrifice in making the weight appeared fruitless as the cherished prize remained out of reach. Disenchanted and desperate, a deal was cut with the mob that controlled boxing. La Motta agreed to take a dive in the Billy Fox contest in exchange for a title fight. Even then La Motta gave up $20,000 in prize money. On June 16, 1949 he met champion Marcel Cerdan in Detroit. The Frenchman retired after ten rounds of hard brawling with an injured arm. La Motta was declared champion at last. He defended his title twice, first against Italy's Tiberio Mitri and then against France's Laurent Dauthuille, where with La Motta trailing on all three scorecards he spectacularly halted his foe with just thirteen seconds of the fight left. The bout was voted the 1950 *Ring Magazine* Fight of the Year. The dramatic fifteenth round also won him the 1950 *Ring Magazine* Round of the Year. La Motta eventually surrendered his crown to Robinson in what was described as boxing's St Valentine's Day Massacre.

La Motta continued boxing as a light-heavyweight and retired in 1952 when suffering his only career knockdown, quitting on the stool. He returned briefly in 1954 and after three more fights finally called it a day. He finished with career record of 106 bouts, 83 wins, 30 by knockout, 4 draws and 19 losses. La Motta was a top ten middleweight for a decade and even secured a top five ranking as a light heavyweight in 1952. It is estimated that La Motta made over $500,000 from boxing and he was in good shape financially. He was elected into the International Boxing Hall of Fame in 1990. In retirement La Motta moved to Miami where he brought a nightclub. He landed in jail for having sex with an underage girl. On his release he appeared in television shows and plays and became a stand-up comic. For a time he was a popular after-dinner speaker. He wrote an autobiography entitled *Raging Bull* and in 1980 film director Martin Scorsese turned it into an award-winning film. Robert De Niro's compelling portrayal has arguably made La Motta into the most famous Italian American boxing name as well as turning him into one of the most enduring sporting figures.

1950–55
JOEY MAXIM [GIUSEPPE ANTONIO BERARDINELLI]
WORLD LIGHT-HEAVYWEIGHT CHAMPION 1950–52

Cleveland's Joey Maxim is remembered as the only man in boxing history to beat Sugar Ray Robinson inside the distance. It happened on June 25, 1952 before a 48,000 crowd at New York's Yankee Stadium. Robinson had won the welterweight and middleweight titles and was gunning for the light-heavyweight crown, but his ambitions were thwarted in New York's summer heat when he failed to come out for the fourteenth round and Maxim was declared the winner. Praise and greatness did not accompany this career-defining victory, nor did it change Maxim's life. Unfortunately the media dwelled on a variety of factors to explain away Robinson's defeat. The most popular alibi was the sweltering heat, which reached 130 degrees at ringside. In a 1996 magazine interview Maxim quipped, before breaking out in laughter: "Some people say Maxim didn't beat Robinson, the heat did. They're right. I never told this to anybody before, but I had air conditioning in my corner in Yankee Stadium that night."[10] In short an overconfident Robinson got his fight tactics wrong, using up a lot of energy and becoming exhausted by the later rounds; and then there were those suggesting

Robinson was a boxer on the slide. Yet he fought on for another thirteen years, capturing the middleweight title in 1955, regaining it in 1957 and winning it again in 1958. Others argued Robinson gave away too much weight—fifteen-and-a-half pounds—to Maxim but the challenge didn't bother Robinson. He had given that much weight to Jake La Motta and still outpointed him. Maxim may not have been in the same class as the "Sugar Man" but then nobody was back then and nobody has been since. Maxim overcame Robinson by displaying strength and durability and demonstrated that he was better than anything in a very competitive light-heavyweight class.

By the time the Robinson bout came around Maxim had also been tangling with the best heavyweights too. He fought Ezzard Charles, the world heavyweight champion, five times. Maxim was an exponent of the defensive art with good technique. He parried incoming blows with startling efficiency, could slip and slide blows and countered strongly. Some said Maxim was slow about the ring and others saw in Maxim the ability to jab with remarkable accuracy, drawing comparisons with a Maxim machine gun. He also possessed a solid chin and was only stopped once. After nine tough years he got his first title shot on January 24, 1950, traveling to England to knock out Freddie Mills in the tenth round at Earl's Court, London. He held the title for three years, successfully defending it twice before losing it to Archie Moore in December 1952. Maxim tried to wrest the title from Moore, but twice lost on points with his last title stab in January 1954.

Throughout his professional career Maxim beat champions and contenders including world heavyweight champions Jersey Joe Walcott and Floyd Patterson, world light-heavyweight champion Gus Lesnevich and an array of headliners like Jimmy Bivins, Irish Bob Murphy, Clarence Brown, Nate Bolden, Lee Oma, Holman Williams, Henry Cooper and Bob Satterfield. Maxim was good enough to be ranked in two divisions simultaneously. In 1950 he not only held the 175-pound title, he was also ranked by *Ring Magazine* as the number three-ranked heavyweight. In May 1951 he met Ezzard Charles for the world heavyweight title, losing by a fifteen round points decision in Chicago. Quite remarkably Maxim was ranked in the world's top ten for thirteen of his eighteen years in the sport. In truth he was underrated and unappreciated and was not a big hit with fans in New York City, appearing there only twice. Low purses dogged his career too, and he picked up only a paltry $19,000 in defeating Mills for the world title. He traveled the length and breadth of the United States just to keep busy.

Maxim was born Giuseppe Antonio Berardinelli on March 28, 1922 in the Collinwood section of Cleveland to Italian parents from the Abruzzi region of central Italy. His interest in boxing was ignited when he went to Vic Raversak's gym and at twelve he started boxing as a flyweight. Maxim, the son of a cement finisher, was soon clinching junior titles and participating in the senior amateur boxing championships, where he won the Cleveland Golden Gloves lightweight title in 1937. A year later he reached the final of the welterweight class. By 1940 he was a full-blown middleweight and performed the clean sweep, capturing the Chicago and Inter-City Golden Gloves championships and National amateur title. He concluded his amateur career with 116 wins out of 121 contests.

In January 1941 he turned professional under the illustrious Jack Kearns, the maker of champions Jack Dempsey, Abe Atell, Mickey Walker, Jackie Fields and Benny Leonard. Following victories over Lee Oma and Red Burman, Maxim forced his way into the annual *Ring Magazine* world rankings after nine months as a professional. In December 1943 he worked as a physical instructor in the Army Air Force. Though boxing activity was restricted he managed to fight six times in 1944 and three times in 1945. It was all systems go from 1946 onwards. After six straight losses Maxim announced his retirement in 1959, finishing with professional career figures of 115 bouts, 82 wins, 4 draws and 29 losses. In retirement Maxim bought a delicatessen store in the Cleveland suburbs. He moved to Miami, where he ran a cab company. He later moved to Las Vegas and worked as a greeter in several casinos before heading back to Cleveland. After suffering a stroke he died on June 2, 2001 in Florida.

ROCKY MARCIANO
[ROCCO FRANCESCO MARCHEGIANO]
WORLD HEAVYWEIGHT CHAMPION 1952–56

With his fighting reputation intact and his legacy assured Rocky Marciano's 49 victories in 49 contests and 43 knockouts is still the yardstick by which future heavyweight champions are judged. Marciano was born Rocco Francesco Marchegiano in Brockton, Massachusetts on September 1, 1923, and was the eldest of six children. Pierino, Marciano's father, left the town of Ripa Teatina in the Chieti province of the Abruzzi region. Marciano's mother, Pasqualina, arrived in the United States in 1916 with her blacksmith father from the village of San Bartolomeo in the Benevento province, near Naples.

For Marciano life was a continuous fight. Afflicted by pneumonia as a child he was given little chance of survival, and somehow miraculously pulled through. Excruciating back pains dogged Marciano's boxing career even before it got started and he waged a tireless battle against the gnawing discomfort, which eventually forced him into retirement. After quitting school at sixteen Marciano worked in a succession of dead-end jobs; firstly as a truckloader, earning $2 a day, followed by stints in a sweet factory and shoe-shining parlor and as a pick-and-shovel laborer for a gas company. In 1943 he was drafted into the United States Army, and on returning home he switched his attention to prizefighting when his dream of becoming a baseball player vanished following an unsuccessful trial with the Chicago Cubs.

After a twelve-fight amateur career, in which he won the New England title, he turned professional on March 17, 1947, announcing his introduction with a third-round knockout. He signed forms with New York fight manager Al Weill, who placed Marciano under the watchful eye of astute trainer Charley Goldman. Marciano signaled his arrival in 1950 when he outpointed unbeaten New York contender Roland La Starza. In the following year he knocked out heavyweight prospect Rex Layne in six rounds, clipped the wings of contender Freddie Beshore and then disposed of his childhood hero Joe Louis in eight rounds. In 1952 he handed Lee Savold the worst beating of his seventeen-year career, hospitalizing him after knocking him out in six rounds in Philadelphia. Then he dispatched Harry "Kid" Matthews in two rounds, in a world title eliminator staged in New York.

On September 23, 1952 Marciano met the 38-year-old champion Jersey Joe Walcott in the Municipal Stadium, Philadelphia for the heavyweight title. Marciano overcame a first-round knockdown and was trailing on points before knocking him out with a pulverizing right in the thirteenth round. A rematch was ordered, and in March 1953 Walcott was blasted out in one round in their Chicago fight. Marciano brought to his fights a ferocious intensity and non-stop action and his punching ability placed him at the very top of the league of heavyweight hitters in history. He knocked out 88 percent of opponents compared to 76 percent by Joe Louis. His devastating power was felt by Carmine Vingo, who ended up in a coma in 1949, while Savold was punched to oblivion and Walcott remained unconscious for two minutes after their first battle. Budd Schulberg, award-winning screenwriter and boxing aficionado, likened Marciano's capability of grinding down an opponent to a "hydraulic drill attacking a boulder." Arthur Daley exalted him as a "perpetual motion punching machine". Marciano's boundless reserves of stamina and remarkable recuperative powers meant he was seldom troubled. He was floored twice in his career; by champions Jersey Joe Walcott and Archie Moore. Marciano made the impossible possible in the first Walcott fight and in the second Ezzard Charles fight.

He was a diligent and dedicated trainer and relished the preparation and honing process accompanying each fight. The arduous gym workouts helped Marciano develop tremendous stamina, which explained his overpoweringly aggressive style. Marciano never suffered from pre-fight nerves and Al Weill referred to Marciano's aura: "Rocky has something you don't see unless you're around him all the time. After a while, you know it's there and so do the guys who get in there with him."[11] Marciano was uncomplicated in the ring. He advanced with real menace and a brawling intensity, and together with his physical strengths this made him an indestructible fighting force. Yet he was not loved by all and frequently felt the full fury of the poison pens of boxing scribes who harped on about Marciano's flaws as a boxer. Unfair comparisons were drawn with Joe Louis, arguably the best heavyweight of all time. In Marciano's defense he fought the best men of his time and none were able to halt the "Brockton Blockbuster's" bandwagon. Whilst it's true that Marciano was neither a stylist nor a polished craftsman he was the best slugger in ring history, able to satisfy the public's yearning for undiluted violence. Marciano was voted three times the *Ring Magazine* Fighter of the Year (1952, 1954, and 1955) and the same journal awarded his involvement in the Fight of the Year for the same period. In 1953 he was named the Professional Athlete of the Year and awarded the diamond-studded belt valued at $10,000. In the *Ring Magazine* 2000 poll, Marciano was voted as the ninth greatest fighter of the twentieth century among all weight classes. Above all, Marciano was a hero to millions of Italian Americans and his high profile and impeccable conduct ensured adulation long after his retirement.

In seven world title fights between 1952 and 1955 Marciano made $1,460,388 from combined purse and television earnings. Almost 260,000 people attended these fights, with total gate receipts of $13½ million. Estimates vary but Marciano made as much money through personal appearances, endorsements and other business transactions, retiring a wealthy man. In retirement he helped charitable causes as well as investing in numerous enterprises, among them a sausage company in Ohio, restaurant in Maryland, bowling alley in Florida and a chain of spaghetti restaurants in Los Angeles. Marciano was killed in a plane crash in Iowa on August 31, 1969 on the eve of his forty-sixth birthday.

CARMEN BASILIO [CARMAN COSMO BASILIO]*
WORLD WELTERWEIGHT CHAMPION 1955–56, 1956–57
WORLD MIDDLEWEIGHT CHAMPION 1957–58

"I've dreamed about being a fighting champion since I was a little boy and I believed it though I was discouraged. I became attracted to it and felt that eventually it had to happen." On June 10, 1955 Carmen Basilio captured the world welterweight title with a dramatic twelve-round knockout of Tony De Marco. Nobody gave more to boxing than the "Canastota Clouter." He embodied the warrior spirit, heart and determination; bloodied, bruised and wounded, but never bowed, Basilio always came to fight. His fighting qualities endeared him to fight fans everywhere, but Basilio suffered plenty of anguish in and out of the ring. He battled against brittle bones, bursitis and wafer-thin skin that cut to shreds when tagged. Under the management of the Amos brothers Basilio was reduced to an ordinary New York club fighter, losing to undistinguished men. His disinterested managers failed to watch him train and rarely put him on main event promotions. Basilio was a poor attraction and at times was not even paid, with friends and family advising him to quit. After losing to Johnny Cesario in June 1951 he temporarily retired, but was back in the ring just to pay his wife's medical bills. For two years he held down a factory job, working days and training nights.

When fight managers John De John and Joe Netro took over Basilio's contract progress ensued. De John, who managed his brother Joey, a big box office attraction from Syracuse, polished up Basilio's natural style and insisted on greater composure from him. Basilio duly obliged and the results followed. In 1952 Basilio found some momentum performing well against the world-rated Chuck Davey and Billy Graham. A year later he beat Ike Williams, former lightweight king, and reversed his defeat to Billy Graham, winning the New York State welterweight title, and later drew the rubber match with Graham. In September 1953 Basilio got his first world title chance against Kid Gavilán of Cuba in Syracuse and was denied by a controversial fifteen-round split points decision. A return match did not materialize and for thirty months Basilio watched from the sidelines as Gavilán lost his title to Johnny Saxton, who in turn lost to Tony De Marco.

In June 1955 Basilio faced De Marco for the 147-pound title and in a sizzling toe-to-toe slugfest the rugged Basilio dropped De Marco twice in the tenth round and then stopped him in the twelfth round in Syracuse. The fight was awarded the 1955 *Ring Magazine* Fight of the Year. Five months later, in his first title defense, Basilio repeated the twelfth-round stoppage in De Marco's hometown of Boston. In March 1956 Basilio lost his title to

Saxton on another controversial fifteen-round decision in Chicago. Basilio won the rematch in Syracuse by a ninth-round knockout. The fight was voted the 1956 *Ring Magazine* Fight of the Year. Basilio met Saxton in Cleveland for the rubber match and again he stopped Saxton.

Basilio was the master of all in the 147-pound division, and with nothing left to prove and beset by weight-making problems he set his sights on the more lucrative middleweight class. On September 23, 1957 he met Sugar Ray Robinson for the 160-pound title at New York's Yankee Stadium before 38,000 fans who paid $560,000, at the time the second largest non-heavyweight gate in boxing history. Basilio picked up a cheque of $215,639. The fight turned out to be one of the greatest boxing matches ever staged. Basilio gave away considerable height and reach to his opponent but outsmarted and outslugged Robinson to win the fight. Respected British writer Peter Wilson of the *Daily Mirror* declared that it was the best fight he had ever watched, pitting the skills and artistry of Robinson against the guts, courage, stamina, durability and body punching of Basilio. This championship contest was awarded the Fight of the Year for 1957 and his peers also voted Basilio the Fighter of the Year. In the March 1958 return match in Chicago, Basilio lost his crown on a split points decision to Robinson. Basilio fought most of the fight with his left eye totally shut. Robinson admitted that it was the toughest fight of all his 202 bouts. This, too, was voted *Ring Magazine* Fight of the Year.

Basilio had three more stabs at the middleweight title, losing twice to Gene Fullmer, both inside the distance, for the first time in his career. In April 1961, following a points defeat to Paul Pender, Basilio announced his retirement, finishing with a record of 79 bouts, 56 wins, 7 draws and 16 losses. He was a two-division world champion and had competed in eleven world title bouts, of which five were voted *Ring Magazine* Fight of the Year.

Basilio was born on April 2, 1927 in Canastota, New York. He was one of ten children, six sisters and four brothers. His father came from the village of Veroli in the Frosinone province near Rome and his mother hailed from Campobasso, Molise region. At seventeen he enlisted in the United States Marines, serving sixteen months in Guam in the Pacific and eight months at Pearl Harbor. He was honorably discharged in November 1947 and went back to amateur boxing, winning the Adirondack Golden Gloves title. After eleven wins in fourteen bouts he turned professional in November 1948. Boxing was not foisted upon him but was a burning passion. He explained:

> I was eight years old and I was just old enough to read the sports pages and about boxing. Jimmy Braddock was my hero. Braddock

was very poor, off relief. I'm talking about he was working for the WPA [worker's relief]. He got $12 a week and made a comeback to win the world heavyweight championship in 1934. I love boxing and that's all I ever wanted to be—a boxer.[12]

In retirement Basilio worked as a physical education instructor at Le Moyne College in Syracuse and as director of sports promotions for a Rochester brewery. Basilio was admired for his work with charitable causes helping deprived children. He died on November 7, 2012.

* Basilio's father Giuseppe changed the family name from Basile to Basilio because it sounded more Americanized. The baptismal name of Carman is almost certainly an Americanized version of the Italian name Carmine. Basilio was taught by his sisters to spell his first name by using the feminine version. The Carmen name stuck with him for the rest of his life.

PADDY DE MARCO [PASQUALE GIUSEPPE DE MARCO]
WORLD LIGHTWEIGHT CHAMPION 1954

Paddy De Marco made a living from bulldozing into his opponents and letting the punches fly at close quarters. Durable and tough, he won the world lightweight title from Jimmy Carter in March 1954. De Marco was born Pasquale Giuseppe De Marco on February 10, 1928 on Sands Street in the Navy section of Brooklyn, New York. De Marco, the son of a solderer, once described the area he grew up in as "simply to walk down the street would be to invite a fight." At sixteen years old he walked into Trinity Gym and put his career in the hands of Jimmy Dixon and trainer Dan Florio, and he never looked back. After a few fights he reached the semi-finals of the New York Golden Gloves Championships.

He made his professional debut on March 20, 1945 and since he was too young to apply for a New York license he fought his first seven bouts in New Jersey. A year later he switched back to New York, where he put together an impressive sequence of results as a featherweight, earning a reputation as one of the grittiest fighters around. Bereft of a big punch, De Marco's methods were not pretty. He relied on roughing up opponents and, blessed with a tremendous fighting spirit, he turned the pressure on with a brand of two-fisted aggression that attracted the nicknames of "Brooklyn Billygoat" and "New York's Baby Bull." De Marco's in-your-face slugging and high work rate unsettled and outmuscled the best featherweights and lightweights around. Top-class boxers like Enrique Bolanos, Humberto Sierra, Billy Graham, Teddy Davis, Eddie Chavez, Orlando Zulueta, Johnny Gonsalves, Henry Davis, Arthur King, Armand Savoie, Tony De Marco and

Ralph Dupas all lost to him. He twice outpointed Sandy Saddler, a feat not even the great Willie Pep could muster. He neutralized Saddler, one of the deadliest hitters in boxing, by covering up against the incoming punches and ploughing in and staying at close range. In their ten-rounds fight staged in Milwaukee in August 1951, De Marco won six rounds and drew one to carry the decision. They met again in December in New York and De Marco once more beat Saddler over the same distance. In April 1953 he strengthened his claim to the world title challenge by outpointing Canadian champion Armand Savoie in Montreal.

De Marco threatened to quit boxing more than once following dubious decisions which derailed his titular ambitions. But in January 1954 the tide finally turned. De Marco entered the lion's den of New Orleans and outpointed hometown favourite Ralph Dupas over ten rounds. After nine years as a professional the removal of this obstacle had finally earned De Marco a world title shot. On March 5, 1954 De Marco won a unanimous decision over Jimmy Carter after fifteen grueling rounds in Madison Square Garden. He hustled and bossed the fight from the first bell until the last. Carter, relying entirely on his left hand, couldn't keep the eager De Marco away, who smartly ducked under his opponent's leads and launched stinging two-fisted assaults to the body. Unfortunately for De Marco, the 5,730 crowd for a world title contest was small and he picked up a paltry sum of $14,000. Eight months later the pair met in San Francisco. De Marco's preparations were disrupted by illness. Weakened by a virus and jaundice an off color De Marco was dropped in the fourteenth round with only the bell saving him. He took more punishment in the last round before the referee signaled the end of the fight. Next De Marco lost ten of his last twelve fights and finally hung up his gloves after being knocked out by Benny Medina in November 1959.

De Marco finished with a fight record of 104 bouts, 75 wins, 3 draws and 26 losses. In retirement De Marco formed one half of a music and comedy double act with boxer Allie Stolz. He also worked as a bartender, construction worker, head waiter and factory operative. For a while he owned a nightclub. In 1968 he moved to Las Vegas and spent the seventies in the casino industry as a dealer and pit boss at Caesars Palace. He relocated to Atlantic City and worked as a casino host before moving back to Las Vegas where he worked until 1985. De Marco died on December 13, 1997 in a Salt Lake City nursing home. He had been suffering from Alzheimer's disease.

TONY DE MARCO [LEONARDO LIOTTA]
WORLD WELTERWEIGHT CHAMPION 1955

Big-punching Tony De Marco almost didn't make it in the professional game but found a way to come back from the brink of anonymity to secure his place among boxing's elite, knocking out Johnny Saxton to clinch the world welterweight title in April 1955. This was a great personal triumph for De Marco, the son of a shoemaker, who had quit the ring at the age of twenty having grown disillusioned with his lack of progress. Handled by Bobby Agrippino, De Marco couldn't get Boston promoters interested. He notched fifteen wins in seventeen fights with both losses coming by way of two cut-eye injuries. De Marco hit the road, traveling to New Jersey, where he scored nine wins out of nine including five knockouts. He uprooted again and this time his destination was Montreal, Canada. It proved to be an unhappy sojourn for the Bostonian, losing both bouts.

De Marco was at a career crossroads. Feeling dispirited and depressed he chose an alternative means of survival. For a time he drove a truck and worked at a fish depot as a freezer storeman, but it was whilst he was in construction that he rediscovered his zest for boxing again. Unable to get any fights in California he headed back to Boston, where he came into contact with Anthony "Rip" Valenti, a familiar fight figure who had owned a boxing gym on Traverse Street since 1920. Valenti took an interest in De Marco and agreed to manage him, placing him under the astute tutelage of trainer Sammy Fuller. Fuller, a former world junior-welterweight champion, knew his way inside the ropes, having shared the ring with the likes of Jimmy McLarnin, Lew Ambers, Billy Petrolle and Barney Ross. Fuller taught the fighter how to use his left hook more fluidly and effectively. When the management team felt De Marco was ready to resume his career they unleashed him.

In 1955 the "Boston Hurricane" blew into championship prominence by recording a two-year unbeaten hot streak, which included fifteen wins and one draw against the best 147-pounders in the world. His victims included notables Terry Young, Paddy De Marco, Teddy Davis, Wilbur Wilson, Carlos Chavez, Johnny Cesario and George Araujo, all of them wilting in the face of De Marco's aggression. His form was such that his titular ambitions could no longer be ignored. On April 1, 1955 the exciting left-hooker got his chance against Johnny Saxton, the African American world champion who had dethroned Kid Gavilán of Cuba. They met in Boston in front of De Marco's fanatical support, and he knocked Saxton out in the fourteenth round of an exhilarating encounter.

After nearly eight years of campaigning as a professional the two-fisted wonder was now king of his class and one of Boston's best attractions, pulling in crowds of over 12,000. Two months after winning the title he defended against the rugged Carmen Basilio in Syracuse, New York, and after a punishing toe-to-toe thriller De Marco lost his laurels by a twelfth-round knockout. Five months later De Marco was given another chance and was again halted by Basilio in the same round. The two-fight series with Basilio were classic slugfests brimming with suspense, blood and thunder. In 1956 De Marco scored victories over world champions Wallace Bud Smith and Kid Gavilán, and following three successive victories in 1957, he took on Virgil Akins for the vacant Massachusetts version of the world title. De Marco lost by a fourteenth-round knockout in the Boston Gardens.

Over the next five years De Marco boxed sparingly in another six fights and with his best days behind him he announced his retirement on March 1, 1962, aged forty. He finished with a career record of 71 fights, 58 wins including 33 knockouts, 1 draw and 12 losses. De Marco was born Leonardo Liotta on January 14, 1932 in Boston's North End to Sicilian immigrants from Sciacca, in the province of Agrigento, Southern Sicily. He was one of four siblings. He fought in the amateur ranks and after twelve wins in fourteen fights he turned professional on October 21, 1948. After boxing De Marco ran a tavern in Phoenix, Arizona and later worked as a court officer in the Massachusetts legislature. Today "Tony De Marco Way," a street in the heart of Boston, honors one of its favorite sporting sons.

Notes

1. Jimmy Johnson quote taken from *Mirror of Life and Boxing World*, September 15, 1923, p. 5.
2. Johnny Brannigan, "Keep 'em laughing Frankie," *Boxing Illustrated*, October 1960, pp. 38–40, 60.
3. John A. Jarrett, "What the Immortal Benny Leonard Said About Tony Canzoneri", *Boxing News*, August 21, 1959, pp. 8–9.
4. Peter Heller, *In this Corner . . . ! Forty World Champions Tell their Story* (London, 1989) pp. 142–148.
5. Nigel Collins, "Mighty Midget," *Boxing News*, June 15, 1990, pp. 22–23.
6. Alan Goldstein, "Where Are They Now?" *Ring Magazine*, April 1980, pp. 74–75.
7. "Willie was a Genius with Boxing Gloves", *Boxing News*, July 24, 1964, pp. 8–10; Joe Duffy, "Epic Moment in a Legendary Career", *The Journal Inquirer*, February 9, 1994, p. 8.
8. Cal Fussman, "Jake La Motta: My Life," *Esquire Magazine*, June 1999, Vol. 131, Issue 6.
9. Sugar Ray Robinson with Dave Anderson, *Sugar Ray: The Sugar Ray Robinson Story* (London, 1992), p. 102.
10. Sean Matheny, "IBD interviews Joey Maxim", *International Boxing Digest*, November/December 1996, pp. 60–61.
11. Budd Schulberg, *Sparring with Hemingway and other Legends of the Fight Game* (London, 1997), p. 116; Russell Sullivan, *Rocky Marciano: The Rock of His Times* (Urbana, IL, 2002), p.177; Tracy Callis, "Rocky Marciano: The Hardest One Punch Slugger," *Wail! The CyberBoxingZone Journal*, October 2000, www.thecyberboxingzone.com (accessed November 20, 2002).
12. Telephone interview with Carmen Basilio, September 9, 1995.

APPENDIX VI: 100 OUTSTANDING ITALIAN AMERICAN PRIZEFIGHTERS 1900–55

RING MONIKER/ REAL NAME	ADDITIONAL INFO	ERA BOXED	BIRTHPLACE/ HOMETOWN
Flyweight (112 pounds)			
Al Battling Murray (Alexander Di Renza)	Contender	1910s/20s	Philadelphia, PA
Jockey Joe Dillon (Giuseppe Capizzi)	Claimed new junior-flyweight title in 1923		BP: Sicily (I) HT: Brooklyn, NY
Patsy Wallace (Pasquale Appalucci)	Contender. American flyweight champ		Philadelphia, PA
Bobby Wolgast (Francesco Giovanni Giordano)	In 1923 he scored a hat-trick of victories over reigning champs, Frankie Genaro, Pancho Villa and Joe Lynch. He never fought for a world title	1920s	BP: Atlantic City, NJ HT: Philadelphia, PA
Bantamweight (118 pounds)			
Al Delmont (Alberto Liberatore Delmonte)	1907 title claimant. Contender & world title challenger	1900s/10s	BP: Grotta Minarda, Avellino, (I) HT: Boston, MA
Joe Wagner (Joseph Valenti)	Contender & world title challenger		Manhattan, NY
Kid Beebe (Frank Boro)	Contender. Claimed to have fought in over 600 bouts		BP: Chicago, IL HT: Philadelphia, PA
Jimmy Kelly (Angelo Iorio)	Contender & world title challenger	1910s	Chicago, IL
Battling Reddy (Luigi Nobile)	Contender & world title challenger	1910s/20s	BP: Salerno, (I) HT: Harlem, NY
Jimmy Murray (Vincenzo Piccoro)	Title claimant & contender. "Bowery Champ"		BP: Genoa, (I) HT: Brooklyn, NY
Carl Tremaine (Carmelo Cantalupo)	Contender. He beat world champions Mike Ballerino, Jack "Kid" Wolfe, Eddie Martin and Bud Taylor. He never got a title shot. "Fists of Steel"		BP: Palermo, Sicily, (I) HT: Cleveland, OH
Terry Martin (Francesco Martino)	Contender. 1922 New England bantamweight champ. "Providence Panther"		BP: Avellino, (I) HT: Providence, RI
Little Jack Sharkey (Giovanni Cervati)	1922 title claimant & contender. "Westside Whirlwind"		BP: Italy HT: Manhattan, NY
Packey O'Gatty (Pasquale Agati)	Contender. "Speed Demon"		BP: Cannitello, Reggio Calabria, (I) HT: Manhattan, NY

RING MONIKER/ REAL NAME	ADDITIONAL INFO	ERA BOXED	BIRTHPLACE/ HOMETOWN
Wee Willie Spencer (William Sperico)	Contender. 1920 New England flyweight title claimant		Manhattan, NY
Tommy Ryan (Charles Marino)	Contender & world title challenger. "McKeesport Bearcat"	1920s	BP: Duquesne, PA HT: McKeesport, PA
Joe Ryder (Giuseppe Gargiulo)	Contender. 1931 New York National Guard featherweight champ. "South Brooklyn Caveman"		BP: Sicily (I) HT: Brooklyn, NY
Mose Butch (Moise Bucci)	1928–29 Pennsylvania bantamweight champ	1920s/30s	Pittsburgh, PA
KO Morgan (Andrew Esposito)	Contender & world title challenger. He beat five world champions	1920s/30s/40s	BP: Stamford, CT HT: Toledo, OH
Tommy Forte	Contender & world title challenger	1940s	Philadelphia, PA

Featherweight (126 pounds)

Eddie Lenny (Edward Setaro)	Contender & title challenger	1890s/1900s	Philadelphia, PA
Benny Yanger (Benjamin Angona)	Title claimant. In 1902 he beat Abe Atell and laid claim to 122 pound title. "Tipton Slasher"		BP: New York HT: Chicago, IL
Frank Carsey (Frank Carsello)		1900s/10s	BP: Naples (I) HT: Chicago, IL
Joe Coster (Giuseppe Agnello)	Contender. In 1911 he laid claim to the 122 pound title		BP: Casteldaccia, Palermo, Sicily (I) HT: Brooklyn, NY
Eddie Marino (Angelo Marino)	Contender		BP: Italy. HT: Georgetown, WA
Young Wagner (Anthony Sarubbi)	Contender. "West Side Slasher"		Manhattan, NY
Patsy Kline (Pasquale Gengaro)	Contender. "Newark Tornado"		BP: Naples, (I) HT: Newark, NJ
Kid Julian AKA Charles Juliano (Angelo Giuliano)	Contender. 1911 "Italian featherweight champion of America"	1900s/10s/20s	BP: Italy HT: Syracuse, NY
Joe Leonard (Giuseppe Leonardi)	Contender. 1922 South West featherweight champ. "Brooklyn Bearcat"	1910s/20s	BP: Sicily (I) HT: Brooklyn, NY
Mike Dundee (Michael Pusateri)	Title claimant at 122 pounds & contender		BP: Italy HT: Rock Island, IL
Andy Martin (Andrea Magri)	Contender. Ex-New England featherweight champ	1920s/30s	BP: Boston, MA HT: New Bedford, MA

RING MONIKER/ REAL NAME	ADDITIONAL INFO	ERA BOXED	BIRTHPLACE/ HOMETOWN
Lew Massey (Louis Masucci)	Contender & world title challenger. "Downtown Latin"		Philadelphia, PA
Johnny Farr (John Farinacci)	Contender & title challenger		Cleveland, OH
Earl Mastro (Vearle Maestro)	Contender & title challenger. "Windy City Buzzsaw"		Chicago, IL
Eddie Shea (Edward D'Onofrio)	Contender & title challenger. 1933 California junior-lightweight champ		Chicago, IL
Petey Hayes (Anthony Ferrara)	Contender. "Saugerties Buzzsaw"		Brooklyn, NY
Roger Bernard (Orazio Bernardi)	Contender	**1930s**	Flint, MI
Lulu Constantino (Carlo Constantino)	Contender & title challenger. "The Candy Kid"	**1930s/40s**	Manhattan, NY

Lightweight (135 pounds)

RING MONIKER/ REAL NAME	ADDITIONAL INFO	ERA BOXED	BIRTHPLACE/ HOMETOWN
Joe Percente I (Giuseppe Persenti)	"Italian Cyclone"	**1890s/1900s**	Kenosha, WI
Kid Thomas (Joseph Tomasullo)	Defeated best lightweights including draw with Joe Gans		Brooklyn, NY
Tommy Daly (Tommaso Brescia)	Contender		BP: San Costantino Albanese, Potenza, (I) HT: New York/ Baltimore, MD
Charlie Sieger (Angelo Sica)	World title challenger. "Hoboken Iron Man"	**1890s/1900s/10s**	BP: Monte San Giacomo, Salerno, (I) HT: Hoboken, NJ
Terry Young (Anthony Samperi)	"Gashouse Terror"	**1900s/10s**	Manhattan, NY
Johnny Marto (Vincent John Marto)	Contender		Manhattan, NY
Kid Locke (Rosario Lucca)			BP: Messina, Sicily (I), HT: Philadelphia, PA
Billy Willis (William Volpe)			Philadelphia, PA
Packey Hommey (Giuseppe Ignazio Benanti)	Contender. "East Side Terror"	**1900s/10s/20s**	BP: Marineo, Palermo, Sicily (I) HT: Manhattan, NY
Johnny Harvey (Giovanni Gallo)	Contender. "Harlem's Belting Coal-Man"	**1910s**	Harlem, NY
Bud Christiano AKA Young Gus Christie (Augustine Christiano)	Contender	**1910s/20s**	Buffalo, NY

RING MONIKER/ REAL NAME	ADDITIONAL INFO	ERA BOXED	BIRTHPLACE/ HOMETOWN
Mickey Donley (Michael Bozza)	Contender		Newark, NJ
Pal Moran (Paul Miorana)	Contender		New Orleans, LA
Phil Logan (Phillip Logandice)	Contender. 1920 Western New York lightweight champ		Jamestown, NY
Jimmy Hanlon (Louis Quaratino)	"Denver Caveman". Also dubbed the "Second Battling Nelson"		Denver, CO
Gene Delmont (Ernesto Barasso)	World title challenger. "Gentleman Gene"		BP: Italy HT: Memphis, TN
Basil Galiano (Basile Galiano)	Contender. 1923 Southern lightweight champ		New Orleans, LA
Lou Paluso (Louis Pagliuso)	Contender. 1926 Pacific Coast lightweight champ. In 1930 he was recognized as world junior-lightweight champ in Utah	1920s	Salt Lake City, UT
Cuddy De Marco (Christopher De Marco)	Contender		Charleroi, PA
Tommy Cello (Edward Tomasello)	Contender & former California lightweight champ		San Francisco, CA
Billy Petrolle (William Michael Petrolla)	Contender. One of the best boxers never to have won a world title. "Fargo Express"	1920s/30s	BP: Berwick, PA HT: Fargo, ND
Tony Falco	Number one contender for Barney Ross's junior-welterweight crown but was never given a title chance. "South Philly Sheik"	1930s/40s	Philadelphia, PA
Eddie Giosa (Armando Giosa)	Contender. He beat four world champions but never got a title shot. "Fistic Comebacker"	1940s	Philadelphia, PA

Welterweight (147 pounds)

Tommy Howell (Antonio Lauletta)	Contender	1900s/10s	BP: Italy. HT: Philadelphia, PA
Paul Doyle (Paolo San Filippo)	Contender. Fought in over 250 bouts and was never knocked out or stopped. "Da Vinci with Boxing Gloves"	1910s/20s	BP: Messina, Sicily (I) HT: Brooklyn, NY

RING MONIKER/ REAL NAME	ADDITIONAL INFO	ERA BOXED	BIRTHPLACE/ HOMETOWN
Bronx Jimmy Kelly (John Picciano)	Contender & world title challenger. "Bronx Tiger"		Bronx, NY
Jack Perry (Antonio Perri)	Contender & world title challenger. "Pittsburgh Whirlwind"		BP: Nicastro, Cosenza (I) HT: Pittsburgh, PA
Eddie Whalen (Colasunno)	1927 New York National Guard welterweight champ & 1930 New York middleweight champ	**1920s/30s**	Brooklyn, NY
Johnny Indrisano AKA Johnny Andrews	Contender. He beat five world champions in non-title bouts. Never fought for the title		BP: East Boston, MA HT: Cambridge, MA
Paulie Walker (Paul Salvatore)	Contender. "Trenton Bulldog"		Trenton, NJ
Jimmy Leto	Contender. He beat six world champions. 1941 Maryland world welterweight title challenger	**1930s/40s**	BP: Bayonne, NJ HT: Hartford, CT
Tony Janiro	Contender. "Babyface Tony"	**1940s**	BP: Springdale, PA HT: Youngstown, OH
Johnny Cesario	Contender. 1947 New England welterweight champ. 1948 New England middleweight champ	**1940s/50s**	Hartford, CT
Tony Pellone AKA Jimmy Pell (Ciro Pellone)	Contender		Manhattan, NY
Charlie Fusari (Calogero Fusari)	Contender & world title challenger. "Fighting Milkman"		BP: Alcamo, Trapani, Sicily (I) HT: Irvington, NJ
Joe Miceli (Joseph Miceli)	Contender. Twice beat world lightweight champs Ike Williams and Wallace Smith and once Johnny Saxton, the welterweight champion. Never given a title shot		Brooklyn, NY

Middleweight (160 pounds)

Al Rogers (Angelo Christiano)	Contender. "Buffalo Iron Man"	**1900s/10s/20s**	Buffalo, NY
Frank Carbone	Contender. 1923 Southern middleweight champ. "The Destroyer"	**1910s/20s**	Brooklyn, NY
Joe Borrell (Joseph Borrelli)	1913–14 title claimant. Scored victory over Harry Greb		BP: New York HT: Philadelphia, PA

RING MONIKER/ REAL NAME	ADDITIONAL INFO	ERA BOXED	BIRTHPLACE/ HOMETOWN
Young Fisher (Charles Fazio)	Contender. "Caveman"		Syracuse, NY
Italian Joe Gans (Anthony Camberlango)	Contender. "Brooklyn Caveman"		Brooklyn, NY
Paul Pirrone	Contender	1920s/30s	Cleveland, OH
Young Terry (Samuel Pane)	Contender & world title challenger. "Trenton Terror"	1930s	Trenton, NJ
Steve Belloise	Contender & world title challenger. "The Spider" & "Ginks"	1930s/40s	Bronx, NY
Tony Martin (Anthony Cianciola)	Contender. 1940 Wisconsin middleweight champ		Milwaukee, WI
Rocky Castellani (Atillio Castellani)	Contender & world title challenger	1940s/50s	Luzerne County, PA
Joey Giardello (Carmine Orlando Tilelli)**	1963 World middleweight champ	1950s/60s	BP: Brooklyn, NY HT: Philadelphia, PA
Joey Giambra	Contender & world title challenger		Buffalo, NY

Light-heavyweight (175 pounds)

Tony Caponi	Contender	1900s/10s	St Paul, MN
Sailor Grande (Charles Grande)	1912 US Navy middleweight champ & 1921 "Panamanian heavyweight champ"	1910s/20s	BP: Paterson, NJ, HT: San Francisco, CA
Young Firpo (Guido Bardelli)	Contender. 1933 Pacific Coast light-heavyweight champ. "Wild Bull of Idaho"	1920s/30s	BP: Barre, VT HT: Burke, ID
Tony Shucco (Anthony Sciucco)	Contender. Between 1932–36 he beat five world champions; Lou Brouillard, Maxie Rosenbloom, Bob Olin and heavyweights James Braddock and Jack Sharkey. Never got a title shot	1920s/30s/40s	Boston, MA
Nick Barone (Carmine Barrone)	Contender & world heavyweight title challenger. "Fighting Marine"	1940s/50s	Syracuse, NY
Willie Pastrano**	1963–65 world light- heavyweight champ	1950s/60s	New Orleans, LA

RING MONIKER/ REAL NAME	ADDITIONAL INFO	ERA BOXED	BIRTHPLACE/ HOMETOWN
Heavyweight (190+ pounds)			
Fireman Jim Flynn AKA Andrew Haymes (Andrew Chiariglione)	Contender. The only boxer to KO Jack Dempsey	**1900s/10s**	Pueblo, CO
Tony Ross (Antonio Molinaro)	Contender. "Italian Bearcat"		BP: Baia e Latina, Caserta (I) HT: Newcastle, PA
Patsy Perroni (Pasquale Pavona)	Contender	**1920s/30s/40s**	BP: New York HT: Canton, OH
Tony Galento (Dominick Galento)	Contender & world title challenger		Orange, NJ
Al Ettore (Albert Dettorre)	Contender	**1930/40s**	Philadelphia, PA
Tami Mauriello (Stefano Mauriello)	Contender & world title challenger. "Bronx Barkeep" & "Fordham Flash"		Bronx, NY
Pat Valentino (Pasquale Guglielmi)	Contender & world title challenger	**1940s**	San Francisco, CA
Roland La Starza	Contender and world title challenger	**1940s/50s**	Bronx, NY

Notes

*The one hundred outstanding Italian American boxers are drawn from a vast pool of headliners and top notchers and exclude world champions and recognized title claimants profiled in this chapter.

** Both Joey Giardello and Willie Pastrano won world titles in the early sixties but they are included as they featured prominently throughout the fifties. Giardello remained the main middleweight contender in the fifties without being awarded a title shot. Similarly Pastrano began his professional boxing career in 1951 and by end of 1955 had fought in 43 bouts, achieving a top ten world ranking in the heavyweight category after beating contender Rex Layne.

Some boxers fought in more than one weight category but they have only been listed once.

Where it has been possible both birthplace/hometown are included.

The fighters are firstly listed by weight category and then by era.

Abbreviation

(I) = Italy

Chapter 5

APPENDIX VII: ITALIAN AMERICAN CHAMPIONS 1900–55: BIRTHPLACE, YEAR OF BIRTH, YEAR AND AGE TITLE WON AND DECENNIAL IMMIGRATION

BOXER	BIRTHPLACE	YEAR OF BIRTH	YEAR TITLE WON*	AGE TITLE WON	DECADE OF MIGRATION**
Hugo Kelly #	Italy	1882	1905	23	1890s
Kid Murphy #	Boston, MA	1886	1907	20	1880s
Frankie Conley #	Italy	1890	1910	19	1890s
Young Zulu Kid #	Italy	1897	1915	18	1890s
Pete Herman	New Orleans, LA	1896	1917	20	1890s
Johnny Wilson	New York City	1893	1920	27	1890s
Johnny Dundee	Italy	1893	1921	28	1880s
Carl Duane	New York City	1902	1923	21	1890s
Lou Bogash #	Italy	1901	1923	21	1900s
Steve Sullivan	New York City	1897	1924	27	1890s
Eddie Martin	New York City	1903	1924	21	1890s
Mike Ballerino	Asbury Park, NJ	1901	1925	24	1890s
Frankie Genaro	New York City	1901	1925	24	1890s
Fidel La Barba	New York City	1905	1925	19	1900s
Rocky Kansas	Buffalo, NY	1895	1925	30	1890s
Sammy Mandell	Italy	1904	1926	22	1900s
Joe Dundee	Italy	1903	1927	24	1900s
Tony Canzoneri	New Orleans, LA	1908	1927	19	1900s
Bushy Graham	Utica, NY	1903	1928	25	1900s
Willie La Morte #	New York City	1904	1929	25	1900s
Battling Battalino	Hartford, CT	1908	1929	20	1890s
Midget Wolgast	Philadelphia, PA	1910	1930	19	1900s
Tommy Paul	Buffalo, NY	1909	1932	23	1890s
Sammy Fuller #	Boston, MA	1906	1932	26	1900s
George Nichols	Sandusky, OH	1908	1932	24	1900s
Lou Scozza #	Buffalo, NY	1905	1932	27	1890s
Young Corbett III	Italy	1905	1933	27	1900s
Vince Dundee	Baltimore, MD	1907	1933	26	1900s
Lou Salica	New York City	1913	1935	22	1900s
Mike Belloise	New York City	1911	1936	24	1900s
Lou Ambers	Herkimer, NY	1913	1936	22	1900s
Tony Marino	Duquesne, PA	1912	1936	24	1900s
Fred Apostoli	San Francisco, CA	1913	1937	24	1900s
Harry Jeffra	Baltimore, MD	1914	1937	22	1900s
Melio Bettina	Little Falls, NY	1915	1939	23	1900s
Pete Scalzo	New York City	1917	1940	22	1900s
Jimmy Perrin #	New Orleans, LA	1915	1940	25	1900s
Izzy Jannazzo #	Ensley, AL	1915	1940	25	1900s
Sammy Angott	Cleveland, OH	1915	1940	25	1900s
Willie Pep	Hartford, CT	1922	1942	20	1910s
Phil Terranova	New York City	1919	1943	23	1910s
Sal Bartolo	Boston, MA	1917	1944	26	1900s
Tippy Larkin	Garfield, NJ	1917	1946	29	1900s

continued on next page

BOXER	BIRTHPLACE	YEAR OF BIRTH	YEAR TITLE WON*	AGE TITLE WON	DECADE OF MIGRATION**
Marty Servo	Schenectady, NY	1919	1946	26	1910s
Rocky Graziano	New York City	1922	1947	25	1910s
Jake La Motta	New York City	1921	1949	27	1910s
Joey Maxim	Cleveland, OH	1922	1950	27	1910s
Rocky Marciano	Brockton, MA	1923	1952	29	1910s
Carmen Basilio	Canastota, NY	1927	1955	28	1910s
Paddy De Marco	New York City	1928	1954	26	1910s
Tony De Marco	Boston, MA	1932	1955	23	1920s

\# Denotes title claimants

* Denotes year of first title captured only. Some boxers listed won more than one title.

** Denotes decade of migration of either the child or the child's parents

DECENNIAL IMMIGRATION OF ITALIAN IMMIGRANTS TO THE UNITED STATES OF AMERICA AND BOXING CHAMPIONS 1900–55

DECADE	HIGHEST RANKING OF MIGRATION	MIGRATION ORIGIN OF BOXING CHAMPIONS (number)	WORLD BOXING TITLES WON (number)	HIGHEST RANKING OF WORLD BOXING TITLES WON
1880–89	7th	2	None	None
1890–99	1st	14	None	None
1900–09	2nd	25	2	5th*
1910–19	1st	9	3	4th**
1920–29	3rd	1	16	1st
1930–39	n/a	n/a	14	1st
1940–49	n/a	n/a	11	1st
1950–55	n/a	n/a	5	2nd

Notes

The Highest Ranking of Migration column refers to the overall position of the Italian American cohort in relation to all other ethnic immigrant groups who traveled to the United States over the decade shown.

The Highest Ranking of World Boxing Titles won refers to the overall position attained by the Italian American cohort in terms of titular success and recognition in professional boxing during the period outlined.

Migration Origin of Boxing Champions column refers to the specific wave of migration the boxing champion belonged to. In the majority of cases the boxer was born in the United States. In these cases the migration of parents is logged instead.

* Denotes that the Italian American cohort was ranked in equal fifth place alongside England and Canada.

** Denotes that the Italian American cohort was ranked in equal fourth place alongside the Jewish American and Wales boxing cohort.

n/a – not applicable for study purposes

Source

Immigration data taken from Thomas Jenkins, "Changes in Ethnic and Racial Representation among Professional Boxers: A Study in Ethnic Succession," (Master's dissertation.,University of Chicago, 1955), p. 31, from Niles Carpenter, *Immigrants and Their Children*, 1920, p. 64; Reports of the Commissioner of Immigration, and the Census of 1930.

APPENDIX VIII^A:
OVERALL WORLD BOXING CHAMPIONS 1900–55*

Ethnic American cohort	1900–09	1910–19	1920–29	1930–39	1940–49	1950–55	TOTAL
Italian	2	3	16	14	11	5	**51**
Irish	12	7	8	4	3		**34**
African	3		1	6	9	9	**28**
Jewish	4	3	12	6			**25**
German	1	5	4	2			**12**
English	3	1	3	1			**8**
Polish	1		1	3	1		**6**
Danish	1	2					**3**
Scottish		2		1			**3**
Czech	1	1					**2**
Lithuanian		1		1			**2**
Mexican					2		**2**
Slovak			1	1			**2**
Swiss	1				1		**2**
Ukrainian				2			**2**
Unknown*	1	1					**2**
Austrian		1					**1**
Belgian		1					**1**
Croatian					1		**1**
Filipino						1	**1**
French	1						**1**
Hungarian					1		**1**
Norwegian				1			**1**
Russian					1		**1**
Swedish						1	**1**
Syrian				1			**1**
Welsh			1				**1**
TOTAL (A)	**31**	**28**	**47**	**43**	**30**	**16**	**195**

continued on next page

Other countries	1900–09	1910–19	1920–29	1930–39	1940–49	1950–55	TOTAL
England	2	6	1	4	1	2	16
France		1	4	3	1	1	10
Canada	2	1	2	2	1		8
Mexico				2	2	2	6
Philippines			1	3			4
Wales	1	3					4
Scotland			1	1	1		3
Australia		1				1	2
Cuba				1		1	2
Germany				2			2
Ireland		1				1	2
South Africa			1			1	2
Argentina						1	1
Austria				1			1
Barbados	1						1
Belgium				1			1
Denmark		1					1
Greece					1		1
Italy				1			1
Japan						1	1
Panama			1				1
Puerto Rico				1			1
Senegal			1				1
Spain				1			1
Tunisia				1			1
TOTAL (B)	**6**	**14**	**12**	**24**	**7**	**11**	**74**
TOTAL (A+B)	**37**	**42**	**59**	**67**	**37**	**27**	**269**

Notes

*Refers to undisputed champions and creditable title claimants, some of whom were either recognized by an American state, national or international sanctioning body. Other criteria considered here is the caliber of opposition, advertised world title contests receiving national or international press coverage.

Under the heading **Unlisted Claimants** is a selection of fighters of excellent, good and fair ability that gained limited exposure as title claimants. These have not been included in the quantitative analysis of this paper and their inclusion merely highlights the common practice in use at the time.

* Some great boxers achieved multiple title captures, sometimes at different weights but for the purpose of this paper only their first title is recorded.
* Unless stated all world champions listed received undisputed recognition.
* The main national and international sanctioning bodies to award titles during the above-mentioned period included NSYAC (New York State Athletic Commission), NBA (National Boxing Association), IBU (International Boxing Union), the European regulatory boxing organization, BBBC (The British Boxing Board of Control. In some cases state/s or individual countries recognized a boxer as their world champion. In these cases the name is bracketed.
* Boxers who were at one time recognized as champions for one sanctioning body and later assumed undisputed titleholder status are listed as undisputed champions only.
* The junior-lightweight championship began in 1924 and ended in 1931 when the weight category fell into disuse. The junior-welterweight class began in 1928 and stopped in 1931. Both classes resumed in 1962.

APPENDIX VIII^B: ITALIAN AMERICAN WORLD BOXING TITLE CLAIMANTS 1900–55

DECADE	NAME	WEIGHT CLASS	TITLE WON
	Hugo Kelly	middleweight (claimant)	1907
	Kid Murphy	bantamweight (claimant)	1907
1910–19	Frankie Conley	bantamweight (California)	1910
	Young Zulu Kid	flyweight (claimant)	1915
	Pete Herman	bantamweight	1917
1920–29	Johnny Wilson	middleweight	1920
	Johnny Dundee	junior-lightweight	1921
	Carl Duane	junior-featherweight	1923
	Lou Bogash	middleweight (NYSAC)	1923
	Steve Sullivan	junior-lightweight	1924
	Eddie Martin	bantamweight	1924
	Mike Ballerino	junior-lightweight	1925
	Frankie Genaro	flyweight	1925
	Fidel La Barba	flyweight	1925
	Rocky Kansas	lightweight	1925
	Sammy Mandell	lightweight	1926
	Joe Dundee	welterweight	1927
	Tony Canzoneri	featherweight	1927
	Bushy Graham	bantamweight (NYSAC)	1928
	Willie La Morte	flyweight (NYSAC)	1929
	Battling Battalino	featherweight	1929
1930–39	Midget Wolgast	flyweight (NYSAC)	1930
	Tommy Paul	featherweight (NBA)	1932
	Sammy Fuller	junior-welterweight	1932
	George Nichols	light-heavyweight (NBA)	1932
	Lou Scozza	light-heavyweight (claimant)	1932
	Young Corbett III	welterweight	1933
	Vince Dundee	middleweight (NYSAC)	1933
	Lou Salica	bantamweight	1935
	Mike Belloise	featherweight (NYSAC)	1936
	Lou Ambers	lightweight	1936
	Tony Marino	bantamweight	1936
	Fred Apostoli	middleweight	1937
	Harry Jeffra	bantamweight	1937
	Melio Bettina	light-heavyweight (NYSAC)	1939
1940–49	Pete Scalzo	featherweight (NBA)	1940
	Jimmy Perrin	featherweight (Louisiana)	1940
	Izzy Jannazzo	welterweight (Maryland)	1940
	Sammy Angott	lightweight	1941
	Willie Pep	featherweight	1942
	Phil Terranova	featherweight (NBA)	1943
	Sal Bartolo	featherweight (NBA)	1944
	Tippy Larkin	junior-welterweight	1946
	Marty Servo	welterweight	1946
	Rocky Graziano	middleweight	1947
	Jake La Motta	middleweight	1949
1950–55	Joey Maxim	light-heavyweight	1950
	Rocky Marciano	heavyweight	1952
	Carmen Basilio	welterweight	1953
	Paddy De Marco	lightweight	1954
	Tony De Marco	welterweight	1955

This list includes Italy-born children who developed their pugilistic skills in American rings and one boxer of mixed Italian-Albanian extraction. *Ring Magazine* recognized Sammy Fuller as the junior-welterweight champion following a twelve-round victory over titlist Jackie "Kid" Berg in May 1932.

APPENDIX VIII^c: IRISH AMERICAN WORLD BOXING TITLE CLAIMANTS 1900–55

DECADE	NAME	WEIGHT CLASS	TITLE WON
1900–09	Terry McGovern	featherweight	1900
	Matty Matthews	welterweight	1900
	Harry Forbes	bantamweight	1901
	James "Rube" Ferns	welterweight	1901
	George Gardner	light-heavyweight	1903
	Frankie Neil	bantamweight	1903
	Jimmy Walsh	bantamweight (claimant)	1905
	Philadelphia Jack O'Brien	light-heavyweight	1905
	Honey Mellody	welterweight	1906
	Mike "Twin" Sullivan	welterweight (California)	1907
	Jimmy Gardner	welterweight (Louisiana)	1908
	Jimmy Reagan	bantamweight (claimant)	1909
1910–19	Jimmy Clabby	welterweight (Australia))	1910
	Jack Dillon	light-heavyweight	1911
	Johnny Kilbane	featherweight	1912
	Mike Glover	welterweight	1915
	Jack Britton	welterweight	1915
	Mike O'Dowd	middleweight	1917
	Jack Dempsey	heavyweight	1919
1920–29	Joe Lynch	bantamweight	1920
	Pinkey Mitchell	junior-welterweight (1)	1922
	Mickey Walker	welterweight	1922
	Mike McTigue	light-heavyweight	1923
	Gene Tunney	heavyweight	1926
	Dick "Honeyboy" Finnegan	featherweight (Massachusetts)	1926
	Jimmy Slattery	light-heavyweight	1927
	Tommy Loughran	light-heavyweight	1927
1930–39	Thomas Freeman	welterweight	1930
	James Braddock	heavyweight	1935
	Freddie Steele	middleweight	1936
	Billy Conn	light-heavyweight	1939
1940–49	Lew Jenkins	lightweight	1940
	Ken Overlin	middleweight	1940
	Freddie Cochrane	welterweight	1941
1950–55	NONE		

This list includes Mike McTigue and George Gardner, both light-heavyweights, who were born in Ireland and came to the USA in their teens. The list does not include Ireland-born world welterweight champion Jimmy McLarnin who immigrated as a toddler to Canada where he served his apprenticeship in boxing before moving to the USA. Jack Dempsey is of mixed Irish-Scotch and Native Indian extraction. Rube Ferns, Jack Dillon and Thomas Freeman are of mixed Irish-Scotch background. One source states Dillon to be of English descent. Ken Overlin is of mixed Irish-English origin.

(1) Pinkey Mitchell, the first junior-welterweight titleholder, only assumed the belt after topping the popular vote conducted by the *Boxing Blade* magazine.

APPENDIX VIII^D: AFRICAN AMERICAN WORLD BOXING TITLE CLAIMANTS 1900–55

DECADE	NAME	WEIGHT CLASS	TITLE WON
1900–09	Joe Gans	lightweight	1902
	Dixie Kid	welterweight	1904
	Jack Johnson	heavyweight	1908
1910–19	NONE		
1920–29	Theodore Flowers	middleweight	1926
1930–39	Young Jack Thompson	welterweight	1930
	William "Gorilla" Jones	middleweight (NBA)	1932
	John Henry Lewis	light-heavyweight	1935
	Joe Louis	heavyweight	1937
	Henry Armstrong	featherweight	1937
	"Tiger" Jack Fox	light-heavyweight (NYSAC)	1938
1940–49	Georgie Pace	bantamweight (NBA)	1940
	Jackie Wilson	featherweight (NBA)	1941
	Beau Jack	lightweight (NYSAC)	1942
	Luther "Slugger" White	lightweight (Maryland)	1943
	Bob Montgomery	lightweight (NYSAC)	1943
	Ike Williams	lightweight	1945
	Harold Dade	bantamweight	1947
	Sandy Saddler	featherweight	1948
	Ezzard Charles	heavyweight	1949
1950–55	Jersey Joe Walcott	heavyweight	1951
	Sugar Ray Robinson	middleweight	1951
	Johnny Bratton	welterweight (NBA)	1951
	Jimmy Carter	lightweight	1951
	Archie Moore	light-heavyweight	1952
	Percy Bassett	featherweight (NBA)	1952
	Teddy "Redtop" Davis	featherweight (NBA)	1953
	Johnny Saxton	welterweight	1954
	Wallace "Bud" Smith	lightweight	1955

African Americans charted only include those born in the United States. Percy Bassett was recognized by the NBA as the "interim champion" whilst titleholder Sandy Saddler was on armed service duty during the Second World War. When John Henry Lewis relinquished his light-heavyweight championship in 1938, "Tiger" Jack Fox won an elimination tournament beating Al Gainer in the final. Though not universally accepted as the light-heavyweight champion, the NYSAC accorded titular recognition to Fox who subsequently lost his crown to Melio Bettina several months later.

APPENDIX VIIIᴱ: JEWISH AMERICAN WORLD BOXING TITLE CLAIMANTS 1900–55

DECADE	NAME	WEIGHT CLASS	TITLE WON
1900–09	Harry Harris	bantamweight	1901
	Abe Atell	featherweight	1904
	Harry Lewis	welterweight (claimant)	1908
	Monte Atell	bantamweight (California)	1909
1910–19	Al McCoy	middleweight	1913
	Battling Levinsky	light-heavyweight	1916
	Benny Leonard	lightweight	1917
1920–29	Jack "Kid" Wolfe	junior-featherweight	1922
	Dave Rosenberg	middleweight (NYSAC)	1922
	Jack Bernstein	junior-lightweight	1923
	Abe Goldstein	bantamweight	1924
	Charley Rosenberg	bantamweight	1925
	Louis Kaplan	featherweight	1925
	Mushy Callahan	junior-welterweight	1926
	Izzy Schwartz	flyweight (NYSAC)	1927
	Pinky Silverberg	flyweight (NBA)	1927
	Benny Bass	featherweight	1927
	Newsboy Brown	flyweight (California)	1928
	Jackie Fields	welterweight	1929
1930–39	Al Singer	lightweight	1930
	Maxie Rosenbloom	light-heavyweight	1930
	Ben Jeby	middleweight (NYSAC)	1932
	Barney Ross	lightweight	1933
	Bob Olin	light-heavyweight	1934
	Solly Kreiger	middleweight (NBA)	1938
1940–49	NONE		
1950–55	NONE		

Jewish American boxers include those who came to the United States as children from Germany, Russia and from Eastern Europe. There is some confusion as to whether Al McCoy is German or Jewish. Boxing historian Tracy Callis states he is German whilst various Jewish organizations say he is Jewish.

APPENDIX VIII^F: UNLISTED CLAIMANTS

ITALIAN AMERICAN

DECADE	NAME	WEIGHT CLASS	TITLE CLAIM
1900–09	Benny Yanger	featherweight (1)	1902
	Al Delmont	bantamweight (2)	1907
1910–19	Joe Coster	bantamweight (3)	1911
	"Fireman" Jim Flynn	light-heavyweight (8)	1911
	Joe Borrell	middleweight (4)	1914
	Frankie Izzo	flyweight (12)	1916
1920–29	Jockey Joe Dillon	junior-flyweight (6)	1920
	Bobby Doyle	junior-flyweight (10)	1921
	Little Jack Sharkey	junior-lightweight (5)	1922
	Mike Dundee	junior-featherweight (9)	1923
1930–39	Lou Paluso	junior-lightweight (11)	1930
	Eddie Shea	junior-lightweight (13)	1930
1940–49	Lou Barbetta	junior-featherweight (7)	1941

(1) Benny Yanger made a tentative world title claim when he was proclaimed 122-pound "Champion of America" by the West End Athletic Club in St Louis, Missouri following a nineteenth round stoppage of world champion Abe Atell.

(2) Al Delmont claimed the bantamweight title when he won a fight on a foul against title claimant George "Digger" Stanley of England in 1907. It has been reported that Delmont won the world 116-pound title.

(3) Joe Coster won a newspaper decision over the officially recognized world champion Abe Atell in 1911. He followed that up by asserting his claim to the 122-pound belt when he beat Frankie Conley in a contest promoted as a world title fight.

(4) Joe Borrell received tentative claimant status in Great Britain when he beat George Bernard of France in a fight billed as a world middleweight title fight in Liverpool, England in 1914. His claim received wider support when he beat future world champ Harry Greb and Frank Mantell, former world middleweight claimant.

(5) Little Jack Sharkey laid claim to the junior-lightweight title in 1922 but it was not taken seriously.

(6) Jockey Joe Dillon was recognized by New York State as the first champion of the newly created junior-flyweight division. He did not fight anyone for the title.

(7) The American Federation of Boxing appointed Lou "Peanuts" Barbetta as the 122-pound junior-featherweight champ. He lost his claim to the title, losing to Davey Crawford in the same year.

(8) "Fireman" Jim Flynn laid claim to the light-heavyweight title without ever defending it.

(9) Mike Dundee of Rock Island, Illinois laid claim to the world junior-featherweight title when he knocked out title claimant Benny Gould of Canada on April 10, 1923 in New York City. His claim was not taken seriously.

(10) Bobby Doyle's claim to the junior-flyweight title was not taken seriously. He won a ten round points decision over Jockey Joe Dillon in Pittsfield, Massachusetts, but he was six pounds over the stipulated championship weight limit.

(11) Lou Paluso, a worthy contender in his own right, was recognized as the junior-lightweight champion of the world by Utah State in 1930 and by the *Ogden Examiner* newspaper. His claim was dismissed outside of the state.

(12) Frankie Izzo of Chicago laid claim to the 105-pound world title in 1916.

(13) On March 28,1930 Eddie Shea convincingly beat Benny Bass, the junior-lightweight champion, on a points decision in St Louis in a no decision bout. Bass title was at risk if he had lost inside the distance. The club staging the contest declared Shea champion but his titlular claim was never accorded general recognition.

IRISH AMERICAN

DECADE	NAME	WEIGHT CLASS	TITLE CLAIM
1900–09	Clarence Forbes	bantamweight (6)	1900
	Johnny Reagan	bantamweight	1900
	Charley McKeever	middleweight	1900
	Tim Callahan	featherweight	1901
	Danny Dougherty	bantamweight (+)	1901
	"Kid" McFadden	bantamweight	1901
	Eddie Hanlon	featherweight (7)	1903
	Tommy Sullivan	featherweight (1)	1904
	Buddy Ryan	welterweight (8)	1904
	Joe Thomas	welterweight (9)	1906
1910–19	Spike Kelly	welterweight	1913
	Gunboat Smith	heavyweight (2)	1914
1920–29	Ritchie Mitchell	junior-welterweight (3)	1920
	Eddie Fitzsimmons	junior-welterweight (3)	1921
	Jock Malone	middleweight (4)	1922
	Dave Shade	welterweight (5)	1925
1950–55	Tommy Collins	featherweight (10)	1952

(+)   Danny Dougherty was acclaimed title claimant following his win over Steve Flanagan in March 1900.

(1)   Tommy Sullivan received claimant status when he beat Abe Atell in a non-title bout.

(2)   Gunboat Smith was a "white heavyweight" world champion. He has been listed as Irish but there is some confusion over his ethnic background. *The Los Angeles Times* reported that Smith is of Norwegian descent and his real name is Edward Eckblad.

(3)   Both Ritchie Mitchell and Eddie Fitzsimmons claimed the junior welterweight title in the early twenties.

(4)   Jock Malone was recognized as a title claimant by Ohio State boxing commission in 1922.

(5)   Dave Shade was recognized by the New York State Athletic Commission as their welterweight title claimant. He lost his claimant status to Jimmy Jones.

(6)   Clarence Forbes was recognized as a world title claimant by the Canadian boxing authority.

(7)   Eddie Hanlon was recognized in California as a world title claimant following his victory over fellow contender Benny Yanger in 1903.

(8)   Buddy Ryan took over Billy "Honey" Mellody's "White" world welterweight title claim in 1904.

(9)   Joe Thomas beat fellow claimant Billy "Honey" Mellody by a knockout, and he laid claim retrospectively when Mellody went on to win the undisputed welterweight title from Joe Walcott.

(10)   Tommy Collins won the NBA world "Interim" featherweight title. The championship was designed to find an active titleholder whilst Sandy Saddler, the undisputed champ, was absent on military duty during the Second World War. Collins's claim was not taken seriously.

JEWISH AMERICAN

DECADE	NAME	WEIGHT CLASS	TITLE CLAIM
1900–09	Tommy Feltz	bantamweight (1)	1902
1910–19	Charley White	lightweight (6)	1914
	Johnny Rosner	flyweight (claimant)	1916
	Artie O'Leary	junior-lightweight (2)	1917
	Joe Burman	bantamweight (5)	1919
1920–29	Oakland Jimmy Duffy	junior-welterweight (claimant)	1920
	Charlie Beecher	junior-featherweight (3)	1922
	Red Chapman	junior-featherweight (4)	1922
	Harry Blitman	junior-featherweight	1923

(1)   Tommy Feltz was born in Poland and claimed the bantamweight title in 1902
(2)   Artie O'Leary is considered the first title claimant of the junior-lightweight category.
(3)   Charlie Beecher laid claim to the 122-pound junior-featherweight title.
(4)   Red Chapman beat Beecher for his version of the world junior-featherweight title as reported by the *Boston Globe*. In 1927 He was recognized by the NBA as featherweight champion.
(5)   England-born Joe Burman claimed the world title when he outpointed champion Pete Herman in 1919. Herman insisted that his title was not at stake and this was generally accepted. In 1923 Burman was again at the centre of a title claim. The New York boxing commission stripped Joe Lynch of his belt for refusing to defend it due to injury. Once the physician's examination revealed that Lynch was probably feigning injury the authorities awarded Burman the title. One day later Burman lost it in a sanctioned title contest to Abe Goldstein who was crowned the new bantamweight champion.
(6)   Charley White, the England-born boxer won a newspaper decision over lightweight claimant Willie Ritchie. The *Milwaukee Free Press* reported White had severely punished Ritchie but he continued as the lightweight titlist.

AFRICAN AMERICAN

DECADE	NAME	WEIGHT CLASS	TITLE CLAIM
1900–09	Denver Ed Martin	heavyweight*	1902
	Young Peter Jackson	welterweight (claimant)+	1904
	Kid Fitzgerald	featherweight (2)	1905
	Sam Langford	heavyweight *	1909
	Sam McVey	heavyweight *	1909
	Joe Jeanette	heavyweight *	1909
1910–19	Harry Wills	heavyweight *	1914
	Bill Tate	heavyweight*	1917
1930–39	George Godfrey	heavyweight (1)	1935
1940–49	Jimmy Bivins	light-heavyweight (3)	1943

All asterisked boxers claimed the "world colored heavyweight championship." A color bar imposed by the boxing establishment following Jack Johnson's reign meant that they were prevented from challenging for the world title.
Canada-born Sam Langford is included in the African American group as he learnt to box in the United States at the age of fourteen and made Boston his home. In addition Langford was acclaimed the IBU light-heavyweight champion in 1911 but his claim went nowhere.
(1)   George Godfrey received IBU world champion recognition when he beat Pierre Charles in 1935. This claim was not taken seriously elsewhere.
(2)   *The Sporting Life* reported Kid Fitzgerald of Baltimore as the American 126-pound world title claimant in 1905.
(3)   With Gus Lesnevich, world light-heavyweight champ, away on military service between 1942 and 1946, Ohio State sanctioned the "Duration" light-heavyweight tournament, and in 1943 Jimmy Bivins won the belt when he outpointed Anton Christoforides. He made one defense of the title but was never able to get a title match with Lesnevich on his return.
+ Young Peter Jackson of Baltimore claimed the world welterweight title when he knocked out champ Joe Walcott in four rounds. The claim was not generally accepted.

APPENDIX IX[A]: OVERALL WORLD TOP TEN RANKINGS 1924–55

1920s (1924–29)

Ethnic American cohort	Fly	Bantam	Feather	Jr-light	Light	Jr-welter	Welter	Middle	Light-heavy	Heavy	**Total**
Jewish	11	9	22	22	18	10	9	8	12		**121**
Italian	19	15	13	13	14	3	10	1	2		**90**
Irish	1	1	3	5	4	1	12	22	23	17	**89**
African		1	1	1	4	4	6	7	1	8	**33**
German			1		1	4	3	5	6		**20**
English (1)	1	4	3	5		1				2	**16**
Unknown*		1			2	1	4	2	4	2	**16**
Slovak (2)							2	1	1	4	**8**
Portuguese			2	2			2				**6**
Welsh	5						1				**6**
Lithuanian										5	**5**
Mexican			2	1				2			**5**
Scotch (5)					4				1		**5**
Polish				2					2		**4**
Czech									3		**3**
Greek					3						**3**
Native Indian	1		1	1							**3**
Syrian (4)		2		1							**3**
Croatian							2				**2**
Norwegian		2									**2**
Armenian					1						**1**
Finnish		1									**1**
French		1									**1**
Hungarian										1	**1**
Swedish								1			**1**
Ukrainian					1						**1**

continued on next page

Other Countries	Fly	Bantam	Feather	Jr-light	Light	Jr-welter	Welter	Middle	Light-heavy	Heavy	**Total**
England	3	6	1	2	1		5	4		1	**23**
Canada	3	2	2	1	1	1	1	1	4	4	**20**
Philippines (3)	5	3	3	1	1	1					**14**
Panama	2	5	2	3							**12**
Cuba	3	1	2		1	1			1		**9**
France	3	4	2								**9**
Chile					4	3				1	**8**
Scotland	3						1	2			**6**
Spain		1					1			4	**6**
Norway								1		3	**4**
Argentina										3	**3**
Belgium							1	2			**3**
New Zealand										2	**2**
Germany										1	**1**
Italy										1	**1**
South Africa		1									**1**
Sweden										1	**1**
Wales								1			**1**
TOTAL	60	60	60	60	60	30	60	60	60	60	**570**

Notes

* Unknown group comprises unidentified white American boxers; bantamweight Joey Rychell, lightweight King Tut, junior-welterweight Tom White, welterweight Ed Roberts, Farmer Joe Cooper, Clyde Hull, middleweight, Harry Ebbets and light-heavyweight/heavyweight contender Young Stribling.

(1)   Junior-lightweight Tod Morgan is reported to be of mixed English-Welsh background. Another source claims Morgan is of Scotch-American descent.

(2)   Welterweight Pete Latzo and heavyweight Johnny Risko are of Carpatho-Rusyn origin, a Slavic people whose home is geographically situated in North Eastern Slovakia.

(3)   Featherweight Johnny Hill was born in the Philippines to an African American father and Filipino mother.

(4)   According to the *Portland Oregonian* the Brazil-born Dixie LaHood (Noman Lahoud) is of Syrian origin.

(5)   One source claims that lightweight Billy Wallace is also of Alaskan Native Indian ancestry.

The Junior-lightweight ratings began in 1924 and ended with the 1931 list when the weight category fell into disuse. The junior-welterweight ratings began in 1928 and stopped in 1931. Both classes resumed in 1962.

1930s

Ethnic American cohort	Fly	Bantam	Feather	Jr-light	Light	Jr-welter	Welter	Middle	Light-heavy	Heavy	Total
Italian	8	17	30	5	23	3	15	19	14	11	**145**
African		4	9		7		12	11	24	12	**79**
Jewish (3)	4	8	3	3	15	5	18	5	11	7	**79**
Irish (2)		1	2	2	8	1	5	16	10	13	**58**
German			11	1	8	1			2	12	**35**
Mexican (1)	4	2	6		3	1	1				**17**
Polish					5		1	7	1	2	**16**
English	3	1	4						6		**14**
Slovak					1			3	2	4	**10**
Unknown*						1	2	3	1	3	**10**
Ukrainian			2		5	1					**8**
Syrian			3	1	2						**6**
Croatian							4		1		**5**
Norwegian		5									**5**
Scotch					1				1	3	**5**
Lithuanian										4	**4**
Russian									4		**4**
Romanian				1	1						**2**
Chinese		1									**1**
Czech									1		**1**
French									1		**1**
Native Indian				1							**1**
Portuguese		1									**1**

continued on next page

Other countries	Fly	Bantam	Feather	Jr-light	Light	Jr-welter	Welter	Middle	Light-heavy	Heavy	Total
England	28	8	10	3	4	2	3	6	10	1	75
Philippines	12	15	1				5	1			34
Canada	2	5	2			1	12	7	3		32
France	14	4	3	1	1		1	8			32
Italy	3	1			5		5	1		6	21
Germany							1	2	3	12	18
Puerto Rico		6			4		3	3			16
Australia		1	1				3	4	5		14
Mexico		4	5		1		3				13
Cuba	2		4	1	2	2		1			12
Spain	3	4	1					1		2	11
Panama		7		1	1						9
Scotland	7		1				1				9
Argentina					1	1				1	3
Belgium	1							2			3
Chile						1				2	3
Guyana	1	2									3
Holland							3				3
Ireland	3										3
South Africa					2					1	3
Wales										3	3
Romania	1	1									2
Tunisia	2										2
Algeria			1								1
Austria	1										1
Belize	1										1
Czechoslovakia							1				1
Finland										1	1
Hungary		1									1
Japan		1									1
Poland							1				1
Venezuela			1								1
TOTAL	100	100	100	20	100	20	100	100	100	100	840

* Unidentified white Americans; middleweight George Black, light-heavyweight Harry Ebbets and heavyweight Young Stribling. No data on welterweight Willard Brown or for middleweight, Marty Sampson.
(1)   Lightweight Tony Herrera (Campbell) is of mixed Mexican-Scottish parentage. Flyweight Jackie Jurich is of mixed Mexican-Irish parentage.
(2)   Henry Hook is reportedly of mixed Irish-Dutch origin.
(3)   Max Baer and Bob Pastor are not Jewish. Baer is of mixed French-German-Scottish origin and is grouped as German. Pastor is of mixed German-Scottish descent and is grouped as Scottish.

1940s

Ethnic American cohort	Fly	Bantam	Feather	Light	Welter	Middle	Light-heavy	Heavy	<u>Total</u>
African (3)		4	15	40	40	28	49	44	**220**
Italian		7	32	12	19	22	6	20	**118**
Irish	1	1	5	6	6	6	6	7	**38**
Mexican (1)	4	9	11	6	1				**31**
Jewish		2	1	4	1	5	1	4	**18**
Polish				2		9	3	1	**15**
Chinese		9							**9**
Russian							9		**9**
Portuguese		7	1						**8**
Unknown*		1	1		2	1	3		**8**
Croatian					6				**6**
Slovak						2		4	**6**
Norwegian								5	**5**
Czech				2			1	1	**4**
Filipino	3	1							**4**
German								4	**4**
Hungarian						3	1		**4**
French			3						**3**
Scotch								2	**2**
Spanish (2)			1						**1**
Ukrainian				1					**1**

continued on next page

Other countries	Fly	Bantam	Feather	Light	Welter	Middle	Light-heavy	Heavy	Total
England	27	14	7	3	3	3	11	4	72
Philippines	8	8	3	3	3	1			26
Scotland	20	5							25
France	10	3	2			8			23
Mexico	2	8	2	9	1				22
Cuba	4	5	6		3	2		1	21
Australia	5	2	1	1	1	3	6		19
Canada		2	2	8	6				18
Puerto Rico			3	2	6	4			15
Ireland	7	1							8
Italy	1	2		1	1	1			6
Wales	4	1						1	6
Belgium	3					1			4
Greece							4		4
Panama	1	2	1						4
Chile					1			2	3
Guyana		2							2
Spain		2							2
Venezuela			2						2
Estonia						1			1
Finland			1						1
South Africa		1							1
Trinidad		1							1
TOTAL	100	100	100	100	100	100	100	100	800

* Unknown group comprises unidentified white American boxers; featherweight Jock Leslie, welterweights Jimmy Garrison and Freddie Archer, middleweight Shorty Hogue and light-heavyweight Tommy Tucker. We have no ethnic origin data on bantamweight Horace Mann.

(1)   There is some confusion as to whether champion featherweight Chalky Wright is Mexican/American or African American. For years it became generally accepted that Chalky Wright, born Albert Wright in Durango, Mexico was the first Mexican to win a world professional boxing title. Researcher Robert Valero claims this is incorrect. What is true is that Wright was black and so ethnically diverse to the Latino-Mexican fighter. His father was called Santiago Wright and to those that knew Wright they all say that his first language was Spanish. For the purposes of this paper Wright remains Mexican. Flyweight Jackie Jurich is of mixed Mexican-Irish parentage.

(2)   Jimmy Hatcher is described by some sources as being of mixed Spanish-Irish-Jewish descent. He has been ranked as Spanish American.

(3)   Middleweight Charley Burley is of mixed African American-Irish parentage. His father was black and mother Irish.

1950–55

Ethnic American cohort	Fly	Bantam	Feather	Light	Welter	Middle	Light-heavy	Heavy	<u>Total</u>
African		2	19	26	20	19	25	27	**138**
Italian			6	3	12	13	13	11	**58**
Irish		2	2	4	8	3	5	3	**27**
Mexican		1	3	7	6				**17**
Portuguese				5					**5**
Swedish (1)						4			**4**
Filipino	3								**3**
French				3					**3**
Unknown*				1	1	1			**3**
German						1	1		**2**
Jewish								1	**1**
Lithuanian								1	**1**
Norwegian								1	**1**
Slovak								1	**1**

Other countries

	Fly	Bantam	Feather	Light	Welter	Middle	Light-heavy	Heavy	<u>Total</u>
France (2)	5	13	6		1	9	1		**35**
England	10	2	3	1		4	3	3	**26**
Cuba	2	2	6	3	7			3	**23**
Australia	4	5			2	2		1	**14**
Italy	2	7	1	2		1			**13**
Philippines	10	1	1						**12**
Scotland	6	5							**11**
Belgium	1	5	2					2	**10**
Germany							7	2	**9**
Mexico	1	4	3	1					**9**
South Africa	4	4				1			**9**
Spain	2	2	3						**7**
Trinidad					1		5		**6**
Argentina	2					2		1	**5**
Japan	5								**5**

continued on next page

Other countries	Fly	Bantam	Feather	Light	Welter	Middle	Light-heavy	Heavy	Total
Wales	2				2			1	5
Canada				2				2	4
Algeria		2							2
Ghana			2						2
Nigeria			2						2
Thailand		2							2
Belize				1					1
Denmark				1					1
Ireland		1							1
Morocco	1								1
Venezuela			1						1
TOTAL	60	60	60	60	60	60	60	60	480

* Unknown group comprises unidentified white American boxers; lightweight Kenny Lane and welterweight/middleweight Bobby Dykes. In summary between 1924 and 1955, twenty boxers in this category notched 38 world top ten rankings. Of these sixteen are of white American background.
(1)   The Hawaii-born Carl "Bobo" Olson is reported to be of mixed Swedish-Portuguese origin.
(2)   Includes Algeria-born and Italy-born boxers who settled and fought for their adopted country.
The world's top ten ratings are based on *Ring Magazine* annual listings based on their overall performances for that year. These were the first boxing ratings and were widely accepted as the official guide to boxing form. These rankings exclude monthly ratings, which later became a regular feature with the magazine.
This data is based on the top ten world ranked fighters including world champion. Where a championship was vacant at the time of the rankings compilation then the top ten challengers are listed.

APPENDIX IX^B: THE MOST PROMINENT ETHNIC AMERICAN GROUPS IN THE WORLD'S TOP TEN RANKINGS ACROSS ALL WEIGHT CATEGORIES 1924–55

1920s [1924–29]

ETHNIC GROUP	TOTAL NUMBER OF BOXERS (IN TOP 10)	TOTAL TOP 10 RANKINGS	OVERALL POSITION
Jewish	61	121	1
Italian	55	90	2
Irish	44	89	3
African	17	33	4
TOTAL	177	333	

1930s

ETHNIC GROUP	TOTAL NUMBER OF BOXERS (IN TOP 10)	TOTAL TOP 10 RANKINGS	OVERALL POSITION
Italian	68	145	1
Jewish	38	79	2
African	36	79	2
Irish	34	59	4
TOTAL	176	362	

1940s

ETHNIC GROUP	TOTAL NUMBER OF BOXERS (IN TOP 10)	TOTAL TOP 10 RANKINGS	OVERALL POSITION
African	98	220	1
Italian	53	118	2
Irish	21	38	3
Jewish	10	18	4
TOTAL	182	394	

1950s [1950–55]

ETHNIC GROUP	TOTAL NUMBER OF BOXERS (IN TOP 10)	TOTAL TOP 10 RANKINGS	OVERALL POSITION
African	65	138	1
Italian	25	58	2
Irish	13	27	3
Jewish	1	1	4
TOTAL	104	224	

DATA SUMMARY 1924–55

ETHNIC GROUP	TOTAL NUMBER OF BOXERS (IN TOP 10)	TOTAL TOP 10 RANKINGS	OVERALL POSITION
African	216	470	1
Italian	201	411	2
Irish	112	213	3
Jewish	110	219	4
TOTAL	639	1313	

APPENDIX IX^C: ITALIAN AMERICANS RATED IN WORLD'S TOP TEN RING MAGAZINE ANNUAL RANKINGS 1924–55

NAME	DECADE/S RANKED	OTHER WEIGHT/S RANKED
Flyweight		
Jimmy Russo	1920s	
Lew Perfetti		Featherweight
Emil Paluso		
Henry "Kid" Wolfe		
Joey Ross		
Willie La Morte		
Frankie Genaro	1920/30s	
Fidel La Barba		Bantamweight/featherweight
Midget Wolgast		Featherweight
Babe Triscaro	1930s	
Bantamweight		
Carl Tremaine	1920s	
Bushy Graham	1920/30s	
Eddie Martin		Junior-lightweight
Andy Martin		Featherweight
Tony Canzoneri		Featherweight/lightweight
Johnny Vacca		
Joey Scalfaro		
Tommy Paul		Featherweight
Harry Fierro	1930s	
Mose Butch		
KO Morgan		
Tony Marino		
Nick Scalba		
Harry Jeffra	1930/40s	Featherweight
Lou Salica		
Tommy Forte	1940s	
Featherweight		
Dom Petrone	1920s	
Mike Dundee	1920/30s	Junior-lightweight
Eddie Shea		
Johnny Farr		Junior-lightweight
Battling Battalino		Lightweight
Earl Mastro		
Frankie Wallace	1930s	Lightweight
Mike Belloise		
Petey Hayes		
Lew Massey		Lightweight
Al Mancini		
Pete Scalzo	1930s/40s	
Jimmy Perrin		
Joe Marinelli	1940s	
Sal Bartolo		
Bobby Ivy		
Mike Raffa		
Charley Constantino		Lightweight
Phil Terranova		
Freddie Russo		
Eddie Compo		
Willie Pep	1940s/50s/60s	
Carmelo Costa	1950s	
Lulu Perez		

NAME	DECADE/S RANKED	OTHER WEIGHT/S RANKED
Junior-lightweight		
Mike Ballerino	1920s	
Carl Duane		
Joey Silvers		
Steve Kid Sullivan		
Tony Vaccarelli		
Lew Paluso	1920/30s	Lightweight
Sammy Fuller		Lightweight
Roger Bernard	1930s	
Joey Costa		
Lightweight		
Johnny Dundee	1920s	
Basil Galiano		
Rocky Kansas		
Sammy Mandell		
Billy Petrolle	1920/30s	Junior-welterweight/welterweight
Sammy Angott	1930/40s	Welterweight
Lou Ambers		Welterweight
Lenny Mancini	1940s	
Chester Rico		
Terry Young		
Tippy Larkin		
Paddy De Marco	1940/50s	
Junior-lightweight		
Jackie Brady	1920s	
Andy Di Vodi		Welterweight
Ralph Lenny		
Welterweight		
Joe Dundee	1920s	
Nick Testo		
Young Corbett III	1920/30s	Middleweight
Vince Dundee		Middleweight
Johnny Indrisano	1930s	
Paulie Walker		
Tony Falco		
Paul Pirrone		Middleweight
Jimmy Leto	1930/40s	
Izzy Jannazzo		
Marty Servo	1940s	
Tony Janiro		
Johnny Cesario		
Tony Pellone		
Ross Virgo		
Ralph Zanelli		
Charley Fusari	1940s/50s	
Carmen Basilio	1950s	Middleweight
Tony De Marco		
Vince Martinez		
Joe Miceli		

NAME	DECADE/S RANKED	OTHER WEIGHT/S RANKED
Middleweight		
Johnny Wilson	1920s	
Young Terry	1930s	
Harry Balsamo		
Vic Dellicurti		
Fred Apostoli	1930/40s	
Steve Belloise	1940s	
Tami Mauriello		Light-heavyweight/ heavyweight
Tony Martin		
Rocky Graziano		
Jake La Motta	1940/50s	Light-heavyweight
Lee Sala		
Rocky Castellani	1950s	
Ernie Durando		
Joey Giardello	1950s/60s	
Joey Giambra	1950s	
Light-heavyweight		
Tony Marullo	1920s	
Lou Scozza	1920/30s	
Ray Actis	1930s	
Tony Shucco		
Carmen Barth		
Melio Bettina	1930/40s	Heavyweight
Ralph De John		
Phil Muscato	1940s	
Joey Maxim	1940/50s	Heavyweight
Nick Barone		Heavyweight
Dan Bucceroni	1950s	Heavyweight
Danny Nardico		
Heavyweight		
Patsy Perroni	1930s	
Charley Massera		
Ray Impelletierre		
Al Ettore		
Tony Galento		
Nathan Mann		
Lou Nova	1930/40s	
Gus Dorazio	1940s	
Pat Valentino		
Roland La Starza	1940/50s	
Rocky Marciano	1950s	
Willie Pastrano		

- Heavyweight Lou Nova is part Italian. His father was of mixed German Italian descent.
+ Lulu (Luis) Perez is of mixed Italian Puerto Rican background.
(1) Junior lightweight Joey Silvers is of mixed Italian-Jewish parentage.

World ranked boxers of Italian parentage hailing from Canada like flyweight Steve Rocco, featherweight champ Jackie Callura, lightweight Johnny Greco and middleweight Frankie Battaglia who spent much of their career inside American rings are not included. Also excluded are Italy-born boxers who boxed in their homeland before arriving in the United States including championship class featherweight Vince Dell'Orto, lightweights Paolo Rosi and Cleto Locatelli, welterweights Saverio Turiello, Werther Arcelli, Michele Palermo aka Mike "Kid" Frattini and Aldo Minelli and middleweight Oddone Piazza. The Italy-born France-based Kid Francis (Francesco Buonagurio), the number one bantamweight and featherweight contender in the early thirties who waged most of his ring battles in the United States, has also been omitted.

APPENDIX X: ITALIAN AMERICANS IN WORLD BOXING TITLE BOUTS 1900–55*

DATE	WEIGHT	CHALLENGER	CHAMPION/ TITLE CLAIMANT	RESULT	VENUE
05/02/00	122–124 pounds	**Eddie Lenny**	Ned "Kid" Broad	Draw Pts20	Brooklyn, NY

'Kid' Broad defends his 124-pound world featherweight title claim.

14/08/00	B	**Casper Leon**	Johnny Reagan	Reagan WPts20	Brooklyn, NY

Johnny Reagan defends his 115-pound world bantamweight title claim.

06/09/00	B	**Casper Leon**	Harry Forbes	Draw Pts20	St Joseph, MO

The 1980 Ring Record Book reported that this was for the vacant world bantamweight championship.

02/04/01	B	**Casper Leon**	Harry Forbes	Forbes WPts15	Memphis, TN

22/04/01	122-pound	**Benny Yanger**	Johnny Ritchie	Draw Pts20	Memphis, TN

Advertised for the 122-pound world title. Chicago Daily Tribune reported that Yanger gave Ritchie "a clever beating". The paper reported that by the end of the fight. Ritchie was "groggy and hanging on the precipice". Ritchie had been knocked down repeatedly and the 1,500 crowd yelled disapprovingly at the referee's decision, reported the paper.

24/04/02	F	**Benny Yanger**	Abe Atell	Yanger WTKO19	St Louis, MO

The St Louis West End Athletic Club boxing club promoter advertised the Yanger-Atell fight for the world featherweight championship. The Chicago Daily Tribune reports that Yanger wins the "legitimate 122-pound American championship".

14/11/02	L	**Charlie Sieger**	Joe Gans	Gans WKO14	Baltimore, MD

Old record books have sometimes recorded this as a world title fight

30/06/03	130-pound	**Benny Yanger**	Eddie Hanlon	Draw Pts20	San Francisco, CA

Billed for the 130-pound world title. Some record books report the above date for the fight but the Chicago Daily Tribune reports that it happened on May 30, 1903.

29/09/03	130-pound	**Benny Yanger**	Eddie Hanlon	Hanlon WPts20	San Francisco, CA

Billed for the 130-pound world title.

10/11/03	L	**Charlie Sieger**	Jimmy Britt	Britt WTKO20	San Francisco, CA

Jimmy Britt defends his "white" world lightweight title claim.

25/04/05	M	**Hugo Kelly**	Philadelphia Jack O'Brien	Kelly WPts20	Indianapolis, IN

Hugo Kelly takes over Philadelphia Jack O'Brien's world middleweight title claim.

07/06/05	M	Tommy Burns (Canada)	**Hugo Kelly**	Draw Pts10	Detroit, MI

Hugo Kelly defends his 158-pound middleweight world title claim.

11/12/05	M	Young Mahoney	**Hugo Kelly**	Draw Pts10	Indianapolis, IN

Hugo Kelly defends his 158-pound middleweight world title claim.

09/03/06	M	Jack "Twin" Sullivan	**Hugo Kelly**	Draw Pts20	Los Angeles, CA

Hugo Kelly defends his 158-pound middleweight world title claim.

15/03/06	F	**Tony Moran**	Abe Atell	Atell WDSQ3	Baltimore, MD

This bout is reported in the Ring Record Book as an American title fight at 126 pounds.

25/06/06	M	Young Mahoney	**Hugo Kelly**	Kelly WKO3	Indianapolis, IN

Hugo Kelly defends his 158-pound middleweight world title claim.

24/08/06	M	**Tony Caponi**	**Hugo Kelly**	Kelly WKO6	Leavenworth, KS

Hugo Kelly defends his 158-pound middleweight world title claim.

02/10/06	H	**"Fireman" Jim Flynn**	Tommy Burns (Canada)	Burns WKO15	Los Angeles, CA

01/03/07	B Vacant (105-pounds)	**Kid Murphy**	Johnny Coulon (Canada)	Kid Murphy WPts20	Milwaukee, WI

DATE	WEIGHT	CHALLENGER	CHAMPION/ TITLE CLAIMANT	RESULT	VENUE
22/04/07	B	**Al Delmont**	Owen Moran (England)	Moran WPts20	London, (UK)

Al Delmont challenged for the English version of the world bantamweight title. Both boxers fought for the vacant crown. After the bout Moran moved up to featherweight.

| 10/05/07 | M | Jack "Twin" Sullivan | **Hugo Kelly** | Draw Pts20 | Los Angeles, CA |

Jack "Twin" Sullivan and Hugo Kelly were the two leading contenders in the middleweight division at the time.

| 07/06/07 | B | **Al Delmont** | George "Digger" Stanley (England) | Delmont WDSQ17 | Liverpool, (UK) |

When Owen Moran outgrew the division "Digger" Stanley made a claim but he lost his disputed claim to the English version of the world title to Al Delmont.

| 30/12/07 | M | Billy Papke | **Hugo Kelly** | Draw Pts10 | Milwaukee, WI |

The two leading lights in the middleweight division met to establish the best claim to the title

08/01/08	B (105-pounds)	Johnny Coulon (Canada)	**Kid Murphy**	Coulon WPts10	Peoria, IL
29/01/08	B (105-pounds)	**Kid Murphy** (Canada)	Johnny Coulon	Coulon WPts10	Peoria, IL
16/03/08	M	Billy Papke	**Hugo Kelly**	Papke WPts10	Milwaukee, WI

With both men reported to be inside the weight limit Papke established leading claim to the 158-pound middleweight title.

| 31/03/08 | B | **Al Delmont** | Jimmy Walsh | Draw Pts12 | Boston, MA |

Delmont challenged for Jimmy Walsh's world title claim

31/07/08	M Vacant	**Hugo Kelly**	Stanley Ketchel	Ketchel WKO3	San Francisco, CA
11/02/09	B (105-pounds)	**Kid Murphy**	Johnny Coulon (Canada)	Coulon WTKO5	New York City
26/03/09	(116-pounds)	**Harry Dell**	Abe Atell	Atell WPts15	San Francisco, CA
18/03/09	F	**Patsy Kline**	Abe Atell	ND10	Brooklyn, NY

This fight is sometimes recorded as a world title fight. With Patsy Kline inside the weight limit this fight is a defense of Atell's crown.

| 02/06/09 | M | **Tony Caponi** | Stanley Ketchel | Ketchel WKO 4 | Schenectady, NY |

This fight is sometimes recorded as a world title fight.

30/06/09	H	**Tony Ross**	Jack Johnson	ND6	Pittsburgh, PA
03/02/10	(116-pounds)	**Frankie Conley**	Danny Webster	ND10	Portland, OR
22/02/10	B (California)	**Frankie Conley**	Monte Atell	Conley WTKO42	Vernon, CA
22/08/10	F	**Eddie Marino**	Abe Atell	Atell WKO3	Calgary (Canada)

Although sometimes recorded as a title fight the match was made at lightweight.

| 13/11/10 | F | **Frankie Conley** | Abe Atell | Draw Pts15 | New Orleans, LA |

Frankie Conley was inside the weight limit and if he had won inside the distance he would have claimed the world title.

| 09/01/11 | F | **Joe Coster** | Abe Atell | ND10 | Brooklyn, NY |

Joe Coster was inside the 122-pound weight limit. This is another title defense made by Abe Atell. Several newspapers report Coster winning the fight convincingly on points whilst another paper gave it to Atell.

| 13/01/11 | F* | **Patsy Kline** | Abe Atell | Atell WPts10 | New York City |

This fight was close with the newspapers divided on who won. The New York Times chose Atell. The Sandusky Star went for Kline and the Associated Press wire service and the Syracuse Herald both agreed on a draw.

| 26/02/11 | B | **Frankie Conley** | Johnny Coulon (Canada) | Coulon WPts20 | New Orleans, LA |
| 28/05/11 | 122-pound | **Joe Coster** | **Frankie Conley** | Coster WPts20 | New Orleans, LA |

This fight was billed for the American (world) title at 122-pounds. Joe Coster claimed the world title upon his victory.

DATE	WEIGHT	CHALLENGER	CHAMPION/ TITLE CLAIMANT	RESULT	VENUE
04/07/11	122-pound	Joe Rivers (Mexico)	**Joe Coster**	Rivers WKO13	Los Angeles, CA

Joe Rivers takes over Joe Coster's world title claim

| 30/09/11 | F | **Frankie Conley** | Johnny Kilbane | Kilbane WPts20 | Los Angeles, CA |

Johnny Kilbane defends his featherweight title claim prior to his title match with champion Abe Atell.

| 01/12/11 | F | **Patsy Kline** | Abe Atell | ND10 | New York City |

Both men were inside the weight limit. If Patsy Kline had won inside the distance he would have claimed the title.

| 03/02/12 | B | **Frankie Conley** | Johnny Coulon
(Canada) | Coulon WPts20 | Vernon, CA |

| 28/05/12 | LH | **Hugo Kelly** | Jack Dillon | Dillon WKO3 | Indianapolis, IN |

Billed as a world light-heavyweight title fight. Jack Dillon claimed the 175-pounds title. He continued to defend his title but received little recognition.

| 02/07/12 | B* | **Joe Wagner** | Johnny Coulon
(Canada) | ND10 | New York City |

| 04/07/12 | H | **"Fireman"
Jim Flynn** | Jack Johnson | Johnson WTKO9 | Las Vegas, NV |

| 04/09/12 | 122-pound | **Johnny Dundee** | Johnny Kilbane | Draw Pts10 | New York City |

Both men were inside the 122-pound weight limit. Kilbane's title was at risk if he lost inside the distance.

| 20/11/12 | B (IBU) | **Battling Reddy** | Charles Ledoux
(France) | ND10 | Bronx, NY |

| 07/03/13 | W | **Tommy Howell** | Spike Kelly | Draw Pts10 | Kansas City, MO |

Spike Kelly defends title claim of American version of world welterweight title

| 29/04/13 | F | **Johnny Dundee** | Johnny Kilbane | Draw Pts20 | Vernon, CA |

| 26/01/14 | M* | **Joe Borrell** | George Chip | ND6 | Philadelphia, PA |

With both men inside the weight limit the champion's title was on the line.

| 26/02/14 | M | **Joe Borrell** | George Bernard
(France) | Borrell WPts15 | Liverpool (UK) |

This fight was billed as a world 160-pound middleweight title fight. Joe Borrell persisted in his title claims following on from his knockout win over Harry Lewis, former world champion. He received little support though.

| 04/06/15 | B* | **Jimmy Murray** | Kid Williams | Williams WPts10 | Baltimore, MD |
| 11/12/14 | M | **Italian Joe Gans** | Al McCoy | McCoy WPts10 | New York City |

Italian Joe Gans weighed inside the weight limit. The champion's title was at risk if he lost inside the distance.

| 25/01/15 | M | **Joe Borrell** | Al McCoy | McCoy WPts6 | Philadelphia, PA |

Al McCoy was inside the weight limit but Joe Borrell is reported to have been just over the 158-pound weight limit. If Borrell had won inside the distance he would have claimed the 160-pound crown.

04/06/15	B*	**Jimmy Murray**	Kid Williams	Williams WPts10	Baltimore, MD
24/07/15	B*	**Jimmy Taylor**	Kid Williams	ND10	Baltimore, MD
13/11/15	M	**Zulu Kid**	Al McCoy	Draw Pts10	Brooklyn, NY

With both men inside the weight limit the champion's title was on the line.

| 07/02/16 | B | **Pete Herman** | Kid Williams | Draw Pts20 | New Orleans, LA |
| 09/02/16 | B | **Terry Martin** | Johnny Ertle | Ertle WPts10 | Brooklyn, NY |

Ertle defends his world bantamweight title claim

| 13/03/16 | B | **Young Zulu Kid** | Johnny Ertle | Ertle WPts10 | Brooklyn, NY |

Ertle defends his world bantamweight title claim

| 28/08/16 | B | **Young Joey
Mendo** | Kid Williams | Williams WRTD5 | Buffalo, NY |

| 18/12/16 | Fly Vacant | **Young Zulu Kid** | Jimmy Wilde
(Wales) | Wilde WTKO11 | London, (UK) |

Young Zulu Kid, generally recognized as the best flyweight in the USA met Jimmy Wilde, the leading European 112 pounder for the inaugural world flyweight championship.

DATE	WEIGHT	CHALLENGER	CHAMPION/ TITLE CLAIMANT	RESULT	VENUE
09/01/17	B	**Pete Herman**	Kid Williams	Herman WPts20	New Orleans, LA
14/05/17	B*	Johnny Coulon (Canada)	**Pete Herman**	Herman WTKO3	Racine, WI
14/05/17	B	**Tony Baron**	Johnny Ertle	Baron WPts6	Pittsburgh, PA

Ertle defends his world bantamweight title claim

DATE	WEIGHT	CHALLENGER	CHAMPION/ TITLE CLAIMANT	RESULT	VENUE
28/09/17	B	**Tony Baron**	Johnny Ertle	Ertle WPts10	Waterloo, IA

Ertle defends his world bantamweight title claim

DATE	WEIGHT	CHALLENGER	CHAMPION/ TITLE CLAIMANT	RESULT	VENUE
05/11/17	B	Frankie Burns	**Pete Herman**	Herman WPts20	New Orleans, LA
05/08/18	B	**Little Jack Sharkey**	Memphis Pal Moore	NC 8	Jersey City, NJ

Memphis Pal Moore defends his world bantamweight title claim

DATE	WEIGHT	CHALLENGER	CHAMPION/ TITLE CLAIMANT	RESULT	VENUE
10/02/19	B*	Patsy Scanlon	**Pete Herman**	Herman WPts20	Pittsburgh, PA
24/03/19	W	**Jack Perry**	Jack Britton	ND10	Pittsburgh, PA
08/05/19	B*	**Patsy Wallace**	Pete Herman	Herman WKO6	Philadelphia, PA
18/05/19	B*	Johnny Solzberg	**Pete Herman**	Herman WPts20	Syracuse, NY
10/06/19	B*	Terry McHugh	**Pete Herman**	Herman WPts20	Allentown, PA
15/08/19	B*	**Little Jack Sharkey**	Pete Herman	ND10	Milwaukee, WI
15/09/19	B*	**Little Jack Sharkey**	Pete Herman	ND10	Detroit, MI
06/05/20	M	**Johnny Wilson**	Mike O'Dowd	Wilson WPts12	Boston, MA
02/06/20	W	**Young Joe Borrell**	Jack Britton	ND8	Philadelphia, PA

Sometimes reported as a world title fight.

DATE	WEIGHT	CHALLENGER	CHAMPION/ TITLE CLAIMANT	RESULT	VENUE
01/07/20	M	Soldier Bartfield	**Johnny Wilson**	Wilson WPts12	Newark, NJ
23/08/20	W	**Lou Bogash**	Jack Britton	Draw Pts12	Bridgeport, CT
08/10/20	W*	**Jack Perry**	Jack Britton	Draw Pts12	Toledo, OH

Sometimes reported as a title fight. Perry, the perennial contender knocked Britton down for an eight count in round three but couldn't finish it off as Britton used his experience and ring nous to avert a knockout defeat. The champion recovered sufficiently to earn a draw.

DATE	WEIGHT	CHALLENGER	CHAMPION/ TITLE CLAIMANT	RESULT	VENUE
22/12/20	B	Joe Lynch	**Pete Herman**	Lynch WPts15	New York City
17/01/21	M	Joe Chip	**Johnny Wilson**	Wilson WPts15	Pittsburgh, PA
10/02/21	M*	Navy Rostan	**Johnny Wilson**	Wilson WKO2	Kenosha, WI
17/03/21	M	Mike O'Dowd	**Johnny Wilson**	Wilson WPts15	New York City
30/03/21	JR-FLY	**Bobby Doyle**	Jockey Joe Dillon	Doyle WPts10	Pittsfield, MA

On winning the contest Bobby Doyle promptly claimed the 108-pounds junior-flyweight title, but the authorities ignored his claim as Doyle was over the stipulated weight limit by six pounds. (Data courtesy of historian Vincent Colitti.)

DATE	WEIGHT	CHALLENGER	CHAMPION/ TITLE CLAIMANT	RESULT	VENUE
25/07/21	B	**Pete Herman**	Joe Lynch	Herman WPts15	Brooklyn, NY
20/08/21	JR-FLY	**Mickey Nelson**	Jockey Joe Dillon	Draw Pts15	Saratoga Springs, NY

On being awarded the newly created 108-pounds junior-flyweight championship Jockey Joe Dillon fought Mickey Nelson in what was billed as a defense of his title claim. Dillon had previously defeated Nelson over fifteen rounds in 1920. (Data courtesy of historian Vincent Colitti.)

DATE	WEIGHT	CHALLENGER	CHAMPION/ TITLE CLAIMANT	RESULT	VENUE
05/09/21	M	Bryan Downey	**Johnny Wilson**	Draw Pts12	Jersey City, NJ

Following Downey's disqualification for a foul blow in their previous bout a rematch was ordered. It ended in a tame draw with Downey recognized as champion by Ohio State and Wilson everywhere else.

DATE	WEIGHT	CHALLENGER	CHAMPION/ TITLE CLAIMANT	RESULT	VENUE
23/09/21	B	Johnny Buff	**Pete Herman**	Buff WPts15	New York City
10/11/21	B	**Little Jack Sharkey**	Johnny Buff	Buff WPts15	New York City

DATE	WEIGHT	CHALLENGER	CHAMPION/ TITLE CLAIMANT	RESULT	VENUE
18/11/21	JR-LW Vacant	**Johnny Dundee**	George "KO" Chaney	Dundee WDSQ5	New York City

Johnny Dundee was crowned the inaugural champion in this newly created division.

DATE	WEIGHT	CHALLENGER	CHAMPION/ TITLE CLAIMANT	RESULT	VENUE
10/02/22	L	**Rocky Kansas**	Benny Leonard	Leonard WPts15	New York City
22/02/22	M(Ohio)	**Frank Carbone**	Bryan Downey	Downey WPts12	Canton, OH
04/04/22	JR-LW	Jimmy Goodrich	**Johnny Dundee**	Dundee WPts10	Toronto, (Canada)

It is sometimes reported as a title defense for Johnny Dundee. Although Goodrich came in one pound over the 130-pound limit the match still went ahead.

DATE	WEIGHT	CHALLENGER	CHAMPION/ TITLE CLAIMANT	RESULT	VENUE
21/04/22	M	KO Jaffe	**Johnny Wilson**	NC 4	Hazelton, PA
04/07/22	L	**Rocky Kansas**	Benny Leonard	Leonard WTKO8	Michigan City, IN
08/07/22	JR-LW	Little Jack Sharkey	**Johnny Dundee**	Dundee WPts15	Brooklyn, NY
15/08/22	F Vacant (NYSAC)	Danny Frush (England)	**Johnny Dundee**	Dundee WKO9	Brooklyn, NY
21/08/22	B	**Frankie Murray**	Joe Lynch	Lynch WKO6	Shreveport, LA
28/08/22	JR-LW	Vincent "Pepper" Martin	**Johnny Dundee**	Dundee WPts15	New York City
10/10/22	W	**Jimmy Kelly**	Jack Britton	Britton WPts12	Havana (Cuba)
09/01/23	M Vacant (NYSAC)	**Lou Bogash**	Charley Nashert	Bogash WTKO11	New York City

Whilst there is some doubt as to whether this was a title fight Sam Cohen of Ring Magazine (September 1978, p. 47) wrote that "Bogash gained recognition as middleweight champ from New York, New England and other states (a total of 32 with boxing commissions), when he stopped Charley Nashert in the eleventh of a New York twelve rounder ending an elimination tourney to decide a successor to Johnny Wilson as middleweight ruler." He received a gold buckle from the Pioneer Athletic Club promoter to honor his win. Later in the year New York stripped Bogash of his title and declared Johnny Wilson their champion.

DATE	WEIGHT	CHALLENGER	CHAMPION/ TITLE CLAIMANT	RESULT	VENUE
19/01/23	JR-LW	Vincent "Pepper" Martin	**Johnny Dundee**	Dundee WPts10	Boston, MA
02/02/23	JR-LW	Elino Flores (Philippines)	**Johnny Dundee**	Dundee WPts15	New York City
01/03/23	Fly	**Frankie Genaro**	Pancho Villa (Philippines)	Genaro WPts15	New York City

Also reported to be for the American flyweight championship. Since both fighters came inside the 112-pound limit Genaro possessed a strong world flyweight title claim especially as three months later Villa knocked out Jimmy Wilde and was recognized world flyweight champion. When Villa suddenly died in 1925 Genaro again made a claim for the world title.

DATE	WEIGHT	CHALLENGER	CHAMPION/ TITLE CLAIMANT	RESULT	VENUE
30/05/23	JR-LW	Jack Bernstein	**Johnny Dundee**	Bernstein WPts15	Brooklyn, NY
26/07/23	F	**Johnny Dundee**	Eugene Criqui	Dundee WPts15	New York City,
29/08/23	JR-FW Vacant	**Carl Duane**	Jack "Kid" Wolfe	Duane WPts12	Long Island City, NY

Record books show that Duane did not make any title defenses and the weight class fell into disuse.

DATE	WEIGHT	CHALLENGER	CHAMPION/ TITLE CLAIMANT	RESULT	VENUE
31/08/23	M	Harry Greb	**Johnny Wilson**	Greb WPts15	New York City
17/12/23	JR-LW	**Johnny Dundee**	Jack Bernstein	Dundee WPts15	New York City
18/01/24	M	Johnny Wilson	Harry Greb	Greb WPts15	New York City
20/06/24	JR-LW	**Steve "Kid" Sullivan**	**Johnny Dundee**	Sullivan WPts10	Brooklyn, NY

Johnny Dundee vacated the world featherweight title on August 10, 1924.

DATE	WEIGHT	CHALLENGER	CHAMPION/ TITLE CLAIMANT	RESULT	VENUE
18/08/24	JR-LW	Vincent "Pepper" Martin	**Steve "Kid" Sullivan**	Sullivan WPts15	Long Island City, NY

DATE	WEIGHT	CHALLENGER	CHAMPION/ TITLE CLAIMANT	RESULT	VENUE
08/09/24	B	**Tommy Ryan**	Abe Goldstein	Goldstein WPts15	Long Island City, NY
15/10/24	JR-LW	**Mike Ballerino**	**Steve "Kid" Sullivan**	Sullivan WKO5	New York City
15/12/24	JR-LW*	**Mike Ballerino**	**Steve "Kid" Sullivan**	Ballerino WPts10	Milwaukee, WI
19/12/24	B	**Eddie Martin**	Abe Goldstein	Martin WPts15	New York City
16/02/25	B*	**Willie Spencer**	**Eddie Martin**	ND12	Portland, ME
20/03/25	B	Charley Rosenberg	**Eddie Martin**	Rosenberg WPts15	New York City

Interestingly "Cannonball" Martin had not lost to Charley Rosenberg in their three previous bouts staged at Madison Square Garden, New York.

01/04/25	JR-LW	**Steve "Kid" Sullivan**	**Mike Ballerino**	Ballerino WPts12	Philadelphia, PA
01/06/25	JR-LW*	Frankie Callahan	**Mike Ballerino**	ND10	Columbus, OH
06/07/25	JR-LW	Vincent "Pepper" Martin	**Mike Ballerino**	Ballerino WPts15	Brooklyn, NY
13/07/25	LH	**Tony Marullo**	Paul Berlenbach	NC 9	Newark, NJ

This fight was billed as twelve- round no-decision fight for the championship. As both men weighed inside the weight limit the title was at stake if the champion was stopped inside the distance.

23/07/25	B	**Eddie Shea**	Charley Rosenberg	Rosenberg WKO4	New York, NY
14/08/25	JR-LW	Billy Henry	**Mike Ballerino**	Ballerino WPts10	Bayonne, NJ

The New York Times reported that this was a successful title defense for Ballerino.

22/08/25	Fly - Vacant (NBA)	**Fidel La Barba**	**Frankie Genaro**	La Barba WPts10	Los Angeles, CA

They fought for the vacant world flyweight title because of Pancho Villa's sudden death. Some record books report that this bout was for the American flyweight championship.

13/11/25	M	**Tony Marullo**	Harry Greb	Greb WPts15	New Orleans, LA
02/12/25	JR-LW	Tod Morgan	**Mike Ballerino**	Morgan WTKO11	Los Angeles, CA
07/12/25	L	**Rocky Kansas**	Jimmy Goodrich	Kansas WPts15	Buffalo, NY
05/03/26	L	Freddie Jacks (England)	**Rocky Kansas**	Kansas WTKO6	Tampa, FL
03/06/26	JR-LW	**Steve "Kid" Sullivan**	Tod Morgan	Morgan WTKO6	Brooklyn, NY
03/07/26	L	**Sammy Mandell**	**Rocky Kansas**	Mandell WPts 10	Chicago, IL
07/07/26	Fly (NBA)	Georgie Rivers	**Fidel La Barba**	La Barba WPts10	Los Angeles, CA
08/10/26	L*	Joe Jawson	**Sammy Mandell**	Mandell WPts10	Rockford, IL
19/10/26	JR-LW	**Johnny Dundee**	Tod Morgan	Morgan WPts10	San Francisco, CA
31/10/26	L*	Clausine Vincent	**Sammy Mandell**	Mandell WPts10	Oklahoma City, OK
19/11/26	JR-LW	**Carl Duane**	Tod Morgan	Morgan WPts15	New York City
21/01/27	Fly	Elky Clark (Scotland)	**Fidel La Barba**	La Barba WPts12	New York City

In August 1927 Fidel La Barba retired from boxing and the flyweight title became disputed for the next ten years.

04/02/27	B (NYSAC)	**Bushy Graham**	Charley Rosenberg	Rosenberg WPts15	New York City

With blatant disregard for the stipulated rules Charley Rosenberg came in four pounds over the 118-pound weight limit and forfeited the title on the scales, but due to the protestations of the crowd and the potential for a riot the authorities allowed the fight to go on.

14/03/27	LW (NBA)	**Andy Di Vodi**	Mushy Callahan	Callahan WKO2	New York City
26/03/27	B Vacant (NBA)	**Tony Canzoneri**	Bud Taylor	Draw Pts10	Chicago, IL

DATE	WEIGHT	CHALLENGER	CHAMPION/ TITLE CLAIMANT	RESULT	VENUE
03/06/27	W	**Joe Dundee**	Pete Latzo	Dundee WPts15	New York City
24/06/27	B Vacant (NBA)	**Tony Canzoneri**	Bud Taylor	Taylor WPts10	Chicago, IL
13/07/27	W	Billy Drako (Germany)	**Joe Dundee**	Dundee WPts10	Cincinnati, OH
16/07/27	L	Phil McGraw	**Sammy Mandell**	Mandell WPts10	Detroit, MI
24/10/27	F Vacant (NYSAC)	**Johnny Dundee**	**Tony Canzoneri**	Canzoneri WPts15	New York City
28/11/27	Fly Vacant (NBA)	Frenchy Belanger (Canada)	**Frankie Genaro**	Belanger WPts10	Toronto, (Canada)

Also reported as a NBA eliminator bout with the right to meet Ernie Jarvis for the title.

06/02/28	Fly (NBA)	Frenchy Belanger (Canada)	**Frankie Genaro**	Genaro WPts10	Toronto, (Canada)
10/02/28	F	Benny Bass	**Tony Canzoneri**	Canzoneri WPts15	New York City
21/05/28	L	Jimmy McLarnin (Canada)	**Sammy Mandell**	Mandell WPts15	New York City
23/05/28	B Vacant (NYSAC)	**Bushy Graham**	Izzy Schwartz	Graham WPts15	Brooklyn, NY

Record books show that Bushy Graham did not defend his title and moved up to the featherweight class and was one of the contenders to compete in the NBA elimination tournament in 1932 designed to find a successor to Battling Battalino.

24/05/28	JR-LW	**Eddie Martin**	Tod Morgan	Morgan WPts15	New York City
07/07/28	W	Hilario Martinez (Spain)	**Joe Dundee**	Dundee WKO8	Barcelona, (Spain)
18/07/28	JR-LW	**Eddie Martin**	Tod Morgan	Morgan WPts15	Brooklyn, NY
23/07/28	Fly (NBA)	Steve Rocco (Canada)	**Frankie Genaro**	Draw Pts10	Toronto, (Canada)
03/08/28	Fly (NYSAC)	**Little Jeff Smith**	Izzy Schwartz	Schwartz WKO4	New York City
28/09/28	F	Andre Routis (France)	**Tony Canzoneri**	Routis WPts15	New York City
15/10/28	Fly (NBA)	Frenchy Belanger (Canada)	**Frankie Genaro**	Genaro WPts10	Toronto, (Canada)
14/12/28	Fly (NBA)	Steve Rocco (Canada)	**Frankie Genaro**	Genaro WDSQ2	Detroit, MI
02/03/29	Fly (NBA)	Emile Pladner (France)	**Frankie Genaro**	Pladner WKO1	Paris, (France)
18/04/29	Fly (NBA)	**Frankie Genaro**	Emile Pladner (France)	Genaro WDSQ5	Paris, (France)

Emile Pladner was disqualified for a low blow.

27/05/29	F	**Buster Brown**	Andre Routis (France)	Routis TKO3	Baltimore, MD
25/07/29	W	Jackie Fields	**Joe Dundee**	Fields WDSQ2	Detroit, MI
02/08/29	L	**Tony Canzoneri**	**Sammy Mandell**	Mandell WPts10	Chicago, IL
22/08/29	Fly (NYSAC)	**Willie La Morte**	Izzy Schwartz	La Morte WPts15	Newark, NJ

This bout was advertised as a world title fight as Izzy Schwartz was recognized by the NYSAC as flyweight champion.

23/09/29	F	**Battling Battalino**	Andre Routis (France)	Battalino WPts15	Hartford, CT
17/10/29	Fly (NBA)	Ernie Jarvis (England)	**Frankie Genaro**	Genaro WPts15	London, (UK)
21/11/29	Fly (NYSAC)	Frisco Grande (Philippines)	**Willie La Morte**	La Morte WTKO7	Paterson, NJ

This fight was billed as a world title fight but lacked official backing.

DATE	WEIGHT	CHALLENGER	CHAMPION/ TITLE CLAIMANT	RESULT	VENUE
18/01/30	Fly (NBA)	Yvon Trevidic (France)	**Frankie Genaro**	Genaro WTKO12	Paris, (France)
08/02/30	B (NYSAC)*	**Johnny Erickson**	Al Brown (Panama)	Brown WDSQ4	New York City
10/02/30	LH (NYSAC)	**Lou Scozza**	Jimmy Slattery	Slattery WPts15	Buffalo, NY
21/03/30	Fly Vacant (NYSAC)	**Midget Wolgast**	Black Bill (Cuba)	Wolgast WPts15	New York City

Wolgast won the final of the NYSAC organized elimination tournament and was recognized as world flyweight champion.

| 28/03/30 | JR-LW | **Eddie Shea** | Benny Bass | Shea WPts10 | St Louis, MO |

Although this was a no decision bout Bass's title was at risk if he had lost inside the distance. Shea won the fight on point's decision but Bass held on to his title.

16/05/30	Fly (NYSAC)	**Midget Wolgast**	**Willie La Morte**	Wolgast WKO5	New York City
29/05/30	LW (NBA)	**Al Delmont**	Jack "Kid" Berg (England)	Berg WTKO4	Newark, NJ
10/06/30	Fly (NBA)	Frenchy Belanger (Canada)	**Frankie Genaro**	Genaro WPts10	Toronto, (Canada)
15/07/30	F	Ignacio Fernandez (Philippines)	**Battling Battalino**	Battalino WKO5	Hartford, CT
17/07/30	L	Al Singer	**Sammy Mandell**	Singer WKO1	Bronx, NY
06/08/30	Fly (NBA)	**Willie La Morte**	**Frankie Genaro**	Genaro WPts10	Newark, NJ

Sometimes reported as a world title bout. The UP wire service reported it was an "unpopular decision".

03/09/30	LW (NBA)	**Buster Brown**	Jack "Kid" Berg (England)	Berg WPts10	Newark, NJ
10/10/30	LW (NBA)*	**Billy Petrolle**	Jack "Kid" Berg (England)	Berg WPts10	New York, NY
14/11/30	L	**Tony Canzoneri**	Al Singer	Canzoneri WKO1	New York City
12/12/30	F	Kid Chocolate (Cuba)	**Battling Battalino**	Battalino WPts15	New York City
26/12/30	Fly (NBA & NYSAC)	**Midget Wolgast**	**Frankie Genaro**	Draw Pts15	New York City

Genaro is the NBA champion and Wolgast the NYSAC titlist. After the contest they retained their respective belts.

| 05/01/31 | JR-LW | **Lew Massey** | Benny Bass | Bass WPts10 | Philadelphia, PA |
| 09/01/31 | W | **Pete August** | Tommy Freeman | Freeman WPts10 | Hot Springs, AR |

Sometimes reported as a world title fight.

26/01/31	L	**Johnny Farr**	**Tony Canzoneri**	Draw Pts10	New Orleans, LA
25/03/31	Fly (NBA)	Victor Ferrand (Spain)	**Frankie Genaro**	Draw Pts15	Barcelona, (Spain)
24/04/31	L & JR-W	Jack "Kid" Berg (England)	**Tony Canzoneri**	Canzoneri WKO3	Chicago, IL
15/05/31	LH	**Don Petrin**	Maxie Rosenbloom	Rosenbloom WPts10	Los Angeles, CA

The weights were announced as 170-pounds and as both fighters were inside the weight limit California recognized this as a world title fight.

| 22/05/31 | F (NYSAC) | **Fidel La Barba** | **Battling Battalino** | Battalino WPts15 | New York City |
| 01/07/31 | F | "Irish" Bobby Brady | **Battling Battalino** | Battalino WPts10 | Jersey City, NJ |

Sometimes reported as a title match. However, the New York Times wrote that Bobby Brady came in half a pound over the 126-pound limit and so breaking the outlined articles of a title contest.

DATE	WEIGHT	CHALLENGER	CHAMPION/ TITLE CLAIMANT	RESULT	VENUE
13/07/31	JR-W	Cecil Payne	**Tony Canzoneri**	Canzoneri WPts10	Los Angeles, CA
13/07/31	Fly (NYSAC)	Ruby Bradley	**Midget Wolgast**	Wolgast WPts15	Brooklyn, NY
16/07/31	Fly - (NBA)	Routier Parra (Argentina)	**Frankie Genaro**	Genaro WKO4	North Adams, MA
23/07/31	F	Freddie Miller	**Battling Battalino**	Battalino WPts10	Cincinnati, OH
27/07/31	JR-W	**Philly Griffin**	Jack "Kid" Berg (England)	Berg WPts10	Newark, NJ
30/07/31	Fly (NBA)	Jackie Harmon	**Frankie Genaro**	Genaro WKO6	Waterbury, CT
10/09/31	L	Jack "Kid" Berg (England)	**Tony Canzoneri**	Canzoneri WPts15	New York City
01/10/31	JR-LW (NBA)	**Joey Scalfaro**	Kid Chocolate (Cuba)	Chocolate WTKO1	Long Island, NY
03/10/31	Fly (NBA)	Valentin Angelmann (France)	**Frankie Genaro**	Genaro WPts15	Paris, (France)
27/10/31	Fly (NBA)	Victor Perez (Tunisia)	**Frankie Genaro**	Perez WKO2	Paris, (France)
29/10/31	JR-W	**Philly Griffin**	**Tony Canzoneri**	Canzoneri WPts10	Newark, NJ
04/11/31	F	**Earl Mastro**	**Battling Battalino**	Battalino WPts10	Chicago, IL
20/11/31	L	Kid Chocolate (Cuba)	**Tony Canzoneri**	Canzoneri WPts15	New York City

This fight is also reported as being for the junior-welterweight title.

DATE	WEIGHT	CHALLENGER	CHAMPION/ TITLE CLAIMANT	RESULT	VENUE
18/01/32	JR-W	Johnny Jadick	**Tony Canzoneri**	Jadick WPts10	Philadelphia, PA
27/01/32	F	Freddie Miller	**Battling Battalino**	NC 3	Cincinnati, OH

This title fight was shrouded in controversy. Firstly it was common knowledge that by 1932 Battalino could no longer make the 126-pound championship weight limit. Secondly both fighters offered little action prompting the referee to call it a no contest. Battalino was subsequently stripped of his title by the NYSAC and officially renounced his claim on the March 1, 1932. An NBA tournament was organized to find a successor to Battalino and this was won by Tommy Paul.

DATE	WEIGHT	CHALLENGER	CHAMPION/ TITLE CLAIMANT	RESULT	VENUE
18/03/32	LH Vacant (NBA)	**George Nichols**	Dave Maier	Nichols WPts15	Chicago, IL

The NBA stripped Nichols of his title for not defending it within eight months.

DATE	WEIGHT	CHALLENGER	CHAMPION/ TITLE CLAIMANT	RESULT	VENUE
26/04/32	M (NBA)	**Young Terry**	William "Gorilla" Jones	Jones WPts12	Trenton, NJ
20/05/32	JR-W	**Sammy Fuller**	Jack "Kid" Berg (England)	Fuller WPts12	New York City

Sammy Fuller claimed the junior-welterweight title following his victory over Jack "Kid" Berg.

DATE	WEIGHT	CHALLENGER	CHAMPION/ TITLE CLAIMANT	RESULT	VENUE
26/05/32	F Vacant (NBA)	**Tommy Paul**	Johnny Pena (Spain)	Paul WPts15	Detroit, MI

Tommy Paul won the final of the NBA elimination tournament designed to find a successor to Battling Battalino.

DATE	WEIGHT	CHALLENGER	CHAMPION/ TITLE CLAIMANT	RESULT	VENUE
31/05/32	LH (NBA)	**Lou Scozza**	**George Nichols**	Scozza WPts10	Buffalo, NY

This was Nichols's first outing since winning NBA title recognition. Scozza made another title claim but the NBA did not accept it.

DATE	WEIGHT	CHALLENGER	CHAMPION/ TITLE CLAIMANT	RESULT	VENUE
14/07/32	LH	**Lou Scozza**	Maxie Rosenbloom	Rosenbloom WPts15	Buffalo, NY

The question of overall supremacy in the light-heavyweight ranks was settled when Maxie Rosenbloom narrowly edged past Lou Scozza.

DATE	WEIGHT	CHALLENGER	CHAMPION/ TITLE CLAIMANT	RESULT	VENUE
18/07/32	JR-W	Johnny Jadick	**Tony Canzoneri**	Jadick WPts10	Philadelphia, PA
04/08/32	JR-LW (NBA)	**Eddie Shea**	Kid Chocolate (Cuba)	Chocolate WPts10	Chicago, IL
04/11/32	L	**Billy Petrolle**	**Tony Canzoneri**	Canzoneri WPts15	New York City
09/12/32	F & JR-LW (NYSAC)	**Fidel La Barba**	Kid Chocolate (Cuba)	Chocolate WPts15	New York City
13/01/33	F (NBA)	Freddie Miller	**Tommy Paul**	Miller WPts10	Chicago, IL

DATE	WEIGHT	CHALLENGER	CHAMPION/ TITLE CLAIMANT	RESULT	VENUE
22/02/33	W	**Young Corbett III**	Jackie Fields	Corbett WPts10	San Francisco, CA
17/03/33	M (NYSAC)	**Vince Dundee**	Ben Jeby	Draw Pts 15	New York City
01/05/33	JR-LW	**Johnny Farr**	Kid Chocolate (Cuba)	Chocolate WPts10	Philadelphia, PA
21/05/33	JR-W (Louisiana)	**Tony Canzoneri**	Battling Shaw (Mexico)	Canzoneri WPts10	New Orleans, LA
29/05/33	W	Jimmy McLarnin (Canada)	**Young Corbett III**	McLarnin WTKO1	Los Angeles, CA
23/06/33	L & JR-W	Barney Ross	**Tony Canzoneri**	Ross WPts10	Chicago, IL
10/07/33	M (NYSAC)	**Young Terry**	Ben Jeby	Jeby WPts15	Newark, NJ
26/07/33	JR-W	**Johnny Farr**	Barney Ross	Ross WKO6	Kansas City, MO
21/08/33	M Pennsylvania	**Vince Dundee**	Teddy Yarosz	Yarosz WPts10	Pittsburgh, PA
12/09/33	L & JR-W	**Tony Canzoneri**	Barney Ross	Ross WPts15	New York City

In an evenly contested title bout Canzoneri lost rounds, six, eight and nine because of low blows. Ross vacated the title on April 15, 1935 and Canzoneri regained the title after winning an elimination tournament designed to find Ross's successor.

30/10/33	M	**Vince Dundee**	Lou Brouillard	Dundee WPts15	Boston, MA
17/11/33	JR-W	**Sammy Fuller**	Barney Ross	Ross WPts10	Chicago, IL
04/12/33	JR-LW	**Frankie Wallace**	Kid Chocolate (Cuba)	Chocolate WPts10	Cleveland, OH
08/12/33	M	Andy Callahan	**Vince Dundee**	Dundee WPts15	Boston, MA
01/05/34	M	**Al Diamond**	**Vince Dundee**	Dundee WPts15	Paterson, NJ
04/05/34	F (NBA)	**Paul Dazzo**	Freddie Miller	Miller WKO6	Louisville, KY
30/08/34	F (NYSAC)	**Mike Belloise**	Baby Arizmendi (Mexico)	Arizmendi WPts15	New York City
11/09/34	M	Teddy Yarosz	**Vince Dundee**	Yarosz WPts15	Pittsburgh, PA
03/05/35	B (California)	**Lou Salica**	**Midget Wolgast**	Salica WPts10	Hollywood, CA
10/05/35	L Vacant	**Tony Canzoneri**	Lou Ambers	Canzoneri WPts15	New York City
11/06/35	B (California)	Pablo Dano (Philippines)	**Lou Salica**	Salica WPts10	Los Angeles, CA
26/08/35	B (NBA)	**Lou Salica**	Sixto Escobar (Puerto Rico)	Salica WPts15	New York City
16/09/35	Fly (NYSAC)	Small Montana (Philippines)	**Midget Wolgast**	Montana WPts10	Oakland, CA

Some record books report this fight as being for the American flyweight title.

04/10/35	L	Al Roth	**Tony Canzoneri**	Canzoneri WPts15	New York City
15/11/35	B (NBA)	Sixto Escobar (Puerto Rico)	**Lou Salica**	Escobar WPts15	New York City
10/02/36	M	**Tony Fisher**	Ed "Babe" Risko	Risko WPts15	Newark, NJ
03/04/36	F Vacant (NYSAC)	**Mike Belloise**	Everett Rightmire	Belloise WTKO14	New York City

The Belloise-Rightmire contest was initially a final eliminator for the NYSAC recognized featherweight title, but over time it has gained acceptance as a title contest. On May 19, 1936 the NYSAC announced Belloise as champion.

29/06/36	B	**Tony Marino**	Baltazar Sangchilli (Spain)	Marino WKO14	New York City
31/08/36	B	Sixto Escobar (Puerto Rico)	**Tony Marino**	Escobar WTKO13	New York City
03/09/36	L	**Lou Ambers**	**Tony Canzoneri**	Ambers WPts15	New York City
04/09/36	F (NYSAC)	Dave Crowley (England)	**Mike Belloise**	Belloise WKO9	New York City

DATE	WEIGHT	CHALLENGER	CHAMPION/ TITLE CLAIMANT	RESULT	VENUE
27/10/36	F (California)	**Mike Belloise**	Henry Armstrong	Armstrong WPts10	Los Angeles, CA

The New York boxing commission still recognized Mike Belloise as champion as they did not view ten round contests as championship bouts, preferring fifteen round fights instead.

27/11/36	W	**Izzy Jannazzo**	Barney Ross	Ross WPts15	New York City
21/02/37	B	**Lou Salica**	Sixto Escobar (Puerto Rico)	Escobar WPts15	San Juan, (Puerto Rico)
07/05/37	L	**Tony Canzoneri**	**Lou Ambers**	Ambers WPts15	New York City
23/09/37	L	Pedro Montanez (Puerto Rico)	**Lou Ambers**	Ambers WPts15	New York City
23/09/37	M (IBU)	**Fred Apostoli**	Marcel Thil (France)	Apostoli WTKO10	New York City

Marcel Thil lost his crown to Fred Apostoli in the ring but ironically boxing politics prevented Apostoli from enjoying champion status. The NYSAC had drafted a pre-fight agreement stipulating that no title was at stake as the commission recognized Freddie Steele as champion. Four months later Apostoli hammered Steele to a ninth round stoppage in a non-title contest to make his point to the commission. Whilst the Ring Recod Book recognize Apostoli as champion from this date, others agree that official recognition came in 1938.

23/09/37	B	**Harry Jeffra**	Sixto Escobar (Puerto Rico)	Jeffra WPts15	New York City
19/02/38	M	**Carmen Barth**	Freddie Steele	Steele WKO7	Cleveland, OH
20/02/38	B	Sixto Escobar (Puerto Rico)	**Harry Jeffra**	Escobar WPts15	San Juan (Puerto Rico)
22/02/38	M	**Young Corbett III**	**Fred Apostoli**	Young Corbett III WPts10	San Francisco, CA

Many viewed Apostoli as the legitimate world middleweight champion having beaten Marcel Thil in New York five months earlier. So, when Corbett III outpointed Apostoli, the California State Athletic Commission moved quickly and declared Young Corbett III as their world middleweight champion on May 5, 1938.

| 23/02/38 | H | **Nathan Mann** | Joe Louis | Louis WKO3 | New York City |
| 01/04/38 | M | Glen Lee | **Fred Apostoli** | Apostoli WPts15 | New York City |

This has been recorded, as a world title fight by Ring Record Book but full championship conditions did not apply as Apostoli weighed slightly over the 160-pound limit.

17/08/38	L	Henry Armstrong	**Lou Ambers**	Armstrong WPts15	New York City
17/10/38	F Vacant (NYSAC)	**Mike Belloise**	Joey Archibald	Archibald WPts15	New York City
18/11/38	M (NYSAC)	**Young Corbett III**	Fred Apostoli	Apostoli WTKO8	New York City

In May 1938 Freddie Steele was stripped by the NYSAC for continually refusing to meet Fred Apostoli. When the fighters met both were recognized as world champion with California bestowing that honor on Young Corbett III.

05/12/38	W	**Al Manfredo**	Henry Armstrong	Armstrong WKO3	Cleveland, OH
03/02/39	LH Vacant (NYSAC)	**Melio Bettina**	"Tiger" Jack Fox	Bettina WTKO9	New York City
02/04/39	B	**KO Morgan**	Sixto Escobar (Puerto Rico)	Escobar WPts15	San Juan, (PR)
28/06/39	H	**Tony Galento**	Joe Louis	Louis WTKO4	New York, NY
13/07/39	LH	Billy Conn	**Melio Bettina**	Conn WPts15	New York City
22/08/39	L	Lou Ambers	Henry Armstrong	Ambers WPts15	Bronx, NY
25/09/39	LH	**Melio Bettina**	Billy Conn	Conn WPts15	Pittsburgh, PA
28/09/39	F	**Harry Jeffra**	Joey Archibald	Archibald WPts15	Washington DC

Jeffra lost on a split points decision. Boxing writers at ringside all agreed that Jeffra had been robbed of victory. In April 1940 Archibald was stripped of his title for continually avoiding leading contender Pete Scalzo, who had knocked out Archibald in two rounds in a non-title bout in December 1938.

| 02/10/39 | M (NYSAC) | Ceferino Garcia (Philippines) | **Fred Apostoli** | Garcia WTKO7 | New York City |

DATE	WEIGHT	CHALLENGER	CHAMPION/ TITLE CLAIMANT	RESULT	VENUE
09/10/39	W	**Al Manfredo**	Henry Armstrong	Armstrong WKO4	Des Moines, IA
17/11/39	B (California)	**Lou Salica**	Tony Olivera	Salica WPts10	Hollywood, CA
04/03/40	B (NBA)	**Lou Salica**	Georgie Pace	Draw Pts15	Toronto, (Canada)

Weight making difficulties had forced Sixto Escobar, the undisputed bantamweight champ to relinquish his belt. In October 1939 the NBA announced George Pace as champion whilst Salica had the support of New York and California.

03/05/40	L Vacant (NBA)	**Sammy Angott**	Davey Day	Angott WPts15	Louisville, KY

The NBA title had been stripped from Lou Ambers for not meeting Davey Day in a title defense.

08/05/40	F (Louisiana)	**Jimmy Perrin**	Bobby Ruffin	Perrin WPts15	New Orleans, LA

Both fighters fought for the vacant Louisiana recognized world featherweight title.

10/05/40	L	Lew Jenkins	**Lou Ambers**	Jenkins WTKO3	New York City
15/05/40	F (NBA)	**Frankie Covelli**	**Pete Scalzo**	Scalzo WKO6	Washington DC

Scalzo was proclaimed champion by the NBA on May 1, 1940.

20/05/40	F	**Harry Jeffra**	Joey Archibald	Jeffra WPts15	Baltimore, MD
24/05/40	W	**Ralph Zanelli**	Henry Armstrong	Armstrong WKO5	Boston, MA
10/07/40	F	**Bobby Ivy**	**Pete Scalzo**	Scalzo WKO15	Hartford, CT
29/07/40	F	Spider Armstrong (Canada)	**Harry Jeffra**	Jeffra WPts15	Baltimore, MD
24/09/40	B	Georgie Pace	**Lou Salica**	Salica WPts15	Bronx, NY
14/10/40	W (Maryland)	**Izzy Jannazzo**	Cocoa Kid (Puerto Rico)	Jannazzo WPts15	Baltimore, MD

This fight was for the vacant Maryland recognized welterweight world title.

28/10/40	JR-W	**Jerome Conforto**	Harry Weekly	Weekly WPts15	New Orleans, LA

This fight was recognized as a world title fight by the Louisiana and Alabama Boxing Commissions.

01/11/40	M (NYSAC)	**Steve Belloise**	Ken Overlin	Overlin WPts15	New York City

An unpopular decision, reported the New York Times

02/12/40	B	Small Montana (Philippines)	**Lou Salica**	Salica WTKO3	Toronto, (Canada)
13/12/40	M (NYSAC)	**Steve Belloise**	Ken Overlin	Overlin WPts15	New York City

Belloise lost on a split points decision.

13/01/41	B	**Tommy Forte**	**Lou Salica**	Salica WPts15	Philadelphia, PA

By outpointing leading contender Tommy Forte, Salica was seen as the undisputed world bantamweight champion.

13/01/41	LH Vacant (NBA)	**Melio Bettina**	Anton Christoforides (Greece)	Christoforides WPts15	Cleveland, OH

Champion Billy Conn relinquished his title, moving up to heavyweight to meet Joe Louis.

17/02/41	H	**Gus Dorazio**	Joe Louis	Louis WKO2	Philadelphia, PA
08/04/41	H	**Tony Musto**	Joe Louis	Louis WTKO4	St Louis, MO
14/04/41	W	**Jimmy Leto**	**Izzy Jannazzo**	Jannazzo WPts15	Baltimore, MD

Izzy Jannazzo defends his Maryland recognized world welterweight title.

25/04/41	B	**Lou Transparenti**	**Lou Salica**	Salica WPts15	Baltimore, MD
12/05/41	F	Joey Archibald	**Harry Jeffra**	Archibald WPts15	Washington DC

Jeffra lost on a split points decision. Jeffra was recognized as world champion by Maryland, Pennsylvania and California states.

19/05/41	F	Phil Zwick	**Pete Scalzo**	Draw Pts15	Milwaukee, WI
16/06/41	B	**Tommy Forte**	**Lou Salica**	Salica WPts15	Philadelphia, PA
01/07/41	F	Ritchie Lemos	**Pete Scalzo**	Lemos WKO5	Los Angeles, CA
26/08/41	LH	**Tami Mauriello**	Gus Lesnevich	Lesnevich WPts15	New York City

Mauriello lost on a split points decision.

DATE	WEIGHT	CHALLENGER	CHAMPION/ TITLE CLAIMANT	RESULT	VENUE
15/09/41	F (Maryland)	**Lou Transparenti**	**Harry Jeffra**	Jeffra WPts12	Baltimore, MD
29/09/41	H	**Lou Nova**	Joe Louis	Louis WTKO6	New York, NY
14/11/41	LH	**Tami Mauriello**	Gus Lesnevich	Lesnevich WPts15	New York City
19/12/41	L	**Sammy Angott**	Lew Jenkins	Angott WPts15	New York City
15/05/42	L	Allie Stolz	**Sammy Angott**	Angott WPts15	New York City

Angott gave up his title in November 1942 because of a hand injury.

DATE	WEIGHT	CHALLENGER	CHAMPION/ TITLE CLAIMANT	RESULT	VENUE
19/06/42	F (NYSAC)	**Harry Jeffra**	Chalky Wright (Mexico)	Wright WTKO10	Baltimore, MD
07/08/42	B	Manuel Ortiz	**Lou Salica**	Ortiz WPts12	Hollywood, CA
25/09/42	F	**Lulu Constantino**	Chalky Wright (Mexico)	Wright WPts15	New York, NY
20/11/42	F (NYSAC)	**Willie Pep**	Chalky Wright (Mexico)	Pep WPts15	New York City
18/12/42	L Vacant (NYSAC)	**Tippy Larkin**	Beau Jack	Jack WKO3	New York City
10/03/43	B	**Lou Salica**	Manuel Ortiz	Ortiz WTKO11	Oakland, CA
08/06/43	F (NYSAC)	**Sal Bartolo**	**Willie Pep**	Pep WPts15	Boston, MA
16/08/43	F (NBA)	**Phil Terranova**	Jackie Callura (Canada)	Terranova WKO8	New Orleans, LA
27/10/43	L (NBA)	Luther "Slugger" White	**Sammy Angott**	Angott WPts15	Los Angeles, CA
27/12/43	F (NBA)	Jackie Callura (Canada)	**Phil Terranova**	Terranova WTKO6	New Orleans, LA
08/03/44	L (NBA)	Juan Zurita (Mexico)	**Sammy Angott**	Zurita WPts15	Los Angeles, CA
10/03/44	F (NBA)	**Sal Bartolo**	**Phil Terranova**	Bartolo WPts15	Boston, MA
05/05/44	F (NBA)	**Phil Terranova**	**Sal Bartolo**	Bartolo WPts15	Boston, MA
29/09/44	F (NYSAC)	Chalky Wright (Mexico)	**Willie Pep**	Pep WPts15	New York City
15/12/44	F (NBA)	Willie Roache	**Sal Bartolo**	Bartolo WPts15	Boston, MA
19/02/45	F (NYSAC)	**Phil Terranova**	**Willie Pep**	Pep WPts15	New York City
01/02/46	W	**Marty Servo**	Freddie Cochrane	Servo WKO4	New York City

In September 1946 Servo was forced to relinquish his title because of a nose injury sustained in a non-title stoppage defeat to Rocky Graziano. He tried a comeback but after two bouts retired permanently. Sugar Ray Robinson went on to win the vacant welterweight crown.

DATE	WEIGHT	CHALLENGER	CHAMPION/ TITLE CLAIMANT	RESULT	VENUE
29/04/46	JR-W Vacant	Willie Joyce	**Tippy Larkin**	Larkin WPts12	Boston, MA
03/05/46	F (NBA)	Spider Armstrong (Canada)	**Sal Bartolo**	Bartolo WKO6	Boston, MA
07/06/46	F	**Sal Bartolo**	**Willie Pep**	Pep WKO12	New York City
13/09/46	JR-W	Willie Joyce	**Tippy Larkin**	Larkin WPts12	New York City
18/09/46	H	**Tami Mauriello**	Joe Louis	Louis WKO1	Bronx, NY
27/09/46	M	**Rocky Graziano**	Tony Zale	Zale WKO6	Bronx, NY

1946 Ring Magazine Fight of the Year

DATE	WEIGHT	CHALLENGER	CHAMPION/ TITLE CLAIMANT	RESULT	VENUE
16/07/47	M	**Rocky Graziano**	Tony Zale	Graziano WTKO6	Chicago, IL

1947 Ring Magazine Fight of the Year

DATE	WEIGHT	CHALLENGER	CHAMPION/ TITLE CLAIMANT	RESULT	VENUE
22/08/47	F	Jock Leslie	**Willie Pep**	Pep WKO2	Flint, MI
24/02/48	F	Humberto Sierra (Cuba)	**Willie Pep**	Pep WTKO10	Miami, FL

DATE	WEIGHT	CHALLENGER	CHAMPION/ TITLE CLAIMANT	RESULT	VENUE
10/06/48	M	Tony Zale	**Rocky Graziano**	Zale WKO3	Newark, NJ
29/10/48	F	Sandy Saddler	**Willie Pep**	Saddler WKO4	New York City
11/02/49	F	**Willie Pep**	Sandy Saddler	Pep WPts15	New York City
			1949 Ring Magazine Fight of the Year		
16/06/49	M	**Jake La Motta**	Marcel Cerdan (France)	La Motta WTKO10	Detroit, MI
20/09/49	F	**Eddie Compo**	**Willie Pep**	Pep WTKO7	Waterbury, CT
14/10/49	H (NBA)	**Pat Valentino**	Ezzard Charles	Charles WKO8	San Francisco, CA
16/01/50	F	Charley Riley	**Willie Pep**	Pep WKO5	St Louis, MO
24/01/50	LH	**Joey Maxim**	Freddie Mills (England)	Maxim WKO10	London, (UK)
17/03/50	F	Ray Famechon (France)	**Willie Pep**	Pep WPts15	New York City
12/07/50	M	Tiberio Mitri (Italy)	**Jake La Motta**	La Motta WPts15	New York City
09/08/50	W	**Charley Fusari**	Sugar Ray Robinson	Robinson WPts15	Jersey City, NJ
08/09/50	F	Sandy Saddler	**Willie Pep**	Saddler WRTD8	Bronx, NY
		Pep was unable to come out for round eight due to an injured shoulder.			
13/09/50	M	Laurent Dauthuille (France)	**Jake La Motta**	La Motta WKO15	Detroit, MI
		1950 Ring Magazine Fight of the Year			
05/12/50	H	**Nick Barone**	Ezzard Charles	Charles WKO11	Cincinnati, OH
14/02/51	M	Sugar Ray Robinson	**Jake La Motta**	Robinson WTKO13	Chicago, IL
14/03/51	W Vacant (NBA)	**Charley Fusari**	Johnny Bratton	Bratton WPts15	Chicago, IL
		Fusari lost on a split points decision.			
30/05/51	H	Joey Maxim	Ezzard Charles	Charles WPts15	New York City
22/08/51	LH	Bob Murphy	**Joey Maxim**	Maxim WPts15	New York City
26/09/51	F	**Willie Pep**	Sandy Saddler	Saddler WRTD9	New York City
		In a dirty fight Pep was forced to retire after nine rounds when leading on all scorecards due to an eye injury.			
16/04/52	M	**Rocky Graziano**	Sugar Ray Robinson	Robinson WKO3	Chicago, IL
25/06/52	LH	Sugar Ray Robinson	**Joey Maxim**	Maxim WKO14	New York City
23/09/52	H	**Rocky Marciano**	Jersey Joe Walcott	Marciano WKO13	Philadelphia, PA
17/12/52	LH	Archie Moore	**Joey Maxim**	Moore WPts15	St Louis, MO
15/05/53	H	Jersey Joe Walcott	**Rocky Marciano**	Marciano WKO1	Chicago, IL
24/06/53	LH	**Joey Maxim**	Archie Moore	Moore WPts15	Ogden, UT
18/09/53	W	**Carmen Basilio**	Kid Gavilán (Cuba)	Gavilán WPts15	Syracuse, NY
		Basilio lost on a split points decision.			
24/09/53	H	**Roland La Starza**	Rocky Marciano	Marciano WTKO11	New York City
		1953 Ring Magazine Fight of the Year			
27/01/54	LH	**Joey Maxim**	Archie Moore	Moore WPts15	Miami, FL
05/03/54	L	**Paddy De Marco**	James Carter	De Marco WPts15	New York City
17/06/54	H	Ezzard Charles	**Rocky Marciano**	Marciano WPts15	New York City

DATE	WEIGHT	CHALLENGER	CHAMPION/ TITLE CLAIMANT	RESULT	VENUE
25/06/54	F (NBA Interim)	**Lulu Perez**	Percy Bassett	Bassett WRTD11	New York City

Lulu Perez, of mixed Italian-Puerto Rican descent was a leading contender for the featherweight title. The NBA sponsored the world "Interim" featherweight championship in the absence of Sandy Saddler, current world champion who was away on military service during the Second World War.

DATE	WEIGHT	CHALLENGER	CHAMPION/ TITLE CLAIMANT	RESULT	VENUE
20/08/54	M	**Rocky Castellani**	Carl Olson	Olson WPts15	San Francisco, CA
17/09/54	H	Ezzard Charles	**Rocky Marciano**	Marciano WKO8	New York City

1954 Ring Magazine Fight of the Year

DATE	WEIGHT	CHALLENGER	CHAMPION/ TITLE CLAIMANT	RESULT	VENUE
17/11/54	L	James Carter	**Paddy De Marco**	Carter WKO15	San Francisco, CA
01/04/55	W	**Tony De Marco**	Johnny Saxton	De Marco WKO14	Boston, MA
16/05/55	H	Don Cockell (England)	**Rocky Marciano**	Marciano WKO9	San Francisco, CA
10/06/55	W	**Carmen Basilio**	**Tony De Marco**	Basilio WKO12	Syracuse, NY
21/09/55	H	Archie Moore	**Rocky Marciano**	Marciano WKO9	New York City
30/11/55	W	**Tony De Marco**	**Carmen Basilio**	Basilio WKO12	Boston, MA

1955 Ring Magazine Fight of the Year.

Notes

* World boxing title bouts include title claims made during the newspaper decision era and prior to the advent of official sanctioning bodies in the United States.

Emboldened typeface indicates boxers of Italian American origin

Unless indicated all contests are for the undisputed title.

Asterisk alongside weight category indicates a no decision bout but the champion's title was at risk if he lost inside the distance.

Where it has been possible to ascertain a fight verdict during the no decision era the outcome has been listed.

NBA - National Boxing Association

NYSAC- New York State Athletic Commission

IBU – International Boxing Union

Occasionally American state/s sanctioned world title bouts. The name of the state is bracketed.

Result abbreviations

WPts – Points winner,

TKO- Technical knockout.Referee stopped contest.

DSQ - Disqualification,

RTD– Boxer retired from contest

KO - Knock out,

ND - Newspaper Decision

Weight abbreviations

Fly –flyweight

B – bantamweight

F – featherweight

JR-F – junior-featherweight

JR-LW – junior-lightweight

L – lightweight

LW – light-welterweight

W – welterweight

M – middleweight

LH – light-heavyweight

H - heavyweight

Source

www.boxrec.com

APPENDIX XI: ITALIAN AMERICANS IN WORLD TOP TEN BOXING RANKINGS 1900–23*

NAME	YEAR/S RATED	STATUS
Flyweight		
Kid Murphy	1906–07	1907 claimant
Young Zulu Kid	1915–17	1915 claimant
Battling Al Murray	1920–21	Contender
Patsy Wallace	1920–22	Contender
Frankie Genaro	1920–23	Contender
Jockey Joe Dillon	1922	1920 junior-flyweight claimant/contender
Joe Colletti	1922	Contender
Terry Martin	1922–23	Contender
Henry Catena	1923	Contender
Bantamweight		
Al Delmont	1904–08	Contender/ claimant
Frankie Conley	1909–11	1910 title claimant
Joe Wagner	1909–11	Contender
Jimmy Murray	1914	Contender
Pete Herman	1915–21	Champion
Little Jack Sharkey	1919–21	Contender/ claimant
Packey O'Gatty	1920	Contender
Carl Tremaine	1920, 1922–23	Contender
Phil Franchini	1921	Contender
Sammy Mandell	1922	Contender
Tommy Ryan	1922–23	Contender
Eddie Martin	1923	Contender
Mike Ballerino	1923	Contender
Bobby Wolgast	1923	Contender
Featherweight		
Eddie Lenny	1901–02	Contender
Benny Yanger	1901–04	Contender/ claimant
Patsy Kline	1910–12	Contender
Joe Coster	1911–12	Contender/ claimant
Johnny Dundee	1912–23	Contender/1921, 1923 junior-lightweight champion/1923 featherweight champion
Steve "Kid" Sullivan	1921–23	Contender
Mike Dundee	1922–23	Contender
Carl Duane	1923	Contender/1923 junior-featherweight champion
Sammy Mandell	1923	Contender
Lou Paluso	1923	Contender
Lightweight		
Charlie Sieger	1902–03	Contender
Frank Picato	1910	Contender
Frankie Russell	1912–13	Contender
Johnny Harvey	1914	Contender
Rocky Kansas	1915–23	Contender
Ralph Brady	1919	Contender
Bud Christiano	1920	Contender
Pal Moran	1920–21	Contender
Phil Logan	1922	Contender

NAME	YEAR/S RATED	STATUS
Welterweight		
Tommy Howell	1913	Contender
Jack Perry	1918, 1923	Contender
Lou Bogash	1920	Contender
Paul Doyle	1921–23	Contender
Middleweight		
Hugo Kelly	1905–11	Contender/ 1905–07/1910 claimant
Joe Borrell	1913–14	Contender
Frank Carbone	1918, 1921	Contender
Johnny Wilson	1920–23	Contender/1920 middleweight champion
Andy Palmer	1922	Contender
Lou Bogash	1922–23	Contender/1923 claimant
Caveman Fisher	1921–22	Contender
Light-heavyweight		
Tony Caponi	1906–07	Contender
Heavyweight		
"Fireman" Jim Flynn	1907–08, 1911–12	Contender
Tony Ross	1909, 1911	Contender

Notes

* With no world ranking system prior to 1924 this special listing is an unofficial classification of Italian American boxers compiled by this author. It is based on overall ability, annual performances and caliber of opposition faced between 1900 and 1923 inclusive.

The column 'Year's Rated' shows year or range of years a boxer merited a top ten listing.

The column 'Status' indicates whether a boxer was a premier contender, a title claimant or champion or all three.

APPENDIX XII: ITALIAN AMERICANS IN RING MAGAZINE'S ANNUAL WORLD TOP 20 RANKINGS 1924–55

NAME	RATING POSITION	YEAR OF RATING	HOMETOWN
Flyweight			
Patsy Ruffalo	16	1928	Mount Vernon, NY
Pete De Gati	16	1932	New York City
Johnny Nate	20		South Bend, IN
Bantamweight			
Vic Burrone	12	1925	New York City
Vic Burrone	13	1926	New York City
Tommy Ryan	15		McKeesport, PA
Tommy Ryan	17	1927	McKeesport, PA
Charley Pinto	16	1928	Buffalo, NY
Johnny Erickson	20		New York City
Georgie Nate	17	1930	South Bend, IN
Dick Welsh	20	1931	Philadelphia, PA
Johnny Gaudes	11	1938	Milwaukee, WI
Johnny Juliano	18	1940	Paterson, NJ
Featherweight			
Petey Mack	12	1925	Jersey City, NJ
Lew Hurley	13		Bronx, NY
Lew Hurley	15	1926	Bronx, NY
Tony Mandell	20	1927	Worcester, MA
Phil Verde	15	1929	Rochester, NY
Tony Leto	19	1930	Tampa, FL
Paul Dazzo	13	1932	Chicago, IL
Frankie Covelli	19	1933	Brooklyn, NY
Paul Dazzo	20		Chicago, IL
Frankie Covelli	18	1934	Brooklyn, NY
Joey Fontana	11	1938	New York City
Frankie Covelli	14	1939	Brooklyn, NY
Billy Passan	19		Philadelphia, PA
Frankie Carto	Group 1*	1943	Philadelphia, PA
Billy Pinti	Group1*		Rome, NY
Bill Bossio	11	1953	Pittsburgh, PA
Junior-lightweight			
Babe Ruth	11	1925	Philadelphia, PA
Phil Verde	15	1928	Rochester, NY
Young Zazzerino	19	1930	Jersey City, NJ
Lightweight			
Tommy "Kid" Murphy	14	1925	Trenton, NJ
Tommy Cello	11	1927	San Francisco, CA
Tommy "Kid" Murphy	16		Trenton, NJ
Matty Mario	17		Staten Island, NY
Eddie Guida	12	1928	New York City
Joey Ferrando	12	1935	Jersey City, NJ
Tony Morgano	14		Philadelphia, PA
Leonard Del Genio	19		New York City
Joey Ferrando	19	1936	Jersey City, NJ
Nick Camarata	15	1938	New Orleans, LA

NAME	RATING POSITION	YEAR OF RATING	HOMETOWN
Nick Camarata	15	**1939**	New Orleans, LA
Pete De Bello	16		Brooklyn, NY
Carmine Fatta	19	**1942**	Brooklyn, NY
Frankie Carto	Group 1*	**1944**	Philadelphia, PA
Mike Delia	Group 1*		Los Angeles, CA
Carmine Fatta	Group 1*		Newburgh, NY
Eddie Giosa	Group 1*		Philadelphia, PA
Al Guido	Group 1*		New York City
Joey Pirrone	Group 1*		Cleveland, OH
Frankie Rubino	Group 1*		Brooklyn, NY
Santa Bucca	Group 1*	**1946**	Philadelphia, PA
Mike Delia	Group 1*		Los Angeles, CA
Johnny Dell	Group 1*		Brooklyn, NY
Eddie Giosa	Group 1*		Philadelphia, PA
Tommy Greb	Group 1*		Boston, MA
Vic Grupico	Group 1*		San Francisco, CA
George LaRover	Group 1*		Philadelphia, PA

Junior-welterweight

NAME	RATING POSITION	YEAR OF RATING	HOMETOWN
Tommy "Kid" Murphy	15	**1928**	Trenton, NJ
Joey Harrison	15	**1929**	Paterson, NJ
Joe Trippe	16		Rochester, NY
Bobby Tracey	20		Buffalo, NY
Young Firpo	11	**1931**	Pennsgrove, NJ
Lew Raymond	16		Baltimore, MD
Philly Griffin	19		Newark, NJ
Eddie Guida	20		New York City

Welterweight

NAME	RATING POSITION	YEAR OF RATING	HOMETOWN
Salvatore "Red" Affinito	19	**1931**	New York City
Andy Saviola	20		Brooklyn, NY
Jimmy Phillips	16	**1932**	Bernardsville, NJ
Frankie Petrolle	19		Schenectady, NY
Al Manfredo	12	**1935**	San Francisco, CA
Mickey Serrian	18	**1936**	Scranton, PA
Leonard Del Genio	19		New York City
Al Nettlow	12	**1939**	Detroit, MI
Tony Marteliano	12	**1940**	New York City
Al Nettlow	14		Detroit, MI
Al Nettlow	No data	**1941**	Detroit, MI
Tony Motisi	16	**1942**	Chicago, IL
Sammy Secreet	19		Pittsburgh, PA
Frankie Wills	16	**1943**	Washington, D.C.
Pete De Ruzza	Group 1*	**1944**	Mamaroneck, NY
Ernie Forte	Group 1*		Providence, RI
Joe Mattone	Group 1*		Newark, NJ
Billy Tordiglione	Group 1*		Boston, MA
Frankie Wills	Group 1*		Washington, D.C.
Bee Bee Wright	Group 1*		Pittsburgh, PA
Sammy Adragna	Group 1*	**1946**	Carnegie, PA
Tony Riccio	Group 1*		Bayonne, NJ
Tommy Rotolo	Group 1*		Rome, NY

Middleweight

NAME	RATING POSITION	YEAR OF RATING	HOMETOWN
Frankie Campbell	13	**1925**	San Francisco, CA

NAME	RATING POSITION	YEAR OF RATING	HOMETOWN
Joe Roche	14	**1926**	San Francisco, CA
Joe Roche	19	**1927**	San Francisco, CA
Vincent Forgione	13	**1929**	Philadelphia, PA
Al Rossi	20	**1933**	Newark, NJ
Johnny Rossi	15	**1935**	Worcester, MA
Johnny Colan	11	**1941**	New York City
Johnny Finazzo	Group 1*	**1944**	Baltimore, MD
Jerry Fiorello	Group 1*		Brooklyn, NY
Larry Fontana	Group 1*		Brooklyn, NY
Ray Rovelli	Group 1*		Newark, NJ
Frankie Terry	Group 1*		Brooklyn, NY
Al Tribuani	Group 1*		Wilmington, DE
Al Priest	14	**1946**	Boston, MA
Joe Curcio	Group 1*		Newark, NJ
Vinnie Rossano	Group 1*		Brooklyn, NY
Izzy Jannazzo	Group 1*		Brooklyn, NY
Joey La Motta	Group 1*		Bronx, NY
Joe Governale	Group 1*		New York City
Jerry Fiorello	Group 1*		Brooklyn, NY

Light-heavyweight

NAME	RATING POSITION	YEAR OF RATING	HOMETOWN
George Nichols	15	**1930**	Buffalo, NY
George Nichols	15	**1931**	Buffalo, NY
George Nichols	16	**1932**	Buffalo, NY
Young Firpo	15	**1933**	Pocatello, ID
George Nichols	20		Buffalo, NY
George Nichols	15	**1936**	Buffalo, NY
Tony Cisco	18	**1940**	Norristown, PA
Johnny Colan	12	**1942**	New York City
Johnny Colan	11	**1943**	New York City
Johnny Colan	11	**1946**	New York City

Heavyweight

NAME	RATING POSITION	YEAR OF RATING	HOMETOWN
Paul Cavalier	18	**1929**	Paterson, NJ
Ralph Ficucello	15	**1930**	Brooklyn, NY
Freddie Fiducia	19	**1941**	Newark, NJ
Tony Musto	17	**1942**	Chicago, IL
Johnny Vorce	Group 1*	**1944**	Detroit, MI
Jimmy Carollo	Group 1*	**1946**	Queens, NY
Joe Muscato	Group 1*		Buffalo, NY
Tony Musto	Group 1*		Chicago, IL

Notes

The table reveals the depth of Italian American boxing talent showing boxers who never achieved an annual *Ring Magazine* world top ten ranking but managed a world top twenty ranking instead.

1925, 1926 – Top fifteen *Ring Magazine* rankings published only.

1943 – Top seventeen in bantamweight rated on ability. Others listed alphabetically.

*Asterisk denotes a Group 1 boxer. In 1941 *Ring Magazine* began listing boxers in groupings based on their ability. Within each group they were listed alphabetically as the editor Nat Fleischer found little difference to award a numerical ranking. A Group 1 boxer contained the best boxer cohort outside top 10 or 15 fighters in each division.

The use of the phrase 'No data' indicates that although boxer was ranked in the world's top twenty it was not possible to offer an exact rating.

Data taken from *Ring Magazine*: 1924–36, 1938–44, 1946, www.boxrec.com: 1937, 1945, 1947–55.

APPENDIX XIII: HEAD TO HEAD CONTESTS BETWEEN ITALIAN AMERICAN AND RIVAL ETHNIC AMERICAN BOXERS LISTED IN THE WORLD'S TOP TEN RANKINGS 1924–55

DATA SUMMARY OF HEAD TO HEAD MATCHES

MATCH-UP	WON	LOST	DRAW	ND	NC	TOTAL
Italian Vs African	223	237	24			484
Italian Vs Jewish	194	228	53	20	4	499
Italian Vs Irish	156	157	29			342
TOTALS	**573**	**622**	**106**	**20**	**4**	**1325**

Notes
All professional boxers included achieved at least one annual world top ten ranking in their career.
The head to head data is based upon the entire professional careers of boxers listed that achieved promotion into the annual world top ten world rankings.

APPENDIX XIV: INTER-ETHNIC RIVALRY IN WORLD TITLE FIGHTS 1900–55*

ITALIAN AMERICAN vs IRISH AMERICAN

DATE	WEIGHT	CHALLENGER	CHAMPION	RESULT
14/08/00	Bantamweight	**Casper Leon**	Johnny Reagan	Reagan WPts20
06/09/00	Bantamweight (vacant)	**Casper Leon**	Harry Forbes	Draw Pts20
02/04/01	Bantamweight (vacant)	**Casper Leon**	Harry Forbes	Forbes WPts15
25/04/05	Middleweight	**Hugo Kelly**	Philadelphia Jack O'Brien	Kelly WPts 20
09/03/06	Middleweight	Jack "Twin" Sullivan	**Hugo Kelly**	Draw Pts20
10/05/07	Middleweight	Jack "Twin" Sullivan	**Hugo Kelly**	Draw Pts20
31/03/08	Bantamweight	**Al Delmont**	Jimmy Walsh	Draw Pts 12
30/09/11	Featherweight	**Frankie Conley**	Johnny Kilbane	Kilbane WPts20
28/05/12	Light-heavyweight	**Hugo Kelly**	Jack Dillon	Dillon WKO3
04/09/12	Featherweight	**Johnny Dundee**	Johnny Kilbane	Draw Pts10
07/03/12	Welterweight	**Tommy Howell**	Spike Kelly	Draw Pts10
29/04/13	Featherweight	**Johnny Dundee**	Johnny Kilbane	Draw Pts20
05/11/17	Bantamweight	Frankie Burns	**Pete Herman**	Herman WPts20
10/02/19	Bantamweight	Patsy Scanlon	**Pete Herman**	Herman WPts20
24/03/19	Welterweight	**Jack Perry**	Jack Britton	ND10
10/06/19	Bantamweight	Terry McHugh	**Pete Herman**	Herman WPts20
06/05/20	Middleweight	**Johnny Wilson**	Mike O'Dowd	Wilson WPts12
02/06/20	Welterweight	**Young Joe Borrell**	Jack Britton	ND8

DATE	WEIGHT	CHALLENGER	CHAMPION	RESULT
23/08/20	Welterweight	**Lou Bogash**	Jack Britton	Draw Pts12
08/10/20	Welterweight	**Jack Perry**	Jack Britton	Draw Pts12
22/12/20	Bantamweight	Joe Lynch	**Pete Herman**	Lynch WPts15
17/03/21	Middleweight	Mike O'Dowd	**Johnny Wilson**	Wilson WPts15
25/07/21	Bantamweight	**Pete Herman**	Joe Lynch	Herman WPts15
18/11/21	Junior-lightweight (vacant)	**Johnny Dundee**	George "KO" Chaney	Dundee WDSQ5
22/02/22	Middleweight	**Frank Carbone**	Bryan Downey	Downey WPts12
21/08/22	Bantamweight	**Frankie Murray**	Joe Lynch	Lynch WKO6
28/08/22	Junior-lightweight	Vincent "Pepper" Martin	**Johnny Dundee**	Dundee WPts15
10/10/22	Welterweight	**Jimmy Kelly**	Jack Britton	Britton WPts12
09/01/23	Middleweight (vacant)	Charley Nashert Fitzsimmons	**Lou Bogash**	Bogash WTKO11
18/08/24	Junior-lightweight	Vincent "Pepper" Martin	**Steve "Kid" Sullivan**	Sullivan WPts15
01/06/25	Junior-lightweight	Frankie Callahan	**Mike Ballerino**	ND10
06/07/25	Junior-lightweight	Vincent "Pepper" Martin	**Mike Ballerino**	Ballerino WPts15
14/08/25	Junior-lightweight	Billy Henry	**Mike Ballerino**	Ballerino WPts10
10/02/30	Light-heavyweight	**Lou Scozza**	Jimmy Slattery	Slattery WPts15
09/01/31	Welterweight	**Pete August**	Tommy Freeman	Freeman WPts10
01/07/31	Featherweight	Bobby Brady	**Battling Battalino**	Battalino WPts10
13/07/31	Junior-welterweight	Cecil Payne	**Tony Canzoneri**	Canzoneri WPts10
08/12/33	Middleweight	Andy Callahan	**Vince Dundee**	Dundee WPts15
19/02/38	Middleweight	**Carmen Barth**	Freddie Steele	Steele WKO7
01/04/38	Middleweight	Glen Lee	**Fred Apostoli**	Apostoli WPts15
13/07/39	Light-heavyweight	Billy Conn	**Melio Bettina**	Conn WPts15
25/09/39	Light-heavyweight	Melio Bettina	Billy Conn	Conn WPts15
08/05/40	Featherweight	**Jimmy Perrin**	Bobby Ruffin	Perrin WPts15
10/05/40	Lightweight	Lew Jenkins	**Lou Ambers**	Jenkins WTKO3
01/11/40	Middleweight	**Steve Belloise**	Ken Overlin	Overlin WPts15
13/12/40	Middleweight	**Steve Belloise**	Ken Overlin	Overlin WPts15
19/12/41	Lightweight	**Sammy Angott**	Lew Jenkins	Angott WPts15
01/02/46	Welterweight	**Marty Servo**	Freddie Cochrane	Servo KO4
22/08/51	Light-heavyweight	Bob Murphy	**Joey Maxim**	Maxim WPts15

ITALIAN AMERICAN vs JEWISH AMERICAN

DATE	WEIGHT	CHALLENGER	CHAMPION	RESULT
24/04/02	Featherweight	**Benny Yanger**	Abe Atell	Yanger WTKO19
15/03/06	Featherweight	**Tony Moran**	Abe Atell	Atell WDSQ3
18/03/09	Featherweight	**Patsy Kline**	Abe Atell	ND10
22/02/10	Bantamweight	**Frankie Conley**	Monte Atell	Conley WTKO42
22/08/10	Featherweight	**Eddie Marino**	Abe Atell	Atell WKO3
13/11/10	Featherweight	**Frankie Conley**	Abe Atell	Draw Pts15
09/01/10	Featherweight	**Joe Coster**	Abe Atell	ND10
13/01/11	Featherweight	**Patsy Kline**	Abe Atell	ND10
01/12/11	Featherweight	**Patsy Kline**	Abe Atell	ND10
11/12/14	Middleweight	**Italian Joe Gans**	Al McCoy	McCoy WPts10
25/01/15	Middleweight	**Joe Borrell**	Al McCoy	McCoy WPts6
13/11/15	Middleweight	**Zulu Kid**	Al McCoy	Draw Pts10
01/07/20	Middleweight	Soldier Bartfield	**Johnny Wilson**	Wilson WPts12
10/02/22	Lightweight	**Rocky Kansas**	Benny Leonard	Leonard WPts15
21/04/22	Middleweight	KO Jaffe	**Johnny Wilson**	NC4
04/07/22	Lightweight	**Rocky Kansas**	Benny Leonard	Leonard WTKO8
30/05/23	Junior-lightweight	Jack Bernstein	**Johnny Dundee**	Bernstein WPts15
29/08/23	Junior-featherweight	**Carl Duane**	Jack "Kid" Wolfe	Duane WPts12
17/12/23	Junior-lightweight	**Johnny Dundee**	Jack Bernstein	Dundee WPts15
08/09/24	Bantamweight	**Tommy Ryan**	Abe Goldstein	Goldstein WPts15
19/12/24	Bantamweight	**Eddie Martin**	Abe Goldstein	Martin WPts15
20/03/25	Bantamweight	Charley Rosenberg	**Eddie Martin**	Rosenberg WPts15
23/07/25	Bantamweight	**Eddie Shea**	Charley Rosenberg	Rosenberg WKO4
04/02/27	Bantamweight	**Bushy Graham**	Charley Rosenberg	Rosenberg WPts15
14/03/27	Light-welterweight	**Andy Di Vodi**	Mushy Callahan	Callahan WKO2
10/02/28	Featherweight	Benny Bass	**Tony Canzoneri**	Canzoneri WPts15
23/05/28	Bantamweight (vacant)	**Bushy Graham**	Izzy Schwartz	Graham WPts15
03/08/28	Flyweight	**Little Jeff Smith**	Izzy Schwartz	Schwartz WKO4
25/07/29	Welterweight	Jackie Fields	**Joe Dundee**	Fields WDSQ2
22/08/29	Flyweight	**Willie La Morte**	Izzy Schwartz	La Morte WPts15
28/03/30	Junior-lightweight	**Eddie Shea**	Benny Bass	Shea WPts10
17/07/30	Lightweight	Al Singer	**Sammy Mandell**	Singer WKO1
14/11/30	Lightweight	**Tony Canzoneri**	Al Singer	Canzoneri WKO1
05/01/31	Junior-lightweight	**Lew Massey**	Benny Bass	Bass WPts10
15/05/31	Light-heavyweight	**Don Petrin**	Maxie Rosenbloom	Rosenbloom WPts10
30/07/31	Flyweight	Jackie Harmon	**Frankie Genaro**	Genaro WKO6

DATE	WEIGHT	CHALLENGER	CHAMPION	RESULT
31/05/32	Light-heavyweight	**Lou Scozza**	Maxie Rosenbloom	Rosenbloom WPts15
22/02/33	Welterweight	**Young Corbett III**	Jackie Fields	Corbett III WPts10
17/03/33	Middleweight	**Vince Dundee**	Ben Jeby	Draw Pts15
23/06/33	Lightweight & Junior-welterweight	Barney Ross	**Tony Canzoneri**	Ross WPts15
10/07/33	Middleweight	**Young Terry**	Ben Jeby	Jeby WPts15
26/07/33	Junior-welterweight	**Johnny Farr**	Barney Ross	Ross WKO6
12/09/33	Lightweight & junior-welterweight	**Tony Canzoneri**	Barney Ross	Ross WPts15
17/11/33	Junior-welterweight	**Sammy Fuller**	Barney Ross	Ross WPts10
04/10/35	Lightweight	Al Roth	**Tony Canzoneri**	Canzoneri WPts15
27/11/36	Welterweight	**Izzy Jannazzo**	Barney Ross	Ross WPts15
03/05/40	Lightweight (vacant)	**Sammy Angott**	Davey Day	Angott WPts15
19/05/41	Featherweight	Phil Zwick	**Pete Scalzo**	Draw Pts15
15/05/42	Lightweight	Allie Stolz	**Sammy Angott**	Angott WPts15

ITALIAN AMERICAN vs AFRICAN AMERICAN

DATE	WEIGHT	CHALLENGER	CHAMPION	RESULT
14/11/02	Lightweight	**Charlie Sieger**	Joe Gans	Gans WKO14
30/06/09	Heavyweight	**Tony Ross**	Jack Johnson	Johnson ND6
04/07/12	Heavyweight	**Jim Flynn**	Jack Johnson	Johnson WTKO9
13/07/31	Flyweight	Ruby Bradley	**Midget Wolgast**	Wolgast WPts15
26/04/32	Middleweight	**Young Terry**	William "Gorilla" Jones	Jones WPts12
23/02/38	Heavyweight	**Nathan Mann**	Joe Louis	Louis WKO3
17/08/38	Lightweight	Henry Armstrong	**Lou Ambers**	Armstrong WPts15
05/12/38	Lightweight	**Al Manfredo**	Henry Armstrong	Armstrong WKO3
03/02/39	Light-heavyweight	**Melio Bettina**	"Tiger" Jack Fox	Bettina WTKO9
28/06/39	Heavyweight	**Tony Galento**	Joe Louis	Louis WTKO4
22/08/39	Lightweight	**Lou Ambers**	Henry Armstrong	Ambers WPts15
09/10/39	Welterweight	**Al Manfredo**	Henry Armstrong	Armstrong WKO4
04/03/40	Bantamweight	**Lou Salica**	Georgie Pace	Draw Pts12
24/05/40	Welterweight	**Ralph Zanelli**	Henry Armstrong	Armstrong WKO5
24/09/40	Bantamweight	**Lou Salica**	Georgie Pace	Salica WPts15
17/02/40	Heavyweight	**Gus Dorazio**	Joe Louis	Louis WKO2
08/04/41	Heavyweight	**Tony Musto**	Joe Louis	Louis WTKO4

DATE	WEIGHT	CHALLENGER	CHAMPION	RESULT
29/09/41	Heavyweight	**Lou Nova**	Joe Louis	Louis WTKO6
18/12/42	Lightweight (vacant)	**Tippy Larkin**	Beau Jack	Jack WKO3
27/10/43	Lightweight	Luther "Slugger" White	**Sammy Angott**	Angott WPts15
15/12/44	Featherweight	Willie Roache	**Sal Bartolo**	Bartolo WPts15
29/04/46	Junior-welterweight (vacant)	Willie Joyce	**Tippy Larkin**	Larkin WPts12
13/09/46	Junior-welterweight	Willie Joyce	**Tippy Larkin**	Larkin WPts12
18/09/46	Heavyweight	**Tami Mauriello**	Joe Louis	Louis WKO1
29/10/48	Featherweight	Sandy Saddler	**Willie Pep**	Saddler WKO4
11/02/49	Featherweight	**Willie Pep**	Sandy Saddler	Pep WPts15
14/10/49	Heavyweight	**Pat Valentino**	Ezzard Charles	Charles WKO8
16/01/50	Featherweight	Charley Riley	**Willie Pep**	Pep WKO5
09/08/50	Welterweight	**Charley Fusari**	Sugar Ray Robinson	Robinson WPts15
08/09/50	Featherweight	Sandy Saddler	**Willie Pep**	Saddler WRTD8
05/12/50	Heavyweight	**Nick Barone**	Ezzard Charles	Charles WKO11
14/02/51	Middleweight	Sugar Ray Robinson	**Jake La Motta**	Robinson WTKO13
14/03/51	Welterweight (vacant)	**Charley Fusari**	Johnny Bratton	Bratton WPts15
30/05/51	Heavyweight	**Joey Maxim**	Ezzard Charles	Charles WPts15
26/09/51	Featherweight	**Willie Pep**	Sandy Saddler	Saddler WRTD9
16/04/52	Middleweight	**Rocky Graziano**	Sugar Ray Robinson	Robinson WKO3
25/06/52	Light-heavyweight	Sugar Ray Robinson	**Joey Maxim**	Maxim WKO14
23/09/52	Heavyweight	**Rocky Marciano**	Jersey Joe Walcott	Marciano WKO13
17/12/52	Light-heavyweight	Archie Moore	**Joey Maxim**	Moore WPts15
15/05/53	Heavyweight	Jersey Joe Walcott	**Rocky Marciano**	Marciano WKO1
24/06/53	Light-heavyweight	**Joey Maxim**	Archie Moore	Moore WPts15
27/01/54	Light-heavyweight	**Joey Maxim**	Archie Moore	Moore WPts15
05/03/54	Lightweight	**Paddy De Marco**	James Carter	De Marco WPts15
17/06/54	Heavyweight	Ezzard Charles	**Rocky Marciano**	Marciano WPts15
25/06/54	Featherweight (NBA 'Interim')	**Lulu Perez**	Percy Bassett	Bassett WRT11
17/09/54	Heavyweight	Ezzard Charles	**Rocky Marciano**	Marciano WKO8
17/11/54	Lightweight	James Carter	**Paddy De Marco**	Carter WKO15
01/04/54	Welterweight	**Tony De Marco**	Johnny Saxton	De Marco WKO14
21/09/55	Heavyweight	Archie Moore	**Rocky Marciano**	Marciano WKO9

SUMMARY OF INTER ETHNIC RIVALRY IN WORLD TITLE FIGHTS 1900–55

MATCH-UP	WON	LOST	DRAW	NC	ND	TOTAL BOUTS
Italian vs Irish	**21**	16	9		3	49
Italian vs Jew	**16**	24	4	1	4	49
Italian vs African	**18**	30	1			49

Notes
World title fights includes title claim defenses made by legitimately recognized title claimants.
Bold denotes Italian American boxer.
ND – Newspaper Decision
RTD – Boxer retired from contest.
NC – No contest
TKO – Technical knockout
KO – Knockout
Pts – Points

APPENDIX XV: WORLD TITLE DEFENSES AND CHAMPIONSHIP TENURE OF THE MAIN ETHNIC AMERICAN COHORTS 1900–55

ITALIAN AMERICAN BOXER

NAME	TITLE/S WON (date/s)	AGGREGATE TENURE OF TITLE REIGN(S) (in months)	TOTAL TITLE DEFENSES	TITLE DEFENSES/ YEAR AVERAGE
Frankie Genaro	1925, 1928–29, 1929–31	45	15	4
Tony Canzoneri	1927, 1928, 1930–33, 1931–32, 1933, 1935–36	60	13	2.6
Willie Pep	1942–48, 1949–50	92	11	1.4
Pete Herman	1917–20, 1921	49	10	2.4
Johnny Dundee	1921–23, 1923	37	8	2.6
Hugo Kelly	1905–07	39	8	2.6
Battling Battalino	1929–32	29	7	2.9
Johnny Wilson	1920–23	41	7	2
Sammy Mandell	1926–30	48	6	1.5
Rocky Marciano	1952–56	39*	6	1.9
Lou Salica	1935, 1940–42	26	6	2.8
Lou Ambers	1936–38, 1939–40	33	4	1.4
Pete Scalzo	1940–41	14	4	3.4
Midget Wolgast	1930–35	72	4	0.6
Fred Apostoli	1937, 1938–39	18	3	2
Mike Ballerino	1925	7	3	5.1
Sal Bartolo	1944–46	27	3	1.3
Joe Dundee	1927–29	25	3	1.4
Vince Dundee	1933–34	11	3	3.3
Harry Jeffra	1937–38, 1940–41	17	3	2.1
Jake La Motta	1949–51	20	3	1.8
Joey Maxim	1950–52	23	3	1.6
Steve Sullivan	1924–25	10	3	3.6

NAME	TITLE/S WON (date/s)	AGGREGATE TENURE OF TITLE REIGN(S) (in months)	TOTAL TITLE DEFENSES	TITLE DEFENSES/ YEAR AVERAGE
Sammy Angott	1940–42, 1943–44	34	2	0.7
Fidel La Barba	1925–27	24	2	1
Willie La Morte	1929–30	9	2	2.6
Rocky Kansas	1925–26	7	2	3.4
Phil Terranova	1943–44	7	2	3.4
Mike Belloise	1936–38	30	1	0.4
Carmen Basilio	1955–56	9*	1	1.3
Melio Bettina	1939	5	1	2.4
Young Corbett III	1933	3	1	4
Paddy De Marco	1954	8	1	1.5
Tony De Marco	1955	2	1	6
Rocky Graziano	1947–48	11	1	1.1
Izzy Jannazzo	1940–41	6	1	2
Tippy Larkin	1946	5	1	2.4
Tony Marino	1936	2	1	6
Eddie Martin	1924–25	3	1	4
Kid Murphy	1907	10	1	1.2
Tommy Paul	1932–33	8	1	1.5
Lou Bogash	1923	-	-	0
Frankie Conley	1910	12	-	0
Carl Duane	1923	-	-	0
Sammy Fuller	1932	6	-	0
Bushy Graham	1928–29	11	-	0
George Nichols	1932	2	-	0
Jimmy Perrin	1940	-	-	0
Lou Scozza	1932	2	-	0
Marty Servo	1946	7	-	0
Young Zulu Kid	1915	12	-	0
AGGREGATE TOTALS		1070	159	**AVERAGE SCORE = 1.8**

Notes

Asterisk indicates the number of months a title was held up to the end of 1955. It does not represent the total aggregated title tenure as boxers like Rocky Marciano and Carmen Basilio continued their championship reigns beyond 1955.

World champions include recognized title claimants.

Frankie Conley, Carl Duane, Lou Bogash, Jimmy Perrin did not make any defenses of their respective titles.

Marty Servo did not make a welterweight title defense as he was forced to retire through injury.

Izzy Jannazzo made one successful defense of his Maryland world welterweight title before abandoning his title claim.

Flyweight Young Zulu Kid was considered the best American flyweight in 1915. He met Britain's Jimmy Wilde for undisputed world title recognition in December 1916 and lost any serious claim to the title.

Bushy Graham did not make any title defenses as he outgrew the bantamweight class and moved up to the featherweight division.

Fidel La Barba relinquished his flyweight title in 1927 to go to university.

Sammy Fuller won recognition as a junior-welterweight title claimant when he beat Jack "Kid" Berg. He did not defend it. Instead six months later he challenged Barney Ross for the undisputed world title, narrowly losing a ten round points decision.

Tippy Larkin defended the 140-pound junior-welterweight title once before abandoning his title.

Light-heavyweight George Nichols was officially stripped of his of NBA title for failing to defend it within the stipulated time period.

Lou Scozza laid claim to Nichols's NBA light-heavyweight title when he outpointed Nichols in his first bout, two months after winning the vacant crown. Scozza's claim was not universally accepted.

AFRICAN AMERICAN BOXER

NAME	TITLE/S WON (date/s)	AGGREGATE TENURE OF TITLE REIGN(S) (in months)	TOTAL TITLE DEFENSES	TITLE DEFENSES/ YEAR AVERAGE
Joe Louis	1937–49	144	26	2.2
Henry Armstrong	1937–38, 1938–40, 1938–39	55	22	4.8
Joe Gans	1902–08	52	16	3.7
Jack Johnson	1908–15	64	9	1.7
Ezzard Charles	1949–51	25	9	4.3
Jimmy Carter	1951–52, 1952–54, 1954–55	36	8	2.7
Sugar Ray Robinson	1946–51, 1951, 1951–52, 1955–57	70*	8	1.4
Ike Williams	1945–47, 1947–51	72	8	1.3
John Henry Lewis	1935–38	36	5	1.7
Sandy Saddler	1948–49,1949–50, 1950–57	64*	5	0.9
Bob Montgomery	1943, 1944–47	47	4	1
Archie Moore	1952–62	36*	4	1.3
Percy Bassett	1952	21	2	1.1
"Tiger" Flowers	1926	9	2	2.7
Beau Jack	1943–44	9	2	2.7
"Gorilla" Jones	1931–32,	5	2	4.8
Georgie Pace	1940	6	2	4
"Young" Jack Thompson	1930, 1931	10	2	2.4
"Jersey" Joe Walcott	1951–52	13	2	1.8
Jackie Wilson	1941–43	13	2	1.8
Johnny Bratton	1951	2	1	6
Harold Dade	1947	2	1	6
Johnny Saxton	1954–55	12	1	1
Wallace Smith	1955–56	14*	1	0.85
"Slugger" White	1943	6	1	2
Teddy Davis	1953	3	-	0
"Dixie Kid"	1904	5	-	0
	AGGREGATE TOTALS	914	145	AVERAGE SCORE = 1.9

Notes

Asterisk indicates the number of months a title was held up to the end of 1955. It does not represent the total aggregated title tenure as boxers like Sugar Ray Robinson, Archie Moore and Sandy Saddler continued their championship reigns beyond 1955.

Although "Dixie Kid" is listed as champion his titular credentials are disputed mainly because the champion Joe Walcott lost on a disqualification in dubious circumstances. When it later transpired that the referee had bet on "Dixie Kid" winning the bout, Walcott continued to defend his title until he lost it officially to "Honey" Melody in 1906. There is no record of any title defenses by Dixie Kid.

Middleweight William "Gorilla" Jones is listed as having two title defenses. His second was a unification title match with IBU champion Marcel Thil.

Featherweight Sandy Saddler made three successful defenses of his title during this period. He also made two defenses of the world junior-lightweight title as recognized by Ohio State.

Featherweight Teddy Davis won the "interim" world title during Saddler's tour of duty in the armed forces. Three months later he challenged Saddler for the title, losing on points. The "interim" title was later abandoned.

IRISH AMERICAN BOXER

NAME	TITLE/S WON (date/s)	AGGREGATE TENURE OF TITLE REIGN(S) (in months)	TOTAL TITLE DEFENSES	TITLE DEFENSES/ YEAR AVERAGE
Jack Britton	1915, 1916–17, 1919–22	67	23	4.1
Mickey Walker	1922–26, 1926–31	96	11	1.4
Mike O'Dowd	1917–20, 1922	30	10	4
Harry Forbes	1902–03	28	9	3.85
Jack Dillon	1911–16	52	8	1.8
Johnny Kilbane	1912–23	111	8	0.9
Jack Dempsey	1919–26	86	7	1
Joe Lynch	1920–21, 1922–24	31	7	2.7
Terry McGovern	1900–01	22	7	3.8
"Rube" Ferns	1900, 1901	16	6	4.5
Tommy Loughran	1927–29	22	6	3.3
Freddie Steele	1936–38	24	6	3
Jimmy Walsh	1905–07	14	6	5.1
"Pinkey" Mitchell	1922–26	48	5	1.25
Billy Conn	1939–40	11	3	3.3
Matty Matthews	1900–01	7	3	5.1
Mike McTigue	1923–25	26	3	1.4
"Honey" Melody	1906–07	6	3	6
Ken Overlin	1940–41	12	3	3
Frankie Neil	1903–04	14	3	2.6
Gene Tunney	1926–28	22	2	1.1
Jimmy Slattery	1927, 1930	8	2	3
Jimmy Gardner	1908	7	2	3.4
Lew Jenkins	1940–41	17	2	1.4
Mike Sullivan	1907–08	19	2	1.3
James Braddock	1935–37	12	1	1
Jimmy Clabby	1910–11	2	1	6
Freddie Cochrane	1941–46	54	1	0.2
Tommy Freeman	1930–31	7	1	1.7
George Gardner	1903	4	1	3
Mike Glover	1915	1	1	12
Jimmy Reagan	1909	1	1	12
Jack O'Brien	1905–12	77	-	0
Dick Finnegan	1926	1	-	0
	AGGREGATE TOTALS	955	154	AVERAGE SCORE = 1.9

Notes

Light-heavyweight Jack Dillon claimed the title as early as 1911 but his claim was only taken seriously in 1915. Although much of his time was spent meeting heavyweights he did defend his title claim eight times.

The record books show that light-heavyweight Philadelphia Jack O'Brien had one of the longest title reigns but in actual fact he never defended his light-heavyweight title and moved up to heavyweight, challenging for the world title.

Light-heavyweight champions, Tommy Loughran and Billy Conn vacated their titles to campaign in the heavyweight division.

Mike "Twin" Sullivan relinquished his claim to the title after two successful defenses due to eye injury.

Featherweight Dick "Honeyboy" Finnegan won the Massachusetts recognized world title. He gave that up without making any defenses.

Heavyweight Gene Tunney retired as champion after two successful defenses.

JEWISH AMERICAN BOXER

NAME	TITLE/S WON (date/s)	AGGREGATE TENURE OF TITLE REIGN(S) (in months)	TOTAL TITLE DEFENSES	TITLE DEFENSES/ YEAR AVERAGE
Abe Atell	1901–12	124	27	2.6
Barney Ross	1933–35, 1934, 1935–38	67	13	2.3
Benny Leonard	1917–25	92	9	1.2
Maxie Rosenbloom	1930–34	53	8	1.8
Monte Atell	1909–10	12	7	7
Battling Levinsky	1916–20	36	7	2.3
Al McCoy	1914–17	43	7	1.9
Izzy Schwartz	1927–29	23	6	3.1
Abe Goldstein	1923–24	14	5	4.3
Benny Bass	1927–28, 1929–31	19	4	2.5
Mushy Callahan	1926–30	41	4	1.2
Jack Bernstein	1923	7	3	5.1
Jackie Fields	1929–30, 1932–33	26	3	1.4
Ben Jeby	1932–33	9	3	4
Louis Kaplan	1925–27	26	3	1.4
Harry Lewis	1908–11	22	2	1.1
Charley Rosenberg	1925–27	23	2	1
Jack Wolfe	1922–23	11	2	2.2
Newsboy Brown	1928	7	1	1.7
Solly Kreiger	1938–39	8	1	1.5
Bob Olin	1934–35	11	1	1.1
Dave Rosenberg	1922	3	1	4
Al Singer	1930	4	1	3
Harry Harris	1901–02	1	-	0
Pinky Silverberg	1927	2	-	0
	AGGREGATE TOTALS	684	120	AVERAGE SCORE = 2.1

Notes
Harry Harris beat Pedlar Palmer in London, England to win the world bantamweight title. He made no title defenses as he could no longer make the 118-pound limit. He abandoned the title.

Lightweight champion Benny Leonard vacated the title when he retired from the sport on January 15, 1925.

Charley Rosenberg forfeited the bantamweight title on the scales when he came in four pounds over the limit in his second title defense against Bushy Graham.

Louis Kaplan vacated the featherweight title after three title defenses when he could no longer make the weight.

Pinky Silverberg won the vacant NBA flyweight title against Ruby Bradley but was stripped several months later when the ruling body sanctioned a flyweight tournament to find an undisputed champion. Silverberg did not make any title defenses.

Barney Ross vacated his junior-welterweight title after his April 1935 title defense against Henry Woods.

APPENDIX XVI: THE AMERICAN BOXER WITH HIGHEST NUMBER OF ANNUAL TOP TEN WORLD RANKINGS 1924–55

NAME	WEIGHT	YEARS RANKED	ERA	ETHNICITY
Joe Louis	heavyweight	16	1930/40/50s	AFRICAN
Archie Moore	middleweight/ light-heavyweight/ heavyweight	15	1940/50s	AFRICAN
Sugar Ray Robinson	welterweight/ middleweight	14	1940/50s	AFRICAN
Willie Pep	featherweight	12	1940/50s	ITALIAN
Joey Maxim	light-heavyweight/ heavyweight	12	1940/50s	ITALIAN
Maxie Rosenbloom	middleweight/ light-heavyweight/ heavyweight	12	1920/30s	JEWISH
Jackie Wilson	featherweight/ lightweight/ welterweight	12	1930/40s	AFRICAN
Tony Canzoneri	bantamweight/ featherweight/ lightweight	11	1920/30s	ITALIAN
Lou Salica	bantamweight	11	1930/40s	ITALIAN
Henry Armstrong	featherweight/ lightweight/ welterweight	11	1930/40s	AFRICAN
Ezzard Charles	light-heavyweight/ heavyweight	11	1940/50s	AFRICAN
Mickey Walker	middleweight/ light-heavyweight/ heavyweight	11	1920/30s	IRISH
Tommy Loughran	light-heavyweight-heavyweight	11	1920/30s	IRISH

Chapter 7

APPENDIX XVII: ITALIAN AMERICAN SIBLINGS IN PROFESSIONAL BOXING 1900–55

NAME	DATES	HOMETOWN	WEIGHT
ADRAGNA, Sammy	1939–48	Carnegie, PA	W
Mimmie	1940–50		W
Jackie	1936–43		F
ALLEN, Joey	1928–43	Camden, NJ	L
Roxie	1925–36		W
AMICO, Mike	1940s*	New York	M
Terry	1940s*		L
AMOS, Babe	1928–36	Syracuse, NY	W
Danny	1930s*		L
APICE, Paris	1929–38	Providence, RI	L
Babe Willard	1920s*		F
Patsy Willard	1920s*		Fl
ASTEY, Dave	1917–25	Manhattan, NY	Fl/B
Willie	1914–21		B
ATTA, Joe	1920s/30s*	Rochester, NY	L
Louis	1920s*		B
Angie	1940s*		F
Augie	1930s/40s*		F
BACCALA, Dom	1941–46	Baltimore, MD	L
Sam	1934–44		W
BALDESINO, Johnny	1940s*	Niagara Falls, NY	W
Al	1943–49		L
BARTO, Mike	1933–38	New Kensington, PA	W
Tommy	1949–55		L
BARTOLO, Sal	1937–49	Boston, MA	F
Dom	1930s/40s*		F
BASILIO, Carmen	1948–61	Canastota, NY	W/M
Joey	1957–70		F
BAZZONE, Mike	1931–38	McKeesport, PA	LH
Joey	1930–41		M
BELLOISE, Mike	1932–47	Bronx, NY	F
Steve	1938–50		M
Sal	1945–52		M/LH
BETTINA, Melio	1934–48	Beacon, NY	LH
Joe	1940s*		H
BLAIR, Mickey	1925–31	Camden, NJ	L
Frankie	1933–39		W
BOGASH, Lou	1916–31	Bridgeport, CT	M
Patsy	1920s*		M
BOVE, Frankie	1938–44	Newark, NJ	F
Mickey	1930s*		F
BRADLEY, Pat	1911–23	Philadelphia, PA	W
Bucky De Carlo	1920s		F
Joe De Carlo	1920s*		L
BRADY, Jackie	1920–33	Syracuse, NY	L
Ralph	1916–25		L
Humbert	1921–27		W

NAME	DATES	HOMETOWN	WEIGHT
CAMARATA, Nick	1933–46	New Orleans, LA	L
Augie	1933–37		F
Jimmy	1933–35		M
Dom	1939–41		F
CAMUSO, Eddie	1950s*	Fall River, MA	H
Freddie	1936–47		W
CANAMARE, Paul	1924–38	Brooklyn, NY	L
Joe	1925–32		W
CAPOBIANCO, Rocky	1940s*	Providence, RI	W
Joe	No data		
CARLINI, Tony	1951–54	Philadelphia, PA	F
Jimmy	1951–54		W
CARR, Paul	1920s*	Buffalo, NY	F
Luke	1919–29		W
CARTO, Frankie	1941–46	Philadelphia, PA	F
Joe	1929–38		W
Nunzio	1946–48		L
CAVALIER, Joe	1922–35	Paterson, NJ	LH
Paul	1922–36		H
CESARIO, Johnny	1943–55	Hartford, CT	W
Sal	1941–48		M
CHRISTIANO, Bud	1917–27	Buffalo, NY	L
Al Rogers	1905–21		M
CIDONE, Vinny	1947–51	Brooklyn, NY	M
Steve	1940s*		M
CISCO, Tony	1935–42	Norristown, PA	M
Hank	1944–47		W
COLLURA, Chang	1930s*	Newark, NJ	L
Ralph	No data		
Phil	No data		
COMPO, Eddie	1944–55	New Haven, CT	F
Johnny	1933–47		F
CONSTANTINO,Lulu	1939–49	Manhattan, NY	F
Bozo	1944–54		W
COPPOLA, Rocky	1940s*	Stamford, CT	F
Fred	1940s*		L
COSTER, Joe	1906–22	Brooklyn, NY	F
Taddo	1910s*		F
DALTON, Charles	1901–20	Los Angeles, CA	L
Steve	1914–23		W
DECERIO, Jimmy	1948–55	Norristown, PA	M
Richie	1950–53		L
DECESARE, Ernie Caesar	1927–34	Philadelphia, PA	L
Bobby Dean	1928–37		F
DE JOHN, Mike	1951–63	Syracuse, NY	H
Joey	1944–55		M
Ralph	1936–47		LH
Carmen	1945–48		LH
DODGE, Joey	1931–36	Sacramento, CA	F
Johnny	1920s/30s*		F
Mickey	1920s/30s*		L
DONLEY, Mickey	1914–24	Newark, NJ	L
Joe	1920s*		W

NAME	DATES	HOMETOWN	WEIGHT
DOYLE, Alex	1937–48	Garfield, NJ	W
Midget	1934–46		L
DUCA, Johnny	1932–40	Paulsboro, NJ	M
Joe	1931–39		M
Mickey	1932–41		L
DUNDEE, Joe	1919–31	Baltimore, MD	W
Vince	1923–37		M
Battling	1916–23		Fl/B
ESPOSITO, KO Morgan	1926–46	Stamford, CT	B/F
Mike	1923–34		F
FARR, Johnny	1922–34	Cleveland, OH	F
Mickey	1920s/30s*		Fl
FISHER, Caveman	1917–28	Syracuse, NY	M
Kid Ritchie	1920s*		F
Mike	1910s/20s*		L
FINAZZO, Eddie	1938–47	Baltimore, MD	M
Johnny	1941–47		LH
Sam	1928–40		W
Joe	1928–45		LH
Victor	1937–42		W
Jack	1938–39		L
Tom	No data		
FONTANA, Joey	1935–47	Brooklyn, NY	F
Larry	1940–47		M
Tommy	1936–41		L
FORGIONE, Vinny	1924–35	Philadelphia, PA	M
Roxie	1935–42		M
FORTE, Tommy	1936–47	Philadelphia, PA	B
Johnny	1939–50		L
FUSARI, Charlie	1944–52	Irvington, NJ	M
Tommy	1939–44		W
GIOSA, Eddie	1943–54	Philadelphia, PA	L
Frankie	1951–55		L
GRAHAM, Bushy	1921–37	Utica, NY	B
Frankie	1920s*		F
GRIFFIN, Mickey	1920s*	Newark, NJ	F
Philly	1924–32		L
GUGGINO, Carl	1930–47	Tampa, FL	L
Gasper	1938–40		L
HAYES, Pete	1930–38	Brooklyn, NY	F
Johnny	1920s*		F
HOWELL, Tommy	1909–14	Philadelphia, PA	W
Frankie	1910s/20s*		W
JOHNSON, Battling	1914–29	Syracuse, NY	L
Patsy	1916–27		B
KANSAS, Rocky	1911–32	Buffalo, NY	L
Joe 'Kid'	1909–19		L
KLINE, Patsy	1907–15	Newark, NJ	F
Nick	1910s*		F
IACOBUCCI, Pat	1945–53	Cincinnati, OH	F
Carmen	1947–59		F
LA BARBA, Fidel	1924–33	Los Angeles, CA	Fl/F
Ted Frenchie	1916–25		B

NAME	DATES	HOMETOWN	WEIGHT
LA MOTTA, Jake	1941–54	Bronx, NY	M
Joey	1945–46		M
LARKIN, Tippy	1935–52	Garfield, NJ	W
Bobby	1930s*		L
LA STARZA, Roland	1947–61	Bronx, NY	H
Jerry	1942–49		M
LENNY, Eddie	1896–1920	Chester, PA	F
Harry	1902–15		L
LEON, Casper	1891–1904	Manhattan, NY	Fl
Benny	1895–1900		F
LETO, Jimmy	1925–43	Tampa, FL	W
Tony	1925–34		F
LONGO, Joey	1942–51	Baltimore, MD	F
Johnny	1942–53		L
Tony	1945–59		F
LUPICA, Sammy	1924–30	Toledo, OH	F
Tony	1922–30		F
Charlie	1923–31		L
MACK, George	1920s*	Jersey City, NJ	F
Petey	1922–30		F
MANDELL, Sammy	1919–34	Rockford, IL	L
Joe	1919–32		F
MARINO, Tony	1930–37	Duquesne, PA	B
Tommy Ryan	1919–29		B
MARTELL, Mickey	1922–31	Philadelphia, PA	W
Richie	1924–32		W
MARTIN, Eddie	1921–32	Brooklyn, NY	B
Gene	1920s*		F
MARTIN, Terry	1915–30	Providence, RI	Fl/B
Harry	1917–29		B
MARTIN, Tony	1936–46	Milwaukee, WI	M
Sam Cianciola	1930s*		M
Matt Cianciola	1925–29		W
MARTZO, Ralph	1920s*	Pittsburgh, PA	W
Sharkey	No data		F
George	No data		L
MASTRO, Earl	1926–32	Chicago, IL	F
Dick	1930s*		F
MICHAELS, Nick	1914–25	Syracuse, NY	L
Patsy	1921–24		F
MORAN, Midget Mike	1919–32	Pittsburgh, PA	B
Tommy	1920s*		L
MORAN, Pal	1914–29	New Orleans, LA	L
Vic	1912–29		L
MOREY, Jesse	1915–20	Buffalo, NY	F
Joe	1919–27		L
MURPHY, Frankie	1920s/30s*	Los Angeles, CA	F
Joe "Dynamite"	1920–32		F
Larry	1920s/30s*		L
MURRAY, Battling	1915–27	Philadelphia, PA	Fl
Tommy	1918–30		B
MUSCATO, Phil	1942–50	Buffalo, NY	H
Joe	1941–49		H
Sammy	1944–53		LH

NAME	DATES	HOMETOWN	WEIGHT
NATE, George	1928–34	South Bend, IN	B
Johnny	1930–33		Fl
O'GATTY, Packey	1915–28	New York City	Fl/B
Jimmy	1910s/20s*		W
PALECCO, Gene	1930s*	Newark, NJ	F
Jack	1920s/30s*		L
Babe	1924–35		W
PALMO, Frankie	1925–38	Cincinnati, OH	M
Joey	1934–46		B/F
PALUSO, Emil	1922–34	Salt Lake City, UT	B
Lou	1919–31		L
PAUL, Tommy	1927–36	Buffalo, NY	F
Frankie	1920s/30s*		B
PETROLLE, Billy	1922–34	Fargo, ND	L
Frankie	1924–34		W
Pete	1921–33		W
PICATO, Babe	1911–29	Los Angeles, CA	L
Charlie	1913–16		L
Frank	1908–16		L
PIRRONE, Paul	1926–39	Cleveland, OH	M
Joey	1940–49		L
PRIEST, Al "Red"	1941–52	Cambridge, MA	M
Johnny	1943–52		L
RAYMOND, Joey	1926–35	Baltimore, MD	W/M
Phil	1924–33		L/W
RASPI, Joe	1930–38	Baltimore, MD	L
Young	1930–40		W
RIZZO, Joe "Twin"	1927–30	Newark, NJ	L
Tom "Twin"	1920s-30s*		L
ROSSANO, Vinnie	1939–50	Brooklyn, NY	M
Rocco	1942–50		W
RUFFALO, Patsy	1927–28	Mount Vernon, NY	L
Jimmy	1926–32		F
SALICA, Jerry	1938–47	Brooklyn, NY	F
Lou	1932–44		B
SHEA, Eddie	1922–34	Chicago, IL	F
Tony	1920s/30s*		F
SINIBALDI, Dom	1942–48	Berlin, NH	W
Al	1938–47		LH
SKYMER, Lew	1920s/30s	Camden, NJ	L
Tommy	1930s*		W
TERRANOVA, Phil	1941–49	Bronx, NY	F
Nat	1946–52		F
Frankie	1931–41		L
Jack	1928–36		L
THOMAS, Dummy	1911–22	San Francisco, CA	F
Frankie	1919–30		W
Paul	1929–33		W
TRABON, Charlie	1920s*	Kansas City, MO	L
Joe	1924–32		L
TRANSPARENTI, Lou	1937–47	Baltimore, MD	B/F
Nick	1934–35		Fl
Joe	1934–38		B
Mike	1930s*		B

NAME	DATES	HOMETOWN	WEIGHT
TRAVERS, Tony	1923–35	New Haven, CT	W
Mickey	1918–31		L
TRIBUANI, Ralph	1931–33	Wilmington, DE	M
Al	1941–49		W
VENDRILLO, Pat	1940–48	Manchester, CT	W/M
Pete	1940s*		L
VIRGETS, Nick	1920–31	New Orleans, LA	F
Phil	1913–21		L
VIRGO, Johnny	1944–46	Rochester, NY	L/W
Ross	1948–52		W
WAGNER, Joe	1903–18	Manhattan, NY	B
Mike	1900s/10s*		F
YANGER, Benny	1899–1910	Chicago, IL	F
Phil	1900s*		F/L
ZILL, Tony	1913–26	Youngstown, OH	L
Al	1910s*		L
Jimmy	1920s*		L

Notes

*Exact dates have not been established. Dates of professional careers is for indicative purposes only. In some cases these might vary depending on sources checked. Fl = flyweight, B = bantamweight, F = featherweight, L = lightweight, W = welterweight, M = middleweight, LH = light-heavyweight, H = heavyweight.

Chapter 8

APPENDIX XVIIIᴬ: ITALIAN AMERICAN NATIONAL (AAU) AMATEUR BOXING CHAMPIONS 1900–55

NAME	WEIGHT CLASS	HOMETOWN	YEAR WON
John Serino	heavyweight (+72kg)	Boston, MA	1911
Jimmy Tomasulo	bantamweight (52,5kg)	Elizabeth, NJ	1917, 1918
John Gaddi	heavyweight (+79,5kg)	New York	1917
James Fruzetti	featherweight (57kg)	Brockton, MA	1918
Ashton Donza	bantamweight (52,5kg)	New Orleans, LA	1919
Samuel Lagonia	middleweight (72kg)	New York	1919, 1920, 1921
AJ De Vito (Frank Genaro)	flyweight (50kg)	New York	1920
Terry Parker	featherweight (57,5kg)	Boston, MA	1923
John Rini	welterweight (67 kg)	Cleveland, OH	1923
Fidel La Barba	flyweight (51kg)	Los Angeles, CA	1924
Salvatore Tripoli	bantamweight (53,5kg)	New York	1924
August Gotto	bantamweight (53,5kg)	Los Angeles, CA	1925
Ray Alfano	featherweight (57,5kg)	St Louis, MO	1925
Patsy Ruffalo	featherweight (57,5kg)	Mount Vernon, NY	1926
Thomas Paul (Papa)	bantamweight (53,5kg)	Buffalo, NY	1927
Christopher Battalino	featherweight (57,5kg)	Hartford, CT	1927
Ralph Ficucello	heavyweight (+79,5kg)	Brooklyn, NY	1929
Alex Santora	lightweight (61,5kg)	Bayonne, NJ	1930
Babe Triscaro	flyweight (51kg)	Cleveland, OH	1931
Joseph Ferrante	bantamweight (53,5kg)	Boston, MA	1931
Anthony Scarpati	featherweight (57,5kg)	Brooklyn, NY	1931
Tony Poloni	light-heavyweight (79,5kg)	Reno, NV	1931
Lou Salica	flyweight (51kg)	Brooklyn, NY	1932
Jimmy Martin (Lombardi)	bantamweight (53,5kg)	Brooklyn, NY	1932
Fred Caserio	middleweight (73kg)	Chicago, IL	1932
Fred Feary (Fioramonte)	heavyweight (+79,5kg)	Stockton, CA	1932
Tony Valore	flyweight (51kg)	Cleveland, OH	1933
Angelo Tardugno	bantamweight (53,5kg)	Washington DC	1933
Louis Barisano	featherweight (57,5kg)	Boston, MA	1933
William Celebron	welterweight (67kg)	Rockford, IL	1933
Armando Sicilia	bantamweight (53,5kg)	Chicago, IL	1934
Danny Farrar (Donato Ferrara)	welterweight (67kg)	Youngstown, OH	1934
Fred Apostoli	middleweight (73kg)	San Francisco, CA	1934
John Marcelline	flyweight (51kg)	Philadelphia, PA	1935
Troy (Troiano) Bellini	bantamweight (53,5kg)	Cleveland, OH	1935
Al Nettlow (Nittlo)	featherweight (57,5kg)	Detroit, MI	1935
Lou Nova*	heavyweight (+79,5kg)	San Francisco, CA	1935
Cozy Storace	welterweight (67kg)	Rome, NY	1939
Angelo Ambrosano	bantamweight (53,5kg)	Philadelphia, PA	1940
Joey Maxim	middleweight (73kg)	Cleveland, OH	1940
Anthony Peppi	flyweight (51kg)	Boston, MA	1943
Joey D'Amato	lightweight (61,5kg)	Warren, OH	1944
Joseph Discepoli	lightweight (61,5kg)	US Marines	1946
Nick Ranieri	middleweight (73kg)	Chicago, IL	1947

NAME	WEIGHT CLASS	HOMETOWN	YEAR WON
Frank Sodano	flyweight (51kg)	Philadelphia, PA	1948
Theodore Fittipaldo	featherweight (57,5kg)	Warren, OH	1948
John L. Cereghin	bantamweight (54kg)	Air Force, Lima, OH	1955

Notes
The National AAU boxing championships began in 1888.
*Lou Nova is of mixed Italian-German and Scotch-Irish origin.
Fred Feary's biological father was Italian. His mother later remarried and her son assumed stepfather's name.

Source: www.boxrec.com

APPENDIX XVIII^B: CHICAGO'S ITALIAN AMERICAN GOLDEN GLOVES CHAMPIONS 1928–55

NAME	WEIGHT CLASS	HOMETOWN	YEAR WON
Nick Fosco	welterweight	Chicago, IL	1928
Paul Dazzo	bantamweight	BP: New Orleans, LA. Chicago, IL	1930
Nick Scialaba	bantamweight	Chicago, IL	1931
Scotty Sylvano	lightweight	Chicago, IL	1931
Fred Caserio	middleweight	Chicago, IL	1931, 1933
Troy Bellini	bantamweight	Cleveland, OH	1934
Al Nettlow	featherweight	Detroit, MI	1934
Patsy Urso	flyweight	Detroit, MI	1935
Mike Gamiere	lightweight	Cleveland, OH	1935
Carl Vinciguerra	light-heavyweight	Omaha, NE	1936
Andy Scrivani	lightweight	Chicago, IL	1935
Linto Guerrieri	light-heavyweight	Rockford, IL	1938
Vic Saccola	flyweight	Detroit, MI	1939
Tony Ancona	featherweight	Detroit, MI	1939, 1940
Saviour Canadeo	welterweight	De Pere, WI	1940
Joey Maxim	middleweight	Cleveland, OH	1940
Sammy D'Errico	featherweight	Cleveland, OH	1942
Tony Janiro	featherweight	Youngstown, OH	1943
Joe Frucci	heavyweight	Gary, IN	1946
Eddie Marotta	featherweight	Cleveland, OH	1947
Nick Ranieri	middleweight	Chicago, IL	1947
Dan Bucceroni	light-heavyweight	Philadelphia, PA	1947

Notes
The *Chicago Tribune* sponsored Chicago Golden Gloves boxing championships have been staged every year since 1928. However, an amateur boxing tournament organized along similar lines was staged five years earlier to test the anti-boxing law and following great opposition organizers decided not to pursue follow-up events. Instead they decided to wait until boxing was legalized in Illinois.

Source: www.goldengloves.com/history

APPENDIX XVIII^C: NEW YORK'S ITALIAN AMERICAN GOLDEN GLOVES OPEN CLASS CHAMPIONS 1927–55

NAME	WEIGHT CLASS	HOMETOWN	YEAR WON
Joe Spatola	lightweight	Long Island, NY	1927
Al Santora	flyweight/ featherweight	Bayonne, NJ	1928, 1929
Tony Caragliano	featherweight	Bronx, NY	1928
Charles Manzy	bantamweight	Jersey City, NJ	1929
Salvatore Affinito	welterweight	Bronx, NY	1929
Ralph Ficucello	heavyweight	Brooklyn, NY	1929
Jimmy Siclari	flyweight	Manhattan, NY	1930
Johnny Mauro	bantamweight	Harlem, NY	1930
Joe Comforti	featherweight	Harlem, NY	1930
Patsy Pasculli	lightweight	Harlem, NY	1930
Andy Melia	middleweight	Long Island, NY	1930. 1931
Tony Scarpati	featherweight	Brooklyn, NY	1931
Lou Salica	flyweight	Brooklyn, NY	1932
Johnny De Foe	bantamweight	Long Island, NY	1932
Henry Balsamo	middleweight	Harlem, NY	1933
Richard Li Brandi	flyweight	Brooklyn, NY	1934
Lou Camps	featherweight	Unionport, NJ	1934
Joseph Ferrone	welterweight	Beacon, NY	1934
Phillip Sommese	light-heavyweight	Westbury, NY	1934, 1935
Pete Scalzo	bantamweight	Brooklyn, NY	1936
Vincent Pimpinella	welterweight	Brooklyn, NY	1936
Salvatore Bartolo	bantamweight	Boston, MA	1937
Joe Matisi	heavyweight	Binghamton, NY	1937
Johnny Aiello	bantamweight	Philadelphia, PA	1938
Tony Sarullo	featherweight	Philadelphia, PA	1938
Tami Mauriello	welterweight	Bronx, NY	1939
Demetrio Carabella	flyweight	New York	1940
Anthony Celentano	welterweight	Davisville, RI	1940
Michael Contestabile	flyweight	Brooklyn, NY	1942
Bally Carubia	welterweight	Long Island, NY	1943
James Carollo	heavyweight	Long Island, NY	1942
Frank Perone	featherweight	New York	1944
Frank Stefano	bantamweight	Farmingdale, NY	1945
Roland La Starza	light-heavyweight	Bronx, NY	1945
Louis Castrilli	featherweight	New York	1946
William Pesante	featherweight	Brooklyn, NY	1947
Tommy Pennino	flyweight	Brooklyn, NY	1948
Enrico Versace	flyweight	White Plains, NY	1949
Carmelo Costa	featherweight	Brooklyn, NY	1952
Anthony Di Biase	welterweight	Stuyvesant, NY	1953
Angelo De Fendis	middleweight	Brooklyn, NY	1953
Tony De Cola	bantamweight	Brooklyn, NY	1954

APPENDIX XVIIIᴰ: NEW YORK'S ITALIAN AMERICAN GOLDEN GLOVES SUB-NOVICE/ ALTERNATE CHAMPIONS 1927–55

NAME	WEIGHT CLASS	BOXING CLUB/ HOMETOWN	YEAR WON
Al Giaco	lightweight	Montrose AC,/Brooklyn	1927
Joseph Siclari	flyweight	Brooklyn, NY	1928, 1929
Teddy Martin	featherweight	Manhattan, NY	1928
Anthony Ventura	featherweight	Paterson, NJ	1929
Al Ragone	flyweight	Unattached	1930
Jerry Mazza	featherweight	Brooklyn, NY	1930
Mike Vetrano	light-heavyweight	Ascension Parish	1930
Sammy Garigliano	flyweight	Yonkers, NY	1931
John Consiglio	welterweight	Brooklyn, NY	1931
Vincent De Lucca	flyweight	Unattached	1932
Peter Caracciola	featherweight	Clark House	1932
Thomas Pontecorvo	heavyweight	Unattached	1932
Harry Mangano	bantamweight	Unattached	1933
Leonard Del Genio	featherweight	Manhattan, NY	1933
Joe Presti	welterweight	Unattached	1933
Joseph Fratello	flyweight	Unattached	1934
Rocco De Cosmo	welterweight	Unattached	1934
Jack Vaccarelli	light-heavyweight	First Avenue Boys	1934
Patsy Erra	bantamweight	Harlem, NY	1935
Joe Comito	welterweight	Unattached	1935
George Maselli	heavyweight	Catholic Boys	1935
Buddy Basilico	featherweight	CYA	1936
Anthony Bianco	featherweight	First Avenue Boys	1937
Sam Di Pasquale	flyweight	Philadelphia Inquirer/ Philadelphia, PA	1938
Armand Dascenza	featherweight	Hudson Dispatch,	1938
Joseph Di Bella	lightweight	Municipal Playground	1938
Jerry Fiorello	welterweight	Trinity Club/ Brooklyn	1938
Felice Corvino	flyweight	Unattached	1939
Lawrence Aglialoro	featherweight	Roman SC	1939
Artie Di Pietro	lightweight	Boys Club	1939
Salvatore Barone	welterweight	Unattached	1939
Joseph Argo	featherweight	Unattached	1940
Rocco Lescio	lightweight	National AC	1940
Nathan Peragine	middleweight	Teasdale AC	1940
Phil Terranova	featherweight	Bronx, NY	1941
Nicholas Picarello	bantamweight	Unattached	1942
Nick Toretto	welterweight	CYO, Bronx	1942
Jerry La Starza	middleweight	CYO, Bronx	1942
Salvatore D'Ambrosio	welterweight	Unattached	1943
Anthony Delicati	featherweight	CYO, Bronx	1944
Dominic Modafferi	middleweight	Trinity Club/ Brooklyn	1944
Roland La Starza	light-heavyweight	CYO, Bronx	1944
Frank Sapone	flyweight	CYO, Bronx	1945
Louis Castrilli	bantamweight	PAL, Bronx	1945
Johnny La Russo	featherweight	Dept of Parks AA/ Bronx,	1945
Angelo Luongo	lightweight	PAL	1945
Michael Tarantino	bantamweight	CYO, Bronx	1946
Carmelo Ippolito	flyweight	Unattached	1947

NAME	WEIGHT CLASS	BOXING CLUB/ HOMETOWN	YEAR WON
Frank De George	featherweight	CYO	1947
Gregory Siragusa	middleweight	Dept of Parks AA/ Bronx	1947
Michael Franco	light-heavyweight	CYO	1947
Michael Figliuolo	heavyweight	PAL	1947
Salvatore Spinelli	flyweight	CYO	1948
Michael Di Pasquale	bantamweight	PAL	1948
Frank Cirillo	featherweight	Trinity Club/ Brooklyn	1948
Hugo Starace	welterweight	Lenox Hill AA	1948
Ernest Toretto	middleweight	CYO	1948
Eugene Darconte	light-heavyweight	Riveredge A&S/ Queens, NY	1948
Carl Antonucci	bantamweight	CYO	1949
Antonio Gandolfo	middleweight	Trinity Club/Brooklyn	1949
Ronald D'Alboro	flyweight	PAL	1950
John Digilio	featherweight	PAL	1950
Ignatius Fugazzotto	welterweight	PAL/Brooklyn	1950
Leonard Florio	light-heavyweight	PAL	1950
Carmelo Costa	bantamweight	PAL/Brooklyn	1951
Nicholas Martino	middleweight	PAL	1951
Joseph Tufaro	lightweight	PAL/Brooklyn,	1952
Anthony Di Biase	welterweight	PAL/Long Island, NY	1952
Tony De Cola	bantamweight	PAL/Brooklyn	1953
Billy Flamio	lightweight	Boy's Club	1953
Anthony Puleo	lightweight	Trinity Club/Brooklyn	1954
Daniel Russo	middleweight	W17th Parks Dept/ Brooklyn	1955

Notes

The inaugural New York Golden Gloves championships began in 1927.

Abbrevations: -

PAL – Police Athletic League

CYO – Catholic Youth Organization

CYA – Catholic Youth Alliance

Unattached signifies the boxer was not a member of a club.

Please note the boxers were primarily from New York's five boroughs. Later boxers from outside the city metropolitan area also competed in these championships.

Source: www.boxrec.com

APPENDIX XVIIIᴱ: PHILADELPHIA'S ITALIAN AMERICAN GOLDEN GLOVES CHAMPIONS 1932–55

NAME	WEIGHT CLASS	BOXING CLUB	YEAR WON
Mickey Grandinetti	welterweight	Germantown	1932
Louis Cinalli	middleweight	Nativity	1932
Joe Maffei	flyweight	Unknown	1933
Gene Gallotto	bantamweight	Unknown	1933
Johnny Marcelline	flyweight	Mason	1934
Gus Dorazio	light-heavyweight	Older Boys Center	1934
Tony Aiello	mini-flyweight	Wilmington, DE	1935
Tommy Forte	flyweight	Mason	1935
Tom Steffanelli	welterweight	Older Boys	1935
Joseph Masciantonio	heavyweight	Older Boys	1935
Johnny Aiello	flyweight/ bantamweight	Wilmington, DE	1936, 1939
Johnny Litto	featherweight	Unattached	1936
Frank Donofrio	light-heavyweight	Seymour	1936
Johnny Forte	flyweight	Unattached/ Pen-Mar	1937, 1938
Tony Sarullo	featherweight	Unattached	1937
Vince Simone	welterweight	Unattached/ Pen-Mar	1937, 1938
Nick Fiorentino	heavyweight	Seymour	1937
Angelo Ambrosano	bantamweight	Corsac	1938
Joe Amico	featherweight	Pen-Mar	1938
Frankie Carto	flyweight/ bantamweight	Unattached/ Crusaders	1939, 1940
Paul Febbo	flyweight/ bantamweight	Pen-Mar	1940, 1942
Eddie Giosa	featherweight/ lightweight	Pen-Mar	1940, 1942
Pat Mattiacci	flyweight	Dunbar	1942
Angelo Sfrisi	light-heavyweight	Pen-Mar	1942

Open category

Vic Capcino	featherweight	Lambs Club	1944
Joe Cuccinotti	flyweight	Pen-Mar	1945
Jimmy Sulla	bantamweight	Southside	1945
Nunzio Carto	featherweight	Pen-Mar	1945
Joe Trofe	welterweight	48th Ward	1946
John Calcinore	light-heavyweight	Pen-Mar	1946
Frankie Sodano	flyweight	34th PAL	1947

Novice silver category

Nunzio Carto	flyweight	Pen-Mar	1944
Vince Di Napoli	bantamweight	Pen-Mar	1944
Frank De Cellano	bantamweight	43rd Ward	1945
Mike Muto	heavyweight	48th Ward	1945
Vince Merollo	lightweight	Pen-Mar	1946
Henry Beltrante	bantamweight	34th PAL	1949

Notes

No data available for 1943 and 1953 Philadelphia Golden Gloves championships.

The Philadelphia tournament changed format in 1944 permitting boxers in all weight classes to compete in an open and novice category.

The cited boxing clubs are all located in Philadelphia. Any boxer outside the area is denoted with place name and state abbreviation.

The *Philadelphia Daily News* sponsored Golden Gloves championships began in 1932.

Source: www.phillyboxing.com

APPENDIX XVIII^F: ITALIAN AMERICAN CHAMPIONS IN THE CHICAGO/NEW YORK INTER-CITY GOLDEN GLOVES CHAMPIONSHIPS 1928–55

NAME	WEIGHT CLASS	TEAM	YEAR WON
Tony Caragliano	featherweight	New York	1928
Charles Manzy	bantamweight	New York	1929
Salvatore Affinito	welterweight	New York	1929
John Mauro	bantamweight	New York	1930
Joe Comforti	featherweight	New York	1930
Patsy Pasculli	lightweight	New York	1930
Nick Scialaba	bantamweight	Chicago	1931
Scotty Sylvano	lightweight	Chicago	1931
Phil Dardell (Ragozzino)	welterweight	New York	1931
Fred Caserio	middleweight	Chicago	1931, 1933
Lou Salica	flyweight	New York	1932
Johnny De Foe	bantamweight	New York	1932
Richard Li Brandi	flyweight	New York	1934
Ario Soldati	light-heavyweight	Chicago	1934
Charles Villareale	bantamweight	New York	1935
Al Nettlow	featherweight	Chicago	1935
Andy Scrivani	lightweight	Chicago	1935
Johnny Brown (Marelli)	bantamweight	Chicago	1936
Vincent Pimpinella	welterweight	New York	1936
Joe Matisi	heavyweight	New York	1937
Johnny Aiello	bantamweight	New York	1938
Linto Guerrieri	light-heavyweight	Chicago	1938
John Forte	flyweight	New York	1939
Demetrio Carabella	flyweight	New York	1940
Frankie Donato	featherweight	New York	1940
Saviour Canadeo	welterweight	Chicago	1940
Joey Maxim	middleweight	Chicago	1940
Tommy Rotolo	featherweight	New York	1942
James Carollo	heavyweight	New York	1942
Tony Janiro	featherweight	Chicago	1943
Bally Carubia	welterweight	New York	1943
Roland La Starza*	light-heavyweight	New York	1945
Eddie Marotta	featherweight	Chicago	1947
Nick Ranieri	middleweight	Chicago	1947
Dan Bucceroni	light-heavyweight	Chicago	1947
Freddie Menna	middleweight	New York	1950
Anthony Di Biase	welterweight	New York	1953

Notes

* Denotes a La Starza victory after his opponent was discovered to have professional status
Only the boxer's team is given and not his hometown.
The inaugural Chicago-New York Inter-City boxing tournament was staged in 1928

Source: www.boxrec.com; www.pagoldengloves.com

Chapter 9

APPENDIX XIX^A: POST-BOXING OCCUPATIONS OF ITALIAN AMERICAN PROFESSIONAL BOXERS 1900–55

EMPLOYMENT	TOTAL
Other small business owner	154
Small business owner: (catering & hospitality)	114
Factory/manufacturing/plant/ refining/processing/brewing etc	100
Boxing-related:	73
Transportation - (bus, truck or cab driver)	43
Law enforcement	40
Construction	34
Tradesman/artisan	26
Municipal/ public sector	24
Security: Company personnel or personal bodyguard	23
Clerical & administration	22
Salesman	22
Docks/ shipyard work	21
Service sector employees	21
Professional	16
Entertainment industry:	15
Racketeer/criminal	11
Union official	11
Sport & leisure related	10
Boxing fatality	9
Education: fitness instructor, high school football coach, sanitation control inspector etc)	9
Fire service	9
Politics	9
Railroad employees	9
Premature death	8
Retail & wholesale (employee)	6
Agriculture	4
Artist	4
Post office work	3
US Armed Forces	3
Charity benefactor	2
Dairy plant production & distribution)	2
Janitorial & cleaning service	2
Disablement	1
Mining	1
Religion	1
TOTAL	862

Notes

The other small business owner category consists of numerous shopkeepers and self-employed individuals. Among them include grocers, shoe repairmen, barbershops, confectionery storekeepers, games room proprietors, auto supplies dealer, gymnasium, hotel, ice cream parlor, shoeshine parlor, delicatessen and macaroni factory owner and bail bondsman business. This category includes former boxing champions who held some level of property ownership and investments.

The small business category owner (catering and hospitality) includes champions Rocky Marciano, Rocky Graziano and Jake La Motta who became media celebrities and wealthy individuals. Marciano achieved fame and fortune as the world heavyweight champion.

The boxing-related roles include manager, referee, judge, trainer, boxing club owner and promoter and state athletic commissioner.

The construction category no longer strictly denotes straightforward laborers as it applied to their fathers. By the time the boxers retired from boxing they developed new found skills and became sought after semi-skilled and skilled construction tradesmen either working as plasterers, bricklayers, structured steel metal workers, moulders and welders or occupied roles as foremen, supervisors and department/section managers.

Railroad employees do not solely denote laborer positions but include various occupations like chief checker, helper and brakeman, boilermaker, tinsmith and locomotion engineer.

The premature death category relates to boxers who met a sudden death at a relatively young age outside the boxing ring.

The disablement category includes a boxer who was injured during the Second World War.

For the purposes of clarity the individual listed under mining was a maintenance foreman and not a miner.

The professional category consists of a banker, tax consultant, flight instructor, physical therapist, and dentist plus three journalists/writers.

The service sector employee category includes bartenders, waiters, ushers and greeters and a restaurant manager.

The entertainment category includes an actor, choreographer, tap dancer and stuntman etc.

The municipal and public sector category denotes individuals who fulfilled a variety of occupations ranging from parks warden, housing inspector and forestry division staff to lift operators in buildings and bridge and street maintenance teams all on the payroll of the respective city council offices.

In cases where more than one sibling boxed the father's occupation is listed once in order to maintain data integrity.

It's important to note that 128 individuals identified as having a main job simultaneously maintained a level of boxing involvement either as a manager, trainer or promoter etc. Thirteen of those included were former world boxing champions.

It is likely that the boxers worked more than one job in post-boxing retirement. Where it is known all positions held are listed.

Of the 51 world champions ten of them retired wealthy. Three were unfortunate victims of the 1929 stock market crash and had their entire savings and stock portfolio wiped out.

APPENDIX XIX[B]: OCCUPATIONS OF WORLD CHAMPIONS 1900–55

NAME	FATHER'S OCCUPATION	PRE-BOXING OCCUPATION	POST-BOXING OCCUPATION
1900s			
Hugo Kelly		Porter, bartender	Retired wealthy. Property owner, joint partner in restaurant and involvement in motion picture business in Illinois
Kid Murphy		Bootblack	Poolroom business owner, factory inspector and boxing manager
1910s			
Frankie Conley			Amateur boxing trainer and gymnasium owner in Kenosha (WI). Spring factory laborer
Young Zulu Kid	Polisher and shop owner	Newsboy	News stand operator – self employed. Also owner of bar & grill
Pete Herman	Banana carrier on Mississippi River	Bootblack	Retired wealthy. Property owner. Owner of nightclub/restaurant in New Orleans. Member of Louisiana State Athletic Boxing Commission
1920s			
Johnny Wilson	Junk man	Postman, sheet metal worker	Retired wealthy. A nightclub owner in New York and Boston. Cigar store owner & bookstore owner. Also involved in boxing promotion
Johnny Dundee	Fish store seller, fishmonger	Fishmonger's assistant	Retired wealthy. Said to have accrued an estimated $400,000
Carl Duane	Jewelry shop owner, bartender	Apprentice jeweler	Bowling alley proprietor
Lou Bogash	Orphaned at fourteen		Wholesale liquor salesman, policeman, and Connecticut State boxing referee
Steve Sullivan	Longshoreman	Shipyard boilermaker	Insurance & real estate interests in Brooklyn, NY. Also boxing manager. Lived in comfortable retirement
Eddie Martin	Café proprietor	Automobile machinist	Longshoreman
Mike Ballerino	Bootblack	US Army	Theater employee
Frankie Genaro		Stable boy, truck driver for butcher	Property owner in New York. Worked for Department of Marine Aviation. Also involved in boxing management

NAME	FATHER'S OCCUPATION	PRE-BOXING OCCUPATION	POST-BOXING OCCUPATION
Fidel La Barba	Railroad laborer	Newsboy	Lost money in 1929 Stock Market Crash. Sports writer, public relations consultant and screenwriter in Hollywood
Rocky Kansas	Laborer		Lost estimated $200,000 in 1929 Stock Market Crash. Cab driver. Also worked in construction for Buffalo City Council
Sammy Mandell	Laborer		Retired with $125,000. Owner of three houses. Lost significant sums in 1929 Stock Market Crash. Later worked in boxing management and promotions. Also worked in a factory and as a bank security guard
Joe Dundee	Fruit store owner. Later a market fruit stallholder	Helped father	Tavern owner in Baltimore. Later shipyard worker
Bushy Graham	Master shoemaker		Retired with $40,000. Owned two buildings. He owned poultry farm and ran a car sales business. He also worked as a boxing trainer
Tony Canzoneri	Grocery shop owner	Bootblack, cigarette, factory operative	Retired wealthy. Lost money through bad investments. He owned a restaurant in New York City. He appeared in Broadway shows and directed a dance band
Willie La Morte	Café/saloon owner	Mill sweeper	Passaic Valley (NJ) Sewer commissioner employee
Battling Battalino		Tobacco factory operative	Made $8,000 loans to friends but were never returned. Bought a farm. Also worked as a construction laborer and physical education instructor at prep school
1930s			
Midget Wolgast	Carpenter and boxer	Newsboy	Squandered riches via playboy lifestyle. Cigar store owner. Worked as a boxing trainer and bartender
Tommy Paul	Boxer		Owned three properties. Owner of a dry cleaning business. Boxing trainer/manager. Also a licensed pilot
Sammy Fuller	Shoe factory machinist	Bootblack	Boxing trainer, delicatessen store owner
George Nichols			Nightclub owner

NAME	FATHER'S OCCUPATION	PRE-BOXING OCCUPATION	POST-BOXING OCCUPATION
Lou Scozza	Cement finisher	Laundry helper	Boxing referee. City of Buffalo court marshall
Young Corbett III	Grape picker	Grape picker, insurance sales	Bar owner, businessman and pin-boy in bowling alley
Vince Dundee	Fruit seller	Helped father	Bar owner
Lou Salica			Owners of several bars in Brooklyn. Later Manhattan fish vendor
Mike Belloise	Carpenter	Assistant camera operator in movie theater	Post office employee. Taxi driver. For a time he owned with his brother Steve, a bed and breakfast hotel
Lou Ambers	Saloon owner	Furniture factory operative, cotton mill worker	Retired wealthy. Property owner. Invested in government bonds and annuities. Restaurant owner. Also involved in public relations
Tony Marino		Apprentice steel mill worker, house painter	Died in the ring in February 1937
Fred Apostoli	Carpenter	Plasterer, sheet metal worker, carpenter's mate, jeweler's messenger boy, hotel lift operator and hotel bellboy	Boxing referee, restaurant owner and sales executive for gift items company
Harry Jeffra	Bus conductor in Baltimore Transit Company	Golf caddy	Property owner, college educated his four children. Later worked as horse jockey's agent and stable manager
Melio Bettina	Railroad laborer	Golf caddy, construction laborer	Businessman, car salesman
1940s			
Pete Scalzo	Construction laborer	Errand boy for tailor, newspaper seller, street entertainer	Worked in construction and as a beer company sales representative. Also worked as a boxing referee and was chief inspector of the New York State Athletic Boxing Commission. Served a stint in show business as a comedy impersonator
Jimmy Perrin	Railroad clerk		New Orleans police officer
Izzy Jannazzo		Business studies high school undergraduate.	General government administrator. Also worked for New York City Department of Sanitation

NAME	FATHER'S OCCUPATION	PRE-BOXING OCCUPATION	POST-BOXING OCCUPATION
Sammy Angott	Coal miner		Manufacturing worker. Devoted much time helping charitable causes
Willie Pep	Construction laborer		Retired wealthy but squandered his riches. Worked as a boxing referee, tax collector, deputy boxing commissioner. Also made numerous appearances as an after dinner speaker
Phil Terranova	Driver		Bar and grill owner, Property investor, textile industry employee, construction laborer, lift operator and fabric inspector in textile industry
Sal Bartolo	Soap factory worker	Bootblack	Bar owner in Boston
Tippy Larkin	Barbershop owner. Later city laborer		Earned an estimated $500,000 but much of his fortune was gone. Worked as a highways supervisor for a New Jersey construction firm
Marty Servo	Grocery clerk		Bar owner, car salesman. Steel mill foreman in Colorado
Rocky Graziano	Boxer and longshoreman	Juvenile delinquent	Retired wealthy. By 1967 he was a self confessed millionaire. Proceeds from film and book rights and appearances in comedy shows, TV ads made this possible. Also an in-demand after dinner speaker. He owned a pizza parlor as well as other enterprises
Jake La Motta	Food peddler from horse drawn cart	Juvenile delinquent	Retired wealthy. Possessed estimated £500,000 fortune. Nightclub owner in Miami, property owner. Like Graziano he benefited from sales of his autobiography and film rights. Involved in various other businesses

1950s

NAME	FATHER'S OCCUPATION	PRE-BOXING OCCUPATION	POST-BOXING OCCUPATION
Joey Maxim	Cement finisher		Delicatessen shop and cab company proprietor. Later worked as a greeter in casinos

NAME	FATHER'S OCCUPATION	PRE-BOXING OCCUPATION	POST-BOXING OCCUPATION
Rocky Marciano	Shoe factory operative	Truckloader, sweets factory worker, bootblack, laborer	Retired wealthy with an estimated fortune between $2–3 million made up of his ring earnings plus personal appearances, endorsements and from other business ventures. He owned a sausage company in Ohio, a restaurant in Maryland, a bowling alley in Florida and a chain of spaghetti restaurants in Los Angeles
Carmen Basilio	Onion farm owner	Onion picker	Retired comfortably. College physical education instructor, Director of sports promotion for brewery. Supported brother's successful sausage making company. Helped numerous charities for underprivileged children
Paddy De Marco	Solderer		Property owner and investments in annuities. Worked in entertainment industry forming part of a comedy double act. Also worked as a bartender, laborer, headwaiter, factory operative and a casino dealer and host
Tony De Marco	Shoe factory operative	Truck driver, construction laborer. Also a freezer storeman at fish depot	Tavern owner. A Massachusetts court officer

APPENDIX XIX^C: OCCUPATIONS OF OTHER ITALIAN AMERICAN PROFESSIONAL BOXERS

NAME	FATHER'S OCCUPATION	PRE-BOXING OCCUPATION	POST-BOXING OCCUPATION
1900s			
Walter Altieri	Postman	Steam fitter, machinist	Motor truck mechanic
Kid Beebe			Refreshments seller at sports venues, coal miner
Tony Caponi			Bartender, stone quarry laborer
Frank Carsey			Chauffeur and car salesman. Also a boxing gym owner
Jack Clifford	Brigadier General in Italian Army		Professional dancer on Broadway and movie actor. Also a boxing instructor and owner of art & design studio in New York
Joe Coster			Investment bank messenger on Wall Street, Also a boxing judge
Tommy Daly			Boxing instructor at West Point military academy
Al Delmont			Gymnasium owner, boxing trainer, manager and matchmaker. Also a café owner
Jim Flynn	Publisher/ writer	Railroad locomotive fireman, blacksmith's helper	Café and beer parlor owner in Los Angeles. Taxicab business owner in Phoenix. Also a boxing promoter
Joe Grim	Baker	Bootblack	Navy yard foreman. Later an industrial plant security guard. Cigar shop manager
Roxy Kanell			Shop owner, factory hand, restaurant dishwasher
Jimmy Kelly		Newsboy	Businessman, boxing manager and politician – New York leader of Second Assembly District
Paul Kelly			Property investor, nightclub owner &, racketeer
Nick Kline			Boxing promoter, saloon owner
Frank Landers	Fruit dealer – self employed	Fruit store clerk	Merchant – self employed
Eddie Lenny			Salesman, pool room clerk
Casper Leon			Cigar maker & shop proprietor, boxing instructor, pool room worker, bowling alley cashier and construction laborer
Kid Locke		Sheet metal worker	Justice of the Peace officer, Police administrator in Clementon (NJ), Publishing house clerk and sheet metal worker

NAME	FATHER'S OCCUPATION	PRE-BOXING OCCUPATION	POST-BOXING OCCUPATION
Lou Magnolia			Businessman. Also became one of the best boxing referees of the twenties
Johnny Marto	*		Grocery store owner and boxing referee
C.M. McCarthy	Saloon keeper	Saloon staff	Salesman, lifeguard
Sledge McCarthy	Saloon keeper	Saloon staff, newsboy	Died young of kidney trouble
Dago Mike (Miglionico)	Ditch digger		Steam roller driver
Dago Mike (Mongone)			Restaurant owner, taxicab company owner and involved in promotions
Joe Percente			Self-employed; news stand proprietor, saloon keeper and bootlegger. Later became an evangelical preacher
Joe Percente II (Balistreri)			Railroad helper & railroad breakman
Nick Santoro			Deputy commissioner of Pennsylvania Boxing Commission
Kid Scaler			Ranch owner, apple grower. Also a gym owner and boxing instructor
Jimmy Sheppard			Medical doctor & chief physician of the New York State Athletic Commission
Lou Sheppard	Food chef		Groundskeeper at General Electric baseball and athletic park
Charlie Sieger	Bootblack		Longshoreman
Kid Stinger		Newsboy, vaudeville stage performer	Self employed. Railroad brakeman
Kid Thomas			Cabaret club owner in New York City
Chick Tricker			Nightclub owner in New York City
Chick Tucker			Saloon owner
Mike Tuths			Boxing manager
Kid Williams			Longshoreman, saloon keeper & lodging house proprietor
Billy Willis	Laborer	Bootblack	Merchant – self employed
Benny Yanger			Boxing referee, boxing instructor & head boxing coach for Chicago Golden Gloves. Also worked as a typesetter

NAME	FATHER'S OCCUPATION	PRE-BOXING OCCUPATION	POST-BOXING OCCUPATION
Terry Young (Samperi)			Water meter company mechanic
1910s			
Johnny Albanese			Butcher
Johnny Alberts			Boxing manager
Kid Andrews			Boxing fatality
Joe Argen			Boxing manager, referee, promoter and New York State Athletic Commission inspector
Al Benedict		Truck driver	Gymnasium owner, bar & restaurant owner. Also boxing manager
Al Blades			Navy yard laborer
Joe Borrell	Retail merchant – self employed	House plumber	New Jersey Police captain, plumber
Pat Bradley (De Carlo)			Lawyer's clerk – Admin & clerical
Chubby Brown			Pool room owner
Young Buffalo			Ironworker
Al Calzone	Foundry laborer		Policeman
Lou Cardell			Police sergeant in Montclair, NJ
Sal Carlo	Sheet metal worker		Shipyard worker
Kid Chicago			Restaurant and hotel owner
Hugo Clement			Restaurant owner, soft drink parlor owner
Jimmy Coffey		Shipyard laborer, fruit dealer & waiter	Construction laborer
Joe Conti			Boxing manager in Rochester (NY)
Frankie Conway		Newsboy	Café and nightclub owner
Freddy Corbett			Businessman - Essington Arena venue owner.
Andy Cortez			Taxicab driver
Charlie Dalton			Shipyard worker
Mickey Dell	Grocery store clerk		Car mechanic, garage owner & mechanic
Gene Delmont		US Army	Actor
Jockey Joe Dillon		Horse racing jockey	Customs office official
Patsy Dugan			Factory hand
Baltimore Dundee	Iron foundry blacksmith	US Navy	1918 flu epidemic fatality
Jimmy Dundee		Newsboy	Tavern owner & boxing manager
Tommy Elm	Dye house dyer	Factory machinist	Boxing referee

NAME	FATHER'S OCCUPATION	PRE-BOXING OCCUPATION	POST-BOXING OCCUPATION
Frankie Fay			Restaurant owner. Also a delivery superintendent for a New York newspaper
Johnny Ford			President & Chairman of Shawmut Dairy Inc. Also Milk Board representative.
Phil Franchini			Tavern owner
Jimmy Fruzzetti	* lived with brother-in-law	Shoe factory operative. Farm laborer	Shoe factory operative
Italian Joe Gans	Concrete worker	Shipyard riveter	Tavern owner, fitness instructor, caretaker, assistant manager in restaurant
Eddie Ganns			Driver
Joseph Gatto			Plumber/steamfitter. Later became well known landscape artist
Charles Grande		Sailor	Nightclub bouncer in New York City
Society Kid Hogan			Racetrack helper and later a horse racing expert
Packey Hommey			Restaurant owner. News stand proprietor
Frankie Izzo		Bricklayer	Bricklayer
Young Joey (Emma) *		Men's clothing store clerk	Tailor. Later worked as a post office guard
Battling Johnson	Factory machinist		Vegetable & fruit huckster –self employed, delicatessen store clerk
Kid Julian			New York Central Railroad police officer
Freddie Kelly			Pool parlor manager, restaurant owner
KO Kid Kelly			Shoe factory operative
Young Hugo Kelly			Restaurant owner. Also a boxing promoter
Johnny Keyes			Boxing manager, businessman
Patsy Kline			Restaurant owner, boxing referee
Joe Lawrence			Boxing manager, promoter & matchmaker
Young Lawrence (Alemi)	Laborer	Machinist	Navy yard machinist
Jack Lee	Banker		Businessman, banker, boxing manager and promoter

NAME	FATHER'S OCCUPATION	PRE-BOXING OCCUPATION	POST-BOXING OCCUPATION
Harry Lenny			Boxing manager, trainer and writer. Masseur/touch healer
Joey Leonard	Self employed grocery storeman		Pool room clerk
Bobby Lincoln			Tavern owner
Tommy Littleton	Grocery store owner		Gymnasium owner in Mobile (AL)
Phillip J. Logan		Newsboy	Barbershop owner
Frankie Mack			Clerical & admin clerk
Frankie Madden			Department of State supervisor
Chick Maglione	Factory worker, shoeshine stand proprietor	Janitor	Real estate salesman
Eddie Marino		US Army, laborer	Gymnasium owner in Georgetown, (WA). A boxing manager, trainer & promoter
Eddie Mason			Boxing trainer
Joe Masterpole			National Guard soldier
Mike Mazie	Hotel owner	Hotel worker	Café owner in Staten Island, NY. Also a boxing referee
Tommy McFarland	Bar owner		Became a Boston governor. A former Massachusetts State boxing commissioner. He owned a tavern and once worked as a department store manager
Young Terry McGovern			Boxing fatality
Nick Michaels	City street laborer	Department of Public Works driver	Bus driver for Syracuse Transit Company. Also worked as foreman for Syracuse parks department
"Diamond" Jim Moran	Vegetable oil importer	Bootblack	Restaurant businessman in New Orleans
Vic Moran	Day laborer		Magazine publisher & writer. Policeman
Jesse Morey	Saloon keeper		Plumber, taxi driver
Al "Battling" Murray	Stepfather – chair factory seat maker		Deputy Pennsylvania State boxing commissioner, Treasurer of National Boxer's Fraternity and Veteran Boxer's Association. Factory hand
Tommy Murray	Stepfather – chair factory seat maker		Chauffeur, taxi driver
Frankie Nelson			Factory machinist
Sam Nolan		Building contractor	Policeman

NAME	FATHER'S OCCUPATION	PRE-BOXING OCCUPATION	POST-BOXING OCCUPATION
Joe O'Brien (Valesano)		House servant, railroad carman	Railroad chief checker
Marty O'Brien	Factory hand. Mother ran grocery store	Apprentice shoemaker	Boilermaker, bartender & fireman
Dom Orsini			Las Vegas casino card dealer
Sailor Pacilio			Worked as rehabilitation officer and jail warden for Oneida County (NY) Sheriff's Department. Also a boxing judge, promoter and instructor
Jack Perry			Boxing manager and actor, making 85 cameo film appearances
Jimmy Phillips			Advertising agent
Frank Picato		Rancher	Rancher in California
Battling Reddy			Tavern owner in New York City
Young Robideau			Businessman - Owner of largest truck fleet in Eastern United States.
Joe "Kid" Post			Pennsylvania railroad employee. Later worked as a riveter at the Ford Rouge plant
Joe "Kid" Rocco			Fireman. Also worked as a boxing referee
Willie Rock	Cabinet maker and confectionery store owner		Pipefitter
Al Rogers			Boxing manager and trainer. Also a defense industry employee
Frankie Russell			Saloon manager – self employed
Doc Schumacher	Doctor	College undergraduate	Dentist. Head of Scimeca family clinic in Kansas
Little Jack Sharkey			Restaurant owner in Greenwich Village, NY
Charlie Sheppard	Restaurant musician		Construction – City of New York
Frankie Stinger			Policeman. Also a used car businessman
Rocky Stramaglia			Factory operative
KO Sullivan			Movie house camera operator
Spike Sullivan	Groceries huckster	Steel mill worker	Fruit store owner
Frank Susnell			Car plant employee. Later became Chrysler Corporation inspector & purchaser
Angelo Taramaschi			Carpenter

NAME	FATHER'S OCCUPATION	PRE-BOXING OCCUPATION	POST-BOXING OCCUPATION
Battling Terry			Construction laborer. Also worked as a factory janitor. At one time he owned a pool & billiards hall
Mickey Travers			Packing house truck driver, rifle factory machinist
Joe Uvanni	Orphaned	Steel mill laborer	For a time worked as a court interpreter. Restaurant owner. Also boxing promoter
Johnny Victor	Liquor store owner	Shipfitter's helper, shop painter	Bookbinder and bindery business owner
Phil Virgets	Saloon merchant		Self employed merchant
Tony Vincent			Poolroom owner, gymnasium owner and boxing manager
Joe Wagner			Boxing manager
Bobby Wilson			Boxing manager
Red Cap Wilson	Bricklayer	Bricklayer	Fish dealer - employee
Tony Zill	Grocery store owner		High school football coach in Ohio. A boxing referee. Also worked in Post Office
Zulu Kid			Sanitaryware factory hand
1920s			
Joe Accetta			Truck driver
Jackie Aldare	Self employed ice and coal dealer		Shipyard worker
Willie Ames	Laborer		Engineering department operative for Summit County (OH)
Sam Anch	Railroad worker		Democrat politician. Also worked as insurance salesman
Nick Antonelli			Homebuilder
Joe Atta	*	Barber	Barber
Louis Atta	*		Barbershop owner
Tony Azzera			Boxing fatality
Pete August	Factory manager	Shipyard laborer	City laborer
Joe Baker			Boxing promoter
Bill Bandy	Stonemason		Nightclub owner, gymnasium owner. Also worked as boxing manager, trainer & cornerman
Lou Barba			Cruise ship physical director
Harry Barone			Construction laborer and foreman. Later became a top national union leader
Nick Bass	Small businessman – partner in tailor shop	Helped in shop	Special licensed police officer. Bouncer. Also worked in the garment industry for 32 years

NAME	FATHER'S OCCUPATION	PRE-BOXING OCCUPATION	POST-BOXING OCCUPATION
Jack Belford	Restaurant owner		Boxing manager, promoter and referee and wrestling judge
Gene Bianco			Hotel employee
Joe Birdie			Nightclub entertainer, tap dancer and master of ceremonies
Patsy Bogash			President and owner of Bogash Insurance Agency business
Joey Bonavita	* Mother ran family grocery store		Restaurant owner in New York City
Pete Bova			Longshoreman, boxing trainer
Humbert Brady	Macaroni factory supervisor		Billiards parlor owner
Jackie Brady	Macaroni factory supervisor owner		Gymnasium owner, restaurant
Johnny Brennan			Restaurant owner in Trenton, (NJ)
Larry Brignolia	Blacksmith & store owner		Blacksmith
Young Britton			Inn owner
Matt Brock	Odd jobs laborer		Food store owner
Billy Brown			Boxing referee and matchmaker
Danny Brown			Barber
Kid Burns (Glorioso)			Factory worker
Vic Burrone	Property investor		Bar owner in New York City
Ernie Caesar			Philadelphia City Hall lift operator
Frankie Campbell	Mercantile business owner, carpenter	Grocery store clerk, laborer	Boxing fatality
Paris Cangey		Student at automobile and electrical school	Steel company worker. Restaurant owner, boxing promoter, trainer and manager
Joe Carlo			School system employee
Luke Carr	Laborer		Tavern owner, City of Buffalo Stadium employee. Boxing referee & boxing trainer
Paul Carr	Laborer	News stand seller, truck driver	Boxing manager. Buffalo parks laborer
Frankie Carter			Restaurant owner. Boxing referee. Also worked as chairman of prison service athletic division
Sammy Caruso			Union executive. President of local UAW CIO. Also worked as TV repairman

NAME	FATHER'S OCCUPATION	PRE-BOXING OCCUPATION	POST-BOXING OCCUPATION
Paul Cavalier			New Jersey chief of professional boxing referees and boxing coach. Education – Attendance officer and later became the chief of attendance section in Paterson, (NJ)
Tommy Cello	Baker & shop owner		Boxing manager
Young Chappie (Capolupo)	Bar & restaurant owner		Bartender – self employed
Angelo Christiano			Boxing manager
Elmer Ciccone	Electrical plant machine hand		Confectionery store owner. Also founder of Mount Pleasant, NY Athletic Club
Young Ty Cobb			Leader of labor union
Joe Colletti	Father died when he was a baby	Newsboy. Vaudeville stage acrobat and tumbler. Later worked as factory machinist	Physical education instructor at a school in Poughkeepsie (NY)
Pascal Colletti			Assistant head at the New Orleans Athletic Club
Marty Collins	Retail merchant, grocery store owner		Bartender and bodyguard
Sammy Compagno	Odd job laborer		Poultry dresser and maker
Anthony Constantino			City of Buffalo worker
Carmen Cook			Stock clerk for Bridgeport Brass Company. Also a boxing promoter & manager
Connie Curry			Nightclub owner. Also worked as a salesman
Georgie Day	Self employed. Mobile fruit seller		Shipping clerk
Frankie De Angelo	Shoemaker & shop owner		Housebuilder company owner
Jimmy De Capua			Police officer. Also a boxing manager
Billy De Foe (Tamburri)	Laborer		Bartender
Harry De Julio			Restaurant owner. Also worked as a boxing referee and was a member of the Connecticut State boxing commission

NAME	FATHER'S OCCUPATION	PRE-BOXING OCCUPATION	POST-BOXING OCCUPATION
Cuddy De Marco	* Mother – retail grocery merchant	Glasshouse box maker	Businessman, car & manufacturer's sales representative. Also worked as a bouncer. Lost much of his wealth in the 1929 Stock Market Crash
Young Jack Dempsey (Amodio)			Barber
Joe Denny	Horse drawn wagon beer distributor, Grocery store owner, Pennsylvania railroad laborer		Bricklayer and building inspector in Wilmington, (DE). Also worked as boxing referee
Jimmy Dixon			Top boxing manager
Mickey Donley		Tailor shop assistant	Boxing referee, police constable. Also worked as steel company laborer
Ashton Donza	Grocery store owner		Grocery store clerk. Boxing referee
Joey Dorando Sr			Restaurant owner
Bobby Doyle			Organized crime henchman
Paul Doyle	*		Bowling alley proprietor, longshoreman, union checker, factory employee and boxing manager
Hoboken Joe Dundee	Pencil factory hand	Railroad machinist	Longshoreman
Mike Dundee	Fruit store owner	Helped father	Restaurant and bar owner. Later moved to California and worked for Hollywood studios as a prop master
Bobby Ertle	Railroad laborer		Railroad boilermaker
Joey Eulo	*		Railroad tinsmith, bar and grill owner
Harold Farese			Works Project Administration construction foreman & sports manager
Johnny Fay			Restaurant owner
Frankie Ferrara			Political campaigner. Boxing manager
Al Ferrone	Factory operative		Bodyguard to New York Mayor Fiorello La Guardia
Ralph Ficucello	Barber shop owner		Car mechanic
Harry Fierro			Gymnasium owner and boxing manager
Young Firpo (Galeazzi)	Odd job carpenter and mason. Mother was a store owner		Factory machinist

NAME	FATHER'S OCCUPATION	PRE-BOXING OCCUPATION	POST-BOXING OCCUPATION
Young Firpo (Locati)	Commercial gardener		Commercial vegetable farm gardener
Caveman Fisher		Iceman	Haberdashery store owner, County Parks department employee
Nick Florio			Boxing trainer
Vince Forgione	Odd job laborer		Florist business owner
Al Frazee			Boxing manager
Steve Galliano			Dye works dyer
Dago Joe Gans	Soft drinks parlor owner		Car plant machinist
Carlo Giannotti			Joint owner of bar
Patsy Gilmore			Restaurant owner
Bobby Gleason			Businessman, gymnasium owner and boxing manager
August Gotto			Early death due to meningitis
Frankie Graham			Self employed barber and later barbershop owner
Frankie Grandetta	*	Newsboy	Movie actor and chauffeur. Private gymnasium owner for high brow businessmen
Mickey Greb	Construction laborer		Newark County courthouse hall of records clerk
Babe Griffin			Box factory laborer. Boxing promoter and manager
Johnny Grosso	Plasterer	Plasterer	Racketeer – shot and murdered in 1932
Midget Guery	Steel plant operative		Insurance salesman, housing board authority member
Phil Gusmano	Factory machinist		Fruit and vegetable salesman – self employed
Jimmy Hanlon	Railroad section man	Bowling alley pin boy	News stand operator
Fighting Pete Harmon			Grocery store owner
Joey Harrison			Boxing referee
Midget Herman			Factory employee
Billy Hill			Barbershop owner. Also a boxing judge
Mike Hogan			Truck driver. Also a boxing referee
Lew Hurley			Laborer
Johnny Indrisano		Caddy, newsboy, and errand boy in Boston, MA	Technical consultant and fight choreographer in Hollywood, (CA). Appeared in over 150 movies as stuntman and extra

NAME	FATHER'S OCCUPATION	PRE-BOXING OCCUPATION	POST-BOXING OCCUPATION
Joe Jackson			Early death - shot to death outside dance hall
Little Jeff	Water company laborer		Shipyard worker, laborer
Buck Josephs	Restaurant owner		Boxing manager
Michael "Kid" Julian	Sewerage contractor		Restaurant owner
Tony Kelly			Businessman, Café and dance hall owner. Also a boxing manager
Sid Kelley			Factory maintenance painter
Lou Kemp			Boxing instructor
Midget Kilburn	Stonemason		New York City chauffeur
Jimmy King	*		Businessman. Owned restaurants and nightclubs on Bourbon Street in New Orleans, LA
Sam Lagonia			Fireman
Frankie Laureate	Policeman	Steel plant laborer	Grill eaterie proprietor
Al Letty	Sculptor & artist. Art studio proprietor		Office clerk
Mickey Lewis			Car dealership proprietor and car salesman
Charlie "Lefty" Longo			Boxing trainer and sport columnist
Charlie Lo Presti			Police Chief of Bergen County, (NJ)
Cowboy Joe Lucignano			Bartender
Charley Lupica	Laborer		Novelty shop collector
Battling Mack			New York City café owner
Petey Mack	*		Factory hand
Joe Malone			Health club operator and boxing instructor
Ernie Mandell	Barbershop owner		Tavern owner
Joey Manuel			Newspaper printer. Also a NYSAC boxing referee
Tony Marano			Former Democratic leader and town councilor in Rome, (NY)
Mike Marcells			Boxing instructor and trainer
Andy Martin	Truck driver	Office boy	Boston school department employee
Charlie Martin			Dairy plant branch manager
Frankie Martin			Steakhouse owner in Pittsfield, (MA)
Joe Martin			Trucking firm owner

NAME	FATHER'S OCCUPATION	PRE-BOXING OCCUPATION	POST-BOXING OCCUPATION
Terry Martin	Bootblack parlor owner	Wood mill hand	Tool factory hand
Harry Martone			Department of Sanitation employee
Tony Marullo	Policeman	Shipyard boilermaker	Businessman – Dance hall and eaterie owner
Johnny Mason			Bank security guard
Gus Masterpole			Welder
Henry Masterpole			Locomotive crane operator
Billy Mastriani	GEC factory worker. Mother ran family grocery store		GEC assembler and welder. Also chief shop steward at his plant. Founder & executive board member of United Electrical Worker's Union. Also a boxing manager
Vito Mazzeo			Boxing referee & judge
Francis McCoy			Owner of trucking company
Kid Terry McGovern			Milkman
Jack McGurn			Joined Al Capone's gang and worked as an enforcer
Jimmy Mendo			Forestry division worker
Joe Messina			Personal bodyguard of Louisiana senator Huey Long
Tony Mike	Saloon keeper		Longshoreman
Al Monaco	Factory operative		Office clerk
Frank Montagna	Butcher & shop owner		Butcher
Joe Monte			Brewery sales representative
Pal Moran			Joint restaurant owner. Also worked as seller at fairgrounds and at racetracks
Bobby Myson			Pizza steak shop manager
Mickey Nelson			Boxing promoter
Young Battling Nelson	Self employed gardener		Gardener
Ralph Nischo			Bouncer and waiter at New York City bar
Bucky Notaro			Maitre D at nightclub. Railroad freight handler
Jimmy Oakland			Stonemason, iron worker
Young O'Connor			Café owner & bar owner
Jimmy O'Gatty	Factory packer & machinist	Factory manager	Sculptor & cameo film actor

NAME	FATHER'S OCCUPATION	PRE-BOXING OCCUPATION	POST-BOXING OCCUPATION
Packey O'Gatty	Factory packer & machinist	Packer	Self employed personal fitness and instructor and trainer. Also a boxing writer and historian
Kid Palmer			Truck driver
Nick Palmer			Massage parlor owner. Also hotel owner in San Juan, Puerto Rico
Philadelphia Jack Palmer		Machinist	Automobile machinist
Emil Paluso	Railroad section man		Office clerk – Administration and clerical
Mickey Pasquale			Department of highways laborer
George Perrotta			Industrial plant security guard. Also worked as a railroad clerk
Kid Pershing	* lived with brother who worked as a cook	Factory hand	Laborer
Carmen Persico			Tavern owner
Billy Petrolle	Railroad laborer	Railroad car checker	Retired with an estimated fortune of $250,000. Owned gift shop selling religious artefacts and a steel foundry in Duluth. Also sat as chairman of the Pioneer National Bank
Frankie Petrolle			Tavern owner
Pete Petrolle	Railroad laborer		Worked for the Los Angeles Police Department traffic division. Also a YMCA boxing instructor
Dom Petrone	Construction laborer		American Labor Party election district captain, Mayor La Guardia's security guard. Also New York Department of Sanitation employee.
Pete Piazza			Café owner
Eddie Pinchot	Construction laborer		Steel plant laborer
Harry Pinti			General Cable Corporation factory employee
Charlie Pinto	Laborer, porter		City of Buffalo Parks Department employee. Also a boxing matchmaker
Sam Pitisci			Boilermaker
Joe Pledge	Grocery store owner	Marble cutter	Bowling alley owner, bookmaker & nightclub owner
Jack Poliseo			Brewery employee
Frankie Porto			Boxing club owner & promoter.
Kid Preston			Factory company president

NAME	FATHER'S OCCUPATION	PRE-BOXING OCCUPATION	POST-BOXING OCCUPATION
Billy Prince			Boxing manager. Later became commissioner of the Connecticut State Athletic Commission & first vice-president of New England Boxing Association. Also a Republican political leader
Jimmy Proto	Fireman	Machinist	Factory operative
Mike Rago			Boxing gymnasium owner. Road construction laborer
Marine Ranieri	Laborer		Ranch laborer
Ernie Ratner	Laborer		Department of Public Works employee
Charlie Ray			Saloon owner
Jack Renzo			Navy guard
Frankie Rex	*	Newsboy	Boxing promoter & manager
Billy Rhodes			Factory machinist
Kid Ritchie			Boxing referee and judge
Joe Rivers (Arpino)			Rope factory hand. President of Textile Workers Union local chapter. Also President of Auburn Housing Authority
Kid Roberts			Laborer. Died at 24 due to tuberculosis
Emmett Rocco	Mill worker	Factory work	Desk sergeant at Ellwood City, (PA) police bureau. Also did shipyard work
Joe Romanelli			Fireman
Frankie Ross			Mill worker, gym owner and tavern owner
Joey Ross			Longshoreman
Pee Wee Ross			Cigar & confectionery store owner, bar owner. Also worked as a welder in Camden, (NJ)
Jack Russo			Boxing manager
Jimmy Russo			Factory hand
Babe Ruth (Schettini)			Taxicab driver
Sammy Sacco			Boxing referee
Phil Salvadore	Railroad laborer	Factory machinist	City fireman. Also motion picture cameraman
Kid Savage	Pump works laborer		Laborer
Johnny Saxon			Grocery store owner
Johnny Scalzi	Factory laborer		GEC factory worker. Also store owner
Phil Scello			Policeman and later detective

NAME	FATHER'S OCCUPATION	PRE-BOXING OCCUPATION	POST-BOXING OCCUPATION
Tony Sciortino			Barbershop owner
Young Peter Sharkey			Factory machinist
Eddie Shea			Cotton Club owner in Chicago, (IL). Also managed hotel-bar establishment. Died aged 42
Lew Skymer	Laborer. Later owned auto supply business	Helped father	Machinist. Took over father's business. Later opened a laundry business
Vincent Sireci			Wholesale manager
Kid Tony Sisti			Artist
Frank Sorci			Shopping center owner
Tony Speno			Police patrolman
John Sposato			Boxing referee
Tony Storace	Stepfather – farm owner		Wire factory operative. Also a boxing promoter
Tillie Taverna			Club bouncer
Nick Testo			Bookmaker establishment owner. Also a boxing manager
George Texas	Laundry presser		Electrical company mechanic. Aircraft instrument manufacturer's employee
Ralph Thomas		Plumber	Boxing fatality
Harry Thorpe	General laborer	Knitting mill laborer	Vehicle mechanic. Owner and operator of Harry's Garage
Dominic Tippero	Coal yard laborer		Boxing fatality
Tony Tin			Company tailor & button hole maker
Charlie Trabon	Grocery store owner		Grocery store owner, boxing manager
Joe Trabon			Kansas City police officer
Bobby Tracey	* lived with brother-in-law who was a newspaper stand owner		Boxing manager & trainer and part owner of taxicab company
Carl Tremaine	Bookbinder	Traveling salesman	Electrician's union affiliate
Joe Triano			Policeman. Also boxing instructor & promoter and co-owner of boxing club
John Triano	Cobbler & shop owner		Maintenance department employee of West Hudson Park, (NJ)
Joe Trippe	Odd job laborer		Factory laborer and blacksmith at Buffalo's waterworks department
Al Tripoli	Stonemason		New York Parks dept employee

NAME	FATHER'S OCCUPATION	PRE-BOXING OCCUPATION	POST-BOXING OCCUPATION
Carmen Tuzzolino	Railroad laborer		Iron foundry worker
Johnny Vacca	Farmer in Italy. In the US he worked as an automobile spray painter		Security guard. Also worked as a private school boxing instructor
Joe Vaccarella	Laborer	Waterboy, ditch digger & seaman	Boxing referee. Later became politician and was elected the Mayor of Mount Vernon, NY in 1951
Johnny Vestri			Shipyard worker
Ralph Villano			Automobile factory operative
Johnny Vito			Liquor hijacker – racketeer
Nick Volpetti	Railroad repairman		Railroad repairman
Jimmy Wilson	Storekeeper		Boxing trainer & cutman
Bobby Wagner	Cobbler, shop owner		Boxing mentor and sponsor of fundraising initiatives to help youth in New York City
Pete Wagner			Boxing referee. Sales manager for national brewery corporation
Patsy Wallace			Janitor
Eddie Whalen	Ice dealer		New York railroad checker
Al Zill			Boxing promoter
1930s			
Nicholas Abate	Factory metalworker		Skilled factory operative
Ray Actis		Caddy	Truck driver
Sal Affinito			Taxi driver.
Roxie Allen	Foreman – construction		Bodyguard
Pasquale A. Amante	Factory laborer, candy company packer		Document clerk at House of Representatives at State House in Boston. Administration-clerical
Babe Amos			Gymnasium owner and restaurant proprietor
Dominic William Angelo			Policeman
Larry Anzalone			Boxing trainer & actor
Joey August			Beer distributor company owner. Also a boxing referee and judge
Louis August			University of Idaho boxing coach. Also a boxing manager
Teddy Baldwin	Factory hand		Street laborer
Phil Baker	Bakery owner		Restaurant owner
Lou Barbetta			Gruman aircraft factory operative

NAME	FATHER'S OCCUPATION	PRE-BOXING OCCUPATION	POST-BOXING OCCUPATION
Carmen Barth			Structural metal worker in construction industry
Sil Barry			Foundry worker
Mike Barto			Police officer and later police chief in New Kensington, (PA). Also ran a boxing gymnasium
Johnny Bassanelli			Boxing referee & judge
Nick Belfiore	Laborer		Gymnasium owner
Mickey Bellero			Packer for manufacturing company
Sam Bennett	Orthopaedic shoe business proprietor	Helped father	Italian bakery shop owner. Shoe factory worker
Nunzio Bisogno			Bus driver
Frankie Blair	*		Bar owner. Barbershop owner. Later became a salesman
Mickey Blair			Bar owner. Murdered in 1941
Johnny Blandino			Truck driver of wholesale produce. Restaurant manager
Charlie Blood			Tavern owner
Johnny Borozzi	Laborer, pipefitter	Newsboy	Tractor trailer driver
Babe Brandelli			Restaurant owner
Billy Brown	Barber	Helped father	Boxing promoter
Buster Brown	Baker		Textile factory laborer
Joey Brown			Boxing referee
Dave Bungy	House painter		General Electric plant operative
Jimmy Burns (Santa Maria)			Café owner
Emil Calcagni			Judge in workmen's compensation court in Newark (NJ)
Savey Canadeo			Salesman
Sal Canata			Factory machine operator. Also a boxing instructor
Tony Cancela			Professional wrestler. Also worked as a boxing manager
Al Capone			Boxing gymnasium owner and later influential union organizer, becoming President of Wrights Aero Union, presiding over 40,000 members
Petey Cara			Madison Square Garden security guard
Richie Carangelo			Electrical technician for Passaic Valley sewerage commission in Newark, (NJ)

NAME	FATHER'S OCCUPATION	PRE-BOXING OCCUPATION	POST-BOXING OCCUPATION
Mario Carbone			Construction foreman
Frankie Caris	Band musician		Gulf Oil company security guard
Paul Carmello			Film actor
Charlie Caserta	Tailor in men's clothing store	Musician	Gymnasium owner, boxing coach
Jimmy Casino			Actor. Also a boxing coach
Tony Catalano			Boxing promoter
Billy Celebron			Boxing promoter and referee
Marty Celeste			Shoe factory worker. Also a NYSAC official
Young Chippy			Deputy sheriff in Poughkeepsie, (NY)
Johnny Ciccone			Early death – shot and murdered on street
Frank Cicero	Cobbler and shop owner	Office clerk	Housing inspector
Jimmy Cirella			Madison Square Garden usher. Also a voiceover artist on TV commercials
George Cirimele			Supervisor at Burgermeister Beer bottling operations in San Francisco
Al Citrino			Newspaper circulation agent – Distribution. Also a boxing instructor
Dom Colan			Factory machinist
Steve Colucci			Ironworker
Johnny Compo			Factory worker
Lulu Constantino			Saloon owner
Jimmy Cosenza	Stepfather – laborer		Boxing promoter
Alfred Croat			Fish and poultry business owner. Later owned a petrol station.
Sammy Crocetti			Executive Director of Boy's & Girls Club of America. Also worked as Brooklyn Dodgers baseball scout
Mike Cusano			Boxing referee
Al Daley	Forge laborer	Carpet factory laborer	Barber
Carlo D'Angelo			Beverage company business owner
Louis D'Arconte	Barbershop owner		Head auditor at state auditor general's office. Also a local democratic political leader

NAME	FATHER'S OCCUPATION	PRE-BOXING OCCUPATION	POST-BOXING OCCUPATION
Gerald D'Elia			Mobile hog dog vendor
Tony De Bellis			Police chief in Orange, (NJ)
Flavio De Bonis	Gardening & landscaping business owner		Florist shop owner. Garden center & nurseries business owner
Vinnie De Cola	Shoe repairer and shop owner		Boxing manager
Patsy De Feo	Coal miner		Self employed carpenter
Joseph De Frank			Cook
Leonard Del Genio	Driver, insurance broker		Internal Revenue Service agent. Also an actor and a boxing manager
Jimmy Del Nero			Farmer
Carl Dell	Railroad laborer		Railroad laborer. Police officer. Also worked as boxing manager/trainer
Petey Della			Boxing referee & judge
Ralph De Luca			Housing authority official
Lloyd De Lucchi	Fruit farm owner		Ship scraperman
Pete De Ruzza			Factory worker
Vince De Santis	Games room proprietor	Chauffeur	Gymnasium owner, part owner of tavern with brother
Mickey Diamond			Boxing manager & trainer
Sam Di Nardo	GEC factory operative		Toolmaker and machinist at GEC plant
Joey Dodge	*	Steel mill worker, car assembly plant worker	Dry cleaning business owner. Salesman. Politician
Alex Doyle			Municipal – Passaic County Department of Bridges employee
Frankie Duane			Owner of glass bottling supply business. Later worked in the department of recreation as community center director and boxing instructor in Elizabeth, (NJ)
Johnny Duca	Laborer		Oil company employee
George Dundee	Barber	Salesman	Boxing promoter and manager
Texas Joe Dundee			Swimming pool lifeguard
Edward Durino			Ironworkers union official
Joe Erne			Office clerk – Administration and clerical
Johnny Farr			Mill operator
Willie Felice			New York City transit system trackman

NAME	FATHER'S OCCUPATION	PRE-BOXING OCCUPATION	POST-BOXING OCCUPATION
Joe Ferrante			Truck driver
Freddie Fiducia	Macaroni factory owner		Ice cream parlor owner, company dispatcher
Sam Finazzo			Boxing manager
Young Joe Firpo (Bracale)	Dye works laborer	Stone quarryman, caddy	Chemical company employee
Young Firpo (Bardelli)	* Mother worked as boarding house keeper	Miner	Boxing referee and promoter. Truck driver
Young Firpo (Rivecca)			Boxing manager
Al Flora	Coal breaker foreman in Wilkes Barre, (PA) mine		Boxing manager, promoter and boxing commissioner. Also gym owner, nightclub and tavern proprietor
Bobby Flynn			Bartender. Boxing manager
Tommy Forte			Bar owner
John Fortuna	Bricklayer		Bricklayer. General Motors plant operative. Later worked as a housing inspector for City of Baltimore, (MD)
Tommy Fusari	Self employed-construction		Self employed heating and air-conditioning engineer
Mike Fusco			Restaurant owner. Democratic Party committee member
Johnny Gaito	Laborer		Parking lot owner in New York City. Also a restaurant owner
Tony Galento	Button factory machinist	Iceman	Tavern owner, professional wrestler
Frank Gaudes			Taxi driver
Mickey Genaro			Boxing manager
Harry Gentile			Hartford, (CT) employee
Nickie Gerard		Butcher	Cigarette vending business employee, boxing manager, Restaurant owner
Ritchie Gibbons			Ironworker
Joey Gimbrone		Construction worker	Truck driver. Also a boxing promoter's assistant & sparring partner. Boxing judge and referee
Ralph Gizzy			Semi-skilled construction worker
Joe Governale			Tax consultant and commissioner of deeds in New York City
Tommy Grady			City employee of water works department. Also worked at electric power plant and foundry

NAME	FATHER'S OCCUPATION	PRE-BOXING OCCUPATION	POST-BOXING OCCUPATION
Joey Greb			Cameo film actor
Phil Guerrera	Railroad car inspector and car repairer		Factory machinist
Lenny Gulotta			Factory security guard
Petey Hayes			Farm owner in Saugerties, (NY). Also worked as travel agent
Tommy Harper			Taxi driver
Tommy Hines			Railroad worker. New Jersey Department of Transportation worker
Nicky Jerome			Factory employee
Casper La Rosa			Bartender
Anthony Laviero	Iron factory moulder helper		Package store owner
Lou Laurie		Petrol station attendant	Boxing referee. Also worked in a factory as a paint sprayer
Pete Leto			Boxing trainer
Frankie Litt	Confectionery store owner	Helped father	Tavern owner, shipyard worker, amusement ride proprietor & truck driver
Johnny Lo Bianco	Barber		Boxing referee, liquor salesman
Al Lo Piano			Bus driver in Connecticut
Tony Mac			Automobile glass company proprietor
Lenny Mancini			Boxing trainer and manager
Joe Maffei	Odd job laborer		Operating engineer
Sam Maltempo			Policeman – became first Police Union President. Also worked as boxing referee, judge and as a deputy boxing commissioner in Manchester, (NH)
Al Mandell			Chemical company watchman
Al Manfredo			Tavern owner
Vito Mangine			President of local chapter of United Gas Coke & Chemical Workers of America.
Nathan Mann		Farm laborer	Tavern owner. Also a liquor salesman
Angelo Manna			Maintenance worker at Worcester City, (MA) hospital
Sammy Marinelli	Factory worker		Police captain in New Britain, (CT)
Larry Marinucci	Factory moulder		New York Communication Worker's Union leader

NAME	FATHER'S OCCUPATION	PRE-BOXING OCCUPATION	POST-BOXING OCCUPATION
Teddy Martin	Baker		Boxing referee and judge. Also a liquor store owner
Fiore Maruco	City laborer		Businessman – Sports arena owner in North Adams, (MA). Boxing and wrestling promoter. Construction ironworker
Nick Masi			Construction worker
Dick Mastro			Radio store owner in Chicago, IL
Earl Mastro		Office boy	Boxing manager. Assistant stage manager for a touring theater company. Steel plant laborer
Teddy Mays	Shoe repairer – self employed		Foundry worker – semi-skilled
Jerry Mazza	Boxer		Tavern owner
Joey Metro			Construction employee. Also a boxing manager
Gene Michelini			Bartender
Frank Mirabile			Electrician. Later worked as a printer
Pete Montesi			Salesman, boxing promoter
KO Morgan	*	Factory messenger, fruit peddler	Restaurant owner. Also a bartender
Ralph Morgan			Fireman
Tony Morgano	Painter	Factory machinist	Iron worker, boxing manager and trainer
Tommy Murphy			Haberdasher
Frankie Murray		Shoe factory operative	Self employed
Sammy Musco			Boxing trainer
Jimmy Musso			Proprietor of beer distribution company and shop owner
Ray Napolitano			Truck driver for meat supply house
Sammy Nebo			Patrolman and later Captain of Atlantic City, (NJ) Police Department
Billy Neri			Truck driver
Al Nettlow			Co-owner of bar with brother in Miami
Joseph Nocella			Business owner
Mickey O'Day			Train factory machinist
Babe Orlando			Boxing magazine publisher and writer. Also a boxing manager
Joe Orsini			Sports shop owner

NAME	FATHER'S OCCUPATION	PRE-BOXING OCCUPATION	POST-BOXING OCCUPATION
Louis "Kid" Oswald			Food produce business in California
Tom Padovano			Longshoreman
Bill Pagani			Barbershop owner
Babe Palecco			Electrical company factory employee
Henry Palmieri			Department store janitor
Biagio Pantano			Restaurant owner. Movie extra
Nick Pastore			Beer salesman. Also worked as a boxing trainer and manager
Frankie Paul			Factory operative and union leader
Johnny Pepe			Bartender
Matt Perfetti	Button factory hand		Bartender
Pete Perrero			Mine maintenance foreman. Later a car salesman
Patsy Perroni			Nightclub owner. Later became a deputy sheriff in Cleveland, (OH). Devoted much time to helping charities for underprivileged children. Also worked as a security guard.
Billy Petrolle II			Factory foreman
Jimmy Phillips			Sales manager. Commissioner of Morristown Airport in New Jersey.
Paul Pirrone	Steel mill laborer		Steamfitter/plumber in construction
Kid Polo			Shoeshine parlor owner
Tony Poloni		University student	Police officer
John Priest			Massachusetts Port Authority security guard
Frankie Rapp	Cobbler, shoe store owner	Helped father	Inherited father's shoe store business
Midge Renault			Union executive. Head of Connecticut's Operating Engineer's Union
Joe Reno (Valeriano)	Truck driver	Employed at uncle's bottling company. Also played semi-pro football.	Police officer and later detective. Also worked as an investigator for the Camden County Prosecutor's Office in New Jersey
Trenton Joe Reno			Boxing manager
Clair Repole	Railroad laborer		Locomotion engineer
Joe Ricciotti			Massachusetts State House court officer. Also worked as a boxing judge

NAME	FATHER'S OCCUPATION	PRE-BOXING OCCUPATION	POST-BOXING OCCUPATION
Tommy Riggi			Water Department clerk
Adolph Ritacco	Furniture factory machinist	Tailor shop helper	Boxing trainer
Joe Rizzo			Welder
Joe Roche	* Mother worked as laundry cleaner		Motorman on street bus
Pee Wee Ross			Cigar and candy store owner, Bar owner
Johnny Rossi			Steel plant worker
Joe Rovelli		Newsboy	Golf club caddy master
Sammy Sacco			City of Buffalo license director
Jerry Salica			Printing plant employee. Also a boxing manager
Jimmy Scaramozi			Boxing referee
Tony Scarpati	Longshoreman	Store worker	Boxing fatality
Alex Scassa	Steel mill laborer	Steel mill chipper	Boxing & wrestling promoter. Boxing manager
Andy Scrivani	Electrician for building contractor		Boxing coach
Louis Severo			Factory operative and boxing manager.
Tony Shucco	Construction laborer		Nightclub doorman
Al Silvani			Boxing trainer, movie actor, stuntman and consultant
Al Sinibaldi			Naval air training station instructor
Phil Siriani			Bottling company truck driver. Also a boxing trainer at Gleason's Gym
Nick Spano			Petrol service station owner. Racetrack clerk. Boxing official
Vince Sposato			Civic politician
Billy Sullivan	Silver plate polisher & jewelry shop employee		Plate polisher & jewelry shop employee
Jackie Tarzan			Maintenance company owner
Danny Tauriello			Newark (NJ) Fire Department Battalion Chief
Al Todisco			Boxing referee
Laddie Tonelli	Coal miner		Plant operative. Boxing trainer
Tony Tozzo			Died young of pneumonia
Joe Transparenti			Highways bureau worker

NAME	FATHER'S OCCUPATION	PRE-BOXING OCCUPATION	POST-BOXING OCCUPATION
Ralph Tribuani	Journalist		Boxing manager/promoter and businessman. Restaurateur & nightclub owner
Babe Triscaro			President of Excavating, Building Material and Construction Drivers Union in Cleveland and Vice President of Ohio Conference of Teamsters
Benny Trotta	Coal miner/ railroad laborer	Worked full-time at Sparrow's Point steel mill before, during and after his boxing career ended.	Boxing trainer, manager and later promoter
Al Turco			Fruit and vegetable dealer
Tommy Zano			Dry cleaning tycoon. Also ran a linoleum and carpet floor covering supplies and fitting business
Max Zona	*		Semi-skilled construction worker
1940s			
Sammy Adragna	Self employed market grocer		Owner of a 34-acre farm. Steel factory worker. Later promoted to head of computerized furnace operations
Peter Agosta			District manager for sales and marketing company in Ramsey, (NJ)
Johnny Aiello		Plumber	Firefighter for the Wilmington (DE) Fire Department. Also worked as a county plumbing inspector. Boxing trainer
Frank Altieri			Cab driver
Tony Amato			Actor and stuntman
Dom Amoroso			Boxing trainer
Jeep Anderson	Chemical plant laborer & city lamplighter		Boxing promoter and businessman
Johnny Andrews			Carpenter
Ozzie Andrews			Beverages company employee
Joey Angelo			Caterer. Coffee shop proprietor. Also worked as Providence (RI) city employee
Larry Anzalone			Cameo film actor
Nick Arcuri			Truck driver & farm owner
Danny Ardito			Director of Golden Age Project in Newark (NJ)

NAME	FATHER'S OCCUPATION	PRE-BOXING OCCUPATION	POST-BOXING OCCUPATION
Arthur Argenti	Streets department laborer		City of Trenton (NJ) streets department operative
Tony Arnone			International Longshoreman's Association of New Orleans employee
Pete Asero			Boxing fatality
Joe Aurillo	Disabled		Tavern owner
Dom Baccala	Bricklayer		Construction contractor, bricklayer
Al Baldesino	Soft drinks store owner		Boxing trainer. Worked for electro-chemical company
Joey Barnum	Racketeer		Boxing manager, Bail bondsman & bodyguard
Nick Barone			Truck driver
Charlie Basile	Steelworker		Barber
Joe Battles			Car salesman
Johnny Bell			Concrete construction company owner
Steve Belloise	Carpenter	Grocery shop assistant	Bartender, bricklayer and city building inspector. Also cameo film actor
Frankie Bove		Newsboy	Shoeshine stand proprietor
Angelo Brocato			Post office employee
Billy Brown			Deputy sheriff – law enforcement. Also owned a billiards and boxing gymnasium in Jacksonville, (FL)
Dan Bucceroni			Boxing manager. Author of boxing instruction manual
Sam Butera	Laborer		Restaurant owner
Lee Campione	General merchandise store owner		Sports bar and grill owner. Wrestling promoter in Owosso, (MI)
Paul Carbetta			Boxing director and instructor
Vic Cardell	Factory machinist		Data processor for Connecticut state – Administration and clerical
Peter Caringi			Tavern owner
Jimmy Carollo			Nightclub owner
Johnny Caruso			Bus driver
Rocky Castellani	Miner	Bootblack, newsboy,	Tavern owner and boxing judge. Also worked as volunteer sports coach
Paul Cavagnaro	Ironmonger and store owner		Police officer

NAME	FATHER'S OCCUPATION	PRE-BOXING OCCUPATION	POST-BOXING OCCUPATION
Al Certo	Musician		Tailor, boxing manager, trainer
Johnny Cesario			Billiards hall owner. Also an actor and charity benefactor
Sal Cesario			Drug dealer
Vinny Cidone	Self employed contractor	Painter	Painter – became Vice-President of Painter's Union
Dom Cirillo	Gangster		Racketeer – Genovese family
Hank Cisco	Shoemaker and shoe repairs shop owner		Policeman and Head of Juvenile Division at the Norristown, (PA) Police Station. Later sports columnist and writer
Johnny Colan	Father sick	Truck driver. Quit textile high school	New York City insurance company investment manager responsible for forty employees. Also a boxing referee
Eddie Compo	Building laborer		Ironworker
Jerome Conforto	Storekeeper		Gymnasium owner and joint owner of bar with Willie Pep in New Orleans
Bozo Constantino			Construction worker
Jimmy Corti			Ironworker
Leo Darcy			Auto body shop repairer. Insurance claims adjuster and examiner
Paul De Bello			Longshoreman – involved in loading operations on Brooklyn waterfront.
Mike De Cosmo			Italian delicatessen shop and restaurant owner
Billy De Foe			Shipyard worker. Also boxing trainer and manager
George De Gidio	Dairy farmer		Farm owner & dog breeder
Ralph De John			Restaurant owner
Vince De Lia			Physical therapist – ran his own practice
Johnny Dell			Boxing gym owner. Car dealership owner
Steve De Luca			New York City police detective in burglary division
Louis De Melo			Farm owner
And De Paul	Crane operator		Professional boxing and wrestling referee. Pennsylvania State Athletic Commission commissioner
Archie De Vino			Equine businessman

NAME	FATHER'S OCCUPATION	PRE-BOXING OCCUPATION	POST-BOXING OCCUPATION
Angelo Di Angelo	Shoe repairer & shop owner		Bartender
Anthony Di Nardo			Welding company owner
Frankie Donato			Salesman
Gus Dorazio	Carpenter	Candy apple and hot waffle seller	Bouncer
Mickey Doyle			Early death – electrocuted in work-related accident
Mickey DuBerry	Grinder, factory operative		Bottling factory supervisor. Licensed boxing referee
Johnny Duke	Road work grader – construction	Bootblack	Boxing club owner, coach and cornerman
Lou Duva	Dye house worker	Bowling alley pin boy, newsboy, bootblack	Boxing manager, trainer and head of Main Events, one of the most successful boxing promotions company in the USA
Phil Enzenga	Shoemaker, shoe shop owner		Boxing trainer and coach
Tony Enzenga			Boxing gym owner
Joey Falco			Nightclub owner
Carmine Fatta			Restaurant owner. Also an ex-government employee
Joseph Ferraiolo			Carpenter
Clem Florio		Horse racing groom. Also attended Brooklyn Technical High School.	Horse racing and boxing writer for *Miami News* and *The News American*
Larry Fontana			Truck driver
Mike Franco			Factory foreman
Charley Fusari	Milkman	Helped father	Restaurant owner. Also worked in public relations for a wholesale liquor company
Patsy Gall	Coal miner	Anthracite rock miner,	Hazelton (PA) City street department employee. Ice business owner
Tony Gartex			Barbershop owner. Also chairman of local Liberal Party
Johnny Giaco			Policeman
Vince Gigante			Racketeer. Later became the head of Genovese family
Mike Gillo			Sanitation department worker in New Haven, (CT)
Johnny Giordano	Railroad repairman		Truck driver

NAME	FATHER'S OCCUPATION	PRE-BOXING OCCUPATION	POST-BOXING OCCUPATION
Eddie Giosa	Barbershop owner	Graduated from vocational school. Metal plater.	Boxing trainer. Metal plater for RCA.Later worked as a mailroom assistant for the *Philadelphia Enquirer*
Tommy Greb			Laborer and painter
Victor Grupico			Truck driver
Al Guido			Dock foreman for fruit company
Tony Janiro			Bartender in New York City. Later worked as a courthouse clerk at Department of Justice & Public Order in Mahoning County, (OH)
Joey Iannotti		Bootblack	Delicatessen store owner. Later worked for national supermarket chain
Johnny Imbrenda	Shoe factory laborer		Tavern owner, longshoreman
Al La Barba		Steamfitter	Supervisor at electrical appliances company
Lenny La Brutto	Painter in construction industry		Ironworker
Joey La Motta	Mobile food peddler		Boxing manager and trainer. Vending machine business owner
Carl La Rocca			Supermarket owner. Doorman security and sheriff's office deputy
Vince La Salva	Shoemaker, self employed tradesman		Restaurant manager
Jerry La Starza	Butcher and store owner		Pilot's assistant in US Air Force
Carmine Lato			Maintenance man for the US Postal Service
Jimmy Letty			Detective
Angelo Luongo			New York Police Department patrolman. Later worked as a private detective and as a security supervisor
Angelo Maglione			Dry cleaning business owner
Sammy Mammone			Construction worker
"Ice" Mancinelli	Small farm owner, grocey shop owner	Newsboy	Worked in the family grocery store
Steve Marcello	Boxer	Barber	Barber

NAME	FATHER'S OCCUPATION	PRE-BOXING OCCUPATION	POST-BOXING OCCUPATION
Tommy Marciano			Factory operative. He became a detective sergeant and later served as Schuylkill Township (PA) police chief
Tony Martin	Wholesale fruit peddler		Casino employee and joint owner of a musical bar
Joe Matisi	Grocery store owner		Construction laborer
Leo Matricciani	Laborer	Attended vocational school	Longshoreman foreman
Tami Mauriello	Orphaned at fourteen. Mother a construction laborer		Restaurant owner. Later worked for a defense contractor. Post-boxing career beset by gambling
Nick Melli			Construction worker
Freddie Menna			Factory worker and union shop steward. Also boxing manager
Leo Micucci			Wholesale food depot proprietor
Marty Monforte			Owner of plumbing and heating company
Paul Mosca			Businessman. Owner of Paul's Service Center.
Pete Muscanera	Businessman	Shoe factory operative	Took over father's business
Joe Muscato	Farm laborer		Professional wrestler
Phil Muscato	Farm laborer		Nightclub owner in Buffalo, (NY). General Motors plant operative
Sam Muscato	Farm laborer		Professional wrestler, boxing judge, referee and timekeeper. Sports instructor for the city of Buffalo Department of Recreation
Vic Nardoni			Bail bondsman. Involved in family business in Los Angeles.
Nello Nucelli			Businessman and civic leader
Johnny O'Keefe			Baker. Part owner of a bakery
Carmine Parella	Railroad foreman		Self employed owner driver of seven-seater limousine
Tony Pellone	Longshoreman	Bootblack	Longshoreman and boxing trainer
Al Pennino	Longshoreman		Longshoreman
Goody Petronelli			Boxing trainer & manager
Vic Pignataro		Painter	Civil service employee at US Military Academy at West Point
Bill Pozza			Policeman in Ellwood City, (PA)

NAME	FATHER'S OCCUPATION	PRE-BOXING OCCUPATION	POST-BOXING OCCUPATION
Mike Raffa			Tavern owner
Lew Raymond	Truck driver. Mother managed family fruit store		Boxing promoter
Chester Rico			Cameo film actor, Taxi driver. Also worked as hotel security guard
Frank Riggi			Actor
Steve Riggio	Grocery dealer – self employed		Cab driver
Kid Sal			Restaurant owner
Mickey Siano			Threading machinist in textile industry
Patsy Spataro			Barbershop owner. Also a boxing trainer
Charlie Spina			Boxing judge
Art Tatta		Bowling alley pinboy	New Haven railroad worker. Also a boxing manager
Charley Titone			Fireman in California
Lou Transparenti			Meat products concession department employee
Al Tribuani	Journalist		Injured in Second World War.
Joe Trofe			Owner of incineration plant
Ralph Troiano	Salesman	Newsboy	Bricklayer
Vince Tumminello	Self employed fruit and veg peddler		Bureau of Highways construction worker
Benny Urso			Boxing coach & trainer
Pat Valentino	Grocery store owner	Helped father	Head-waiter at top restaurant at San Francisco's Fisherman's Wharf
Lenny Vendrillo	Silk mill weaver		Meter reader for Connecticut power company
Pat Vendrillo	Silk mill weaver		Sheet metal worker. Telephone company lineman
Smoky Joe Ventafido	Shoe factory laborer		Tavern owner
Vinnie Vines			General Electric plant operative
Pete Virgin	Electricity company laborer		Boxing trainer and manager
Ross Virgo			Restaurant owner
Sal Voccia			Post office employee
Frankie Wills	Miner	Miner	Taxi driver & tile setter
Babe Wolf			Restaurant owner
Terry Young			Criminal, robber. Also a nightclub bouncer

NAME	FATHER'S OCCUPATION	PRE-BOXING OCCUPATION	POST-BOXING OCCUPATION
Ralph Zanelli	Farm laborer	Street fighter, newsboy	Construction laborer. Brewery employee
1950s			
Frank Alotta			Businessman
Ritchie Astone			Singer/actor/choreographer in Hollywood and in Las Vegas
Mike Bazzone			Boxing manager and trainer. A gymnasium owner
Billy Bossio			Bartender
Mario Calandra			Construction company owner
Frank Cappuccino			Boxing referee. Also Board of Education sanitation control inspector
Johnny Cesario	Shop proprietor		Concessions director at Hartford Civic Center in Connecticut
Joe Curcio			Bar owner with Ernie Durando
Vinnie De Carlo			Actor
Angelo De Fendis	Fruit store owner		Racketeer
Joey De John			Groom at horse racing track
Mike De John			Bartender
Joey Dorando Jr.			Bail bondsman businessman
Ernie Durando	Hod carrier - construction		Bar owner with Joe Curcio, Hollywood restaurant owner. Safety co-ordinator at New Jersey Turnpike Authority. Also a boxing judge
Tony Esperti			Organized crime henchman
Frank Favaro			Farm owner; Horse breeder and vintner
Joe Fusco			Construction laborer
Lou Filippo			Boxing manager, trainer and referee and judge. Also worked for an electrical components company
Tony Gagliardi			New York City Police officer. Later became private detective
Jimmy Gambino	Confectionery shop owner	Store clerk	Drug dealer. Post-boxing career beset by heroin addiction. 'T' shirt and socks seller
Joey Giambra	Unemployed. On welfare support	Newspaper seller, saloon singer, bootblack	Boxing referee, casino greeter, cab driver
Joey Giardello	Department of Sanitation supervisor		Insurance salesman. Also worked as a distributor for a chemical company. Noted for his work with special needs children

NAME	FATHER'S OCCUPATION	PRE-BOXING OCCUPATION	POST-BOXING OCCUPATION
Tommy Giorgio			Professional wrestler
Frankie Ippolito			Manhattan College graduate. High school physical education instructor
Peter Ippolito			Roofer in construction industry
Jackie La Bua			Security guard
Roland La Starza	Butcher shop owner	Helped father	Flight instructor – licensed pilot, cattle ranch owner. TV and film actor
Joey Lupo			Businessman – Owner of fitness centers in Miami, FL. Personal fitness trainer
James Malatino			Federal government worker
Dicky Manzi			Farm owner
Vince Martinez	Laborer		Hotel business owner. Later worked in the computer business
Joseph Marino			Public works department employee and entertainer
Peter Marino Sr.			Landscaping and masonry company owner
Joe Miceli			Truck driver. Odd job man and entertainer
Tony Miragliotta		University student	Vocational rehabilitation officer at the Vocational Rehabilitation Office in Berkley (VA)
Danny Nardico			Athletic director of Nevada State Prison at Carson City
Willie Pastrano	Laborer, ship cook.		Bouncer, casino greeter. Also worked as a boxing trainer and manager. Post boxing career beset by heroin and alcohol addiction
Lou Pelosi			Policeman
Al Priest	Roofer in construction industry	Newsboy	Businessman – owner of several bars. Restaurant owner
Joe Rindone	Laborer		Painter
Mickey Rosati			Auto mechanic. Also a boxing club owner
Lee Sala	Bricklayer		Whisky distribution salesman. Later worked as deputy sheriff. A boxing referee
Gene Tortorice			Construction work, boxing trainer

| Chico Vejar | University undergraduate | Actor. A major national campaigner in cerebral palsy fund-raising initiatives. Also worked as executive assistant at Hartford, (CT) Athletic Division |

Notes

* Denotes fathers who were either deceased or absent from the home.

All names are listed alphabetically under each decade heading.

The decade does not rigidly represent the complete career of each boxer listed. It merely serves to indicate that the boxer fought most of his professional boxing contests during that period.

Only the known occupations of the boxers are cited and it does not purport to be a comprehensive list of all activities undertaken throughout a persons working life.

APPENDIX XX: LIFE EXPECTANCY OF THE ITALIAN AMERICAN BOXING COHORT 1900–55

Life expectancy of Italian American champions and title claimants

NAME	YEAR OF BIRTH	YEAR OF DEATH	AGE
Hugo Kelly	10/02/1882	Unknown	
Kid Murphy	02/05/1886	10/10/1963	77
Frankie Conley	04/10/1890	August 1952	61
Johnny Wilson	03/07/1893	08/12/1985	92
Johnny Dundee	22/11/1893	22/04/1965	71
Rocky Kansas	21/04/1895	10/01/1954	58
Pete Herman	12/02/1896	April 1973	77
Young Zulu Kid	22/04/1897	April 1977	80
Steve "Kid" Sullivan	21/05/1897	September 1979	82
Lou Bogash	24/02/1901	07/03/1978	77
Mike Ballerino	10/04/1901	04/04/1965	64
Frankie Genaro	26/08/1901	27/12/1966	65
Carl Duane	25/06/1902	June 1984	82
Eddie Martin	26/02/1903	27/08/1966	63
Joe Dundee	16/08/1903	31/03/1982	78
Sammy Mandell	05/02/1904	07/11/1967	63
Willie La Morte	16/06/1904	06/02/1990	85
Lou Scozza	15/04/1905	30/11/1967	62
Young Corbett III	27/05/1905	20/07/1993	88
Bushy Graham	18/06/1905	05/08/1982	77
Sammy Fuller	10/06/1906	30/05/1979	73
Fidel La Barba	29/09/1906	03/10/1981	76
Vince Dundee	22/10/1907	27/07/1949	41
Battling Battalino	18/02/1908	25/07/1977	69
George Nichols	09/07/1908	October 1986	78
Tony Canzoneri	06/11/1908	10/12/1959	51
Tommy Paul	04/03/1909	28/04/1991	82
Midget Wolgast	18/06/1910	19/10/1955	45
Mike Belloise	18/02/1911	02/06/1969	58
Tony Marino	18/05/1912	01/02/1937	24*
Lou Salica	16/11/1912	30/01/2002	89
Fred Apostoli	02/02/1913	29/11/1973	60
Lou Ambers	08/11/1913	24/04/1995	81
Harry Jeffra	30/11/1914	September 1988	73
Sammy Angott	17/01/1915	22/10/1980	65
Izzy Jannazzo	31/01/1915	18/06/1995	80
Jimmy Perrin	03/02/1915	14/04/1997	82
Melio Bettina	18/11/1915	20/12/1996	80
Pete Scalzo	01/08/1917	15/06/1993	75
Sal Bartolo	05/11/1917	19/02/2002	84
Tippy Larkin	11/11/1917	December 1991	74
Phil Terranova	04/09/1919	16/03/2000	80
Marty Servo	03/11/1919	09/02/1969	49
Jake La Motta	10/07/1921	Alive	(93)
Rocky Graziano	01/01/1922	22/05/1990	68
Joey Maxim	28/03/1922	02/06/2001	79
Willie Pep	19/09/1922	23/11/2006	84
Rocky Marciano	01/09/1923	31/08/1969	46
Carmen Basilio	02/04/1927	07/11/2012	85
Paddy De Marco	10/02/1928	13/12/1997	69
Tony De Marco	14/01/1932	Alive	(82)

Notes

Hugo Kelly's year of death is unknown.
Boxers Jake La Motta and Tony De Marco are still alive respectively and for the purposes of this study their current ages are bracketed.
*This list contains one boxing fatality and this is denoted in the age column.

Life expectancy of Italian American contenders/headliners/other professional boxers

NAME	YEAR OF BIRTH	YEAR OF DEATH	AGE
Joe Thomas	1878	24/12/1923	45
Dago Mike (Mongone)	05/07/1879	01/11/1966	87
Fireman Jim Flynn #	24/12/1879	12/04/1935	55
Charlie Sieger #	07/02/1880	29/03/1951	71
Joe Grim	14/03/1881	19/08/1939	58
Benny Yanger #	18/02/1882	15/04/1958	76
Jimmy Kelly	1883	09/01/1948	64
Charlie "Kid" Dalton	24/02/1884	31/03/1951	67
Harry Lenny	22/05/1884	March 1963	78
Al Delmont #	05/07/1884	October 1963	79
Terry Young I #	01/09/1884	1956	72
Eddie Marino #	1885	23/05/1949	64
Frank Landers	05/04/1885	10/12/1954	69
Kid Stinger	25/11/1886	19/05/1966	79
Kid Locke	06/03/1887	June 1966	79
Joe Uvanni	27/07/1887	22/08/1956	69
KO Sullivan	22/08/1887	December 1968	81
Lou Sheppard	25/09/1887	July 1974	86
Tony Ross #	October 1887	31/08/1941	53
Frankie Nelson	08/01/1888	15/08/1971	83
Al Rogers #	12/04/1888	08/10/1959	71
Frank Picato	11/10/1888	06/07/1960	71
Marty O'Brien	1889	24/01/1969	80
Joe Coster #	26/01/1889	20/06/1974	85
Patsy White	25/03/1889	17/11/1964	75
Battling Terry	01/01/1890	December 1973	83
Johnny Harvey	04/05/1890	1965	74
Italian Joe Gans #	16/02/1891	25/08/1953	62
Angelo Taramaschi	26/04/1891	26/11/1960	69
Joe Percente	15/11/1891	23/03/1993	101
Kid Julian	15/12/1891	June 1969	77
Patsy Kline #	1892	25/09/1950	58
Joe Borrell #	21/06/1892	31/12/1978	86
Freddie Kelly	27/06/1892	01/12/1973	81
Packey Hommey	24/07/1892	February 1981	88
Phil Virgets	1893	24/10/1926	33
Joe Clifford	22/01/1893	October 1979	86
Babe Picato	01/02/1893	December 1966	73
Spike Sullivan	02/03/1893	May 1975	82
Sam Nolan	05/08/1893	20/12/1975	82
Mike Mazie	15/10/1893	April 1973	80
Battling Reddy #	01/03/1894	July 1977	82
Pat Bradley	20/03/1894	1977	83
Hugo Clement	12/04/1894	January 1975	80
Paul Carr	20/06/1894	16/05/1996	101
Steve Dalton	26/12/1894	27/03/1962	67
Ralph Thomas	1895	27/10/1924	29*
Al Blades	03/02/1895	17/04/1987	92
Gene Delmont #	25/03/1895	01/09/1987	92
Jimmy Coffey	05/04/1895	January 1972	77
Frankie Murray #	27/05/1895	December 1984	89

NAME	YEAR OF BIRTH	YEAR OF DEATH	AGE
Willie Ames	15/08/1895	14/05/1967	71
Joe O'Brien	23/11/1895	26/11/1969	74
Young Lawrence	06/12/1895	March 1974	78
Tommy McFarland	1896	01/10/1954	58
Phil Franchini	15/01/1896	June 1984	88
Johnny Victor	29/02/1896	June 1977	81
Rocky Stramaglia	14/03/1896	November 1964	68
Tony Zill	15/03/1896	26/10/1958	62
Mickey Donley #	21/08/1896	22/02/1944	47
Jimmy Musso	09/10/1896	03/01/1982	85
Jimmy Hanlon #	12/11/1896	August 1977	80
Red Cap Wilson	01/12/1896	06/02/1966	69
Pep O'Brien	1897	28/03/1950	53
Paul Doyle #	18/01/1897	October 1972	75
Young Terry McGovern	19/02/1897	21/12/1918	21*
Jockey Joe Dillon #	03/05/1897	January 1973	75
Bud Christiano	15/05/1897	24/08/1964	67
Phil Salvadore #	27/09/1897	12/06/1945	47
Italian Jack Herman	1898	06/12/1941	43
Patsy Rubino	1898	14/07/1969	71
Mickey Carroll	14/02/1898	October 1967	69
Jimmy Dundee	15/05/1898	26/08/1966	68
Ralph Brady #	29/06/1898	August 1966	68
Joe "Kid" Kansas	14/08/1898	01/06/1980	81
Bobby Ertle	03/10/1898	24/03/1984	85
Jimmy Dixon	1899	21/11/1953	54
Patsy Wallace #	17/02/1899	October 1965	66
Patsy Bogash	04/03/1899	01/11/1969	70
Young Remsey	06/03/1899	May 1983	84
Louis Atta	22/04/1899	15/02/1991	91
Mickey Travers	29/04/1899	03/09/1982	83
George "Kid" Texas	07/07/1899	January 1978	79
Ted Frenchie	31/07/1899	1968	68
Jimmy Fruzzetti	20/10/1899	September 1979	79
New Haven Joe Currie	25/12/1899	October 1971	71
Marty Collins	1900	August 1984	84
Sonny Compagno	1900	July 1937	37
Babe Orlando	03/02/1900	March 1976	76
George Fitzsimmons	12/02/1900	July 1968	68
Frankie Rex	06/03/1900	1983	83
Hoboken Joe Dundee	15/03/1900	June 1987	87
Nick Michaels	18/03/1900	June 1988	88
Young Carmen	25/03/1900	10/01/1972	71
Frank Susnell	17/05/1900	25/11/1981	81
Packey O'Gatty #	03/06/1900	10/10/1966	66
Kid Leonard	10/06/1900	March 1974	73
Battling Al Murray #	06/07/1900	31/12/1979	79
Al Cook	10/07/1900	December 1971	71
Tiger Johnny Cline	27/09/1900	07/07/1964	63
Billy Prince	28/09/1900	15/06/1968	67
Basil Galiano #	1901	21/08/1939	38
Charlie Trabon	1901	04/04/1990	89
Philadelphia Jack Palmer	10/01/1901	January 1968	67

NAME	YEAR OF BIRTH	YEAR OF DEATH	AGE
Tommy Murray	07/02/1901	March 1991	90
Kewpie Collins	02/03/1901	July 1982	81
Tony Marullo #	03/06/1901	01/02/1984	82
Humbert Brady	16/01/1901	July 1977	76
Tommy Cello #	18/01/1901	01/03/1969	68
Willie Spencer #	09/02/1901	October 1970	69
Racehorse Roberts	13/02/1901	28/01/1949	48
Kid Pershing	04/03/1901	14/04/1986	85
Andy Thomas	04/07/1901	05/02/1923	21*
Harry Martin #	02/12/1901	06/02/1934	32
Frankie Brown	1902	25/12/1971	69
Willie Curry	1902	1983	81
Eddie Shea #	1902	11/02/1947	44
Bucky Josephs	19/03/1902	28/03/1983	81
Morris Meola	26/05/1902	19/06/1991	89
Joe Paglina	02/08/1902	21/12/1982	80
Mike Dundee #	04/08/1902	October 1977	74
Ashton Donza	27/08/1902	06/10/1952	50
Dago Joe Gans	19/03/1903	12/09/1988	85
Tony Vaccarelli	22/03/1903	31/10/1990	87
Bobby Tracey	24/09/1903	18/03/1989	85
Joe Roche #	23/10/1903	December 1982	79
Matty Mario	1904	03/10/1994	90
Don Tippero	1904	1925	21*
Johnny Saxon	12/01/1904	24/11/1984	80
Harry Thorpe	12/02/1904	April 1978	74
Vic Burrone	27/02/1904	February 1977	73
Jack Coburn	28/02/1904	17/02/1996	92
Joe Azzarella	26/04/1904	01/12/1966	62
Frankie Campbell	May 1904	26/08/1930	26*
Pete Bova	11/05/1904	July 1993	88
Andy Martin #	28/05/1904	23/02/1987	82
Mickey Bellero	16/06/1904	07/07/1994	90
Paul Cavalier	16/06/1904	20/07/1993	89
Joey Manuel	25/06/1904	13/07/1971	67
Jimmy Wilson	07/09/1904	26/10/1958	54
Phil Gusmano	05/11/1904	10/11/1971	67
Al Tripoli	27/11/1904	07/03/1990	85
Johnny Grosso	1905	14/10/1932	27
Jack McGurn	1905	15/02/1936	30
Billy Petrolle #	10/01/1905	14/05/1983	78
Tony Mandell	14/02/1905	September 1979	74
Johnny Mason	03/03/1905	15/05/1990	85
Bert Visconi	01/05/1905	January 1984	78
Carl Cavelli	28/05/1905	28/12/1980	75
Babe Ruth	02/06/1905	June 1971	66
Patsy Ruffalo	04/06/1905	02/11/1990	85
Mike 'Kid' Julian	03/08/1905	20/02/1977	72
Lou Paluso #	16/08/1905	February 1981	75
Frankie Grandetta	26/11/1905	January 1984	78
Al Gracio	03/12/1905	01/12/1977	72
Midget Herman	30/12/1905	27/06/2000	94
Al Ferrone	1906	1998	92

NAME	YEAR OF BIRTH	YEAR OF DEATH	AGE
Mickey Taylor	1906	August 1960	54
Andy Di Vodi #	19/01/1906	05/02/1989	83
Johnny Ceccoli	28/08/1906	November 1980	74
Johnny Vacca #	03/09/1906	April 1983	76
Johnny Indrisano #	01/11/1906	09/07/1968	61
Gene Stanton	08/11/1906	August 1978	72
Frankie Rapp	09/11/1906	April 1982	75
Emmett Rocco	18/12/1906	01/12/1961	55
Roger Bernard #	1907	17/09/1954	47
Johnny Pepe	1907	April 1988	81
Young Zazzarino	1907	31/12/1948	41
Lew Massey #	04/01/1907	01/08/1993	86
Matty White	07/01/1907	March 1980	72
Larry Marinucci	09/02/1907	April 1982	75
Billy Mastriani	04/03/1907	09/02/1967	59
Young Firpo (Bardelli) #	25/04/1907	August 1984	77
Emil Paluso #	17/06/1907	March 1980	72
Tony Marano	27/06/1907	21/04/1998	90
Tony Poloni	28/09/1907	May 1983	75
Charlie Young	07/10/1907	08/11/1997	90
Nick Antonelli	22/10/1907	21/11/2005	98
Vincent Sireci	15/12/1907	December 1978	71
Eddie Frisco	17/12/1907	25/06/1968	60
Carmen Tuzzolino	31/12/1907	25/10/1981	73
Ernie Mandell	19/01/1908	18/12/1993	85
Earl Mastro #	29/02/1908	23/12/1993	85
Ralph Ficucello	02/03/1908	April 1988	80
Billy Angelo	21/04/1908	July 1987	79
Joe Trippe	10/05/1908	10/05/1987	79
Mickey Terry	10/06/1908	04/04/1996	87
Frankie Petrolle	18/06/1908	August 1967	59
Don Petrin #	09/10/1908	October 1979	71
Angelo Puglisi	16/11/1908	19/06/1977	68
Paul Negri	22/11/1908	04/10/1993	84
Jimmy Russo	1909	1977	68
Johnny Gaito	14/01/1909	13/12/1991	82
Phil Guerrera	24/02/1909	April 1980	71
KO Morgan #	12/05/1909	01/03/1976	66
Jimmy Phillips	08/09/1909	12/04/1998	88
Joey Harrison	24/10/1909	26/03/1995	85
Buster Brown #	02/01/1910	December 1991	81
George Annarino	22/01/1910	November 1984	74
Young Firpo (Bracale)	10/02/1910	January 1976	65
Tony Galento #	12/03/1910	22/07/1979	69
Joey Dodge	19/03/1910	28/01/1988	77
Paul Pirrone #	28/04/1910	10/07/1988	78
Tony Shucco #	13/06/1910	February 1983	72
Mose Butch #	24/08/1910	29/07/1991	80
Billy Celebron	10/09/1910	11/12/1987	77
Hank Palmeri	10/09/1910	June 1985	74
Johnny O'Keefe	1911	May 1989	78
Johnny Nelson	08/01/1911	19/02/1989	78
Salvatore Affinito	17/01/1911	July 1964	53

NAME	YEAR OF BIRTH	YEAR OF DEATH	AGE
Teddy Martin	12/03/1911	18/12/1983	72
Milo Milletti	15/03/1911	16/05/1999	88
Johnny Duca	28/03/1911	28/12/2001	90
Al Citrino	11/04/1911	15/06/1993	82
Tony Scarpati	21/04/1911	21/03/1936	24*
Young Terry #	17/05/1911	31/12/1977	66
Clair Repole	22/05/1911	October 1986	75
Jay Macks	24/06/1911	August 1979	68
Young Al Mellow	26/06/1911	02/06/1994	82
Vince De Santis	01/07/1911	September 1987	76
Phil Baker #	01/08/1911	27/11/1996	85
Ray Actis #	26/08/1911	14/02/1997	85
Tony Falco #	05/10/1911	June 1974	62
Patsy Pasculli	05/11/1911	17/02/1991	80
Mickey DuBerry	17/11/1911	23/01/2001	89
Jimmy Leto #	27/11/1911	01/06/1986	74
Johnny Lucas	1912	01/07/1988	76
Laddie Tonelli	19/01/1912	07/06/1992	80
Patsy Perroni #	03/02/1912	01/10/1987	75
Mickey Marchitto	04/02/1912	June 1984	71
Jimmy Tramberia	17/02/1912	04/06/1988	76
Ralph Fulton	18/03/1912	25/12/1994	82
Harry Little	16/04/1912	07/03/2003	90
Paul Dazzo #	08/08/1912	07/06/1992	79
Al Manfredo #	22/08/1912	16/01/1990	77
Paris Apice	28/08/1912	24/07/1961	49
Carmen Barth #	03/09/1912	18/09/1985	73
Bucky Keyes	24/11/1912	December 1982	80
Tony Celli	1913	21/09/1952	39
Frankie Blair #	22/03/1913	22/03/1994	80
Benny Trotta	08/07/1913	25/07/1971	68
Tony Morgano #	August 1913	02/02/1985	71
Fiore Maruco	18/08/1913	19/05/2003	89
Frankie Caris	09/09/1913	07/01/1987	73
Freddie Fiducia	12/10/1913	10/05/1966	52
Sal Canata	13/10/1913	26/11/1991	78
Al Ettore #	19/11/1913	15/11/1988	75
Freddie Camuso	1914	December 1991	77
Lou Lombardi	1914	1986	72
Frankie Sagilio	25/03/1914	31/03/1997	83
Carl Guggino	12/04/1914	19/02/1988	74
Harry Balsamo #	10/05/1914	14/10/1991	77
Al Spina	05/07/1914	19/07/1987	73
Joe Maruco	09/10/1914	27/11/1996	82
Carl Vinciguerra	19/10/1914	10/11/1997	83
Frankie Gallucci	28/12/1914	June 1981	66
Joe Erne	1915	01/06/2007	95
Sal Baccala	04/01/1915	17/09/1967	52
Tommy Grady	21/02/1915	04/03/1992	77
Ralph Gizzy	12/03/1915	July 1986	71
Patsy Gall	24/03/1915	12/01/2008	92
Nick Camarata	18/04/1915	07/01/1996	80
Nathan Mann #	03/05/1915	26/10/1999	84

NAME	YEAR OF BIRTH	YEAR OF DEATH	AGE
Tony Cisco	11/05/1915	21/10/1974	59
Leonard Del Genio #	07/06/1915	09/08/1991	76
Joey Zodda	08/07/1915	28/08/2007	92
Joey August	12/08/1915	23/11/1996	81
Young Chappie	02/09/1915	June 1965	49
Al Mancini #	28/09/1915	25/07/1992	77
Joe Wagner	28/09/1915	April 1982	66
Ralph Zanelli #	02/10/1915	29/11/2006	91
Johnny LoBianco	07/10/1915	16/07/2001	85
Emil Calcagni	21/11/1915	19/11/2002	87
Tony Musto #	03/12/1915	30/09/1994	78
Gene Palecco	04/03/1916	19/07/1988	72
Carl Dell	03/05/1916	22/01/2009	92
Mickey La Marr	17/05/1916	23/05/1995	79
Gus Dorazio #	04/07/1916	September 1969	69
Armando Sicilia	06/09/1916	31/12/1984	68
Joe Transparenti	21/09/1916	19/06/1999	83
Pete Galiano	07/01/1917	December 1980	63
Carmine Parella	16/01/1917	14/07/2009	92
Salvy Saban	19/01/1917	February 1969	52
Richie Gibbons	16/03/1917	21/04/1999	82
Ralph Vona	17/03/1917	September 1964	47
Savey Canadeo	27/04/1917	07/11/1993	76
Johnny Barbara	18/05/1917	December 1977	60
Chester Rico #	28/05/1917	June 1981	64
Carmine Fatta #	22/07/1917	29/05/2008	90
Joe Matisi	23/08/1917	07/07/1997	79
Johnny Aiello	27/08/1917	06/04/2005	87
Gaspar Abruzzo	10/10/1917	May 1981	63
Lou Laurie	19/11/1917	26/12/2002	85
Patsy Spataro	27/12/1917	August 1993	75
Mickey Doyle	1918	21/10/1950	32
Frank Wills	12/04/1918	30/07/1980	62
Vince Pimpinella	20/05/1918	23/03/1994	75
Lou Transparenti #	06/07/1918	21/08/2008	90
Carmen Notch #	17/07/1918	21/01/1991	72
Jerome Conforto	28/08/1918	15/07/1988	69
Eddie Ganns	06/11/1918	01/10/1961	42
Tommy Forte #	22/11/1918	15/01/2001	82
Vic Nardoni	27/11/1918	March 1974	55
Steve Belloise #	16/12/1918	February 1984	65
Matt Perfetti	28/12/1918	12/02/2002	83
Nick Fiorentino	02/01/1919	07/02/1999	80
Nick Castiglione	17/02/1919	17/04/1978	57
Frankie Rubino	14/05/1919	August 1980	61
Nick Spano	19/05/1919	July 1981	62
Lenny Mancini #	12/07/1919	29/11/2003	84
Tony Motisi #	17/09/1919	29/04/1997	77
Joe Muscato	22/11/1919	08/12/1977	58
Sammy Adragna	02/12/1919	25/10/1999	79
Pete Asero	1920	16/07/1940	20*
Al Guido #	1920	1961	41
Pat Valentino #	25/01/1920	25/07/2008	88

NAME	YEAR OF BIRTH	YEAR OF DEATH	AGE
Big Boy Carilli	12/02/1920	06/04/2006	85
Lee Campione	09/03/1920	22/04/2008	88
Al Priest #	03/06/1920	31/12/2001	80
Sammy Secreet #	13/06/1920	02/08/1999	79
Leo Micucci	02/09/1920	07/06/1997	76
George De Gidio	08/09/1920	08/05/2007	86
Jimmy Casino	10/10/1920	06/09/1999	78
Joey Iannotti	21/10/1920	13/01/2008	87
Victor Grupico	25/01/1921	20/01/1993	71
Lulu Constantino #	10/02/1921	06/07/1981	60
Al Tribuani #	15/02/1921	16/11/1995	74
Terry Young II #	27/04/1921	05/11/1967	46
Baby Galento	09/06/1921	February 1977	55
Ernie Petrone	29/07/1921	07/03/1997	75
Tom Altieri	02/08/1921	20/01/2006	84
Dom Baccala	16/08/1921	29/07/2006	84
Vince La Salva	01/09/1921	02/12/2009	88
Johnny Brenda	30/01/1922	12/03/2007	85
Billy Brown	04/03/1922	21/12/2001	79
Dom Sinibaldi	30/03/1922	December 1983	61
Joe Aurillo	14/06/1922	25/01/2008	85
Vinny Cidone	21/08/1922	19/11/2008	86
Frankie Carto	08/10/1922	22/02/2005	82
Jimmy Carollo	1923	November 1998	75
George La Rover	11/01/1923	02/03/1991	68
Phil Muscato #	15/03/1923	07/07/1991	68
Johnny Potenti	13/05/1923	March 1981	57
Bobby Zollo	31/07/1923	18/11/1988	65
Tami Mauriello #	18/09/1923	03/12/1999	76
Eddie Giosa #	13/03/1924	18/02/2007	83
Johnny Duke	18/05/1924	05/03/2006	81
Tommy Greb	19/08/1924	10/09/1987	63
Charley Fusari #	20/08/1924	01/11/1985	61
Freddie Russo #	03/10/1924	1987	62
Joey Angelo	1925	24/08/2005	80
Pat Vendrillo	27/01/1925	December 1981	56
Tommy Ciarlo	27/02/1925	24/05/1987	62
Santa Bucca	28/02/1925	31/01/1997	71
Ernie Durando #	07/04/1925	May 1992	67
Joe Curcio #	19/04/1925	December 1979	54
Pete Virgin #	27/06/1925	25/09/2004	79
Lou Filippo	01/12/1925	02/11/2009	83
Johnny Cesario #	11/12/1925	15/10/1997	71
Joe Rindone	01/02/1926	29/11/1998	72
Nick Barone #	12/06/1926	12/03/2006	79
Joe Griffo	26/12/1926	17/01/2004	77
Joey De John #	1927	09/05/2008	81
Eddie Compo #	04/01/1927	03/01/1998	71
Roland La Starza #	12/05/1927	30/09/2009	82
Rocky Castellani #	28/05/1927	31/08/2008	81
Tommy Bazzano	07/10/1927	02/09/1991	63
Tony Janiro #	27/10/1927	21/02/1985	58
Tony Pellone #	27/10/1927	05/07/1995	67

NAME	YEAR OF BIRTH	YEAR OF DEATH	AGE
Vic Cardell #	12/11/1927	31/08/1987	59
Dan Bucceroni #	03/12/1927	16/04/2008	80
Sam Butera	11/12/1927	15/02/2006	78
Archie De Vino	20/12/1927	22/01/2009	81
George Baltieri	22/02/1928	28/10/2005	79
Joe Miceli #	08/01/1929	19/07/2008	79
Eddie Marotta	22/02/1929	26/05/2002	73
Clem Florio	21/07/1929	25/05/2008	78
Carmine Fiore	05/08/1929	29/08/1992	63

Notes

# Denotes contender in the name column

* Denotes boxing fatality in the age column

This list contains seven boxing fatalities.

In some cases dates of birth and death vary depending on source checked.

Boxers are arranged in order of year of birth with the earliest dates first.

Boxers have been randomly selected from available source material.

a) **Average life expectancy of Italian American champions, title claimants, contenders and other boxers combined**

BOXER CLASS	TOTAL (number of boxers)	AGGREGATE AGE (Years)	AVERAGE LIFE EXPECTANCY (Years)
Champion/title claimant	51*	3575**	70.1
Contender	103	7427	72.1
Headliners & other category boxers	275	20060	72.9
TOTAL	**429**	**31062**	**72.4**

Notes

* Denotes that two champions are still alive. No data is available for Hugo Kelly.

** Denotes the current ages of two champions still living.

b) **Average life expectancy of Italian American professional boxers by decade**

DECADE (birth of boxer)	TOTAL (number of boxers)**	AGGREGATE AGE (Years)	AVERAGE LIFE EXPECTANCY (Years)
Pre 1890*	30	2092	69.7
1891–1900	80	5833	72.9
1901–10	125	8991	71.9
1911–20	132	9644	73
1921–30	61	4421	72.3
1931–40	1	81	81
OVERALL TOTAL	**429**	**31062**	**72.4**

Notes

* The pre-1890 category includes boxers born outside the ten-year period range.

** Total number of boxers includes champions, claimants and contenders and other professional boxers

APPENDIX XXI: ITALIAN AMERICANS IN WORLD BOXING TITLE BOUTS 1955–2014

DATE	WEIGHT	CHALLENGER	CHAMPION	RESULT	VENUE
14/03/56	Welterweight	Johnny Saxton	**Carmen Basilio**	Saxton WPts15	Chicago, IL
12/09/56	Welterweight	**Carmen Basilio**	Johnny Saxton	Basilio WKO9	Syracuse, NY

Voted 1956 Ring Magazine Fight of the Year.

DATE	WEIGHT	CHALLENGER	CHAMPION	RESULT	VENUE
22/02/57	Welterweight	Johnny Saxton	**Carmen Basilio**	Basilio WKO2	Cleveland, OH
23/09/57	Middleweight	**Carmen Basilio**	Sugar Ray Robinson	Basilio WPts15	New York City

Carmen Basilio relinquished the welterweight crown when he won the middleweight title from Robinson and a series of eliminators were organized to find a successor. Voted 1957 Ring Magazine Fight of the Year

DATE	WEIGHT	CHALLENGER	CHAMPION	RESULT	VENUE
29/10/57	Welterweight	**Tony De Marco**	Virgil Akins	Akins WKO14	Boston, MA
21/01/58	Welterweight	**Tony De Marco**	Virgil Akins	Akins WTKO12	Boston, MA

The above contests between Tony DeMarco-Virgil Akins were only recognized as 'world title' matches by the Massachusetts sanctioning body.

DATE	WEIGHT	CHALLENGER	CHAMPION	RESULT	VENUE
25/03/58	Middleweight	Sugar Ray Robinson	**Carmen Basilio**	Robinson WPts15	Chicago, IL

The NBA stripped Robinson of his title thirteen months later for his refusal to sign for a defense against arch rival Carmen Basilio. The sanctioning body proceeded to match Basilio and Gene Fullmer for their version of the vacant title. Voted 1958 Ring Magazine Fight of the Year.

DATE	WEIGHT	CHALLENGER	CHAMPION	RESULT	VENUE
06/06/58	Welterweight (Vacant)	**Vince Martinez**	Virgil Akins	Akins WTKO4	Los Angeles, CA
11/02/59	Lightweight	**Johnny Busso**	Joe Brown	Brown WPts15	Houston, TX
28/08/59	Middleweight (NBA Vacant)	**Carmen Basilio**	Gene Fullmer	Fullmer WKO14	San Francisco, CA
20/04/60	Middleweight (NBA)	**Joey Giardello**	Gene Fullmer	Draw Pts15	Bozeman, MT
29/06/60	Middleweight (NBA)	**Carmen Basilio**	Gene Fullmer	Fullmer WKO12	Sat Lake City
22/04/61	Middleweight	**Carmen Basilio**	Paul Pender	Pender WPts15	Boston, MA
20/10/62	Light-middleweight	**Joey Giambra**	Denny Moyer	Moyer WPts15	Portland, OR

This contest was for the inaugural vacant WBA world light-middleweight title.

DATE	WEIGHT	CHALLENGER	CHAMPION	RESULT	VENUE
16/02/63	Junior-lightweight	**Johnny Bizzarro**	Flash Elorde (Philippines)	Elorde WPts15	Manila, (Philippines)
01/06/63	Light-heavyweight	**Willie Pastrano**	Harold Johnson	Pastrano WPts15	Las Vegas, NV
07/12/63	Middleweight	**Joey Giardello**	Dick Tiger (Nigeria)	Giardello WPts15	New York City
10/04/64	Light-heavyweight	Gregorio Peralta (Argentina)	**Willie Pastrano**	Pastrano WKO6	New Orleans, LA
30/11/64	Light-heavyweight	Terry Downes (England)	**Willie Pastrano**	Pastrano WTKO11	Manchester, (England)
14/12/64	Middleweight	Rubin Carter	**Joey Giardello**	Giardello WPts15	Philadelphia, PA
30/03/65	Light-heavyweight	Jose Torres (Puerto Rico)	**Willie Pastrano**	Torres WKO9	New York City
21/10/65	Middleweight	Dick Tiger (Nigeria)	**Joey Giardello**	Tiger WPts15	New York City
20/06/66	Lightweight	**Johnny Bizzarro**	Carlos Ortiz (Puerto Rico)	Ortiz WTKO12	Pittsburgh, PA
22/01/69	Light-heavyweight	**Frank De Paula**	Bob Foster	Foster WKO1	New York City
03/12/70	Welterweight	**Billy Backus**	Jose Napoles (Cuba)	Backus WTKO4	Syracuse, NY

DATE	WEIGHT	CHALLENGER	CHAMPION	RESULT	VENUE
04/06/71	Welterweight	Jose Napoles (Cuba)	**Billy Backus**	Napoles WTKO8	Inglewood, CA
16/06/72	Welterweight	**Billy Backus**	Hedgemon Lewis	Lewis WPts15	Syracuse, NY
08/12/72	Welterweight	**Billy Backus**	Hedgemon Lewis	Lewis WPts15	Syracuse, NY

The Backus-Lewis contests were sanctioned as world title fights by the New York Boxing Commission only. This was a response to Napoles who refused to give a Backus a return match following the latter's twelve round win over top contender Danny McAloon in April 1972.

DATE	WEIGHT	CHALLENGER	CHAMPION	RESULT	VENUE
30/06/75	Middleweight (NBA)	**Tony Licata**	Carlos Monzon (Argentina)	Monzon WKO10	New York
23/05/76	Lightweight (WBA)	**Lou Bizzarro**	Roberto Duran (Panama)	Duran WKO14	Erie, PA
16/10/76	Light-welterweight (WBA)	**Tony Petronelli**	Wilfredo Benitez (Puerto Rico)	Benitez WTKO3	San Juan (Puerto Rico)
20/05/78	Welterweight (WBA)	**Billy Backus**	Pipino Cuevas (Mexico)	Cuevas WTKO2	Los Angeles, CA
09/09/78	Welterweight (WBA)	**Pete Ranzany**	Pipino Cuevas (Mexico)	Cuevas WTKO2	Sacramento, CA
15/09/78	Light-heavyweight (WBA)	**Mike Rossman**	Victor Galindez (Argentina)	Rossman WTKO13	New Orleans, LA
05/12/78	Light-heavyweight (WBA)	Aldo Traversaro (Italy)	**Mike Rossman**	Rossman WTKO6	Philadelphia, PA
15/04/79	Light-heavyweight (WBA)	Victor Galindez (Argentina)	**Mike Rossman**	Galindez WRT9	New Orleans, LA
30/06/79	Middleweight	**Vito Antuofermo**	Hugo Corro (Argentina)	Antuofermo WPts15	Monte Carlo, (Monaco)
04/08/79	Lightweight (WBA)	**Johnny Lira**	Ernesto Espana (Venezuela)	Espana WTKO9	Chicago, IL
30/11/79	Middleweight	Marvin Hagler	**Vito Antuofermo**	Draw Pts15	Las Vegas, NV
16/03/80	Middleweight	Alan Minter (England)	**Vito Antuofermo**	Minter WPts15	Las Vegas, NV
28/06/80	Middleweight	**Vito Antuofermo**	Alan Minter (England)	Minter WTKO8	London, (England)
13/06/81	Middleweight	**Vito Antuofermo**	Marvin Hagler	Hagler WRT4	Boston, MA
03/10/81	Lightweight (WBC)	**Ray Mancini**	Alexis Arguello (Nicaragua)	Arguello WTKO14	Atlantic City, NJ
07/11/81	Light-middleweight (WBA vacant)	**Rocky Fratto**	Tadashi Mihara (Japan)	Mihara WPts15	Rochester, NY
13/02/82	Lightweight (WBC)	**James Busceme**	Alexis Arguello (Nicaragua)	Arguello WTKO6	Beaumont, TX
08/05/82	Lightweight (WBA)	**Ray Mancini**	Arturo Frias	Mancini WTKO1	Las Vegas, NV
24/06//82	Lightweight (WBA)	Ernesto Espana (Venezuela)	**Ray Mancini**	Mancini WTKO6	Warren, OH
13/11/82	Lightweight (WBA)	Duk Koo Kim (South Korea)	**Ray Mancini**	Mancini WTKO14	Las Vegas, NV

Kim died four days later of his fight injuries. The WBC ordered all future bouts to be restricted to twelve rounds.

DATE	WEIGHT	CHALLENGER	CHAMPION	RESULT	VENUE
15/09/83	Lightweight (WBA)	Orlando Romero (Peru)	**Ray Mancini**	Mancini WKO9	New York
14/01/84	Lightweight (WBA)	Bobby Chacon	**Ray Mancini**	Mancini WTKO3	Reno, NV
29/01/84	Light-welterweight (WBC)	**Billy Costello**	Bruce Curry	Costello WTKO10	Beaumont, TX

DATE	WEIGHT	CHALLENGER	CHAMPION	RESULT	VENUE
15/04/84	Lightweight (WBC)	**Harry Arroyo**	Charlie Brown	Arroyo WTKO4	Atlantic City, NJ
01/06/84	Lightweight (WBA)	Livingstone Bramble (Virgin Islands)	**Ray Mancini**	Bramble WTKO14	Buffalo, NY
16/07/84	Light-welterweight (WBC)	Ronnie Shields	**Billy Costello**	Costello WPts15	New York
01/09/84	Lightweight (WBC)	Charlie Brown	**Harry Arroyo**	Arroyo WTKO8	Youngstown, OH
03/11/84	Light-welterweight (WBC)	Saoul Mamby (Jamaica)	**Billy Costello**	Costello WPts15	New York
12/01/85	Lightweight (WBC)	Terrence Alli (Guyana)	**Harry Arroyo**	Arroyo WTKO11	Atlantic City, NJ
16/02/85	Light-welterweight (WBC)	Leroy Haley	**Billy Costello**	Costello WPts12	New York
16/02/85	Lightweight (WBA)	**Ray Mancini**	Livingstone Bramble (Virgin Islands)	Bramble WPts15	Reno, NV
06/04/85	Lightweight (WBC)	Jimmy Paul	**Harry Arroyo**	Paul WPts15	Atlantic City, NJ
29/06/85	Super-middleweight (IBF)	**Vinnie Curto**	Chong-Pal Park (South Korea)	Park WPts15	Seoul, (South Korea)
22/08/85	Light-welterweight (WBC)	Lonnie Smith	**Billy Costello**	Smith WTKO8	New York
11/04/86	Super-middleweight (IBF)	**Vinnie Curto**	Chong-Pal Park (South Korea)	Park WKO15	Los Angeles, CA
06/09/86	Light-welterweight (WBA)	**Brian Brunette**	Patrizio Oliva (Italy)	Oliva WTKO3	Naples, (Italy)
06/09/86	Light-heavyweight (IBF)	**Bobby Czyz**	Slobodan Kacar ((Yugoslavia)	Czyz WTKO5	Las Vegas, NV
26/12/86	Light-heavyweight (IBF)	David Sears	**Bobby Czyz**	Czyz WKO1	West Orange, NJ
21/02/87	Light-heavyweight (IBF)	Willie Edwards	**Bobby Czyz**	Czyz WKO2	Atlantic City, NJ
04/05/87	Light-heavyweight (IBF)	Jim McDonald	**Bobby Czyz**	Czyz WTKO6	Atlantic City, NJ
02/06/87	Lightweight (IBF)	**Vinny Pazienza**	Greg Haugen	Pazienza WPts15	Providence, RI
29/10/87	Light-heavyweight (IBF)	Charles Williams	**Bobby Czyz**	Williams WRTD9	Las Vegas, NV
06/12/88	Lightweight (IBF)	Greg Haugen	**Vinny Pazienza**	Haugen WPts15	Atlantic City, NJ
07/11/88	Light-welterweight (WBC)	**Vinny Pazienza**	Roger Mayweather	Mayweather WPts12	Las Vegas, NV
08/11/88	Middleweight (WBA)	**Doug DeWitt**	Sumbu Kalambay (Italy)	Kalambay WTKO7	Monte Carlo, (Monaco)
04/03/89	Light-heavyweight (WBA)	**Bobby Czyz**	Virgil Hill	Hill WPts12	Bismarck, ND
06/03/89	Light-welterweight (WBO vacant)	**Ray Mancini**	Hector Camacho (Puerto Rico)	Camacho WPts12	Reno, NV
18/04/89	Middleweight (WBO)	**Doug DeWitt**	Robbie Sims	DeWitt WPts12	Atlantic City, NJ

This bout was for the inaugural vacant WBO world middleweight title.

DATE	WEIGHT	CHALLENGER	CHAMPION	RESULT	VENUE
25/06/89	Light-heavyweight (IBF)	**Bobby Czyz**	Charles Williams	Williams WTKO10	Atlantic City, NJ
15/01/90	Middleweight (WBO)	Matthew Hilton (Canada)	**Doug DeWitt**	DeWitt WRTD11	Atlantic City, NJ

DATE	WEIGHT	CHALLENGER	CHAMPION	RESULT	VENUE
03/02/90	Light-welterweight (WBO)	**Vinny Pazienza**	Hector Camacho (Puerto Rico)	Camacho WPts12	Atlantic City, NJ
29/04/90	Middleweight (WBO)	Nigel Benn (England)	**Doug DeWitt**	Benn WTKO8	Atlantic City, NJ
01/12/90	Light-welterweight (WBA)	**Vinny Pazienza**	Loreto Garza	Garza WDSQ11	Sacramento, CA
09/03/91	Cruiserweight (WBA)	**Bobby Czyz**	Robert Daniels	Czyz WPts12	Atlantic City, NJ
09/08/91	Cruiserweight (WBA)	Bash Ali (Nigeria)	**Bobby Czyz**	Czyz WPts12	Atlantic City, NJ
01/10/91	Light-middleweight (WBA)	**Vinny Pazienza**	Gilbert Dele (France)	Pazienza WTKO12	Providence, RI
08/02/92	Middleweight (IBF)	**Dave Tiberi**	James Toney	Toney WPts12	Atlantic City, NJ

A controversial decision. Dave Tiberi never fought again.

DATE	WEIGHT	CHALLENGER	CHAMPION	RESULT	VENUE
08/05/92	Cruiserweight (WBA)	Don Lalonde (Canada)	**Bobby Czyz**	Czyz WPts12	Las Vegas, NV

Bobby Czyz forfeited his version of the cruiserweight title in September 1993 due to inactivity.

DATE	WEIGHT	CHALLENGER	CHAMPION	RESULT	VENUE
09/06/92	Light-middleweight (WBO)	**Pat Lawlor**	John David Jackson	Jackson WRTD9	San Francisco, CA
28/01/95	Super-featherweight (WBC)	**Fred Liberatore**	Gabriel Ruelas (Mexico)	Ruelas WRTD2	Las Vegas, NV
20/05/95	Light-heavyweight (WBO)	**Paul Carlo**	Dariusz Michalczewski (Poland)	Michalcczewski WKO4	Hamburg, (Germany)
24/06/95	Super-middleweight (IBF)	**Vinny Pazienza**	Roy Jones Jr	Jones Jr WTKO6	Atlantic City, NJ
26/08/95	Welterweight (WBO)	**Tony Gannarelli**	Eamonn Loughran (Northern Ireland)	Loughran WTKO6	Belfast, (Northern Ireland)
30/09/95	Cruiserweight (WBO)	**Marc Randazzo**	Ralf Rocchigiani (Germany)	Rocchigiani WPts12	Hannover, (Germany)
3/03/96	Cruiserweight (WBA)	**Brian La Spada**	Nate Miller	Miller WTKO9	Miami, FL
02/12/97	Super-middleweight (IBF)	**Joey De Grandis**	Charles Brewer	Brewer WPts12	Philadelphia, PA
20/08/99	Lightweight (Vacant IBF)	Israel Cardona	**Paul Spadafora**	Spadafora WPts12	Chester, VA
17/12/99	Lightweight (IBF)	Renato Cornett (Australia)	**Paul Spadafora**	Spadafora WTKO11	Pittsburgh, PA
15/01/2000	Light-heavyweight (WBA/WBC/IBF)	**David Telesco**	Roy Jones Jr	Jones Jr WPts12	New York City
03/03/2000	Lightweight (IBF)	Victoriano Sosa (Dominican Republic)	**Paul Spadafora**	Spadafora WPts12	Verona, NY
06/05/2000	Lightweight (IBF)	Mike Griffith	**Paul Spadafora**	Spadafora WTD10	Pittsburgh, PA
16/12/2000	Lightweight (IBF)	Billy Irwin (Canada)	**Paul Spadafora**	Spadafora WPts12	Pittsburgh, PA
08/05/2001	Lightweight (IBF)	Joel Perez	**Paul Spadafora**	Spadafora WPts12	Pittsburgh, PA
01/03/2002	Super-middleweight (WBC)	**Vinny Pazienza**	Eric Lucas	Lucas WPts12	Mashantucket, CT

Notes

Chapter 1

1. "The Renaissance, Floats, Symbols and Colors 1400–1500," http://www.comune.siena.it (accessed September 20, 2005).

2. "Battling at the Bridge: Stick Fights and Boxing Spectacles in Renaissance Venice", p. 4, http://www.thehaca.com (accessed June 15, 2005).

3. "Boxing in Italy – An Antiquity," *Ring Magazine*, March 1926, p. 21.

4. http://www.comune.siena.it (accessed September 20, 2005).

5. Denis Mack Smith, *Mussolini* (Milan, 1981), pp. 128–131, 149; Carole C. Gallucci and Ellen Nerenberg, *Writing Beyond Fascism: Cultural Resistance in the Life and Words of Alba de Cespedes* (Madison, NJ, 2000), p. 66.

6. John Bodnar, *The Transplanted: A History of Immigrants in America* (Bloomington, 1985), p. 20, quoting John W. Briggs, *An Italian Passage: Immigrants to Three American Cities 1840–1930* (New Haven, CT, 1978), pp. 2–12.

7. *Ibid.*, quoting Donna Gabaccia, "Houses and People: Sicilians in Sicily and New York," Ph.D. dissertation, University of Michigan, 1979, pp. 125–127.

8. Thomas Kessner, *The Golden Door: Italian and Jewish Immigrant Mobility in New York City 1880–1915* (New York, 1977), pp. 28, 31–33.

9. Maldwyn Jones, *Destination America* (London, 1976), p. 199; Gary Ross Mormino, *Immigrants on the Hill: Italian Americans in St Louis 1882–1982* (Urbana, 1982), p. 96.

10. Gene P. Veronese, "Anti-Italian Sentiment in America," Chapter 6 in *Italian-Americans and Their Communities of Cleveland* (Cleveland, 1977), pp. 141–142, quoting E. Ross, *World's Week*, Vol. 27, No 4, August 1914, pp. 278–279, available at http://www.clevelandmemory.org/italians (accessed October 6, 2003).
11. *Ibid.*, p. 128 quoting *New York Times*, March 16–17, 1891.
12. David Pacchioli, "Dark Legacy," http://news.psu.edu/story/140775/2004/05/01/research/dark-legacy (accessed November 14, 2004).
13. Veronese, "Anti-Italian Sentiment in America," pp. 123–124, quoting James Zander, *American Minority Relations*, quoted by Richard Gambino, *Blood of My Blood: The Dilemma of the Italian Americans* (New York, 1975), pp. 253–254, available at http://www.clevelandmemory.org/ italians (accessed October 6, 2003).
14. *Ibid.*, pp. 130–131, quoting Salvatore LaGumina, *Wop!: A Documentary History of Anti-Italian Discrimination in the United States* (New York, 1973), p. 72.
15. Everett Skehan, *Rocky Marciano* (London, 1989), p. 5.
16. Richard Gambino, *Blood of My Blood: The Dilemma of the Italian Americans* (New York, 1975), pp. 119–123.
17. Jerre Mangione and Ben Morreale, *La Storia: Five Centuries of the Italian American Experience* (New York, 1992), p. 129.
18. Personal interview with Enrico Vecchione, New York City, September 15, 1995.

Chapter 2

1. John Bodnar, *The Transplanted: A History of Immigrants in America* (Bloomington, 1985), p. 76, quoting Steven Dubnoff, "The Family and Absence From Work," Ph.D. dissertation, Brandeis University, 1976, pp. 254–258.
2. Gene P. Veronese, "The Distant Magnet: Italian Immigration to America 1570–1970," Chapter 5 in *Italian-Americans and Their Communities of Cleveland* (Cleveland, 1977), p. 109, quoting Reports to the US Immigration Commission 1912, available at http://www.clevelandmemory.org/italians (accessed October 6, 2003).
3. Personal interview with Hank Kaplan, Miami, August 17, 2005.
4. Don Majeski, "A History of Boxing Economics Part III," *International Boxing Digest Magazine*, August 1998, p. 52.
5. Veronese, "The Distant Magnet," p. 109, quoting from Reports to US Immigration Commission 1912; Steven A. Riess, "Sport and the American Dream: A Review Essay," *Journal of Social History*, 1980, Vol. 14, p. 297.

6. *Chicago Daily Tribune*, September 30, 1903, p. 6.

7. *National Police Gazette*, December 11, 1920, p. 14.

8. *The All New Ring 1980 Record Book* (New York, 1980); *New York Times*, September 16, 27, 28, 1937.

9. "Interview with NBA President Fred Saddy," *Ring Magazine*, September 1950, pp. 5, 36; Willie Pep and Robert Sacchi, *Willie Pep Remembers Friday's Heroes* (New York, 1973), p. 51.

10. Silvano M. Tomasi and Madeleine Engel, *The Italian Experience in the United States* (New York, 1970), p. 127 quoting Jeremiah W. Jenks and W. Jett Lauck, *The Immigration Problem: A Study of American Immigrant Conditions* (New York, 1917) and Robert F. Foerster, *Italian Emigration of our Times* (Cambridge, 1919).

11. Peter Heller, *In This Corner. . . ! Forty World Champions Tell their Stories* (London, 1989), p. 48.

12. Humbert Nelli, *The Italians in Chicago: A Study in Ethnic Mobility 1880–1930* (New York, 1970), p. 67, quoting Frank Beck, *The Italian in Chicago: Bulletin of the Department of Public Welfare* (Chicago, February 1919).

13. Alan M. Kraut, *The Huddled Masses: The Immigrant in American Society 1880–1921* (Arlington Heights, 1982), p. 139, quoting Thomas Kessner, *The Golden Door: Italian and Jewish Immigrant Mobility in New York City 1880–1915* (New York, 1977).

14. Frank Edwards, "Battling Reddy – Veteran East Sider, NY fought world's best bantams and feathers", *Ring Magazine*, October 1949, p. 27.

15. Gary Ross Mormino and George Pozzetta, *The Immigrant World of Ybor City 1885–1985: Italians and their Latin Neighbours* (Urbana, 1987), p. 288, quoting Miriam Cohen, *Changing Educational Strategies*.

16. Telephone interview with John De John, September 16, 1995.

17. Nelli, *Italians in Chicago*, p. 153.

18. Tomasi and Engel, *The Italian Experience*, p. 60.

19. Nelli, *Italians in Chicago*, Chapter II, "What it means to be living in a slum", quoting Anthony Sorrentino, p. 68.

20. Nathan Glazer and Daniel Moynihan, *Beyond the Melting Pot: The Negroes, Puerto Ricans, Jews, Italians and Irish of New York City* (Cambridge, MA, 1963), p. 199.

21. Richard Alba, Albert J. Raboteau and Josh DeWind, *Immigration and Religion in America: Comparative and Historical Perspectives* (New York, 2009), p. 44.

22. Personal interview with Angelo Dundee, Miami, August 17, 2005.

23.   Telephone interview with Tony De Marco, September 25, 1995.

Chapter 3

1.   Personal interview with Joey Cilione, New York City, September 15, 1995.
2.   Personal correspondence from Vince Colitti confirms Jim Flynn's story, October 30, 2005, p. 5.
3.   Personal interview with Angelo Dundee, Miami, August 17, 2005; Angelo Dundee and Mike Winters, *I Only Talk Winning* (London, 1988), p. 28.
4.   Carmelo Bazzano letter and sample research paper to boxing historian Hank Kaplan, March 31, 1992.
5.   *New York Herald,* June 9, 1919, p. 7.
6.   Telephone interview with John De John, September 16, 1995.
7.   *Chicago Daily Tribune,* December 30, 1909.
8.   *Philadelphia Evening Public Ledger,* August 24, 1916, p. 10.
9.   Telephone interview with Willie Pep, September 23, 1995.
10.   Everett M. Skehan, *Rocky Marciano* (London, 1983), pp. 97–98.
11.   H.L. Mencken, *The American Language* (New York, 1936), p. 493.
12.   Michael La Sorte, *La Merica: Images of Italian Greenhorn Experience,* (Philadelphia, 2003), pp.154–156.

Chapter 4

1.   Elliott Gorn, *The Manly Art: The Lives and Times of The Great Bare-Knuckle Champions* (London, 1986), p. 46.
2.   Herbert Asbury, *The Gangs of New York* (London, 2002), p. 265.
3.   *National Police Gazette,* August 22, 1903, p. 3.
4.   Casper Leon data from *National Police Gazette,* April 28, 1897 and December 3, 1921, p. 7; *Ring Magazine,* March 1925, p. 19; July 1926, pp. 6, 9; July 1943 pp. 8, 42; *New York Times,* May 9, 1926.
5.   *National Police Gazette,* September 30, 1905, p. 10.
6.   Wilbur Wood, "Boxers of Italian Descent Invade Realm of Fistiana in Ever Increasing Numbers", *New York Herald,* January 27, 1924, p. 3; *Boxing,* May 4, 1921, p. 182.
7.   Ted Carroll, "The Golden Age of Bantamweight Boxing", *Ring Magazine,* December 1953, pp. 12–13.
8.   *New York Times,* January 12, 1935, p. 20.
9.   "Willie was a Genius with Boxing Gloves", *Boxing News,* July 24, 1964, pp. 8–10; Joe Duffy, "Epic Moment in a Legendary Career", *The Journal Inquirer,* February 9, 1994, p. 8.

10. Gene P. Veronese, "Anti-Italian Sentiment in America," Chapter 6 in *Italian-Americans and Their Communities of Cleveland* (Cleveland, 1977), p.154, available at http://www.clevelandmemory.org/Italians (accessed October 6, 2003); National Italian American Foundation.
11. Thomas Hauser and Stephen Brunt, *Italian Stallions: Heroes of Boxing's Glory Days* (Toronto, 2003), p. 11.
12. Nat Fleischer, *Ring Record Book and Encyclopaedia* (New York, 1959), pp. 477–801, 903–919.

Chapter 5
1. S. Kirson Weinberg and Henry Arond, "The Occupational Culture of the Boxer," *American Journal of Sociology*, Vol. 57, March 1952, pp. 460–469.
2. Thomas Jenkins, "Changes in Ethnic and Racial Representation in Professional Boxers: A Study in Ethnic Succession," Master's dissertation, University of Chicago, 1955.
3. Telephone interview with Barry Hugman, December 8, 1995.
4. "Interview with NBA President Fred Saddy," *Ring Magazine*, September 1950, p. 5.
5. Bernard Postal, *The Encyclopaedia of Jews in Sports* (New York, 1965), p. 117; Ken Blady, *The Jewish Boxers Hall of Fame* (New York, 1988), p. 209; Allen Bodner, *When Boxing was a Jewish Sport* (Westport, CT, 1997), p. 2; Bert Sugar, *The Ring All New 1980 Boxing Record Book* (New York, 1980), p. 434; http://www.jewishsports.net; Harold Ribalow, *The Jew in American Sports* (New York, 1948), p. 98.
6. Robert Strauss, "In this Corner," *The Inquirer*, December 30, 2004, http://articles.philly.com/2004-12-30/news/25387146_1_boxing-maccabee-tribe-of-jewish-warriors (accessed 4 June 2014); Nat Bodian, "Remembering Newarkers from the Golden Age of the Jewish Boxer," December 28, 2004, http://newarkmemories.com/memories/540.php (accessed February 28, 2005); Bodner, *When Boxing was a Jewish Sport*, pp. 10–11.
7. Peter Levine, *Ellis Island to Ebbets Field: Sport and the American Jewish Experience* (New York, 1992), Chapter 10, pp. 190–215, quoting from Heywood Broun and George Britt, *Christians Only: A Study in Prejudice* (New York, 1931) and Stephen Steinberg, "How Jewish Quotas Began," *Commentary*, September 1971, pp. 67–76.
8. Levine, *Ellis Island to Ebbets Field*, p. 91.
9. Lionel Maldonado and Joan Moore, *Urban Ethnicity in the United States: New Immigrants and Old Minorities* (Beverley Hills, CA, 1985), p. 251.

10. Boxing Illustrated, June 1950.

11. Personal interview with Hank Kaplan, Miami, August 17, 2005.

12. S.A. Riess, *City Games: The Evolution of American Urban Society and Rise of Sports* (Urbana, 1991), p. 116.

13. Jeffrey Sammons, *Beyond the Ring: The Role of Boxing in American Society* (Urbana, 1990) pp. 139–141, quoting from *New York Times*, March 8, 1952, *IBC vs. US cited in Carbo Hearings*.

14. Levine, *Ellis Island to Ebbets Field*, p. 188.

15. Sammons, *Beyond the Ring*, p. 90.

16. Personal interview with Dennie Mancini, London, July 25, 1995.

Chapter 6

1. *New York Times*, February 18, 1900.

2. Jerre Mangione and Ben Morreale, *La Storia: Five Centuries of the Italian Experience* (New York, 1992), p. 331.

3. Gary Ross Mormino, "The Playing Fields of St. Louis: Italian Immigrants and Sports 1925–41," *Journal of Sport History*, Vol. 9, No. 2, Summer 1982, p. 13.

4. William J. Baker, *Playing With God: Religion and Modern Sport* (Cambridge, MA, 2007), p. 178.

5. Thomas Jenkins, "Changes in Ethnic and Racial Representation among Professional Boxers: A Study in Ethnic Succession," Master's dissertation, University of Chicago, 1955, pp. 102, 112, 123.

6. Gerald R. Gems, Linda J. Borish and Gertrud Pfister, *Sports in American History: From Colonization to Globalization* (Champaign, IL, 2008), p. 233.

7. Jenkins, "Changes in Ethnic and Racial Representation," p. 60.

8. "Religion: The Bishop's 25th", *Time*, May 11, 1953, http://content.time.com/time/magazine/article/0,9171,935339,00.html (accessed June 4, 2014).

9. Robert Orsi, *The Madonna of 115th Street: Faith and Community in Italian Harlem 1880–1950* (New Haven, CT, 2002), p. 35.

10. Mormino, "The Playing Fields of St Louis," p. 8.

11. Martin Sánchez-Jankowski, *Islands in the Street: Gangs and American Urban Society* (Berkeley, CA, 1992), pp. 24–26.

12. Frederick Thrasher, *The Gang: A Study of 1,313 Gangs in Chicago* (Chicago, 1963), pp. 13, 48, 52, 60.

13. Thomas J. Ferraro, *Feeling Italian: The Art of Ethnicity in America*, (New York, 2005), p. 220.

14. William Foote Whyte, *Street Corner Society: The Social Structure of an Italian Slum* (Chicago, 1943), p. 273.

15. Telephone interview with Tony De Marco, September 25, 1995.

16. Nathan Glazer and Daniel P. Moynihan, *Beyond the Melting Pot: The Negroes, Puerto Ricans, Jews, Italians and Irish of New York City* (Cambridge, MA, 1968), pp.188–189, quoting Herbert J. Gans, *Urban Villagers: Group and Class in the Life of Italian Americans* (New York, 1962) and Robert Foerster, *The Italian Emigration of our Times* (Cambridge, MA, 1919).

17. Telephone interview with Joey Fariello, New York City, September 24, 1995.

18. Dennis Marconi, email message to author, December 23, 1999.

19. *Chicago Daily Tribune*, September 2, 1902 and November 26, 1902.

20. *Bridgeport Herald*, July 17, 1904; *Newcastle News*, May 5, 1905; *National Police Gazette*, 1905; *Utica Daily Press*, November 3, 1956, p. 6.

21. *Philadelphia Evening Public Ledger*, March 29, 1917; Christopher Sterba, *Good Americans: Italian and Jewish Immigrants during the First World War* (New York, 2003), p. 136.

22. Jenkins, "Changes in Ethnic and Racial Representation," p. 55, quoting Caroline F. Ware, *Greenwich Village, 1920–1930* (Boston, 1935).

23. "Settlement Movement Provides Athletics for the Working Boys," *New York Times*, May 12, 1907, http://query.nytimes.com/gst/abstract.html?res=980CEFDE1539E733A25751C1A9639C946697D6CFS (accessed March 5, 2011).

24. Harry P. Kraus, *The Settlement House Movement in New York City 1886–1914* (New York, 1980), pp. 223–224.

25. Michael T. Isenberg, *John L. Sullivan and His Times* (London, 1988), pp. 39–59; Madelon Powers, *Faces Along the Bar: Lore and Order in the Workingman's Saloon 1870–1920* (Chicago, 1999), p. 152.

26. Carlo Rotella, *Good with their Hands: Boxers, Bluesmen and Other Characters of the Rust Belt* (Berkeley, CA, 2002), pp. 23–24.

Chapter 7

1. Gratiolet quote taken from John Milton Hoberman, *Darwin's Athletes: How Sport has Damaged Black America and Preserved the Myth of Race* (New York, 1997), p. 189.

2. *New York Evening World*, Night Edition, October 21, 1903, p. 12.

3. Patrick B. Miller, "The Anatomy of Scientific Racism: Racialist Responses to Black Athletic Achievement," *Journal of Sport History*, Spring 1998, pp. 129–134; Hoberman, *Darwin's Athletes*, pp. 189, 193, 214.

4. *Boxing*, May 4, 1921, p. 182.
5. DeWitt Van Court, "American Boxers Lead World in Gameness", *Ring Magazine*, October 1923, p. 14.
6. Wilbur Wood, "Boxers of Italian Descent Invade Realm of Fistiana in Ever Increasing Circles", *New York Herald*, January 27, 1924, p. 3.
7. Michael Oriard, *King Football: Sport and Spectacle in the Golden Age of Radio, Newsreels, Movies and Magazines, the Weekly and the Daily Press* (Chapel Hill, NC, 2001), p. 256, quoting Elmer D. Mitchell, "Racial Traits in Athletics," *American Physical Education Review*, Vol. 27, March, April, May 1922, pp. 93–99, 147–52, 197–206.
8. Thomas Hauser and Stephen Brunt, *Italian Stallions: Heroes of Boxing's Glory Days* (Toronto, 2003), p. 11.
9. Personal interview with Angelo Dundee, Miami, August 17, 2005.
10. Personal interview with Hank Kaplan, Miami, August 17, 2005.
11. Toynbee quote taken from *Ring Magazine*, August 1950.
12. David E. Ruth, *Inventing the Public Enemy: The Gangster in American Culture 1918–34* (Chicago, 1996), p.9 2; Kevin P. Murphy, *Political Manhood: Real Bloods, Mollycoddles and Politics of Progressive Era Reform* (New York, 2008), pp. 83–84.
13. Gail Bederman, *Manliness and Civilization: A Cultural History of Gender and Race in the United States 1880–1917* (Chicago, 1995), pp. 11–15.
14. Hardwin Ferrand, "Fighting for his Family," *Arena Boxing Magazine*, October 1929, pp. 24–25.
15. Russell Sullivan, *Rocky Marciano: The Rock of our Times* (Urbana, IL, 2002), pp. 19–20.
16. Joe Sarge Kinney and Adolph Caso, *Young Rocky: A True Story of Attilio Rocky Castellani* (Brookline Village, MA, 1985), pp. 62–63.
17. Gary B Youmans, *The Onion Picker: Carmen Basilio and Boxing in the 1950s* (Syracuse, NY, 2007), back cover.
18. Jake La Motta with Joseph Carter and Peter Savage, *Raging Bull: The True Story of a Champ* (New York, 1980), pp. 64–65.
19. Telephone interview with Jake La Motta, September 20, 1995.
20. Richard Gambino, *Blood of My Blood: The Dilemma of the Italian Americans* (Toronto, 2000), p. 130.
21. Telephone interview with Carmen Basilio, September 21, 1995.
22. Personal interview with Dennie Mancini, London, July 25, 1995.
23. Telephone interview with Steve Corbo, August 7, 2005.
24. Personal interview with Herb Goldman, New York City, September 15, 1995.

25. Thomas Jenkins, "Changes in Ethnic and Racial Representation among Professional Boxers: A Study in Ethnic Succession," Master's dissertation, University of Chicago, 1955, p. 126.
26. Personal interview with Hank Kaplan, Miami, August 17, 2005.

Chapter 8
1. Ciro Poppiti's assertion that Italians made a bigger contribution in American football is contained in George Kirsch, Othello Harris and Claire E. Nolte, *Encyclopaedia of Ethnicity and Sports in the USA* (Westport CT, 2000); Lawrence Baldassaro's claim that Italians made the biggest impact in baseball is contained in the essay "Before Joe D: Early Italian Americans in the Major Leagues," in Lawrence Baldassaro and Richard A. Johnson (eds), *The American Game: Baseball and Ethnicity* (Carbondale, IL, 2004), pp. 92–115; Joe DiMaggio data taken from Donald Dewey and Nicholas Acocella, *The Biographical History of Baseball*, (New York, 1995), pp. 113–115.
2. Gary Ross Mormino and George Pozzetta, *The Immigrant World of Ybor City 1885–1985: Italians and their Latin Neighbors* (Urbana, 1987), pp.188–192, quoting Steven Riess, *Touching Base: Professional Baseball and American Culture in the Progressive Era* (Westport, CT, 1980).
3. Steven A Riess, *The American Sporting Experience: A Historical Anthology of Sports in America* (New York, 1984), p. 297.
4. Mormino and Pozzetta, *The Immigrant World of Ybor City*, p. 251. Data taken from scrapbook belonging to Arturo Camero in Ybor City.
5. Baldassaro and Johnson, *The American Game*, pp. 92–115.
6. Steven Riess, *Touching Base: Professional Baseball and American Culture in the Progressive Era* (Westport, CT, 1980), pp. 191,192.
7. Dan Hunt, Dan Holmes and Kirk Robinson, "The History of African Americans in Organized Baseball," October 3, 2005, http://www.thebaseballpage.com (accessed February 10, 2006).
8. New research data computed in 2014 by the author from http://www.baseballcube.com, http://www.baseball-almanac.com and http://www.baseballlibrary.com.
9. *Time Magazine*, May 30, 1938.
10. Thomas Jenkins, "Changes in Ethnic and Racial Representation Among Professional Boxers: A Study in Ethnic Succession," Master's dissertation, University of Chicago, 1955, pp. 102–104.
11. *New York Times*, May 3, 1932, p. 28
12. Personal interview with Arthur Mercante, New York City, July 28, 2005.

13.   Personal correspondence from Vince Colitti, September 12, 2007; *Auburn Citizen*, September 14, 1982, p. 12.

14.   Michael Oriard, *King Football: Sport and Spectacle in the Golden Age of Radio and Newsreels, Movies and Magazines, the Weekly and Daily Press* (Chapel Hill, NC, 2001), pp. 33–34.

Chapter 9

1.   Gary Ross Mormino, *Immigrants on the Hill: Italian Americans in St Louis 1882–1982* (Urbana, 1982), p. 92, quoting from J.S. Woodworth, *Strangers within our Gates* (Toronto, 1909). The Italian brought $13 and the English and German immigrants brought $64 and $58 respectively.

2.   S. Kirson Weinberg and Henry Arond, "The Occupational Culture of the Boxer," *American Journal of Sociology*, Vol. 57, March 1952, pp. 49–67.

3.   *The Story of Raging Bull*, BBC Radio 5 Live, December 21, 2010, 9.00 p.m.

Bibliography

Books

Alba, Richard, Albert J. Raboteau and Josh DeWind, *Immigration and Religion in America: Comparative and Historical Perspectives*, New York: New York University Press, 2009.

Anderson, Dave. *Ringmasters: Great Boxing Trainers Talk about Their Art*, London: Robson, 1991.

Andrews, T.S. *World's Annual Sporting Records*, Milwaukee, WI: TS Andrews Record Book Co. 1906–34.

Asbury, Herbert. *The Gangs of New York*, London: Arrow, 2002.

Ashe, Arthur. *A Hard Road to Glory: The African American Athlete in Boxing*, New York: Amistad Press, 1988.

Baker, William J. *Playing With God: Religion and Modern Sport*, Cambridge, MA: Harvard University Press, 2007.

Baldassaro, Lawrence and Richard A. Johnson. *The American Game: Baseball and Ethnicity*, Carbondale, IL: Southern Illinois University Press, 2002.

Ballarati, Giuseppe. *I campioni del passato, Vol. 1*, Roma, Italia: Ballarati, 1983.

Bederman, Gail. *Manliness and Civilization: A Cultural History of Gender and Race in the United States 1880–1917*, Chicago, IL: University of Chicago Press, 1995.

Blady, Ken. *The Jewish Boxers Hall of Fame*, New York: Shapolsky Books, 1988.

Bodnar, John. *The Transplanted: A History of Immigrants in Urban America*, Bloomington, IN: Indiana University Press, 1985.

Bodner, Allen. *When Boxing was a Jewish Sport*, Westport, CT: Praeger, 1997.

Bondanella, Peter. *Hollywood Italians: Dagos, Palookas, Romeos, Wise Guys and Sopranos*, New York: Continuum International, 2004.

Brady, Jim. *Boxing Confidential*, Manchester, UK: Milo, 2002.

Candeloro, Dominic. *Chicago's Italians: Immigrants, Ethnics, Americans*, Mount Pleasant, SC: Arcadia, 2003.

Cavaioli, Frank, Angela Danzi and Salvatore J. LaGumina. *Italian Americans and Their Public and Private Life*, Staten Island, NY: The American Italian Historical Association, 1993.

Court, Dewitt Van. *The Making of Champions in California*, Los Angeles, CA: Premier Printing Co, 1926.

Davis, R.C. *The War of the Fists: Popular Culture and Public Violence in Late Renaissance Venice*, New York: Oxford University Press, 1994.

De Marco, William M. *Ethnics and Enclaves: Boston's Italian North End*, Ann Arbor, MI: UMI, 1981.

Dewey, Donald and Nicholas Acocella. *The Biographical History of Baseball*, New York: Carroll & Graf, 1995.

Dundee, Angelo with Mike Winters. *I Only Talk Winning*, London: Robson, 1988.

Duranti, Emilio. *I grandi della boxe italiana*, Firenze, Italia: Editoriale Olimpia, 1966.

Fair, James. R. *Give Him to the Angels: The Story of Harry Greb*, New York: Smith and Durrell, 1946.

Ferraro, Thomas J. *Feeling Italian: The Art of Ethnicity in America*, New York: New York University Press, 2005.

Fitch, Jerry. *Cleveland's Greatest Fighters of All Time*, Mount Pleasant, SC: Arcadia, 2002.

Fleischer, Nat. *Black Dynamite: The Story of the Negro in the Prize Ring From 1782–1938 Vol. I–V*, New York: Ring Publishers, 1938.

Fleischer, Nat. *Ring Record Book and Encyclopaedia*, New York: Ring Publishing, 1941–80.

Freundlich, Larry. *Reaching for the Stars: A Celebration of Italian Americans in Major League Baseball*, New York: Ballantine, 2003.

Gallucci, Carole and Ellen Nerenberg. *Writing beyond Fascism: Cultural Resistance in the Life and Words of Alba de Cespedes*, Madison, NJ: Fairleigh Dickinson University Press, 2000.

Gambino, Richard. *Blood of My Blood: The Dilemma of the Italian Americans*, Toronto: Guernica Editions, 2000.

Gans, Herbert. *Urban Villagers: Group and Class in the Life of Italian American's*, New York: Free Press of Glencoe, 1962.

Gems, Gerald R., Linda J. Borish and Gertrud Pfister, *Sports in American History: From Colonization to Globalization*, Champaign, IL: Human Kinetics, 2008.

Giambra, Joey and Fred Villani. *The Uncrowned Champion*, Las Vegas, NV: Joey One Inc, 1979.

Glazer, Nathan and Daniel P. Moynihan. *Beyond the Melting Point: The Negroes, Puerto Ricans, Jews, Italians and the Irish of New York City*, Cambridge, MA: MIT Press, 1963.

Gorn, Elliott. J. *The Manly Art: The Lives and Times of the Great Bare-Knuckle Champions*, London: Robson, 1986.

Graziano, Rocky with Ralph Corsel. *Somebody Down Here Likes Me Too*, New York: Stein and Day, 1981.

Gurrardo, L. *Italia, Ventesimo Secolo*, Milano, Italia: Reader's Digest, 1985.

Hauser, Thomas and Stephen Brunt. *Italian Stallions: Heroes of Boxing's Glory Days*, Toronto: Sport Classic Books, 2003.

Heller, Peter. *In This Corner . . . !: Forty World Champions Tell Their Story*, London: Robson, 1989.

Hoberman, John Milton. *Darwin's Athletes: How Sport Damaged Black America and Preserved the Myth of Race*, New York: Marriner, 1997.

Holli, Melvin. G. and Peter d'A Jones. *Ethnic Chicago: A Multicultural Portrait*, Grand Rapids, MI: William B. Eerdmans, 1995.

Hugman, Barry J. *International Boxing Yearbook*, London: Macdonald & Queen Anne Press; 1989.

Hugman, Barry. J. *The British Boxing Board of Control Yearbook*, London: Robson, 1996.

Isenberg, Michael. T. *John L. Sullivan and His Times*, London: Robson, 1988.

Johnston, Alexander. *Ten and Out: The Complete Story of the Prize Ring in America*, New York: Ives Washburn, 1947.

Jones, Maldwyn. *Destination America*, London: Weidenfeld and Nicolson, 1976.

Kessner, Thomas. *The Golden Door: Italian And Jewish Immigrant Mobility In New York City 1880–1915*, New York: Oxford University Press, 1977.

Kinney, Joe Sarge and Adolph Caso. *Young Rocky: A True Story of Attilio Rocky Castellani*, Brookline Village, MA: Branden, 1985.

Kirsch, George, Othello Harris and Claire E. Nolte. *Encyclopaedia of Ethnicity and Sports in the USA*, Westport, CT: Greenwood Press, 2000.

Klapp, Orrin E. *Heroes, Villains and Fools: The Changing American Character*, Englewood Cliffs, NJ: Prentice Hall, 1962.

Kraus, Harry P. *The Settlement House Movement in New York City 1886–1914*, New York: Arno Press, 1980.

Kraut, Alan. J. *The Huddled Masses: The Immigrant in American Society 1880–1921*, Arlington Heights, IL: Harlan Davidson, 1982.

La Motta, Jake with Joseph Carter and Peter Savage, *Raging Bull: The True Story of a Champ*, New York: Bantam, 1980.

La Sorte, Michael. *La Merica: Images of Italian Greenhorn Experience*, Philadelphia: Temple University Press, 2003.

Leibling, A.J. *The Sweet Science*, London: Sportsman Book Club Edition, 1958.

Levine. Peter. *Ellis Island to Ebbets Field: Sport and the American Jewish Experience*, New York: Oxford University Press, 1992.

Lowenthal, Leo. *Literature, Popular Culture and Society*, Palo Alto, CA: Pacific, 1968.

Mack Smith, Denis. *Mussolini*, London: Weidenfield and Nicolson, 1981.

Maldonado, Lionel and Joan Moore. *Urban Ethnicity in the United States: New Immigrants and Old Minorities*, Beverly Hills, CA: Sage, 1985.

Mallett, M.E. *Mercenaries and their Masters: Warfare in Renaissance Italy*, Totowa, NJ: Rowman and Littlefield, 1974.

Mangione, Jerre and Ben Morreale. *La Storia: Five Centuries of the Italian American Experience*, New York: Harper Perennial, 1992.

Manzello, Nick. *Legacy of the Gladiators: Italian Americans in Sport*, Worcester, MA: Ambassador, 2002.

Maselli, Joe and Dominic Candeloro. *Italians of New Orleans*, Mount Pleasant, SC: Arcadia, 2004.

Mencken, H.L. *The American Language*, New York: A.A. Knopf, 1936.

Mormino, Gary Ross. *Immigrants on the Hill: Italian Americans in St Louis 1882–1982*, Urbana, IL: University of Illinois Press, 1986.

Mormino, Gary Ross and George Pozzetta. *The Immigrant World of Ybor City 1885–1985: Italians and Their Latin Neighbors in Tampa*, Urbana, IL: University of Illinois Press, 1987.

Morrison, Ian. 1988, *Boxing: Records, Facts and Champions*, London: Guinness Books, 1988.

Mullan, Harry. *The Great Book of Boxing*, New York: Crescent, 1987.

Murphy, Kevin P. *Political Manhood: Real Bloods, Mollycoddles and Politics of Progressive Era Reform*, New York: Columbia University Press, 2008.

Myler, Patrick. *The Fighting Irish: Ireland's Role in World Boxing History*, County Kerry, Ireland: Brandon, 1987.

Nash, Roderick. *The Nervous Generation: American Thought 1917–30*, Chicago, IL: Elephant Paperbacks, 1970.

Nelli, Humbert. *Italians in Chicago: A Study in Ethnic Mobility 1880–1930*, New York: Oxford University Press, 1970.

Odd, Gilbert. *The Hamlyn Encyclopaedia of Boxing*, London: Hamlyn, 1990.

Oriard, Michael. *King Football: Sport and Spectacle in the Golden Age of Radio, Newsreels, Movies and Magazines, the Weekly and the Daily Press*, Chapel Hill, NC: University of North Carolina Press, 2001.

Orsi, Robert. *The Madonna of 115th Street: Faith and Community in Italian Harlem 1880–1950*, New Haven, CT: Yale University Press, 2002.

Pep, Willie and Robert Sacchi. *Willie Pep Remembers Friday's Heroes*, New York: Friday's Heroes Inc, 1973.

Postal, Bernard. *The Encyclopaedia of Jews in Sports*, New York: Bloch Publishing, 1965.

Powers, Madelon. *Faces Along the Bar: Lore and Order in the Workingman's Saloon 1870–1920*, Chicago: University of Chicago Press, 1999.

Ribalow, Harold. 1948, *The Jew in American Sports*, New York: Bloch Publishing, 1948.

Riess, Steven A. *The American Sporting Experience: A Historical Anthology of Sports in America*, New York: Leisure Press; 1984.

Riess, Steven A. *City Games: The Evolution of American Urban Society and the Rise of Sports*, Urbana, IL: Illini Books ed. University of Illinois Press, 1991.

Riess, Steven A. *Sports and the American Jew*, New York: Syracuse University Press, 1998.

Riess, Steven A. *Touching Base: Professional Baseball and American Culture in the Progressive Era*, Westport, CT: Greenwood Press, 1980.

Ripley, R. *Everlast Boxing Record*, New York: Everlast Sports Publishing Company, 1925.

Roberts, J. Alexander Skutt. *The Boxing Register: International Boxing Hall of Fame Record Book*, Ithaca, NY: McBooks Press, 2006.

Roberts, Randy. *Jack Dempsey: The Manassa Mauler*, London: Robson, 1987.

Robinson, Sugar Ray with Dave Anderson. *Sugar Ray: The Sugar Ray Robinson Story*, London: Robson, 1992.

Romano, John. *Post Boxing Record*, New York: New York Post Publishing, 1934.

Ross, Barney and Martin Abramson. *No Man Stands Alone: The Story of Barney Ross*, Philadelphia, PA: J.B. Lippincott Co., 1957.

Rotella, Carlo. *Good with their Hands: Boxers, Bluesmen and Other Characters of the Rust Belt*, Berkeley, CA: University of California Press, 2002.

Ruth, David E. *Inventing the Public Enemy: The Gangster in American Culture 1918–34*, Chicago: University of Chicago Press, 1996.

Sammons, Jeffrey. T. *Beyond the Ring: The Role of Boxing in American Society*, Urbana, IL: University of Illinois Press, 1990.

Sánchez-Jankowski, Martin. *Islands in the Street: Gangs and American Urban Society*, Berkeley, CA: University of California Press, 1992.

Schulberg, Budd. *Sparring with Hemingway and other Legends of the Fight Game*, London: Robson, 1997.

Skehan, Everett M. *Rocky Marciano*, London, Robson, 1983.

Smith, Kevin. *Boston's Boxing Heritage: Prizefighting from 1882 to 1955*, Mount Pleasant, SC: Arcadia, 2002.

Sori, Ercole. *L'emigrazione italiana dall'unità alla seconda guerra mondiale*, Bologna, Italia: Editore Mulino, 1979.

Spivey, Donald. *Sport in America: New Historical Perspectives*, Westport, CT: Greenwood Press, 1985.

Sterba, Christopher. *Good Americans: Italian and Jewish Immigrants during the First World War*, New York: Oxford University Press, 2003.

Sugar, Bert. *The Ring All New 1980 Boxing Record Book*, New York: Ring Publishing, 1980.

Sugden, John. *Boxing and Society: An International Analysis*, Manchester, UK: Manchester University Press, 1996.

Sullivan, Russell. *Rocky Marciano: The Rock of His Times*, Urbana, IL: University of Illinois Press, 2002.

Thernstrom, Stephan. *Harvard Encyclopaedia of Ethnic Groups*, Cambridge, MA: Harvard University Press, 1980.

Thernstrom, Stephan. *The Other Bostonians: Poverty and Progress in the American Metropolis 1880–1970*, Cambridge, MA: Harvard University Press, 1973.

Thrasher, Frederick M. *A Study of 1,313 Gangs in Chicago*, Chicago, IL: University of Chicago Press, 1927.

Tomasi, Silvano and Madeleine Engel. *The Italian Experience in the United States*, New York: Centre for Migration Studies, 1970.

Turpin, G. *Forgotten Men of the Prize Ring*, San Antonio, TX: Naylor Co, 1963.

Veronese, Gene P. *Italian-Americans and Their Communities of Cleveland*, Cleveland, OH: Cleveland State University, 1977.

Walsh, Peter. *Men of Steel: The Lives and Times of Boxing's Middleweight Champions*, London: Robson, 1993.

Waxman, Maurice and Charlie Vackner. *Bang Boxing Record, 1938*, New York: Bang Magazine, 1938.

Whyte, William F. *Street Corner Society: The Social Structure of an Italian Slum*, Chicago, IL: University of Chicago Press, 1943.

Youmans, Gary B. *The Onion Picker: Carmen Basilio and Boxing in the 1950s*, Syracuse, NY: Syracuse University Press, 2007.

Articles

Ackerman, Meyer. "New Faces," *Ring Magazine*, July 1937.

Albertanti, Francis. "Italy Proud of its Fighting Sons," *Ring Magazine*, October 1922; "From Jeweler to Top Notch Boxer: Story of the Rise of Carl Duane, the Bronx Steam Roller," *Ring Magazine*, March 1924; "From Bananas to Boxing Gloves – The Colorful Story of Joe Dundee, Pride of Baltimore," *Ring Magazine*, March 1926; "Tony Canzoneri Seeks to Emulate Teacher, Pete Herman, Former Champion," *Ring Magazine*, July 1927.

Ballard, Duke. "Boxing's Whirlwind," *Ring Magazine*, April 1935.

Bazzano, Carmelo. "Willie Pep: Last Sport Hero of Hartford's Little Italy," University of Massachusetts, Boston, 1993.

Brannigan, Johnny. "Keep'em Laughing Frankie," *Boxing Illustrated*, October 1960.

Bromberg, Lester. "The Top Ten Italian-Americans of All Time," *Ring Magazine*, May 1977.

Brown, Ned. "Links Lure Jeffra," *Ring Magazine*, December 1937.

Callis, Tracy. "Rocky Marciano: The Hardest One Punch Slugger," *Wail! The CyberBoxingZone Journal*, October 2000, http://www.cyberboxingzone.com.

Carroll, Ted. "Maxim Cashing in Decade's Effort," *Ring Magazine*, August 1949; "The Golden Age of Bantamweight Boxing," *Ring Magazine*, December 1953; "Italians Make Ring History," *Ring Magazine*, July 1956.

Casey Mike. "Man of Granite with Heart to Match, Rise and Fall of Basilio, One of The Great Champions," *Boxing News*, 2 October 1987.

Cohen, Sam. "Lou Bogash – What a Fighter!" *Ring Magazine*, September 1978.

Crussan, Milton. Sammy Fuller article, *Arena Magazine*, April 1930, p. 29; Lou Scozza article, *Arena* Magazine, June 1930.

Daley, Arthur. "What Makes Sammy Run?" *New York Times*, June 1, 1943; "Jimmy Johnston goes High Hat," *New York Times*, January 7, 1944; "Brother Act," *New York Times*, August 17, 1945; "The Split Decision Kid," *New York Times*, September 18, 1947.

Davis, Luckett V. "Tony Canzoneri Biography," *America National Biography Online*, http://www.anb.org.

Davis, Robert. "The Police and the Pugni: Sports and Social Control in Early Modern Venice," *Stanford Humanities Review*, Vol. 6.2, January 1, 1998.

Duffy, Joe. "Epic Moment in a Legendary Career," *The Journal Inquirer*, February 9, 1994, p. 8.

Edwards, Frank. "Battling Reddy – Veteran East Sider, NY fought world's best bantams and feathers," *Ring Magazine*, October 1949.

Ewart, Gar. "Midget Wolgast Seeks Clear Claim to Crown," *Arena Magazine*, Vol. 2, No 10, July 1930.

Ferrand, Hardwin. "Fighting for his Family," *Arena Boxing Magazine*, October 1929.

Fisher, Ray. "Tommy Paul, Buffalo Lad Makes Good," *Ring Magazine*, September 1931.

Fitzgerald, Joe. "Piece of History Buried with Boxer," *Boston Herald*, February 23, 2002, http://www.bostonherald.com.

Fleischer, Nat. "Bat Battalino Crowned Featherweight King," *Ring Magazine*, November 1929; "Nat Fleischer Says . . .," *Ring Magazine*, September 1931; "Billy Petrolle: The Man with the Iron Fist," *Ring Magazine*, May 1932.

Hamill, Don. "54 Straight and the Title," *Ring Magazine*, February 1943.

Heller, Peter. "Meet the Champs – Then and Now – Petey Scalzo," *Boxing Illustrated*, January 1971; "Meet the Champs – Then and Now – Fred Apostoli," *Boxing Illustrated*, July 1972.

Jarrett, John A. "Meet Tony De Marco: New World's Welter Champ," *Boxing News*, April 15, 1955.

Jenkins, Thomas. "Changes in Ethnic and Racial Representation among Professional Boxers: A Study in Ethnic Succession," Master's dissertation, University of Chicago, 1955.

Kaplan, Hank. "Italian-Americans Honor Their Fistic Greats," *Ring Magazine*, February 1978; "Petey Scalzo: The Greek Ambassador," *The Sweet Science*, November 10, 2005, http://www.thesweetscience.com/article-archive/2005/2854-petey-scalzo-the-greek-ambassador; "Sal Bartolo: The Maritime Champ," *The Sweet Science*, November 16, 2005, http://www.thesweetscience.com/article-archive/2005/2871-sal-bartolo-the-maritime-champ.

Keating, Frank. "Recalling the night, 50 years ago when a Casablanca butcher's son took on a Raging Bull," *The Guardian*, June 7, 1999.

Kieran, John. "Honey Lou, Accompanied By the Clarinet," *New York Times*, March 1, 1935.

Lawrence, Jack. "Tony Canzoneri: The Lad Who Smiles at Reverses," *Ring Magazine*, January 1930.

Lieb, Frederick G. "The Italian in Sport," *Ring Magazine*, March 1924.

Linn, Ed. "Carmen Basilio Reaches For The Jackpot," *Sport Magazine*, October 1957 in Thomas Hauser and Stephen Brunt, *The Italian Stallions: Heroes of Boxing's Glory Days*, Toronto: Sport Classic Books, 2003.

Mahoney, Billy. "The Orphan Boy Who Became a Champion . . . The Rags to Riches Story of Fred Apostoli," *Boxing Illustrated*, 1969.

Majeski, Don. "A History of Boxing Economics Part III," *International Boxing Digest Magazine*, August 1998.

Mandell, Richard. "I'm Proud That Sammy Mandell was my Dad," *Boxing Illustrated*, 1968.

Markson, Harry. "Starts as a Heavyweight Stars as a Middleweight," *Ring Magazine*, April 1944.

Martinelli, Phyllis and Leonard Gordon. "Italian Americans Across Half a Century," *Ethnic and Racial Studies*, Vol. II, No. 3, July 1988.

Merrill, Eddie. "Pep Versus Bartolo," *Ring Magazine*, August 1944.

Miller, Bill. "Fighting Italians," *Ring Magazine*, January 1933.

Moran, J.R. "Boston's Strong Boy," *Ring Magazine,* June 1932.

Mormino, Gary Ross. "The Playing Fields of St. Louis: Italian Immigrants and Sports 1925–41," *Journal of Sport History*, Vol. 9, No. 2, Summer 1982.

Olver, Ron. "Slam Bang TV Champ," *Boxing News*, June 3, 1955.

Perno, Albert. "Luck Important Factor in Fight Game," *Ring Magazine*, June 1928.

Queijo, Joe. "From Hoodlum to Hero: Rocky Graziano", *Secondsout.com*, May 21, 2002, http://www.secondsout.com/legends/legends-update/from-hoodlum-to-hero-rocky-graziano.

Riess, Steven A. "Sport and the American Dream: A Review Essay," *Journal of Social History*, Vol. 14, 1980.

Roberts, Randy. "Eighteenth Century Boxing", *Journal of Sports History*, Vol. 4, No. 3, 1977.

Scutari, Ferdinando. "Johnny Dundee – da pescivendolo a campione mondiale", *Lo Sport Illustrato,* July 1915; "Hugo Kelly," *Lo Sport Illustrato*, Year III, No. 5, March 15, 1915.

Smith, Harry B. "Coast Fans Rave over New Middleweight Find – Fred Apostoli," *Ring Magazine*, January 1937.

Thorne, Harvey. "Melio Bettina is 'Beacon' in Light-Heavyweight Fog," *Ring Magazine*, November 1938.

Van Court, DeWitt. "American Boxers Lead World in Gameness," *Ring Magazine*, October 1923.

Vigeant, Billy. "Boxing's Little Giant: Willie Pep Will 'O the Wisp," *Ragtyme Sports Magazine*, April 1995.

Waxman, Maurice. "Another Amateur Makes Good," *Ring Magazine*, December 1935.

Weinberg, Kirson S. and Henry Arond. "The Occupational Culture of the Boxer," *American Journal of Sociology*, Vol. 57, 1952.

Weston, Stanley. "Those Fighting Italians: Italians Who Held World Championships", *Boxing Illustrated*, June 1963.

Wood, Wilbur. "Boxers of Italian Descent Invade Realm of Fistiana in Ever Increasing Circles," *New York Herald*, January 27, 1924.

Interviews

Steve Acunto	September 21, 1995
Carmen Basilio*	September 21, 1995
Al Certo	September 20, 1995
Steve Corbo	August 7, 2005
John De John*	September 16, 1995
Tony De Marco	September 25, 1995
Angelo Dundee*	August 17, 2005
Joey Fariello*	September 24, 1995
Joey Giardello*	August 8, 2005
Herb Goldman	September 15, 1995
Hank Kaplan*	August 17, 2005
Jake La Motta	September 20, 1995
Dennie Mancini*	July 25, 1995
Arthur Mercante*	July 28, 2005
Harry Mullan*	July 20, 1995
Dan Muscato	August 6, 2005
Willie Pep*	September 23, 1995

Notes

* Deceased.

All the September 1995 interviews were conducted in the United States between September 13 and 27, 1995. Further interviews were recorded with L.I.R.A. Italian community centre residents in Mott Street and in Mulberry Street, Lower East Side Manhattan, New York. All 2005 interviews were conducted in the United States between July 25 and August 20, 2005. Interviews with Harry Mullan and Dennie Mancini were carried out in London, England.

Newspapers and journals
Arena Boxing Magazine
Baltimore Sun
Boston Globe
Boston Post
Boxing
Boxing Blade
Boxing Illustrated
Boxing News
Boxing World and Athletic Chronicle
Brooklyn Daily Eagle
Chicago Daily Tribune
International Boxing Digest
La Gazzetta dello Sport
Mirror of Life and Boxing World
National Police Gazette
New York Evening Telegram
New York Herald
New York Times
Philadelphia Evening Public Ledger
Philadelphia Inquirer
Ring Magazine
San Francisco Chronicle
The Knockout Magazine
The Veteran Boxer

Websites

http://www.clevelandmemory.org/italians
http://www.ibroresearch.com
http://www.jewishsports.net
http://www.baseballcube.com
http://www.baseball-almanac.com
http://www.baseballlibrary.com
http://www.databasefootball.com
http://www.ncaa.com
http://www.nfl.com
http://www.goldengloves.com
http://www.pagoldengloves.com
http://www.amateur-boxing.vip.interia
http://www.boxrec.com
http://www.ancestry.com
http://www.thehaca.com
http://www.comune.siena.it
http://www.newslibrary.com
http://www.fultonhistory.com
http://www.cyberboxingzone.com
http://www.legacy.com
http://www.secondsout.com
http://www.ibhof.com
http://www.thesweetscience.com
http://www.anb.org